The History of

MODERN FASHION

Daniel James Cole and Nancy Deihl

The History of

MODERN FASHION

FROM 1850

Laurence King Publishing

LAURENCE KING

Published in 2015 by
Laurence King Publishing Ltd
361–373 City Road
London EC1V 1LR
United Kingdom
Tel: +44 20 7841 6900
Fax: +44 20 7841 6910
email: enquiries@laurenceking.com
www.laurenceking.com

Designer Grita Rose-Innes
Picture Researcher Heather Vickers
Development Editor Anne Townley
Senior Editor Felicity Maunder

Frontispiece A ready-to-wear dress by Alexander McQueen,
2009, photographed by Surachai Saengsuwan.
© Surachai Saengsuwan

Printed in China

Contents

Chapter Contents

Chapter 13
The 2000s *Mixed Messages* 417

Introduction

From a 21st-century viewpoint, the clothing of the late nineteenth century seems to epitomize "old-fashioned." The hoop skirts, restrictive corsetry and the abundance of trimming on women's clothing, and the somber, tailored coats and stiff top hats worn by men, all appear impractical, formal, and decidedly un-modern. However, these styles reflected not just current taste, but also incorporated the latest in technology: new dyes and fabric finishes, innovative construction methods, and industrial garment production.

What was true in 1850 remains valid now: fashion consistently reflects technological innovations and economic and political developments, and relates to prevailing styles in the fine and decorative arts. We start this history of fashion in 1850 – and call it "modern" – for several reasons. During this period, mechanized production, including power looms and the widespread use of the sewing machine, transformed the manufacture of clothing. Fashions evolved rapidly and fashionable clothing became available to a wider public. Concurrent technical improvements in printing also allowed for expansion of the fashion press for an ever-growing audience. Additionally, the development of the designer system, and the role of the fashion designer as a catalyst of stylistic change, laid the foundation for the universe of designers and brands integral to today's fashion industry.

After the opening chapter, the text is organized into chapters dealing with individual decades. This might seem an arbitrary structure; after all no one flips a switch to introduce a new fashion on the first day of the first year of a decade. However, with few exceptions, we have found that there is a spirit that prevails through each decade. And human beings (especially fashionable beings) tend to identify those ten-year periods with their individual clothing perceptions. There is

also a marked tendency for fashion writers to work in decades – forecasting a coming decade or summing up as it comes to a close. Fashion writers also refer to the past in decade style, associating particular "looks" with these ten-year periods.

This book treats fashion as a phenomenon interlocked with other cultural forms. Each chapter offers a concise summary of political and social changes in the decade under consideration. Important works in the visual and performing arts are presented and, where possible, illustrated, highlighting the crucial role performers (whether international opera stars or self-made internet sensations) have played in setting and popularizing fashions. It also exposes patterns in the way fashions rise and fall, acknowledging the interlinked roles of designers, celebrities, the media, even exhibitions – ranging from the great international expositions of the late 19th and early 20th centuries to major museum shows of contemporary designers. While celebrity culture is often discussed as a recent social trend, for example attributing the popularity of early 2000s "Boho-chic" to actress Sienna Miller, the same mechanism was well in place in the late 19th century, such as Princess Alexandra's contribution to the acceptance of tailored ensembles for women.

The History of Modern Fashion is based on scholarship, but it is not intended only for scholars. General readers, students, anyone interested in the history and dynamics of fashion will discover more in-depth information about fashion movements and "moments" that may be somewhat familiar; learn about designers who were prominent in their own time but have not received their due from history; and will find also some long-standing myths – Poiret eliminated the corset! Chanel invented the black dress! – dispelled or corrected. An extensive bibliography suggests resources for further research on specific designers, topics, and decades. Readers will note the growth of the fashionable world over time. Early chapters present haute couture in Paris as the source of style; by the start of the 2000s, Asia's influence is significant. This book is intended to expand the narrative and dialogue of modern fashion, a vibrant, rapidly changing cultural form that is an important component of the increasingly globalized world.

Acknowledgements

During the years of researching and writing this book, we were assisted and encouraged by friends and family, colleagues and students.

We'd like to recognize the inspiring research presentations of Clara Berg, Audrey Chaney, and Larissa Shirley, all FIT graduates and myth-busters, ably guided by Lourdes Font, our esteemed colleague. We also acknowledge the support of fellow FIT faculty Michael Casey, Chloe Chapin, Sheila Marks, Pamela Synder-Gallagher, and Nan J. Young. Elyse Carroll, another FIT alumna, established initial picture organization. At New York University, Elizabeth Marcus and Elizabeth Morano were encouraging colleagues; Damien Davis and Vonetta Moses were consistently helpful; and Felicity Pitt, NYU alumna, assisted with the bibliography.

Elaine Maldonado, Jeffrey Riman, and Celia Baez of the Center for Excellence in Teaching at FIT were unfailingly supportive. We acknowledge encouragement from IFFTI (International Foundation of Fashion Technology Institutes). Lee Ripley was an early supporter of the project. The Metropolitan Opera Archives, and Eugenia Bell at The Richard Avedon Foundation generously assisted in our quest for images, as did Renaldo Barnette, Nooraliff Bin Ismael, Manya Drobnack, Krystal Fernandez and Babette Daniels, James Houser, Yuniya Kawamura, Melanie Reim, Alexandra Armillas, and Steven Stipelman. Kien Chan, John Paul Rangel, Idham Rously, Auguste Soesastro, and Vivienne Aurheum Yoou provided research assistance. Clare Sauro of the Robert and Penny Fox Historic Costume Collection at Drexel University and Cynthia Cooper of the McCord Museum of Canadian History offered insights and expertise.

Without the Gladys Marcus Library Special Collections & College Archives, this project would not have been possible. We are grateful to the entire staff there, past and present, including Juliet Jacobs, Tess Hartman Cullen and Ashley Kranjac, but especially Karen Trivette Cannell and April Calahan.

At Laurence King Publishing, we have benefited from the patience, knowledgeable guidance and remarkable expertise of Anne Townley and Felicity Maunder. Heather Vickers, picture editor extraordinaire, secured amazing images that enliven these pages. The sophisticated design by Grita Rose-Innes brought this story to life. We are also grateful to the anonymous reviewers who offered so many helpful insights and suggestions.

Special thanks for particular support and encouragement are due to the following exceptional individuals: Steve Deihl, Ford Deihl, Jeanne Golly, Pamela Grimaud, Desirée Koslin, Bradford S. Martin, David Roberts, Surachai Saengsuwan, and Felix Xie.

Finally, during our years of teaching, we have had the pleasure of working with many dedicated and persistent students whose interesting research has deepened our appreciation for and knowledge of the history of fashion. We are grateful for what we have learned from them – as much as we hope they have learned from us.

In memoriam Elaine Stone

Chapter 1

1850–1890

The Dawn of Modern Clothing

Fashion in the period 1850–1890 reflected the latest developments in engineering, chemistry, and communications. During the second half of the 19th century, the growth of photography and inventions such as aniline dye and the sewing machine all had impact on the design, manufacture, and distribution of clothing. This period witnessed the development of the "fashion designer" as a profession, and the birth of the haute couture system. Family businesses dominated the fashion world. Worth, Creed, Redfern, and Doucet were all dynasties that lasted through several generations. International politics and social and economic fluctuations strongly affected fashion as well; changes in government and trade relations, urbanism, and increased social mobility all influenced dress. Visitors to any of the international expositions of the

Opposite Realistic details in James Tissot's *The Shop Girl* (1885) convey the pleasures of shopping in the late 19th century. Holding a carefully wrapped parcel, a *modiste* in a simple black dress opens the door for a departing client, while well-dressed passersby appreciate the shop's enticements.

Right By the 1850s the use of sewing machines in the commercial manufacture of clothing was widespread, and models for home use, as shown here, were widely marketed as well.

1850s – including the Great Exhibition in London's "Crystal Palace" in 1851, the subsequent Great Exhibition in New York in 1853, or the Exposition Universelle of 1855 in Paris – could not have failed to notice that the world of material pleasures was rapidly expanding.

The Road to 1850

By the late 18th century the phenomenon of fashion had developed into a progression of silhouettes that typically evolved from the previous style; these silhouettes began to change at a faster rate than ever before in the history of fashion. Style setters such as Queen Marie Antoinette of France and George, the British Prince Regent, wore fashions that were quickly copied by others. Subsets of fashionable people devoted to a particular look were well established, and popular culture influenced clothing as the stylish imitated famous performers and fictional characters. Colored fashion plates were significant to the development of a fashion press.

From the beginning of the 19th century historicism and orientalism were recurrent themes in fashion and the arts. Influences from India and Central Asia were popular, and styles of the past (including the Middle Ages, the Elizabethan era, and the 17th century) were revived. The lure of the exotic and of the past were by-products of the prevailing artistic movement, Romanticism. Fashion leaders for women included Joséphine Bonaparte, Empress of France, and Dolley Madison, wife of the American president. Men's fashion was dominated by two personalities and their contrasting points of view: George Bryan "Beau" Brummell was known for tailored restraint, while Lord Byron advocated a poetically disheveled look. The progression of styles for men and women produced periodic undulations in skirt shapes and lengths, necklines, sleeves, waists, shoulders, and cravats.

1837 saw the beginning of the sixty-three-year reign of Queen Victoria, the most powerful and influential monarch in Europe, who set social standards until her death in 1901. For her marriage to her cousin, Albert of Saxe-Coburg and Gotha, on February 10, 1840, Victoria chose a white wedding dress and orange blossoms, solidifying an important dress custom. Victoria's emphasis on conservative social values represented a pendulum swing from the permissive society of the Regency period in Britain. The impact of the Industrial Revolution, and economic depressions in parts of the world (including Australia and the United States) were reflected in clothing of the 1840s. Silhouettes for both men and women became simpler, and decoration and colors became more subdued. Modesty was a priority and sartorial sobriety was typical, especially in the United Kingdom and the United States.

During the 1840s, women's clothing was characterized by a jewel neckline and long sleeves. Sleeves were commonly simple and straight; as the decade progressed bodices sometimes had flared sleeves, with cotton or linen undersleeves, usually with a matching collar. Décolletage was seen in women's eveningwear, but was most often in the form of a wide bateau neckline and seldom showed cleavage. Skirts became longer, usually reaching the floor, after shorter lengths had been popular in the 1830s, and petticoats maintained a bell-shaped silhouette. The waist was slightly dropped and bodices typically came down to a center front point. The poke bonnet was the dominant hat style and its closely fitted sides and brim were in keeping with the prevailing focus on modesty.

Men typically wore the frock coat; trousers were straight with fly fronts. Colors were dark and somber. For formal wear (outside of court dress), black tailcoats were the standard of elegance, sometimes still worn with knee breeches although long pants began to be common in the evening as well. The top hat was the most widespread hat style.

Social and Economic Background

In Britain, under the long rule of Queen Victoria, industrialization continued at a rapid pace. The development of railroads, the migration of workers into cities, and

An illustration from *American Fashions* from 1847 depicts a family in styles typical of the mid-19th century.

the expansion of colonial influence in China, Africa, Southeast Asia, and India all contributed to the prosperity and self-image of the British and were important to evolutions in taste. The scope of the British Empire was reflected in the availability of goods from all over the world and the adoption of particular items of dress. By the mid-19th century Paris was the undisputed center of fashion despite the turbulent state of French politics.

The Second Empire began in 1852 when President Louis-Napoléon Bonaparte proclaimed himself Emperor Napoleon III. Members of the French court, especially Napoleon's attractive wife, Empress Eugénie, were influential in matters of style. Other European royals, including Elisabeth, Empress of Austria, and Princess Pauline Metternich, the wife of the Austrian ambassador to the French court, were also fashion leaders. However, the aristocracy vied with new fortunes made in finance, real estate, transportation, and manufacturing. Royals, aristocrats, and nouveaux riches all took part in the spectacle of fashionable life in Paris, which was transformed into a modern city of wide boulevards and impressive open spaces. Following the Franco-Prussian War in 1870 the Second Empire came to an end, and by 1872 the Third Republic was in place. Elsewhere in Europe, following a series of upheavals in 1848, the various small kingdoms of Germany were consolidated under Chancellor Otto von Bismarck. In Italy, the Third War of Independence in 1866 made Giuseppe Garibaldi a national hero.

Other parts of the world experienced similar disruptions. Changes in international relations affected technological developments and trade. The American Civil War

JENNY LIND

Swedish soprano Johanna Maria "Jenny" Lind (1820–1887) was known for her concert performances in Europe during the 1840s and the United States during the early 1850s, the latter produced by flamboyant circus promoter P. T. Barnum. Lind was contracted for previously unheard-of fees. Barnum orchestrated remarkable advance publicity and succeeded in creating a cult figure playing to sold-out houses on her American tour. The "Lindomania" (or "Jenny Rage") caused by her American popularity led to frantic audiences and rioting in oversold concert halls. One night when Lind's veil fell off the stage and into the audience "it was ripped to shreds by relic hunters."[1] Jenny Lind's style was widely imitated by fashionable women, and some fashion historians have even credited her with popularizing the style for the three-tiered skirt of the early 1850s. The media circus surrounding Lind, her rabid fan base, and the official souvenir merchandise were unprecedented for a musician, anticipated only by the enthusiasm that had surrounded pianist Franz Liszt in Europe the decade before. Lind's career is especially important as a prototype for pop culture iconography, and the extent of this extreme musical fandom and hype foreshadows the "Beatlemania" of the 1960s and other similar 20th-century phenomena.

An album of "Jenny Lind Music," c. 1850, published in Boston.

(1861–1865), and the abolition of slavery, had a significant impact on the American economy, westward expansion, and the textile industry. During the war, the mobilization of over three million servicemen necessitated the mass production of clothing and led to the beginnings of industry sizing standards. In addition, profits generated by the war helped establish a new class of wealthy industrialists. Unable to import cotton from America during the Civil War, Britain turned to Australian sources, giving a boost to cotton production in the colony.

In one of the most significant global events of the 19th century, Japan opened its borders in 1853–1854. The end of more than 250 years of relative isolation led to new diplomatic missions and had a notable impact on Western tastes. Trade treaties were signed with the United States, followed by other major countries, and several Japanese port cities became open to trade. Japanese goods entered the Western market.

The Arts

While this period was marked by a spirit of experimentation – even rebellion – in the arts, historicism and orientalism continued to be major factors in art and design. The Académie des Beaux-Arts of Paris and the Royal Academy of Arts in London promoted history painting as the most important genre, while depictions of contemporary life were considered the lowest level of endeavor. In a gesture of independence from the academy, the Impressionist movement officially began in Paris in 1874 with an exhibition organized by the Anonymous Society of Artists, whose members included Claude Monet, Edgar Degas, Pierre-Auguste Renoir, Gustave Caillebotte, and Berthe Morisot. Taking their subject matter from the world around them, these artists created scenes of boating parties, people at the beach, vibrant views of the countryside, and images of the movement and sparkle of life in their fast-paced world. Just as synthetic dyes made mid-century fashions brighter, new chemical pigments became available for artists who exploited spectacular new hues. Fashion was integral to modern life and the Impressionists captured stylish men and women at sun-dappled picnics, cafes, theaters, and racetracks.

Romantic artists such as Eugène Delacroix and Jean-Léon Gérôme perpetuated a romanticized view of Asia as well as Egypt and North Africa. Performing arts contributed to the orientalist vogue. In 1871 Italian composer Giuseppe Verdi created his idealized version of ancient Egypt in *Aida*. The Parisian taste for theatrical excess was whetted by Jules Massenet, who took audiences to South Asia with *Le Roi de Lahore* (1877) and to Byzantium with *Esclarmonde* (1889). Giacomo Meyerbeer's *L'Africaine* (1865) and Léo Delibes' *Lakmé* (1883) depicted forbidden love between European men and Eastern women. Ballet also contributed to the trend of orientalist entertainments: among many such productions, Cesare Pugni's *The Pharaoh's Daughter* (1862) was particularly ludicrous, involving opium-induced hallucinations and reanimated mummies.

Portrait photography became increasingly popular not just among the wealthy but also among the growing middle class. Celebrities such as the Countess di Castiglione and Lillie Langtry understood the power of photography as a means of manipulating public image. French photographers such as Nadar chronicled the age, while Julia Margaret Cameron captured the Aesthetic dress of the British intelligentsia. Even ordinary citizens posed for their local photographer and the resulting *cartes de visite*, portraits, and group photos record the enthusiasm for this new medium.

The Fruits of Industry

While a rigid social hierarchy was still in place in Europe, North America experienced greater social mobility. In the United States, only one hundred years old in 1876, social position was increasingly determined by wealth, rather than birth. Though descended from Dutch farmers in colonial New York, the Vanderbilts established themselves as leaders of New York society. Likewise, the Astors, originally a merchant family from Germany, created an important real estate empire. These prominent families constituted a sort of American equivalent to Old World aristocracy. The Astors, Vanderbilts, and other prominent New Yorkers such as J. P. Morgan were instrumental in the founding of major cultural institutions. Throughout North America fashion leaders emerged from fortunes made in a great variety of industries; they were important to Paris fashion. Isabella Stewart Gardner of Boston was the heiress to a textile and mining fortune. Chicago society followed Mrs. Cyrus (Nettie) McCormick, whose husband invented a mechanical reaper, and Bertha Honoré Palmer, wealthy from her husband's real estate empire. Potter Palmer founded a dry goods store, Potter Palmer and Co., that became retail giant Marshall Field & Co. American millionaires married their heavily dowered daughters into aristocratic European families. Titles ennobled the sometimes ill-gotten gains of the wealthy "Robber Baron" families and American "Dollar Princesses" brought much needed capital to impoverished aristocrats.

Industrialization also contributed to the growth of cities and an urban middle class. Improvements in production methods led to an unprecedented choice of consumer goods. The first practical sewing machine came from Elias Howe (1819–1867). Howe received a patent in 1846 and steadily improved his model. When Howe's competitor John Bachelder sold his patent to I. M. Singer (1811–1875) in the early 1850s, the machine had been improved to the point where Singer could successfully modify and actively market it. Commercial models were in use during the 1850s and the first Singer model for the home, the "Grasshopper," was offered in 1858. Aggressive marketing of the new device insured success in the domestic realm; young ladies demonstrated the machine in well-appointed showrooms. Sewing machines were designed to fit in with the aesthetic of the mid-century with painted floral decoration and curved iron treadle tables. Special attachments for ruffling, binding, hemming, and buttonholes expanded the range of the home sewer, encouraging a taste for more elaborate apparel. By the time of I. M. Singer's death in 1875, his company was selling over 180,000 machines a year.

The establishment of department stores in major cities added another dynamic aspect to fashion. These impressive buildings, built with up-to-date amenities, were stocked with enticingly displayed goods. The new department stores were vast emporia where items were offered for sale with visible price tags, and uniformed salespeople demonstrated their products. The department stores included restaurants and cafes, staged art exhibitions and often stayed open until ten o'clock in the evening. Seasonal fashions were featured on racks and live models. Buyers could purchase ready-made dresses, outerwear, lingerie, and accessories as well as textiles and trim; shopping became an exciting new urban pastime. Parisians enjoyed sophisticated shopping at several stores: Le Bon Marché opened in 1852, Le Printemps in 1865 and La Samaritaine four years later. Emile Zola's 1883 novel, *Au Bonheur des Dames*, chronicled the seductive aspect of consumption as well as its less pleasant side effects, including the long hours of the workers, the elimination of small specialty stores, and even shoplifting by desperate female customers. The influence of Paris' department store culture was felt worldwide. Montreal's largest and most fashionable store, Morgan's, was established in 1860 on McGill Street. It grew so rapidly that James and Henry Morgan erected a four-story building in 1866 to better serve the carriage trade, wealthy clients who arrived in private carriages. Holt Renfrew began in the 1830s in Quebec City as a hat shop, and later expanded into fur and received a royal warrant from Queen Victoria during the 1880s. America led the world in the continued development of the department store. After twenty years in the dry goods business, the Irish immigrant Alexander Turney Stewart built his Marble Dry Goods Palace in 1848 at Broadway and Chambers Street in New York City. His next store, opened in 1862 further uptown, was a six-story structure that featured open floors, a grand staircase, and a glass-domed rotunda. Steam-powered elevators were installed later. Arnold Constable & Co. opened a huge store on Fifth Avenue in 1877 that offered a full range of merchandise. Two important names, Lord & Taylor and Macy's, also established their flagship stores during this crucial period of retail expansion. John Wanamaker's store at Thirteenth and Market Streets in Philadelphia, known as the Grand Depot, opened in 1876. It was renowned for its luxurious interior details that included stained glass skylights and a central counter, measuring 90 feet (over 27 meters) in circumference, that surrounded a gaslit "dark room" for the display and sale of evening silks.

By the 1870s, ready-made goods of all sorts were available through mail-order catalogs. In 1872, Aaron Montgomery Ward issued his first catalog, under the business name of Montgomery Ward. His early circulars were one-page listings of items that ranged from hoop skirts to handkerchiefs, most of which were priced at one dollar each. Ten years later, the Montgomery Ward catalog listed over 10,000 items in 240 pages. Doubtless inspired by Ward's success, Richard Sears, who started out selling watches, teamed up with Alvah Roebuck and the first Sears Roebuck catalog went out to American consumers in 1893. Even rural areas were served by the mail-order businesses. Used clothing represented another important sector, and a lively market in second-hand clothing existed in most urban areas. Clothes were sold to be worn as-is or were restyled to follow changes in fashion.

Fashion Media

French publications were particularly influential worldwide, but every major city had periodicals that documented changes in fashion. Typically printed in tabloid format, most publications included descriptions of the latest modes with editorial commentary, advice on health and beauty, household hints, and serialized fiction. The fashion plates, illustrations contained in each issue, offered pictures of new styles in dress, accessories, and hairstyles and reinforced prevailing standards of beauty. *La Mode Illustreé*, *Le Moniteur de la Mode*, *L'Art et la Mode*, and *La Mode Pratique* were some of the most popular French journals. In Britain, women read *The Queen*, *Ladies' Newspaper* and the *Englishwoman's Domestic Magazine* among others. Berlin's *Der Bazar* chronicled developments in Parisian style and the activities of the elite, as did *La Moda Elegante*, published in Madrid. In the United States, *Harper's Bazar* began publication in 1867 as "A Repository of Fashion, Pleasure, and Instruction" and joined other female-oriented magazines such as *Godey's Lady's Book and Magazine*, *Peterson's Magazine* and *Demorest's Monthly Magazine and Mme. Demorest's Mirror of Fashions*.

Paper patterns for dresses and ensembles were distributed via the magazines beginning in the 1850s. "Madame" Demorest sold ungraded paper patterns, initially through Godey's and then Demorest publications. She also had 300 shops that operated in the United States and abroad under the name of Madame Demorest's Magasins des Modes. An improvement on the one-size system came in 1863 from Ebenezer Butterick, a tailor who responded to his wife's wish for graded patterns. The first Butterick patterns were for men's and boys' garments. In 1866, women's dress patterns were offered. By 1876, Butterick had created several publications to highlight new fashions and sell patterns, which were available by mail order and at branch stores throughout North America and Europe.

These periodicals were important transmitters of ideas and practices to an increasingly fashion-conscious public. Writers and editors for major fashion publications acknowledged their responsibility to their readers with "Letters from Paris" and similarly titled features. Fashion vocabulary used in magazines of the time often included the words "toilet," "toilette," and "costume" to describe an ensemble. As *Le Moniteur de la Mode* of January 1869 noted, "the difference between the toilets for friendly calls and toilets for ceremonial ones, for dancing parties or for balls, are equally marked. It is a perfect code which the Parisian knows by heart."

The Fashionable Elite

Napoleon III married a Spanish countess, Eugénie de Montijo. Schooled in France and familiar with French society, as Empress of France she became one of the most important cultural figures of the mid-19th century. Although she was shorter and stouter than the prevailing female ideal, Eugénie was nonetheless considered beautiful and possessed a remarkably poised and graceful demeanor. She brought significant glamour to the French court of the Second Empire and her fashion influence and style were rivaled only by Empress Elisabeth of Austria. Eugénie maintained pre-eminence in fashion until the fall of the Second Empire. Her portraits, painted by Franz Xaver Winterhalter, recorded in detail not only her beauty but also her exquisite taste in clothing. Many styles were associated with Eugénie, including the cage crinoline, and her appearance in a new fashion gave it a stamp of approval and guaranteed its success. At the court of the Second Empire, Eugénie presided over fashionable women who wore the work of elite Parisian dressmakers; particularly important among them were Princess Pauline Metternich, the wife of the Austrian ambassador, and the Countess di Castiglione, wife of the Italian ambassador.

In the United States, Harriet Lane was the first woman titled "First Lady," even though she was not married to the president. Harriet served as the official White House hostess for her bachelor uncle, James Buchanan, during his presidency of 1857–1861. Earlier, during Buchanan's time as a senator and then Secretary of State, Harriet was befriended and mentored by a former president's wife (and fashion leader), Dolley Madison. When Buchanan was appointed minister to the Court of St. James in 1853, Harriet accompanied her uncle to London where she earned the favor of Queen Victoria, and traveled to Paris to procure a wardrobe befitting her

Franz Xaver Winterhalter's 1855 painting *The Empress Eugénie Surrounded by Her Ladies in Waiting* depicts the tulle fabric, wide necklines, and extremely full skirts fashionable at the French court.

THE COUNTESS DI CASTIGLIONE

Virginia Oldoini, Countess di Castiglione (1837–1899), was an Italian aristocrat at the court of Emperor Napoleon III. She became notorious for her affair with the emperor, and for her passion for Italian independence and unification. She was a femme fatale of great fascination to the press, and her appearances at court masquerades were legendary. Prior to arriving in Paris, the countess was celebrated in Turin, where she and her husband, Francesco Verasis, Count di Castiglione, were presented at the court of Vittorio Emanuele II. Realizing her potential, the Italian prime minister sent the Castigliones to Paris in 1855, where the countess started to advocate for the cause of Italy – and became involved with Napoleon III. French society shunned the countess after Italian men attempted to assassinate the emperor as he was departing her home one night, and she left France. She returned to Paris in 1863 when she re-entered the court and appeared at a fancy dress ball at the Tuileries dressed as the "Queen of Etruria," emphasizing her role in the liberation of Italy. Her striking costume was slit from the hem up the side and revealed glimpses of her bare leg underneath; her loose mane of hair added to her wild appearance. Although she was not a style setter in the league of Empress Eugénie or Elisabeth of Austria, her lavish clothes were celebrated; she was typically dressed by Mme. Roger, a popular dressmaker of the day. The countess is perhaps even more memorable for her ornate hairstyles and for frequently coloring her hair.

Fascinated by photography and enamored with her own beauty, she developed an obsession for sitting for the camera. Beginning in 1856, she collaborated with photographer Pierre-Louis Pierson, often acting as her own stylist and supervising the retouching and alteration of the photographs. Together they experimented with new directions for both the camera and the pose, even creating a series of rather scandalous images of her feet and legs. Consciously documenting her appearance for posterity, she understood the power of photography as a means of manipulating her image as a celebrity. In the 21st century, this idea is taken for granted, but in her time it was groundbreaking.

Mocking her own vanity, the Countess di Castiglione, c. 1865, coyly plays with her reflected image.

diplomatic obligations. When he was elected president in 1856, Buchanan brought Harriet back to Washington to serve as White House hostess. Soon she was referred to as "America's First Lady." She encouraged eveningwear styles with a wide off-the-shoulder neckline and a décolletage cut low for America at that time.

A new style setter emerged in 1863 when Alexandra of Denmark married Edward, Prince of Wales. Tall and slender, Alexandra contrasted with the rather stocky family into which she married. Her influence on fashion was significant and would extend through the following decades. Soon after her marriage to Edward, an "Alexandra" jacket (a precursor of later tailored styles) was a fashion item, one of many fashions she encouraged. Between her marriage in 1863 and the spring of 1871, Alexandra had six children, and her pregnancies reduced her place in the spotlight. But the birth of her sixth child – and her return to more society exposure – coincided with the end of the Second Empire. During the years following the Franco-Prussian War, the Paris fashion industry rebounded, but the new Third Republic did not provide the fashionable world with an elegant empress to emulate. As a result, many looked to Britain and greatly magnified Alexandra's role in fashion during the 1870s and 1880s. Self-conscious about a scar at the front of her neck, Alexandra popularized chokers that not only covered the scar, but flattered her long, slender neck. Her chokers were frequently black velvet ribbon, but soon included jeweled collars and her signature pearls.

Above For her obligations as White House hostess for her uncle, President James Buchanan, Harriet Lane (shown here in her inaugural gown in 1857) impressed Washington society with her wardrobe procured in Paris.

Right Style setter Frances Folsom Cleveland (the much younger wife of President Grover Cleveland) is seen here c. 1886 in an evening gown typical of her elegant fashion sense.

Photographed by James Russell & Sons in 1876, Alexandra, Princess of Wales, wears a tailored style for outdoor activity, one of many fashions that she helped popularize. The casual appeal of the handkerchief in her pocket attests to the ensemble's emphasis on practicality over artifice.

The term "Professional Beauty" – a woman famous purely for her physical charms – coincided with the development of photography and the demand for *cartes de visite* and cabinet photographs of well-dressed, beautiful women. The popularity of the "PBs" (as the plural was frequently abbreviated) was also encouraged by the Prince of Wales and idle, wealthy men of his circle. The PBs were not aristocratic ladies of the court, but typically actresses, wives of wealthy merchants, and mistresses of nobles. Perhaps the most notable of these ladies was Lillie Langtry. Born Emilie Le Breton on the island of Jersey, she married Edward Langtry in 1874, and the couple took up residence in the Belgravia area of London. She debuted in London society while in mourning for a close relative, wearing a simple black dress that became her trademark look for some time. Her marriage proved unhappy and she soon caught the eye of the Prince of Wales and became his mistress. The voluptuous Lillie contrasted with the lithe Alexandra. On account of her birthplace, she was nicknamed the "Jersey Lily" and was immortalized holding a lily in her portrait by the Pre-Raphaelite painter John Everett Millais. She was also a pioneer in the arena of public image and probably the first celebrity product model in history, notable for endorsing Pears soap, and a cleverly designed collapsible bustle that became known as the "Langtry Bustle." Falling into dismal financial straits in 1880, Lillie embarked on a career as an actress. Her stage clothing was obsessively documented in the fashion press and she frequently appeared in gowns designed by Parisian dressmakers. Her celebrity extended to the United States where she toured as an actress and continued her product endorsements.

Upon her marriage to sitting President Grover Cleveland on June 2, 1886, twenty-two-year-old Frances Folsom became the youngest First Lady in American history. Tall and beautiful, the Buffalo native became an instant sensation: her image filled magazines, fan mail inundated the White House, and her style – including even her facial expressions in photographs – was enthusiastically copied. "Frank" (or "Frankie"), as she was nicknamed, married Cleveland, a friend of her family, soon after she completed college. The wedding in the White House had a small guest list, but was widely publicized. The bride wore a dress from the House of Worth. As First Lady, Frances kept a simple hairstyle, and when she shaved the back of her neck to create a cleaner line and better highlight her chignon, women did their own hair "à la Cleveland." *Carte de visite* reproductions of her photograph were very popular, and her portrait image was used (without permission) to endorse a wide range of products.

One of the best known of the "Professional Beauties" – and sometime mistress of the future King Edward VII – Lillie Langtry is shown here reclining in an opulent gown from the House of Worth, c. 1888.

Opposite left A plate from *Graham's Paris Fashions* features eveningwear of the early 1850s. 18th-century revival influence is seen in the overskirt effect of the yellow dress while the tiered style of the white gown was a popular fashion for several years. For evening, women accented their center-parted hairstyles with flowers and ribbons, and carried folding fans.

Opposite center An 1857 fashion plate from *Magasin des Demoiselles* shows daywear ensembles, both with jacket bodices and *basquins*, pagoda sleeves, and white *engageantes*. Both women wear indoor bonnet styles, and the child's dress reflects the influence of adult fashion.

Opposite right Two day dresses, c. 1855, from the Metropolitan Museum of Art. Both have pagoda sleeves and are made of cotton mousseline, one printed à la disposition (left) and the other featuring a prominent paisley motif (right).

The Elements of Women's Fashion, 1850s and 1860s

The first layer of clothing for the well-dressed woman included drawers and chemise. The corset, worn over a chemise, provided the defined waist, well-supported bust and curved hipline necessary for a fashionable figure, but was also considered essential for good posture. Corsets were stiffened with materials that ranged from wood to bone to metal and extended from the breasts to just below the waist. The corset cover (a lightweight sleeveless garment) was worn over the corset. On top of this, one or more petticoats were worn. Women wore a wrapper for breakfast and the morning hours at home.

As the 1850s opened, the silhouette consisted of a bell-shaped skirt, attached to a fitted bodice that ended in a slight point center front. Colors, fabrics, trims, and dressmaker details were more opulent than in the 1840s. Fashionable women often had interchangeable bodices created from the same fabric as one skirt, to multipurpose the dress for different occasions: one modest for daytime formal wear or dinner and another, short-sleeved and décolleté, for evening formal events, such as opera and balls. Some women ordered three bodices, for even more specifically delineated usage. As the fashionable large skirts required large amounts of fabric, this was an economical practice and may also have been influenced by packing for travel. Bodices showed a great variety of details of cut and decoration. The "jacket bodice" became popular, simulating a jacket over a blouse. This was achieved with a chemisette at the center front and sometimes with a mock man-styled waistcoat. It was often styled with large peplums, called *basques* or *basquins*. Bodices often showed faux yoke details with self appliqué or trim, and contrasting trim was very popular. Bodices often had center front openings with decorative buttons, which were frequently anchored in place by split pins that allowed the wearer to change the buttons quickly. Sleeves ranged from the prim straight style of the 1840s to full flared "pagoda" sleeves and many other variations. By the 1850s, *engageantes* were sometimes quite full and frilled. The "Marie" sleeve, with its multiple puffs and a ruffled flounce at the wrist, was also popular. For evening, the sleeves were typically small puffs, and the bodice cut to the shoulder points or off the shoulder. As the 1850s progressed, the evening neckline became a wide, usually shallow V shape and cleavage was sometimes exposed, and often an applied bertha collar was added. *Canezous* (soft garments for the upper body, including chemisettes, unstructured lace and mousseline jackets, and dickeys) were used to augment both day and evening bodices.

The skirt was created with panels of fabric gathered at the waist, usually with shirring or cartridge pleats. A trend for flounces on the skirt was usually seen as three large tiers, or sometimes in groups of small ruffles, or also a cluster of smaller flounces toward the hem. As the decade progressed, skirts became fuller and additional layers of petticoat were required to maintain the silhouette, leading to other solutions to support the shape. Woven horsehair (known in French as *crin*) was often used as skirt lining, and stiff horsehair petticoats called *jupons de crinoline* or *jupes de crin* were used to create a fuller silhouette. Petticoats fully lined with horsehair, and petticoats with horizontal strips of horsehair, were the beginning of what would become a hooped undersupport.

This hooped understructure – the cage crinoline – was introduced around 1855. The term crinoline to describe a frame hoop skirt developed from the *jupon de crinoline* style petticoat. The new structure was actually sold with a variety of names including "spring skirt," "hooped petticoat," "skeleton skirt," and, in reference to the empress, even the "Parisian Eugenie Jupon Skeleton." The exact origin of the hoop skirt is not clear, but the fashion probably began in France, though it was promptly adopted elsewhere. Some accounts tell of Eugénie wearing the crinoline at a diplomatic visit to Windsor Castle, and of its enthusiastic reception by the British court. Numerous patent applications in the United States demonstrate the enthusiasm for the cage crinoline there. While some versions used stiffened rope, caning, or whalebone to form the hoops, the newly invented flexible steel was the most common as well as

INTERPRETATIONS OF THE CRINOLINE

When it was in fashion, in addition to countless cartoons lampooning the style, the cage crinoline was nicknamed the "birdcage skirt," mocking its shape but also commenting on the caged state of the woman wearing it. Since its time, fashion historians and theorists have offered a variety of interpretations of the crinoline and its place in a larger cultural context. C. Willett Cunnington, writing in the 1930s, saw it as an expression of the women's rights movement: women were now "determined to occupy a larger space in the world." James Laver, in 1968, offered a few different insights. First, he interpreted the vessel-like shape of the crinoline as a mark of female fertility and linked it to population growth in England, epitomized by the family values of Victoria, herself the mother of nine children. Laver also noted that the crinoline symbolized the "supposed unapproachability of women"; the size of the skirt kept men at arm's length. But, he further suggests, this symbolic barrier was "a hollow sham"; the crinoline was "an instrument of seduction" with its swinging motion in a "constant state of agitation." Teresa Riordan in her 2004 book *Inventing Beauty* compared the crinoline to the dome of the United States Capitol that was constructed during renovations to the building during the mid-1850s. Images of the dome in partial state were widely circulated and "… what did the undressed iron dome look like? Exactly like a gigantic hoop skirt, hovering over the national seat of the American government." Riordan even asserts that the images of the partially constructed dome may have contributed to the idea of the cage crinoline.

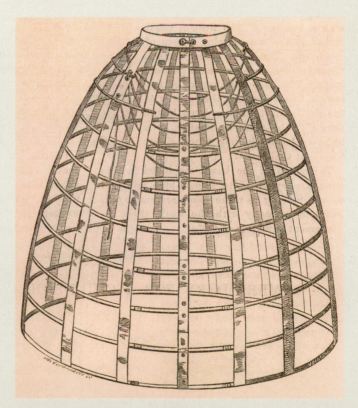

The structure of the cage crinoline clearly delineated by an advertisement for Douglas & Sherwood in *Godey's Lady's Book*, 1858.

the most technologically progressive material. There were two typical constructions of the cage crinoline: one style was created by suspending the hoops from fabric tapes attached to a waistband, and the other was a fabric petticoat with casings that held the hoops in place. On occasion, suspenders were worn to transfer the weight of the hoops from the waist to the shoulders. Sometimes flounces or a row of quilting finished the edge to soften the hard line created by the bottom hoop. A woman typically wore a lightweight petticoat over the crinoline to minimize the ridges, and sometimes a small petticoat was worn underneath the crinoline to prevent sunlight from revealing the shape of legs through a lightweight dress outdoors. A tip of the crinoline could be shockingly immodest, and drawers or "pantalettes" became essential. But despite concerns of modesty, the crinoline also helped promote an allure for legs and feet. The crinoline was in almost continuous motion, and some movements – such as sitting, climbing stairs, or stepping up into a carriage – offered tantalizing glimpses of a woman's legs. Accordingly, women's fashions placed more emphasis on stockings, often colored and embroidered. The newly revived heeled shoe became even more important and provocative short boots were popular in brightly colored leathers. Sitting in the crinoline posed a challenge, but was accomplished by collapsing up the back of the hoops. Some crinolines had such flexible hoops that advertisements showed a woman sitting directly on them. The crinoline was not universally worn; it was high fashion. Some women of modest means certainly wore the style, as the crinoline was affordable and not reserved for the wealthy, but many women continued to wear multiple petticoats instead. The largest crinolines were reserved for court appearances, balls, and other formal events, with smaller versions worn for day-to-day life.

The crinoline was the object of great derision, as seen in countless satirical cartoons; many newspapers and magazines barely printed one issue without lampooning the style. Contemporary accounts described the crinoline as jerky and machine-like, because the flexible steel hoops made a slight mechanical, metallic noise as a woman walked. The crinoline was in one way a definite improvement over heavy layers of petticoats, but it was also awkward, inconvenient, and very dangerous as a woman was not always aware of the space she occupied. Many factories forbade their female employees to wear the cage crinoline to work as women could be caught in machinery, and crinolines were sometimes tangled in the wheels of carriages. But fire was the primary hazard, as a woman could easily back into a fireplace or jostle a small table and tip over a burning candle. This was compounded by the flammability of fabrics, and the air under the skirt that encouraged fire to rapidly engulf a dress. Frances Appleton Longfellow, the wife of American poet William Wadsworth Longfellow, died of burns sustained when her crinoline-supported skirt caught fire.

During the late 1850s, a new dress construction emerged in which the customary bodice and skirt division was replaced by a cut that used continuous panels from shoulder to hem with no waistlines. Various terms including *robe Gabrielle* and "Isabeau style" were appearing in the fashion press by 1859 to designate this style, eventually called *robe en princesse* or princess style. Dresses of this type were sometimes loosely fitted, and intended for some measure of physical activity, falling into the category known as walking costumes. Some examples in fashion plates and photographs displayed details such as military-inspired plastron panels, or a row of buttons. The fullness of the skirt was achieved with the shaping of the princess seams, and sometime inverted box pleats. Princess-line construction had significant impact on fashions in the next few years, and the term would also eventually be used to describe bodices with similar vertical seaming.

By the mid-1860s some fashionable women gave up the crinoline, possibly because it was now mass-produced and no longer the latest word in fashion. Other women wore new shapes of crinoline, as it moved toward the back and became smaller, and some examples arched a bit over the buttocks. With the diminution of the crinoline came a short-lived fashion for a raised waist, and for a brief time around 1867, the excesses of the large skirt and Second Empire exaggerations were countered

ENCORE UNE CRINOLINE !!!!!

Above left A fashion plate from *La Mode Illustrée*, 1867, shows the influence of the Moyen Age revival taste on high fashion, with details such as pendant sleeves and dagged edges. The new, smaller crinoline shape creates a leaner silhouette.

Above right The relative simplicity of some late 1860s fashions is exemplified by this silk taffeta afternoon dress from the collection of the McCord Museum of Canadian History.

with an elegant simplicity. Typically, gored skirts created a graceful A-line shape, and trim was usually subtle and restrained. But soon a revivalist sensibility returned and both day and evening styles reflected strong influences from the 18th century as polonaise skirt styles, often over contrasting underskirts, were popular. Extra padding on the buttocks, sometimes referred to as "dress improvers," combined with skirt fullness gathered and draped to the back, formed a decisive enhancement of the derrière. And as the back gained importance, some underskirts were "half-crinolines," with the hoops going only from side to side around the back, with curved shaping at the top.

Court dress retained the traditional trains, fashionable in France since the First Empire, and popular in Great Britain, Austria, and throughout Europe. White was commonly worn by young ladies making their debut at court, and in fact some young women restyled their wedding gowns for court presentations. For her wedding to Edward, Prince of Wales, in 1863, Princess Alexandra followed the example her mother-in-law, Victoria, had set twenty-three years earlier. Her white satin dress was flounced with lace and tulle and heavily decorated with orange blossoms, which also adorned her hair. Such fabrics were typical for brides, although some wedding gowns were made of fine cotton mousseline. Alexandra's bridesmaids also wore white tulle, common for bridesmaids at the time, with floral circlets on their heads. Often bridesmaids wore white veils like those worn by brides.

Fitted and semi-fitted jackets and coats in a variety of lengths went by such names as *paletot*, *pardessus*, and *pelisse*. Mantles were loosely fitted coats with wide bodies and wide sleeves, and were frequently thigh to knee length. Circular cloaks called "talma cloaks" were worn, and variations on these styles received hybrid names such as "pelisse-mantle" or "talma-mantle." A fancy cloak for formal evening dress in luxurious fabric was called *sortie de bal*. Paisley shawls – the genuine Indian versions, those made in France, and the copies woven in Paisley, Scotland – remained highly desirable accessories through the 1860s. Other fashionable shawls were made of silk crepe or lace; a triangular shape was preferred.

Gloves were essential for leaving the house. Reticules were carried, and for daytime, decorative detachable pockets were attached to waistbands. The woman of the house

often wore a chatelaine, a collection of keys, small tools, and even sometimes a small notebook hung stylishly from chains attached to the waistband. A parasol was an essential accessory for a lady when outdoors in the sunshine. The poke bonnet was still in fashion during the 1850s, but other less concealing styles of hats became fashionable. Hats were often worn further back to show more of the face and hair. Soft cloth bonnets were sometimes worn indoors during daytime hours. Center parts of the hair continued from the 1840s but with less severity, and during the course of the decade were sometimes replaced and the hair swept back. Side curls were popular early on but soon a neater waved style prevailed. Chignons in the back were sometimes contained in snoods, and this style continued into the 1860s. Following the symmetrical lines of the hairstyles, ribbon bows decorated either side of the head, often combined with small bouquets of flowers.

Matched sets of evening jewelry completed the highly embellished look for formal dressing. The expanse of skin exposed by evening décolletage provided a setting for fine jewelry as society women became display mannequins exhibiting the extent of their husbands' fortunes. Decorative combs and other hair ornaments were frequently added for evening. Evening gloves or mitts were often made of lace or net. Formal dress during the early 1850s called for short evening gloves, leaving an expanse of naked arm between the short sleeve and the glove. A variety of decorative fans were popular with evening dress.

The Elements of Women's Fashion, 1870s and 1880s

With the Franco-Prussian War and the end of the Second Empire, the fashion trade in France came to a standstill and Paris' domination of fashion was threatened. But after the war the garment industry of Paris was booming once again; couture not only survived the crisis, it grew. With couture houses such as Worth, Pingat, Laferrière, and Félix at its pinnacle, Paris was the fashion center of not only Europe, but of the Western world. By 1870 a new silhouette had crystallized and it held for a few years. Corsetry continued to develop and the waist and torso became more defined, and another understructure – the bustle – became the mode. The following two decades of women's fashion were defined by the bustle: its presence, its absence, its return, and ultimately its fall from favor. High fashion, depicted in fashion plates and photographs, showed a delineation of three phases: a first bustle period, the cuirasse bodice silhouette, and a second bustle period. Vernacular fashions of the time showed these same phases, but the distinctions were more subtle.

The range of bustle undersupports in use at the time was wide and varied. Different styles and shapes went by a number of different names, often trade names. The term "dress improver" continued to be used frequently, as were *tournure*, *panier crinoline*, and *jupon*. The support was constructed in a variety of ways including pads on fabric tapes tied around the waist or attached to petticoats, graduated half-rings of sprung steel, or rows of horsehair ruffles attached over the buttocks and sometimes down the back of the petticoat. Some small cage crinolines were still worn shaped into the form of the new silhouette. Pads made of wire braided into a net were promoted as healthy alternatives as the open work of the structure allowed air to pass through, eliminating the discomfort of an overheated backside.

The combination, an all-in-one piece that combined pantalettes and chemise, usually of cotton or linen, was introduced to lingerie. Another new development in lingerie and loungewear was the tea gown, commonly worn in the afternoon hours (during tea time) while a lady took a break from her corset, but might receive callers. Rich in trimmings and dressmaker detail, the tea gown combined the ease of a wrapper with the elegance of eveningwear. The notable couture houses showed this new style alongside their other offerings of evening gowns and afternoon toilettes.

The first bustle period, which continued until about 1877, was characterized by an emphasis on femininity in fashion. The polonaise-style overskirt was ubiquitous, giving women a puffy – almost fluffy – effect to the hips and buttocks. Bows and fabric flowers were common decorative details, and ruching and ruffles in great profusion

Below left By 1870, the cage crinoline had been replaced by a new understructure that emphasized the buttocks: the bustle. This advertisement for the "Alaska Down Bustle" from 1877 also shows a camisole, corset, and petticoat.

Below right A promenade dress from the Los Angeles County Museum of Art, of violet-colored silk taffeta, decorated with pleated self trim and silk macramé fringe, provides a subtle example of the new silhouette of the early 1870s.

were typical. While the pastels typical of the Second Empire continued, more vibrant colors were featured as well. Dresses were often created in contrasting shades of the same color; however, bold contrasts of color, texture, and pattern were often used in a single ensemble. Necklines changed from previous years as a slight V shape became an option for daytime. These V necklines were usually shallow, but sometimes deeper and filled in with ruffles or a fichu. Square necklines were given a similar treatment. Daytime sleeves were usually long, but three-quarter lengths were also common. Evening dresses also featured a variety of sleeves and necklines, including revealing off-the-shoulder and sleeveless styles.

As the decade wore on, the size of the bustle decreased, and by 1878 a new silhouette had solidified of which the most important feature was the utilization of vertical seamed construction in the princess style. The entire silhouette was influenced by the bodice, which elongated to a dropped waist, often descending as far as the hip, then often becoming more exaggerated to the knee, and then to the floor. At floor length, the bodice became a dress, and a new version of the *robe en princesse* was created, now sleek and fitted. Although the dress was molded to the figure, the waist was often left unaccented by structural or design details such as seaming, belts, or sashes. As the bustle decreased in size and the dress became more fitted, skirt fullness was concentrated toward the floor, and the dresses often fanned out into dramatic fishtails. Overskirt drapery was still sometimes seen, but with far less fullness and puffiness. Corsetry was especially important to this style; the hip area was molded as well to maintain the fashionable line. The petticoat, often eliminated because of the tight fit through the hips, was replaced by tiers of lingerie ruffles that attached to the inside bottom of the skirt and could be detached for easy cleaning. Silhouettes for evening were essentially the same as those for day and the modes for ruffles

James Tissot's *Too Early* (1873) typifies the styles of the first bustle period, with feminine details and profusion of ruffles. The fashion for a ribbon tied around the neck has been attributed to Alexandra, Princess of Wales.

Above Parisian fashions, as illustrated in *Peterson's Magazine* in July 1880, show a variety of womenswear styles from the years between the two bustle periods.

Opposite left A cover image from *Harper's Bazar*, August 17, 1877, depicts a "seaside dress"; its cuirasse form with smooth fit through the body utilizes the princess line, and is cut continuously across the waist, emphasizing a tight fit through the hips that flares into the full hem. Dust ruffles attached to the inside of the skirt finish the ensemble along with requisite accessories such as a parasol and decorated hat.

Opposite right A fashion plate from *La Mode Illustrée* in 1887 features two women in toilettes typical of the second bustle period, with their striking geometric form and strong contrasts.

Opposite bottom The variety of women's footwear needed for a fashionable wardrobe – including riding boots – is depicted in this illustration from *Harper's Bazar*, May 25, 1889.

and bows continued, as did the sleeve and neckline shapes. Asymmetry, something not frequently seen in the 19th century, was popular both day and night. Daytime decoration included geometric inspiration, and masculine and military influence. Colors were often darker than in the previous years, with plaids popular. Hems were sometimes accordion-pleated in a style called "kilting."

The sleek elegance of this "cuirasse" style lasted only a few years. By 1882 a little more drapery had asserted itself over the hips and began to inflate once again, and during 1883 and 1884, the bustle was back – and larger than before. Many of the elements of this second bustle period stood in contrast to the first period. The bustle shape was rigid, like a shelf projecting out of the back of the woman at a ninety-degree angle. The color story continued along the darker lines of the cuirasse period, although summertime modes were often white with black or blue trim in the style of sailor uniforms. Trains at the backs of skirts were now almost nonexistent, appearing only in the most formal evening or court dress. Often hems were off the floor. Pleats and pleated ruffles replaced the gathered ruffles previously popular.

The fit of the cuirasse bodice corresponded to the tailoring techniques used in the emerging "tailor-made" costume. Derived from menswear and equestrian styles, the newly popular jacket and skirt combination was referred to as a tailor-made; the designs of John Redfern advanced the style. Princess Alexandra preferred the tailor-made instead of typical toilettes for morning attire as its practicality suited her sense of stylish simplicity. Masculine aspects of clothing applied not just to the newly popular tailor-made costumes but to toilettes as well. Military and menswear influence was suggested by trim and details including epaulette-like tabs (not always on the shoulders) and decorative cockades. Though bodice and skirt combinations typically replaced princess-line dresses, the bodice was molded and longer and unbroken across the waist, continuing the cuirasse look. But during 1888 and 1889 the bustle once again went out of fashion and *The Daily Telegraph* in London documented its demise in florid terms: "Ladies' dress improvers are, according to an unwritten law

which is said to have been lately promulgated in the academics of fashion, to be rigidly relegated in future to the limbo of relics of the past."[2] By the end of the 1880s, a softer look had begun, often still incorporating an underskirt and overskirt combination. Sleeves developed a slight puff at the sleeve cap, and the seeds of the 1890s silhouette were sown.

Outerwear styles were largely unchanged from the previous decades and many of the same terms applied, such as *paletot*, *pelisse*, *mantelette*. But, significantly, more fitted jackets and coats developed in relation to the silhouette. The dolman was a jacket that was cut or gathered up in the back to accommodate the bustle shape, often hanging down longer in front. A decorative detail was often placed at the small of the

back to highlight the silhouette. It was popular in both day and evening forms, and versions with longer backs were common during the cuirasse period. The development of outerwear styles, including "waterproofs" and more tailored coats, offered practical options to the dressier coats and cloaks. The Ulster, a long coat, particularly popular during the lean cuirasse silhouette period, incorporated men's tailoring techniques; the long clean lines of princess-line construction were utilized, and the Ulster frequently had detachable shoulder capes.

Hats in a wide variety of shapes were in vogue throughout these years. Bonnets with small brims were worn toward the back of the head, the brims sticking up. Masculine inspiration also applied to hats. Some were shaped like derbys or top hats. A variation on the top hat shape quite popular during the second bustle period put the crown at a sharp angle, giving the look of an inverted flowerpot. Although masculine in inspiration, women's hats were often decorated with flowers and frills. Hair styling, too, was playful as curls of hair were worn cascading down, mirroring the ornate drapery of the skirts. Sometimes bangs were cut and curled into a little mop. Shoes continued along the same lines as in earlier decades. The popular Louis heel became slightly higher and boots more sleekly fitted through the ankle. Long gloves offset the short-sleeved and sleeveless styles for evening.

Designers and Dressmakers

Charles Frederick Worth (1825–1895) was born in England in 1825. After working in a fabric and drapery business in London, he arrived in Paris in 1846 and within two years was working at Gagelin-Opigez et Cie. Gagelin-Opigez was a high-quality, diverse apparel business dealing in fine fabrics, women's accessories, and *confection* (ready-mades), and had expanded into made-to-measure dressmaking. The company was awarded a medal for dressmaking at the 1851 Crystal Palace Exhibition in London and reportedly supplied some of the fabrics used in Empress Eugénie's trousseau in 1853. During these years, Worth may have designed dresses under their house label. At the 1855 Exposition Universelle, a court train from Gagelin-Opigez, designed by Worth, won the first class medal in its category. Worth married Marie Vernet, a model at the store, and designed dresses for her to showcase his skills. Eventually Worth left Gagelin-Opigez and went into business with a partner, Otto Gustave Bobergh, who probably provided most of the capital and business management. The two set up shop together under the label "Worth et Bobergh" at 7 rue de la Paix. Marie Worth, working alongside her husband and Bobergh, was also a significant contributor to the business in its early years. Worth et Bobergh was an emporium that, in addition to offering custom dressmaking, sold fabrics, shawls, and *confection*.

Much of the mythology of Worth's early years comes from the memoirs of Princess Pauline Metternich. She arrived in Paris in 1859 with her husband Prince Richard von Metternich, the ambassador from Austria. Pauline soon became a fixture at the court and included in Eugénie's closest circle. According to the princess, Madame Marie Worth paid a call with a folio of sketches from the house and the princess ordered two dresses, one of which she wore shortly thereafter to a ball at the Tuileries Palace:

> I wore my Worth dress, and can say with truth that I have never seen a more beautiful gown, or one that fitted more beautifully. It was made of white tulle strewn with tiny silver discs (a fashion which, just then, was at its height), and trimmed with crimson-hearted daisies that nestled among little tufts of feathery grass; these flowers were all veiled in tulle. A broad white satin sash was folded round my waist.[3]

According to Metternich's account, Eugénie instantly noticed her gown, and was so impressed that she summoned Worth to the palace the following morning and their collaboration began, thus catapulting Charles Frederick Worth to success.

This legend created by Metternich's retrospective account (and reinforced by Worth's son's later memoirs) is contradicted by other factors. Worth does not receive important mention in the French fashion press prior to 1863. Furthermore, Worth et Bobergh did not use the designation "*Breveté de S. M. l'Impératrice*" until 1865, indicating the royal warrant of Empress Eugénie was granted that year.[4]

Nonetheless, Worth et Bobergh eventually became responsible for much of Eugénie's wardrobe, including court dress, eveningwear, and "fancy dress," and the rapidly growing business gained the patronage of many other women of the French court. Worth's designs for Eugénie reinforced national pride, as they not only showcased the work of the Paris dressmaking industry but also promoted French luxury textiles from Lyons.

Worth was nicknamed a "man milliner," a term for a fastidious man in the fashion business. Part of Worth's appeal was his novelty; his English-accented French was considered charming, and his luxurious showroom was decorated as an elegant court salon and staffed by well-dressed young men with similar English accents. The house developed an impressive list of clients through the 1860s including Elisabeth of Austria

EMPRESS ELISABETH OF AUSTRIA

Empress of Austria and Queen of Hungary, Elisabeth was one of the most significant fashion setters of the 19th century. An 1865 Winterhalter portrait of Elisabeth in an exquisite tulle gown attributed to Worth conveys an image of elegance and serene beauty. Her actual life story, however, was not the fairy tale one might assume from the painting.

"Sisi" grew up a duchess in Bavaria in a setting far from the rigid manners of court. Her older sister was originally intended to be the wife of their first cousin, Franz Joseph, Emperor of Austria, but he cast his sights on Elisabeth. He had already been emperor for six years when they were married in 1854; she was just sixteen, and he twenty-four. Her tiered and embroidered white moiré wedding dress was reproduced in the French fashion periodical *L'Iris*. The marriage quickly became unhappy, in part because of his mother, Archduchess Sophie, who continually criticized Elisabeth. Elisabeth had not been given a sophisticated education; she was unprepared for Viennese society and her ignorance of protocol made her unpopular with the aristocracy.

Eventually, her dislike for court and her unhappy marriage led her to make few public appearances. She often left Vienna, usually under the pretense of seeking relief from some illness, real or imagined. The press frequently commented on her absences, her travels without her husband, and her illnesses and their odd cures. Rumors of mental illness were fueled by the eccentricities of her cousin Ludwig II of Bavaria, implying that madness ran in the family. Tall and slender with a very small waist, Elisabeth became obsessed with her appearance, exercised compulsively, and developed an eating disorder. An avid horsewoman, she set styles in equestrian wear. She was famous for her dark and wavy hair, so long that it came down to her knees. Other women throughout Europe copied her large, full chignons, but most needed the addition of hairpieces to simulate the volume of Elisabeth's hair.

Despite her dislike for court life her glamour was significant and helped establish the Austrian court as a rival to Second Empire France. Even Empress Eugénie, her greatest competitor as a fashion icon in Europe, noted Elisabeth's remarkable beauty. Elisabeth was a Worth customer but was often dressed domestically by clothiers within the empire. She promoted nationalistic and regional styles of dress. At an official court reception the night before her wedding she wore a white organdy dress embroidered in green and gold metallic thread with Arabic text from the Qur'an, an excellent example of "Ottoman" influence in fashion. She generated much popularity on a visit to the Tyrol by wearing clothes inspired by traditional dress of the region. When Franz Joseph and Elisabeth were crowned King and Queen of Hungary in 1867 (an act that recognized political equality for Hungary within the empire) she wore a Worth creation in the style of the Hungarian gala costume, white with silver embroidery, pearl details, and a black velvet bodice. She loved the Hungarians, and she was as popular in Budapest as she was disliked in Vienna. Elisabeth frequently retreated to her Hungarian castle where, as she said, "I am not continually under a microscope and where I can fancy that I am a woman like all others, and not some extraordinary insect created for the malicious investigations and observations of the public."[5]

Many aspects of Elisabeth's life – unhappy marriage, strained relationship with her mother-in-law, eating disorder, and media fascination – anticipate the life of a royal style icon of the late 20th century, Diana, Princess of Wales. Elisabeth came to a tragic end when she was assassinated by an Italian anarchist on September 10, 1898.

Empress Elisabeth of Austria, wearing the Charles Frederick Worth gown created for her coronation as Queen of Hungary, June 8, 1867.

and Louise, Queen of Norway and Sweden. Worth also dressed some of the glamorous *demimondaines* of Paris, and gained the custom of nouveau riche Americans, including Isabella Stewart Gardner. Worth et Bobergh closed its doors during the Franco-Prussian War, but Worth, without Bobergh, reorganized and continued designing into the following decades.

The business operated after the war as the **House of Worth**, and Worth's sons Gaston (1853–1924) and Jean-Philippe (1856–1926) eventually joined their father's business. Gaston was the businessman, while Jean-Philippe was creative, becoming the lead designer of the house when his father retired around 1889–1890. These were years of great success for the House of Worth. The Worth men were influential in the development of Le Chambre Syndicale de la Haute Couture Parisienne, founded in 1868. Gaston served as its president from 1885 to 1887. The association set standards for the couture business and was concerned with issues of design piracy. During this period Charles Frederick Worth affected an "artistic" look for himself, purportedly wearing a loose velvet dressing gown and soft beret even for business; his self-styling helped create the image of the designer as distinct from the dressmaker.

Emile Pingat (1820–1901) began his business at roughly the same time as Charles Frederick Worth. Although a smaller operation, his house created many fashionable toilettes worn at society and court soirées, including tulle gowns that rivaled those from Worth et Bobergh. Pingat too counted notable European aristocracy and wealthy Americans among his discerning customers. Many of them revered Pingat's creations as the finest and most elegant available at any house in Paris, made with unsurpassed construction technique. His work often incorporated elements of historic and orientalist inspiration.

In these years several other businesses were well established and vital to the Paris fashion industry. **Maison Félix** began operation in the 1860s and the young designer probably provided some of Empress Eugénie's wardrobe and that of other ladies of the French court. "Even in the palmiest days of Worth ... the house of M. Felix could boast a proud supremacy. Its list of patrons included ... the most beautiful women among royalty and the leaders of fashion on both sides of the Atlantic."[6] Félix was a particular favorite with well-dressed women of the stage, and his clients included Lillie Langtry, Ellen Terry, and operatic star Sybil Sanderson. He was known for his quality and for his high prices. **Madeleine Laferrière** (c. 1825–c. 1900), whose business began mid-century, was recognized for her fine workmanship. Her establishment also contributed to the wardrobe of Empress Eugénie, and her clientele included not only women of the court, but also famous courtesans and actresses, who often sought her expertise for stage costumes. She is credited with having created many costumes for actress Sarah Bernhardt, and the business grew notably during these decades. Dressmakers **Mlle. Palmyre**, **Mme. Vignon**, and **Mme. Roger** all contributed to the trousseau or wardrobe of Empress Eugénie, and were important for other ladies of society. Milliner **Caroline Reboux** created sought-after hats for an elite clientele that included Eugénie.

The house of **Doucet** had already played an important role in fashion in Paris for several decades. Founded in the early years of the 19th century, Doucet was also a multi-generational family business that specialized in many areas of clothing, particularly lingerie, accessories, and men's furnishings. Napoleon III and other European royalty favored Doucet's shirts. Jacques Doucet (1853–1929) joined the business during the 1870s and in the following years the house of Doucet grew to include ladies' couture with Jacques as the designer. Jacques transformed the business into one of the leading couture houses of the day.

In England, a drapery house in Cowes on the Isle of Wight, run by **John Redfern** (1820–1895), made the transition into dressmaking during the 1860s. Taking advantage of its proximity to one of Queen Victoria's official residences, and to the lively yachting activities frequented by a wealthy international set, Redfern created both sport and dress clothes for well-dressed women. By the late 1860s Redfern was well established and the empire built by the house over the next few decades ultimately rivaled Worth's in its importance, and had an even greater international presence.

Sailors' uniforms served as inspiration for Redfern for women's seaside and yachting clothes, and became a fashion staple. In addition to ensembles for resort wear and yachting, Redfern was a leader in sports apparel including tennis and equestrian outfits.

Redfern created jersey bodices for tennis and other activities, and both Alexandra and Mrs. Langtry were fundamental to introducing this style. The gradual growth of women's tailor-made ensembles involved fashion trends, royal style setters, sport, and leisure (and the women's rights movement) and Redfern did more to develop and promote this style than any other designer of the time.

Encouraged by the patronage of his elite clientele, Redfern expanded his empire, and a London establishment was opened in 1878, run by Frederick Bosworth Mims. A Paris branch, with Charles Pennington Poynter (1853–1929) at its helm, opened in 1881, and soon Poynter oversaw the opening of other stores in France. Both Mims and Poynter took the name Redfern for public relations purposes. A New York City store on Fifth Avenue and Broadway opened in 1884 with Redfern's son Ernest Arthur as its director. The urban branches sold not only the sport and resort clothes that had secured the firm's reputation, but also Redfern toilettes for afternoon and evening wear. Building on the company's origins in a resort town, branches of **Redfern and Sons** opened in Newport, Rhode Island, and Saratoga Springs, New York. They also did profitable mail-order business.

In addition to procuring fashionable clothing abroad, prominent American women patronized private dressmakers. Born into slavery in Virginia, **Elizabeth Keckly** (1818–1907) was able to purchase her freedom by 1852 and established a dressmaking business in Washington D.C. Her most famous client was First Lady Mary Todd Lincoln and she counted politicians' wives among her customers, including Mrs. Jefferson Davis and Mrs. Robert E. Lee – representing both sides in the years of great tension between North and South.

John Redfern's 1885 designs for the trousseau of Queen Victoria's daughter Princess Beatrice were widely covered by the press on both sides of the Atlantic. Four of the ensembles are shown here as illustrated in *Harper's Bazar*, May 16, 1885.

Fashion Fabrics and Textile Technology

Women's fashion fabrics concentrated on decorative effects. Historic and oriental inspirations were common in patterns and the paisley motif enjoyed continued popularity. Border prints, also known as "à la disposition," especially popular in the 1850s and 1860s, suited the edges of ruffles and pagoda sleeves. Moirés and large-scale brocades were popular in eveningwear, especially when flounces were not used. Bold floral patterns reminiscent of the mid-18th century were also common in evening dresses. Ribbon and fringe, manufactured to coordinate with specific fabrics, were important to the luxurious look of fashion. Passementerie, braid, cording, and ball fringe were used. Taffeta and velvets were popular in both day- and eveningwear. Plaids and stripes were perennial fashion staples. The jacquard loom, introduced at the beginning of the century, was in widespread use. In addition to floral motifs, jacquard-woven patterns featured foliage and feathers, swags and arabesques, often in large scale, by the 1880s. Machines for producing bobbinet had been invented several years earlier, and by the 1850s tulle was essential – used in evening, bridal, and summer formal daytime toilettes. The technology of the net machine allowed the manufacture of machine-made lace; however, handmade lace was still a mark of gentility and pieces of heirloom lace were often picked off of garments to be reused on others. Parisian designers, in particular Worth, enjoyed collaborative relationships with the luxury textile mills of Lyons, France. The textile companies had representatives in Paris and consulting services gathered swatches and trim and ribbon samples from leading manufacturers for distribution to other fashion centers.

Innovations in print and dye technology also had an indelible impact on fashion, especially the development of aniline dye. Prior to this time, dyestuffs were derived from plants, insects, and minerals, some of which were unhealthy, even toxic. Bright green dyes, in particular compounds known as "Scheele's green" and "Paris green,"[7] were based on arsenic and was in wide use for clothing – even hosiery – and paper and silk flowers used to embellish fashionable dresses and decor. Other dyes, including shades of red and dark blue, also contained arsenic, causing illness with symptoms that ranged from skin eruptions to delirium. In 1856, William Perkin, an eighteen-year-old English chemistry student, synthesized a dye from coal tar. The first color available became the most famous shade, a jewel-tone purple that Perkin named "mauveine," eventually shortened to "mauve." Synthesized aniline dyes were colorfast – they would not fade from washing or sunlight – and produced vivid, saturated colors. The mauve dress that Queen Victoria wore to the wedding of her daughter, Victoria, the Princess Royal, was featured in the press and soon England, and the rest of the fashionable world, was caught up in "mauve mania." Cementing its popularity, Empress Eugénie also wore the color. Perkin was eventually knighted for his accomplishments, which furthered the relationship between advances in chemistry and textiles. John Mercer, another English chemist, had already developed "mercerizing," using sodium hydroxide to strengthen and add luster to cotton fibers, and refinements to the mercerizing process continued. As the 20th century approached, the example set by aniline dye and mercerizing led to further advances in textile processing.

The Cult of Mourning

During the mid-19th century, mourning practices became increasingly precise and prescribed. Black armbands and hatbands, worn with dark clothing, became the norm for men. But a highly specific code governed mourning apparel for women, especially widows. The first stage of mourning required dresses that were often literally draped in black crepe. After the initial period, a widow remained in black but could move on to more luxurious fabrics and trim, with black lace,

Because of societal conventions in the Victorian age, mourning clothes were an essential part of women's wardrobes. This example, c. 1865, from the collection of the National Gallery of Victoria in Melbourne, combines black taffeta with a Middle Ages-inspired dagging appliqué in black velvet, and was likely worn for the second stage of mourning.

Top Masquerade balls were so popular that leading fashion magazines featured costume designs for such occasions, with exotic and historic inspiration. *La Mode Illustrée* presented these ensembles in 1864.

Above The "Dolly Varden" fad of the early 1870s (illustrated here on a piece of popular sheet music) was inspired by a Charles Dickens character, and revived styles of the 1780s.

fringe, and jet beading. In the last stage of mourning, the color palette expanded to include shades of gray, purple, lavender, and white. Accessories, jewelry, trim, and dressmaker details were all addressed in mourning conventions. As pearls, bright metals, and gemstones were considered inappropriate, special mourning jewelry was worn and often included the name or image of the deceased. Other pieces of jewelry displayed "relics" of the departed loved one, most often locks of hair. The entire process exceeded two years for a widow, who was typically expected to spend a year and a day in the first stage of mourning dress. Women were advised not to change into the next stage of mourning on the earliest day allowed by the custom, to avoid appearing over-eager to move quickly through the process. Shorter periods of mourning were also prescribed on the death of other relatives. At the death of members of the royal families or heads of state, mourning was imposed at court, and even the general public was expected to participate in "General Mourning" and dress accordingly. Periodicals, advertisements, and catalogs indicated that mourning styles reflected the general movements of fashion. Many dressmakers specialized in mourning clothes, and some stores sold only black goods.

While the Western world at large participated in these customs, they were at their most extreme in Britain. This was certainly true of Victoria herself. Her mother, the Duchess of Kent, and her husband, Prince Albert, died within ten months of one another in 1861. The devastated Victoria would wear black mourning for the rest of her life and some widows followed her example. While few made Victoria's commitment to mourning, many people followed the progression from black to gray and purple. Jay's Mourning Warehouse in London was a prominent purveyor of proper attire. The demand for crepe mourning fabric was a boon to the textile industry in England. The Courtauld Company found great success selling heavily crimped black silk mourning crepe, some of which was even waterproof for outerwear.

In the United States, the Civil War's 600,000 casualties provided the dressmaking industry with countless widows and bereaved mothers, who typically followed customs similar to Britain. During the war years, President and Mary Todd Lincoln lost their eleven-year-old son William from typhoid in 1862, garbing Mrs. Lincoln in mourning for a child for the second time (they had lost another son, Edward, in 1850). Following President Lincoln's assassination in 1865, Mrs. Lincoln (like Victoria) spent the rest of her life in mourning. Not long after the war ended, *Harper's Bazar* published its debut issue in 1867 – illustrating mourning wear on its cover.

Historic and Exotic Influences

Fancy dress was popular from early in Victoria's reign and fashion magazines often included masquerade costumes, including neoclassic, medieval, 18th-century, and orientalist modes. European royalty and nobility were often painted in their masquerade costumes, reinforcing the costumes' importance to fashion. But these tastes were not limited to fancy dress; the interest in historic and exotic modes was strongly reinforced by Paris couture, and these tastes also reflected the historicist and orientalist currents in the arts.

From the early 1850s through the 1880s, 18th-century revival styles were important to women's fashion in some form or another. Open-front skirts with underskirts, bows on the center front of bodices, and 18th-century-style sleeve ruffles were evident. Most notable was the looping up of skirts to reveal underskirts, reviving the polonaise style, and overskirt styles with drapery on each side were named "pannier" after the 18th-century understructure. The "Dolly Varden" costume, a fad of the early 1870s, was inspired by a character from Charles Dickens' novel *Barnaby Rudge*, set in 1780. Though the novel was published in 1841, an illustration of Dolly Varden was among items from Dickens' estate for sale after his death in 1870 and this widely reproduced image promptly inspired the fashion trend. The Dolly Varden look revived the shepherdess style of Marie Antoinette, with a polonaise-style overskirt. It was often made up in a printed cotton fabric similar to the chintzes of the 18th century. A 1780s-style hat, typically of straw, usually completed the ensemble.

Claude Monet's 1876 painting *La Japonaise* depicts his red-haired wife, Camille, in an elaborate formal kimono holding a folding fan, reflecting the taste for Japonisme in the West that followed the establishment of trade with Japan.

In addition to 18th-century influence, classical ideals were seen, especially in jewelry and trimmings in a Greco-Roman mode. In the 1850s and early in the 1860s, it became fashionable to decorate hems with Greek key borders, usually in large scale to match wide, crinoline-supported skirts, and the motif also adorned the edges of pagoda sleeves. The medieval period was also continually revived with pendant sleeves, scalloping, and dagging, often in the form of appliqué. Renaissance style also made contributions, seen in the popularity of heart-shaped bonnets, called "à la Marie Stuart" in reference to the 16th-century queen.

Cashmere paisley shawls had already been in fashion from the early 1800s, but provide a benchmark for Asiatic taste in Western fashion, which also typically included Chinese and Ottoman elements. But Japonisme – the passion for all things Japanese – surpassed the popularity of the Indian-, Chinese-, and Ottoman-inspired styles. Both sexes adopted loosely draped, kimono-inspired dressing gowns for at-home wear (some made in Japan for export markets) and some women had custom-made dresses that combined a fashionable Western silhouette with imported kimono silks. Japanese motifs such as chrysanthemums, cherry blossoms, and irises were popular in textile design and as embroidered embellishment on dresses, and Japanese fans were a common accessory. Japanese style (both real and imagined) had an enormous impact on popular culture. A delegation of seventy samurai who traveled to New York in 1860 caused a sensation – New Yorkers staged a parade and had their photos taken with the exotic visitors. Gilbert and Sullivan's *The Mikado* (1885) used an ersatz Japanese setting and kimono-clad cast to poke fun at the British aristocracy.

European regional dress provided another inspiration. Stylistic features of folk costume, particularly from Central Europe (such as dirndl bodices), found their way into fashionable womenswear and childrenswear. One such example was the Swiss belt (called *corsage suissesse* or *ceinture suissesse*), a wide, shaped and stiffened belt or sash, often made of black velvet, that typically had points at both the top and bottom of the center front, and was usually worn with a skirt and blouse combination. Spain also provided romantic and exotic inspiration as fashionable women adopted lace mantillas, tassel or ball fringe and soutache trim, resembling the decoration on torero jackets. Bolero variations were referred to as "Figaro" jackets, after *The Barber of Seville*, or "senorita" jackets. Spanish inspiration was particularly evident in fashion but also in literature and the performing arts. This taste for Spanish style culminated in 1875 with Georges Bizet's French opera *Carmen*.

The Zouaves, a battalion of Algerians fighting in the French Army, inspired braid-trimmed jackets worn by women and children. Coming from Turkey and Central Asia via the Crimean War, the burnoose, which was a tasseled and hooded cloak, came into fashion in the 1850s. From the Italian wars, the revolutionary leader Giuseppe

Right A boy in a Zouave-style jacket, photographed c. 1865–1868, indicates that the vogue for European national folk costume included childrenswear, and spread to North America.

Far right A fashion plate from *L'Illustrateur des Dames* (c. 1867) shows two dresses with distinctive features: the blue dress at right features asymmetrical details, a decorative apron panel, and a detachable hanging pocket; the apricot-colored dress on the left includes Spanish inspiration in the torero-style trim on the yoke.

A lithograph by Noyce, c. 1850, illustrates Amelia Jenks Bloomer, along with two young women, all wearing her reform-style dresses and loose trousers.

Garibaldi became the most unlikely of fashion icons when full-cut blouses, called Garibaldis, became fashionable. Garibaldi blouses were frequently the vivid red worn by his followers, the Garibaldinis, but were also worn in "magenta" and "solferino" – two vibrant shades of aniline dye named for his battles – and also in white and off-white. A Garibaldi-style pillbox hat also entered the fashion repertoire of women and girls and red Garibaldi jackets trimmed in gold braid came into style. In another fashionable political statement, Italian women wore domestically produced black velvet to *vestire alla lombarda* – dress in the Lombard style – promoting native material rather than wool imported from Austria or Germany.

Dress Reform and Aesthetic Dress

Opposition to current fashion focused on health, hygiene, women's rights, and aesthetics. Advocates of dress reform reacted to the possibly unhealthy effects of corsets, weighty layers of petticoats, and trailing hemlines. In the 1850s, women's rights activists in the United States, led by Elizabeth Smith Miller, Amelia Jenks Bloomer, and Elizabeth Cady Stanton, proposed clothing for women that included pajama-like trousers under a skirt. The ensemble was worn without rigid foundation garments. Bloomer's support of the new look in the feminist journal *The Lily* led to the label "Bloomer Costume" for the distinctive ensemble. Several religious sects adopted clothing that included some variation on trousers for women, but the Bloomer Costume was the first attempt to popularize an alternative to the artificial silhouette imposed by fashion. The loose trousers of the Bloomer Costume vaguely resembled Turkish costumes. Reform dress was also associated with the healthful benefits of therapeutic "water-cure" communities, and calisthenic exercise, especially at schools for girls and young women. Supporters banded together to form various committees including the National Dress Reform Association. Around 1859, Bloomer abandoned the trousers she made famous, not only because she found that a recent innovation – the cage crinoline – made conventional dress more comfortable, but because the focus on her outfits distracted from more important issues.

By the 1870s, reformers on both sides of the Atlantic advocated shorter skirts, more practical stockings and undergarments, shoes with broad soles and low heels, washable materials, and the elimination of veils, heavy hats, and false hair. In a series of lectures given in Boston in 1874, speakers made repeated references to non-Western and antique practices, calling the dress of "Siamese women," "Greek and Roman maids," and Hawaiians more pure and graceful. The reform agenda stressed social equality and the costume of the former "Bloomerites" evolved into the American Costume. The American Costume, which was adopted by a small number of forward-thinking professional women – including the physician Harriet N. Austin and the politician Marietta Stow – resembled Amelia Bloomer's ensemble, but with masculine straight-cut trousers.

"Rational Dress," the British term for dress reform, developed significantly. The 1884 International Health Exhibition held in London promoted a range of Aesthetic and reformist apparel including Dr. Gustave Jaeger's wool clothing system. As a professor at Stuttgart Royal Polytechnic, he formulated a philosophy of dress that led to a line of garments for men, women, and children. Jaeger ascribed unusual properties to wool – he believed that wool attracts a pleasure-producing substance, as opposed to cotton, linen, and silk, which accumulated contamination. He advocated natural, undyed knitted wool undergarments to be worn daily and simple T-shaped gowns for leisure wear. The Jaeger Company was founded by a British devotee of the professor's system (not by Jaeger himself) and opened its first store in London in 1884. Through catalogs and stores, Jaeger offered form-fitting wool shirts and other garments, and promoted breeches for men. Jaeger's visibility – loyal customers included playwright George Bernard Shaw – and commercial success helped legitimize the Rational Dress movement. While the initial impact of Jaeger and other early dress reformers was not widespread, such innovations in dress affected clothing for sports and leisure activities.

Aesthetic dress, another reaction to prevailing fashion, originated in England with the artists of the Pre-Raphaelite Brotherhood in the 1850s. Rejecting what they called the artificiality of contemporary dress, they advocated medieval-style dresses for women and a return to knee breeches and blouson shirts for men. Artists including Dante Gabriel Rossetti and William Holman Hunt copied clothing of the past to dress their models in simple, flowing gowns worn without corsets, crinolines or bustles. The Pre-Raphaelites carried this interest into their own lives and wore variations on historic dress. William Morris, his wife Jane, and others involved in the Aesthetic and Arts and Crafts movements, also looked to historic sources for design inspiration. They, too, promoted simpler clothing, softer materials, natural dyes, and simple hairstyles. Aesthetic dress came to show influence not only from medieval and Renaissance style but ancient Greece and Rome as well as peasant traditions, and occupied a niche in fashion favored by ladies with artistic inclinations. The notable British actress Ellen Terry adopted Aesthetic elements (medieval-style gowns, and kimonos for at-home wear) in her daily dress and cropped her hair years ahead of the trend. Julia Margaret Cameron photographed her relatives and friends wearing loosely draped robes and flowing hair to express an Aesthetic mood. Oscar Wilde proved a remarkably idiosyncratic representative for the male version of Aesthetic dress. For Wilde, alternative dress was aligned with progressive social causes, in particular

Below left Autumn by G. F. Folingsby (c. 1882) captures a female Aesthete in a high-waisted dress and hair tied up with a Greek-style *fillet*. The Australian setting of the painting attests to the reach of Aesthetic tastes.

Below right Oscar Wilde, photographed by Napoleon Sarony in 1882, embodied the ultimate in Aesthetic styles for men, although he wielded little actual influence on menswear.

Above In *Frozen Out* by George Dunlop Leslie (1866), two women wear looped-up skirts showing colorful petticoats underneath, a style especially popular and practical for outdoor activity that also reflected the revival of 18th-century tastes.

Below Bathing costume for women and children, illustrated in *Der Bazar*, June 26, 1871, showed significant resemblance to the reform dress advocated by Amelia Jenks Bloomer.

women's issues and sexual emancipation for men and women. Pushing artistic style to the extreme, Wilde adopted long hair, knee breeches, and velvet jackets, truly dressing the part of the unconventional, witty man of letters.

Devotees of Aesthetic style patronized Liberty of London, founded in 1875 by Arthur Lazenby Liberty. The company began as an importer of Eastern goods and had occasional exhibitions of historic textiles. By the 1880s it had become one of the most fashionable shops in London with departments for carpets, rugs, furnishing fabrics, dress fabrics, embroideries, jewelry, and decorative objects in Arts and Crafts and Aesthetic style. Liberty participated in the 1884 exhibition of Reform Dress in London and in that same year opened their "costume" department offering artistic clothing.

Women's Sports Clothing

More practical clothing for physical activity became important. Casual dress styles, often with princess-style construction, were given designations such as "walking costume" and "seaside costume." Croquet, a popular sport for women and men to play together, and other outdoor activities encouraged a new, practical shorter skirt length around 1860. The overskirt was looped up with a series of internal fabric tapes and loops, a device commonly called a "dress elevator." The looping up of the overskirt placed new importance on the petticoat, calling for decorative bands or trim around the bottom. Skating ensembles also used shorter hemlines. By the 1860s, bathing costume bore a strong resemblance to Amelia Jenks Bloomer's reform costume (which had been ridiculed ten years earlier) with full trousers and a tunic in the shorter length, as the ideals of dress reform encouraged sensible sport clothes.

Women's equestrian clothes were typically made by men's tailors, not dressmakers. Developments in men's tailoring during the 19th century were applied to women's equestrian wear, adding to the development of the "tailor-made" costume for women. Riding costume usually included a jewel-neck jacket bodice with a center front opening over a habit shirt (typically a sleeveless dickey). Equestrian skirts were often cut with long trains to insure an attractive drape when the wearer was seated sidesaddle on the horse. Skirts were frequently so long that a woman required assistance to mount and dismount. The ensemble was completed with a beaver, felt or silk top hat that followed menswear style, but was often adorned with a tulle veil that fluttered elegantly behind as she rode. Both Victoria and Eugénie favored riding apparel from the British tailoring firm Creed, which had served men since 1710. In 1850, Henry Creed, the great-grandson of the founder, opened a Paris branch and soon expanded the offerings of the company to include tailored clothing for women. Equestrian skirts narrowed through the hips during the late 1870s, mirroring the silhouette of fashion. The jackets, while comfortable through the chest with a bit of wearing ease, were usually nipped into a tight waist, often utilizing boning to help achieve the shape.

As tailored costume began to emerge, some dressmakers created jacket and skirt ensembles in lighter-weight fabrics worn for warm weather outdoor activities. Important style icons, including Princess Alexandra, Lillie Langtry, and Elisabeth of Austria, were active in sports and their sport clothes set styles for other women. Golf, tennis, and shooting were all popular. Elisabeth wore tailored coats with matching ankle-length skirts for her frequent recreational hiking, and a similar ensemble could be worn for shooting. Ensembles with full trousers (again resembling the Bloomer Costume) were sometimes worn for tennis but, more often, dresses were seen, frequently with the kilted skirt used in fashionable dress, while the jersey styles advocated by Redfern became more common. While archery was a popular pastime for young women, they often participated

in the sport in fashionable afternoon dresses, and not specific sports clothes. Beginning in the 1870s, the word "polonaise" was used again to describe a coatdress, gathered up to calf length in polonaise style, that was worn with a coordinating underskirt, often for skating and other outdoor activities.

Menswear

As women's clothing grew more complicated, men's clothing simplified into a columnar shape. Unlike women's fashion, which was in constant flux, menswear during this forty-year period showed only slight periodic variations and set a pattern for the next hundred years of men's fashion. Uniformity, quiet elegance, and adherence to standards were important in men's apparel. High-quality fabrics distinguished better clothing and revealed the affluence and social position of the wearer. While women's clothing was marked by an abundance of trimmings and an extensive color palette, men tended to dress in darker colors, favoring black, dark blue, and shades of brown and gray. Men of the time wore a standard daytime "suit" composed of coat, trousers, and waistcoat. During the 1850s these three key pieces were usually of different fabrics, but in the succeeding decades one fabric was used, creating a matched ensemble.

The first layer of clothing consisted of drawers and an undershirt (commonly known as a "vest") made of cotton, linen, machine-knitted wool or, for the very wealthy, silk. Loose, drawstring-waist drawers reached to above the knee. Some men preferred tighter drawers that covered the entire leg, ending in ribbing at the ankle. The vest had short or long sleeves and a round neckline that buttoned halfway down the chest. In the 1860s "combinations" were introduced that joined vest and drawers into one garment.

In general, shirts were white cotton or linen with flat fronts, detachable collars, and slightly gathered sleeves ending in a buttoned cuff; they had very little decorative

An advertising poster promoting dress and casual wear for men for fall and winter 1864–1865, from New York clothier Genio C. Scott. Bold checks mark sturdy, loose-cut sack suits for country walks and outdoor activities, while town wear is delineated by more conservative and formal options.

Gustave Caillebotte, *Oarsman in a Top Hat*, 1877–1878. Having shed his coat, but still in top hat and waistcoat, a young man in a jaunty striped shirt tries his hand at rowing.

detail for day. As ready-made garments became more popular, custom-made shirts for evening began to show more detail such as very narrow tucks or intricate embroidery, indicating higher quality and laborious maintenance. When a man was properly dressed, only the collar and upper chest of the shirt were on display. Stripes and colors were worn for sporting activities or in the country. Neckwear, knotted around the collar, took many forms including four-in-hand ties, stocks, ascots, string ties, bow ties, and lavalieres – wide cravats tied in a soft bow. Men of the professional class, including office workers, wore dark ties for day. The best neckwear was made of silk, often patterned with dots, stripes and small foulard patterns. Artists and writers distinguished themselves with original neckwear choices, but most men opted for one of three prevailing styles: bow tie, four-in-hand or, for formal occasions, ascot. Truly fashion-conscious men tied their own neckwear, but by the 1870s pre-tied cravats were available.

The waistcoat (vest) was essential to a man's ensemble. From 1850 on, double-breasted waistcoats reaching to a little below the natural waist were popular. The desired tight, smooth fit was achieved through precise cutting and with a strap and buckle arrangement, or ties, in back. Usually chosen to contrast with coat and trousers, waistcoats were worn in a variety of fabrics. Wool (in plain colors, checks, tweed, or plaid), silk satin or brocade, and cotton in different weaves and finishes were all popular. With notched or smooth lapels, pocket welts or flaps and, sometimes, embroidery and stamped metal buttons, waistcoats provided color and distinction in the otherwise somber male ensemble.

During the 1850s, trousers were slightly loose around the hips, with pleats at the waist, tapering at the bottom. They were held up by suspenders (braces) and had buttoned fly fronts. From the 1860s until 1890, trousers narrowed to a stovepipe silhouette; in combination with the emerging preference for matching coat and trousers this created a fitted, lean effect.

Several styles of jacket were seen, but the frock coat was the most popular style for day wear. The wardrobe of a fashionable man also included the tailcoat for formal evening wear, and the sack jacket, which began to move from sporting activities into everyday apparel by 1890. The frock coat had a fitted body extending into skirts that usually reached to just above the knee. Customarily made of black or blue-black wool, it had notched lapels or smooth lapels. Later frock coats were made without a waistline; the silhouette was straighter and more columnar but still quite long. The

Right An illustration featuring vests for day and evening wear from 1887 attests to the continued importance of the vest to the man's ensemble in a variety of fabrics and styles.

Below Gentleman's Magazine of Fashion in March 1877 showed the three dominant coat styles of the late 19th-century gentleman: (left to right) the sporty and less formal sack jacket; black tailcoat for evening; and the frock coat, worn with coordinating trousers.

Bottom Gentleman's Magazine of Fashion in October 1876 illustrated a man in a casual short overcoat, and riding clothes for both a man and a woman; the military-style frogging on the front of the woman's bodice was a particularly popular detail.

cutaway coat evolved from equestrian wear. This association with riding, a morning activity, led to the cutaway's designation as the proper jacket for what became known as a morning suit.

The sack jacket or sack coat, also referred to as a lounge jacket, provided a less formal alternative to the frock coat. Shorter (reaching to upper or mid-thigh) and looser, with notched lapels, no waistline shaping, and pocket flaps, the sack jacket was seen in single- and double-breasted variations and buttoned high up the chest. The sack jacket became the dominant form in menswear as the century progressed.

The black tailcoat, cropped to the waist in front with two "tails" that descended from the waist seam to the backs of the knees, was the preferred style for evening. In the most luxurious examples, the lapels of tailcoats were faced with satin or velvet. In their dark eveningwear, men provided a background for the extravagance of ladies' dress: *Le Moniteur de la Mode* of April 1869 deemed the dark clothes of men at a ball to be a bit "dismal" – but added that they gave "great relief to the ladies' toilets." The tuxedo emerged in 1860 as a daring evening alternative. Edward VII, the *bon vivant* eldest son of Victoria and Albert, was reputedly the first to wear the tuxedo, created for him by his tailor Henry Poole of Savile Row. The tailless dark jacket with satin-faced lapels was worn with matching trousers with a satin stripe down the outseam of each leg. The tuxedo was accessorized with a black tie, instead of the white tie that was customary with the tailcoat. Originally the tuxedo was worn with a waistcoat, but the vest atrophied to a pleated cummerbund by the 1880s. Also known as a dinner suit, the tuxedo gained its most common name from its association with Tuxedo Park, a wealthy community in New York State, where an American socialite boldly wore the style he had seen in England to an evening at the Tuxedo Park Club, and the new fashion became popular.

The ceremonial clothing of male royalty, and for those associated with the court, showed influence from military uniforms, replacing existing forms of court dress based on the styles of the 18th century. For their weddings, royals wore full military regalia with the addition of white satin bows at their shoulders. Queen Victoria instituted uniforms for members of the royal household and for many in civil service, with high collars and quantities of gold braid that signaled the wearer's rank. In 1854, James Buchanan, American minister to the Court of St. James (and future president), bristled at the formality of court rules. After much negotiation with the master of

In *Fops at the Mabille Ballroom* (c. 1865–1870) the full skirts swirl up to provocatively display ankle boots, stockings, and petticoats in a public ballroom. On the left is a young man in a sack suit, a remarkably informal style in such an evening setting.

ceremonies at the court, Buchanan appeared in what he described as "the simple dress of an American citizen ... a black coat, white waistcoat and cravat and dress boots." In 1869, in an acknowledgment of changing times, the court announced that gentlemen to be presented at Levées were to wear trousers, but for Drawing Rooms, another category of presentation, knee breeches were still expected.

Continuing the tradition developed at the beginning of the 19th century, the best men's clothing was English. Even in France, the acknowledged center of fashion, English tailors were held in high esteem. Fine wools and alpaca were used for elegant outerwear in tweeds, grosgrains, superfines, and countless other weaves and finishes. Variations in outerwear included *paletots*, loose overcoats ending mid-thigh; circulars, wide capes often lined with fur; and raglan capes with sloping shoulders. In 1856, Thomas Burberry opened a shop in Basingstoke, Hampshire, England, that grew to become an important supplier of clothing for outdoor activities. Burberry developed a tightly woven, weatherproof wool twill called gabardine that was used in its products beginning in the 1880s.

Accessories completed the look of the well-dressed man. The top hat was the style seen most often in town, but other hats were available: derbys, straw hats, and unstructured caps. Shoes and boots were made of leather, or combinations of leather and fabric, with toes that ranged from broad to pointy and with one-inch (2.5-centimeter) heels. Most were laced or buttoned, although above-the-ankle boots were available with elastic gussets. Gloves were worn in public and watches on chains were common. Individuality was expressed through the great variety of grooming styles for hair and whiskers. While hairstyles were short, very few men were clean-shaven; most sported some combination of beard, mustache, and sideburn.

The Golden Jubilee Drawing Room at the Court of St. James (as shown in the *Illustrated London News*, 1887). Queen Victoria presides at a reception, her customary black dress contrasting with the pale court toilettes of the women. The anachronistic court attire for men featured knee breeches and heavily decorated coats.

In 1850, ready-to-wear garments for men included unfitted overcoats, shirts, and some trousers. Innovative clothiers such as New York's Brooks Brothers, founded in 1818, offered off-the-rack suits as early as 1845. By the 1880s, a man could be completely outfitted in ready-made clothing. Catalogs indicated the impressive variety of styles, colors, and materials that added appeal to standard items. For example, a catalog of the New York clothier Brill Bros. described drawers and vests available in "Cotton, Balbriggan, Lisle thread, Merino Wool and Silk." The company offered an innovative "coat shirt" which buttoned all the way down the front "to be put on and taken off in the same manner as a coat" that they recommended for "Professional men who must dress quickly."

Blue jeans made their first notable appearance in California as a result of the "gold rush" that began in 1848 and continued for almost forty years. Men who flocked to the San Francisco area to prospect for gold needed durable trousers. Levi Strauss, an immigrant from Bavaria, spent six years in New York where he worked with his brothers at their dry goods business. He continued west to San Francisco in 1853 and set up a business outfitting the prospectors. After selling work pants made by others, in 1873 he began manufacturing specialty trousers that were noteworthy for strong fabric, reinforced seams, and riveted pockets – a detail that was patented that same year. The pants became known as "Levi's" or jeans, referring to the denim twill-weave fabric, also called "jean." Many other companies throughout the United States produced work clothes but Levi Strauss & Co. grew into a particularly well-respected and profitable business. The number 501XX was assigned to the basic design around 1890. Strauss' design for jeans established a standard; blue jeans were fundamental to the development of an American aesthetic in dress.

Children's Fashion

The Victorian emphasis on family life as well as a burgeoning consumer culture encouraged a focus on children's clothing and grooming. Children were shown alongside adults in fashion plates, and women's magazines featured pictures and patterns of fashionable clothes for the young. Illustrations often presented children at play, in games of London Bridge or blind man's buff in domestic settings. Fashion illustrations and many group portraits of the era show siblings in matching dresses, a visual expression of their familial ties. The convention of matching dresses continued into young adulthood as sisters and best friends sometimes wore "companion" styles.

As with adults, clothing for children was governed by social conventions. Particular styles were associated with specific ages and were based on changes in body shape, activity, and social roles. Infants were dressed in long gowns that facilitated bathing and hygiene. Toddlers of both sexes wore waistless dresses and smocks that were usually gathered from a shoulder yoke. Young boys were "breeched" some time between the ages of three and eight, meaning that they were moved from skirts into

pants, usually short pants or "knickerbockers," loose knee-length pants gathered onto a band at the knee. This transition was obviously related to toilet training children, but it also symbolized the start of a boy's identification with male society. Boys' hair was worn short and neatly parted. Tailored suits for boys, including short pants or trousers, waistcoat, and jacket, reflected adult men's fashion. White shirts and bow ties were worn for dressed-up occasions. Tweed suits with tailored jackets and knickerbockers were worn for outdoor sports and country life. Sailor suits were an established tradition for boys by mid-century and the sailor suit was available in summer and winter versions.

Girls always wore dresses or skirt and blouse combinations, never pants. From about six years old, girls wore dresses that reached a little below the knee and had more shape than those they wore as toddlers. Their skirts were bell-shaped from about 1850 to 1870 and more triangular following that period, reflecting the evolution of women's fashion. For girls out of early childhood, the waistline was often defined by a sash. Petticoats worn under the skirt helped add volume, as did child-sized crinolines when they were fashionable for adult women. As adult fashion moved into the bustle period, around 1870, girls' dresses responded with drapery at the rear. Throughout the period, ruffles and trim were popular. Many sleeve variations existed, again mirroring the variety of women's fashion. Teenage girls wore structured, fitted bodices. Long, wavy hair was prized and girls wore their hair long, often accented with a hairband or ribbon, until their late teens, when they were considered adults and put their hair up.

Other influences on adult fashion were seen in children's clothing as well. Historic inspiration and folk and national styles were particularly favored. The Garibaldi blouse and Zouave jacket were popular for children. Some dresses of the time showed folkloric touches such as gathered sleeves and laced-up bodices. Scottish style also influenced fashion in the form of kilt suits for boys and both sexes wore tartan-patterned ensembles.

Underwear consisted of drawers, with loose knee-length legs, and an undershirt or vest. The two pieces were sometimes attached to form a one-piece garment. Made of cotton, linen, or wool, summer versions were sleeveless and longer sleeves were worn for cold weather. Corsets for children were common. Advertising and books of advice emphasized the healthful benefits of corsets. Their purpose was less to mold the body into a fashionable shape than to provide support for growing muscles and improve posture. During the time of wide bell-shaped skirts, children wore pantalettes, long

An 1881 illustration from *Revue de la Mode/Gazette de la Famille* shows a variety of options for a boy's wardrobe, including the continued popularity of sailor styles.

drawers often finished with decorative edging, that were visible beneath their skirts. Pantalettes also took the form of tubes of fabric that tied on with drawstrings above the knee. Children wore knee-length stockings made of knitted wool or cotton, usually in gray, black or white. Flat-soled, ankle-height boots were common for all ages. Girls also wore thin-soled slipper-like shoes with special occasion dresses. Hats were always worn outdoors and were available in many variations including bonnets, wide-brimmed styles, and soft caps. For dressy occasions, girls had decorative hair ribbons and lace headdresses.

Fabric was determined by season and occasion. Dark velvets and wools were used for winter clothes. Spring and summer fabrics included airy cottons in white, pastel colors, and small floral prints with abundant lace trimming for girls. Boys' clothes were made in lightweight wools, linen and cotton twills, with tailoring details such as soutache braid and topstitching.

The Growth of the Fashionable World

Centers of fashion and culture emerged in Australia and North and South America. New York City, Philadelphia, and Chicago continued to grow, as did Montreal and Toronto, Sydney and Melbourne, and Buenos Aires. The upper class of emerging countries yearned for the sophistication of Europe, but confronted frontier situations with surprising new challenges. Ladies of large cities were attuned to the latest developments from Worth and Pingat, while women in the countryside, especially in colder areas of the American West, Canada, and Alaska, actually wore trousers in their hardworking daily lives. In Australia, some of the cultured urban elite fashioned themselves along British Aesthetic lines, while pioneers in the outback were a world away from such affectation. Some cultural standards in the New World had been set by immigrants from previous generations, as in Roman Catholic French Canada and Puritan Massachusetts, and occasionally European traditions clashed with the realities of life in a growing country. An odd instance of such conflict and contrast between the Old and New Worlds occurred in November 1878. Canada's new Governor General and his wife, Princess Louise, bungled their initial official appearance with the citizens of Montreal. Specifying that female guests attending a reception wear the low-necked dresses expected for such an event in Europe, they did not take into consideration the dress standards typical of this largely Roman Catholic population, and the economic conditions that prevented many local women from owning formal dresses, not to mention the cold weather in November. Women were allowed a slight reprieve if a "medical certificate" could be produced. The press described the incident as a major political faux pas and criticized the couple for their ignorance of Quebec's culture.[8]

European fashion influence extended even to Asia. Mongkut, King Rama IV of Siam, made strong efforts toward Westernization during his reign in the 1850s and 1860s that included Western-style dress worn by the royal family. During the reign of Emperor Meiji of Japan, Western styles of clothing influenced the wardrobes of wealthy and fashionable Japanese aristocrats. The Rokumeikan, a Western-style reception hall near the imperial palace, opened in 1883 and served as the setting of European-style balls and musicales. Shortly afterward the empress consort, Ichijo Haruko, known as Empress Shōken, adopted Western dress for her public appearances. Despite some backlash against the Western styles and customs, the empress continued to wear the styles, as did the women of the court, and their clothing choice would influence the future of style in East Asian cultures.

Toward 1890

During these forty years, Parisian fashion was considered the epitome of elegance but ready-made clothing, made possible by inventions such as the sewing machine, was also important. The market for fashion expanded through the growth of department stores and mail order. The evolution from the crinoline silhouette to a more streamlined shape and the development of the tailor-made emphasized an evolving attitude to practicality, and ideas from dress reform had impact on subsequent styles. Menswear reflected standardization in sizes, production, and form. Photography was used to promote celebrity and record fashion and other phenomena of modern life. The Eiffel Tower rose on the Paris skyline in 1889, built for that year's Exposition Universelle. The Exposition, which included a Galerie des Machines that displayed hundreds of new mechanized inventions, opened one hundred years after French revolutionaries brought the Ancien Regime to an end. The Eiffel Tower became the focal point of the city that had so successfully merged Old World elegance with a spirit of modernity, a combination which represented the fashionable world in general.

An 1888 *ukiyo-e* print by Yoshu Chikanobu depicts Western ballroom dancing at the Rokumeikan in Tokyo, where the Japanese upper class learned Western customs and manners, and dressed in Western styles.

Chapter 2

The 1890s

Extremes of the Gilded Age

As the final decade of the century opened, the continued propriety of the Victorian age was in some ways merely a thin veneer masking a hedonistic society. Likewise, in fashion, the late 19th-century taste for extravagance contrasted with hints of a more modern simplification. Practical, tailored looks emerged from sports clothing and through women's "borrowings" from the male wardrobe, especially influencing clothing worn by women entering the workplace. In this period, often known as the Belle Epoque or the Gilded Age, high fashion represented a culmination of the refinement of Parisian dressmaking as it had developed over the last forty years. Haute couture customers embraced the luxurious creations of the Parisian houses with lavish colors, ornate decoration, and striking proportions such as the leg-of-mutton sleeve

Opposite Primrose and Feather (1899) by Alphonse Mucha, a Czech artist who also worked in Paris, exemplify the art nouveau aesthetic and capture the age's ideal of feminine beauty. The upswept hairstyles, pearly color palette and sinuous silhouette reflect fashion ideals.

Right Pierre-Victor Galland's depiction of Parisian nightlife, *The Bar at Maxim's* (c. 1899), vividly illustrates the attitudes and styles associated with *fin-de-siècle* decadence.

and conical skirt. Orientalism and historicism were combined with the emerging style, art nouveau. The staid demeanor of Queen Victoria and Princess Alexandra expressed proper womanhood, while the "Gibson Girl" embodied a wholesome, active beauty. But the fashionable world was equally influenced by women whose allure communicated sexual power: *demimondaines* were an important social institution and, while such women could be considered vulgar, many were cultured, compelling fashion leaders.

Social and Economic Background

Victoria's reign continued, but her son and heir Albert Edward, Prince of Wales, was the dominant figure in British society. Under the Third Republic (in place since 1870), France lacked the court structure that had provided a splendid, sparkling focus for fashion during the Second Empire. However, Paris retained leadership in fashion, design, and the arts despite turmoil in government resulting from the rapid turnover of leaders, as well as strained relations with Italy and Germany. Cultural life and fashion in Vienna were in a period of decline at the beginning of the decade. Following the death of her son, the Crown Prince Rudolf, Empress Elisabeth of Austria abandoned fashion and dressed in black mourning for the remainder of her life (until her assassination in 1898), casting a pall over the empire of Austria-Hungary.

The United States, Canada, and Australia benefited from waves of immigration that populated their expanding territories, where political stability was associated with industrial growth. Although most nations experienced periodic economic downturns, prosperity and steady improvements in technology – especially in the realms of transportation, energy, sanitation, and communication – suffused the period with an atmosphere of determination, ardor, gaiety, and confidence in the future.

Developments in manufacture, distribution, and advertising, as well as a generally higher standard of living for the middle class, increased the consumption of fashion. Shopping centers such as The Arcade in Cleveland and Moscow's Glavnyi Universalnyi Magazin opened early in the decade, featuring many stores under one roof. Great department stores and smaller emporia catered to customers from all social strata with appeals to the many sides of consumer desire: for the latest style, good quality,

An intricate dinner bodice (1897) from the Montreal merchant Vere Goold, with black accents over a warp-print silk taffeta, suggests the effects of iridescent favrile glass from Tiffany and filigree ironwork patterns, embodying the 1890s taste for opulence.

unique features, or bargain pricing. Greatly increased production was often the result of poor working conditions for garment laborers, which became the target of public scrutiny. Jacob Riis' *How the Other Half Lives*, published in 1890, detailed the struggles of the largely immigrant lower class in New York, including stories of tenement dwellers, often women and children, who worked in sweatshops or did sewing work at home for pitiful wages.

The Arts

Post-Impressionism was the prevailing experimental movement in painting (although the term was not coined until 1910), dominated by French painters including Georges Seurat, Paul Gauguin, Paul Cézanne, and Henri de Toulouse-Lautrec. Reacting to Impressionism with bolder colors, abstracted shapes, and challenges to conventional perspective, they broke new ground and laid the cornerstones of modern art. Jean Moréas' Symbolist manifesto, published in *Le Figaro* in 1886, crystallized the Symbolist movement, which had been in development for several decades (with debt to the Romantics and the Pre-Raphaelites). During the 1890s, the otherworldly images of artists including Gustave Moreau, Odilon Redon, Pierre Puvis de Chavannes, Arnold Böcklin, and Edvard Munch contributed to the impact of Symbolism.

Art nouveau provided the predominant influence on fashion from the visual arts. Art nouveau tendencies (including stylized natural

Lillian Russell, 1893.

Nellie Melba, c. 1890.

DIVAS OF THE GILDED AGE

American singer and actress Lillian Russell (1861–1922) was one of the most visible personalities of the time. Russell's career was primarily in operetta, variety, and vaudeville, in both the United States and Britain. Living through four marriages, Russell's most remembered relationship was with her longtime gentleman friend, American millionaire James "Diamond Jim" Brady. The affair earned her the nickname "Diamond Lil" as his wealth provided her with many of the luxuries that typified the excesses of the American nouveaux riches. The full-figured Russell was celebrated as a great beauty; bound into her tight corsets, the proportions of her voluptuous figure suited the hourglass silhouette of the time, and anticipated other curvaceous ladies that followed, including Mae West and Marilyn Monroe.

Nellie Melba (1861–1931) was the most remarkable opera singer of the decade. Born Helen Porter Mitchell near Melbourne, Australia, she began her career in the early 1880s. Taking as her stage name Nellie Melba in honor of Melbourne,

she set off for Europe and soon achieved great success that solidified her international career. During the 1890s she was the toast of Paris and Monte Carlo, New York and Chicago, receiving unprecedented fees, and she was among the first singers to be recorded. One of the best-dressed women of her day, Melba was an important couture client, particularly at the House of Worth, and she considered Jean-Philippe to be a superior designer to his father.[1] Worth created many of her stage costumes in addition to her fashionable clothing. Her celebrity extended beyond the stage: French chef Auguste Escoffier created recipes in her honor, including Peach Melba and Melba toast; her endorsement appeared on many advertisements, and other products were named after her including a one-piece combination undergarment. Her greatest achievement was becoming Australia's first global celebrity and style setter. In 1918 Melba was made Dame Commander of the Order of the British Empire.

forms and Japonisme) represented an important step toward modernity in the arts. Art nouveau's presence can be detected in the undulating line of women's dresses, and the luminescent surface decoration of jewelry and accessories. While the description *art nouveau* had been in use since the 1880s, the term solidified with the opening of Siegfried Bing's gallery named "L'Art Nouveau" in Paris in 1895. The sensual, exotic stylization of art nouveau frequently included beautiful women as decorative elements. Fashionably dressed (or undressed) females were featured in advertisements for a variety of products. In subtle, pearly tones the Czech artist Alphonse Mucha depicted languid, curvaceous women on posters, calendars and other works. Mucha's output included images of the actress Sarah Bernhardt that epitomized the exotic, stylized aspect of art nouveau. Using bold compositions and vivid primary colors, Jules Chéret portrayed another side of the *fin-de-siècle* woman: visible, energetic, and active. In the United States, Louis Comfort Tiffany and his studio produced important decorative arts, including stained glass windows, mosaics, favrile glass lamps and other objects. Art nouveau was known as *Jugendstil* in Germany after the journal *Jugend* founded in 1896, and *Arte Nuova* or *La Stile Liberty* in Italy (acknowledging the influence of the British retailer Liberty of London). Certain cities became hotbeds of art nouveau with decorative arts and public architecture in this style, including Paris, Barcelona, and Vienna.

Despite the decline in court life, Vienna emerged as a site of exciting activity in the arts with the establishment of the Vienna Secession in 1897 under the leadership of prominent artists including Josef Hoffmann, Gustav Klimt, Koloman Moser, and Joseph Maria Olbrich, and later Otto Wagner. Reacting against the conservative spirit of the established Vienna Künstlerhaus, the artists of the Secession brought exhibitions of challenging art and design to the Viennese public, including Impressionist painting. With the aim of unifying fine and decorative arts and architecture, the Secessionists, and other decorative artists who followed their ideas, developed a style that was initially informed by art nouveau but shortly took on a more austere, geometric rigor.

Russia experienced a high point in art and music. The coronation of a young new tsar, Nicholas II, took place in 1894. At that time a trend for reviving the empire's pre-Westernized past, in fine and decorative arts and in performance, was in full force – the "Neo-Russian" movement. Painters such as Mikhail Nesterov, Viktor Vasnetsov, and Ilya Repin presented scenes from Russian folk tales and history. Onstage, opera composers contributed to the trend with such works as Alexander Borodin's *Prince Igor* and Nikolai Rimsky-Korsakov's *Sadko*. But Western European influences were still present, as Pyotr Ilyich Tchaikovsky continued his Romanticist output with the ballets *Sleeping Beauty* and *The Nutcracker*. His *Swan Lake* reflected a Symbolist aesthetic with a fantastical tale of forbidden passion. The young Sergei Rachmaninoff, a protégé of Tchaikovsky, continued his mentor's Romantic styles into the next century.

Similar Romantic and nationalistic sentiments flavored orchestral music throughout the rest of Europe in the work of great composers such as Antonin Dvořák, Gustav Mahler, Edvard Grieg, and Gabriel Fauré. On the opera and ballet stages, opulent, lurid forms of historicism and orientalism continued to fascinate audiences along with works on more conventionally Romantic themes. Jules Massenet's opera *Thaïs* told of an Egyptian courtesan during the Byzantine era, based on a scandalous novel by Anatole France. Massenet also premiered his opera based on Goethe's *The Sorrows of Young Werther*. A naturalistic slice-of-life style known as *verismo* began to dominate opera in Italy. Giacomo Puccini created *La Bohème*, a story of impoverished artists and a seamstress dying of tuberculosis. Pietro Mascagni's popular *Cavalleria Rusticana* and Ruggero Leoncavallo's *Pagliacci* set tales of passionate love triangles and murder among the lower class.

Popular entertainment featured in the music halls in major cities often included provocative female singers and dancers, circus-style gymnast acts and outrageous mock-oriental sketches. In the United States and Canada, a new style of entertainment emerged as vaudeville. But nightlife was at its most decadent and star-studded in

Above Fantasy and stylization characterize this brooch by Eugène Feuillâtre (gold, enamel, and moonstones). The butterfly wings and female face represent two motifs frequently used in jewelry and accessories.

Above right Aubrey Beardsley's black and white illustrations for Oscar Wilde's controversial *Salome* – including "The Peacock Skirt" seen here – offer a striking, graphic version of the art nouveau aesthetic.

Paris, where performers such as can-can star La Goulue and music hall singer Yvette Guilbert entertained aristocrats as well as *demimondaines* in spectacular venues such as the Folies Bergère and the Moulin Rouge. On the Parisian stage, American Loie Fuller was a significant pioneer in the world of dance. Fuller experimented with new technologies in theatrical lighting and expressed Greco-Roman inspiration in her movements. In some dances she twirled large expanses of fabric to create cloud- and flower-like formations under vividly colored lights – an expression of art nouveau in movement. Artists of the day were fascinated by her and depicted her image in painting, graphic arts, and sculpture.

Oscar Wilde's comedies, including *The Importance of Being Earnest* and *Lady Windermere's Fan*, lampooned the manners of British society. Wilde's novel *The Picture of Dorian Gray* and his French-language verse play *Salome* (which offered a particularly sordid version of the biblical tale) expressed the fevered decadence of the age. Although performances of the work were banned in England, a published edition of *Salome* featured illustrations by the remarkably talented and short-lived Aubrey Beardsley (1872–1898) and immortalized the talents of both the writer and the illustrator. *The Yellow Book*, a quarterly published in England from 1894 to 1897, included work by artists and writers including Beardsley and Walter Crane, H. G. Wells and Henry James, and helped popularize Aesthetic and art nouveau taste. The journal's yellow cover was chosen in imitation of salacious French novels that arrived wrapped in yellow paper; although published for only a short period, the journal was emblematic of the spirit of the decade.

The Elements of Women's Fashion

Upper-class social etiquette determined proper attire based on season, time of day, activity, and location. The wardrobe of a socially prominent woman was large and addressed many activities, occasions, and specific customs. A ritualistic series of changes throughout the day had evolved during the last several decades, and the couture system and fashion press helped encourage all of them. The lady of society began her day in a luxurious at-home wrapper, changed into a tailored walking suit for morning errands or visits, put on a subtle afternoon dress for socializing, and a tea gown for late afternoon relaxation in her rooms, taking a break from her corset. The ritual of daily dressing culminated in elaborate dinner or evening dress, with specific

Above Foundation garments, including corsets and petticoats, continued in much the same vein as in earlier decades, with the bustle or "improver" still present in a smaller, vestigial form, as illustrated in the Jordan Marsh catalog, 1890.

Right Stylish daytime ensembles, c. 1891, are shown in a plate from *La Moda Cubana*, featuring fuller sleeves, shoulder emphasis, and flat-brimmed hats.

styles for balls and receptions. Jewelry and accessories were donned or removed according to time of day as well.

As the decade of the 1890s began, the woman's silhouette consisted of a deflated version of the 1880s second bustle period, often retaining the relationship of an underskirt and overskirt, but without the aggressive silhouette of a bustle. The back of the skirt continued to be augmented, although in a much slighter way, with small pads or net cage dress improvers merely rounding out the rear, no longer projecting it. The sleeve continued a development from the late 1880s, with gathered fullness across the top that became more pronounced quickly into the next few years. Corsetry, already very tight and constricting, resulted in a pronounced "hourglass" shape, with the breasts and the hips full and rounded, in contrast to a tightly bound waist, often referred to as a wasp waist. The combination of a large sleeve, a constricted waist, and a skirt that flared out sharply created a very distinctive silhouette, and the "hourglass" of the corseted midsection was in fact repeated in the overall entire form.

Princess dresses still were part of the fashion repertoire at the beginning of the decade, and their vertical piecing likely contributed to the revival of gored skirts. The gores were repeated triangular-shaped panels that when sewn up created a conical skirt, often with a slight train in the back. As the overskirt and underskirt combination went out of vogue early in the decade, the popularity of the gored skirt shape increased. Petticoats were also gored and the overall look was one of geometric

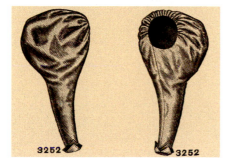

Above Two variations of leg-of-mutton (or gigot) sleeve from *The "Standard" Designer* in 1896 illustrate different construction methods for this popular fashion detail.

Right A fashion plate from *Le Moniteur de la Mode*, 1893, features a day dress in the hourglass silhouette, with enormous gigot sleeves and wide gored skirt.

sharpness and stiffness. Linings and interfacings, such as woven horsehair, were often used to mold the skirt into the desired shape, and the hem of the skirt was usually faced with additional stiffening.

The sleeve fullness continued to increase and by 1893 the leg-of-mutton (or gigot) sleeve, a feature of 1830s fashion, was back in vogue. While variations of the leg-of-mutton sleeve were referred to by a variety of different names, this style took two principal forms. One was a large spherical upper sleeve that seamed near the elbow to a tightly fitted undersleeve; the other was one continuous piece that tapered from a full top to a tightly fitted wrist. For evening, the sleeves were sometimes just as large as the daytime versions, ending at the elbow and worn with long gloves, but often the size was significantly reduced, or sleeveless styles were worn. The shoulders were highly emphasized in eveningwear, and when the sleeves were not large, they were often heavily decorated at the shoulder with swags of fabric, ribbons, and fabric flowers. In some instances projecting epaulettes provided shoulder emphasis on a sleeveless dress.

Evening necklines showed much variety; the square neckline was very popular, but rounded and V shapes were also frequently seen. For daytime, collars began to grow upward, extending nearly to the top of the neck over the decade. As the collars grew, various means to keep them stiff and supported were utilized, including bones, horsehair lining, and wires. Often the collar was decorated with trims and satin ribbons.

Below The Gibson Girl, the creation of illustrator Charles Dana Gibson, was often shown in practical tailored separates enjoying outdoor sports.

The fashion press and the industry used a wide variety of names for daytime dresses including "carriage dress," "walking costume," "afternoon toilette," "calling suit," and other terms. These appellations were more a product of the fashion system than actual reflections of such specific dressing. However, while dresses continued to be worn for day, women's daytime apparel began to offer other options and greater variety. The tailor-made suit became a staple during this decade, and examples were included in the output of the major designers. The "promenade" suit, a term in use since the 1860s, featured prominently in this decade for formal daytime town wear; it was essentially a woman's tailor-made costume fabricated from dress fabrics, rather than men's suiting, and often utilizing more ornate, feminine trims and details.

By 1897 and 1898, the prevailing silhouette in fashionable womenswear transformed once again, this time softening the extremes of the leg-of-mutton sleeve and the hard angles of the gored skirt. The sleeve became smaller, with small puffs replacing the large spheres. The use of epaulettes continued, but they also diminished in size and often took the form of small ruffles at the shoulder. As the sleeve grew smaller, the skirt took on a more elegant shape created by extra flare at the bottom of the gores. Commonly called a "trumpet line skirt," the shape also resembled a lily, and showed the influence of the curvilinear forms of art nouveau. As the skirt shape changed, petticoats adapted to support the transformed line.

The increasing presence of women in certain occupations – such as stenographers and telephone operators – contributed to a simplification of fashion. A new career look emerged, essentially an American style, consisting of a shirtwaist blouse combined with a separate gored skirt. The concept of sportswear separates emerged, even though that term would not be applied for years to come. The shirtwaist blouse borrowed from the man's wardrobe and responded to a utilitarian emphasis in fashion. This decade marked significant efforts in women's rights; the seeds were being sown for widespread reform attempts, and fashion reflected that sentiment.

The Gibson Girl

Charles Dana Gibson's artistic creation, "The Gibson Girl," crystallized the image of this new woman into iconic form. Gibson was an illustrator, commissioned by some of the most important American magazines of the time. His 1895 marriage to society heiress Irene Langhorne provided added inspiration to the development of the female characters he illustrated, as Gibson used Irene and her sisters as models. The tall and athletic Gibson Girl was the archetype of a new woman who embodied changes in society, and dressed in the new, practical separates. Frequently, the Gibson Girl was shown wearing her gored skirt with a shirtwaist blouse and straw boater, enjoying leisure activities. Gibson's cartoons were widely distributed and became part of the popular culture of the United States, and their popularity extended to Europe. A wide variety of merchandise was decorated with the Gibson Girl's image. Gibson's style was imitated by other artists and was influential on a generation of American illustrators.

Outerwear and Millinery

Women's outerwear continued in the wide variety typical of previous decades, and much the same terminology was used to describe these various forms. Capes were particularly popular as they accommodated the leg-of-mutton sleeve, and sometimes included extra fullness gathered in across the shoulder that mimicked the silhouette of the leg-of-mutton. Short capelets were often worn, for sport, town, and evening with different details and trimmings. Evening styles were frequently heavily decorated, and often included a ruffled pierrot-style collar. Coats, when worn, needed a large sleeve to accommodate the sleeves of the garment underneath. More masculine varieties were worn in recreational and country contexts, continuing the trend for borrowing from menswear.

Above A seaside costume shows the transition at the end of the decade as full leg-of-mutton sleeves reduced in size, often accompanied by trim epaulette details. Hats accommodated ever-widening hairstyles, and wearing entire taxidermied birds was not uncommon.

Right Popular styles of outerwear included a full-sleeved coat and a cape as pictured in *La Mode Pratique* (1892). Both accommodated the fashionable large sleeves.

Increased participation in outdoor activities called for specialized sports clothing. The *Journal des Demoiselles et Petit Courrier des Dames Réunis* featured these hunting costumes for women in September 1891.

Right Men and women took to the road on bicycles in a variety of sportswear styles. Many women wore daring bifurcated outfits, such as those seen in this 1897 illustration of cycling in Ostend by Belgian artist Carl Hermann Kuechler.

Opposite Millinery was particularly decorative, with trimming that ranged from lace to feathers to artificial flowers. An illustration from *The Delineator* (1897) shows the broader brims that developed by mid-decade, a trend that would continue to grow until the early 1910s.

Larger saucer-shaped hats developed, replacing the perched styles popular in the 1880s, and some tricorne styles were also popular. By mid-decade hats had increased in size, and with this enlargement, hairstyles became larger as well, reviving the look of the 1780s as captured in the paintings of Gainsborough. These fuller hairstyles often required hairpieces to fill out the proportion. Materials that had been popular hat trimmings during the previous decades became even more indispensable as the size required an increased amount of decoration. Feathers, particularly from ostriches and egrets, became essential, and the sale and trading of feathers exploded into a large industry. Entire wings of birds – or, in some cases, entire birds – dramatically decorated hats. In addition to the vast array of feather decoration, bows and fabric flowers added to the adornment. While feathers defined millinery fashion, the Audubon Society and other groups protested the slaughter of birds for use on hats.

The Influence of Sport

Women's sports costume became more precisely delineated and readily available. Leisure-time activities, including cycling, golf, and tennis, required apparel that had been previously restricted to the aristocracy but was now more accessible to the middle class, and increasingly influenced fashionable clothing. Bathing costume continued along the lines that had developed earlier in the century. Shooting and hiking outfits that frequently included a short skirt above the ankles met with more widespread acceptance. Women's sweaters were increasingly popular for recreational wear. A new emphasis on exercise at women's schools required sports-specific clothing.

The bicycle craze was particularly important. The new invention was promoted as a way to enjoy the countryside and enthusiastic men and women turned bicycle riding into a sport. Women dressed for the new pastime in several novel ways, challenging existing ideas of modesty. Many wore tailored jackets and above-the-ankle skirts with laced-up boots. But the more adventurous donned a bifurcated, bloomer-like costume, exhibiting one of the first mainstream applications of dress reform ideals. This development in fashion was of such note that a woman in a bifurcated bicycle suit was featured on the cover of *Harper's Bazar* in 1894. In 1897 Boston's Jordan Marsh department store prominently featured "The Anna Held Cycling Suit." Named after

An evening gown in an art nouveau-patterned coral silk by Jean-Philippe Worth for the House of Worth, c. 1898–1900 (top), and Jacques Doucet's iridescent gown, of sheer silk over lamé, c. 1898–1900 (above), demonstrate the elegant silhouette of eveningwear. While skirts were long and flowing, shoulders and décolletage were often exposed.

the shapely and well-dressed performer, the outfit appeared to be "an ordinary skirt when the wearer is off the wheel," but it "gracefully conceals the seat when riding." A "bicycle chatelaine" described in the press in 1896 was to be attached to the handlebars and contained "a card-case, scent bottle, pin cushion, and space for handkerchiefs, and other et caetera which milady may desire to carry on the trip."[2] Images of women on bicycles permeated popular culture, suggesting new possibilities of speed, freedom, and modernity. By 1890 Butterick was regularly publishing patterns for divided skirts as well as jackets and blouses for sports.

Designers

During this period, the couture designation distinguished the clothing of the affluent from ready-made merchandise, as the handwork and unique creations from "name" designers held a prestige not found in mass-produced clothing. Couture garments were distinguished by their custom fit and distinctive decorative detail. While sewing machines were used for much of the basic construction of a dress or ensemble, finishing was done by hand by specially trained workers. Embroidery and trimmings were crucial to the look of fashion and took the form of profuse application of passementerie, lace, beading, sequins, and synthetic stones. Parisian couturiers attracted affluent clientele from all over Europe, North America, and Britain, including members of the European aristocracy and nouveau riche Americans, as well as opera singers, dancers and actresses, and the mistresses of wealthy and powerful men. The couture system combined the particular vision of the designer, the luxury textile industry, the skills of the couture workshops, and the specific tastes of the customer. The 19th century's two most important fashion innovators – Charles Frederick Worth and John Redfern – both died in 1895, leaving their businesses to sons and junior partners. These successful fashion dynasties demonstrate the robustness of the industry in which an established name could survive the passing of its founder.

Textiles were produced in the wide variety necessary to accommodate the caprices of fashion and included many weights and weaves of wool, silk, linen, and cotton. Many were given descriptive names that alluded to novelty and exoticism, piquing the interest of fashionable customers. In addition to the more usual fabrications such as duchesse satin, peau de soie and moiré, dresses were offered in Hindu crepe and Persian taffeta. Velvets and other pile weaves were particularly popular and offered in a variety of surface treatments. Wool textiles were woven with metallic threads, lending luster to even the most serviceable materials. A general trend for pale, pearly colors permeated fashion especially toward the end of the decade. Sometimes dark accents anchored light pink, ivory, and peach-toned silk.

Well before his death in 1895, **Worth** had brought his sons into the business. As Charles Frederick took less and less responsibility in the business and spent his later years in semi-retirement, Jean-Philippe proved to be a talented designer, perhaps more "artistic" and original than his father. While continuing to cater to the established customer base, Jean-Philippe introduced many stylistic innovations into the work of the house, such as incorporating influences from Aesthetic dress, Japonisme, and art nouveau. Worth opened a London office in 1897.[3]

Emile Pingat was still in operation in this decade. With an international clientele of discerning and elegant women, Pingat was a master of the use of art nouveau inspiration in his creations. In 1896, after being active for nearly forty years, Pingat merged with another dressmaking business, A. Wallès & Cie.

Under the direction of Jacques Doucet, the house of **Doucet** was increasingly important. Doucet's most famous client was the celebrated Parisian actress Gabrielle Réjane, but he outfitted other entertainers and *demimondaines*. Doucet designed the wedding gown for Consuelo Vanderbilt's marriage to Charles Spencer-Churchill, the Duke of Marlborough, in 1895. Although the gown was fabricated in New York by a society dressmaker, Mrs. Donovan, the press emphasized Doucet's design contribution.⁴ As with Worth and Pingat, his designs were often inspired by historic fashion and included many details drawn from the 18th century. As he prospered in fashion, Doucet established himself as a discerning and adventurous art collector and initially concentrated on fine and decorative arts of the 18th century. Doucet's leading designer, José de la Peña de Guzman, was important to the quality and reputation of the house.

The house of **Paquin** was opened in 1891 by Isidore René Jacob, who had assumed the surname Paquin for business purposes. In the same year, he married Jeanne Marie Charlotte Beckers (1869–1936), who was trained as a seamstress and became the design mind of the business. M. and Mme. Paquin quickly became very successful, even expanding to a London branch in 1897.

Also among the established houses were **Laferrière** and **Félix**, both firms that had contributed to the wardrobes of Second Empire court ladies and were still flourishing. Joining these established design houses were the young German-born **Gustave Beer** (active c. 1890–1929), who would make a strong mark on the next two decades, and **Callot Soeurs**, a new house opened around 1895 by four sisters from an artistic family: Joséphine Callot Crimont, Marie Callot Gerber, Marthe Callot Bertrand, and Regina Callot Tennyson-Chantrelle.

By the 1890s, **Redfern and Sons** had achieved genuine international success, growing from a respected tailoring house into a fully fledged couture establishment. While other couturiers typically expected their clientele to come to them at their Paris ateliers, Redfern took its style and innovations outside of London and Paris to the fashionable world via eleven stores in Britain, France, and the United States, becoming the first transatlantic couture business. Following the death of founder John Redfern, the international fashion empire was under the direction of the founder's son Stanley Redfern with Charles Poynter and Frederick Mims. Poynter, responsible

Below left Short capes were an essential part of a well-dressed woman's wardrobe. This fashionable and ornate cape from French designer Emile Pingat, c. 1895, in white duvetyne heavily embellished with satin, gold braid, sequins, and pearl and crystal beads, is from the collection of the Philadelphia Museum of Art.

Below right A jacket from a walking costume by Emile Pingat, c. 1893, from the Brooklyn Museum Costume Collection at the Metropolitan Museum of Art, exemplifies the lavish combination of materials and orientalism often seen in his work.

SARAH BERNHARDT

Sarah Bernhardt (1844–1923) was perhaps the greatest actress of the late 19th century. Beginning her career at the Comédie-Française in the 1860s, she became known for the remarkable tone of her voice, often compared to the luster of precious metals. Her career blossomed in the 1870s and 1880s, and she performed for many of the crowned heads of Europe – and possibly had an affair with the Prince of Wales. During her sixty-year career, "The Divine Sarah" toured much of the Western world, including Europe, Britain, and the Americas. Celebrated especially as a tragedienne, Bernhardt's great roles included Joan of Arc, Medea, and Cleopatra. Near the end of her career, she starred in silent films, the first major stage actress to do so.

Typical of the female celebrities of her day, Bernhardt used photography to enhance her public persona, and the great French photographer Félix Nadar created many images of her, sometimes merely draped in fabric instead of actual clothes. Her portrait was painted to great acclaim. The popularity of her image reached its zenith in the 1890s with the widely circulated and now iconic posters of Alphonse Mucha featuring Bernhardt – still beautiful in middle age. Bernhardt also posed for renowned photographer Napoleon Sarony. It is these representations from the 1890s that crystallized her image for generations to come. Her appearance, uncorseted, in flowing clothing and provocative poses, "gave an impression of mysterious and probably forbidden passions."[5] Bernhardt was often depicted in a reclining position, reflecting the sinuous curves of art nouveau but also suggesting a predatory snake or a tigress. Such poses emphasized Bernhardt's sexuality, independence, and disregard for social conventions.

Bernhardt's clothing was created by major couture houses, with her own significant design input. When she achieved stardom in the 1870s, her stage costumes were created by Mme. Laferrière. Later in her career, Bernhardt established her own costume atelier. While Bernhardt was an advocate of artistic dress reform, her clothes were markedly different from Rational Dress societies' concern with health, or the historic stylings of the Aesthetics. She took the ideas of Aesthetic dress and realized them in a flamboyant, Mannerist style. With her looser-fitting gowns she rejected some trappings of high fashion – corsetry and bustles – but held on to the lavish dressmaker details and fabrics. Bernhardt had a love for flowing gowns, cut in one piece in the style of the *robe en princesse* and ending in a long and opulent train, and she frequently used strong vertical details such as lace ruffles down the side-front. These styles emphasized and celebrated her slender proportions. Bernhardt was an early convert to trousers in her real life, in the spirit of the dress reformers but with more stylistic savvy. She often wore a pajama suit around her home, and was so fond of the ruffled pierrot collar that she incorporated it into many of her dresses. This collar became a feature of mainstream fashion. Her frizzy hair was frequently copied, and avant-garde women of high society even imitated her walk, her gestures, and her facial expressions.

With an over-the-top public image, Bernhardt relished outrageous publicity. She sometimes performed *en travesti* (young man's parts) and these cross-dressed roles briefly encouraged rumors that she was actually a transvestite man. She was famously photographed in a coffin at her home – she claimed that lying there helped her to understand the subtexts of her tragic roles – which encouraged speculation that she actually slept in it. In both her fashion and decorating choices, Bernhardt embodied the decadent perfumed world of orientalist stage spectacles, and the hallucinatory visions of Symbolist painter Gustave Moreau.

Sarah Bernhardt as Cleopatra in 1891, photographed by Napoleon Sarony.

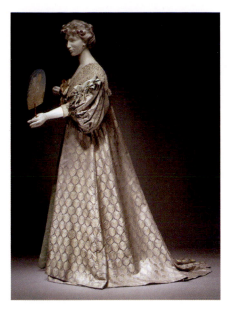

primarily for the Paris branch, was the most important design leader in the company and operated with the adopted surname Redfern. The house's daywear and sportswear offerings had expanded into evening clothes, court dress, stage costumes, and lingerie, and they continued to include British and European royalty in their clientele. Their continued relationship with the British fashion periodical *The Queen* was significant to their success.

A new British designer emerged in the 1890s, one who would achieve great prominence and influence in the following two decades: **Lucile** (1863–1935). Born Lucy Sutherland in London, she married James Wallace in 1884, but they divorced in 1890. To provide financial support for herself and for her daughter Esme, she began working as a dressmaker out of her home under the name Mrs. James Wallace, and (by her own account later in life) cut the fabric for her creations on her dining room floor. In time, many commissions from society women developed her business. By 1894 she opened Maison Lucile in London's West End, and soon her creations were being featured in important fashion magazines such as *The Queen*.

Further Influence of Dress Reform

The ideals of dress reform continued into the 1890s. While still somewhat avant-garde, the reform fashions were less shocking as time went on. They sometimes reflected elements of nationalist dress, such as peasant-style blouses. These ideas, although initially outside of the mainstream, developed in the 1890s as a recognized niche market. In London, Jaeger continued operation, and Liberty of London's catalogs made such fashions more accessible. Members of the Vienna Secession encouraged dress reform ideas in Austria.

Dresses with an Empire, or raised, waist were briefly fashionable during the early years of the decade, and showed the growing influence of Aesthetic dress on mainstream fashion. First Lady Frances Folsom Cleveland wore an Empire-style dress to the inauguration ball at her husband's return to the presidency in 1893. Although the style did not gain mass appeal, it foretold the popularity of a raised waistline that emerged toward the end of the next decade. Other elements of Aesthetic dress affected fashion: most important was the growing popularity of the tea gown. By the 1890s the style was still slightly novel, and fashion magazines were still promoting it as a relatively unfamiliar mode, but even major couture houses offered the tea gown fashioned on Aesthetic lines.

Top Aesthetic dress influenced high fashion, as demonstrated in a Worth tea gown from 1894 with its loose silhouette and celery green color – a favorite of the Aesthetes often parodied as "greenery-yallery."

Above A plate from *New York Fashions*, c. 1895, depicts a man and woman in practical daywear. The increased popularity of women's tailored ensembles and men's sack suits pointed to greater modernization in dress as the new century approached.

Right An American family in Oregon, c. 1892. Their clothing was probably a combination of ready-made, home-made, and constructed by dressmakers and tailors. Details such as a pierrot collar show how high fashion was interpreted in mainstream dress. The men exhibit a variety of coat styles.

Menswear

The rules that applied to women's clothing controlled masculine dress as well, but menswear exhibited much less stylistic variety. Men's clothing emphasized quality tailoring and well-dressed men obtained their clothing in Britain or from British tailors in other countries. Men adhered to the details established over the course of the 19th century: good wools, impeccable linen, and precise fit. But elements of "dash" in accessories and grooming were appreciated: well-groomed mustaches, hothouse flowers worn as boutonnières, and monocles slung on long ribbons. No man was judged properly dressed without an appropriate hat, well-polished shoes, and a distinctive walking stick. Posture was important and supportive corsets for men were worn to achieve "soldierly bearing." After fifty years of uncreased trousers, and a short-lived fashion for side-to-side creases, trousers began to be worn with a center crease, another example of how details defined male fashion. Cuffs (also known as turn-ups) were becoming common in menswear by the 1890s; while practical, cuffs represented a controversial addition to town wear because of their association with muddy ground and country dress. The frock coat began to appear old-fashioned and was increasingly replaced by the sack jacket, worn over matching trousers. The tuxedo (known as the dinner jacket) increasingly challenged the tailcoat for evening events.

Over their suits, men wore capes and overcoats, some known as Ulsters and reefers. The influence of sports clothing on men's town wear was noticeable; waterproof coats were seen on city streets and stores featured Mackintoshes and other rainwear. Burberry's Tielocken, a belted raincoat, was introduced in 1895, and worn by British officers during the second Boer War (1899–1902), furthering the company's reputation for practical, English style. The Norfolk jacket, named after the English county where Edward, Prince of Wales, had his country home, became popular for activities such as hunting and golf. Often made of traditional wool tweed in heathery tones, the thigh-length loose-fitting jacket had back pleats for easier movement and vertical bands applied to the front to protect the body of the jacket from the abrasion of slings and straps. Roomy flapped or patch pockets could be used for golf balls or

Top Summer looks for men, as shown in *New York Fashions*, June 1896, often emphasized light colors for clothing and accessories.

Above Loungewear included smoking jackets and luxurious wrappers, here illustrated in *New York Fashions*.

Right A sample book from New York's Edward Hart Mammoth Tailoring Establishment shows a variety of styles for men for spring and summer 1898.

EDWARD, PRINCE OF WALES

Albert Edward (1841–1910), the eldest son of Victoria, finally ascended to the throne in 1901 as King Edward VII. But in the latter half of the 19th century, the heir apparent, known as "Bertie," was greatly influencing public taste. Indifferent toward his studies, Edward's real talent lay in the realm of social relations. During the years before he became king, he traveled widely. A charming and diplomatic representative of Great Britain, he was welcomed in North America, the Middle East, and throughout Europe. Before his 1863 marriage to Alexandra of Denmark, Edward's romantic exploits caused great family stress. Queen Victoria blamed Edward for Prince Albert's death in 1861 from an illness Albert contracted during a visit to Cambridge to confront Edward about his bad behavior.

Throughout his life, despite his marriage with Alexandra (which produced six children), Edward was romantically linked to a series of glamorous, prominent women including Lillie Langtry and Jennie Churchill. Edward's vigor extended to sports and leisure pursuits, especially horse racing and hunting. At his country retreat at Sandringham in Norfolk, Edward favored Norfolk jackets often made up in tweeds and worn with matching vests and knickerbockers. He had a particular enthusiasm for boldly checked tweed outerwear. In the 1860s Edward's tailor invented the style that became known as the tuxedo. After a visit to Homburg, Germany, in 1889 Edward adopted the Homburg hat with its stiff, creased crown and shaped brim and this style was picked up by other well-dressed men. A taste for high living (or at least hearty eating) led to two other sartorial innovations associated with "Bertie" – the unbuttoned frock coat held together with a decorative chain, and the practice of wearing a waistcoat with the bottom button unfastened. Although this last detail was certainly seen before his time, Edward's appearance legitimized the look, which remains to this day an important detail. Despite his portly physique, Edward's sporty, often showy taste was very influential and his impact on men's fashions was surpassed only by his grandson, the future Duke of Windsor.

Edward, Prince of Wales, in 1891.

other equipment. The style became established as a wardrobe staple associated with affluent country leisure.

The light-colored clothing previously only worn for tennis, cricket, and boating infiltrated men's fashion. Off-white wool flannel pants were teamed with both matching and contrasting single-breasted blazers and worn for social occasions. Moving from resort to town wear, the immaculately kept white suit, in lightweight wool or crisp linen, became a familiar summer look for men.

Indoors, gentlemen relaxed in full-length wrappers (or robes), often made of fine wool, with loose cord waist ties and quilted satin cuffs and collar. Smoking jackets were by now an essential part of a gentleman's wardrobe; originally intended to save evening jackets from cigar and cigarette smoke, they were worn for after-dinner tobacco and increasingly for informal entertaining. They were available in velvets, soft silks, and brocades. These wrappers and jackets were worn over shirt, tie, and trousers. Smoking jackets and wrappers were influenced by Asian style in details such as frogged or scrolled closures.

Children's Fashion

Many items of children's dress continued unchanged from earlier decades. Descriptions in magazines and catalogs emphasized dressing children "properly" with an emphasis on practicality and style. Parents were urged to prepare their children for the upcoming season with practical pieces for everyday, outfits for specific sports and dressy ensembles for social occasions. Corsets for children were still widely accepted. Some models had elastic stocking supporters attached.

The prevailing styles of adult fashion found their way into children's clothes. Smocks and dresses for young boys and girls featured large, gathered sleeves, similar to the gigot sleeves worn by women. School-age girls wore gathered, triangular skirts and flat hats trimmed with flowers and ribbons – the youthful versions of their mothers' gored skirts and decorative platter-shaped millinery. Jackets for boys often resembled the popular Norfolk jacket and were worn with knickerbockers, known as "knickers." Leggings (sometimes also called leggins) were buttoned leg warmers made of leather, heavy cloth or, for the most dressed-up occasions, black velvet. Combined with supportive, laced-up ankle boots, the leggings were worn by boys too young for trousers.

Right Foundation garments for children were worn for posture training, and readily available through department stores and catalogs. These examples were offered by Jordan Marsh in spring/summer 1897.

Far right The Norfolk jacket popular for menswear was also often seen on young boys, here worn with leather leggings for cold weather in an illustration from 1896.

Above left & right The *Journal des Demoiselles* illustrated a range of children's styles in 1891. Of particular note are the floral "Greenaway" dress and the Russian-style tunic on the boy in brown knickers.

Sailor suits had become standard for boys and girls. Boys wore sailor blouses with knee-length knickers and dark wool stockings that covered the knee. Soft, banded berets or upturned, ribbon-trimmed straw hats often completed the outfit. Girls' sailor blouses were worn over pleated or gathered skirts. In keeping with the maritime origins of the style, a palette of white, navy, and light blue predominated. By fourteen, girls wore dresses that were just above ankle length and reflected current adult trends, with a marked waistline and trimmer skirt. Boys wore two-piece outfits consisting of blouses or jackets with knee- or mid-calf-length trousers. On reaching adolescence, they wore long trousers.

A trend for the picturesque influenced children's dress. Exotic and historical touches were popular for dressy outfits in particular. Little girls were sometimes dressed in ankle-length Empire-waisted gowns referred to as "Greenaway" dresses, making reference to the popular illustrator of children's books Kate Greenaway, and the term "Russian" described any number of variations on shirts for boys and dresses for girls that featured band collars, asymmetrical buttoning and embroidered yokes.

Tattooing in Fashion

Tattooing, practiced throughout Europe for centuries, had by the mid-19th century become marginalized to sailors, circus performers, and prison convicts. The British and American navies in particular drew inspiration from the cultures of the South Pacific they encountered. In Japan, the practice was outlawed, in part to encourage Westernization by suppressing the "barbaric" custom. Japanese tattooing went underground and became associated with organized crime. In coastal towns, however, tattoo art flourished as many tattoo parlors still operated. The laws that governed tattooing allowed Japanese practitioners to tattoo non-Japanese foreigners, usually sailors, but also curious and daring civilians. Following the example of their father, Edward (who had been tattooed in Jerusalem in 1862), Prince Albert Victor and Prince George Frederick (later King George V) received tattoos in Yokohama during the 1880s. The Tsarevich Nicholas (later Nicholas II of Russia) followed the lead of his lookalike British cousins and also got a Japanese tattoo. Other European aristocrats soon followed the fashion.

EUGEN SANDOW

Eugene Sandow. [*sic*] – Just two words but what a wealth of romance and magic is woven around them. As the mind ponders upon that name it drifts back to mythology, where the lords of Valhalla hold sway with the legendary heroes of Rome and Greece. It hardly seems possible that the material world of the twentieth century ever accepted a living individual, and cloaked him with the same glamour. But it did. Eugene Sandow is not a myth, he was a living, breathing being of flesh and bone like you and me. Yes, but such flesh and bone!

Eugen Sandow, c. 1900.

So proclaimed George F. Jowett in a tribute to Eugen Sandow in the March 1927 issue of *Strength*. Such lofty and mythic language was, and still is, part of the Sandow legacy.

Eugen Sandow (1867–1925) was born in Königsberg, Prussia. A weak and sickly child, he defied conventional wisdom of the time that held that one had to be born strong to be strong as an adult; he built up his body and became known as a competitive wrestler. Rising to prominence through strength competitions, Sandow began his stage performances in London in 1889. He came to the attention of impresario Florenz Ziegfeld Jr., who exhibited him at Chicago's Columbian Exhibition in 1893, and in vaudeville.

Before Sandow, strongmen were commonly circus and sideshow attractions. Whereas other performing strongmen of the time were noteworthy for their feats of strength, Sandow's popularity was achieved not by his lifting prowess but by his posing and flexing. In sculpting his own body, Sandow became a scholar of ancient Greek and Roman statuary. Studying the proportions of the ideal classical physique, he incorporated poses from antiquity into his performances. He served as an artist's model, and was famously photographed mimicking well-known antique sculptures, notably the Dying Gaul.

This "Father of Modern Bodybuilding" played an important role in its development as a competitive sport, and recorded his methods in how-to books that were landmarks in the field. He encouraged a more sporty, athletic male image that thrived at the end of the 19th century, and his physical achievements influenced the modern ideal of the gym-toned physique. Embodying the extremes of the decade, during the 1890s his raw, if contrived, form of masculinity stood in sharp contrast to Oscar Wilde's effeminate aestheticism, but also to the stylish and rakish dandyism of Edward, Prince of Wales. As Oscar and Edward were defined by their clothing, Sandow was defined by his nakedness. Jowett, in the article quoted above, declared: "As Moses led the children of Israel from bondage, this man led humanity from the stranglehold of Victorian foppery."

By the 1890s the practice became increasingly widespread in Europe and the United States, encouraged by the invention of the electric tattoo machine by Samuel O'Reilly, a tattoo artist working in New York's Bowery neighborhood. While the aristocracy, both male and female, got tattooed, major newspapers reported on the trend as alarming and decadent and identified tattooing as "foreign." Although the middle-class public flocked to see full-body-tattooed circus performers such as "La Belle Irene" or Barnum's "Constantine," the trend was disturbing outside of the bounds of these socially marginalized groups. Social arbiter Ward McCallister referred to the trend as "vulgar and barbarous" as it gained popularity among "The Four Hundred," New York's 400 most prominent socialites.

Looking Toward a New Century

As the year 1900 and a new century came closer, the world anticipated with uncertainty a future of new inventions and technologies. Science fiction flourished in this decade, notably through the popular works of British author H. G. Wells, whose novels *The Time Machine* and *The War of the Worlds* presented threatening scenarios of alien visitors and menacing machinery. But in reality, what had seemed like fantasy was taking shape in the form of developments in motion pictures, sound, and transportation. By 1899, preparations were underway for the Exposition Universelle of Paris of 1900, a momentous event that would herald and celebrate emerging technologies and inventions, and showcase them to a world hungry for the new. The exposition featured the work of many of the leading couture houses. Fashion anticipated the new century as dressing for high society, once determined by the time of day, was increasingly influenced by technology and activity, indicating fashion's response to the modern way of life.

A picture of tattoos in the *New York World*, August 29, 1897, accompanied an article that dubbed tattooing a "startling French fad."

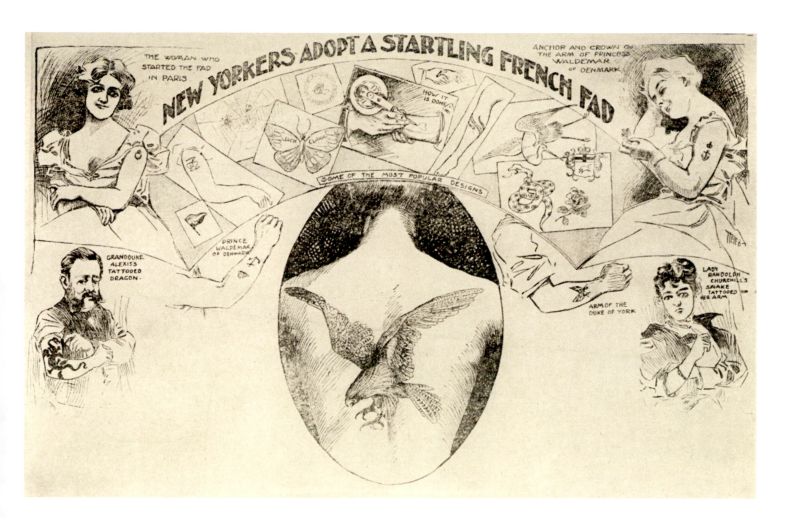

Chapter 3

The 1900s

A New Century

The Western world entered the new century celebrating modernity and innovation. Devices and processes created over the previous twenty years achieved widespread usage and visibility, and the average man or woman of 1900 may have witnessed the telephone and telegraph, the gramophone and the automobile. The first successful powered flight in 1903 showed that air travel could be a reality. Electricity was a novelty when it illuminated the Eiffel Tower in 1889, but by 1900 it was in many homes, even changing the way clothes were maintained as electric irons became common and electric washing machines were introduced.

This sense of innovation was reflected in the continued development of practical, modern fashions. While the look of women's clothing was still defined by corsetry until the end of the decade, the fashions that emerged encouraged a more natural line. Menswear dispensed with some of the 19th-century formalities in favor of more functional styles. Practical work clothing and recreational attire became more important categories of fashion.

Opposite Illustrator J. C. Leyendecker (1907) captures the excitement of the newly available automobile, which required special clothing for drivers and passengers.

Right Wilhelm Gause's painting *Ball der Stadt Wien* depicts the elan of the Belle Epoque, with pastel gowns and formal menswear at an official reception in 1904.

Top Pablo Picasso's *Woman with a Cape* (1901) pictures fashionable dress through the lens of his emerging modern art style.

Above This cigarette case from Fabergé, with its dragonfly motif, exemplifies the continued taste for art nouveau. It was a gift from Empress Alexandra of Russia to her brother, Ernst Ludwig, Grand Duke of Hesse.

Social and Economic Background

The start of the new century saw the United States coming into its own as a world power, as a producer of capital goods, a consumer of luxury items, and still a destination for struggling emigrants from the Old World. With immigration, the populations of North American cities mushroomed. Although the new arrivals frequently lived in poverty, industrial activity was thriving in growing cities such as New York, Chicago, Montreal, Philadelphia, and Boston. New cultural institutions blossomed, often financed by successful industrialists who exploited the cheap immigrant labor.

Continued growth in garment manufacturing led to increased unionization on both sides of the Atlantic. In New York City, organizing efforts of workers, often Mediterranean and Eastern European immigrants, were important in the formation of the International Ladies' Garments Workers' Union (ILGWU), founded in 1900. A strike in Paris in 1901 involved several thousand tailors who served the most prominent Parisian couture houses. The strike emphasized the divisions between the tailoring and dressmaking segments of the industry as the tailors, predominantly male, sought to bring the female dressmakers on board with the effort to organize. The aims of the strikers included reductions in working hours and the establishment of wage standards. In New York in 1909, 20,000 shirtwaist makers went on strike, affecting the middle-priced sector of the industry.

This period was also marked by growing international tensions. Following in the wake of the assassination of Elisabeth of Austria in 1898, several heads of state were killed early in the decade. In Italy, King Umberto was shot by an anarchist in 1900, a murder that possibly inspired an American anarchist to shoot President William McKinley in 1901. In Serbia, in 1903, a group of dissidents savagely murdered King Aleksander and Queen Draga. Britain, France, and Russia enjoyed a solid alliance, while Germany and France continued bitter resentments, left over from the Franco-Prussian War. Germany's relations with both Britain and Russia were also strained – ironically, as the royal families were all related through the family line of Queen Victoria. In Africa, disagreements over African territories brought European powers into conflict. In the Pacific arena unrest brewed while Japan continued to westernize and grow in influence and military strength. Other European nations were involved in colonial conflicts in Southeast Asia.

The United States' aggressive defense of Cuban independence from Spain resulted in the Spanish-American War of 1898, and American success added the gloss of military victory to its growing reputation for industrial might. As a result Cuba, Puerto Rico, Guam, and the Philippines were released from Spanish control. Theodore Roosevelt emerged from the war a popular public figure, the embodiment of national capability and a symbol of a new masculinity.

The Arts

Henri Matisse, André Derain, Maurice de Vlaminck, and others used exciting, unexpected color and brush strokes in their vivid depictions of people and places for expressive effect and became known as Fauves. In 1907, Pablo Picasso painted *Les Demoiselles d'Avignon* using Fauvism and African art as springboards to a new style. Georges Braque created artworks that incorporated found materials in Cubist interpretations of still lifes, landscapes, and portraits.

Contemporary art and decor in art nouveau, *Jugendstil*, and Arts and Crafts style appealed to an artistic elite. The popular new Mission style, a North American manifestation of Arts and Crafts, was marked by simplicity and "honest" lack of decoration. Frank Lloyd Wright's innovative "Prairie" style was informed by the ideals of Mission. However, the revival styles of the previous generation were still in circulation; prominent architects such as New York's Stanford White championed the Beaux-Arts aesthetic.

Art nouveau was still popular in Europe, particularly in luxury decorative items. Cartier, Fabergé, and Lalique created exquisite objects including jewelry, cigarette

Top Poster of the original 1900 Opéra-Comique production of *Louise* by Gustave Charpentier.

Above Ivan Bilibin's costume design for *Le Coq d'Or* (1908) exemplifies the trend for Russian folkloric revival in art and stage works and anticipates fashion trends of coming years.

cases, and decorative accessories. French watchmaker Louis Cartier created what were probably the first wristwatches, for aviator Alberto Santos-Dumont, in 1904, and the style eventually replaced the pocket watch. The House of Fabergé won renown for the spectacular Easter eggs commissioned by the Russian royal family. With several stores in Russia and in Britain, Fabergé also sold a wide variety of jewelry and accessories. René Jules Lalique achieved lasting fame for his glass designs, but also created jewelry and decorative objects, often including darkly romantic, almost gothic, snakes and bats.

Fiction writers as diverse as Marcel Proust, Jack London, Joseph Conrad, Thomas Mann, and Sidonie-Gabrielle Colette were creating new work that sharply contrasted to the fiction of the 19th century. In Great Britain, Harley Granville Barker wrote *The Voysey Inheritance*, a drama of familial manners, while in the United States, Langdon Mitchell examined issues of divorce in his play *The New York Idea*. John Millington Synge put the gritty aspects of Irish life on the stage, to both comic and tragic effect. As both playwright and producer, David Belasco presented a new, more naturalistic type of drama on the Broadway stage, including *Madame Butterfly* and *The Girl of the Golden West*. Florenz Ziegfeld premiered his first Follies on Broadway in 1907, a lavish production that would come to define the genre.

In Vienna, following in the tradition of the immensely popular Johann Strauss II, Franz Lehár composed *The Merry Widow*, a charming treatment of the problems of the old-fashioned aristocracy. The work premiered to great success in Vienna in 1905, and other productions around Europe soon followed. Lehár's frothy work contrasted with more modern currents in Vienna, where Sigmund Freud's development of psychoanalysis and the Wiener Werkstätte's advanced design stimulated the cultural scene.

Opera continued to flourish in this decade. Richard Strauss adapted Oscar Wilde's *Salome* in 1905, continuing the scandal associated with the work. Puccini adapted David Belasco's play *Madame Butterfly* in 1904. Puccini's version experimented with a new naturalistic dramatic style on the operatic stage but, with its kimono-clad heroine, also continued the taste for orientalism. Gustave Charpentier's *Louise* depicted life in the French dressmaking industry, while French composers Claude Debussy and Maurice Ravel explored new tone colors that followed movements in the visual arts. Italian tenor Enrico Caruso was the first superstar of recorded sound; the Victor Victrola, which debuted in 1906, was the earliest record player to become widely successful.

In the United States, ragtime, an early form of jazz, combined an African-influenced, syncopated beat with romantic-style melodies and influence from European polka. Ragtime's most important composer was Scott Joplin (c. 1867–1917), who was influenced by both his African American heritage and his German piano teacher in synthesizing a style that had a major impact on the history of popular music. To the mainstream white public, ragtime was both infectious and subversive.

Film, which had debuted as a novelty in the 1890s, was now a popular form of entertainment and an international industry. Georges Méliès' *Le Voyage dans la Lune* (*A Trip to the Moon*) (1902) and Edwin S. Porter's *The Great Train Robbery* (1903) were among the most successful early films. By 1905, movie houses became more common. In 1906, the Australian Charles Tait directed the first feature-length (70 minutes) film, *The Story of the Kelly Gang*. Individual film actors and actresses were not yet "stars" but a few, including the on-screen cowboys Gilbert Anderson and Tom Mix, drew devoted fans.

During the reign of Nicholas II in the 1900s, Russian artists and designers continued to develop the Neo-Russian style. For a 1903 masquerade, the imperial court and their guests wore costumes inspired by Old Russia. This taste was also seen onstage, where the designs of illustrator Ivan Bilibin, inspired by Russian folk art, were particularly noteworthy. The style was elevated further by Léon Bakst, who became the principal set and costume designer for the Ballets Russes, a spectacular dance company that debuted in Paris in 1909 under impresario Serge Diaghilev. Their work

furthered the Neo-Russian movement and also embraced avant-garde sensibilities with sensual dance style and vivid productions.

Fashion and Society

For the fashionable upper classes the international social whirl continued, given added steam by Edward VII's ascension to the British throne. As the king and queen, Edward and Alexandra's impact on fashion continued, although they were some of the most mature style setters that the 20th century would know. The country observed a lengthy state mourning following the death of Victoria, so they had served as king and queen for more than a year by the time that they were officially crowned in 1902. Alexandra's wardrobe for the mourning period consisted primarily of black, purple, lavender, and white toilettes, liberally decorated with jet. Maud of Wales, the daughter of Edward and Alexandra, became Queen of Norway in 1906. Maud's style was as remarkable as her mother's; she possessed exquisite taste and her clothing was supplied by important court dressmakers and couturiers.

Other women also exerted great influence on the tastes of the day. The elegant Italian opera singer Lina Cavalieri (1874–1944) was often referred to as the most beautiful woman in the world, celebrated for her remarkable looks and her lithe wasp waist. Cavalieri was painted by great artists of the day, and her elegant couture wardrobe was pictured in alluring *carte de visite* images.

The popularity of the Gibson Girl image continued, and the typical separates ensemble had been adapted into mainstream style. But onstage a different interpretation of the character was popularized when London producer Seymour Hicks presented "The Gibson Girls," competitors to popular chorus-girl ensembles including the "Gaiety Girls" and the "Florodora Girls." Belgian-born Camille Clifford (1885–1971) was selected as the ultimate example of the Gibson Girl in a highly publicized competition that involved Charles Dana Gibson himself. She performed as the Gibson Girl in both New York and London. Her image was reproduced in many souvenir photographs where she copied poses and scenes from the original Gibson Girl cartoons. Ironically, with her extreme wasp waist, sculpted princess-line dresses and Gainsborough-style headdress, Clifford's version of the Gibson Girl deviated significantly from the original character.

Progressive American women, such as Alice Roosevelt, were more accurate exemplars of the modern, liberated spirit of Gibson's original creation. Another such woman was American stage actress Ethel Barrymore (1879–1959). Barrymore changed the perception of actresses, and encouraged the theatrical world to take her, and her profession, more seriously, without the artifice of the prevailing star system. Barrymore rejected the frilly styles of the day in favor of sartorial simplicity. She preferred uncomplicated hairstyling and streamlined dresses, disliking the changes of dress during the course of the day that high fashion dictated.

Great portrait artists such as Giovanni Boldini, Paul César Helleu, and Philip Alexius de László captured prominent women in the luxurious fabrics and glittering jewels of the Edwardian age. Conversely, the cartoons by Georges Goursat, under the pen name Sem, poked fun at the leisured class. Despite increasing political turmoil, the spirit of the Belle Epoque continued through the decade. The wealthy frequented luxurious hotels and resort areas such as the Riviera. Financing this lifestyle required money, and wealth began to outshine titles in the social scheme. Wealthy American heiresses married into prominent, but insolvent, European families. Women such as Consuelo, Duchess of Marlborough (née Consuelo Vanderbilt), and the Princesse de Polignac (the former Winnaretta Singer, an heiress to the Singer sewing machine fortune) were international fashion leaders whose patronage was essential to the couturiers. The tastes of Americans visiting Paris haute couture houses had a significant impact, leading Isadore Paquin to remark that "fashions are made by the Americans."[1] Despite the increasingly global influence of the United States, no American designer rose to the level of fame of the French or British designers, although some articles of the time indicate the presence of American business efforts in Paris' fashion industry.

Top Italian opera singer Lina Cavalieri, here painted by Giovanni Boldini c. 1901, was often touted as the most beautiful woman of the age. Her distinctive center-parted hair differed from the prevailing pulled-back hairstyle.

Above Photographed here for the cover of *Theatre* magazine, actress Ethel Barrymore favored simple styles.

Alice Roosevelt, the eldest daughter of Theodore Roosevelt, photographed in 1902.

ALICE ROOSEVELT

Photographs of Alice Roosevelt (1884–1980) show a slender young woman with perfect posture, thick chestnut hair, and a determined countenance. The oldest child of Theodore Roosevelt, she was chronicled during her father's terms as Governor of New York and then President of the United States, she fascinated the American public and inspired other young women to imitate her style. During her father's presidency, Alice was the most photographed woman in America. She was presented to society at a White House ball and the event sparked her resolve to "have a good time," as she later wrote in her memoirs; the rebellious Alice partied enthusiastically, smoked in public, and socialized with an international group. On an official trip to Asia, Alice met Nicholas Longworth, a congressman from Ohio, and they were married in 1906. The public devoured details of Alice's American-made white silk wedding dress and the press followed the couple on their honeymoon to Cuba. In tribute to her influence on fashion, she was immortalized in popular music with the 1919 song "Alice Blue Gown." Marriage to a politician kept her in the public eye and Alice maintained her stylish appearance and interest in fashion. The large hats that were fashionable during her youth became a signature look throughout her life.

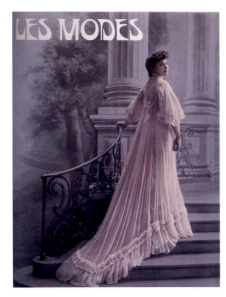

Above Singer and actress Gabrielle Réjane wearing a *robe d'intérieur* by the house of Doucet on a 1902 cover of *Les Modes*, the most prestigious French fashion magazine of the decade.

Below left to right Dresses from Boué Soeurs, Ernest Raudnitz, and L. Perdoux et Cie., as illustrated in the fashion folio created by the Paris couture syndicate for the 1900 Exposition Universelle.

Opposite A group of tailor-mades and promenade suits are illustrated in *Façon Tailleur* magazine c. 1902. A variety of hat shapes are shown, including 18th century-inspired tricorne styles.

Fashion Media

Periodicals covered both high society and developments in fashion. The fashion press in the United States grew with the debut of the fashion supplement section of the *New York Herald* on Sunday January 7, 1900. *Harper's Bazar* continued as an important fashion magazine, while *Ladies' Home Journal* covered fashion along with other household topics. *Les Parisiennes*, published by American Fashion Co. in New York, offered readers "the very latest Paris modes" and included descriptions in English, French, and German. In 1909, American businessman and publisher Condé Nast purchased the society weekly *Vogue* and repositioned the journal as a fashion magazine. The fashion press began to incorporate photography, a medium whose presence in fashion grew steadily for several decades. *Harper's Bazar* began including photographs in the late 1890s. Photography was particularly important in *Les Modes*, the French fashion publication that included numerous photographs of the work of the French design houses. Each issue featured a cover and some interior photos that were evocatively colorized.

The Paris Exhibition of 1900

The 1900 Exposition Universelle was a remarkable event in many ways. The second modern Olympic Games were held in conjunction with the exhibition and the fair was an important factor in the development of the Paris Métro. A huge stone sculpture representing *La Parisienne* – with "clothes" designed by Mme. Jeanne Paquin – was perched atop the main entrance and welcomed visitors to the fair. Fifty-eight countries participated and exciting emerging technologies were displayed. Fair attendees could circle the grounds on a *trottoir roulant*, a moving sidewalk loop over a mile and three-quarters (three kilometers) in length, and the electric light of the brightly illuminated fairgrounds was dramatically reflected in the River Seine. While the fair offered the latest technology, the design scheme represented art nouveau at its apogee.

Most of the leading fashion designers of the day were represented at the Exposition in a presentation organized by Mme. Paquin. The fashions featured in the Exposition were displayed on forms and lavishly reproduced in folios. The House of Worth's exhibit featured wax figures in a theatrical-style setting that suggested the typical activities of fashionable women.

The Elements of Women's Fashion

The *Pictorial Review* of January 1901 stated that the tailor-made costume was "a faithful reflection of modern manners and customs." Its casualness and practicality were by now more appreciated and the suit was established as a mainstream component of

831   832   833   834

B. FINKELSTEIN & BRUDER

831

832

833

834

Above The exquisitely fashionable Queen Maud of Norway casually glances at the newspaper, wearing a gown by the Parisian couture house Laferrière.

a woman's wardrobe. This emphasis on practicality also reflected the changing role of women, as efforts for women's rights grew more assertive. The popularity of the shirtwaist blouse also continued; simple styles were featured along with more decorative options and often all types of blouses were referred to as "waists." The promenade suit, the more decorative version of the tailor-made, continued to grow in popularity.

Although vivid colors continued in vogue, strongly reasserted at the end of the decade, a refined and delicate color story enjoyed great popularity in both day and evening dress. While simplicity and modernity were important, a taste for decoration still dominated fashionable ladies' clothing, but was more delicate than the rather drastic, high-contrast extremes of the mid-1890s. Dresses were detailed with a profusion of ornament, such as beadwork, passementerie trim, soft self bows, ruffles and puffs, appliqué, exotic tassel fringe, and contrasting fabric textures. A nautical color theme, inspired by sailor uniforms, also enjoyed widespread popularity. Mothers walking through the park often coordinated charmingly with their children clad in sailor-style middy blouses, as the navies of Great Britain, the United States, Japan, and Russia were all powerful forces across the seas. Even evening gowns reflected the trend.

New developments in corsetry achieved the prevailing bodice shape, often called pouter pigeon style. Bodices were usually fitted across the back, but very full in the front with fullness gathered into the neck or a yoke, and gathered again into the waistband. The skirt maintained the trumpet shape that evolved in the late 1890s, becoming even more fitted through the hips, further approaching an art nouveau-inflected lily shape. Skirt length varied, ranging from trained to slightly off the floor depending on formality and activity. Sometimes skirts and bodices were joined together, a construction that became more common.

Collars continued to be very high and stiffened, and any open neckline during the daytime, no matter how slight, was quite unusual. For evening, square, gently rounded, and V necklines all continued from the 1890s, and the bateau style was also

Above An American bride and groom pose for their wedding portrait in 1901. The bride wears a lingerie-style dress made of silk, with her headdress decorated with orange blossoms.

Below This advertisement for Royal Worcester and Bon-Ton Corsets features the exaggerated S-curve shape that came into fashion around 1900.

Opposite bottom Sailor influence on womenswear can be seen with these two dresses, the left for afternoon illustrated in *La Mode Illustreé*, and the right for evening, shown in *Le Bon Ton*, both 1903.

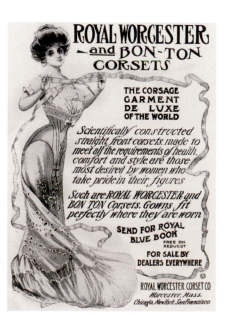

popular. As the decade started, sleeves were often simple and fitted, with small puffs at the shoulder. The most important sleeve development was the popularity of a looser sleeve that was more fitted at the top and became full at the wrists, gathered into a cuff, commonly known as a bishop sleeve. Sometimes, especially in tailor-made and promenade suits, the sleeve of the jacket was straight or slightly flared, ending at three-quarter length, exposing the bishop-style sleeve of an underblouse. Evening bodices were often sleeveless and worn with long gloves, but other evening styles show elbow-length puffed sleeves, or narrow upper sleeves ending in an 18th-century-style ruffle. Sometimes formal afternoon dresses featured elbow-length sleeves and were also worn with long gloves.

Experimentation with the position of the waistline was characteristic of this period. Short-waisted bodices, beginning shortly after 1900, showed a waistline at the mid-ribcage. Some dresses had a two-waistline effect that was created with both construction and trim detail. Princess-line dresses returned to fashion around 1905, often for daytime dress occasions such as the promenade, and in eveningwear. Some examples actually combined princess-line panels in one area (usually down the front) with waist seams on other parts of the dress. A raised waist became typical by 1908.

"Lingerie dresses" were made of cotton, linen, and sometimes plain silks, with underwear details, such as inset rows of lace, tucks, and small ruffles. A trend that had its roots in late 19th-century styles, lingerie dresses were worn for any number of occasions, particularly in spring and summer seasons. Especially delicate and detailed versions were worn for daytime formal events, including receptions, garden parties, and school graduations, and lingerie dresses became very common for wedding gowns. The lingerie dress was also sometimes worn for casual summertime eveningwear.

Foundations and Lingerie

Changes in corsetry at the very end of the 1890s led to the popularity of the S-curve (or S-bend) shape by 1900. The S curve was created by a stiff busk down the center front that tilted the top of the ribcage forward and caused the pelvis to tilt backward. Some corsets in this new line were initially promoted as "healthier" as they reduced the amount of pressure on the sides of the waist. In reality, this "health benefit" was offset by the strain of the unnatural posture. The fully S-curve shape was often achieved with additional foundation pieces. Small dress improver pads continued to be worn on the buttocks and "bust improvers" filled in the space between the breasts, to enhance size and encourage a low placement of the bust point. The beauty ideal was that of an ample-bosomed, mature woman, reflecting the aging of full-figured celebrities including Frances Folsom Cleveland, Nellie Melba, and Lillian Russell. Corset covers, camisoles, and drawers were worn, and combinations were popular. Petticoats were gored and had elaborate ruffles to create extra flare at the bottom of the skirt. In 1907 the DeBevoise Company advertised its "Brassiere" as a "close-fitting, bust supporting corset cover." Such early forms of the brassiere were substantial in size and sometimes called "bust bodice." Stockings, although largely hidden in daily life, were often very ornamental. Knitted of silk, cotton, or fine wool, often in lacy patterns, stockings were available in a variety of colors and were decorated with embroidered tendrils, bows and other fanciful motifs.

Maternity and Plus-Size Clothing

In 1904, Lena Himmelstein Bryant opened her store on Fifth Avenue in New York, and, because of a clerical error, the business became known as Lane Bryant. Lane Bryant specialized in fashion for "stout" figures and offered maternity clothes. At the time pregnancy was seen as a private, and not very fashionable, state and Lane Bryant's offerings represented the beginning of an important specialty market.

Maternity corsets were very widely advertised. The Berthe May Company of New York claimed its maternity corset "insures ease and comfort to the mother and safeguards the life of the expected child. It allows the mother to dress as usual and to preserve a normal figure."[2]

Outerwear and Millinery

Coats and jackets were essential parts of women's wardrobes in the colder seasons. Full length, three-quarter, mid-length, and waist length were all available options. The coats also reflected the stylish silhouettes of the garments underneath. Often military influence could be seen in the trimming. New looser-fitting styles of outerwear included short boxy unfitted jackets. *La Mode Illustrée* in 1903 featured an illustration of a *jaquette mi-ajustée*, a semi-fitted, hip-length jacket for informal walking and town attire. Longer coats, often between knee and calf length, were loose in an almost A-line shape with wide flared sleeves. This style became known as the "kimono coat" and, although it was by no means the authentic T-shaped garment of Japan, the loose fit suggested a resemblance to its namesake. Kimono coats were available in a variety of fabrics for day and evening and had a strong impact on coat style that grew into the 1910s.

Hats continued to grow in size during this decade. Eighteenth-century portraits often reproduced in fashion magazines served as inspiration for millinery and underscored the similarity of styles between the two eras. As the hats grew even larger, the amount of trims increased and the effect was even more striking and dramatic than before. Hat-wearing protocols changed somewhat as hats became such a prominent feature of fashion; they were seen indoors even in evening-dress situations. Fashion illustrations and society portraiture often featured women in evening dress with large and aggressively plumed hats. Paintings by artists as diverse as Picasso and William Merritt Chase demonstrate their fascination with the period's outsize millinery creations.

Fur Outerwear

Fur outerwear for women became especially popular and an important component of Edwardian style. An increased taste for fur clothing in this decade was probably influenced by the Franco-Russian Alliance dating from 1892; not only was Russia a major supplier of pelts, but fur fashions were already common there. Leading furriers exhibited at the 1900 Exposition and important French couturiers offered fur pieces. Men's winter coats in this period were trimmed and lined in fur, with fur collars, revers, and cuffs. However, the most spectacular furs were worn by women: seal, fox, sable, otter, ermine, skunk, and squirrel were all utilized, frequently in combinations with one fur for the main body and another contrasting type as trim. Heads and especially tails were very popular as trimming on all types of fur pieces.

Canada and Russia were the most important sources of fur. The center of the Russian trade was in the Siberian Urals. Revillon Frères, a transatlantic fur company from Paris, set up a number of trading posts in northern Canada, and along with the Hudson Bay Company (already established there) furnished great quantities of fur for the fashionable in European and North American urban centers. Holt Renfrew continued to specialize in furs, and by 1900 the company had expanded from its Quebec City location to include stores in Montreal and Toronto.

Designers

As the Exposition Universelle indicated, the French fashion industry was a well-organized and creative universe. Most of the couture houses maintained well-appointed salons, now typically electrified and very frequently decorated in Louis XVI style. Salespeople and models (referred to as mannequins) were present at the front of the house, with the designer or design personnel accessible to greet important clients and supervise fittings. Usually the large workrooms were on the premises but hidden from the public. In addition to the top level of couture houses, there were

dressmakers, tailors, milliners and furriers, and the many suppliers necessary for the creation and sale of their output. French fashion periodicals of the time indicate that a very wide variety of specialists advertised in the important magazines. Many of the top couturiers of Paris were profiled by Frederic Lees in *Pall Mall*, a British general-interest arts and lifestyle periodical, in 1902. Lees' article recounts his travels around Paris' fashion district, paying calls at several of the leading houses including Paquin, Redfern, Laferrière, Beer, and Worth.

The **House of Worth** was rather tied to the past, as its established client base had grown older, and was still stylistically more in sympathy with the 1880s and 1890s than with the new century. Sometimes this old-fashioned conservatism was noted in the press. But more often, whether or not the ideas were fresh, the House of Worth was still regarded as a major force in fashion and the source of elegant creations. Their London presence expanded with a full service branch in 1902.[3]

The first years of the 20th century represented the zenith of the house of **Doucet**. Its remarkable output included creations made of soft, often diaphanous, fabrics embellished with lace, ribbon, and floral embroidery in a low-contrast, refined color palette with elements of Japonisme. During this decade, Doucet himself took less involvement in the house and continued to concentrate on his art collection. The design direction of the house was in the hands of longtime Doucet employee José de la Peña de Guzman.

Redfern Ltd., as it was now called, was at the height of its success and stylistic influence. The Cowes branch that had begun the fashion empire closed during this decade. The focus moved more toward couture: while the London store was considered the place to purchase the very English tailor-made and sports styles, Redfern's Paris store was highly regarded for its superb couture creations. In truth, both types of clothing could be had at either store. Paris was now the dominant branch and Charles Poynter Redfern of the Paris store became the head of all of Redfern Ltd. in 1902. Poynter Redfern was instrumental in keeping the taste for the 18th century popular

in fashion, with Watteau-style pleats on mantles and tea gowns and white mousseline "Romney frocks." He also endorsed the Empire-style elevated waist as an option to other styles. Poynter Redfern was creating "à la Grecque" and Directoire dresses early in the decade.

Laferrière was by this time a very old and venerable house; when the founder of the house, Madeleine Laferrière, passed away is unclear, but contemporary accounts indicate that the business was continuing without her by this decade. The house was under the directorship of Arsène Bonnaire, who was active in the administration of the Chambre Syndicale. The look was subtle, elegant, and exquisitely detailed. According to Lees, Maison Laferrière was the most important supplier of gowns to the British court, and Laferrière was well represented in the wardrobes of both Queen Alexandra and her daughter Queen Maud of Norway.

Gustave Beer enjoyed great attention from the fashion press of the time, including *The New York Times* and *Les Modes*. With great skill and remarkable taste and artistry, Beer was a notable supplier of gowns to well-dressed noble clients including the Empress of Germany, the Queen of Portugal, and Russian duchesses. Lees' article in *Pall Mall* stated that "beside being the most aristocratic, he is the most expensive house in the world." Beer opened other salons in towns popular with his elite clientele, including Monte Carlo.

Paquin had grown a great deal in only a decade with success in both their Paris and London branches. Isidore Paquin remained the visible sales and business manager, and the design contributions of Jeanne were widely acknowledged, thanks in part to her significant involvement in the Exposition Universelle. In the early years of the 1900s, Paquin emphasized Directoire-style toilettes in soft supple fabrics often using layers of delicate materials, an emerging trend that both defied the stiffness of the 1890s and looked to the future.

Callot Soeurs were known for highly refined work, frequently decorated and delicately embroidered. Their mother was a lacemaker, and the Callot sisters often included lace in their work to ethereal effect. They embraced art nouveau and exotic Asiatic influences. **Marie Callot Gerber** (c. 1870–1927) emerged as the lead designer, noted for her technical expertise as well as an experimental aesthetic.

The Orient Express connected Western Europe to Central Europe and the Balkans. The March run of the train earned the nickname "*train des couturières*" because it carried the principal designers and saleswomen from the top Eastern European fashion houses to Paris, where they picked up the newest styles for clientele in Vienna, Budapest, and Sofia. Among the most notable Eastern European designers was the Vienna-based Baron Christoph von Drecoll. "His house enjoyed the favour of southeastern Europe and the Levant – upper class Roumanians and Serbians, rich Greeks, the *chic* of Alexandria and Cairo, French cities both. In his employ was a young and ambitious Austrian pair, Monsieur and Madame Wagner."[4] M. and Mme. de Wagner opened a branch of **Drecoll** in Paris under a licensing agreement, with him as business manager and her as designer.

Lucile made an advantageous marriage to Lord Cosmo Duff Gordon in 1900. Lady Duff Gordon, as she became known, grew the business significantly in this decade: Lady Gordon's younger sister, the author Elinor Glyn, wore Lucile clothes and Glyn's society connections attracted clients to Maison Lucile. Lucile added many women of royalty and nobility to her client list. In 1905 she reorganized the business, incorporating as **Lucile Ltd.** She began to experiment with themes that would characterize her work: exoticism and romanticism. Detailing was refined and feminine and her style was naturally suited to luscious and graceful tea gowns. Strongly disliking the practice of labeling prototypes with numbers, Lucile frequently gave provocative names to her designs – such as "Passionate Longing" – and thought of her designs in romantic emotional contexts. These theatrical qualities attracted successful actresses to the house, and Lucile was often commissioned for stage costumes, including those for British actress Lily Elsie in a 1907 production of *The Merry Widow*. Among the costumes was a hat that was just a little wider and just a little higher than the prevailing mode. The slight but noticeable exaggeration of current fashion was quickly and widely adopted, and the new larger hat style was often referred to as the "Merry Widow Hat." Lucile's innovative, theatrical fashion presentations contributed to the establishment of runway fashion shows in years to come.

British retailer **Liberty of London** was still an influential distributor of Aesthetic styles and the influence of Aesthetic ideals on mainstream fashion was more widely accepted. This was especially reflected in the work of Paul Poiret and Mariano Fortuny.

Paul Poiret (1879–1944) began his career as a sketch artist, selling his designs to couture houses. He became an assistant at Maison Doucet, which was followed by a position as a staff designer at Worth. Poiret was hired to create daywear, but tested his boundaries with garments such as his overtly orientalist and extremely full "Confucius" coat. According to the designer's memoirs, the avant-garde coat elicited an outraged response from an important Worth client, but Poiret caught the eye of longtime Worth customer Lillie Langtry.

Upon leaving Worth, Poiret established his own house in 1903. With his simpler aesthetic, Poiret offered something new that was refreshing to an adventurous customer, and less expensive than the established houses. However, it was not until 1908 that Poiret truly asserted his aesthetic. For his collection of dresses that year, Poiret issued a striking limited edition folio; he chose twenty-five-year-old Paul Iribe to create the illustrations for *Les Robes de Paul Poiret*. With their graphic abstractions, bold geometries and Fauvist color story, Iribe's pochoir prints departed from current

A fabric design from the Wiener Werkstätte swatch book, for a pattern named "Gazelle."

WIENER WERKSTÄTTE

With striking geometric motifs, bold colors, and avant-garde silhouettes, the fabric and clothing designs from the Wiener Werkstätte (Vienna Workshop) appealed to an elite and progressive clientele. The Wiener Werkstätte was founded in 1903 by Josef Hoffmann and Koloman Moser who, inspired by the British Arts and Crafts movement, believed in social change through design reform and the unification of the fine and decorative arts. Like the Vienna Secession, they were aware of Aesthetic developments in Europe and were influenced by the work of the architect and designer Charles Rennie Mackintosh. The workshop produced graphics, wallpaper, furniture, metal ware, jewelry, clothing, and textiles, and sold the products through Wiener Werkstätte shops in Vienna and, later, Germany, Switzerland, and New York.

Wiener Werkstätte designers believed that a good design was suitable for many uses and that all individuals involved in the creation of a product should be credited. While the styles of individual designers varied, the workshop aesthetic was often described as "severe" and architectural, but references to folk art motifs and Expressionist styles were also seen, especially in the textiles. The colorful, eye-catching patterns suited the simplified shapes of Viennese Reform dress and the effect was recorded in Gustav Klimt's paintings of his mistress, fashion designer Emilie Flöge, and other socially prominent women. Despite the founders' intention to democratize good design, expensive materials and careful production values kept costs high, making the products quite exclusive. The Wiener Werkstätte continued in operation until 1932.

Above left High-waisted neoclassic dresses and 18th-century-style tousled hair and headwraps were typical features of the 1908 collection from Paul Poiret, illustrated in a folio of pochoir prints by Paul Iribe, *Les Robes de Paul Poiret.*

Above right With their distinctive pleats and exotic and antique references, Mariano Fortuny's Delphos gowns appealed to an artistic clientele.

conventions in fashion illustration and prefigured the *moderne* style (later known as art deco). The dresses depicted featured a looser, columnar Directoire-inspired silhouette, free from the corseted S-curve shape. Poiret mixed Directoire details (such as raised waistlines and bandeaux) with elements of Japanese and Middle Eastern style.

Color was of great importance to Poiret, and while other designers including Paquin, Doucet, Callot, and Redfern were already moving to a new palette, he claimed credit for the shift in taste as if it were his own invention. As he wrote in his memoirs:

> the taste for the refinements of the eighteenth century had led all the women into a sort of deliquescence, and on the pretext that it was "distinguished," all vitality had been suppressed. Nuances of nymph's thigh, lilacs, swooning mauves, tender blue hortensias, niles, maizes, straws, all that was soft, washed-out, and insipid, was held in honour. I threw into this sheepcote a few rough wolves; red, greens, violets, royal blues, that made all the rest sing aloud.[5]

Poiret promoted the abandonment of the corset more overtly than any other designer. The fashion designs of the young Poiret gained a select following and early support in the fashion press. Word of mouth among adventuresome well-dressed women spread, and by 1909 Countess Margot Asquith (the wife of Prime Minister Herbert Asquith, and a notable style setter) invited Poiret to show his designs at 10 Downing Street. This elicited an outraged response from the British press, which nicknamed the official residence "Gowning Street."

In Venice, the multifaceted Spanish-born designer **Mariano Fortuny y Madrazo** (1871–1949) created garments and fabrics influenced by a number of sources. He embraced many of the same innovations as Poiret, but Fortuny was outside of the mainstream, operating in a more artistic arena. Wealthy, chic, and artistically inclined women wore his dresses.

Top British actress Lily Elsie in stage clothes for *The Merry Widow* designed by Lucile, including one of the celebrated large hats.

Above Milliner Jeanne Lanvin expanded into childrenswear and womenswear during this decade, and her work was often marketed in "mother–daughter" vignettes, such as this 1909 photograph from *Les Modes*.

The son of a painter, Fortuny was successful in a wide variety of artistic endeavors including fine art and theatrical design. He established his fashion and textile business in 1906. He also worked in interior design and became famous for his lamps, and his fabric designs were used in both clothing and decor.

Fortuny drew inspiration from a variety of sources including ancient art in museum collections. He utilized styles from the ancient world much more authentically than other designers of the decade. Fortuny also looked to North African, Far Eastern, and Near Eastern sources, and was especially inspired by the Italian medieval and Renaissance periods, following literary trends exemplified by the works of Gabriele D'Annunzio.

The Delphos was his signature design, taking its name from the ancient Greek sculpture, the Charioteer of Delphi. A columnar sleeveless one-piece dress, pleated in Fortuny's exclusive method, with very small, slightly irregular accordion pleats, the Delphos gown trailed evenly around front, sides, and back, achieving the look of an inverted morning glory blossom. Venetian glass beads usually ran down the two side seams. The Delphos was belted in a variety of ways, including stenciled self belts, cording, and sashes in various placements, often inspired by Greek sources. Delphos gowns were frequently worn with matching pleated overtunics. The Knossos scarf, a large rectangle of fabric (often printed in ancient-inspired designs), was typically draped over the Delphos. T-shaped tunics with both narrow and wide sleeves, batwing coats, flowing overblouses, and dresses were also available in luxurious velvets, brocades, and printed fabrics from Fortuny. Fortuny continued to produce most of the same designs for several decades.

French designer **Madeleine Vionnet** (1876–1975) had her first important job in London in the 1890s, working for a court dressmaker, Kate Reily. When she returned to her native Paris in 1901, Vionnet found work as a *vendeuse* for Maison Bechoff-David, and was later employed at Callot Soeurs. Throughout her life, Vionnet praised the excellent training she received at Callot and her subsequent career was influenced by their refined taste and quality of workmanship. She joined Maison Doucet in 1907. Her first diaphanous dresses at Doucet were shown on barefoot, uncorseted models, showing a spirit of innovation that rivaled Poiret's. Vionnet was popular among Doucet's avant-garde *demimondaine* and actress clientele, but her ideas were at odds with the established image of the house. Eventually she left the firm, setting up her own business early in the following decade.

Jeanne Lanvin (1867–1946) began her career as a milliner in 1890, and started designing dresses when some of her friends and millinery clients admired the clothes that she made for her daughter. Soon she received commissions for girls' dresses and coordinating mother–daughter ensembles. Lanvin's work at the close of the decade was very forward-thinking, including loose T-shaped dresses with ancient or medieval themes. Admitted to the Chambre Syndicale de la Haute Couture in 1909, she began to receive steady coverage in the French fashion press at about the same time.

The fashion press and advertising attests to the activity and popularity of other houses in Paris at this time, including **Maison Rouff**, **Martial et Armand**, **Maison Raudnitz**, and **Maison Perdoux**. New designers emerged that would figure strongly during the next decade, including **Boué Soeurs**, **Maison Chéruit**, and **Georges Doeuillet**, and there is evidence that at least two Americans (J. Green and Weeks) had established couture businesses in Paris by the late years of the decade.[6]

Beauty Treatments and Body Shaping

In addition to corsets, fashionable women followed various "flesh reducing" measures; some involved rubber undergarments or elastic "reducing bands" worn around the midriff, or bath tonics and slimming drinks. The desired effect was often described as "Greek" and the sculpture of Venus de Milo was considered an image of female perfection. One beauty writer declared that "even roly-poly plumpness takes all the youth out of a woman's face and step; and every ten pounds added beyond plumpness

Above A group of swimmers in Asbury Park, New Jersey, 1905, enjoy the waves, and exhibit the more modern swimwear common by this decade.

Below Tennis clothes are featured in this print from the Viennese folio *Der Tag einer Dame* by Stephanie Glax.

ages her."[7] Ladies turned to exercise for more graceful posture, equilibrium, lung expansion, and better digestion. Massage was recommended to tone the facial muscles; wrinkles were treated with home-made concoctions or commercial preparations. Recipes to correct complexion problems were widely available and called for surprising combinations of ingredients – one lotion mixed almonds, distilled water, and bichloride of mercury. But for serious facial problems such as moles and discolored spots, electrolysis was in use. Synthetic hair dye was introduced in 1907.

Sports Clothing

By 1900, automobiles were being produced in Europe and the United States, and by 1910 were manufactured in many other parts of the world. Early automobile owners were affluent but the introduction of Ford's Model T in 1908 made the invention accessible to middle-class households. Dusty roadways combined with the open design of early autos demanded special clothing, and a new category of apparel was created. Drivers and passengers wore long, loose coats known as dusters. Department stores and specialty suppliers stressed the combination of "fashionable appearance" and durability. Long rubber "auto shirts" with back closures, capes and ponchos were also worn. Women commonly donned heavy veils over their driving hats. Other headgear completely encased the head with openings only for the eyes and with gauze at the mouth for filtration. Driving gloves and goggles and masks made drivers resemble early aviators.

Women's bathing costumes were sometimes fabricated with bloomer or knickerbocker bottoms attached to the blouse. They often had a calf-length skirt that was worn

over the one-piece combination. Sailor collars, middy ties, and blue and white color schemes followed the trend for nautical inspiration in women's fashion. There were also variations available in men's bathing suits. In some areas, men swam in trunks – usually only in the company of other men. More commonly, men wore one- or two-piece suits made of dark knitted wool, often accented with stripes. While women often wore laced-up swimming sandals and dark stockings with their bathing suits, men usually went barefoot. A major change in attitude toward women's swimwear was developing, inspired by newly prominent female swimmers, particularly Annette Kellerman from Sydney. Nicknamed "The Australian Mermaid," Kellerman developed practical one-piece swimsuits for her competitions by attaching stockings to a boys' knit swimsuit – a shocking but advantageous innovation.

Menswear

Menswear showed a continued progression toward informality. One of the best indicators of stylistic change was evident in hats. While not entirely banished, the top hat (a signifier of elegance during the 19th century) was seen mainly on older gentlemen, for very formal occasions, or with riding dress; the top hat seemed incompatible with the practical, more casual mood in menswear. Black felt bowlers (known as derbys in the United States) became the daytime standard for town wear. In summer, straw boaters and Panama hats were seen everywhere. Continuing the sports-inflected direction of fashion, shoes were increasingly laced up, in contrast to earlier buttoned closures. Two-tone looks were popular, often achieved with fabric spats.

The more modern sack (or lounge) suit worn by most men, especially in the cities, continued to replace the frock coat. The suit consisted of jacket, vest, and trousers and was standard for professional men, whose ranks increased with the growth of office work and administrative positions. Fashions in men's jackets showed slight changes from season to season. Single- or double-breasted, with turned-back, notched lapels, the sack jacket was worn over a matching V-necked vest and straight-cut trousers. Suits were worn by men of all walks of life for important social, religious, and civic events. Ready-made suits were increasingly available through department stores and men's clothiers. Tailors, whether independent or employed by the store, provided the alterations necessary to make an off-the-rack suit fit the customer. British tailoring

Above The Chicago Monarch Tailoring Company offered these conservative suit styles for smartly attired businessmen in 1900.

Right The American outlaw gang The Wild Bunch photographed in 1900 by John Swartz. In addition to tailored menswear, each man wears the "derby," as this rounded hat was called in the United States.

THE ARROW COLLAR MAN

The Arrow Collar Man was the creation of Joseph Christian Leyendecker (1874–1951) for Cluett, Peabody, and Co., the manufacturer of Arrow collars. When he received the Arrow commission, J. C. Leyendecker was already well known as an illustrator, prominently featured in American magazines including *The Saturday Evening Post*. The maintenance of men's shirts was hard work, and a new detachable collar provided a clean, crisp look every day. The Arrow Man was introduced in 1907 and continued through the transition from Arrow collars to Arrow shirts, contributing greatly to the success of

the brand. Often regarded as the male equivalent of the Gibson Girl, he embodied an emerging American masculine ideal that emphasized chiseled good looks, broad shoulders, and physical fitness – athletic but elegant. The Arrow Man was dapper in every situation – playing golf, in eveningwear, even reading the newspaper – and his meaningful gaze thrilled customers for several decades. Although he was actually modeled on Charles Beach, Leyendecker's business manager and romantic companion, the Arrow Man won the hearts of American women – even receiving fan mail and marriage proposals.

A typical example of Leyendecker's Arrow Collar Man.

continued to be held in the highest esteem, but the less formal American style made inroads. While mass-produced suits lacked the distinction of custom or made-to-order clothing, they allowed even working-class men to look fashionable.

Shirts worn for business were usually white with stiff detachable collars that were cut quite high on the neck through the decade, mirroring the upright look of women's necklines. The four-in-hand tie gained more popularity, replacing the more complicated variations of the previous period.

The emergence of the "blazer," a tailored jacket worn with trousers of a different color, represents another instance of sports and leisure influence. Navy blue blazers were worn for tennis and yachting by participants and spectators and acquired upper-class leisure connotations, even after sporting attire eliminated jackets in favor of less restrictive apparel. Jodhpurs, a trouser style with flared thighs adopted from East Indian dress, offered an alternative to breeches for riding gear. Their slightly military air, especially in khaki or brown, corresponded with a more rugged sensibility (as embodied by Theodore Roosevelt).

Outerwear continued to be available in many variations, cut to fit over suit jackets. Some styles were intended for rough, country wear and others were for town. The Chesterfield coat, single-breasted and loosely or semi-fitted, below the knee, with a front placket and velvet collar, was a popular overcoat for business wear. Black derbys and dark Chesterfields created a modernized visual equivalent of the top hat and frock coat of the preceding generation.

Children's Fashion

As in the past, children's clothes showed influence from the fashions of adults. There were marked distinctions in children's clothing between school clothes, play clothes, and special occasion dressing. Attitudes toward health, hygiene, and exercise were revealed in the presentation of children's clothes; even the natural shape of baby shoes was an important consideration for mothers. In general, little girls and toddlers of both sexes wore low-waisted dresses. As they matured, girls adopted clothing that suggested aspects of grown-up style, in particular the loose bodices, high collars, and profuse trimmings of current women's fashion.

Schoolwear for a boy often consisted of a cotton shirt and knee-length trousers or knickerbockers worn with a practical, boxy jacket and a matching cap. Dark stockings and ankle boots were worn virtually all year, except for summer. Boys also wore knitted pullovers or vests. School clothes for girls were simple in style. Young girls, up to about ten, often wore aprons or pinafores over their cotton or wool dresses. Aprons were also worn over skirt and blouse outfits. Typically made of two panels, front and back, the aprons were attached at the sides and offered a practical solution to the problem of keeping kids' clothes clean. Play clothes were described in terms such as "tumble-dresses" and "knock about suits," and magazines and pattern companies emphasized the use of durable, washable fabrics.

Special occasions and ceremonies called for more fantasy. For young boys, a "Little Lord Fauntleroy" look was promoted consisting of two-piece velvet suits – a straight single-breasted jacket over knee-length velvet shorts or breeches. Wide ruffled collars and thin-soled shoes, sometimes with rosettes, and long hairstyles completed the look. Other picturesque styles included "Van Dyck" outfits – complete with child-size cavalier details, capes for boys and lacy aprons for girls.

Distinctive accessories added touches of charm to children's outfits. Hair ribbons, usually tied in a bow to one side, were a favorite with the carefully curled hairstyles of well-dressed girls. Boys wore soft caps or, with the perennially popular sailor suits, curled-brim straw hats. Girls' hats were surprisingly large and got larger as the end of the decade approached.

The End of the Decade

During the last few years of the decade, changes were in the air. In silhouette, the waist was moving up, the skirt was narrowing, and the uncorseted figure was endorsed by several designers. The corsetry industry responded with new, less restrictive, more flexible versions; advertisements featured models in exaggerated back-bending poses. But the S-curve shape still remained. The 1908 Exposition de Toilettes at the recently established Hôtel des Modes exhibited the work of a variety of Paris designers displayed on wax figures and dress forms. A transitional silhouette was apparent; the elevated waist was teamed with an S-curve posture and the low padded bust, creating a very matronly effect.

Foretelling the next decade, on October 3, 1909, *The New York Times* reported on Paris fashions for the season. The full-page article focused on exotic influences, citing Byzantine, Indian, Egyptian, and most especially Russian styles. It profiled the major houses, and even asserted that the source of the Russian style was Charles Poynter Redfern: "Redfern is a master at these Russian effects, which he is using very much this season for street costumes. He has just returned from Russia whither he goes almost every summer." Velvets and lush brocades, black and dark blue satins were noted as the fabrics of the season. T-shaped, looser-fit dresses, based on medieval prototypes, were described as "tunic gowns." The exoticism and historic influence present in 1909 set the stage for the prevailing aesthetic of the following decade.

Wax figures display the designs of Paris couture houses at the Hôtel des Modes, with paintings by Giovanni Boldini displayed behind. This 1908 exhibition captures fashion in transition, as the elevated waist, prevalent at the end of the decade, is combined with the S-curve foundation which had been present for several years by this time.

Chapter 4

The 1910s

Exotic Fantasy, Wartime Reality

Opposite Ernst Ludwig Kirchner's *Two Women* (1911–1912) portrays a pair of seamstresses on a Berlin street. Despite the expressionistic interpretation of the scene, the details of the women's outerwear are typical of the decade: large hats and ankle-length straight coats with fur collars.

Below A 1911 illustration from the French magazine *Femina* shows a group of fashionable women in afternoon toilettes, exemplifying the variety of hat and dress styles visible during the early years of the decade.

The story of the years between 1910 and 1920 is one of transition and contrast. The decade provided a capstone to previous eras but also forged the way for the radical changes of the 1920s. At the beginning of the decade the pleasure-focused mood of the Edwardian era continued and exoticism and romance took various forms. Both new designers and established houses supplied elegance and elan to the fashionable world in a variety of styles. Luxuriant orientalism and romantic historicism continued to influence fashion as designers dressed stylish ladies for Arabian harems or 18th-century courts. But the onset of World War I extinguished the frivolity and imposed a new order. Men from many nations and all social classes were thrown together in the armed services, helping to dissolve the rigid social hierarchy of the Edwardian era. Women's role in public life was enlarged; their participation in the war effort aided the cause of women's voting rights. In general, the evolution of fashion during the decade reveals a move away from rigid social conventions toward a new simplicity.

Social and Economic Background

The 1912 sinking of the RMS *Titanic* on its much publicized maiden voyage resulted in the loss of more than 1,500 lives. The defining event of the decade was World War I, the result of tensions in Europe that came to a head with the assassination of Austrian Archduke Franz Ferdinand on June 28, 1914. Owing to a complicated web of alliances, the resulting response by Austria-Hungary involved most European nations as the Central Powers (Austria-Hungary, Germany, and their allies Bulgaria and the Ottoman Empire) were opposed by the Allied Powers (the United Kingdom, Russia, and France). Over the next four years, a generation of young men went to war and the casualties were unprecedented. New weapons and lethal chemical agents transformed modern warfare.

Because of their participation in the conflict, Australia and Canada emerged as mature nations, more significant to the international community. The United States joined the Allies in 1917 and further solidified its role as a world power. The aftermath of the war brought an end to monarchies in Germany and Austria and altered class relations throughout Europe. The 1917 Russian Revolution signaled the end of another monarchy and shook the social structure, sending many wealthy Russians into Western Europe. The ensuing changes laid the foundation for the Soviet system that dominated Eastern Europe for much of the 20th century.

The Arts

This decade was exceptionally exciting in the visual and performing arts. Avant-garde movements pushed forward conceptual innovations and questioned the role of art in modern society. Kees van Dongen captured the exaggerations of clothing in his Fauvist portraits of fashionable women. Pablo Picasso and Georges Braque took painting further into the realm of abstraction, and aspects of these Cubist works found their way into other art forms including sculpture, graphic arts, and even fashion illustration. The controversial 1913 Armory Show expanded New York City's role in the art world. Alfred Stieglitz's "291" gallery presented exhibitions of American modernists, including Marsden Hartley and Georgia O'Keeffe.

Artists based in Zurich during the war years, including Tristan Tzara and Jean Arp, developed ideas and practices that became known as Dada. Rejecting traditional

MARCHESA CASATI

Luisa Casati embodied an extreme version of the exoticism of the era. Born into a wealthy Milanese family in 1881, Luisa was an artistic child and her unconventional interests were indulged. At nineteen, she married the Marchese Camillo Casati Stampa di Soncino, but the couple lived together for only a few years. Her long affair with the Italian poet Gabriele D'Annunzio deepened her appreciation of the exotic. The perennially insolvent D'Annunzio considered Casati a muse (one of many), and referred to her as "Kore," the queen of the underworld in Greek mythology. The two shared a love of masquerade, and dabbled in the occult.

Casati was a couture customer, favoring the creations of Poiret and Fortuny. But her appearance could be described as outrageous rather than fashionable: she wore layers of trailing black fabric, accessorized with strings of pearls that reached her hemline and, on at least one occasion, a necklace of live snakes. She defied even the most tolerant beauty standards with flame-colored dyed hair and a face powdered deathly white. To enhance her large green eyes, she used clouds of kohl and long false eyelashes, sometimes wearing patches of velvet on her eyelids and strips of black tape as eyebrows.

Casati was in every sense an exhibitionist, wearing fur coats over her pale nude body for moonlit strolls in Venice to walk her pet cheetahs. She mingled with an international crowd of artists and writers and had herself painted and photographed many times by artists as varied as Giovanni Boldini and Augustus John, Adolph de Meyer and Man Ray. Until 1930, she divided her time between Rome, Venice, Paris, and Capri, but then retreated to London where she died in 1957, millions of dollars in debt, having spent her immense wealth on clothes, jewelry, extravagant homes, parties, and luxuries such as diamond-studded leashes for her cheetahs.

Casati's greatest contribution to fashion may be posthumous: her eccentric, extravagant style inspired modern fashion designers including John Galliano for Dior and Tom Ford for Yves Saint Laurent. The Marchesa line of eveningwear designed by Georgina Chapman and Keren Craig was named in homage to Luisa Casati.

Marchesa Luisa Casati, by Giovanni Boldini.

art forms, the Dadaists produced collages and photomontages and staged provocative events including war protests – deliberate nonsense that reacted to the chaos and upheaval of the war. The Italian Futurists, who sought to convey the dynamism of modern life in works of painting, sculpture, and poetry, included fashion in their artistic vision. Giacomo Balla's 1914 manifesto on men's dress called for an end to somber colors and severe tailoring. Balla proposed asymmetrical jackets in collages of shocking saturated colors to make menswear relevant to modern life. Another Italian, Ernesto Michahelles (known as Thayaht), invented and promoted a utilitarian jumpsuit, the "tuta."

On the theatrical stage, the revolutionary playwright George Bernard Shaw premiered many important works including *Pygmalion* and *Heartbreak House*. In France, the production of Guillaume Apollinaire's play *The Breasts of Tiresias* was seminal to the emerging Surrealist movement. Escape artist Harry Houdini elevated his stunts to a sensational level of performance art. Austrian Richard Strauss premiered the ultra-romantic opera *Der Rosenkavalier* in Dresden in 1911. Giacomo Puccini's opera *The Girl of the Golden West* (based on Belasco's play) premiered in New York in 1910 and depicted a slice of 1849 Gold Rush life. Modern composers Igor Stravinsky and Erik Satie were so assimilated into the cultural landscape of Paris that their works were profiled in leading fashion magazines. Jazz continued to develop as songs such as William Christopher Handy's "The Saint Louis Blues" and Irving Berlin's "Alexander's Ragtime Band" brought the previously marginalized African American idioms into the mainstream.

The Ballets Russes had a strong influence on design. The company's repertoire included exotic folk tales with Arabian, Persian, and Russian settings aided by the evocative designs of Léon Bakst. Lead dancers of the Ballets Russes, especially Vaslav Nijinsky (the undisputed star of the company), were celebrated in French society. The company presented notable collaborations and innovative, if sometimes scandalous, repertoire. *The Rite of Spring* (1913), with music by Stravinsky, choreography by Nijinsky, and designs by Russian artist Nicholas Roerich, caused rioting at its premiere as the audience reacted to the production's shocking music and staging.

While most industrialized nations were producing movies, Hollywood became the world's largest center of film production, taking over from New York. A number of talented directors debuted during this decade. D. W. Griffith and Cecil B. DeMille established standards for visual opulence with epics such as *The Birth of a Nation* and *Male and Female*. Mack Sennett's Keystone Film Company became famous for producing the "Keystone Cop" comedies, and films featuring the "Sennett Bathing Beauties." The popularity of movies spawned related businesses including fan magazines and even make-up.

Fashion and Society

With the death of King Edward VII on May 6, 1910, the British Empire was thrust into a period of national mourning for several months. The "Black Ascot" races of 1910 were attended by spectators in various degrees and colors of mourning, and French fashion houses actively advertised their mourning styles to the wealthy bereaved of Britain. *The Queen* immediately published suggestions for fashionable mourning attire. The new Queen Consort of Great Britain, Mary of Teck, was promoted as a style leader in the press, but by the end of the decade her staid look no longer represented current fashion. Other European royals, such as Alexandra of Russia and Marie of Romania, showed a much more decisive flair.

Wealthy and independent-minded American women increasingly exerted influence on fashion. Gertrude Vanderbilt Whitney, both an artist and patron of the arts, expressed her modern spirit in her wardrobe as well as her art acquisitions. She combined French couture with pieces from Asia and was an early fan of pajamas and trousers. Rita de Acosta Lydig, a New Yorker of Cuban and Spanish heritage, was known for her dramatic, original style. Lydig wore exotic creations from Callot

– including pajamas – many of which were embellished with antique lace from her collection. Lydig had hundreds of shoes handmade by Pietro Yantorny of Paris.

As the cause of women's suffrage (votes for women) intensified, crusaders realized the power of a unified image. British "suffragettes" adopted the color scheme of white, purple, and green, which symbolized purity, loyalty, and hope. American suffrage advocates demonstrated in white and purple with gold or yellow. Many suffragists were also often seen in tailor-made suits, conveying a serious, businesslike impression.

While Paris continued to dominate high fashion taste, domestic garment industries were developing worldwide. The United States, in particular, continued to build its garment business, made possible through the availability of raw materials, technological development, and the continued influx of immigrant labor. However, while America pursued its goal of good fashion for everyone, several aspects of industry practice were called into question including working conditions and design piracy. In 1911, the Triangle Shirtwaist Factory fire in New York caused the deaths of 146 workers, mostly young immigrant women. The American industry was also known for unauthorized copying of designer originals and outright piracy. During his 1913 trip to the United States, Paul Poiret was furious to see mediocre dresses and hats labeled with his own name. High-end manufacturers responded with new labeling practices. The manufacturing and distribution capability of the United States was significant, but America was still strongly dependent on France for design inspiration.

Mary Pickford in her typical girlish style with long ringlets.

Theda Bara in *Cleopatra*, 1917.

SCREEN BEAUTIES

As film eclipsed other forms of popular entertainment, the cinema became a new place to showcase style. In this decade the "movie star" was born – and the movie star as style icon. The public read about their favorites in fan magazines and the fashion press, and actresses endorsed fashion and beauty products.

Leading the pack of female stars was Canadian-born Mary Pickford (1892–1979), the biggest box office draw of the decade, nicknamed "America's Sweetheart" for her sympathetic roles. Noted for her romantic fashion sense, Pickford often dressed in Lanvin and Lucile, and her style was covered in magazines and widely imitated. Lucile created Pickford's wardrobe for *Rebecca of Sunnybrook Farm*, although the dresses said more about Pickford's love of clothes than the character. Pickford was also a skilled businesswoman and negotiated contracts that set precedents for actresses in the industry, and in 1919 was one of the co-founders of United Artists studios.

Sisters Lillian Gish (1893–1993) and Dorothy Gish (1898–1968) maintained a *jeune fille* (young girl) style similar to Pickford. However, both included Fortuny creations in their personal wardrobes. Gloria Swanson (1899–1983) developed a glamorous persona while still a teenager, and despite diminutive stature was known for her lavish ensembles. She starred in several spectacular productions from Cecil B. DeMille, including the exotic *Male and Female*. As the public's interest shifted from stage to screen, the career of singer-turned-actress Geraldine Farrar (1882–1967) was emblematic of that shift. A star of the Metropolitan Opera, Farrar attracted the attention of DeMille, who starred her in a silent film adaptation of *Carmen*, and epic vehicles *Joan the Woman* and *The Woman God Forgot*.

Theda Bara's (1885–1955) seductive femme fatale image led to her being known as the "Vamp" (short for vampire), and she enhanced this persona with shockingly revealing costumes. Though she was really Theodosia Goodman from Ohio, her studio's publicity department spun exotic stories about her, including that she was of Egyptian birth, an image she cultivated with kohl-lined eyes and dark lips.

The increased prominence of cosmetics in film influenced the general public. Maksymilian Faktorowicz (1875–1938) was the pre-eminent Hollywood make-up artist. Known as Max Factor, he was instrumental in developing the looks of many actresses. His invention "flexible greasepaint" was an important achievement in screen make-up, and he encouraged the use of the word "make-up" as a noun (it was previously used only as a verb).

This perceived inferiority, compounded by limited interaction with Europe during the war, prompted measures such as the "Designed in America" competition initiated by *Women's Wear* in 1916, which encouraged American designers to look to American cultural resources for inspiration.

By this time, every major city had a choice of large department stores contributing to the expansion of the fashionable world. London's most important store, Harrods, opened a branch in Buenos Aires in 1914, its only overseas location. Australia saw the growth of the Myer stores, with the establishment of a branch in Melbourne, and the expansion of the David Jones Company.

Fashion Media

The fashion media was expanding and specialized publications targeted diverse regions, interests, and incomes. Photography grew significantly as a means to transmit fashion, but illustration was especially sophisticated in this decade. Paul Iribe's career continued and other important French fashion illustrators emerged, especially George Barbier, Georges Lepape, and Etienne Drian. In contrast to the fashion plates of earlier years, their stylish illustrations often included witty or provocative narrative content.

French magazines were particularly influential and the most luxurious was *La Gazette du Bon Ton*, which showcased the work of leading designers in an artistic context. It was founded in 1912 by publisher Lucien Vogel with the participation of six couturiers, Chéruit, Doeuillet, Doucet, Lanvin, Poiret, and Worth, with Paquin and Redfern joining shortly afterward. Printed on high-quality paper, the monthly edition featured illustrations of couture fashions rendered by the leading illustrators of the day including Barbier, Lepape, Drian, and Louis Maurice Boutet de Monvel. In the French tradition of elite journals, the *Gazette* was fully illustrated, reacting to the growth of photography in other magazines. *Les Modes* provided an elegant,

Below left George Barbier's illustration for the cover of *Les Modes*, April 1913, depicts an evening dress from Boué Soeurs in a fanciful setting.

Below right Early Surrealism influenced graphic art and design, as seen in George Wolfe Plank's cover for *Vogue*, November 1, 1914.

if conservative, presentation of fashion for the genteel and well-to-do woman. *Les Modes* continued its frequent use of colorized photographs in a tasteful and elegant layout. *Femina* was geared to a middle-class readership, with chatty depictions of sports stars and theatrical performers. *Femina* included "how to" fashion tips, and ran a column of beauty secrets from the glamorous opera singer Lina Cavalieri entitled "*L'Art d'être belle.*" Both *Les Modes* and *Femina* included work from great illustrators.

The Queen continued as the most important ladies' magazine in Britain. Nearly every category of women's clothing was included, along with children's fashion, and uniforms for domestic help. Housewares and food were covered, along with travel, and pets – including cat shows and the dogs of the royal family. Fashions were reproduced in illustrations and in photographs, and columns such as "The Court Chronicle" and "*Causerie de Paris*" ("The Talk of Paris") kept the reader updated on the latest styles. Occasional articles gave tips on how to adapt the latest modes to suit the Antipodean seasons for the growing fashionable elite in Australia.

In the United States, the *Ladies' Home Journal* and its competitor *McCall's* featured fashion content and household coverage. *The Delineator: A Journal of Fashion Culture and Fine Arts* also continued as a major fashion periodical. *Vogue* and *Harper's Bazar* both grew in importance and contributed to the growth of American fashion illustration. *Vogue*'s evocative covers were created by several great illustrators including Helen Dryden, E. M. A. Steinmetz, George Wolfe Plank, and F. X. Leyendecker (the brother of J. C. Leyendecker).

But photography increasingly conveyed the story of fashion and important artists emerged in the medium. Edward Steichen was already a commercial photographer by the 1890s. His reputation for elegant fashion work began in 1911 when he photographed Poiret's models for *Art et Décoration* and introduced an artistic "mood" to fashion photography. Adolph de Meyer was the chief photographer for *Vogue* from 1913 to 1921 and worked for *Harper's Bazar* after that. His portraits of socialites and celebrities conveyed the languor and elegance sought by the fashionable women of the time.

Bohemians and "Couture Bohemians"

Bohemians, subsets of society that flouted conventional lifestyle, were flourishing in San Francisco, Paris, and other urban centers. In New York City, intellectual women walked the streets of Greenwich Village in loosely fitting blouses and shapeless full skirts, with sandals and unkempt flowing hair, while their male counterparts favored loose open-necked shirts without ties. Important circles had developed in Britain among the intellectual elite including the "Coterie" and the "Bloomsbury Group." The bohemian trends of the 1910s were in some ways a revisiting of Aesthetic dress ideals of earlier years, and in fact this generation of bohemians included children and grandchildren of earlier Aesthetes. Like other eccentricities of fashion in the past, bohemian style was fodder for much lampooning: "Some day, when fate has delayed your laundry … go down and take a try at being Bohemian," quipped Robert Benchley in *Vanity Fair* in March 1916.

Dorothy "Dorelia" McNeill, the second wife of British painter Augustus John, was perhaps Britain's greatest exponent of bohemian style. Rejecting petticoats and foundations, Dorelia dressed in "gypsy"-inspired style, with loose blouses and draped peasant shawls, floral-print skirts, kerchiefs, and folk-art beads. Dorelia further flouted convention by tanning her skin. Women who emulated her style found regional clothing and fabrics in import stores. By mid-decade, the fashion magazines were advocating shapeless skirts, peasant smocks, and sandals for gardening and at-home attire, showing the effect of the bohemian aesthetic on casual clothing for the mainstream.

Some British women kept one foot in society and one in the bohemian world. Perhaps most notable was Lady Diana Manners (later Lady Diana Cooper). A true style setter, she was considered one of the most beautiful English girls of her generation and appeared as a model, including on the cover of *The Queen*. Active in

Vogue promoted smocks for gardening in 1914, taking a bohemian style into high fashion.

the intellectual "Coterie," she also worked as an editor for *Femina* for a short time after the war. Her later acting career assured her place in 20th-century popular culture. With her unconventional lifestyle, Manners anticipated the new liberated women that would typify the younger generation of the 1920s.

The Elements of Women's Fashion

Womenswear showed endless variation and constant flux of silhouette. Although neutrals were in style, the color palette also included vivid colors and strong contrasts. Despite movements toward modernization, the decade was also marked by three particular inspirational modes: orientalism, 18th-century revival, and a melange of ancient and medieval.

The decade's taste for orientalism encompassed a wide range of influences including Turkish, North African, Egyptian, Persian, and Far Eastern. Fashion magazines were filled with features on Eastern themes, and exotic locales provided settings for fashion illustrations. Draped shawls, brocaded fabrics, beads, and fringes all contributed to a world of exotic fantasy. In the earlier years of the 1910s, Directoire influence

An illustration from *Femina*, May 15, 1910, presented dresses for attending horse races. The narrow skirts feature a variety of details including pleats, draping, embellished borders, and rows of decorative buttons.

was seen in soft mousseline dresses, described with terms such as "Mme Recamier style," "Josephine frock," and "Empire gown." Louis XVI styles were revived with striped cotton dresses and ruffled *engageantes*; exaggerated revers and jabots recalled 18th-century menswear. Fichus added a romantic touch to necklines. Ancient and medieval influence was particularly strong at the beginning of the decade and the press often used phrases such as "Byzantine" to describe the styles. Greco-Roman looks for evening presented women as veiled heroines from antiquity, and Greek keys were popular as a decorative element. Dresses with simple T-shaped construction were referred to as "tunic" gowns.

The S-curve silhouette was all but gone by 1911. At the beginning of the decade, the most important news was the narrowing and straightening of the silhouette, and simpler, straighter construction of garments. The waistline moved higher up the body. Bodices were less fitted through sides and back but lost their fullness in the front, eliminating the matronly blouson effect of the previous decade. Sometimes bodices featured raglan sleeves and no shoulder seams. The new narrow skirt advocated most strongly by Poiret – the hobble skirt – was the dominant style, although less adventurous women continued to wear full skirts. Frequently, a pleat down the center back provided ease of movement. The basic skirt shape was fitted and straight to the instep, with many variations and accents including horizontal bands, gathering, and pleats near the hemline. Other styles used details on the skirt such as tabs, rows of buttons, and draped panels. Tailor-made suits grew in popularity as the hobble skirt was teamed with a jacket that came down over the hips. Dresses were often fabricated to look like suits, a style that recalled the jacket bodices of the 1850s.

Elegant spring looks, suggested by *Femina* (November 15, 1913) for a formal wedding, include tunic and pannier effects, diagonal tiers, and fishtail hems.

Cotton lingerie dresses were also still popular. While skirts were simple, blouses were highly decorated and available in numerous variations. The word "blouse" was used to describe different styles, ranging from soft and flowing versions to more fitted bodice-like garments, and the word "shirtwaist" was still used to describe blouses with a masculine style. The rigid collars of the 1900s went out of fashion and smaller turned-down collars lay down on the shoulders. Simple jewel and V necklines were featured, and (for the first time since the 1880s) necks and collarbones were visible in the daytime. Cotton jabots sometimes emerged asymmetrically from plackets. Sleeves for daytime shortened with three-quarter lengths and elbow lengths common.

Eveningwear styles showcased lush fabrications, and rich colors enlivened fashionable nightlife. Evening gowns showed more fluidity (as new foundation garments emphasized youth over maturity) and long necklaces accentuated the elongation of the body. Some young women wore diaphanous harem pants for evening. Sashes were very popular for both day and evening, and drew on orientalist and ancient inspirations. Fashion magazines featured the latest variations of *ceintures à la mode*, often wrapped repeatedly and stylishly knotted, with decorated and draped ends.

During 1912–1913, styles became unusual and varied. Bodices were often very full and continued the T-shaped form. Poiret's "Minaret" dress was influential on even the most conservative design houses. Variations were seen as well: what Poiret showed with a stiff hooped hem transformed into a soft peplum. Other skirts were cut with fullness at the hips that tapered to the hem, a shape referred to as "peg top." Skirts were often covered with tiers of ruffles and bubble puffs that concentrated on the hip area or gradually became smaller toward the hem. Controlled fullness on each hip

was known as "pannier" drapery, but sometimes skirts featured irregular drapes and swags. Such silhouettes looked either soft or crisp, depending on fabric. Some looks featured trains, often in a fishtail form that emerged from a narrow hem. Hems rose slightly, revealing more ankle, and some wrap-front skirts gave occasional glimpses up the calf.

By the war years, hems rose to their highest level since the 1830s, and skirts flared once again. The full skirts, often tiered, were sometimes supported with an understructure. With the new silhouette, Louis XVI inspiration was particularly pronounced. Skirts often showed fancy details, with polonaise drapery and hip emphasis. Tighter bodices often accompanied the fuller skirts. In February 1916, American *Vogue* declared "that tight bodices will point the way to Louis Seize Fashions, that skirts will puff 1870-wise at the hips above 1916 ankles." According to the *New York Times*, designers in 1916 individually promoted a wide range of fashions: Doeuillet and Redfern maintained "soberness in style," Paquin showed the season's shortest skirts, and Worth reveled in historic influence including "the days of Empress Eugenie."[1] Mme. Gerber at Callot showed full skirts and a great deal of silver and gold embroidery. Reflecting the war, women's tailor-mades showed a military

Top E. M. A. Steinmetz's illustration on the cover of *Vogue* in August 1915 conveys the romantic silhouette of the mid-decade. Hints of 18th-century revival are seen in the full skirts, wide-brimmed hats, fichu-like scarves, and Louis heels.

Above A George Barbier illustration of an evening dress highlights the provocative low back and swinging beaded tassels. The dragon and lacquer-red mirror in the background emphasize the exotic appeal of this design by Parisian couturiere Jenny.

Right Women's suits offered in the Sears catalog in 1919 show a loose, almost shapeless, silhouette with hemlines just above ankle length. Smaller hats were seen in a wide variety of shapes.

By 1918, barrel-shaped skirts were seen for both day and evening, as shown in these two promotional plates for spring fashions from Cheney Silks.

influence, combining regimental jacket styles with the fashionable full skirts. Practical modernism coexisted with romanticism and often a woman dressed in military style one day, and in girlish "Marie Antoinette" mode the next.

As the war drew to its close, the silhouette changed once again. The waist moved back up and the torso resumed a looser fit. The skirt, still at mid-calf length, retained fullness around the waist but narrowed around the hem. The resulting silhouette was barrel-shaped and pervaded day dresses, suits, and eveningwear. The 1910s ended with a narrow silhouette once again, but now with a higher hemline and less defined body and an ambiguous waistline. This shapelessness took the form of chemise dresses, straight tubes of fabric often loosely belted. Eveningwear regained some of the panache of the pre-war years. Long fishtailed sheath dresses, undulating fringe and halter tops celebrated the end of the war, and the coming of a new decade.

Court presentation gowns still featured trains and long veils. Wedding dresses were in keeping with fashionable afternoon or evening frocks, and white had become fully established as the standard color. Typically wedding dresses had enormously long trains and veils. Bridesmaids were still sometimes dressed in white, but colors were coming into use. The vogue for large hats also affected bridesmaids' attire, and gigantic hats – as large as any in fashion – were worn for indoor church weddings; 18th-century-inspired mobcaps were another option.

Outerwear

As the decade began women's overcoats for day were typically tubular and reflected the straightening and narrowing of the silhouette. Kimono- and burnoose-style coats were especially popular for evening. Cocoon coats were featured for both day and evening. *Manteaux de théâtre* and *manteaux de soir* were luxurious versions of kimono and cocoon styles, showpieces of a woman's wardrobe and designers' collections. These were sometimes worn open, but often had a surplice front buttoned low on the hip.

For spring and summer, Spencer jackets were often worn over high-waisted chemise-style dresses, as were a variety of lightweight wraps. As the decade continued into the war years and women's skirts took on a wider shape, outerwear was cut full through the body to accommodate the silhouette. Evening coats maintained an exotic allure. By the end of the decade, outerwear narrowed once again to follow the form of the dresses underneath.

A wide variety of practical outerwear was available at Burberry and Aquascutum among other companies, with London-based companies leading the market. Some offered tweeds with waterproof finishes. Fashionable women continued to include fur in their wardrobes in the form of coats, hats, boas, scarves, and muffs. Many furriers offered restyling of older furs into more fashionable styles. By mid-decade, fashion showed a shift toward more exotic furs such as leopard, zebra, and monkey, and the popularity of Persian lamb increased. Dog fur from Asia, sometimes referred to as "Manchurian dog," was an economical option. Full animal skins were draped over the shoulders. Fur trim was common on cloth coats, and small strips of fur frequently decorated dresses.

Millinery and Accessories

Hats were essential to fashion and millinery was prominently featured in illustrations on the covers of fashion magazines. By 1910 the dominant hat style was a wide-brimmed shape, and oversized hats were perched atop wide hairstyles. The wide hats contrasted with the narrow lines of the hobble skirt, and the overblown scale of the hats was satirized by contemporary cartoonists.

A large platter shape was the most common, but many styles showed large brims turned up in unusual positions. Convertible hats featured brims that could be pinned up in a variety of ways. The straw boater continued to be worn, often trimmed with nothing but a striped ribbon. Hats were heavily trimmed and decoration frequently took on architectural form; bows were often large in scale, sometimes as broad as the

Below A cocoon-shaped theater coat designed by Jeanne Paquin, in the collection of the Western Reserve Historical Society (left), was depicted by J. Gose for *La Gazette du Bon Ton* in 1912 (right).

Opposite top A page from the John Wanamaker spring/ summer catalog of 1918 offers a wide variety of bust bodices, brassieres, dress shields, and other lingerie options.

brim itself. Ostrich feathers were still popular and egrets, used for their distinctive white feathers, were hunted nearly to extinction. Feathers sometimes projected up like horns, and entire bird wings were used as decoration. Aigrettes, single or double feathers that pointed straight up from the hat, were frequently used. Bunches of faux grapes were a common trim, and fabric flowers, particularly Asian varieties such as irises and cherry blossoms, were popular.

New shapes emerged as fashion magazines devoted space to the different virtues of *chapeaux plats* and *chapeaux hauts* (oversized turbans, bonnets, high pillbox shapes, and brimless toques), and by 1913 the new shapes began to prevail. During the war years, hats showed masculine influence as top hat and derby shapes often accompanied menswear-inspired suits. Some women's hats resembled the helmets of men's battle dress, with crowns that came down over the head for the first time in recent history. Wide-brimmed hats, now with deeper crowns and less decoration, accompanied the more romantic-style dresses that were also being worn. Headdress was also extremely important to eveningwear. Turbans were often seen for evening and ornamented headbands, often trimmed with aigrettes, were also commonly worn.

The shorter hems that fashion dictated placed added emphasis on shoes, and more decoration was required to keep a fashionable foot. Heels were often square, but curved Louis heels were the most popular shape. The vamps of women's shoes were frequently decorated with bows, rosettes, and buckles. Straps across the top of the foot became popular, influenced by new trends in dancing. Short boots were sometimes constructed in two-toned styles with canvas tops. Purses with long straps became very popular, and were sometimes worn suspended from the shoulder. Fans and parasols were still popular and available in a variety of materials. Umbrellas were important accessories that elegantly coordinated with fashionable ensembles.

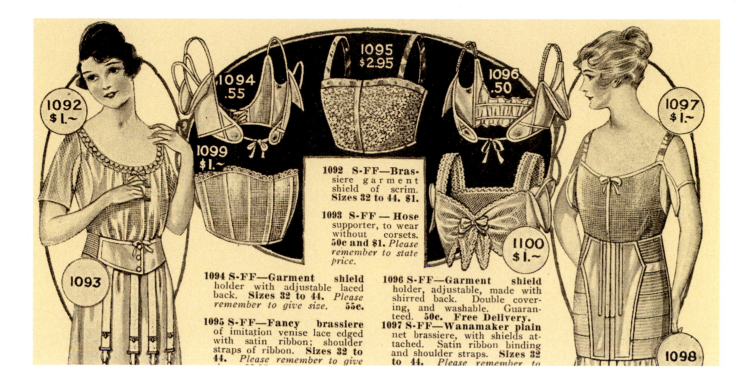

1092 S-FF—Brassiere garment shield of scrim. Sizes 32 to 44. $1.

1093 S-FF — Hose supporter, to wear without corsets. 50c and $1. *Please remember to state price.*

1094 S-FF—Garment shield holder with adjustable laced back. Sizes 32 to 44. *Please remember to give size.* 55c.

1095 S-FF—Fancy brassiere of imitation venise lace edged with satin ribbon; shoulder straps of ribbon. Sizes 32 to 44. *Please remember to give*

1096 S-FF—Garment shield holder, adjustable, made with shirred back. Double covering, and washable. Guaranteed. 50c. Free Delivery.

1097 S-FF—Wanamaker plain net brassiere, with shields attached. Satin ribbon binding and shoulder straps. Sizes 32 to 44. *Please remember to*

Foundations and Lingerie

Camisoles, corset covers, drawers (or knickers), and combination suits were still worn at the beginning of the decade. With narrower skirts, petticoats narrowed and lost their tiers of ruffles at the hem. The narrow hobble skirt sometimes necessitated the "hobble garter," a narrow strap that wound around the calves to restrict a woman's stride to prevent her from ripping her skirt with a vigorous step.

The S-curve shape lingered briefly but was soon outmoded and a straighter posture was advocated. The new silhouette of women's dresses required support for the breasts and a smoothing effect over the waist and hips. Corsets were softer in construction and often incorporated elastic materials. Adjustable models used lacing to alter the proportions to suit the wearer, and webbing styles were sold for maternity wear. "Corset belts" emerged early in the decade; they covered only from the bottom of the ribcage to the hips and were similar to what would later be called a girdle. Many of the new corset styles began below the breasts and were worn in combination with the brassiere. Brassieres took many forms, usually worn for control and shape but sometimes designed with more solid structures to minimize the breasts. Other less structured styles, known as "bandeaux," were more common toward the end of the decade. As underwear reduced, underarm dress shields became an important item in a woman's wardrobe.

Satin camisoles and knickers became more common, and were sometimes combined into "cami-knickers." Similarly, petticoat and camisole were combined into a slip-style chemise by the end of the decade. Mid-decade, petticoats became shorter and wider, to support the silhouette of the war years; often flounced with ruffles, these full petticoats were stiffened, sometimes even hooped, earning the nickname "war crinoline." Many stockings were still quite decorative and, aside from beachwear, legs were always covered. Hose supporters with rubber buttons became widespread for women (as well as men and children) to hold up their stockings.

The term "tea gown" was still used but, with less restrictive corsetry and fit, the ritual associated with it was less profound.

Below Weingarten Bros' "Reduso" corsets, here advertised in the *Ladies' Home Journal*, promoted a smooth silhouette that was straighter than the S-curve seen in the early 1910s.

Other terms such as afternoon gown, rest gown, dressing gown, and *robe d'intérieur* were used. Liberty continued to advertise its "artistic creations" for home wear. T-shaped dressing gowns that pulled over the head, including offerings from Jaeger, reflected the medievalist trend in dressmaking. Women's nightdresses were becoming lighter and more simplified, but were not the only sleepwear option. In December 1911 *The Queen* featured a pair of pajamas described as "sounding the utilitarian note with much precision … a pajama sleeping suit for ladies, quite a novel departure, and one that is steadily gaining ground."

Sports Clothing

The modern Olympic Games elevated public interest in sports. Women competed in a number of categories, necessitating activity-specific clothing. Other international sports tournaments, especially in tennis and golf, received a great deal of media attention. Publications as wide ranging as *La Gazette du Bon Ton* and the Sears catalog featured sports clothes for a variety of activities. Increasingly, women took part in more physically strenuous sports activities and approached them more vigorously than before. Genteel sportswomen wore fashionable "sport gowns," or *toilettes de sport*, for activities that ranged from badminton to shooting. Freedom of movement for many sports was achieved simply by wearing a flared, ankle-length skirt with a knit sweater. Even polo, aviation, fencing, and motorcycling were embraced by some sports-obsessed women. Among the particularly adventurous, trousers were worn for hiking and similar pursuits. Athletic footwear was developed to suit specific activities.

As with outerwear, London led the way in sports clothing and retailers advertised "everything for the sports woman." Tailored sports suits sometimes combined three-quarter-length coats with ankle- or calf-length skirts, often kilted or with concealed bifurcations. Sweaters were advertised in most major fashion magazines and several manufacturers featured knitted coats designed for golf and other sports. Skiwear for women included a long skirt and a sweater or knit coat; similar ensembles were worn for other winter activities including sledding and skating. Special underwear for sports continued to develop. However, some women still wore rigid corsetry even for athletic activities.

Field hockey players dressed in skirts and blouses, often with ties, and similar outfits were sometimes worn for golf and tennis. By the end of the decade women's sports attire reflected the change in fashionable dress and shorter, more practical skirts were increasingly accepted. Women's swimwear was affected by the gradual acceptance of more women actually swimming instead of merely "bathing." Another important development occurred in the United States in Portland, Oregon. Carl Jantzen and John Zehntbauer of the Portland Knitting Company created knit suits for a men's rowing club, and by the end of the decade had turned this idea into ribbed-knit swimsuits for men and women.

Most horsewomen continued to ride sidesaddle in skirts and jackets, sometimes with pants worn under the skirt. Along with the traditional top hats and derbys, tricorne hats were sometimes worn, showing the taste for 18th-century style. A few years into the decade, reflecting an emancipated tone in dress, women in breeches began to ride astride in riding clothes indistinguishable from men's; this fashion appears to have been accepted more quickly in the United States.

Designers

The well-established houses of Worth, Doucet, and Redfern all participated in *La Gazette du Bon Ton*, and the sophisticated, modern illustrations of the journal instilled a freshness to the output of all three. The **House of Worth**, now under the leadership of Charles Frederick Worth's grandson Jean-Charles Worth (1881–1962), continued to be

The dagged points and layered skirt of this Lucile evening dress, from *Les Modes*, June 1914, anticipated the handkerchief hems popular in the 1920s.

highly respected. At **Doucet**, de la Peña remained the de facto creative leader. **Redfern Ltd.** was still in operation in both Paris and London as well as other branches.

By 1910 Lady Duff Gordon had opened a branch of **Lucile Ltd.** in New York to take advantage of the lucrative American market. In 1911 she opened a branch in Paris, later stating, "The idea of invading the very temple of fashion and setting up my altar there appealed to me enormously."[2] Her Paris atelier received prompt and significant coverage in the French fashion magazines, *Les Modes* in particular. But the time was also tainted with scandal. Opening her New York salon required transatlantic travel and on April 14, 1912 Lucile, her husband, and their secretary were aboard the doomed RMS *Titanic*. The lifeboat that the three boarded was purportedly the first to leave the sinking ship and at less than half-capacity; rumors circulated that Lord Duff Gordon had bribed the crew. The incident caused great personal difficulty for the couple.

The designer continued to promote a highly romantic image for herself and her clientele, who included notable stage performers such as Hungarian cabaret stars The Dolly Sisters, and American dancer Irene Castle. Lucile's work was typified by diaphanous gowns in flowing sheer fabrics, orientalist fantasies, and an emotive historicism. But the designs were also sometimes suffused with modernity. As she developed her theatrically styled fashion shows, Lucile elevated the role of the fashion model.

Lucile chose to live in New York from 1914 to 1919 to escape the war, and opened a store in Chicago in 1915. While in the United States she created ready-to-wear designs for Sears and wrote columns on style for *Harper's Bazar* and *Ladies' Home*

Isadora Duncan, c. 1915　　　　　　　　　Irene Castle, c. 1918

DANCE AND FASHION

Dance and dancers influenced the style of the decade. The Ballets Russes was particularly important from its Paris debut in 1909, but other dancers and other types of dance also exerted strong influences.

Modern dancer Isadora Duncan (1877–1927) was frequently inspired by ancient Greece. In performances she often wore recreations of Greek dress, merely pinned at each shoulder and tied at the waist; part of the thrill of seeing her perform was the possibility of tantalizing glimpses of her body that occurred with the movement and slippage of her costume. Duncan also wore Greek-inspired styles in her daily life. Although her direct impact on fashion was not felt beyond bohemian circles, her style reflected the Greek modes in high fashion, and her dances were even imitated in fashion shows. Duncan loved Fortuny gowns and even dressed her children in them. Extremely fond of long flowing scarves and shawls, Duncan was strangled by one in a freak accident in 1927, making her a fashion victim in the literal sense of the word.

The most important change in social dancing involved dances from South America, in particular the tango, from Buenos Aires, and the Maxixe from Rio di Janeiro. Both were derived from working-class dances. Reflecting changes in popular music, new dances were characterized by a physicality that contrasted with the erect postures of the late 19th century. Women's eveningwear addressed the needs of these new dances with shorter hem lengths, slit skirts, and harem pants worn under skirts (a style known as *robe en culotte*). Corset advertisements emphasized their suitability for these new dances, even using "X-ray" views in illustrations. The dance floor became a popular setting for fashion illustrations. Covers of fashion magazines sometimes featured dancing couples, and diagrams of dance steps were published in their pages. Designers conceived of dresses in motion, with trims that moved with the body. The word "tango" was even used for the color orange in fashionable applications. The tango affected fashionable postures, and as columnist Francis de Miomandre quipped in the pages of *Femina* in 1911:

> As a result of their devotion to this dance, our *elegantes* have developed the habit of standing that way in all other situations of life. And so it is tangoing that they enter the room, that they take tea, that they listen to intelligent men, get into the car, try on dresses, wait for the tennis ball, in short – live.

With the new dances came ballroom-dancing stars, most important the husband and wife team of Vernon and Irene Castle. After moving to the United States in 1906, the British Vernon married the American-born Irene Foote in 1911. Performing together in Paris, the couple introduced dances with jazz rhythms to Europe. Returning to the United States, they operated a dance school and starred on Broadway. They danced their own version of the tango along with their signature dance, the "Castle Walk." When Irene cut her hair in 1915 her "Castle bob" was widely imitated, as were her headbands, known as "headache bands." Her elegant gowns were frequently from Lucile and Callot, but Irene also designed some of her own clothes. Vernon, a fighter pilot in the war, was tragically killed in 1918, but Irene continued to perform and her fame – as both a dancer and a style setter – followed her into the coming decades.

Journal. She also continued her career as a costume designer, creating costumes for the Ziegfeld Follies and feature films. By the end of the decade she began to sell off portions of her business, which ultimately led to the decline of the house.

With his distinctive, avant-garde styles and his gift for flamboyant self-promotion, **Paul Poiret** had ascended to a very prominent place in the fashion world. By 1910 he was frequently featured in major fashion publications and was particularly noted by American journalist Anne Rittenhouse. He presented himself and his work as part of a world where taste, luxury, fine art, and culture were all linked together, and developed relationships with many notable artists of the day. Poiret worked with the Fauve artist Raoul Dufy on fabric designs; Georges Lepape created another important folio of Poiret's designs, *Les Choses de Paul Poiret* (1911), and designed distinctive stationery for the *maison*. Poiret incorporated fabrics from the Wiener Werkstätte and Fortuny in his collections. In 1911 he designed costumes for *Nabuchodonosor* followed by another Middle Eastern-themed production, *Le Minaret*, of 1913. For his famous soirée, the Thousand and Second Night Party of June 24, 1911, Poiret turned the grounds of his house into "Aladdin's palace," with mounded silk cushions, multicolored fountains, and fireworks. Guests were required to wear "Persian" style and, if not properly dressed, were directed to a chamber where they were put into costumes designed by Poiret. During the 1910s Poiret's work included the *robe-pantalons*, also known as *robe sultane* or pantaloon gown, a dress composed of loose harem-style trousers attached to a long tunic, and the Byzantine-style tunic dress. The

A group of mannequins model Poiret designs, showing a range of styles from 1910.

Minaret tunic (taking its name from the stage production of *Le Minaret*) grew out of Poiret's explorations of Eastern style and was worn by young women at his parties, and it soon became part of his fashion offerings.

Poiret traveled throughout Europe giving lectures and showing his models. On a 1913 trip to America, he was welcomed as the prophet of fashion. Wanamaker's department store produced an elaborate presentation highlighting Poiret's work. Poiret was also active in perfume and cosmetics, and interior design. In 1911, using the name of one of his daughters, Poiret started to produce his Rosine line of perfumes. In the same year he established the Ecole d'Art Décoratif and the Atelier Martine, named after another daughter. The school provided art training to young girls of modest means. Their designs in turn were the basis for the decorative arts objects, including wallpapers, rugs, and cushions, available through Martine. Poiret designed costumes for several films, including *Les Amours de la reine Elisabeth* (1912) starring Sarah Bernhardt.

In his 1914 satire of current fashion (which winks at Poiret's styles), *Le Vrai et le Faux Chic*, the cartoonist Sem referred to **Jeanne Paquin** as "*La Reine de la Rue de la Paix*" (essentially "The Queen of Fashion"), and his opinion was widespread. The sudden death of Isadore Paquin in 1907 at age forty-five led the *New York Times* to predict the demise of the house. But Jeanne Paquin maintained the business, and in 1911 she was joined by her half-brother, Henri Joire, and his wife, Suzanne. Maison Paquin took part in many international exhibitions in this decade. Paquin's most impressive showing was at the Turin exhibition of 1911 where the house had its own pavilion built in neoclassic style. The display featured dancers in Greek-style garments and bare feet, and wax figures wearing Paquin creations. The Paris branch concentrated on couture, while the London store also carried sports clothes. Known

Above left Paquin's tunic-style dress, featured on the cover of *Les Modes* in May 1914, shows ancient and medieval influence in styling and construction.

Above right A photo by Talbot for *Les Modes*, May 1912, featured an evening dress by Lanvin with striking contrast in color and trim.

for dressing European royalty, Paquin set her sights on the new money of the New World. By 1912 Paquin was represented in New York by Paquin & Joire, a separate business directed by one of her relatives. In 1915 a store opened in Buenos Aires, taking advantage of the city's growth as a center of fashion and wealth. Madrid was also added to the fashion empire.

Like Poiret and Lucile, Paquin staged dramatic fashion shows. The house of Paquin was lauded for the variety of its output. Mme. Paquin preferred shorter, ankle-length hems for freedom of movement, as in her *robes de tango*. In an example of Paquin's forward-thinking elegant practicality, Geraldine Farrar modeled the "day into evening dress" in 1913 in the fashion press. Paquin encouraged black as a fashion color, and cultural references from all over the globe found their way into her designs. Mme. Paquin also collaborated with Iribe, Barbier, and Lepape to produce luxury items. She fabricated Iribe's costumes for *Rue de la Paix*, a play about the fashion industry presented in Paris in 1912. The designer also collaborated with Léon Bakst on a collection with neoclassic and exotic elements. While many of the established houses of the time were ready to offer their clients harem pants in the manner of Poiret, Paquin steadfastly opposed them. Jeanne Paquin received the *Légion d'honneur* award for commerce in 1913, a moment that firmly established and recognized the role of women in fashion design for the rest of the century. This was followed by her term as president of the Chambre Syndicale de la Haute Couture from 1917 to 1919.

Jeanne Lanvin's move to couture continued with great success. Her work was often represented in fashion magazines with pictures of mothers and daughters together. But by around 1911 her women's fashions were pictured by themselves, confirming Lanvin's success as a couturiere. Like other designers of this period who successfully changed with the times, she was able to provide a variety of looks for a variety of tastes,

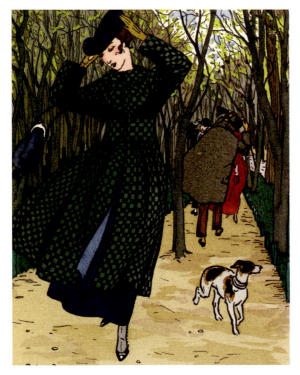

Top A. E. Marty illustrated a tiered afternoon dress by Georges Doeuillet for *La Gazette du Bon Ton*, May 1914; the silhouette was typical of Doeuillet's work.

Above A full-skirted coat by Madeleine Chéruit, a style favored by the designer, was pictured by Brissaud in *La Gazette du Bon Ton*, April 1914.

Opposite An afternoon dress from Drecoll, shown in *Les Modes*, July 1910, featured soft pleating and a tunic effect.

including the prevailing orientalist and romantic trends. Lanvin's soft colors in diaphanous fabrics showed inspiration from the Impressionist painters. She often incorporated graphic patterns realized with appliqué, embroidery, and beading. Her international presence was enhanced with her participation in the Panama-Pacific Exposition of 1915 in San Francisco.

Callot Soeurs moved to new premises in Paris during 1914, and expanded their operation to stores in Biarritz, London, and Nice. The creations of Callot Soeurs were considered among the finest available. Under the direction of Marie Callot Gerber, the house experimented with sleek, streamlined modern looks and continued their use of fine fabrics utilizing laces, lamé, and brocades embellished with exquisite detail to create a sense of overt elegance and luxury. Orientalism continued to be a recurrent theme, and they showed avant-garde pajama ensembles as early as 1911.

Georges Doeuillet (1865–1929) trained with Callot during the 1890s, and began his own house in Paris in 1900, participating in the Paris Exposition Universelle that same year, and quickly became noted for his "delicacy of design and exquisiteness of finish."[3] Doeuillet was one of the participating designers in *La Gazette du Bon Ton*. He often favored neoclassic looks as well as tiered skirts that narrowed to the hem. He was credited with the popularity of the "barrel" silhouette at the end of the war and some of his designs looked to the modernity of the 1920s.

Madeleine Chéruit (d. 1935) opened her own house in 1906, having previously worked at Maison Raudnitz. By the 1910s she had proven herself a force in Paris couture, and *La Gazette du Bon Ton* documented her sophisticated designs. In the headline of a fashion story in 1914, the *New York Times* credited her with creating the new full-skirted style that led to the prevailing silhouette of the war years. Chéruit was often described as an elegant and beautiful woman, and she used her striking appearance to showcase her style: "Mme. Cheruit dresses herself with elegance, and the world of fashion watches with interest every gown and hat and wrap she wears to the races, to the opera, to the theatre."[4]

Gustave Beer maintained operation with stores throughout Europe and was prominently featured in the press. Early in the decade he created remarkably elegant gowns in the draped neoclassic mode. By the end of the decade, Beer incorporated a sleek *moderne* style into his work, an aesthetic that continued with his output into the 1920s.

Drecoll continued under the leadership of M. and Mme. de Wagner. *Les Modes* frequently included numerous photographs of their designs that indicate a consistently elegant aesthetic on the leading edge of the time. The **Boué Soeurs**, Sylvie and Jeanne, began their business around the turn of the century, and were well established by this decade. With a very romantic aesthetic, their signature style included lace, sheer fabrics, and ribbon rosettes, and they also created very popular lingerie. A New York store, established by 1915, proved very successful into the next decade, and stores in London and Bucharest were also opened. The house of **Bechoff-David** created clothes that often took a significant amount of influence from Poiret. Their work included a culotte-style divided skirt or "pantaloon gown" in 1911, that adapted Poiret's rarified harem idea for street wear. The work of the house was very visible in the fashion press of the time, with images often included in the *New York Times*, *Les Modes*, and *Femina*. Other prominent names in Paris fashion of the decade included **Mme. Jenny**, **Maison Agnès**, **Maison Rouff**, **Martial et Armand**, and **Cauet Soeurs**. Many of these houses continued to hold a place of some importance into the following decade.

Top Eduard Wimmer-Wisgrill's sketch for the fashion department of the Wiener Werkstätte, c. 1913, exemplifies the geometric aesthetic associated with the Vienna workshop's output.

Above A sketch from the American firm Max Meyer of an early Gabrielle Chanel design highlights her use of nautical and military inspirations, c. 1916.

Arriving in Paris in 1911, a young Russian designer, Romain de Tirtoff (1892–1990), took the pseudonym **Erté**, derived from the French pronunciation of his initials. Shortly afterward, he gained employment as an assistant and sketch artist for Poiret. When Poiret closed his house in 1914 because of the war, Erté went to work designing for American retailers, notably Henri Bendel's and Altman's. Also in 1914 he was secured by *Harper's Bazar* as an illustrator to compete with the prodigious talents that were creating the covers of *Vogue*.

In addition to his Venetian palazzo, **Mariano Fortuny** maintained stores in Paris, London, and New York. The Delphos gown, adopted as a tea gown by fashionable women in the previous decade, was now worn for evening and American women were the first to wear the style outside the home as eveningwear.[5] Styles comparable to Fortuny's were being produced by **Maria Monaci Gallenga** (1880–1944), who featured similarly luxurious and historically inspired fabrics, and pleated sheath dresses with ancient-style tunics. Another designer, **Vitaldi Babani** (active 1895–1940), working in Paris, also created similar work with overt ethnic inspiration including kaftans and kimonos.

The Wiener Werkstätte added a fashion department, headed by **Eduard Josef Wimmer-Wisgrill** (1882–1961). Wimmer-Wisgrill was highly adept at realizing the latest Parisian silhouettes in fabric designs from the Viennese workshop. His elegant and fashion-forward dresses and suits earned him the nickname "the Poiret of Vienna."

While living in an orphanage as a teenager, **Gabrielle Bonheur Chanel** (1883–1971) was trained to sew by nuns and later had her first job working for a dressmaker. At a young age she showed a taste for simpler dressing, and an affinity for menswear that she incorporated into her own wardrobe. While romantically involved with a wealthy horse breeder, Chanel showed a taste for riding astride and for men's-style equestrian clothes. Also at this time she was decorating store-bought hats, and by 1909 she had begun a small millinery business in Paris. In 1910 she moved to a larger storefront on rue Cambon, naming her store Chanel Modes. Her work as a milliner was promptly successful, gaining the attention of fashion magazines and the custom of a number of notable Parisian actresses and *chanteuses*. Chanel's lease on the rue Cambon premises prohibited her from making dresses in the space, to protect the interests of another dressmaker tenant established in the building. Wishing to add clothing to her business, she opened a boutique in the resort town of Deauville. A favorite vacation spot of Jeanne Paquin, Deauville also boasted a branch of Redfern Ltd. specializing in sports clothing. Deauville was the perfect place for Chanel to test her ideas, and she was able to build a small but growing clientele for her sportswear designs among the wealthy vacationers. She opened her first couture house in Biarritz in 1915, and the affluent clientele built her business quickly. With stores in three cities, Chanel's fashion empire was established.

Sportswear and menswear (including military uniforms) would inform Chanel's style; she carried simplicity even into her couture designs. Although she did use a wide range of colors, her taste for neutrals developed early on in her career. Her creative work with the fabric gained Chanel a reputation as the "Jersey House." Likewise, she elevated knit sweaters further into fashionable women's daywear. A synchronicity between Chanel's taste and a new simpler lifestyle at the end of the war propelled her career forward. Coverage in American fashion magazines contributed enormously to her success. Her personal grooming and lifestyle choices – sunbathing and tanning, cutting her hair short – became news. Surrounded by celebrities, by 1919 Chanel was a star herself.

The Beauty Industry

The elaborate hairstyles of the Belle Epoque were abandoned during this decade, and by mid-decade hair became tighter to the head. Even if they retained their long hair in back, women increasingly had their hair cut short around their faces and across the forehead. The permanent wave was introduced in London in 1904, and by the 1910s

the practice was widespread. By the end of the decade short haircuts, often known as "bobs," were quite common and the fashion for bobbed hair insured that frequent haircuts and styling sessions became part of women's beauty routines.

Attitudes toward the use of cosmetics were changing as well. In October 1913, *Vogue* asserted that hiding the rouge pots and powder puffs was part of the "old order" and stated that the cosmetics were "every woman's privilege, nay duty." The popularity of products and treatments is evident in the great numbers of advertisements in the press, as well as the noticeable make-up on fashion models, society women, and performers in photographs. The fashionable face that developed over the decade, with darkened arched eyebrows, smudged eyes, pink cheeks, and a rosebud mouth, was created with cosmetics.

Three female entrepreneurs provided a base for the growth of the modern beauty industry. Helena Rubinstein (1870–1965), an Australian of Polish birth, began marketing a face cream in Melbourne, taking advantage of lanolin from Australia's sheep industry, and by 1915 had a thriving cosmetics business with salons in London, Paris, and New York. Rubinstein established a chain of salons (some with spa features) across the United States. Her fortune supported lavish acquisitions of fashion and art and a program of international philanthropy. Rubinstein's rival Elizabeth Arden (1884–1966) also offered products and treatments through a network of salons and was the first to promote the idea of the "makeover." Arden was born Florence Nightingale Graham in Ontario, Canada. Having restyled herself "Elizabeth Arden" she opened the first of her "Red Door" salons – on New York's fashionable Fifth Avenue – in 1910 and continued to expand internationally for the next fifty years. Born Sarah Breedlove in Louisiana, Madam C. J. Walker (1867–1919) built an empire on haircare products specifically formulated for African Americans. Between 1910 and 1920, Madam Walker's Indianapolis-based business included a factory, training school and salon, and a network of representatives, all black women like her. She finally settled in New York where she became active in Harlem's political scene and a leading philanthropist. These three pioneers – Rubinstein, Arden, and Walker – applied science to beauty and stressed the high quality of their products through attractive packaging and trained representatives; in each case, the founder's image was vital to the identity of the company.

The War and Fashion

The war's impact on fashion was widespread and took many forms. Because textiles were needed for military use, civilians were urged to conserve fabric. The color palette of fashion changed, in part as clothing reflected the somber realities of wartime, but also because of the lack of synthetic dyes previously exported from Germany. Labor shortages also had an impact. Elaborate dressing rituals – such as the custom of upper-class women changing outfits three times a day with the help of a maid – seemed obsolete. Military uniforms influenced civilian fashion. Women dressed in masculine styles as they took on wartime jobs replacing men who had gone to war. Prominent women who served in organizations such as the Red Cross and service auxiliaries wore uniforms, sometimes created for them. Innovations used in the military included the "separable fastener", invented by Gideon Sundback in 1913 and patented in 1917. The trench coat, a belted overcoat that developed from Burberry's famous Tielocken, took its name from trench warfare. With its combination of heroic associations and practical features, the style was adopted by civilians and became a permanent part of the modern wardrobe for men and women.

The luxury industries were disrupted by the military service of proprietors (including Poiret) and workers and also the reduction of their accustomed international clientele. Manufacturers, retailers, and the fashion press often used references to the war to sell products. *Vogue* featured articles such as "Dressing on a war income." Even corsets were marketed to appeal to wartime sensibilities, as in the "New Military Curve" from Royal Worcester. Wanamaker's "Win-the-War" catalog for

Above A British army officer wears a trench coat, a style that made a rapid transition from military use to civilian wardrobes.

spring and summer 1918 offered merchandise targeted to a patriotic clientele, from "Women's Suits, After the Fashion of the Army Uniforms" to "War-Time Simplicity in Babies' Dresses!" Customers were reminded that "wool will win the war," encouraging women to buy silk or cotton instead, saving wool for the military. A "woman-all" jumpsuit was available to "the patriotic woman eager to do her bit in kitchen or garden." Some aspects of the war had surprising effects on fashion later in the century. Camouflage, probably influenced by Cubism, was first developed in France for World War I. Reconstructive plastic surgery on men injured in the war became the basis of many of the cosmetic surgery procedures that grew increasingly widespread and fashionable during the following decades of the 20th century.

The overwhelming casualties of the war made the public question established mourning customs. Mourning as an institution had to be abandoned; the potential for an unprecedented number of bereaved women wearing black – young widows, mothers, and sisters – threatened to darken further the public consciousness already devastated by the war itself.

Menswear

This period saw the end of the 19th-century aesthetic in men's fashion. Hugh Cundry of Henry Poole, the renowned Savile Row tailoring firm, said that 1914 marked "the end of civilization."[6] Practicality was promoted and styles associated with a leisured or elite lifestyle became outmoded.

Due to the disruption of wartime, fashions for men did not undergo major fluctuations during the decade. However, the silhouette of the lounge suit continued to streamline and usage of older styles such as the frock coat and morning suit declined further. A slim silhouette prevailed. Suit jackets, whether single- or double-breasted, were extremely trim with nipped-in waists and narrow sleeves. Trousers were also

Opposite bottom A plate from *American Gentleman*, a tailoring trade publication, illustrates a range of menswear styles for autumn/winter 1917–1918. The prevailing silhouette was slim and shaped, and a variety of hats was promoted.

Below left A 1911 illustration of a young man in a khaki-colored suit from a Parisian retailer emphasizes the sporty styling of his jacket and accessories.

Below right A Dannenberg illustration from c. 1914 shows the generous cut of men's overcoats, worn with dashing accessories.

narrow, with flat fronts and sharp center creases. Some had cuffs; the customary length was rather short, ending above the instep. Fabrics ranged from plain wools to woven patterns including pinstripes and chalk stripes, windowpane checks, and geometric-patterned tweeds. Outerwear was sometimes more generously cut as A-line overcoats flared out over the narrow suits.

A vogue for khaki suits reflected further influence from uniforms and also signaled the acceptance of more casual standards. Faced with the decline in civilian orders, tailors compensated for the loss of business by making military uniforms, especially for officers, in accordance with government specifications made available to the tailoring trade. In 1917 the trade journal *American Gentleman* declared that "anything that smacks of military dress is bound to be popular with both old and young." The same magazine claimed that a scarcity of imported silk "brought the bow tie into prominence as an all-year-around vogue." While bow ties and other variations were seen, the four-in-hand tie was the dominant style. A slightly puffed version was popular. Wristwatches were increasingly worn, as driving and soldiering made the pocket watch inconvenient. Fedoras and even Stetson-style hats were frequently worn for all but the most formal occasions.

For the signing of the Treaty of Versailles on June 28, 1919, Prime Ministers David Lloyd George of the United Kingdom and Georges Clemenceau of France, and President Woodrow Wilson of the United States of America wore morning suits with cutaway jackets. Prime Minister Vittorio Emanuele Orlando of Italy wore a sack suit, like many other members of the various international delegations. The *New York Times* noted that the "black coats" of the Allied leaders provided a sharp contrast with another ceremony that took place at Versailles in 1870, dominated by Chancellor Otto von Bismarck in an ornate white uniform.[7] The *Times* underlined how this reinforced a move from the old order into a new world.

A LA GRANDE MAISON :: PARIS

Below American children in typical attire, c. 1916. The perennially popular sailor suit takes on added poignancy as the United States is on the verge of entering the war.

Children's Fashion

The contrast between practical and decorative that characterized women's clothing was seen in children's clothes as well. While freedom of movement was stressed, training corsets were still used for proper posture. As in past decades, young children wore smocks and loose dresses. Teenage girls' clothing reflected the dominant styles in womenswear. Boys out of early childhood increasingly wore knickerbockers instead of short pants and transitioned into long trousers at a younger age than in the past. Children's fashion also felt the influence of military styling. This was augmented by the growth of the Scouting movement for boys and girls throughout the English-speaking world. Scouts wore uniforms in shades of khaki, brown, and green with large pockets and ranger hats. Groups of young girls and boys in their uniforms mirrored adults who were serving in the military or involved in the war effort.

By this time, sailor looks were more popular than ever, for all ages from toddlers to teenagers. Boys and girls wore pull-over blouses, often called middies, with sailor collars, ties, and other nautical details. Sailor blouses and suits were available in casual and dressy styles and were even a popular style for swimwear. While combinations of blue and white were the most common, a range of other colors was seen including stripes, khaki, and even pink and white. Outerwear followed the lines of adult fashion and hats were worn outdoors. For boys, soft caps were the most popular style for daily wear.

Magazines continued to recommend historic looks for special celebrations, such as pageboy costumes for little boys and lingerie-style dresses for young girls. Light colors predominated for dressy clothing in warm weather. As in the past, children wore distinctive hats for special occasions. Girls' hats were often very ornate and varied. Even little girls wore astonishingly large hats. Following the fashions in women's hat styles, oversize mobcaps, wide brims, and high crowns were seen. Straighter, knee-length dresses with low waistlines, bobbed hair, and even bare legs, seen on girls in the 1910s, emerged as important elements of women's dress in the following years.

The End of the Decade

At the end of the 1910s, the overall simplification of fashion seemed appropriate to post-war society. Two French designers began their careers in the late years of the decade promoting a simplified aesthetic: Jean Patou and Lucien Lelong. Jean Patou (1880–1936), the son of a prosperous tanner in Normandy, founded a fashion business in Paris around 1910. Patou was ready to show his first couture collection in 1914, but the war forced him to change his plans. He served in the army, and reopened in 1919. From the beginning, Patou emphasized simplicity and favored shorter skirts; he was crucial to the development of the sporty, pared-down styles of the 1920s. Lucien Lelong (1889–1958) was the son of couturiers Arthur and Eleanore Lelong, whose house, while small, was well established. In 1918 Lucien, a wounded war veteran, returned home and took over the business. Lucien's modern aesthetic radically changed the house, and would have a great impact on fashion in the coming years.

World War I irrevocably changed the world order. Nowhere was this more evident than in the way men and women dressed. Following the war, an influenza epidemic killed millions. During its peak years of 1918 and 1919, the flu epidemic was especially severe in Europe but the effects were felt worldwide. Civil workers wore respiratory masks and women's hats with protective veiling were marketed to shield wearers from contagion. This was the culminating devastation of a decade that had experienced more than its share of tragedy. As men returned from battle, Western society attempted to resume "normalcy." A truly modern lifestyle was taking shape and a fresh aesthetic accompanied this development: Lepape's crisp graphics, Wimmer-Wisgrill's bold patterns, and Chanel's relaxed designs were evidence of a new sensibility.

Opposite top left Uniform influence and the trend for khaki in menswear also affected boys' clothing, as seen in this illustration from the John Wanamaker catalog, 1918.

Opposite top right Girls' fashions illustrated in *Pictorial Review* in 1916 show a variety of styles for different ages. Toddlers wear smock-like dress and young girls have dropped waistlines that anticipate adult styles in the following decade. Whimsical hats are shown for all ages.

Below Home from the war, a French soldier's children are ready to welcome him back into civilian clothes. "A Soldier's Homecoming" by A. E. Marty, from *Les Modes et Manières d'Aujourd'hui*, 1919.

Chapter 5

The 1920s

Les Années Folles

A pleasure-filled, exuberant spirit shaped the 1920s, often referred to as the Jazz Age, the Roaring Twenties or *Les Années Folles*. After an initial stage of economic uncertainty following the war, a sense of relief, even euphoria, took hold. Dark events at the beginning and end of the decade – the Great War and the economic crash of 1929 – contributed to the fun, frivolous image of these years between. Tangos and foxtrots shared the dance floor with new energetic steps including the Charleston, Blackbottom, and Shimmy. Stylish men wore tails and tuxedos for evening, escorting ladies in shimmering sheath dresses, illuminated by the glimmering lights of big cities at night. Automobiles were faster and more available, contributing to the popularity of outdoor activity; as new designs featured roofs and windshields, special driving clothes became obsolete. Changes in fashion reflected the growing influence of the automobile on daily life and the auto became a symbol of sophistication in fashion photography.

Opposite The glittering nightlife of newly electrified cities reflected the energetic and modern spirit of the age, as exemplified by Georges Lepape's cover for *Vogue*, March 15, 1927, depicting model Lee Miller.

Right George Barbier's "Au Revoir" depicts the end of an elegant soirée, showing a variety of formal evening styles for men and women. The rendering of the automobile's wheels and the streamlined sculptures flanking the arched windows reflect the art deco aesthetic.

Social and Economic Background

More than 10 million died in the war. In addition to the emotional effect of such devastation, the survivors confronted shortages and the need to rebuild. The Treaty of Versailles changed the power structure of Europe, as empires were broken up and smaller, independent countries emerged. The League of Nations was established as an international overseer. Germany was required to pay reparations, as the Allies were intent on limiting economic growth in Germany.

Women's voting rights were achieved in Canada and Scandinavia by 1918, in Germany by 1919, in the United States by 1920, and in Great Britain by 1928. Of the major European countries, only Spain, France, and Italy held back. Alcohol prohibition emerged in several nations during the 1910s and the United States government ratified the Eighteenth Amendment in October 1919, prohibiting the production and sale of liquor. Americans still found ways to drink, ranging from home-brewed "bathtub gin" to prescription "medicinal" liquor. Speakeasies, nightclubs that illicitly served alcoholic beverages, contributed to the celebratory spirit of these years, placing women in a previously male-only drinking environment.

The Arts

Dada laid the foundation for Surrealism, one of the most influential art movements of the 20th century. The Surrealists, an international group of artists including Max Ernst, Man Ray, Salvador Dalí, and René Magritte, explored the uncanny quality of dreams and the subconscious. Orphism, an offshoot of Cubism, used color to celebrate the dynamism of modern life, as seen in the work of Robert and Sonia Delaunay. Other painters applied the faceted forms of Cubism to realistic depictions of cities and landscapes, including Americans Charles Demuth and Georgia O'Keeffe and Canadian Lawren Harris. The pleasures and anxieties of the period were expressed in literature by D. H. Lawrence, F. Scott Fitzgerald, Virginia Woolf, and Ernest Hemingway. Contemporary society was critiqued in the works of William Faulkner, Sinclair Lewis, and Theodore Dreiser while T. S. Eliot and James Joyce experimented with new literary forms. In the theater, challenging dramas from Eugene O'Neill contrasted with the stylish drawing-room comedies of Noël Coward.

Jazz dominated popular music. "Negro orchestras" were featured in many of the best-known nightclubs in America and Europe. Performers Louis Armstrong, Ma Rainey, and Bessie Smith helped forge a fashionable image of African Americans. In the early years of the "Harlem Renaissance," the New York City neighborhood saw a burst of creativity in the arts. Black performers were also particularly popular in Paris, where American-born Josephine Baker became famous for her energetic dance style and exotic costumes. In a famous number, she danced nearly nude in only a "skirt" made of faux bananas. One of the most charismatic performers in Paris, Baker emerged as a fashion icon and her beauty was captured by the great photographers of the time and immortalized in the posters of Paul Colin.

George Gershwin's *Rhapsody in Blue* (1924) and *An American in Paris* (1928) fused jazz rhythms with classical format. His *Blue Monday*, a jazz opera with a Harlem setting, was produced on Broadway in 1922. The musical theater offered amusing glimpses of contemporary life in musicals such as Gershwin's *Lady, Be Good* (1924) and *No, No, Nanette* (1925) with music by Vincent Youmans. Sheet music spread popular songs, including selections from musicals, and was also important for transmitting fashion information.

The film industry offered a variety of entertainments ranging from comedies starring Charlie Chaplin or Buster Keaton to Cecil B. DeMille's biblical epic *The Ten Commandments* (1923) and Walt Disney's popular animated character, Mickey Mouse. D. W. Griffith's *Orphans of the Storm* (1921) and Abel Gance's *Napoléon* (1927) brought grand production values to historical subjects. Tales of the exotic East continued with Rudolph Valentino as *The Sheik* (1921) and with *Thief of Bagdad* (1924) starring Douglas Fairbanks. *The Jazz Singer* (1927), starring vaudeville star Al

CHICAGO

(That Toddling Town)

Words & Music
by
FRED FISHER

HENLO
U.S.A

Published by FRED FISHER INC. 224 W. 46TH St. New York.

Above left Josephine Baker, an American singer, actress, and cabaret performer, wears a clutch coat and the short, pomaded hairstyle she favored (photographed by Emil Bieber c. 1925).

Above right A young couple in evening clothes are seen against the Chicago skyline on the sheet music to a popular 1922 hit song.

Jolson in blackface, was the first major feature-length film with synchronized sound – a breakthrough in filmmaking technology that ushered in "Talkies." The Academy of Motion Picture Arts and Sciences was founded in 1927, and the first Academy Awards were presented in a fifteen-minute ceremony on March 16, 1929. Janet Gaynor became the first woman to win the Academy Award for Best Actress and, although not the most glamorous actress of the day, she set into motion the phenomenon of Best Actress "Oscar" winner as style setter.

The 1925 Exposition and Art Deco

The Exposition Internationale des Arts Décoratifs et Industriels Modernes was held in Paris from April to October of 1925. The momentous exhibition featured innovative displays including Le Corbusier's Pavillon de l'Esprit Nouveau and a crystal fountain by Lalique. The commonly used term "art deco" was coined in the 1960s based on the title of this exposition, giving a name to the style on view at the show. Art deco, a sleek, polished aesthetic, was influenced by a number of sources including Cubism, the ancient Near East, and pre-Columbian design, and was characterized by the use of geometric shapes, repeats, and gradation. Typical motifs include classical-inspired figures and streamlined animals such as gazelles and impalas. Art deco's influence on fashion was seen in jewelry, accessories, and textile patterns. Many prominent fashion designers participated in the Exposition including Louiseboulanger, Callot, Doeuillet, Jenny, Lanvin, Lelong, Poiret, Vionnet, and Worth. The French textile industry showed particularly beautiful designs from Rodier, Cornille Frères, and Bianchini-Férier. The deco aesthetic reflected current beauty ideals, exemplified in the almost Cubist physique of bodybuilder and model Tony Sansone and the lean elegance of Josephine Baker.

Rudolph Valentino

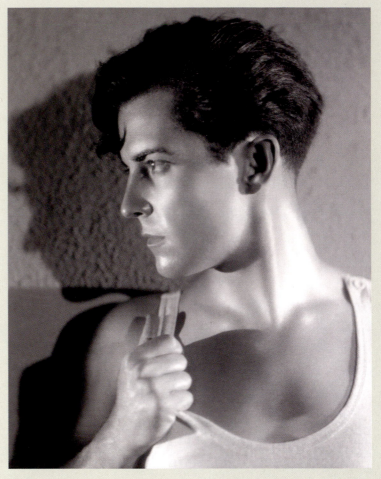

Ramón Novarro

MATINEE IDOLS

Movie screens were filled with the images of handsome, charismatic actors – "matinee idols" – whose style was emulated by men throughout the Western world. The suave Wallace Reid was dubbed "the screen's most perfect lover" and dashing John Gilbert was described in equally hyperbolic terms. Japanese American Sessue Hayakawa, often cast as the dangerous exotic lover, became an unlikely matinee idol.

Douglas Fairbanks began his career as a stage actor, but soon went to Hollywood and enjoyed a rapid rise to fame. The husband of Mary Pickford and a founding member of both United Artists studios and the Academy of Motion Picture Arts and Sciences, he earned the nickname "King of Hollywood." His films, including *The Mark of Zorro*, *Robin Hood,* and *The Black Pirate*, were typical of the "swashbuckling" genre of which Fairbanks was king. He became famous for his work in period-costume drama, managing to look manly even in tights. Fairbanks and Pickford were the first to be immortalized with their handprints and footprints in cement at Grauman's Chinese Theater.

Born in Italy, Rudolph Valentino worked as a taxi dancer and operetta performer in New York before arriving in Hollywood to become one of the biggest box office draws of the decade. Although famous for his "Latin Lover" persona, his films such as *The Young Rajah*, *Blood and Sand*, and *The Sheik* included Eastern locales and storylines. Valentino was magnetic to the ladies, attracting a large female fan base. While men sometimes found his meticulous sartorial sense effeminate, they were jealous of his appeal to women. His hair, slicked back with pomade, was widely emulated, earning his imitators the collective nickname "Vaselinos." Valentino was known for his complicated love life, and his most famous relationship was his tempestuous marriage to designer Natacha Rambova. Valentino's premature death caused widespread public mourning, pushing his female fans into hysterical behavior.

The muscular and handsome Ramón Novarro was Valentino's closest rival as Hollywood's Latin Lover. Born José Samaniego in Durango, Mexico, Novarro arrived in Los Angeles in 1913, and within a few years was cast in small parts. During the early 1920s, he graduated to larger roles, in such films as *Scaramouche* and *The Arab*. His most famous performance was in the title role of *Ben-Hur* for which he wore costumes that highlighted his athletic physique, impacting the image of male sexuality in film.

Chinoiserie and Egyptomania

A taste for chinoiserie continued, often in outrageous forms, ranging from the popularity of mah-jong, the Chinese tile game, to Puccini's spectacular last opera, *Turandot*, a passionate tale set in legendary Peking. Grauman's Chinese Theater in Hollywood opened in 1927 with imported Chinese artifacts including a 30-foot (9-meter) stone dragon. Cartier decorated objects and jewelry with motifs such as dragons and lotus blossoms. Fashion reflected the style with embroidery and beaded motifs on eveningwear and pajamas.

On November 4, 1922, British archaeologist Howard Carter and his team discovered the entrance to the tomb of King Tutankhamun. Images of the treasures found inside flooded the news media and a craze for Egyptian style – "Egyptomania" – gripped popular culture, influencing architecture, interior design, and decorative arts. The fashion industry exploited the trend, producing garments printed and embroidered with Egyptian motifs. Egyptian-style jewelry and accessories were popular at all market levels.

In addition to Chinese and Egyptian, many other regional styles were used as inspiration. The taste for Russian folk art continued in fashion, as a large number of Russians displaced by the 1917 revolution had settled in Paris. Embroidery and appliqué, accessories and silhouettes were all strongly influenced by the trend. Spanish inspiration took many forms, in both clothing and architecture, as did Arabian styles. American Indian, Aztec, and Mayan forms influenced design, and aspects of African style were also inspirational.

Above Ernst Dryden's 1927 illustration, painted on Asian newspaper, of two fashionable women in lounging pajamas, captures the orientalist taste of the period.

Below A Tutankhamun-inspired evening jacket of beaded lamé (France, c. 1922–1925) displays Egyptian motifs including lotus blossoms, falcons, and fanciful hieroglyphic-inspired details.

Lyubov Popova's design for a day dress (1923–1924) utilizing fabric of her own design reflects the Constructivist aesthetic.

Russian Art and Style

The Russian Revolution was followed by several years of civil war that ended with Soviet control in 1923. During the revolution, many Russian artists and designers fled, but for those who stayed in Russia, the years were momentous as art and design flourished. A group of innovative artists and designers built on artistic styles of the pre-revolutionary years. Their work was influenced by Cubism and Futurism, leading to the development of a specifically Russian style of painting and architecture, Constructivism. A leading figure of the movement was Lyubov Popova (1889–1924). In addition to her large output of paintings, she designed fabrics, theatrical costumes, and clothing. Her fashion designs often used large squares of fabric with simple construction. Constructivist painter Aleksandra Ekster (1882–1949) applied the principles of the movement to striking theatrical set and costume designs. Her work was an original fusion of Futurist and folkloric influences. Leading the creative burst of the early 1920s was the multi-media artist Aleksandr Rodchenko (1891–1956). Rodchenko was a key figure in the cultural life of the Soviet Union. With a group of artists known as Productivists, he sought to incorporate design into everyday life in the new society, creating jumpsuits that he called "production clothing." He also created textile designs incorporating geometric and interlaced guilloché (repeating wavelike) patterns.

German Culture

Following the war, the German Empire was replaced with a new government, referred to as the "Weimar Republic." The short-lived, liberal government encouraged social freedoms, racial diversity, and alternative lifestyles. But this period was also characterized by social unrest, extreme inflation, and economic depression. A lively, decadent nightlife developed and cabarets and jazz clubs flourished. Berlin became one of the most important cultural centers of the Western world, rivaling New York and Paris.

The Neue Sachlichkeit ("New Objectivity") developed from German Expressionism, which had flourished during World War I. Artists including George Grosz, Otto Dix, and Christian Schad chronicled the dissolute world of Jazz Age Berlin in realistic, often disturbing, paintings. The Bauhaus, a design school that began operation in Weimar in 1919, founded by architect Walter Gropius, was influential in the applied arts and was known for a simple streamlined aesthetic. Filmmaking in Germany entered an Expressionist phase. *The Cabinet of Doctor Caligari* (1920), *Nosferatu* (1922), and *Metropolis* (1927) featured bold cinematography and highly stylized production design. *Pandora's Box* (1929), the tale of an amoral, sexually liberated woman, included an emblematic performance by American actress Louise Brooks. Playwright Bertolt Brecht collaborated with composer Kurt Weill on musical works which often included Marxist messages. Austrian Ernst Krenek incorporated jazz into his opera *Jonny spielt auf*. Premiered in Leipzig in 1927, its title character was a black jazz musician played by a white singer in blackface. The wildly successful work, produced in Europe and New York, featured a Dada sensibility with musical saws, alarm clocks, and sirens in the orchestration.

Fashion Media

La Gazette du Bon Ton continued to publish until 1925. *L'Officiel de la Couture et de la Mode*, which covered the leading Parisian designers, began publication in 1921. Styles of the Russian avant-garde were showcased in *Iskustova Odevastia*, and the German fashion press included *Styl* and *Die Dame*. In Canada, the women's magazine *Chatelaine* debuted in 1928. Menswear was featured in *L'Homme Elegant* and *Monsieur*, which were launched in Paris in January 1920. Both *Vogue* and *Harper's Bazaar* flourished and attained dominant roles on both sides of the Atlantic. *Vogue* continued to feature remarkable illustrated covers including work by Georges Lepape, and Erté continued his association with *Harper's Bazar* (which became *Harper's*

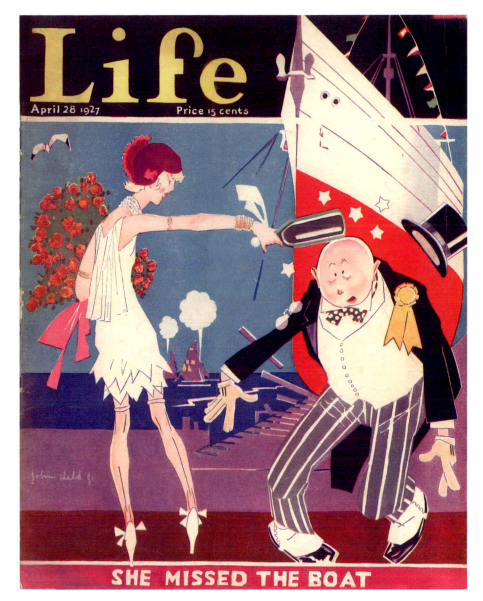

Above The 1929 German film *Pandora's Box* starred Louise Brooks as the amoral seductress Lulu, seen here in a poster for the French release of the movie. Brooks' on-screen style encouraged the popularity of her geometric bobbed haircut.

Right Known for witty illustrations of "flaming youth" at play, John Held Jr. created a vivid, fun-loving flapper in handkerchief hem dress, cloche hat, and stockings rolled to her knees, for the cover of *Life* magazine, April 28, 1927.

Bazaar in 1929). The art deco style of Spanish illustrator Eduardo García Benito took inspiration from a variety of sources including Renaissance art and the work of the painter Amedeo Modigliani. Austrian artist Ernst Dryden, a student of Gustav Klimt, began his career working as a fashion and graphic designer in Vienna and Berlin, and in 1926 began work with *Die Dame* as a fashion illustrator. Dryden's elegant, chic style incorporated orientalist and Surrealist elements. While illustration was vital to this decade, fashion photography was coming of age. Edward Steichen continued his work in fashion photography for *Vanity Fair* and *Vogue*. Multi-media artist Man Ray became an important fashion photographer. Russian-born George Hoyningen-Huene established his career working for French *Vogue*, his style marked by a striking chiaroscuro and a neoclassic sensibility.

La Garçonne and the Flapper

Whether they were called *garçonnes* or flappers, fashionable young women of the period set new standards for female freedom and style. Their behavior could be read as a reaction to the seriousness of the suffragettes: with the vote obtained, these young women set their sights on their next demand – sexual liberation. Some emerged from bohemian circles, and embraced the avant-garde, liberal politics, or hedonistic lifestyles. A new group of bold beauties including Tallulah Bankhead, Nancy Cunard,

Above Clara Bow, in a still from the 1927 film *It*, exemplified the North American flapper.

Below Popular fashions available from catalogs reflected trends from high fashion as seen in these modestly priced dresses from 1923.

Marion Davies, Zelda Fitzgerald, and Colleen Moore provided sharp contrast to the girlish femininity of Mary Pickford and the Gish sisters.

The term *garçonne* (a play on the French word for boy) derived from Victor Margueritte's controversial 1922 novel *La Garçonne*, whose heroine cut her hair short, dressed in mannish clothes, and led a sexually liberated life which included lesbian affairs. *Garçonne* was used to denote a style that was lean and androgynous. By mid-decade, the look was popular on both sides of the Atlantic, in a range of styles from sporty ensembles to near cross-dressing. In Paris and Berlin, extreme forms of the *garçonne* image were often linked to alternative lifestyle subcultures. Couturieres Madeleine et Madeleine produced a tuxedo for women in 1926.[1] Some American periodicals and manufacturers were uneasy with the French term and used the description "boyish" to market the clothing in this new style.

Although flappers are sometimes described as the American and Canadian version of the *garçonne*, there were differences. While the origins of the term "flapper" are uncertain, it was already in wide usage by 1920. The characteristic posture of these young women, the "flapper slouch," conveyed a casual and carefree manner, and evening clothes trimmed with fringe and beads were emblematic of their lively attitude. Cartoonist John Held Jr. created the archetypal image of the flapper on magazine covers and posters. Held depicted her as free-spirited, flippant, and boisterous. A short-lived magazine, *The Flapper*, appealed to these girls, billing itself as "not for old fogies." Two popular novels featured heroines in the flapper mold. Anita Loos' *Gentlemen Prefer Blondes*, published in 1925, was also adapted for the Broadway stage. Elinor Glyn's *It* (1927) was quickly made into a hit movie starring Clara Bow, whose captivating performance defined the flapper. "It" was a euphemism for sex appeal, and Bow was dubbed the "It Girl."

The Elements of Women's Fashion

The styles of the 1920s developed from innovations of the previous decade. Simplified wardrobes, sleeker shapes, and more body exposure became the norm. The boyish figure was the ideal by 1925. Although images in magazines featured a sleek and elegant look, real women in these styles often failed to achieve the lean, attenuated aesthetic promoted by high fashion. Unlike the endless silhouette undulations of the 1910s, the prevailing silhouette of the 1920s showed only minor, gradual changes. The decade began with shapeless "chemise" styles: tubular, T-shaped sheaths, with loose belts indicating ambiguous waistlines, sometimes high, sometimes low, and hems usually at calf length. Tops were typically loose, and often cut without shoulder seams. Some skirt and top combinations were created with the skirt attached to a slip that was covered by an overblouse. Uncomplicated construction was common. Designers often responded with decorative surface details and used printed fabrics. Geometric motifs were created by piecing together contrasting fabrics, especially for sportswear. Asymmetrical details in both cut and decoration were frequently seen.

Following the shorter lengths and slit dresses of the 1910s, legs became a focus of fashion. During the decade, hemlines fell and rose – and fell again. With the hemline fluctuations, a variety of hem treatments developed including handkerchief point, paneled, scalloped, and uneven and asymmetrical styles. Hemlines reached their lowest point, at the ankle, by autumn 1922. Following this low ebb, hemlines began to steadily rise, and by 1926 most fashionable women's skirts were just below the knee where they remained for a few years.

Beginning early in the decade, the prevailing fashionable waistline was at the pelvis or further down on the hip. As the hemline solidified at just below the knee, this lower placement of the waist prevailed. While fashionable waistlines were usually dropped, some women belted their dresses at the natural waist, as seen in photographs of prominent style setters including Louise Brooks, Josephine Baker, Colleen Moore, and Clara Bow.

While much of fashion strove toward sleek simplicity, the *robe de style*, a full-skirted dress worn for both dressy daywear and for evening, maintained genuine femininity and even old-fashioned elegance. Associated especially with Jeanne Lanvin, but also available from other houses, the *robe de style* was a continuation of the romantic full skirt of the middle war years, now with a looser bodice and a lowered waist. Undersupports of petticoats, even hooped cages, were used to create the silhouette, and the fuller skirts were decorated with a variety of details, often tiers of ruffles or petals.

Tailored ensembles and knit separates were very popular for daytime, worn often with matching pleated skirts. Jackets were typically hip length and were sometimes belted or buttoned low, with a loose fit through the torso. In addition to the trendy *garçonne* look, some ensembles showed influence from uniforms and men's sportswear. Skirts were straight, without pleats, or featured a group of pleats positioned to one side. A knit ensemble, in the style of Chanel or Patou, was essential to the wardrobe of a young woman of fashion; it provided ease of movement and showcased a fashionable boyish figure.

Blouse and skirt combinations were popular. Blouses, nearly always three-quarter or long-sleeved, were varied, including sailor and peasant styles and more masculine button-front looks. They were usually worn as overblouses covering the upper hip area. The blouse provided the fashionable dropped waistline, and some blouses were worn with belts near the bottom or tucked in, with a deep blouson.

Daytime dresses were usually simply fashioned as well, made of a variety of knit and woven fabrics. Simple bodices with long sleeves were common, but occasionally sleeveless and short-sleeved versions were seen. Necklines were usually relatively modest, often decorated with pin tucks, collars, ruffles, or trim. Ensembles of dresses with matching or coordinating coats also became popular as another option for town wear. In imitation of this look, some dresses had faux "coat fronts" emerging from the side and shoulder seams.

Below left Gordon Conway's illustration shows another side of 1920s fashion – emphasizing the soft styling, uneven hemline, and bold art deco floral print of a chiffon garden party dress from 1929.

Below right The romanticism of the mid-1910s continued with the *robe de style*, here illustrated for the cover of *Vogue* by Helen Dryden (February 15, 1921).

Overleaf With advances in transportation, the theme of travel became increasingly popular in fashion illustration. Pierre Mourgue's 1927 image depicts two Chanel coat and dress ensembles described as "semisports wear." Both wool coats were lined with woolen materials; the striped jersey used for the top was also used to line the coat seen on the right, producing the striking effect of matching striped revers.

THE HEMLINE

Hemline fluctuations, and the public's reaction to them, proved to be one of the 20th century's most important fashion themes. Although the undulations of the hemline in the 20th century really began in the 1910s, in the 1920s hem lengths became an object of significant social and media attention, even prompting attempts at legislation. Reactions to hemline changes in the 1920s predicted similar changes and responses in the late 1940s and early 1970s. While the 1920s are frequently stereotyped as a time of knee-length skirts, this length actually prevailed for only a few years of the decade.

The drop of the hemline in 1922 (back to its lowest level since before World War I) provoked strong but varied reactions. Within ten days during August 1922 the *New York Times* ran two stories that chronicled contradictory responses.

> Because short skirts are cheaper to make, the dresses worn by inmates at the State Reformatory for Women at Bedford [New York] are not to be made longer to conform to the new styles worn by women outside. Some of the prisoners, anxious to be in style, asked attendants to allow longer dresses. The new uniform one-piece dress decreed for prisoners a few days ago comes down to within a foot of the ground. Although this is lower than Bedford women formerly wore their skirts, matrons admitted that it only strikes a happy medium between the extremely short skirts formerly affected outside and the long skirts now in

vogue. "The new regulation is more economical," said Major Amos T. Barker, Superintendent, today. "We won't keep up with the styles here."[2]

Meanwhile, about 300 miles (480 km) to the north, a different reaction was taking shape in Canada:

> Twenty of Montreal's smartest and prettiest girls, rebelling against the attempt of style creators to foist long skirts on women, have formed a "No-Longer-Skirt League." Members are pledged to cling to the abbreviated variety and do all they can to induce other young women to keep their skirts short.[3]

In 1926, following the rise of the hemline to just below the knee, the American economist George Taylor studied the popularity of quality silk hosiery as an expression of affluence, as stockings were well exposed by shorter skirts. Taylor's work has been misinterpreted as creating the "Hemline Index," a popularly held economic myth that maintains that with prosperity come shorter hemlines, and that recession brings longer lengths. While it has been repeated ever since, the maxim is easily disproved when the relationship between the hemline and the economy is clearly examined. Ironically, as the "Hemline Index" was developing it also disproved itself: at the height of prosperity two years *before* the Stock Market crash of 1929, Paris couturiers were already showing longer lengths.

Models outside a fashion exhibition in Holland Park, London, display a range of hemlines fashionable at the same time in 1925.

Right George Barbier's 1921 illustration for the luxury fashion publication *La Gazette du Bon Ton* renders a beaded cherry blossom motif in art deco style on a Gustave Beer gown with dramatic trailing panels.

Far right Maison Callot was renowned for its striking color schemes and distinctive embroidery, which was appreciated by its discerning clientele. The bold floral motif on this dress from c. 1922–1925 also reflects the aesthetic seen on luxurious shawls of the time.

Shorter hemlines prevailed, and long dresses all but disappeared for the theater, bridal wear, horse races, garden parties, and even balls, opera, court dress, and formal affairs of state. As with smart daytime dresses there were many hemline variations. Handkerchief hems were especially popular by mid-decade, and by decade's end skirts were sometimes knee length in front cascading to longer lengths in back, often touching the floor; panels, often extended sashes, trailed theatrically.

Early in the decade, evening dresses often featured dramatic hip emphasis, especially "pannier"-style drapes on both sides, or large poufs of fabric in asymmetrical arrangements. The *robe de style* was popular for evening, but by mid-decade many evening dresses were simple sleeveless sheaths, with decorative details at the hips.

Arms were exposed as long gloves were rarely worn. Evening necklines, often in simple round shapes at front and back, were much more revealing than previous fashions. Voided chiffon velvet, satins, crepes, and georgettes, usually in neutrals or jewel tones, were used, as were lamé and metallic shot fabrics. Evening styles were also frequently beaded and sequined. Fringe, tassels, feathers, and other dangling trims became more prevalent on dancing dresses in response to the movements of popular steps; such styles were popularized on-screen in musical numbers, as seen on Joan Crawford in *Our Dancing Daughters* (1928).

Daytime formal wear typically featured soft styles that resembled the silhouettes of evening clothes, but provided more coverage. Formal daytime dresses often had circular, petal or long sheer sleeves, and separate bertha collars in lace or chiffon were worn over sleeveless dresses. Some dresses of the period blur distinctions between formal daytime and simpler evening styles. Depending on the time of year and the occasion, the same dress could be worn for afternoon or evening with a change of accessories.

Wedding and bridesmaid dresses were also typically styled in the manner of evening clothes, and again the *robe de style* was popular, as were handkerchief and other hem treatments. Wedding dresses were often sleeved with lace and tulle, and sleeveless versions were also worn. Trains came not from the dresses but from the veils, as the enormously long veils popular in the 1910s were still fashionable: now with shorter skirts the veil was the only element of the ensemble that trained. For court dress and state occasions, some older aristocrats and royals, including Queen Mary, continued to wear long dresses. However, short dresses became standard for these occasions, teamed with long trailing veils or trained capes.

Above left **A fashionable gentleman and ladies arriving at a cricket match in 1928 in daytime formal wear with accessories carefully chosen for such an occasion.**

Above right **Consuelo Vanderbilt, the daughter of William Kissam Vanderbilt II, pictured here dressed for her 1926 marriage, was described as "a bride of importance" when this photograph by Edward Steichen appeared in *Town and Country* (February 1, 1926).**

Outerwear

Unbelted shapeless styles were popular for coats at the beginning of the decade, with more defined shapes in later years. Coats were often cut in one-piece panels from shoulder to hem, but others were pieced with "waistbands" at hip level. Some fashionable coats featured long lapels or self scarves. Coats fastened with low buttons or a belt at hip level. Trench coats were adapted to the fashionable silhouette. Some coats were short enough to allow skirts to peek out at the bottom. "Clutch coats" were without closures and needed to be held closed by the wearer; although impractical they were also popular. Fur coats were still essential to a well-dressed woman's wardrobe, with fox, Persian lamb, and exotic pelts popular. Furs at the fashionable short length were usually seen with oversized collars that framed the face. Stoles, capes, and tippets were worn, and toward the end of the decade, single or paired fox pelts became popular. Cloth coats were frequently trimmed with fur collars, cuffs, and bands at the hems. Evening outerwear was luxurious. Kimono and cocoon shapes continued, shorter to conform to the new skirt lengths. Panné velvets and brocades were typical for capes and wraps, often trimmed with fur. Evening versions of the clutch coat were common, as were narrow capes held closed in the same manner. Crepe shawls with large embroidered floral motifs and long fringe were also popular for evening. Although essentially Latin in inspiration, most of these shawls were manufactured in Asia and were often referred to as Chinese shawls or "Manila" shawls.

Millinery and Accessories

Shoes with T-straps and instep straps were common for both day and evening. Sandal styles were also worn. In the daytime, pumps and Oxfords, often with Louis heels, were popular. Two-toned looks were common in a variety of leathers and fabrics. Heels became a vehicle for decoration, often bejeweled in art deco motifs, continuing the look of glittering dresses. "Russian boots," calf- or knee-high boots with low heels, were popular, appearing even with cocktail dresses for après-ski attire. Occasionally, even short, crushed boots were worn. Galoshes were stylish, not just for rainy days, but worn by young women as a whimsical fashion statement. Commonly worn undone, they made a flapping noise as the wearer walked.

The cloche, a tight bell-shaped hat, was the most prevalent style, its popularity related to the fashionable shorter hairstyles. The cloche was pulled low on the forehead, even covering the eyebrows. Women's knit caps were made to fit in the same manner. Turbans continued into the 1920s, especially for evening, but the scale and fit reflected the lines of the cloche. Hats were less decorated than in the past; trims were often simple, geometric details. Large plumes were no longer popular, severely impacting the feather industry. Wider-brimmed hats, sometimes called picture hats, were worn especially at formal daytime occasions and often decorated with fabric flowers. Berets became fashionable at the end of the decade, their popularity encouraged by actresses Janet Gaynor and Clara Bow. Headbands and aigrettes were worn for evening, while tortoiseshell combs decorated with faux stones adorned hairstyles. Tall "Spanish" combs were placed in chignons by women who had left their hair long.

Small handbags were popular, ranging from framed styles to drawstring versions. Leather or fabric envelope bags were typically known as pochettes or "clutches." Handbags were often decorated with geometric details, or reflected ethnic influences or Egyptomania, and were typically beaded for evening. As women now smoked openly, cigarette cases and cigarette holders became essential accessories and often showed art deco styling. Feathered fans continued to be used at court, and were also seen with eveningwear. Gloves, notably absent at night, were worn in short lengths for daytime, and wristwatches became increasingly common.

Long strings of beads accessorized evening clothes and added to the elongation of the silhouette; sometimes multiple strands were worn. Dangling earrings and button styles were popular, and bangle bracelets were often worn in groups. Often shorter strings of beads with matching earrings completed a day ensemble, and small brooches were also popular. Influences from Cubism and historic modes strongly influenced jewelry design.

Foundations and Lingerie

While rigid body-shaping foundation garments diminished in popularity, the figure was still controlled and body smoothing was essential. Curvaceous women were shaped by boned corsetry to minimize their proportions. Foundations covered the breasts, but slender women who could achieve the fashionable "boyish" look without corsetry typically wore brassieres. Rather than enhance, brassieres contained the breasts; but by the end of the decade, more breast-shaping styles were introduced. The slip continued in popularity but cami-knickers were also worn, as were combinations of camisoles and drawers. New terms for underwear included "step-ins," "teddies," and "panties." Delicate feminine details often decorated lingerie.

Nightgowns and peignoir sets were simple, usually in pastel colors, with dainty decorative details. Pajamas continued to be worn for sleepwear, and were popular loungewear. Most top couturiers included pajamas in their offerings and they were celebrated in the media: Gertrude Lawrence made news wearing Molyneux pajamas on stage, and Maria Falconetti wore a Chinese-inspired pajama set by Martial et Armand in *La Garçonne*. In 1928 *L'Officiel* featured chic beach pajamas worn in Venice, declaring that "undress has left the intimate domain of bedroom and boudoir."

Nude-colored stockings became fashionable as more leg was exposed by mid-decade. Silk was preferred, but rayon was also widely used. Stockings were commonly held up by suspender garters attached to foundations, but some adventurous young women rolled their stockings to just above the knee, where they were held with elastic garters. The most daring of "flappers" rolled them to below the knee.

Fashion Fabrics

At the beginning of the decade, luxury fabrics were in short supply but the manufacture of quality silks, wools, cottons, and linens was resumed by 1923. At the war's end, Germany was forced to surrender many patents, including those for dyes and synthetic fibers. This led to advances in textile technology, especially in Britain and the United States. Rayon, the first manufactured fiber, in development since the late 19th century,

was promoted as a cheaper alternative to silk. It was often called artificial silk or "art
silk" until it was named "rayon" in 1924. Throughout the decade, the emphasis was
on supple, lightweight fabrics, and the simple cuts of women's fashions called for
interesting textile designs. Geometric designs such as zigzags and stripes worked
well with the narrow silhouette. Floral patterns were stylized and flattened, and
other prints showed scenes from modern life – tennis and other sports, automobiles,
and cityscapes. Edward Steichen, Raoul Dufy, John Held Jr., George Barbier, and
even tennis star Helen Wills all designed textile prints that featured contemporary
themes. Other fabrics incorporated metallic threads for a shimmery effect, combining
lamé with other embellishments such as beading and sequins, often in geometric art
deco motifs.

Designers: France

Several of the great houses of the turn of the century continued into the 1920s.
Worth, now directed by the third generation of Worth men, was still considered
important. Gaston's son, Jean-Charles, who had taken on design directorship a few
years earlier, appeared on the cover of *Time* magazine in 1928. By 1920 **Redfern Ltd.**
closed the New York store and several British locations, and the Paris and London
branches financially separated in 1923. The same year Charles Poynter Redfern
employed young French designer Robert Piguet at the Paris store, and he brought
modern ideas to the house. **Doucet** persisted into the 1920s, with the patronage
of many long-term clients, who, like the house, were now in advanced years. In
1929 Jacques Doucet died, and his house and clientele were absorbed by Georges
Doeuillet. **Drecoll** continued operation until 1929, when it merged with the
prestigious Maison Beer. In 1920 **Jeanne Paquin** retired, leaving Madeleine Wallis
as design director. But the house did not maintain its prominence under Wallis.
By 1923 **Lucile Ltd.** was sold and restructured; Lady Duff Gordon stopped designing

 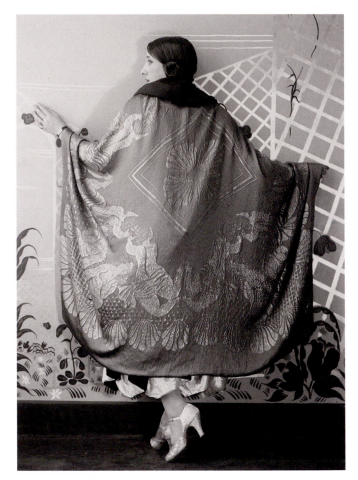

Above left Glamorous actress and designer Natacha Rambova wearing a fringed and embroidered shawl.

Above right This lavish evening cape by Poiret from 1926 utilizes a textile designed by Raoul Dufy, here photographed against a backdrop created by Poiret's Atelier Martine.

for the company, although she continued work with private clientele and ready-to-wear labels.

Paul Poiret's house resumed operations when the war concluded and his participation in *La Gazette du Bon Ton* continued to keep his work exposed in an elegant context. Poiret favored a lush color palette and eschewed the black and neutrals favored by other designers. He continued to create inventive and attractive clothes – experimenting with cut and drape – while maintaining his aesthetic informed by historicism and exoticism. He continued to utilize Raoul Dufy's evocative fabric designs for luxurious garments. The stage clothing he created for Josephine Baker exemplified his exotic taste. Poiret also continued to operate the Rosine and Martine companies. The perfumes and cosmetics from Rosine had exotic names, such as Nuit de Chine and Maharadjah, and were presented in opulent packages usually designed by Martine. At the 1925 Exposition, Poiret made an extravagant presentation with three barges, named *Amours*, *Délices* and *Orgues*, anchored along the left bank of the Seine, promoting Rosine and Martine. But his lavish display bankrupted his business; his financial woes and his reduced relevance to fashion were underscored when he and Denise, his wife and great muse, were divorced in 1928.

Marie Callot Gerber, the director of **Callot Soeurs**, was often regarded as the grande dame of Parisian couture. Gerber took advantage of the simple lines of fashion to display a wide variety of exotic Asian-inspired textiles and details. Chinese silk brocades were used, and the ancient Near East inspired decorations including beading and the house trademark, embroidery. Callot's output continued the lush aesthetic of the 1910s while still embracing more Modernist trends. When Mme. Gerber died in 1927, the house continued under the direction of her sons Pierre and Jacques. The younger generation sustained the luxurious style, but the label lost its relevance during the 1930s.

Jeanne Lanvin expanded her business considerably. She continued the romantic styles she created during the war, and was especially known for her versions of the *robe de style*, often with beautiful embellishments including beading, embroidered medallions, lace flounces, and ribbon and appliqué flowers. But her wide variety of output also included the sleeker, modern silhouette. In 1920 she formed an interior decor division, Lanvin-Décoration, with architect and designer Armand-Albert Rateau. In 1923 additional boutiques were opened in Cannes and Le Touquet, followed by numerous international locations. Drawing inspiration from the soft hues of Impressionism, Lanvin established her own dye house in 1923 devoted to the creation of unique colors. She also began a menswear department under the direction of nephew Maurice Lanvin. Perhaps most important for the long-term impact of the house was the development of fragrance laboratories Lanvin Parfums, which launched Mon Péché (My Sin) in 1925 and Arpège in 1927. Rateau designed the round black glass bottle for Arpège, which included a golden stopper in the form of a raspberry and was decorated with a mother–daughter logo that had been designed by Paul Iribe. In 1925, Lanvin served as the vice president of the Pavillon d'Elégance at the Paris Exposition and in 1926 was awarded the *Légion d'honneur*.

In 1912 **Madeleine Vionnet** opened her Paris house, where she continued the soft unstructured styles that had characterized her work at Doucet. Vionnet closed shop during the war, but reopened in 1918; by 1920 her point of view had evolved, marked by an original use of geometry and innovative cut. Vionnet typically "sketched" her designs, not only in pencil and paper, but also in muslin on half-scale dress forms. During the early 1920s, images of her dresses were frequently featured in fashion magazines, often illustrated by Thayaht. In 1922 Vionnet moved to grander premises with an elegantly decorated salon and larger workrooms for her sizable staff. She expanded to New York in 1924, and Biarritz in 1925.

Above Vionnet maintained detailed photographs of each piece in her collections in her ongoing efforts to prevent design piracy. The dress shown here (1929) illustrates her continuing exploration of "Grecian" inspiration.

Below In a sophisticated black satin ensemble for spring/summer 1920, probably intended for late day dressing, Chanel makes refined use of black glass buttons as a subtle embellishment.

Vionnet created soft blouson and T-shaped dresses with classical and medieval inspiration. She often featured asymmetry, and placed unusual attention on the back of the dress. Scarves that matched or coordinated with the dresses were integral to the designs, and often attached. Vionnet was very creative with sleeves, using wing-like shapes, or kimono styles. Although much of her work in the 1920s utilized the straight grain of the fabric, she also experimented with the bias. Vionnet exploited its potential like no one before, and was its greatest exponent. In the 1920s she often combined straight and bias grain in one dress to capitalize on the effect each provided. Vionnet frequently used repeating shapes, a design element typical of art deco. Fabric roses became a recurrent theme; clusters of roses adorned the shoulders of evening capes, and dresses were covered with big rosettes. Full-skirted dresses were formed from repeated "petals" of fabric, and resembled upside-down flowers. Other signature details included cutwork and lattice openwork, pin tucks, ribbon, and fabric appliqués. Embellishment often included ancient Egyptian and Greek motifs, sometimes designed in collaboration with Thayaht. Embroidery and beading were frequently executed by embellishment house Maison Lesage, where new techniques were developed to accommodate Vionnet's use of the bias. Although Vionnet's reputation was made with her dresses, the output of the house also included tailored ensembles, outerwear and fur, sport clothes and accessories. Like other designers, Vionnet was concerned with design piracy, and to protect her work she stamped the labels of her clothes with her own fingerprint. Madeleine Vionnet was awarded the *Légion d'honneur* in 1929.

Gabrielle Chanel solidified her reputation with two-piece ensembles in wool jersey, cardigan suits, simple black dresses, and distinctive accessories such as costume jewelry and two-tone shoes. Chanel followed the trend for diversification with the 1921 launch of her fragrance Chanel No. 5, created by chemist Ernest Beaux. Chanel No. 5, in its *moderne* bottle, represented a significant step in the development of designer fragrances, and the eventual financial success of the scent (and other cosmetics) built her fortune. Her couture clientele at this time included European royalty, but Chanel was especially favored by actresses, including Gertrude Lawrence and Ina Claire. Chanel maintained a mystique, cultivating an aloof persona even with her most famous clients.

Early in the decade, Chanel featured pieces with Russian influence including two-piece ensembles with tops based on the *roubachka*, a traditional peasant-style blouse. Embroidered Russian motifs decorated many pieces. These collections reflected her affair with the expatriate Grand Duke Dmitri Pavlovich. The extensive decoration necessitated a separate embroidery workshop that was supervised by Pavlovich's sister, the Grand Duchess Maria Pavlovna. In addition to Russian inspiration, Chanel also followed the vogue for Asian styles.

As the decade continued other influences prevailed and her designs were sleeker with simpler embellishment. By around 1923, Chanel's work was typified by straight sheath dresses, often with topstitching or simple self details. These simple looks often featured Chanel's taste for black, beige, and other neutrals, but she also used a variety of colors in her collections, favoring shades of red, from burgundy to scarlet to pink, especially in eveningwear. She strongly promoted the dress and coat ensemble for smart daywear, which became a signature look for the house. Her spare styles and borrowings from menswear contributed to the development of the *garçonne* look. Her jersey pieces were in such demand that she opened her own mill, Tricots Chanel, in order to meet the need. A woven fabric mill, Tissus Chanel, was also opened.

Also fundamental to the Chanel look was the black dress, produced in many variations, including jersey sport versions, woven fabrics for day, and beaded and sequined sleeveless styles for eveningwear. The concept of the "little black dress," which became associated with Chanel, had many precedents. In 1922 Mme. Charlotte at the house of Premet, known for very modern clothes, designed a simple black dress, "La Garçonne," that featured a white collar and cuffs like a maid's uniform. Charlotte's dress was widely imitated, and a likely inspiration for Chanel's black dresses. Other designers

THE CHANEL LEGEND

The reputation of Coco Chanel has magnified in the years since her death in 1971, establishing her in the public consciousness as perhaps the most influential designer of the 20th century. While many of the styles associated with Chanel are part of the contemporary wardrobe, her innovations have become overstated as inventions, with claims that include "Chanel invented jersey," "Chanel invented black dresses," "Chanel invented costume jewelry" – even "Chanel invented modern clothing."

She was not the most famous designer of her day, sharing the spotlight with Lanvin, Lelong, Patou, and Vionnet, and her designs built on the work of other designers. But Chanel's continuing appeal owes much to her rags-to-riches life story. The social-climbing couturiere often obscured her humble origins, a fact that has frustrated biographers and added

Gabrielle Chanel wearing a jersey ensemble of her own design.

to the Chanel mystique. Sent to an orphanage at the age of twelve by her widowed father, she was educated by nuns. At seventeen, she moved to the town of Moulins and attended a convent school. Afterward, she worked as an assistant in a shop that sold lingerie, and sang in a cafe frequented by army officers. Her most popular song, "*Qui qu'a vu Coco?*", was the source for her nickname, "Coco." At this time, she met Etienne Balsan; independently wealthy from a family textile fortune, Balsan bred horses on his nearby estate. Chanel went to live with him there in 1907 and the equestrian atmosphere and Balsan's social circle were fundamental to her education in the ways of the world. Through Balsan, Coco met her next lover, Arthur "Boy" Capel, a British polo player and businessman. Chanel began a millinery business, operating out of a Paris apartment. Capel helped her expand into her own millinery shop and then into a clothing store in Deauville, and a couture house in Biarritz. With her move to 31 rue Cambon, Paris, in 1919, she was able to operate a fully fledged *maison de couture*.

Although she was reported to have spent little time in the workrooms, Chanel had definite ideas about construction; she obsessed over details and demanded endless fittings. Although taught to sew by the nuns at the orphanage, she had no genuine training in couture and this often caused disagreements with her skilled workers, whose knowledge of garment construction exceeded her own.

During the Nazi occupation of Paris, Chanel lived with Hans Günther von Dincklage, a German officer, at the Ritz hotel where she kept a suite, and it was perhaps only her friendship with Winston Churchill that saved her from deportation or imprisonment after the war. The fact that her personal politics could be troubling added to Chanel's contradictory, unconventional image. Chanel was also famous for being less than gracious with her colleagues. She took pot shots at Poiret, famously saying publicly that designing "Scheherazade is easy, a little black dress is difficult." But in her personal life and her career, Coco Chanel exemplified a certain kind of woman who, by her own account, lived the life of the 20th century: decisive, sexually liberated, self-made, and successful.

Above Smart day dresses by Lelong and Patou depicted in *Art Gout Beauté*, July 1929, show the prevailing lean line of fashion. Despite the consistency in overall silhouette, necklines, sleeve shapes, and other details provided variety.

Opposite top Edward Molyneux excelled at creating shimmery evening sheaths such as this dress from 1925, made even more dynamic with long strands of beads hanging below the hem.

Opposite bottom Fashion model Marion Morehouse in a fluffy feathered sheath dress from Louiseboulanger, photographed by Edward Steichen, 1926.

were known for similar black dresses, particularly Germaine le Comte, who opened her house in 1922. But Chanel's 1926 long-sleeved jersey version was perhaps the benchmark of the style, and American *Vogue* compared the simple dress to the utilitarian Ford automobile. However, it is noteworthy that *Vogue* also illustrated a black dress from Drecoll on the opposite page in that issue.

Chanel's boutiques in Deauville and Biarritz continued their success, buoyed by the post-war boom in leisure activity. Chanel's own lifestyle contributed to the popularity of her sport clothes and she encouraged the suntan for women as a mark of leisure and affluence. Chanel wore her own designs and she wore them well, adding the force of her personality to the simple styles she promoted. In 1928 Chanel installed the famous mirrors in her salon, creating one of the most recognizable images of French couture of the 20th century. The sleek, modernist design would figure prominently in years to come in photography of her work, and of the woman herself.

From the time he opened his couture house in 1919, **Jean Patou** was known for simplicity of line and a "pure" approach. Patou hired the architects Süe et Mare to redesign the interiors of his 18th-century *maison* in luxurious, *moderne* style. Dapper, energetic, and very Parisian, Patou declared in 1923 that his aesthetic emphasized harmony and ease, in contrast to the excesses of the previous decade. As with Chanel, Patou's collections from 1920 to 1922 combined simple silhouettes with Russian folkloric details. Patou was a great innovator in knit separates and his so-called "Cubist knits" featured stripes and geometric designs. Many of his designs show bold graphic contrasts. Patou collaborated with French fabric houses to achieve unusual color effects; an especially deep blue, known as *bleu Patou*, debuted in 1923. For evening, Patou adorned his simple silhouettes with asymmetrical ruffles, feathers, and glittering embellishments.

In a widely publicized episode, Patou traveled to New York in 1924 to find long-legged, athletic American models to bring back to Paris. He increasingly designed for swimming, skiing, and tennis as active sports became more popular with high society. These clothes were sold through Le Coin des Sports (his Paris sportswear shop, located on the ground floor of his couture house) and his boutiques in Deauville and Biarritz. He added his monogram to many of the simple pieces, making them instantly identifiable as designer sportswear. Patou offered perfumes, including Le Sien, a fresh scent that could be worn by men and women, possibly the first unisex fragrance. Patou's suntan oil, Huile de Chaldée, was especially popular on the French Riviera. In 1928 he outfitted the Vicomtesse de Sibour (daughter of Gordon Selfridge, of department store fame) with a small, versatile traveling wardrobe for her around-the-world airplane trip with her husband; both the trip and the wardrobe were widely covered in the press. Other prominent clients included the Dolly Sisters as well as American actresses Constance Bennett and Louise Brooks.

The house of **Lucien Lelong** became one of Paris' most prominent couture businesses and his designs were at the forefront of fashion. From the beginning, Lelong's designs were geared toward an active modern woman. From 1920 to 1921, the house was known as Lelong et Fried, but by 1922 it was operating as Lucien Lelong. In 1924 his move to 16 rue Matignon helped raise the house's profile. The elegant setting housed his growing business, which expanded to a staff of about 3,000 including a team of designers that he supervised. A profile in *Vogue* in 1925 described him as "the *animateur* of his collections ... the one who imposes his taste and thus brings about artistic unity." He offered simple styles and repeatedly claimed to be inspired by only one epoch – his own. Lelong's designs showed a linear emphasis with straight cuts, narrow pleats, and supple fabrics. He embraced a Cubist aesthetic with geometric

prints and graphic knits for day and art deco-style beading for evening. Lelong and his design team considered motion an integral part of modern fashion and by 1926 the house was known for "kinetic" design. In 1927 he further developed the kinetic idea with "kinoptic" designs – combining kinetics and optics. For example, he created pleats that looked monochrome at rest but opened when the wearer walked to reveal a second color underneath. The effect was enhanced with slight changes in silhouette as Lelong subtly tightened the waistline and added more fullness to skirts.

In 1925 Lelong was sent to the United States by the French government to analyze labor practices and production methods and to study the role of women in the American fashion industry. He launched his perfume line in 1926 with three perfumes known as A, B, and C, all intended for different moods and times of day. His next two perfumes were J for Jasmine and N, named for Natalie Paley. His 1927 marriage to Paley, an exiled Russian princess, cemented his ties to high society. Known for her beauty and style, Princess Paley modeled for Lelong before their marriage and continued to wear and be photographed in his clothes until their divorce in 1937. Lelong was awarded the *Légion d'honneur* in 1926.

The Irish-born **Edward Molyneux** (1891–1974) began his career as a sketch artist for Lucile, and later designed at her Paris branch. Serving in the British Army during the Great War, Molyneux rose to the rank of captain and was wounded, losing sight in one eye. He continued to be referred to as "Captain Molyneux" for the remainder of his career in fashion. Molyneux quickly asserted an aesthetic that was often sleek and understated and appealed to a woman of individual refinement. Subtle and elegant, Molyneux's designs were perfectly suited to the spirit of the post-war age; he combined restraint with perfect taste while avoiding the sparse simplicity advocated by others. His shimmering dresses for evening enhanced the glittering nightlife of the age. His good taste and chic aesthetic attracted many aristocratic and royal women to his salon. Divorced after a brief marriage, Molyneux embraced the increasing acceptability of divorce by creating second-marriage wedding dresses for divorcees, often in pastel colors.

Louise Melenot (1878–1950) began her career as a teenager in a dressmaker's studio. She later continued with Maison Chéruit, working as a staff designer. After marrying Louis Boulanger, she opened her salon with him in 1927, and combined her names to form **Louiseboulanger**. The new house was promptly successful and gained a reputation for being ahead of the trends. Her use of color and fabric was praised for its elegance and chic. Louiseboulanger's evening dresses were very popular and often featured dramatic trimming. She was innovative with uneven hemlines, and also created dresses with a pouf-style skirt similar to the *robe de style*. Necklines sometimes featured scarves swathed to the back, and cowl drapery. Like her former employer, Madeleine Chéruit, Mme. Boulanger was celebrated for her beauty and striking personal fashion sense.

Sonia Delaunay (1885–1979) was a painter who turned her talents to fabric and fashion design. Born Sonia Terk in Ukraine, she moved to Paris and married Robert Delaunay in 1910. Together, they explored color as its own subject in a style they termed "Simultaneity." In the 1910s Delaunay created Simultaneous outfits for herself and her husband and made a multicolored quilt for her son that was a pivotal piece for her design career. During the war years Delaunay opened a boutique, Casa Sonia, in Madrid where she sold furnishings, accessories, and clothes for adults and children. Returning to Paris in 1920, Delaunay began designing for private clients, and was also commissioned in 1923 to design textile patterns for a fabric manufacturer. The simple, unfitted shapes of fashion provided a perfect canvas for her vivid, painterly designs of disks, zigzags, and geometric shapes. At the 1925 Exposition, Sonia Delaunay collaborated with furrier Jacques Heim on their Boutique Simultané. Delaunay designed coats, caps, and other pieces completely embroidered in wool and silk in gradated tones, producing an *ombré* effect. Her custom work appealed to forward-thinking clients including Gloria Swanson and Nancy Cunard. With her husband,

Painter and fashion designer Sonia Delaunay applied the aesthetic of Orphic Cubism to her innovative swimwear designs.

Delaunay invented and marketed the *tissu-patron* or fabric pattern, apparel fabric printed with outlined pattern pieces ready to cut and sew. Sonia Delaunay was an active participant in the Parisian avant-garde; her circle included painters, poets, and composers. The Delaunays were commissioned by Diaghilev to design the Ballets Russes' production of *Cléopâtre* and other projects included collaborations with writer Tristan Tzara, as well as designs for film.

Following in the footsteps of her brother, Paul Poiret, **Nicole Groult** (1887–1967) opened a couture house during the 1910s. Groult was the wife of a noted furniture designer and cultivated an artistic circle, and by 1920 her business was well established, with a celebrity clientele, and her work also sold in the United States. Groult espoused a modern but artistic aesthetic and was often notably featured in fashion magazines. Nicole Groult also worked as a theatrical costume designer.

Several other Paris designers, although smaller in output, were also notable. From her house on the avenue des Champs-Elysées, **Mme. Jenny** offered a full range of clothes including dresses, coats, lingerie, and furs. Her creations were often described as youthful and original and received significant press coverage. **Jane Regny** began her career as a tennis player and made the move from sport to clothing. She opened her couture house in 1923, riding the wave of the sports clothes trend that was cresting with Chanel and Patou. Regny specialized in sportswear, knits, and sweaters that often featured graphic patterns in the art deco style, and also designed eveningwear. **Salon Myrbor**, managed by Marie Cuttoli, offered artistic creations by several designers, most notably the Russian avant-garde painter Natalia Goncharova (1881–1962), who was known for appliqués and embroideries in Cubist, Fauve and Constructivist style. The renowned milliner **Suzanne Talbot** offered apparel with regional themes including pieces inspired by African, Southeast Asian, and Russian influences. The two sisters of photographer George Hoyningen-Huene both opened couture businesses. Helen worked in both France and the United States using the name **Helen de Huene**. More notable was Elizabeth, who designed under the name **Yteb**, a backward misspelling of her nickname Betty. The house featured rich surface embellishment and embroidery with some of the designs created by the designer's brother.

Designers: United States

While European designers had already discovered the importance of the American market, during the 1920s a handful of American designers and retailers began to develop the high fashion industry in New York. **Jessie Franklin Turner** (1881–1956) began her career designing for Bonwit Teller and opened her own house in 1922 on Park Avenue. Turner was known for luxurious eveningwear and tea gowns. She often drew upon broad cultural sources in her work, studying the collections of New York's museums for inspiration. Franklin was praised as the most original of American fashion designers at this time, consistently creating her own ideas. **Madame Frances** was an important dressmaking company, operating on West 56th Street. Owner Frances Spingold (1881–1976) also wrote a fashion column and was a noted art collector.

Other New Yorkers, some of them recent immigrants, asserted their own fashion aesthetics. Born Henrietta Kanengeiser in Vienna, **Hattie Carnegie** (1889–1956) began her career as a milliner, and opened a dress shop in New York in 1923. Carnegie acted as a creative director, orchestrating the talents of her design staff (who included some of the great talents of the next generation of American designers). Never trained in dressmaking but gifted with excellent taste, she maintained a boutique that catered to a discerning clientele, where she sold not only her own label, but imported French apparel. **Mariska Karasz** (1898–1960) moved to the United States in 1913, and soon found some success as a fashion designer creating unusual custom pieces. Karasz drew heavily upon the folk art of her native Hungary, and was also attuned to the innovations of the avant-garde artists of Europe. Later, Karasz was better known as a textile artist applying the same fusion of styles to her work.

Born in Kiev, Valentina Nicholaevna Sanina Schlee (c. 1899–1989) was known professionally as **Valentina**. Her habit of spinning tales throughout her life obscured many details of her early years, including her actual date of birth. She maintained that she met George Schlee at a Russian train station as she was fleeing the revolution carrying the family jewels. The Schlees (who may or may not have actually married) lived in Athens, Rome, and then Paris before arriving in New York in 1923. Valentina soon caught the notice of New York society with her own very individual style; she diverged from the prevailing look by wearing her hair long with a full-length black velvet dress of her own design. Valentina opened a store in 1928 on Madison Avenue in partnership with Sonia Levienne, a fellow Russian, where she espoused a theatrical style influenced by her experiences as a performer in Europe. In addition to their clothing, Sonia and Valentina also sold imported regional costume pieces, such as embroidered shawls. While against the current of mainstream fashion, her style was discovered by a small clientele of individualistic women whose numbers soon grew.

Costume Design and Fashion

Costume design for stage and film exerted a strong influence on fashion. Period pieces were still widely popular, often costumed in strikingly inauthentic "historic" styles. But a large number of plays, musicals, and films featured contemporary stories that required current fashions for their costuming. Several of the most notable designers transitioned between the worlds of fashion and entertainment. Female stars looked to designers and dressmakers for their stage clothes and retailers used cross-promotions linked to stage productions. Fashions worn in the movies were exposed to a wider audience, and gowns worn by popular actresses were reproduced as paper dolls in fan magazines. *Motion Picture* magazine declared in 1925, "Styles are dictated in Hollywood and Paris designers follow them." A new wave of costume designers emerged in Hollywood and the studio system repeatedly paired designers with the same actresses to dress.

French illustrators Paul Iribe and George Barbier were hired as film costume designers. Erté entered into a much publicized contract with Metro-Goldwyn-Mayer where he designed costumes for several films, but the arrangement proved

Actress Alla Nazimova wears a rubber thigh-length dress designed by Natacha Rambova for the 1923 film adaptation of Oscar Wilde's *Salome.*

unsuccessful. American costume designer Gilbert Adrian (1903–1959) arrived in Hollywood in 1924 where he became head costume designer at MGM after the departure of Erté. Adrian was immediately successful and developed a career that would help define fashion in the coming decade. Howard Greer (1896–1974) began his career working for Lucile in her American stores, and worked in Paris for other notable designers. He designed for Paramount Studios, and maintained his own fashion line. Travis Banton (1894–1958), a former employee of both Lucile and Madame Frances, was noticed when Mary Pickford wore one of his designs for her 1920 marriage to Douglas Fairbanks. Banton's couture background was showcased with his first film *The Dress Maker from Paris* (1925). The act of fashionable shopping was central to *Why Change Your Wife?*, a 1920 film starring Gloria Swanson with costumes by Clare West.

Natacha Rambova (1897–1966), born Winifred Shaughnessy in Utah, was best known for her three-year marriage to Rudolph Valentino. An actress, producer, and designer, she designed costumes for some of her husband's films. Perhaps her greatest achievements were set and costume designs for a film version of Oscar Wilde's *Salome* (starring Alla Nazimova) inspired by Aubrey Beardsley's 1894 illustrations. Among the costumes were two thigh-length dresses that anticipated the "mini dress" of the future. For several years in the late 1920s and early 1930s, Rambova also worked as a fashion designer with a studio and store in New York.

The flamboyant costumes of follies and revues reflected and inspired fashion trends. Erté was particularly renowned for his showgirl costumes on Broadway and in Paris. British designer Dolly Tree (1899–1962) created follies costumes for productions in Paris, London and on Broadway. Among her designs, she developed boned strapless bodices, a style which crossed over into mainstream fashion.

Hair and Beauty

Continuing a tendency begun in the late 1910s, hair was cut close to the head in various styles known as "bobs," "shingles," and "crops." Marcel waves, formed using a heated curling iron, offered a softer alternative to boyish haircuts. Many fashionable women were known for their distinctive short hairstyles, for example Louise Brooks' geometric bob, Gertrude Lawrence's slightly waved style, and Josephine Baker's flat shiny curls.

Make-up was now firmly part of fashion. Women imitated the make-up of their favorite film stars, hoping to achieve Mae Murray's "bee-stung" lips or Clara Bow's smoky eyes. Applying make-up in public gained acceptance; lipstick cases and compacts for face powder and rouge were attractive fashion accessories. Kohl was popular for emphasizing the eyes and eyebrows were plucked to thin, arched lines. In October 1925 *Vogue* advised readers that "time and place should be taken into consideration in make-up almost as much as they are in costume," urging readers to heighten make-up for the afternoon and to go "vivid" for evening. Nail polish was a new addition to the dressing table and became available in a range of colors. Clear lacquer added a well-groomed touch, but more daring women grew their nails long and applied deep shades of pink, red, and even purple and green to coordinate with their outfits.

Beyond cosmetics, more extreme measures were employed. A dimple-producing appliance was patented in 1921, to add flirtatious indentations to cheeks. Also in 1921 the American Association of Plastic Surgeons was founded, indicating the growth of the specialty and the need to enforce standards. The youthful ideal in beauty helped popularize early versions of the facelift. Other procedures, especially nose jobs, flourished in a culture increasingly influenced by Hollywood standards of glamour, and the spread of psychology, which held that physical "defects" could result in social anxiety and should be corrected. In 1924 the *New York Daily Mirror* ran the "Homely Girl Contest," which sought the homeliest girl in New York to reward her with the services of a plastic surgeon who would make her a beauty.

Sports Clothing

The growing popularity of sporting activities necessitated specialized clothes, but sportswear also influenced street wear. Celebrity athletes inspired ordinary men and women to imitate their dashing looks and sporty clothing. Fashion was influenced by tennis greats Suzanne Lenglen and Helen Wills, and champion swimmer Gertrude Ederle. At the designer level, Lelong, Patou, Chanel, and Regny promoted especially relaxed and modern sports clothes. Chanel's designs for the Ballets Russes' production of *Le Train Bleu*, named after the luxury train that carried passengers to resorts in the south of France, and choreographed by and starring Bronislava Nijinska, put activewear onstage as theatrical costumes, as the production depicted the French upper class in sport activities. Nijinska's costume in the ballet showed inspiration from the outfits worn by Suzanne Lenglen, the reigning French tennis champion. Known for her aggressive playing style, Lenglen wore smart white knit separates designed by Patou, who also dressed her off the court. In March 1926, *L'Officiel* reported on an upcoming match between Lenglen and American Helen Wills in fashion terms, wondering which would prevail: "The silk headband of Suzanne Lenglen or the canvas visor of the young Californian?"

Aside from major French designers, other companies were important in the development of the sportswear category. In 1920 Jantzen launched the red diving girl logo and in 1921 began to use the word "swimsuit." The West Coast Knitting Mills (later Cole of California) began in 1923; Pacific Knitting Mills in California took the name Catalina, and in 1928 Australia's MacRae Knitting Mills changed its name to Speedo. The trend in swimwear for both men and women was briefer cut, as the demand for physical freedom increased and modesty became less important. Stockings with swimwear went out of style, and swim tops were cut with larger openings for more movement and for tanning. However, the newer fashions challenged existing decency laws and occasional arrests occurred. Wool dominated swimwear, and rayon and silk jersey were also used. Loose bathing ensembles continued to be worn by older, more conservative women, who were not interested in tanning or actually swimming. A vogue for "poolside" attire (for women who did not get wet) created a fad for wearing fine jewelry with swimwear at Riviera resorts.

Golf became even more popular, and golf clothes for women resembled daytime ensembles with pleated jersey skirts and knit tops. Pants and overalls for the beach,

Below left Tennis star René Lacoste poses in 1924 with champion Suzanne Lenglen, who is wearing sportswear by Patou.

Below right Innovative swimwear from Lucien Lelong, photographed by George Hoyningen-Huene, 1929.

gardening, and other outdoor activity were increasingly accepted. Women wore pants for winter sports, including skiing, replacing the long skirts that had been worn in the previous decades. Young college girls wore men's-style knickers in active situations such as hiking and camping.

Menswear

Menswear was marked by experimentation and informality. Fine tailoring continued to be important but individual touches were welcomed, as breaking – or at least bending – sartorial rules was part of being stylish. Fashionable young men adapted traditional British styling to their faster-moving lifestyle, producing variations that shocked their elders. What might have been considered garishly "loud" in the pre-war era was seen as fresh and youthful in the 1920s, and elegance was defined by a new nonchalance. Styles were set on college campuses and athletic fields. Tennis continued to influence menswear; star player René Lacoste's clothes were particularly noted. But more rugged style prototypes emerged as fashionable men imitated sports heroes such as baseball player Babe Ruth and boxer Jack Dempsey. The predominance of sports even influenced how underwear was constructed; it was now designed to allow for more freedom of movement.

Men wore sweaters in every shape and style. V-necks were worn with shirts and ties, sometimes layered with a jacket. Turtlenecks, crew necks, and shawl collars were also popular. Argyle and Fair Isle patterned knits were adopted by many men following the lead of the dapper Edward, Prince of Wales, who like his grandfather was known for his love of outdoor sports and adventurous fashion taste. Brightly colored knit pullovers, vests, and socks were popular. They were commonly paired with plus-fours, the baggy, knee-length pants originally worn by golfers and then more generally accepted for casual wear. As with women's fashion, vibrant textile patterns also enlivened menswear. Bright, contemporary designs were seen on leisure clothing, especially casual shirts and dressing gowns, ranging from colorful geometrics to collage-style prints with witty motifs.

With the new focus on swimming (and inspiration from star swimmers such as Johnny Weissmuller), beach and resort wear became an important category of clothing. Swimsuits for men resembled those of women, knitted wool one- and two-piece suits that had scooped necks and cutaway armholes, a waistline marked with

Above The lively, decorative print on this boxer-style dressing gown reflects the influence of Dufy and Léger, evidence of the whimsical spirit that occasionally infiltrated menswear. Similar styles were worn as beach wraps by both sexes. *Le Gout du Jour*, 1920.

Below The creative team at Walt Disney studios (with Disney himself at center left next to starlet Margie Gay), photographed in 1926, in plus-fours and sporty knits.

Above left A British man in the wide trousers known as Oxford bags, c. 1925.

Above right Silent film actor Ben Lyon cavorts on skis wearing a raccoon coat, a style particularly associated with collegiate fashion, c. 1925.

stripes or a belt, and shorts that reached just to the upper thigh. In these wet wool suits, swimmers' physiques were clearly on display. In addition to influence from athletic wear, styles drawn from workwear gained favor. Bulky knit pullovers and cardigans were worn over round-necked jerseys and open-collared shirts with baggy pants for country occasions and at the beach. In the resorts of France, vacationers donned local clothing – striped sailor jerseys, espadrilles, and straw hats. More formal beach areas – such as Palm Beach and Newport – called for light-colored suits or blazers in linen and tropical-weight wool.

However, not all men abandoned traditional suits and jackets. At the beginning of the decade, short, cuffed, creased trousers were still in style. Jackets and blazers were fitted and worn buttoned high on the chest over waistcoats, stiff-collared shirts and ties, often worn with collar bars. By mid-decade, a bolder approach was in full swing. In keeping with the new focus on youth, a collegiate look emerged that combined traditional styles such as tweeds, sweaters, and striped silk ties, with unexpected youthful touches. Tweed jackets were cut close to the body, with sloping shoulders and very narrow sleeves. Pants widened to an extreme in a style known as Oxford bags, appearing in 1925 at the university of the same name, and adopted by faddish college men at other British schools and in America. In the widest versions, Oxford bags had a hem circumference of 40 inches (101 centimeters).[4] While the scale of Oxford bags was an extreme style, even mainstream trousers showed a looser fit by the late 1920s. Raccoon coats, often worn with fedoras, became the unofficial "uniform" of college boys. In another adaptation of sporting style, striped blazers, derived from tennis and cricket, were worn with white flannel pants with light-colored or two-tone shoes.

Grooming also emphasized a youthful appearance. Men wore their hair slicked back from a side or center part, in imitation of movie stars such as Rudolph Valentino. Although some cultivated thin mustaches, in the style of Douglas Fairbanks, most men favored a clean-shaven, polished look, which was accentuated by the fashion for suntanned skin.

Children's Fashion

By this time children's fashion was a distinct sector of the fashion industry. Fashionable clothing for children was available in department stores and specialized retail shops. Women's magazines continued to advise on children's clothing and showcased seasonal offerings. Clothes were advertised in magazines and newspapers, often linked to special events such as back-to-school and holidays. As with women's fashion, French influence was highlighted. Magazines consistently noted trends from Paris in their coverage of developments in children's fashion. Several couture houses offered clothing for children, most notably Lanvin; Mignapouf specialized in high-quality childrenswear. While photographs were increasingly included in fashion publications, delightful illustrations showed children in the simple cuts of the time, rendered in vivid graphics. Little girls wore very short dresses with no waistlines and simple surface decoration. Young boys wore shorts, often with tunic-like tops. The

The newsboy cap and chunky knit sweater show the influence of active outdoor sports and present a contrast with the fitted tailored three-piece suit of the adult, who continues the aesthetic of the Arrow Collar Man.

vogue for sweaters and athletic influences seen in menswear also affected clothing for boys. Both sexes had bobbed hair. As with adult fashions, comfort and mobility were emphasized; even in the highest price range, children's clothing was simply styled and easy-fitting in silhouette. Choice of fabric delineated the difference between daywear and special occasion clothes. Versatile and washable, cotton was the favorite fiber for children's clothing. Linen and lightweight wools were also common. While occasions such as weddings and parties called for elaborate, sometimes whimsical, dress, the trend for dressing children in antique styles and decorative frills had largely passed. Soft pastel versions of the *robe de style* were common for teenage girls for special occasions.

Buttoned boots were almost universally abandoned in favor of flat shoes. The new fashion also eliminated the dark stockings that had been worn almost year-round. Children wore bare legs with white knitted knee socks or crew socks. Overall, children were less covered on a daily basis; their clothing was trimmer, shorter, and less voluminous. There were fewer occasions when hats were required and gloves were rarely worn. Underwear for the young followed the trend of adult underwear. Lightweight clothing and a straight silhouette called for an end to frilled petticoats for girls, and to corsetry for children. The practice of dressing little boys in dresses was virtually abandoned. Even as toddlers they wore rompers and short shorts. Outerwear, too, reflected the move toward simplicity. Double-breasted coats and jackets, often with piping and appliqué, reinforced the geometric styling. Mini cloches over short bobs and shingle-cuts made little girls – from toddler age through the teen years – look as modern as their mothers.

Illustrations from *Les Enfants très parisiens*, 1925, show high-style children's fashions. Girls of all ages wore shift dresses with flat shoes and tightly fitting hats, similar to the cloches of adult women. The straight silhouette and trend for geometric pattern are also seen in the boys' shorts ensembles.

The Growth of the Fashionable World

Following the Allied partitioning of the Ottoman Empire and the ensuing Turkish War of Independence, the Republic of Turkey was officially declared in 1923. Mustafa Kemal (later known as Atatürk) became the first president. Kemal put forth reforms to position this new nation as a modern secular state. His reform agenda called for the Westernization of clothing and reacted against the Islamic dress customs of the Ottoman period. The 1925 "Hat Law" suppressed the wearing of fez hats and encouraged Western styles. Kemal himself sported a Panama hat for a public appearance that year. Kemal also advocated Western-style clothing for women, relaxing the religiously based modesty laws, and discouraging the wearing of headscarves. In the Kingdom of Iran during 1923, Reza Pahlavi (later known as Reza Shah) was strongly influenced by the ideologies of Kemal. Although some forms of Westernization in dress had occurred earlier, Reza Shah's 1928 clothing reform laws mandated the adoption of many Western styles and restricted female head coverings; these and other reforms caused significant conflict with religious fundamentalists. Reza Shah continued his reforms and eventually the chador (the traditional full-body covering for women) was forbidden by law.

The End of the Decade

By 1929, films with sound began to dominate cinema and even television existed in a rudimentary form. Soviet leader Joseph Stalin continued to institute collectivist reforms, and liberal attitudes embraced in Germany during the 1920s ignited a conservative backlash, as the National Socialist German Worker's Party was gaining strength. Of all these changes and transitions, the most important was the crash of the New York Stock Exchange on October 24, 1929.

As the decade drew to a close, many changes to the female silhouette marked a transition. A downward movement of the hemline and more shaping of the torso began as early as 1927, and changes could be detected in the work of Lucien Lelong and other designers. Both of these elements – length and fit – developed further in 1929. Patou's autumn/winter collection of that year, while interpreted by some in the media as a radical departure, crystallized trends that were already in the air. Skirts were growing longer, the silhouette was more molded and feminine, and the placement of the waist was varied and undecided. As the aesthetic of the 1930s emerged from the envelope of the 1920s, modesty was reasserted while decoration decreased. Just as in the world in general, fashion expressed both transformation and uncertainty.

Miss C. Dawes of Montreal, photographed by the prestigious Wm. Notman & Son studio in 1929, wears an evening gown showing transitional elements of the last years of the 1920s.

HARPER'S BAZAAR
INCORPORATING "VANITY FAIR"
AUGUST, 1934
HOLIDAY FICTION AND FASHIONS
EVELYN WAUGH
FORD MADOX FORD
ROSITA FORBES
MARGERY SHARP
HAROLD NICOLSON
TWO SHILLINGS NETT

Chapter 6

The 1930s

Aspirations of Glamour

Opposite An Erté cover for *Harper's Bazaar*, August 1934, captures the glamorous mood of the decade.

Below American labels Hattie Carnegie, Bergdorf Goodman, Sally Milgrim, Jay Thorpe, and Bendel are featured in these daytime ensembles illustrated in *Vogue*, March 1, 1932.

The Stock Market Crash of 1929 sent much of the Western world into an economic depression with impact on many industries, including fashion and international trade. Despite the economic downturn, skyscrapers thrust into the skies, many in art deco style. The completion of the Empire State Building, the Chrysler Building, and the Rockefeller Center established New York as a center of Modernist architecture. Glamour and exotic locales featured in Hollywood film, and even the Surrealist dreamscapes that dominated visual art offered escapist fantasies. The final sequence of the 1933 film *King Kong* combined these varied cultural currents – desperate times, glamorous fashion, Surrealism, and art deco – as a giant ape dangling from the Empire State Building held in his gargantuan hand actress Fay Wray, in a lamé evening gown.

Social and Economic Background

In many parts of the world, the decade was largely defined by economic hardship. Unemployment was high and governments responded with relief programs. In the

161

United States, Franklin D. Roosevelt, elected president in 1932, initiated the "New Deal," a series of measures intended to stimulate recovery. A drought in the midwestern United States displaced hundreds of thousands of people. In Great Britain "Hunger Marches" brought attention to unemployment and poverty there. Other parts of the world, including Australia and Canada, were similarly affected. Dire economic conditions combined with unresolved tensions after World War I set the stage for totalitarian governments in Germany and Italy. The rise of the National Socialist Worker's Party in Germany put an end to the liberal democracy of the Weimar Republic and, in Italy, Benito Mussolini became increasingly militant in promoting Italian imperialism. Japan's expansion into Chinese territory in the Sino-Japanese War increased tensions in Asia, and Japan established the puppet state Manchukuo in Manchuria. In 1939, Prime Minister Plaek Phibunsongkhram established Thailand as the official name of his country (formerly known as Siam) and enacted measures to enforce Westernization of clothing for the masses. The *Hindenburg* disaster in 1937 destroyed hopes for the development of the passenger airship as a mode of civilian transportation.

The Arts

Surrealism continued, and was influential on decorative arts and fashion. Prominent artists including Giorgio de Chirico and Pierre Roy created illustrations for fashion magazines. Dreamlike landscapes and portraits were created by American Magic Realists Paul Cadmus and Ivan Albright. Tamara de Lempicka combined the mood of Magic Realism with an art deco sensibility in her paintings of elegant women in sleek dresses.

Art deco influence was widespread in architecture and the decorative arts. The style evolved from its luxurious, exotic beginnings into a more cubic and volumetric phase, described as Streamline. Modern industrial designers streamlined appliances, furniture, even jewelry, to make products more modern and desirable.

Carel Willink's *Wilma* (1936) presents high fashion in the context of the Magic Realist painting style.

Musical landmarks included Gershwin's opera *Porgy and Bess* (1935), which featured an entirely African American cast. Broadway audiences attended Cole Porter's musicals *Gay Divorce* (1932) and *Anything Goes* (1934), and *Babes in Arms* (1937) and *The Boys from Syracuse* (1938) by Rodgers and Hart. *Me and My Girl* (1937) popularized a new dance step, "The Lambeth Walk." Noël Coward's comedies included *Private Lives* (1930) and *Design for Living* (1932). Drama was also well represented onstage; Robert Sherwood's 1936 *Petrified Forest* depicted disillusionment in rural America, and in London, *Love on the Dole* (1934) featured a working-class girl forced to support her family as a bookie's mistress. Dance in performance ranged from the emotional works of modern dance pioneer Martha Graham to popular revivals of romantic ballets.

Film was affordable entertainment; movie attendance soared, encouraged by the new technology of talking pictures. By 1935 the Technicolor process was introduced. The newly enacted Motion Picture Production Code restricted sex and violence on-screen. Popular genres included musicals (*Top Hat*, 1935); witty comedies (*Dinner at Eight*, 1935); romances set in exotic locales (*Shanghai Express*, 1932); gangster movies (*The Public Enemy*, 1931); and historical dramas (*Queen Christina*, 1933). But while glamour was the rule, films such as *An American Tragedy* (1931) and *Of Human Bondage* (1934) broke new ground in realism.

Art and Politics

Art and politics were strongly linked. In the United States, the Works Progress Administration employed artists as diverse as Ben Shahn and Diego Rivera to create murals and other public artworks in realistic styles. Under government sponsorship, photographers Dorothea Lange and Walker Evans created memorable images of the Great Depression.

A crepe dress fabric printed with hydrangea blossoms in an art deco abstraction.

Political changes in Germany directly affected cultural life, as a campaign of censorship declared certain works *Entartete Kunst* ("Degenerate Art"), including many of the Weimar period's most notable achievements. Artists and composers whose work had been labeled "Degenerate" emigrated to the United States, including George Grosz, Ernst Krenek, and Kurt Weill. Some of these talents flourished in Hollywood. Architects and designers associated with the Bauhaus also emigrated. The officially approved German art emphasized tradition, propagating wholesome "Aryan" imagery in representational sculpture and painting. Music by earlier German composers, especially Beethoven and Wagner, was revived. Leni Riefenstahl's films propagated German myth making, including *Triumph of the Will* (1934) and *Olympia*, her documentary of the 1936 summer Olympic Games (which ironically highlighted black American Jesse Owens' four gold medals).

In the Soviet Union, the creative burst of the early 1920s was suppressed by reforms. Modern art styles were declared "bourgeois," and artists, including the once avant-garde Aleksandr Rodchenko, were put into service creating propaganda for the new government. Socialist Realism emerged, emphasizing the heroism of the worker and everyday life. Symbols of progress – tractors, grain, and the hammer and sickle emblem of the state – were incorporated into graphics and even fabric design.

Fashion and Society

With the repeal of Prohibition, glamorous clubs such as El Morocco, 21, and the Stork Club in New York became centers of nightlife, and at the Savoy Ballroom and the Cotton Club in Harlem, couples danced to swing music by Duke Ellington and Count Basie. London society revolved around evenings at the theater, dinners at the Savoy Grill, or screenings at the Curzon Cinema. In Paris, international "cafe society" patronized clubs such as the Boeuf sur le Toit. Cruise ships combined luxurious accommodations with travel to exotic areas. India, New Zealand, and South America were among the newly fashionable destinations promoted in evocative travel advertising.

The public was fascinated with each season's debutantes. Margaret Whigham, daughter of a rayon tycoon, was London's "Deb of the Year" of 1930. Woolworth heiress Barbara Hutton had four orchestras and singing sensation Rudy Vallée at her coming-out party in 1932. Media favorite debutante Brenda Frazier appeared on the cover of *Life* magazine in 1938, and was dubbed a "celebutante." The boisterous and immodest flapper image was left behind and even debutantes strove for a veneer of mature sophistication. In 1937 *Vogue* advised: "Look like a woman of the world, a woman of poise and experience."[1]

Wallis Simpson epitomized the new "hard" chic, before and after her marriage to Edward, the former Prince of Wales. When he became King Edward VIII in January 1936, he was already known for his jaunty taste and playboy lifestyle. Within a year he gave up the throne to his younger brother (who became George VI) in order to marry Mrs. Simpson, an American divorcée. The Duke and Duchess of Windsor, as they were known after their June 1937 wedding, were important fashion icons. For their wedding, the Duchess of Windsor wore a simple Mainbocher dress in pale blue, dyed to match the interior of the wedding chapel. A valued couture client, the duchess was known for a style that was restrained, almost severe. Her simple ensembles from Mainbocher, Schiaparelli, Balenciaga, and other designers provided a background for her spectacular collection of jewelry. While the duchess' style was based on discipline, the duke was known for his sporty and relaxed approach, which was influential on menswear. Faced with a life of enforced leisure after his abdication, Edward and his duchess considered the cultivation of style a vocation.

Fashion Media

Magazines offered fantasy and escape and powerful fashion editors such as Carmel Snow, who began working at *Harper's Bazaar* in 1933, molded the magazines' point of view. The press gave luxury products a hard sell, and described fashions with very specific delineations such as "bridge frock" or "luncheon frock," encouraging larger wardrobes to boost the fashion industry. Diana Vreeland's whimsical "Why Don't You?" columns for *Harper's Bazaar* were typical of fashion's emphasis on fantasy. But magazines also published money-saving tips, reflecting economic realities. Selected dog breeds were profiled as if they were yet another accessory. Celebrity tie-ins were numerous, including modeling and product endorsements. Two new men's fashion magazines were launched: *Apparel Arts* in 1931 and *Esquire* in 1933.

Photography and illustration shared the pages of the major publications. The striking images of Edward Steichen and George Hoyningen-Huene set the standard for the industry. In July 1932 a Steichen swimsuit photo was the first color photographic cover of French *Vogue*. Horst P. Horst began photographing for *Vogue* in 1931. Other great talents emerged: John Rawlings' photographs were first featured in *Vogue* in 1936; Louise Dahl-Wolfe, who operated her own studio in New York, began working for *Harper's Bazaar*; and New Yorker Toni Frissell joined *Vogue* in 1931. Martin Munkácsi, who had worked for *Die Dame* in Berlin in the 1920s, joined *Harper's Bazaar* in 1934, bringing his background as a sports photographer to his fashion work. German-born Erwin Blumenfeld began his career as a fashion photographer in Paris and George Platt Lynes contributed photos to several magazines. Designer and photographer Cecil Beaton, who began working for *Vogue* in the late 1920s, was also known for photographing the British royal family.

Despite the growth in fashion photography, great illustrators contributed to the overall fashion consciousness. Fashion illustration's biggest stars continued to be Erté at *Harper's Bazaar*, and Georges Lepape and Eduardo García

Edward, Prince of Wales (briefly King Edward VIII), and his wife, American divorcée Wallis Warfield Simpson – shown here at Balmoral Castle in 1936 – were important fashion setters for high society during the decade.

Benito at *Vogue*. Emerging new talents promoted a gestural style that departed from the prevailing look of the 1910s and 1920s. Chief among them were Christian Bérard, Marcel Vertès, Carl Erickson (known simply as "Eric"), and René Gruau.

Fashion Technologies

The slide closure became a more important factor in fashion during the 1930s. It was often marketed under brand names such as the "Talon slide fastener," or "lightning fastener," but the term "zipper" was eventually adopted in vernacular use. The name was inspired by galoshes from B. F. Goodrich that had debuted the previous decade. They closed with slide fasteners and were named "zippers." Women's foundation garments used zippers, and the fitted upper body shapes of dresses also encouraged their use. Front zipper closures allowed children to fasten their own garments. Zipper fly fronts on men's trousers became widespread by the end of the decade. Colored zippers were used to match dress fabrics, but some designers exploited their decorative potential and featured contrasting zippers.

Synthetic fabrics continued to develop. Rayon and acetate were common, and were often used as substitutes for silk, especially in lingerie. At the high end, designers used novelty fabrics, such as the textured rayons favored by Elsa Schiaparelli. Cellophane was also trendy, lending sparkle, particularly to eveningwear. Lastex, a spun elastic yarn, was important for sportswear, foundations, and hosiery. Artificial wools were also offered. Nylon, the most important textile innovation of the decade, appeared in 1939. In development since the mid-1920s, DuPont's strong lightweight fiber revolutionized hosiery.

The Elements of Women's Fashion

Neoclassic styles were the prevailing mode early in the decade; white and ivory columnar bias-cut evening dresses often featured Greek details such as cowl or cascade drapes. Fashion magazines compared dresses to Greek architecture and photographers juxtaposed models with ancient columns and sculptures. Turn-of-the-century "lingerie" styles contributed larger hats, ruffled blouses, gored skirts, and white cotton dresses, with *Vogue* hailing "The Modern Gibson Girl" in 1932. As the decade continued other influences emerged, and in 1934 *Time* noted three dominant looks: medieval, crinoline, and Empire. The medieval style featured long gothic lines, flaring skirts, dagging, and scalloping; the crinoline style was marked by full skirts, often tulle, and romantic details; the Empire style featured high waists and small puffed sleeves. Fashion writers noted other historic influences such as bustle drapery, present by mid-decade. By the end of the decade, military inspiration, both historic and contemporary, was prevalent.

Regional inspirations were strong and varied, encouraged by exotic destinations and the Exposition Coloniale Internationale in Paris in 1931. China, India, and Southeast Asia were of great importance. Fashions of Mexico and the American Southwest were adopted. American heiress Millicent Rogers wore tiered skirts and American Indian "squash blossom" necklaces, and the style of Mexican painter Frida Kahlo, wife of Diego Rivera, was also inspirational. The popularity of tourist "dude" ranches in the western United States encouraged cowgirl looks. In addition, European

Augustabernard, rivaled only by Vionnet in her expertise with the bias cut, promoted neoclassic style, as seen in this illustration by Georges Lepape.

CRÉATION

HH 339

GIBSON GIRL BLOUSED
COAT IN TWO TONES
OF GREY
DARKER TONE IS USED
FOR SKIRT

Top A French fashion plate
from early in the decade shows
transitional elements – ambiguous
waistline, modified cloche hat
– that indicate the dividing line
between late 1920s and early
1930s styles. The silver fox stole
became a key look of the 1930s.

Above The "Gibson Girl" revival
is evident in this industry sketch
for New York City fashion house
André Studios in 1938.

folkloric styles continued in peasant blouses, aprons, and other details. Gypsy looks were featured later in the decade with full, colorful striped skirts, and *Harper's Bazaar* quipped in 1937:

> Someone met a gipsy, someone thought of gipsy stripes and tossed them through Paris … Else how can you account for the wild gipsy mood that runs through all the spring collections?

The big news for color was a decline in the popularity of black at the start of the decade, leading *Vogue* to remark in June 1931: "It would appear that white has sought to fill the place left vacant by black." White was common for evening, for daytime formal occasions, and town wear. But black continued to be worn, often combined with icy pastels or hot saturated colors. A range of colors was seen in both day- and eveningwear with sophisticated tertiary shades popular. Popular prints included florals and polka dots, and stripes and plaids cut on the bias to form diagonals.

Many fashion elements were universal to both day and evening. The boyish figure of the twenties was outmoded and the line of fashion, while still lean, allowed for a more mature femininity, emphasizing natural curves. The body-hugging fit was frequently enhanced by the bias cut. Waists were defined once again, sometimes with structure and darting, sometimes with belts and sashes. During the early 1930s multiple waistlines were in evidence, marking the transition from the 1920s silhouette. Yokes at the top of the skirt indicated both a natural waist and a hip emphasis; similarly placed decorative details on both waist and hips created the same effect. Sometimes wide waistbands extended from the pelvis to below the bust. Hemlines dropped for both day and evening, and skirts were commonly bias-cut or constructed with gores and godets. Bateau necklines were popular for both day and evening, and low-cut backs were not only featured for evening gowns but in formal day and cocktail looks.

Embellishment was reduced during the early 1930s, with visual interest often provided by details: asymmetrical piecing, tucks, self scarves, oversized bows, pelerines, fichus and jabots, and peplums. Later in the decade, bold graphic trims were applied, and symmetry was once again common. With the early sleek silhouette, sleeves provided variation, even flights of fancy, in both day and evening clothes. Victorian leg-of-mutton sleeves (sometimes crisp, sometimes soft) were popular, often slit with peekaboo shoulder exposure. Fluttery circular sleeves, capelet, and petal styles were common, and bishop, pagoda, kimono, and dolman "batwing" styles were available. As the decade progressed, padded shoulders and large sleeves balanced wider or boxier skirts.

For daytime dressing, two moods prevailed: tailored and smart, and soft and graceful. Suits and dress ensembles continued to be popular, as was the *robe tailleur* (tailored dress). Matching coats were worn over suits, and coat and skirt sets worn with soft blouses expressed the tailored theme. Jackets, sometimes fitted and sometimes loose and cinched in, were very popular over dresses, a trend *Vogue* referred to as "jacketeering." Although the bias cut was typical, skirts on the straight grain were also worn, often with insets of box pleats. Longer skirts were the norm by 1931, reaching approximately 10 inches (25 centimeters) from the floor. Hems for daytime began to rise during the mid-1930s, and skirts became either fuller or straighter, losing the sleekness of earlier years. By 1939, a shorter length, slightly below the knee, was standard. Many blouses and dresses contrasted the tailored mode with fluttery details such as ruffles, oversized bows and tie necks, and varied sleeve shapes. Shirtwaist fronts were popular, showing Edwardian influence. Surplice front closures were seen on day dresses, and were especially popular for maternity clothes because of their easy adjustability.

Knit dresses and separates were also closely fitted; sweaters, often with bold designs and bright colors, were widespread. The term "sportswear" began to be used for casual

Above Marlene Dietrich in one of her signature pants ensembles.

Below left "The dinner dress grows more invaluable," declared *Vogue* (October 15, 1932), illustrating gowns by (left to right) Maggy Rouff, Maison Mirand, and Lucile Paray.

Below right Two British gowns with matching millinery for the Ascot races in 1933.

daytime clothing. Pants for women, sometimes known as "slacks," increased in popularity, encouraged by the media presence of prominent actresses Katharine Hepburn and Marlene Dietrich, and aviatrix Amelia Earhart. In the most casual of circumstances, even blue jeans were now acceptable.

For evening, glamour prevailed, and women of all economic strata looked to leading designers and Hollywood for inspiration. When embellishment was seen, bugle beads and sequins were often used, as were fringe, fur, and marabou, and other surface treatments included trapunto (quilting) and appliqué. Evening fabrics ranged from matte crepe, panné velvet, and charmeuse, to ciré satin and lamé. Lace was popular, and as the decade progressed organza and taffeta achieved the fuller silhouettes. By 1931 evening hemlines were down to the instep or the floor. Necklines were "demurely high or wickedly low."[2] Halternecks and T-strapped backs were typical, along with fichu styles and fluttery ruffled necklines. Rounded and sweetheart shapes were seen at decade's end. Although frequently skirts were sleek and unadorned, often flounces and ruffles wrapped around the body. Evening jackets, from bolero to mandarin shapes, were commonly worn, not as outerwear but to coordinate with dresses. Suits for evening, with matching long skirts and jackets, were also featured. The concept of transitional late day, cocktail, and dinner dresses continued to expand, with the term "after five dressing" coming into common usage. Full mid-calf-length cocktail and dancing styles became popular by the end of the decade. Slinky styles were compared to nightgowns, with the press declaring negligees "come down to dinner" in 1931.[3]

Court activities were greatly reduced throughout Europe, and the fossilized court dress no longer had an effect on fashion. However, daytime formal occasions, such as horse races and garden parties, required romantic and stylish long gowns (often in silk, cotton organza, or dotted Swiss), usually with wide-brimmed picture hats. Guests at other society occasions wore similarly lavish ensembles. Wedding dresses were affected by the historic modes of the day, with the long lines, high waists and puffy sleeves of Empire especially typical in white and ivory satin and charmeuse. Other brides chose fuller lines in organza and tulle. Veils continued much of the grandiosity of previous decades, often long and training. Bridesmaids' dresses typically followed the style lines of the bride's, in softly colored shades; frequently circlets of flowers or veils were worn.

Above Skiing grew markedly more popular outside of its original territory in Alpine and Nordic countries. Fashion magazines frequently illustrated styles for the slopes, such as this illustration from *Adam*, November 15, 1934, which features styles for men and women.

Opposite "Sandscapes of 1932" *Vogue* captioned this illustration (January 1, 1932), which shows Riviera beachwear and resort wear, including designs by Parisian Jane Regny. The style of a halter top created by draping a man's handkerchief (lower left) was embraced by the most adventurous French women.

Sports Clothing

Skiwear blossomed in this decade, reflecting the increased popularity of the sport, now available to more middle-class enthusiasts and encouraged by the 1932 and 1936 Winter Olympic Games. It was fully acceptable for women to wear pants on the slopes, and skiwear styles were often featured in the fashion press. Skating clothes were also promoted with profiles of Olympic champion Sonja Henie. Equestrian clothes followed trends in menswear with women riding astride in tweed jackets.

The term "play clothes" began to be used for leisure clothing that could transfer from beach to sport to gardening. Tennis and golf clothes for the serious player continued the practical styles of the 1920s, but the fashionable dilettante's clothes reverted to less practical forms as, following daywear fashions, longer hems and woven fabrics were often worn. Some practical styles continued to develop, such as bifurcated skirts for many activities.

Swimwear developed both technically and stylistically. The elastic yarn Lastex was used in swimsuits, and improved fit. Suits with adjustable backs promoted tanning with fewer tan lines, and halter styles were offered. Swim cap manufacturers noted improved designs for keeping hair dry. Two-piece swimwear was common, with exposed midriffs but covered navels. Animal and batik-style prints were used on woven fabrics, as well as satin finishes. Reflecting the trend for celebrity endorsement, tennis star Helen Wills "designed" a line of swimwear for the BVD label. Pajamas grew in popularity for beach lounging and some daring women wore them with bandeau tops, or even large handkerchiefs folded and tied as halter tops.

Above left Fitted coats with large fur collars were a ubiquitous item in the well-dressed woman's wardrobe during the 1930s.

Above right As the decade began, the dominance of cloche hats and berets gave way to a wide variety of hat styles, often including dramatic wide brims.

Outerwear

Outerwear followed the lines of daywear. As the decade began, sleeker, more fitted styles were worn, often with full sleeves. As the silhouette transformed, coats changed with it, with padded shoulders and shorter lengths by the end of the decade. Textured fabrics such as tweed and bouclé were frequently used. Trench coats were worn as rainwear, as were styles created using the latest waterproof fabrics.

Mink and sealskin were especially popular for fur coats. Cloth coats, and sometimes suits, featured fur cuffs and collars made of mink, leopard, or Persian lamb. But the real vogue was the fox stole, worn over either a coat or a dress. Often large fox collars were attached to coats, mimicking the proportion of the popular stoles. The use of large collars was so common that dog fur continued as a lower-priced substitute, euphemistically identified to create a more exotic (and acceptable) product.

Spectacular drapey coats were worn to match evening dresses, often trimmed with fur. Capes in both short and floor lengths were worn, in fabrics ranging from panné velvet to taffeta. Sometimes dramatic Elizabethan-inspired ruffled collars were seen.

Millinery and Accessories

A wide range of hat options was fashionable. *L'Officiel* declared in 1930: "The greatest charm of the present day fashion is its infinite variety."[4] Hat makers Talbot and Reboux continued to dominate Paris, while French-born Lilly Daché was the leading milliner in New York. Medium- and wide-brimmed hats were worn on a diagonal slant. Hats that were merely tightly fitted crowns with projecting details were common early in the decade; they were worn sharply angled with one eyebrow obscured. Pillbox shapes and fedoras were worn at angles and sometimes decorated with a single pheasant feather. High "cossack" hats were usually made of fur. Phrygian caps were seen, as were turbans. Some shapes and decorations reflected a taste for Surrealism.

Berets continued to be worn, and were especially popular in the early years of the decade. So was the "slouch hat," a loose cloche that pulled down over the forehead, popularized by Greta Garbo's casual off-screen style. By the mid-1930s, snoods were in vogue, encouraged by the medieval trends in fashion. As the decade drew on, hats were sometimes small and boxy, worn centered on the forehead and tilting forward, often with substantial floral decoration. Picture hats, often ringed with lace ruffles or covered with bouquets of faux flowers, conjured images of Empress Eugénie's court. In 1938 *L'Officiel* commented once again: "Never has millinery been more eclectic than at the present time and a woman has no excuses for not being hatted according to her type and personality." Further development of late day and cocktail dressing encouraged hats for evening, sometimes referred to as "dinner and dancing hats." Decorative combs, diadems, and bandeaux of feathers were also worn for evening.

A perfectly chosen handbag was considered the finishing touch for an outfit. Pochette and clutch-style handbags continued from the 1920s, now usually in larger versions, sometimes decorated with art deco-style details. Minaudières, small decorative cases, were often carried as evening bags, sometimes fitted with matching containers for cosmetics and cigarettes. Although dresses often featured attached scarves, separate scarves were everywhere, and were available in a wide variety of shapes. Scarves developed as luxury items; Hermès introduced their *carrés*, beautiful printed silk squares often made in limited editions. Self belts and sashes were also common on dresses, but contrasting fabric and leather belts (including many novelty leathers) were often used to complete an ensemble, with wider widths becoming more prevalent during the course of the decade. Muffs were featured, sometimes in fabric to match an outfit, though fur versions were widespread (some with dangling

Vogue featured these "Gallic Gaieties" (October 15, 1934), a collection of accessories and separates essential for the season. The "dachshund" muff, earrings, sweater, and pink chenille evening jacket were by Elsa Schiaparelli.

tails). In keeping with the Surrealist mode, Schiaparelli offered one in the shape of a dachshund. Combination "muff bags" did double duty.

Gloves were essential to a smart day ensemble, and also returned to use for evening. While discreet short styles, including crochet, were common, gauntlet styles, reminiscent of the 17th century, became chic and were often decorated with studs, cutwork, and embroidery. Long gloves for evening and special occasions were available, but most women continued the bare-arm style of the 1920s, as shorter gloves, below the elbow, were more stylish.

Different shoe styles were worn for various occasions, ranging from flat brogues to very high heels for evening. Most daytime shoes had some heel, and many fashionable shoes were colorful and eye-catching. Even rain boots were shaped to sleekly cover heeled shoes. Two-tone spectator styles were especially popular, and some had small peep-toe openings. For summer, sandals for town had heels and cut-outs. Huaraches and espadrilles were popular for resort areas. During the course of the decade, shoes became more chunky. The most daring women wore platform shoes, introduced in 1937 by Wally di Castelbarco, the daughter of conductor Arturo Toscanini, who brought the beach style from Venice to New York.

Spectacular brooches in the shape of animals or flowers provided a focal point for simple dresses and daytime suits, a style favored by the Duchess of Windsor. The crystalline forms of art deco also continued to influence jewelry and pins, and earrings resembled skyscrapers. Bracelets were often very large and extravagant; bangles were popular, as were charm bracelets and strands of pearls wrapped around the wrist, even over gloves. Jewelry with monograms and text was also popular. Diamanté buckles and dress clips frequently adorned evening dress.

Foundations and Lingerie

As the waist returned to its correct anatomical placement, a lean but shapely figure was the ideal. Some trim young women went without underwear beneath soft bias-cut evening clothes, emphasizing neoclassical beauty and avoiding bra and panty lines. But most women used foundations to achieve smooth contours. Advertisements often depicted women as lithe art deco goddesses. Reflecting both the desired silhouette and the taste for the exotic, Princessa foundations promised "bamboo slimness." Larger women required more sturdy foundations for the fashionable silhouette. In 1934 *Fashions Art* asserted:

The woman with the most perfect figure in the world can't hope to wear today's streamline fashions without some sort of foundation garment. Today, the discovery of two-way stretch elastic makes it possible for a woman to eat her cake and keep her youthful figure also.

Slide closures were used in foundations, and Lastex was crucial to "unboned" girdles that often went well down the thighs or were even bifurcated. They were still often referred to as corsets in advertising, but other evocative trade names such as "beautifiers," "flexees," or "foundettes" were used by some manufacturers.

Brassieres were made with separating cups in forms that ranged from lightweight and silky to strong and supportive. Nicely shaped breasts were needed for higher-waisted styles. Spiral stitching began to be used for shaping. "Bras," as they were sometimes called, were available with versatile straps to accommodate back- and shoulder-baring dress styles. The Maidenform company debuted, and included larger sizes in their offerings. Some slips had built-in bras and control panels to minimize lines and produce a sleek silhouette. Corsets with attached flounces eliminated the need for a slip. Separable foundations that attached a long-line bra to a panty girdle were also available.

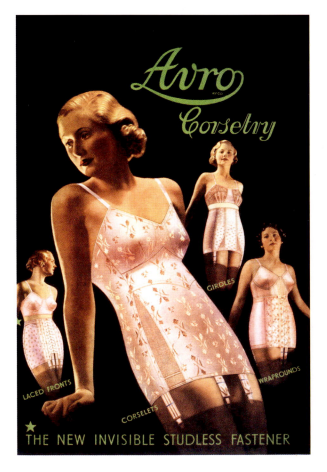

An underwear ad from Avro Corsetry shows the typical foundation of the time. The fashion photography exhibits the stylistic influence of German Expressionist cinema.

Be sure to remember these things

9535

Take your neckline seriously. wear your waistline high and low, slash your sleeves, but keep them voluminous, and you are ready for the smartest Spring gatherings.

Home sewing was emphasized; often local newspapers offered paper pattern services to enable the home sewer.

Stockings were usually plain, sometimes with clocks and occasionally lace or patterned. They were worn in a variety of colors based on skin tones and marketed with evocative names. Stockings were made of silk or rayon until the introduction of nylon in 1939. More advanced sizing of stockings was introduced, and knee-high styles were popular with the mid-calf hem lengths of fashionable daywear.

Camisoles and tap pants were still part of the range of underwear; a "dance set" consisted of a bra with matching tap pants. Silky wide-legged pajamas were increasingly worn not just for sleep but also for loungewear. The bias cut was also used in slips and nightwear; some nightgowns were nearly indistinguishable from sleek evening gowns. Conversely, lingerie and loungewear exerted a strong influence on fashion. Fluttery, lightweight materials were popular for dresses, lending a boudoir look to many ensembles, especially for summer.

Designers: France

Time magazine summed up French haute couture in 1934:

> Couturiers may be divided roughly, and not without argument, into three groups. First are the older houses who are heavy with prestige but exercise comparatively little authority over fashion trends. In this class are Worth, Paquin, Callot Soeurs and Redfern. Next is a large group of comparatively young houses or old ones which have passed their prime, not at present the most dominant influence in fashion. Preeminent among them are Lelong, Chanel, Louiseboulanger, Jane Regny, Martial & Armand, Marcel Rochas, Maggy Rouff, Alix, and Jean Patou. Finally there is a handful of houses now at or near the peak of their power as arbiters of the ultra-modern haute couture. Regardless of who else might be included nearly every fashion expert would agree that in this group the following houses most decidedly belong: Vionnet, Lanvin, Augustabernard, Mainbocher, Molyneux and Schiaparelli.

The bias cut that **Madeleine Vionnet** explored during the 1920s became not only a signature of her designs, but dominated fashion during the first half of the 1930s. Like the art of Brancusi and Lalique, Vionnet's work was both sculptural and fluid, and her white and ivory dresses were the zenith of the neoclassic style. The press held her aloft saying:

> No one else can do what she can with materials ... She has a classic feeling for the pure poetry of the body and for line at the expense of color. She disregards fashion. When Chanel was "in," Vionnet was "out." Today their positions are reversed. But whether she is in or out, her collections retain a classic elegance which is the very pinnacle of the dressmaker's art.[5]

Vionnet worked directly with textile manufactures to develop fabrics with enhanced bias properties. Diagonal and asymmetrical style lines, and extraordinary feats of piecing, characterized her work for both day and evening. Some gowns featured suspended pieces of fabric that the wearer wrapped around her body to complete the look. Hoyningen-Huene captured the spirit of her neoclassic designs in his "Bas Relief" photographs, immortalizing Vionnet's connection to ancient Greece.

In 1934 Vionnet moved away from her focus on ancient inspiration, and incorporated the emerging romantic styles. Striking surface treatments such as tufts and plissé decorated full skirts; one such taffeta dress was described as "full and quilted like the gowns La Pompadour wore."[6] Second Empire metallic flecked nets were used, and large skirts were sometimes decorated with horizontal details that resembled the cage crinoline. But neoclassic styles continued to be offered, and some designs cunningly merged both neoclassic and romantic inspirations. In the late years of the decade, Vionnet was attracted to the trend toward bold contrasts of graphic prints and appliqué details. At the end of the most important decade of her career, Vionnet retired in 1939.

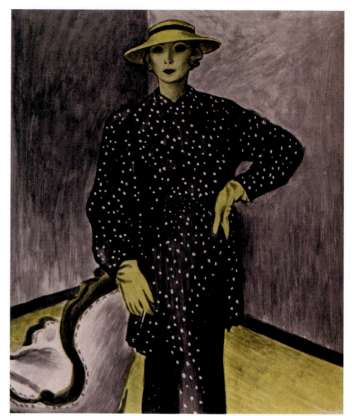

Above left A typically chic ensemble from Mainbocher with a wide pleated bertha collar and slim skirt, accessorized with sharply angled hat and gauntlet gloves.

Above right A 1934 fashion plate features a Molyneux ensemble combining polka dots – a popular motif – with vibrant, striking yellow accessories.

Jeanne Lanvin, "one of the most striking and individual personalities in the creative fashion world,"[7] never lost her view of femininity. In the 1930s she continued to turn out graceful romantic styles with flow and drape in lightweight materials with beautiful embellishments. But she was also able to adapt to the evolving version of "feminine" that included a more sophisticated chic. Many of her evening gowns featured low décolletages and slit skirts and contrasted areas of lamé or paillettes with matte fabric, conveying the essence of art deco at its apogee.

Born in Provence, Augusta Bernard (1886–1946) began her career as a dressmaker copying the work of other well-known designers. She opened her house in 1923 calling her label **Augustabernard** and her most significant work came during the early 1930s. Her work with the bias cut was in many ways the equal of Vionnet's, and Augustabernard was known for elegant eveningwear in the neoclassic mode; her gowns typically featured sleek fit to the hip, then flared to billowing fullness. She also featured smart daywear. For day and evening, decoration was often achieved with simple details such as topstitching, piecing and self trim. Augustabernard enjoyed significant press coverage: *Time* magazine declared in 1934, "she is noted for her superb technique which makes her dresses the favorites of connoisseurs." Unable to maintain financial success during the hard economic times, Bernard closed her doors by 1935.

Main Rousseau Bocher (1890–1976) was born in Chicago in 1890. After working as the editor of French *Vogue*, Bocher opened his couture house in Paris in 1930, an unusual venture for an American. Perhaps taking his cue from Louiseboulanger and Augustabernard, he combined his first and last names as **Mainbocher**. Throughout the 1930s, he presented understated, luxurious collections to an international clientele. Ensembles were closely fitted and often featured contrasting light-colored details (such as buttons or collars, ruffles or revers) on navy blue or black. Mainbocher also favored two-color prints in dark blue or black with white. He was a favorite designer of Wallis Simpson, the future Duchess of Windsor, and as well as designing her wedding dress he continued to dress her in later years. As World War II loomed, Mainbocher closed his Paris house in 1939 and moved his business to New York.

Alix was one of the most creative drapers in Paris. A deftly draped afternoon dress featured in *L'Officiel* in 1933 exemplifies her skill.

Irish-born **Edward Molyneux** often utilized discreet prints, dots, and checks in black and white for day dresses and sport ensembles. Simply cut evening gowns often featured interesting fabric treatments such as pale watery prints or panels that contrasted matte and shine. The gowns he designed for Gertrude Lawrence in *Private Lives* (1930) set a standard for elegance in a decade in which fashion and costume were interdependent. Molyneux designed the bride's gown and trousseau for the 1934 wedding of Princess Marina of Greece to the Duke of Kent. Molyneux was also known for trim suits with short jackets over skirts or three-quarter-length coats worn over matching dresses, and even designed evening suits.

Originally from Rome, **Elsa Schiaparelli** (1890–1973) moved to Paris in 1922 with a young daughter. After a short period of working as a freelancer for other designers, Schiaparelli began her career with a collection of novelty sweaters introduced in 1927. By 1929 Schiaparelli was known for her striking suits and sport clothes. In 1931, Schiaparelli wore a divided skirt of her own design in London, and created similar culottes for Spanish tennis star Lili de Alvarez, generating much reaction from the British press.

Schiaparelli experimented with innovative materials and used zippers as functional and decorative elements. From the early 1930s, she often used shoulder pads, constructing a boxy silhouette that became influential by the end of the decade. Amusing details – such as buttons shaped like snails or cockroaches – enlivened her well-tailored pieces. Her provocative accessories included the convertible knit "Mad Cap" and a black felt hat shaped like a shoe. Accessories and separates were available at the "Schiap Shop," a retail boutique she opened in 1935 on the ground floor of her couture house at 21 place Vendôme, Chéruit's former premises. Schiaparelli's many perfumes included Shocking, Sleeping, and Snuff (for men), all presented in whimsical artistic packaging.

Schiaparelli was known for her collaborations with contemporary artists, especially the Surrealists; Jean Cocteau designed embroidery for several pieces. Her collaborations with Salvador Dalí were particularly noteworthy. In 1936–1937 she offered "Surrealist" suits inspired by Dalí's paintings of figures with drawers projecting from their torsos: the suit jackets had pocket flaps with plastic "drawer handles." Further work with Dalí resulted in other extraordinary designs including a silk evening dress with a large lobster motif, and another evening dress with a printed motif of ripped flesh. Schiaparelli's stylish clients included the prominent art collectors Marie-Laure, Vicomtesse de Noailles, Mme. Arturo Lopez-Willshaw, and socialite and fashion editor Daisy Fellowes.

Lucien Lelong continued to be a dynamic force in Paris couture. In 1934 he established Lucien Lelong Editions, the first genuine ready-to-wear line by a Parisian couturier. This step exemplified his bold approach to business and reflected his admiration for the American fashion system. Pieces from the Editions line were featured in middle-of-the-road fashion publications, fulfilling Lelong's desire to reach a larger audience. His Modernist aesthetic was reflected in the stylish design of his salons. The house had approximately 1,000 employees producing garments for illustrious clients who included Marlene Dietrich, *Vogue* editor Bettina Ballard, and Princess Liliane "Baba" d'Erlanger. In 1937 Lelong was elected president of the Chambre Syndicale de la Haute Couture Parisienne.

Chanel's was an individual aesthetic that, while keeping with the times, still followed themes present in her work since the beginning. Her jersey and woven suits, with belts cinching jackets at the waist, were still popular, as were her tennis clothes and beachwear. Although she avoided the bias cut, in keeping with the prevailing taste, Chanel created white, ivory, and pastel evening dresses in markedly feminine designs of lace and tulle, often tiered; black was still shown, as were vivid jewel tones. Silver and gold lamé were also featured, and sequins were used on evening sheaths and pajama suits. She used bows as a recurrent theme, for hairbands, dresses and jewelry.

Bold, often whimsical prints displayed across full skirts were a trademark style for Elsa Schiaparelli.

Seeking a Paris fashion connection to keep ahead of trends, movie producer Samuel Goldwyn hired Chanel to design both on- and off-screen wardrobes for several of his studio's major actresses, offering her a staggering one million dollars per year. But she ultimately designed for only three films during 1931 and 1932 and the experience was not wholly successful. Chanel continued to work in costuming in France, designing film costumes for director Jean Renoir. She also collaborated with Jean Cocteau on stage and screen, often paired with the fashion illustrator Christian Bérard working as set designer.

Jewelry figured prominently in the output of the house, and Coco Chanel herself was often heavily bedecked in her own product. The pearls and beads of the 1920s were still important to the Chanel look. She collaborated with illustrator Paul Iribe (who became her fiancé) on remarkable diamond jewelry until his sudden death in 1935. Chanel also collaborated with Fulco di Verdura, who designed the baked enamel cuff that became a signature Chanel look. In keeping with the *moyen age* (medieval) themes influencing fashion, Verdura took inspiration from the Byzantine Empire, and used the Maltese cross as a signature motif. The collaboration continued until Verdura departed for the United States in 1934, launching his own line in New York.

The house of Chanel weathered the economic crisis thanks to an international clientele, including women from the increasingly fashionable South American and Indian markets, and new business ventures and collaborations. Her 1931 collection featured cotton piqué, organdy, and other cotton fabrics for evening dresses in a promotion with the British textile manufacturer Ferguson Brothers Ltd., and she created designs for other British manufacturers in the ready-to-wear market. By 1932 she had opened "Au 23," a boutique that *Vogue* described as a "female haberdashery shop." However, Chanel's fragrances and cosmetics continued to be the most profitable venture of her various enterprises.

A very important designer in the 1920s, **Louiseboulanger** continued her success as a significant member of the Paris couture scene into the 1930s. The house featured elegant designs for day and evening, and was also known for luxurious dressing gowns. She maintained an aesthetic that simultaneously combined Old World elegance and modernity. Louiseboulanger was described as a "daringly original designer who creates extreme styles in unusual and exclusive materials"[8] and praised for her "unique feeling for fabrics."[9] She closed her house in 1939.

Maggy Rouff, born Marguerite de Wagner (1896–1971), was the daughter of the directors of Drecoll. She joined the family business in 1920 and designed for the label, but when Drecoll merged with Maison Beer in 1929, she left to join the long-established house of Rouff. With the new partnership, she took the name "Maggy Rouff." Rouff offered evening and day dresses, lingerie, and sportswear. Her customers sought chic sophistication, and Rouff provided ensembles that were striking but not overdone. Her dresses in the 1930s featured a sleek fit that embodied the smooth elegance of the decade. Known for her skilled use of fabric and color, she used smartly pieced geometric details, and trademark drapery that often defined the torso and waist with wrapped treatments. Rouff was also known for her creative sleeves and dramatic necklines. Rouff drew from history with inventive tailored pieces described in the press as "Jacobin" and "Directoire." She licensed designs to McCall's for paper patterns. Rouff was awarded the *Légion d'honneur*, and published commentaries on fashion, including *Ce que j'ai vu en chiffonnant la clientèle* (1938) and *La philosophie de l'élégance* (1942), which defined her viewpoints on style.

Germaine Emilie Krebs (1903–1993) began her long career in the early 1930s, designing under the names **Alix Barton** and, as of April 1934, **Alix**. She was often referred to as a designer of extreme originality whose work evoked the lines of Gothic and antique statuary. Descriptions of her collections noted her technical finesse, rivaling those of Vionnet and Augustabernard. Alix's day dresses and ensembles often featured unique construction details with tied panels, cowl necks, crossover bodices, and bell-bottom sleeves. Her eveningwear was varied and often showed cut-out areas of exposure at the shoulder, midriff, or lower back. Alix enthusiastically adopted new materials including tissue lamé, cellophane, rayon, and stretch velvet. She produced evening dresses in her own version of the classical mode. While other designers draped their clients in clinging bias-cut silk charmeuse, Alix swathed women in yards and yards of jersey worked into hundreds of tiny pleats.

Jean Patou began the decade with a new fragrance, Cocktail, introduced in 1930. One of the first to transition to a new silhouette before the end of the 1920s, Patou explored a streamlined look with slender skirts and dresses for day, often with diagonal details such as surplice bodices and angular piecing at the hipline. His sportswear was still in demand; ski ensembles paired loose trousers with fitted jackets, often trimmed with fur or knit ribbing and worn with scarves marked with Patou's logo. *Vogue* described Patou's fashion shows as "among the social events of Paris." Shortly after the presentation of his 1936 spring/summer collection, Jean Patou died suddenly. The business remained in his family for several years and the numerous Patou fragrances were important to its success.

Cristóbal Balenciaga Eizaguirre (1895–1972) was born in Getaria, a fishing village in the Basque region of Spain. His mother was a seamstress and Balenciaga learned to sew at an early age, acquiring skills that would enable him to succeed as a couturier: he learned French and worked with both a tailor and a dressmaker. In 1919 he opened his own boutique in San Sebastián, a fashionable resort, with the backing of the Marquesa de Casa Torres, who had known him as a child. A branch in Madrid followed and he expanded into Barcelona by 1935.

Below left Madeleine Vionnet's output during the decade was remarkably varied. Here she combines luxurious fullness of skirt with a Surrealist print in an image captured by the lens of Man Ray.

Below right Shown in one of his earliest Paris collections, Cristóbal Balenciaga's Infanta dress exhibits inspiration from 17th-century Spanish court dress enlivened with an art deco sensibility.

Above left A Nina Ricci ensemble illustrated by Pierre Mourgue. Of the many ethnographic influences in fashion, Russian inspiration was particularly popular.

Above right A markedly chic Parisian woman crosses the Pont Alexandre III in a stylish ensemble by couturier Robert Piguet.

As growing political tensions led to the Spanish Civil War, Balenciaga left for Paris and established his house there, first showing in 1937. Vladzio d'Attainville, an employee and family friend, followed him to Paris and became his business partner. Although the Spanish branches remained open, Balenciaga based himself in Paris for the rest of his career. His first collection in Paris did not attract significant press attention, but via word of mouth he swiftly established an influential clientele. Important New York stores, including Bendel's and Saks, began to feature his smart tailored pieces and striking eveningwear. He repeatedly looked to Spain for inspiration, including the costumes of bullfighters, the *majas* in the paintings of Goya, and the peasants of his native Getaria. Velázquez's portraits of 17th-century princesses were the inspiration for Balenciaga's Infanta dresses of 1939, ivory and pastel satin gowns with black velvet trim in baroque motifs. Balenciaga was also known for deep black evening gowns inspired by the elegant black clothes of 16th-century Spain. His Diablo line featured nipped-in waists and padded hips. In the world of Paris fashion, Balenciaga cultivated an aloof persona, and shied away from personal publicity.

Nina Ricci (1883–1970) was born Maria Nielli in Torino and nicknamed Nina as a child. Her family moved to Paris when she was a teenager. In 1904, while employed by a Paris couturier, she married jeweler Louis Ricci. She opened her own house in Paris at the age of forty-nine in 1932, at 20 rue de Capucines, joined by her son Robert who managed the business. The house grew from 25 to 450 employees by 1939; while this was actually only a mid-sized operation by the standard of the French couture industry, the house attracted a large clientele. An elegant woman herself, Ricci designed feminine and alluring clothes that were simultaneously conservative yet dramatic. She often used striking contrasts and large-scale details, featuring sophisticated treatments such as *nervure* (cording) and trapunto. Ricci reinterpreted the neoclassic mode in bold, graphic form with notes of fantasy.

After earlier employment with Poiret and Redfern, **Robert Piguet** (1898–1953) opened his couture house in 1933. Piguet was known for dramatic designs often in

Elizabeth, the Queen Consort of Great Britain, wears a romantic ensemble from her 1937 "White Wardrobe" by Norman Hartnell, reminiscent of mid-19th-century tulle dresses from couturiers such as Charles Frederick Worth and Emile Pingat.

deep, saturated colors and, his favorite, black. Wide bands of ruffles or pleats at shoulder or hem added emphasis to simpler silhouettes. Coats were often cut with swing at the back or with scarves that crossed diagonally. Historic references also appeared frequently as high collars and leg-of-mutton sleeves. His success was aided by a new assistant designer, Christian Dior, who joined the house in 1938. Dior's historic influences meshed with Piguet's and designs from late in the decade featured tightly fitting buttoned bodices and ruffled petticoats under crinoline-shaped skirts.

Other designers also figured noticeably in the Paris fashion scene including Bruyère, Groupy, Paray, Borea, and Premet. Drecoll, having merged with Beer in 1929, merged again in 1931 with Maison Agnès, becoming **Agnès-Drecoll**. **Doucet-Doeuillet** also continued during this decade, while the venerable **Martial et Armand** provided classic tailored pieces among its offerings. The last of the Creed family to work in the business, **Charles Creed** (1909–1966) offered smart suits to a discerning clientele. **Sonia Delaunay** closed her dressmaking business in 1929, but continued to design inventive fashion fabrics for the Amsterdam store Metz & Co. Delaunay's one-time collaborator, the furrier **Jacques Heim** (1899–1967), expanded into cloth coats and dressmaking, with stores in both Paris and Biarritz, advertising what *Vogue* called "architecturally conceived" couture. **Marcel Rochas** (1902–1955), whose house was established in 1925, offered day and evening clothes, often with dramatic contrasts and historical inspiration. **Jane Regny** continued her work in colorful Modernist separates and sportswear and activewear.

Designers: Britain

Worth's London branch continued to do steady business with conservative designs, while the London branch of Redfern merged with Ernest (which had been founded by John Redfern's son Ernest in the 1910s) under the label **Ernest and Redfern**. Other established companies, such as **Burberry** and **Jaeger**, were still thriving with traditional products, but younger talents were asserting their importance. Although rightfully considered among the French designers of the time, Edward Molyneux opened a London store in 1932, with John Cavanagh as his assistant. South African immigrant **Victor Stiebel** (1907–1976), after assisting court dressmaker Reville, opened his shop in 1932 and quickly became known for elegant and restrained dresses. The label **Lachasse** was founded in 1928 with Digby Morton as its design director; when Morton left to launch his own label in 1934, Hardy Amies filled his position.

Norman Hartnell (1901–1979) sketched dresses as a child, later saying, "my interest in fashion began with a box of crayons."[10] He began his studies in architecture at Cambridge in 1921 but he aspired to become a theatrical costume designer. Dropping out of Cambridge, he went to work for Madame Désirée, a court dressmaker in London. Soon Hartnell struck out on his own, and, with the financial backing of family members and his sister Phyllis acting as business manager, he opened his own small operation in Mayfair in 1923. By the late 1920s he had a sizable and notable clientele, and had shown in Paris. Hartnell gained a reputation for clothes that were romantic and chic, and early on began using tulle, which was rather unfashionable as a dress fabric at the time. He provided stage wardrobe for leading actresses, including Gertrude Lawrence (costuming her in Noël Coward's *Tonight at Eight-Thirty* among other productions) and the Parisian music hall star Mistinguett. He also dressed the young British writer Barbara Cartland, who would remain his client until the end of his career. Hartnell began selling to an American clientele, primarily through Bonwit Teller in New York, and was prominently featured in both British and American *Vogue*.

In 1934 Hartnell moved to stylish new premises at 26 Bruton Street. The same year, he received his first commission from the royal family, the wedding dress and trousseau of Lady Alice Montagu-Douglas-Scott for her marriage to Prince Henry, Duke of Gloucester. Among the bridesmaids, whom he also dressed, were the young princesses Elizabeth (later Queen Elizabeth II) and Margaret. Following the abdication

Hattie Carnegie's suit, seen on the cover of *Vogue*, September 1, 1932, included a stylish jacket with unusual clip closures, a torero-inspired hat, and oversized fur muff.

of Edward VIII, Hartnell was secured to design the dresses of the ladies-in-waiting for the coronation of George VI, and soon after began dressing Elizabeth, the Queen Consort. In his designs for the queen, Hartnell made reference to the full-skirted tulle gowns of the mid-19th century. According to his memoirs, during a visit to Buckingham Palace in 1937, he was encouraged by King George himself to look at Winterhalter's portraits of royal ancestors for inspiration for the queen's gowns.

This "crinoline" look became a trademark for Hartnell, and was popular for eveningwear and debutante dresses in London society. Elaborate embroidery and beading also became a signature look, in motifs and patterns that he created inspired by historical sources. While many of the French designers outsourced such work to embellishment houses such as Lesage, Hartnell maintained his own workshop.

Designers: United States

Several industry groups were formed to promote New York couture, including the Fashion Group and the Fashion Originators' Guild. Founding members of the Fashion Group included cosmetics giant Elizabeth Arden, Lord & Taylor executive Dorothy Shaver, *Harpers Bazaar* editor Carmel Snow, and emerging designer Claire McCardell. The Fashion Originators' Guild was formed to protect the work of American designers. Neiman Marcus, the Texas retailer founded in Dallas in 1907, began presenting its annual fashion awards in 1938.

Hattie Carnegie maintained her store on East 49th Street to great acclaim. She still offered Parisian couture, but featured elegant gowns and daywear under her own label, as well as luxurious fur pieces, and expanded into accessories, costume jewelry, and cosmetics. She included the Duchess of Windsor among her clients, and her studio continued to incubate future American talents. **Jessie Franklin Turner** continued in business, by 1932 operating out of 25 East 67th Street. Her advertising announced tea gowns and unusual and distinctive designs. Her designs were striking and maintained her bohemian aesthetic. Having established her business in the 1920s, **Nettie Rosenstein** (1890–1980) opened a store on West 47th Street in 1931 where she sold her high-quality day- and eveningwear and accessories, and her clothes were retailed around the country. She was one of the recipients of the Neiman Marcus Fashion Award in its inaugural year, 1938. The private couture salons at the Henri Bendel and Bergdorf Goodman department stores, with high-quality dresses derived from French designer models, were the choice of many women of society.

The idiosyncratic **Valentina** was still active in the 1930s. She had a gift for self-promotion and often acted as her own model. Perhaps more than any other New York designer, she attracted a glittering celebrity clientele and was of extreme importance to American high style. Valentina separated from her business partner Sonia Levienne, with whom she had opened a store in 1928 on Madison Avenue. While her work in the 1920s was against the mainstream, in the 1930s Valentina was more relevant to current trends, albeit with her own creative and individual vision. She rejected "fashion" in favor of "style" and sought to create clothes with lasting appeal. Her workshop was known for its superb construction and her use of grain and drape was sophisticated. She experimented with neoclassic and *moyen age* modes and asserted a theatrical aesthetic. With her early training as a dancer, motion and the potential for grand gesture were of great importance to her. Eccentric headwear appealed to Valentina. She created "coolie"-style hats worn for day and night, was one of the first designers to

Soprano Lily Pons costumed for *Lakmé* at the Metropolitan Opera, c. 1932.

LILY PONS AND THE MIDRIFF

French soprano Lily Pons (1904–1976) debuted at the Metropolitan Opera in 1931, creating an immediate sensation. She performed roles that showcased both her spectacular singing and attractive appearance, including the title character of Delibes' *Lakmé*. Dressed in sumptuous costumes based on traditional South Asian attire, the petite Pons appeared in revealing clothes featuring her bare midriff in the manner of the Indian *choli*. Critics noted her costuming as much as her singing, observing Pons "went to the Hindus themselves and succeeded in finding the materials for her wraps."[11]

Indian impact on fashion was widespread and varied. The "exotic" Princess Karam of Kapurthala figured importantly in the smart set of London and Paris, and was frequently featured in fashion magazines dressed by leading couturiers. Schiaparelli, Alix, and Valentina designed dresses with Indian inspiration. References to the splendor of India appeared in

advertisements for products ranging from jewelry to luxury automobiles. Midriffs had already started to peek out into fashion, especially for leisurewear and swimwear. Perhaps encouraged by Pons' costumes, the bare midriff became more frequent for eveningwear during the 1930s. Joan Crawford in *The Women* (1930) was costumed in a spectacular lamé evening gown, with midriff cut-outs, reflecting the South Asian trend.

During the course of the 1930s, Pons turned to Valentina for a new set of Lakmé costumes and wardrobe for other roles; for the Queen of Shemakan in *The Golden Cockerel* Valentina once again revealed Pons' midriff. Pons was very visible in the fashion press as a celebrity endorser and model. She went to Hollywood, and made three films for RKO. *I Dream too Much* (1935) cast her as an opera singer opposite Henry Fonda and included sequences of her as Lakmé, exposing her midriff to a wider audience and preserving it for posterity.

Muriel King sketched this zebra-striped resort dress in 1934.

embrace medieval-style snoods, and featured a variety of peculiar fabric coifs. She noted that her earliest memories were of Russian Orthodox nuns and she incorporated veils and wimples into her designs. During the early 1930s, Valentina began designing theatrical costumes. Her stage clients included Metropolitan Opera stars Rosa Ponselle and Lily Pons, and actresses such as Lynn Fontanne, Katharine Cornell, and Katharine Hepburn. Valentina designed Hepburn's clothes for the Broadway premiere of *The Philadelphia Story*. Her stage costumes were known for their remarkable chic and inventiveness but often markedly departed from historical accuracy.

Sally Milgrim (c. 1890–1994) began her business in Manhattan's Lower East Side, and by 1927 had established a store at 6 West 57th Street. She promoted the new concept of ready-to-wear designer fashions at her shop, but also offered custom creations. Her work was typified by chic, crisp styles, and included suits and furs along with elegant eveningwear in rich colors. She attracted notable celebrity clients to her store, and one of her most famous designs was the light blue gown worn by First Lady Eleanor Roosevelt for the 1933 inaugural ball. During the course of her career, she opened several stores throughout the United States. During her college education at Vassar in the 1920s, **Elizabeth Hawes** (1903–1971) began making her own designs and interned at Bergdorf Goodman. Leaving for Paris in 1925, she held several jobs in the French fashion industry, including assisting Nicole Groult. Returning to New York in 1928, she opened her own store, but traveled again to Paris in 1931 to show her very "American" collection. Like Milgrim, she contributed to the development of designer ready-to-wear at her store and included accessories in her line. Hawes also advocated trousers for women. Her 1938 memoir *Fashion is Spinach* offered a sharp critique of the industry in which she worked. **Muriel King** (1900–1977) opened a couture salon in New York in 1932, and the same year established a line of high-priced ready-to-wear through Lord & Taylor. Trained as a painter, King was a fashion illustrator in the 1920s and then turned her talent to designing. King's meticulous sketches were turned over to her dressmakers who constructed the garments, producing simple, well-made clothes prized by her socialite clients. Muriel King worked occasionally in film costumes, beginning in 1935 by dressing Katharine Hepburn in *Sylvia Scarlett*. **Clare Potter** (1903–1999), in her association with Lord & Taylor, added to the development of distinctly American sportswear. She won the Neiman Marcus award in 1939.

Hollywood Costume Design

Hollywood costume designers drew heavily from Paris and London, but were also innovators, creating gowns that were imitated the world over. Film stars embodied high style and their costumes were important to their appeal. Myrna Loy in *The Thin Man* (1934), costumed by Dolly Tree, epitomized the sophisticated lady. Fred Astaire and Ginger Rogers personified elegance, with Astaire typically dressed in black tails and Rogers often in swirling white gowns. Knock-offs of Hollywood styles were easily available, and references in advertisements, paper patterns, and catalogs promised the consumer would look like their favorite star.

Warner Brothers maintained an impressive stable of designers, notably John Orry-Kelly, who made Bette Davis chic for *Fashions of 1934*. Walter Plunkett at RKO

ANNA MAY WONG AND THE CHEONGSAM

Born in California, Anna May Wong (1905–1961) had her first film role at fourteen. Her Chinese heritage provided an entrée into the film industry but also proved to be her greatest barrier to true stardom. Wong appeared in a number of successful films including *Daughter of the Dragon* (1931) and *Shanghai Express* (1932). The characters she played were typically one of two stereotypes: betrayed Butterfly or sinister Dragon Lady. In either case, she was doomed to die at the end of the film. For most of her forty-year career, the film industry prohibited "interracial" love scenes and Wong never received an on-screen kiss from a white actor. She often lost leading roles to Caucasian actresses in "yellow face."

Wong was considered one of the best-dressed women in the world but her style was unconventional, reflecting her Chinese heritage and Western lifestyle. Wong navigated between current fashions and Chinese tradition, amassing an impressive collection of Chinese clothes. Publicity photos showed her in outfits ranging from bathing suits to cheongsams. Traditionally a loose-fitting robe, the cheongsam (or *qipao*) became fitted and sleek in versions favored by fashionable women in Shanghai. The cheongsam transferred easily to Western taste and Wong's association with the style helped popularize the dress as a staple. Wong's image in the 1930s was reinforced by Travis Banton's interpretation of the cheongsam for *Limehouse Blues* (1934), which covered Wong in a spangled dragon.

Wong was said to have the most beautiful hands in Hollywood, and her hairstyle, with straight-cut bangs, was widely imitated. She can be considered the first fashion icon of Asian descent and opened the door to more inclusive standards. Anna May Wong made Asian beauty glamorous.

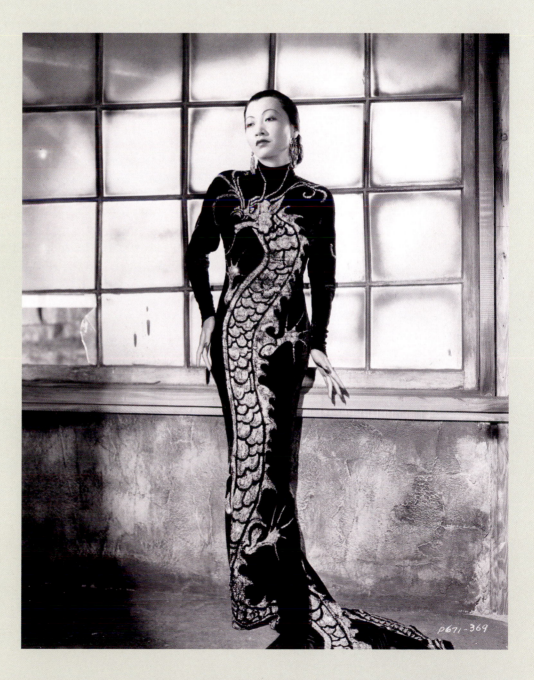

Anna May Wong, costumed by Travis Banton in a dragon-decorated adaptation of the cheongsam, for the film *Limehouse Blues* (1934).

preferred designing period films: his inaccurate but influential 19th-century costumes for *Gone With the Wind* (1939) inspired designer collections.

Travis Banton, the lead designer at Paramount, dressed Claudette Colbert, Marlene Dietrich, Carole Lombard, Mae West, and Anna May Wong. His costumes for Colbert's interpretations of Egypt in *Cleopatra* (1934) featured the queen of the Nile in bias-cut lamé gowns. Among Banton's designs for Dietrich was the white, masculine-tailored formal wear for *Blonde Venus* (1932). The costume was scandalous, but Dietrich was also known for wearing trousers in her real life. Banton also guided the early career of Edith Head (1897–1981), who joined Paramount in 1924 as an assistant. Head's career grew quickly, aided by the departure of Banton, and she achieved widespread recognition for Dorothy Lamour's costumes in *The Jungle Princess*.

The most influential Hollywood costume designer was Gilbert Adrian at MGM, often billed simply as Adrian. For *Dinner at Eight* (1934) he dressed Jean Harlow, the "Blonde Bombshell," in white bias-cut charmeuse gowns that derived inspiration from Vionnet and Augustabernard. Harlow's gowns were so sleek to her body that she wore no underwear, and frequently was not able to sit down between takes; rather, she reclined on specially created "slant boards." Joan Crawford's Adrian wardrobe was widely copied, from films such as *Grand Hotel* (1932) and *The Bride Wore Red* (1937). Among her costumes for *Letty Lynton* (1932) was a white organza dress with puffy and ruffled sleeves that exemplified turn-of-the-century inspiration. The dress was widely copied and sold in retail stores; Macy's in particular reportedly sold thousands. Paper patterns allowed home sewers to make their own. Other dresses that merely featured frilly sleeve details were still dubbed "Letty Lynton Style." Adrian's use of shoulder emphasis on Crawford anticipated the wider shoulder of the 1940s. Greta Garbo was glamorized by Adrian in *Inspiration* (1931), and he created an outrageous orientalist wardrobe for her in *Mata Hari* (1931). *The Women* (1939), starring Crawford and Norma Shearer, was perhaps the pinnacle of Hollywood fashion. The cast was decked out in fabulous Adrian gowns,

Below left Actress Jean Harlow wears one of the stunning white bias-cut gowns created for her by designer Gilbert Adrian, here in the film *Dinner at Eight.*

Below right Adrian was also known for his designs for Joan Crawford, shown here in the 1932 film *Letty Lynton.* This dress, dubbed the "Letty Lynton" dress, was one of the most copied garments of the decade, selling thousands of copies at Macy's alone. The decorated puffed sleeves were of particular influence to fashion.

and though primarily shot in black and white, the film included a Technicolor fashion show sequence.

Despite the depth of design talent in Hollywood, several studios actively courted French fashion houses. For example, the 1938 film *Artists and Models Abroad*, while credited to Edith Head at Paramount, also listed contributions from Alix, Lanvin, Lelong, Paquin, Patou, Rouff, Schiaparelli, and Worth.

Vernacular Fashion

Despite the background of economic distress, keeping up with fashion was a concern for all but the poorest people and being attractively dressed was important for maintaining respectability. Retailers provided many ways for the mainstream public to dress fashionably, offering "smart but thrifty" styles and promoting versatile separates. A trickle-down system was in place as average citizens aspired to high fashion. Authorized copies of Paris originals occupied a niche at the high end of retail. Large stores and mail-order houses featured celebrity endorsements and references to name designers. Sears sold "Autograph Fashions" – dresses, separates, and accessories labeled with the names of stars including Fay Wray, Loretta Young, and Claudette Colbert. Other pieces made reference to Paris fashion, such as "Vionnet Drape" dresses of 1938.

Mainstream clothes kept up with changes of silhouette and detail, but in less luxurious fabrics (such as rayon instead of silk) and many dresses were washable, eliminating dry-cleaning costs. Most women, even those working in manual jobs, continued to wear dresses (except for hard physical labor). Home sewing provided an option for less expensive fashion. Many major designers worked with pattern companies to make versions of their designs available. The phenomenon of "finish at home" and "semi-made" dresses, including those available through Sears, offered mainstream customers slightly more custom-made clothing than normal retail goods.

Below left An example of the widespread, mainstream impact of the Letty Lynton dress can be seen here.

Below right Two women in cleaning smocks, c. 1935. While glamour was exalted in the media, everyday wear for most women was simpler and made of practical materials, yet showed elements of the fashionable silhouette.

DOROTHY LAMOUR AND THE SARONG

Hollywood offered a wave of exotic island and jungle dramas including *King Kong*, *The Most Dangerous Game*, and *Tarzan*. *The Jungle Princess* (1936) launched the career of American actress Dorothy Lamour (1914–1996). The white, New Orleans-born Lamour played "Ulah," a Malaysian woman living in the jungle with her pet tiger. The gorgeous Lamour was clad in strapless wrapped dresses that costume designer Edith Head based on the indigenous garment of maritime Southeast Asia, the *sarung*. A length of fabric, sometimes sewn into a tube and typically batik-dyed, the traditional *sarung* usually wrapped around the body as a skirt. The word literally means "sheath" in the Malay and Indonesian languages and the garment is usually called "sarong" in English. In *The Hurricane* (1937) Lamour portrayed a Polynesian island princess, once again costumed by Head. The sarong-style dresses in these two films caused a sensation, and were an important step in both Head's and Lamour's careers. Southeast Asian inspirations were already creeping into fashion. *Vogue* observed as early as January 1933 (with erroneous geography), "Java is influencing our shores – some of the new beach clothes are of materials similar to the glamorous stuff Bali natives wear," noting tied-on wrap skirts and simple rectangular tops with rope drawstrings. But such styles were encouraged further by the popularity of Lamour's films. Sarong skirts, typically in large-scale tropical floral prints, became resort wear and leisurewear staples for Western women, often worn over swimsuits poolside; some evening designs of the period also reflected the wrapped style. Several more "sarong films" followed for Dorothy Lamour, culminating in her 1952 appearance in *Road to Bali*, and earning her the nickname "Sarong Queen."

Hair and Beauty

Although women cut back on fashion expenses, hairstyling and cosmetics remained important. *Vogue* magazine counseled, "when you can't go to a party in a new dress, you do your hair in a new way." Products were available at all price levels, so everyone could enjoy a new lipstick, fragrance, or hairstyle. Maybelline cake mascara and Tangee lipstick offered glamour at low cost. Cosmetic and fragrance advertisements consistently promised escape and transformation. A 1932 advertisement for Lelong's Murmure declared, "feel at your best, or perhaps a bit above it ... just the thing for a year like this." Eyeshadow (some with an iridescent effect) joined brow pencil, mascara, and eyeliner in many beauty kits. But *Vogue* warned that "you can go wrong-er with your eye make-up than you can with any other thing you put on your face!" and urged readers to apply eye make-up first before making their rouge and lipstick decisions. Face powder and foundation were so accepted that cosmetic companies developed products to prime the face for application of foundation. Cosmetic surgery procedures continued to develop and facelifts became more common. Opera star Nellie Melba and society decorator Elsie de Wolfe were early facelift recipients.

For most of the decade, hair was worn close to the head in waves that ranged from softly brushed back to tight and lacquered. The Frederics Vita-Tonic Process, one of many permanent wave solutions, was endorsed by glamorous actresses including Constance Cummings and Jean Harlow. With movie stars known for their striking hair color, hair dye became less covert. Dyeing the hair platinum blonde was particularly popular, a look especially inspired by Jean Harlow. Salons advertised hair coloring by many different manufacturers. Nail polish continued to be popular; one fashionable manicure style left the "moon" and tips white with a swipe of vivid color only in the center. Inexpensive brands such as Cutex and Lady Lillian offered nail polish in shades to match the wearer's complexion or her outfit.

More overt advertising of feminine hygiene products brought them into the realm of beauty aids. While sanitary pads had been commercially available at least since the 1890s, listed among the lingerie in mail-order and store catalogs, the new advertisements for Kotex appeared in fashion magazines and presented the product as an innovation that could help women participate fully in an active, and fashionable, life.

Menswear

Following the playful, collegiate extremes of the 1920s, menswear became sleeker and more shaped, influenced by developing technologies as well as by celebrities such as film stars, musicians, and sports figures. Fashionable menswear projected a classic look with references to English sportswear. The silhouette for tailored clothing featured jackets with a slightly high waist and broad shoulders; double-breasted styles were popular. Trousers were also high-waisted, with pleats in front. Trouser legs were frequently wide and often featured cuffs. Formal wear was dominated by the dark evening tuxedo; for warm nights and resort areas, the white dinner jacket worn with dark trousers was increasingly popular. Topcoats adhered to a wide-shouldered silhouette and trench coats remained popular as outerwear. Accessories followed established categories from previous decades. Neckties were frequently striped and geometric, often unlined.

Entertainers exerted significant influence on menswear. Some men emulated idiosyncratic styles such as the tie-as-belt worn by Fred Astaire, and Duke Ellington's silk suits. While film studios spent freely on actresses' gowns, male stars were often expected to provide clothes from their personal wardrobes. Actors such as Cary Grant, James Stewart, and Gary Cooper were identified with specific menswear styles. Gangster films recorded the exaggerated look of notorious figures such as Chicago mobster Al Capone: boldly striped double-breasted suits with big shoulders, silk shirts, short wide ties, and angled fedoras.

Below A fashionable couple epitomizes the crisp and sophisticated style of the decade.

Bottom Actor James Stewart in 1935. His sporty but elegant separates demonstrate the wide reach of the Duke of Windsor's style.

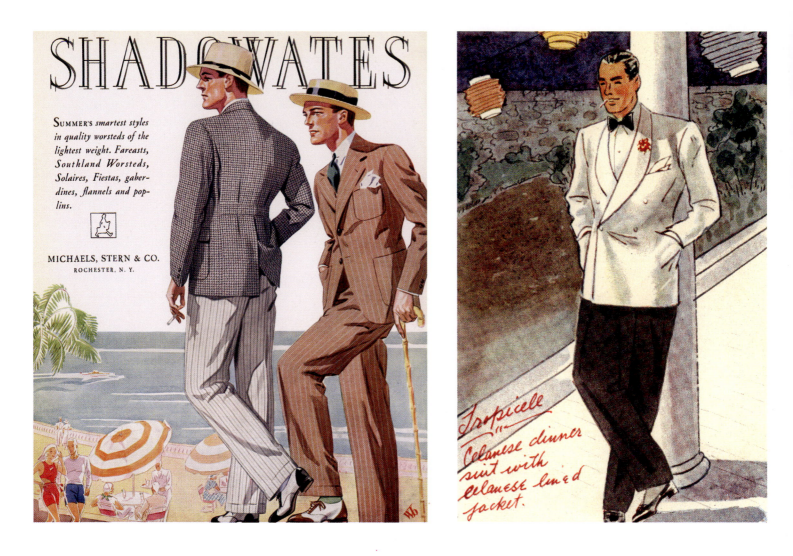

SHADOWATES

SUMMER'S *smartest styles
in quality worsteds of the
lightest weight. Fareasts,
Southland Worsteds,
Solaires, Fiestas, gaber-
dines, flannels and pop-
lins.*

MICHAELS, STERN & CO.
ROCHESTER, N. Y.

Tropicale
*Celanese dinner
suit with
celanese lined
jacket.*

Above left Resort wear for men as advertised in *Apparel Arts*, summer 1932, reflects the continued influence of styles from earlier decades, with such details as the back belt on the sport coat.

Above right White, cream, and pastel dinner jackets enjoyed significant popularity, as seen in this 1934 *Apparel Arts* illustration.

Opposite top A men's locker room at a golf club was a typical scenario to advertise men's underwear. Singlets, often worn with yoked boxer shorts, were common offerings from the Mansco brand.

Opposite bottom A variety of outfits for boys are playfully illustrated in *Apparel Arts*, 1935.

A well-groomed look was fashionable. Hair was sharply parted or slicked back. Most men were clean-shaven, striving for a polished look, although thin mustaches, such as those worn by Clark Gable and William Powell, were also fashionable. After Gable appeared without an undershirt in *It Happened One Night* (1934), sales of men's undershirts allegedly dropped. While it is impossible to pinpoint Gable's true effect on undershirts, clothing sales fluctuated during the decade, and the menswear industry felt pressure from customers who questioned the necessity of certain items of clothing – a phenomenon dubbed "Go-withoutism" in the apparel trade press – including undershirts, sock garters, and hats. While "going without" could be read as a symptom of economic hardship, changing attitudes were also important. American underwear manufacturer Coopers introduced a revolutionary style in 1935; their Jockey brief provided support and comfort with a Y-shaped fly and snug fit.

During the summer of 1932, many men in Britain and North America adopted the European custom of swimming shirtless. Soon the style was accepted in Palm Beach, and became widespread. Recognizing the trend, in 1934 Jantzen offered "The Topper," a bathing suit that connected top and trunks with a zipper at the waistline. Resort wear emerged as an important category, ranging from light-colored linen suits for more elite areas to informal sailor-style jerseys and knit polo shirts. Tennis star René Lacoste introduced knit shirts with his crocodile logo in 1933. For skiing, men wore knickers or loose pants (gathered at the ankle) with colorful sweaters and a variety of jackets, some buttoned or zip-front in wool, others with military details or fuller anorak styles. The Champion company introduced a hooded sweatshirt for workwear that was later adopted for sports. Easy-care properties and reliable fabric

finishes were emphasized. "Quick dry Celanese" was used for pullovers, swim trunks, athletic shirts, and underwear. Lastex, added to many garments, was especially important to socks. Talon mounted an aggressive advertising campaign to convince men the zipper fly was better than buttons.

The Duke of Windsor was responsible for setting many menswear styles. Working with his London tailor, Frederick Scholte, the duke popularized styles such as: ink blue for evening formal wear; less constructed but strong-shouldered "English Drape" suits; trouser cuffs; and even zippered flies. Many casual styles were also associated with him including Fair Isle knits, tartan, bold pattern combinations, and extremely baggy plus-fours that he called "plus-twenties." He also favored wide-spread shirt collars, and thick tie knots. The duke's daring combinations were widely imitated. Checks, tweeds, and windowpane plaids were popular for suits. Men wore colorful combinations and mixed assertive patterns freely, even adopting fancy vests in bright colors and surprising textures.

Children's Fashion

As with women's fashion and menswear, one of the major factors in children's fashion was the influence of celebrities. Child star Shirley Temple, one of Hollywood's top earners, endorsed a complete wardrobe for girls available through Sears. The clothes ranged from day dresses in petite prints to an all-wool snowsuit and were based on her film costumes. Freddie Bartholomew, the popular child star of 1937's *Captains Courageous*, endorsed a line of sportswear for boys. The young English princesses Elizabeth and Margaret were frequently photographed on special occasions, but also in play clothes. They were usually dressed in identical outfits, and their side-parted hair, smocked dresses, pleated skirts, and double-breasted coats with matching hats were widely imitated.

Above Pajamas for girls, shown in *La Mode Enfantine*, a Parisian fashion magazine for childrenswear.

Right La Mode Enfantine offers a variety of daywear options for girls of several ages.

Denim jeans were available for children and adolescents, and were acceptable for play and chores. Girls of young school age wore dresses with no waistlines and similarly styled jumpers over printed blouses with round collars or jewel necklines. Skirts often had pleats and godets and were worn with sweaters or tucked-in blouses. Plaid was very fashionable and some dresses played the diagonal lines of bias-cut skirts against the straight grain of the bodice. For special occasions, similar styles were worn in more delicate fabrics, often with scalloped hems and embroidered details. Sailor styles for boys and girls were still popular. Middy tops and double-breasted jackets in a red, white, and blue palette were combined with pleated skirts for girls, or shorts for boys. Young boys were dressed in suits with short pants, often in wool tweed or corduroy for winter or cotton twill for summer. For teenagers, influence from adult styles was especially notable and rules about proper dress applied. Teenage girls' dresses showed smooth waists and hips, with fluttery neck and shoulder details including scarves, capelet sleeves, and bows. A diagonal emphasis was achieved with crossed scarves and off-center buttoning. Coats often featured fur collars. Fashion for teenage boys included formal wear, usually tuxedo-style dinner jackets.

The preoccupation with a smooth figure reached even into the children's market. *Vogue* urged readers in 1937 to consider a girdle for girls as young as nine, as soon as they start to develop a "tummy." In general, underwear for girls was a bit less geometric than before and lots of pink was used for undershirts, panties, slips, and nightgowns. Socks for children of both sexes reached the knee, or just below, often in white but also ribbed with Fair Isle bands. Teenage girls wore stockings. The general fashion for knit and crochet hats was especially appropriate for children, and little berets and brimmed styles were popular for girls. Boys wore soft caps. Shoes for children included lace-up ankle boots for both boys and girls, brogues for boys, and Mary Janes for girls.

The End of the Decade

The 1939 World's Fair in New York, "The World of Tomorrow," showcased technologies including television, fluorescent lighting, color photography, air conditioning, and nylon. Connecting fashion with the fair, *Vogue* commissioned outlandish futuristic ensembles created by leading industrial designers. The fair celebrated Surrealism, including a fanciful installation by Salvador Dalí. But the confidence expressed at the fair did not reflect the world at large. Although the United States looked to an optimistic future, dramatic events in Europe and Asia brought uncertainty to daily life. Germany invaded Austria, Poland, and Czechoslovakia; Italy invaded Albania; Japan continued to grow its foothold in China. The "Pact of Steel" between Italy and Germany promised mutual defense and other nations watched as the lines of confrontation were delineated. In September 1939 Great Britain and France declared war on Germany.

Men throughout the world hung their fashionable clothes in the closet, and put on uniforms. Paris houses were showing the last collections the outside world would see for several years; wary of the risk, many American buyers did not attend. Some designers showed unabashedly sentimental designs, dressing women as romantic heroines in the face of coming dangers. But while some clung to obsolete visions of a romantic past, other women's fashions mirrored the look of uniforms. Skirts were shorter and straighter, and shoulders broadened, as tailored silhouettes became more widespread. The shape of the early 1940s was already in place.

French periodical *Idées Sports* featured these ensembles for summer and autumn 1939, clearly indicating the shape of fashion in the coming years.

Chapter 7

The 1940s

War and Recovery

The 1940s present a study in contrast: a contrast between war and peace, and between the patriotic austerity of the war years and the joyful opulence of the post-war period. Within these ten years, fashion offered opposing images of women – exemplified by masculine "Utility" fashions and the buoyant femininity of the "New Look." But even during wartime the importance of appearance was stressed, as in Elizabeth Arden's cosmetic advertisements declaring "Beauty marches on." As significant numbers of men throughout the world were involved in the war, they, too, experienced the division, going into uniforms and then back to civilian clothes by decade's end. The restrictions of World War II had an impact on many aspects of fashion, limiting the usual evolution of styles. However, the war's end restored much of the fashion system to its pre-war order.

Social and Economic Background

By 1940, war was underway and involved two opposing forces. The Axis Powers consisted of Germany, Italy, and Japan, led respectively by Adolf Hitler, Benito

Opposite Two coats by Marcel Rochas worn with striking millinery, illustrated by Pierre Mourgue in 1943, are typical of fashion in occupied Paris, where despite wartime deprivations a number of couture houses managed to remain open.

Right British singer Vera Lynn, known as "The Forces' Sweetheart," celebrates the opening of a YMCA tea car in London in June 1942 that served refreshments to military personnel.

Mussolini, and Emperor Hirohito. After the Japanese attack on Pearl Harbor, on December 7, 1941, the United States entered the conflict, joining what came to be known as the Allied nations. These comprised France, Great Britain and the Commonwealth nations, the Union of Soviet Socialist Republics, and China. Resistance movements in occupied countries also joined the fight against the Axis Powers. Concentration camps in Germany, Austria, Poland, and other areas of Europe were part of the German strategy of exterminating Jews and other minority groups, including homosexuals, Jehovah's Witnesses and European Roma (Gypsies). Concentration camps were also used in other parts of the world; Japan held prisoners in China, Java, and Sumatra. Japanese Americans were forcibly interned in camps in the western United States, while people of German ancestry or origin were interned in Great Britain and Canada. Major battles were fought in Europe, Asia, and North Africa. The war in Europe ended with V-E Day on May 8, 1945. On September 2, after the US bombing of Hiroshima and Nagasaki, Japan surrendered, an event known as V-J Day or Victory in the Pacific Day.

Civilian involvement in the war was significant. Conscription meant that millions of families had brothers, sons, husbands, and fathers in the armed services. Governments expected civilians to support troops by buying war bonds and conserving and recycling materials. Even before it joined the war, the United States was called upon to supply its allies; the economic activity generated by this wartime production helped end the Depression. Many women saw their roles change as some joined female branches of the military or worked in jobs related to military production. Some women also filled civilian jobs left vacant by men who were serving in the armed forces.

In the aftermath of the war, the map of the world was again redrawn, with the help of the newly chartered United Nations. Germany was divided, its eastern section controlled by the Soviet Union, emblematic of the post-war divide between capitalism and communism. Physical rebuilding was accompanied by economic recovery. Damage to infrastructure and agriculture was especially severe in Europe, and displaced peoples struggled to return to their homelands. Of the major powers, the United States and Canada, which had not been the site of battles, had the most rapid recovery. From 1947 to 1951, the US Marshall Plan aided European nations with food, fuel, and machinery.

The Arts

Surrealism continued, frequently with a darker tone, and remained particularly influential on fashion photography and illustration. Realist styles appealed to another part of the art market, exemplified by the American scenes of Edward Hopper, Andrew Wyeth, and self-taught painter "Grandma" Moses. In New York, a group of artists including Mark Rothko, Adolph Gottlieb, and Jackson Pollock experimented with abstraction influenced by Jungian psychology, the beginnings of Abstract Expressionism. During the first half of the decade, the Streamline style continued to influence the design of furniture, automobiles, and other products. Major architectural projects were delayed because of the war. The art deco style declined in architecture, replaced by the simpler, more rectilinear International Style. In 1944 fashion historian Bernard Rudofsky curated *Are Clothes Modern?* at the Museum of Modern Art, the museum's first exhibition of fashion.

Current events provided compelling material for literature, stage, and screen, including Arthur Koestler's *Darkness at Noon* (1940), a novel about the dangers of dictatorship, and Ernest Hemingway's *For Whom the Bell Tolls* (1940), set during the Spanish Civil War. Lillian Hellman's timely play *Watch on the Rhine* premiered in 1941 and a film version soon followed. *Mrs. Miniver* (1942) and *Casablanca* (1942) offered other views of the war. Even Disney's animated feature *Fantasia* (1940) included a sequence that alluded to the struggle between good and evil, and the studio's Oscar-winning cartoon short *Der Fuehrer's Face* (1943), starring Donald Duck, lampooned

Lauren Bacall and Humphrey Bogart in *The Big Sleep* (1946).

FILM NOIR

The film noir aesthetic of the 1940s made a lasting impact on visual culture. The term "film noir" was coined by French film critics in the post-war period to describe dark-themed thrillers produced by American studios starting around 1940. Often based on popular crime stories, sometimes called "hard-boiled fiction" or "pulp fiction," movies such as *Double Indemnity* (1944) and *Murder, My Sweet* (1944) explored the dark underside of the American dream. In striking cinematography influenced by German Expressionism, the angles and shadows of the modern city combined with the hard lines of contemporary fashion to underscore a dark view of contemporary life.

Themes of betrayal, violence, and sexual obsession were central to many of the films and the female characters were costumed to reflect their deadly allure, from menswear-inspired daywear to figure-molding evening dresses. The femmes fatales of films such as *The Glass Key* (1942) and *The Woman in the Window* (1944) presented wicked counterparts of the strong women of wartime – using their beauty to ensnare unsuspecting men. One of the leading ladies of film noir, Barbara Stanwyck embodied the hard look with a wardrobe of sharp-shouldered suits and coats, dark lipstick, and lacquered blonde hair.

The look of film noir was influential beyond the movie screen. Fashion photography showed influence from the style. During the heyday of film noir, fashion images used deeply shadowed interiors, lit through venetian blinds, to convey both glamour and mystery. Film noir style continues to inspire fashion designers, stylists, and photographers into the 21st century.

Nazi propaganda. Alfred Hitchcock directed the war-themed *Foreign Correspondent* and the suspenseful *Rebecca*, both in 1940. Film noir thrillers presented dark dramas, reflecting the paranoia of the period. In the post-war years, the use of color continued to propel film design, as seen in *Black Narcissus* (1947), *The Red Shoes* (1948), and *The Pirate* (1948). Other important films included *The Best Years of our Lives* (1946) and *Gentleman's Agreement* (1947). In a turn away from their war-focused offerings such as *Nine Men* (1943), Britain's Ealing Studios produced comedy features such as 1949's *Kind Hearts and Coronets*.

Popular music was dominated by big band swing. The careers of vocalists Ella Fitzgerald, Vera Lynn, Bing Crosby, Frank Sinatra, and others blossomed during the decade. In addition to live performances, record sales were increasingly important to their success. Many performers were called upon to entertain the armed forces throughout the world. On the Broadway stage, two works with musical scores by Richard Rodgers were notable. *Pal Joey* (1940), with lyrics by Lorenz Hart, captured the sardonic spirit of the late Depression years. But during the peak of the war in 1943, Rodgers, working with lyricist Oscar Hammerstein II, created *Oklahoma*. The folksy story of farmers and cowboys echoed the patriotic mood of the country and *Oklahoma* was awarded a special Pulitzer Prize in 1944. The same year Betty Comden, Adolph Green, and Leonard Bernstein created *On The Town*, a story about three sailors on shore leave in New York City. The Tony Awards, honoring excellence in the American theater, were established in 1947; Arthur Miller's drama *Death of a Salesman* (1949) won a Tony in 1949. Two outstanding productions, *Mister Roberts* (1948) and *South Pacific* (1949), demonstrated the continued appeal of wartime stories.

American composer Aaron Copland also wrote music that reflected patriotic themes. His *Fanfare for the Common Man* (1942) was dedicated to the American soldier, and was inspired by a speech from Vice President Henry Wallace. Copland's ballets *Rodeo* (1942), choreographed by Agnes de Mille, and *Appalachian Spring* (1944), choreographed by Martha Graham, reflected regionalist subjects. Songs of the times – both "art song" and popular – often used the war as subject matter. French composer Francis Poulenc set to music Louis Aragon's poem *Fêtes Galantes*, which described Parisians fleeing the approaching Nazi troops. Songs ranging from the Andrews Sisters' upbeat "Boogie Woogie Bugle Boy" to Vera Lynn's poignant "The White Cliffs of Dover" carried the wartime themes into popular music.

Fashion Media

While some of the magazines' early response to the war verged on frivolous – such as "Blackouts bring out white accessories"[1] – fashion magazines helped their readers adjust to changing times. Magazines presented fashion as an antidote to the horror of war, and a necessary part of maintaining morale. Under the direction of longtime editor Edna Woolman Chase, American *Vogue* added features on canned foods and advised its readers to get involved with the war effort. The war provided illustrators with new inspiration for imagery, and offered magazines new editorial content and advertisements. War-themed covers appeared on all major magazines with striking graphics and patriotic colors.

Lee Miller (already known as a fashion model) emerged as an important photographer, and Audrey Withers, the editor of British *Vogue*, was one of the first to recognize Miller's talent. Miller's shocking photos of the war's devastation, including images of the liberation of the Buchenwald concentration camp, were published in both American and British editions. The work of Toni Frissell was also significant to the diffusion of war images in fashion periodicals, featuring the Red Cross and the Women's Army Corps. Established photographers Erwin Blumenfeld, John Rawlings, and Louise Dahl-Wolfe continued to be important figures in fashion media. New talents in photography included Irving Penn and Richard Avedon. Illustrators René Gruau, Jacques Demachy, Eric, and Vertès created dramatic fashion images. Lisa Fonssagrives represented a new generation of fashion "models" (a term that began to

An editorial from *Harper's Bazaar*, April 1943, shows the cinematic influence of film noir on fashion photography.

replace "mannequin" in English-language publications) who enjoyed name recognition with the fashion-conscious public.

Many magazines interrupted publication during the decade. French *Vogue* did not publish for some time during the war. The British edition offered less frequent issues. *L'Art et la Mode*, a French magazine that offered extensive couture coverage, reduced the number and size of its issues and added captions in German. September 1944 saw the debut of *Seventeen*, the first American magazine aimed at high school girls, and Hearst's *Junior Bazaar* targeted young women, an important emerging market.

At the end of the war, magazines appealed to their readers to rediscover their femininity. In January 1946 *Vogue* declared, "Back on the pedestals, ladies" and "Fashions are here to help women remember their sex." The return to romance influenced cover design. In contrast to wartime images of stoic women, fashion magazines alluded to the presence of men. A *Vogue* cover from March 1, 1948 with a photograph by Irving Penn showed an elegantly dressed woman smiling into a mirror, with a man's accessories on the edge of her dressing table. The issue featured "Fashions chosen with a man in mind." After the war, *L'Officiel* featured several cover illustrations of well-dressed couples, emphasizing post-war "togetherness."

Fashion and Society

Many society women engaged in war relief work preparing medical supplies, sewing, and knitting for soldiers, and raising money for charities. American socialites Mrs. Harrison Williams and Mrs. Ector Munn organized *Paris Openings*, a 1940 exhibition at Wanamaker's in New York to benefit the Colis de Trianon, a charity headed by the Duchess of Windsor and Lady Mendl. The show featured beautiful couture evening dresses from the wardrobes of the organizers and their friends, and celebrated the frivolity of pre-war life and the artistry of French couture. The Victory Debutante Cotillion and Ball on December 21, 1942 highlighted the New York social season. For this group presentation of debutantes at the Ritz-Carlton, families introducing their daughters were asked to purchase war bonds instead of hosting private parties. The patriotic decor mixed holiday greenery with flags of the United Nations, and debutantes, dressed in white and silver, danced with their uniformed escorts to popular songs (including Frank Loesser's "Praise the Lord and Pass the Ammunition").

The War and Fashion

Fashion, on its many fronts, was subject to the problems and priorities of wartime. Some designers were drafted into the military. Others designed uniforms for branches of the armed services. German forces occupied Paris from June 1940 to August 1944. The normal flow of fashion – from Paris to the rest of the world – was disrupted. Because of the interruption in communications and trade between North America and Europe, the three largest fashion centers – Paris, London, and New York – created for their own markets. As a result, the American fashion industry experienced a period of unprecedented development and expansion.

On each front, fashion served as propaganda and expressed nationalism, and civilians felt the impact on their wardrobes. As resources were directed to the war

effort, the governments in North America and Britain regulated the production and consumption of clothing. Equipping armies required enormous resources; textiles were essential for uniforms, tents, parachutes, and other supplies, limiting the amounts available for civilians. Wool was especially in demand, but cotton, linen, and silk were also restricted. Dyes were not as plentiful, limiting the color range of materials. White fabric and leather were not as bright because bleaching agents were in short supply. Copper, brass, and tin – used for costume jewelry and accessories – were diverted to war production.

Perhaps the most dramatic impact was felt in women's hosiery. In France, women made gaiters to match their outfits. As early as September 1941 (even before the United States entered the war), the American government embargoed Japanese silk, causing hoarding of silk stockings. In response, many stores limited the number of pairs sold to each customer. At that point, nylon accounted for about 25 per cent of stocking sales and was expected to be available indefinitely. In October 1942 nylon was in short supply. A price ceiling was placed on nylon stockings and they were virtually unobtainable by 1943. The stocking shortage even inspired a popular song, "When the Nylons Bloom Again," by Fats Waller and George Marion Jr. Women everywhere had to wear stockings made of wool, cotton, or rayon, or apply make-up to their legs.

Paris Fashion under the German Occupation

By 1941 clothing restrictions were in place in France, limiting consumer purchases and the amount of fabric that could be used. However, the French couture industry was affected differently. At the beginning of the decade, French couturiers designed for their own domestic market, creating pieces that responded to the war. Air raids, known as *alertes* in French, inspired practical clothes and accessories. Creed offered an "*alerte* plaid" shawl with big pockets. Molyneux showed black silk pajama pants with a hooded jacket and "*bleu alerte*" sash. Piguet and Schiaparelli designed

Above left The short fur coat, elaborate hat, and platform shoes of this woman in occupied Paris contrast with the more practical clothing of the woman in the background.

Above right Rebellious French youth known as "Zazous" sported loud suit styles, exaggerated accessories, and sunglasses. Photo by Albert Harlingue, 1944.

jumpsuits for bomb shelter dressing. Coats and jackets with hoods and large pockets became fashionable. French women adopted an everyday look of tweed suits worn with low-heeled leather shoes and snoods or berets. For their many clients forced to ride bicycles because of gas rationing, Piguet and Balenciaga designed culottes hidden under skirts. Hermès offered zippered belts to conceal valuables and shoulder bags that resembled hunting pouches. When electricity was unreliable, French hairdresser Gervais powered his hair dryers with bicyclists pedaling in the basement, while some women took to their own bicycles using fresh air to dry and set their hair.

In early 1940, some couturiers presented fashion shows in Amsterdam or participated in trade fairs in Spain, one of the few European countries not involved in the war. The French fashion press was filled with patriotic appeals to consumers: *L'Art et la Mode* declared, "Supporting luxury industries is the duty of all French citizens."[2] With the German occupation of Paris, the situation became complicated. Designers and workers were drafted and high-quality materials were not available. The couture clientele changed as international socialites were replaced by entertainers, the wives and mistresses of Nazi officers, and wealthy collaborators. Some French women were still able to buy, but because of rationing, they had to receive permission from the Germans to purchase from designers.[3] Many couture houses stayed open, including Lelong, Piguet, Patou, Lanvin, Ricci, Worth and Rochas, most with reduced work forces. Balenciaga and Molyneux were shut down by the Germans. After she showed a *tricolore* collection flaunting French patriotism, Alix (now using the name Madame Grès for her business) was closed as well, but reopened later. Schiaparelli fled to the United States before the occupation but her house remained open. Chanel closed her couture business but kept her boutique open and lived in the Ritz with her Nazi officer lover during the war.

Recognizing the economic and cultural value of French couture, Hitler wanted to move the entire industry to Berlin or Vienna, a plan that horrified the couturiers. Lucien Lelong, the president of the Chambre Syndicale de la Haute Couture Parisienne, negotiated with the Germans and managed to reach an agreement whereby the houses remained open in Paris (or reopened if they had closed) and continued to produce luxury clothing, most of which outfitted German women. The number of models in each collection was limited by the Germans. Consequently, from 1940 to 1944 Parisian couture worked in isolation, its creations unpublicized even in the rest of France.

Styles evolved from the practicality of the early decade as the visions of the designers were reasserted. Working from the romantic styles of the late 1930s, designers offered dresses with defined waists, and full skirts and sleeves. While some of the pieces were executed in low-quality fabrics, femininity and decoration were emphasized. Even average Parisian women strove to maintain a fancy, feminine image in the face of hardship. Hats were particularly extravagant, as milliners made imaginative use of whatever materials were available. When Paris was liberated in 1944, photographs of dressed-up Parisiennes were circulated outside the city. In Britain and the United States, people were shocked at the frivolity of French fashion. It was still wartime, and accusations were made that the fashion industry had collaborated with the Nazis.

Enthusiasts of American swing music (which the German occupiers had forbidden), Parisian "Zazous" represented a rebellious youth culture. Zazou men wore long jackets, pants wide at the top and tight at the bottom rolled up above the ankle, bright socks, and large sunglasses – day and night. Their female companions wore jackets with extremely wide shoulders and flippy skirts. Zazous of both sexes had elaborately styled hair, with high rolls in front.

Fashion in Fascist Italy

During his rise to power, Mussolini incorporated fashion into his political agenda, attempting to develop a truly Italian style. Italians were urged to purchase clothing made in Italy. The attempt to purge Italian fashion of foreign influences even led to the publication of a "dictionary" of fashion that suggested Italian equivalents for French words and phrases.[4] The regime encouraged uniforms for various occupations and glorified traditional regional clothing. Italy had a small high fashion industry, but Italian designers were challenged by material shortages. These were especially severe in the prestigious accessories market, where restrictions on leather forced designers such as Salvatore Ferragamo and Guccio Gucci to create pieces in alternative materials including cork, plastics, and fabric. Nonetheless, Fontana, one of the most important fashion houses of Italy, developed during this period. The three Fontana sisters, Zoe, Micol, and Giovanna, worked in the family dressmaking business in Traversetolo, near Parma, until the mid-1930s. They moved to Rome, and in 1943 established their fashion house.

Fashion in Nazi Germany

While the Nazi regime obviously appreciated the French fashion industry, it also tried to forge a German style. One important mechanism was the Deutsches Mode-Institut, of which Magda Goebbels, the wife of Hitler's Minister of Propaganda, was appointed the first director. In keeping with the focus on German history and tradition, women were urged to rediscover folk styles such as dirndl skirts and embroidered blouses, and to pursue knitting and other handicrafts. Hearty, athletic models were presented as examples of wholesome womanhood – a reaction to the slender, sophisticated Parisian beauty standard that had dominated since the 1920s. The heroic medieval tales depicted in Richard Wagner's operas also provided fashion inspiration. Germany received the bounty of French textile mills and also had a well-developed textile industry of its own, so did not experience the material constraints of other countries during most of the war years.

A photo by Sonja Georgi of a young woman posing outdoors in a suit inspired by traditional dress appeared in *Die Dame* in 1940.

Three young women model Utility dresses from the British Birketex label in June 1943. Each dress has short sleeves, minimal shaping and restrained details.

Rationing and Utility in Britain

Early responses to the war in Britain included "siren suits" – jumpsuits that could be pulled on quickly during air raids.[5] In June 1941 clothing rationing began, based on coupons. In the first year of the program, every adult was allotted sixty-six coupons. The coupons were not used as cash, but were intended to control the purchase of clothing, shoes, and household textiles. For example, seven coupons were needed to obtain a dress and fourteen for a coat. Because of the severity of shortages, the annual coupon allotment was reduced each year until 1945, when it was down to twenty-four coupons per person. Certain items were exempt, including second-hand clothes and work clothing. Supplies for home sewing were also exempt and the government encouraged conservation through the "Make Do and Mend" campaign. In posters and brochures, the fictional "Mrs. Sew-and-sew" offered tips on how to darn socks, mend everything from panties to coats, and use pajama legs to make children's undershirts. Some form of rationing was in place until 1949.

The Utility Scheme was instituted in 1941 to insure the manufacture of non-wasteful clothing. Utility clothing followed the general lines of fashion. Cuffs, wide belts, and other details were eliminated. Small prints and checks made matching patterns easier. The Incorporated Society of London Fashion Designers (INSOC), founded in 1942 (on the model of the Paris couture syndicate), consulted on Utility clothing designs, some of which went into manufacture, marked with the "CC41" (Civilian Clothing 1941) label. The participating designers included Norman Hartnell, Hardy Amies, Digby Morton, Peter Russell, Victor Stiebel, Bianca Mosca, Worth of London, Edward Molyneux, Charles Creed, and fashion editor Daisy Fellowes. The

The fashion that L-85 built

This is the Man (Donald Nelson)
who made the rule
that sent Design
to a strict new school.

This is the Skirt
and these the Shears
that narrow the line
to lean war years.

This is the Tunic
that's smooth over hips
that are cased in skirts
that are close as slips

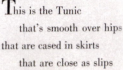

This is the Jacket
that's boxy and square
that tops the tight skirts
that all of us wear.

This is the Cap Sleeve
next summer will bring;
it's best above skirts
that are slim as a string.

This is the Coat
that's belted and shorn
that always looks better
when tight skirts are worn.

queen encouraged Hartnell's participation, saying, "You have made so many charming things for me that if you could do likewise for my countrywomen, I think it would be an excellent thing to do."[6] Government programs urging hard work and responsible clothing choices were amplified by two important role models: Princess Elizabeth and Princess Margaret. Elizabeth served in the Auxiliary Territorial Service, and images of her wearing an auto mechanic's uniform were especially powerful propaganda.

North American Fashion "On Its Own"

Throughout the war years a nationalistic fervor characterized press coverage of American fashion. Journalists declared that Americans were the best-dressed people in the world thanks to the highly industrialized and democratic fashion system. The September 1, 1940 issue of *Vogue* proclaimed, "For the first time, the fashion center of the world is here – in America." As the United States could not look to Paris for design direction, American designers were aggressively promoted. American fashion had different tiers, ranging from "high couture," often available through the custom departments of high-end stores, to mass market. Lord & Taylor featured ten designers in their new "Designers Shop," reflecting the commitment to local talent promoted by Dorothy Shaver, the store's vice president. An exhibition at the Metropolitan Museum in 1942 featured evening gowns by American designers. The Coty Awards debuted in 1943 to honor excellence in American fashion design; a $1,000 war bond was awarded to Norman Norell, and hat designers Lilly Daché and John-Frederics each received a $500 war bond.

Starting on April 8, 1942, American fashion was shaped by General Limitation Order L-85, which regulated the amount of materials used by clothing manufacturers. Almost as soon as the United States entered the war, the War Production Board asked

Stanley Marcus (of Neiman Marcus) to devise a program that would conserve fabric without introducing major stylistic changes, so as not to encourage consumers to discard what they already had. The severest restrictions concerned wool clothing: maximum jacket length was 25 inches (63.5 centimeters), and skirts had to be no more than 28 inches (71 centimeters) in length with a circumference of 64 inches (162.5 centimeters). Some styles and details were forbidden altogether, including French cuffs and dolman sleeves. Wool evening dresses and skirts were banned. Hems were 2 inches (5 centimeters) and most patch pockets were forbidden. Clothing made of fabric other than wool was less restricted. Sheer fabric, such as chiffon, was unaffected and was highlighted for evening and bridal looks. In addition, ration coupons were issued to households; women were limited to three pairs of leather shoes per year. Unrationed shoes included ballet flats, espadrilles, and rubber overshoes. Stores merchandised rationed and unrationed goods separately.

The fall 1942 collections were the first created under the regulations, and designers showed simple styles with innovative touches: drawstrings instead of metal fasteners, fur linings in place of wool, and highlights of sequins and braid. A trend toward informality influenced eveningwear in the United States. Knee-length dinner dresses, and even some evening dresses, were seen. Simple short-sleeved sheath dresses for evening were promoted as elegant "backdrops" for jewelry and accessories.

Canada created the Wartime Prices and Trade Board (WPTB) to deal with shortages of labor and materials. The WPTB enacted manufacturing guidelines similar to L-85 with even more stringent restrictions on evening and bridal fashions. Fashionable clothing in Canada followed the lean wartime silhouette.

Overt exoticism in fashion declined, in part because of the prevailing emphasis on practicality. Any reference to Japanese style was avoided and, instead, the public was urged to consider styles from America's "friends": China, South America, Mexico, and Greece.[7] Colorful dress prints with tropical motifs of llamas, palm trees, and bananas were called "Good Neighbor" prints. While most women did not want to look like "Rosie the Riveter" – the archetypal masculinized war worker – separates and sportswear gained favor. Trousers were increasingly seen, especially in the country and on bicycles. *Vogue* offered "A Primer on Pants" in 1941, advocating tailored, fly-front trousers as the most flattering.

The Elements of Women's Fashion 1940–1946

By 1939 womenswear had evolved into a style that emphasized a defined shoulder, tailoring, and shorter skirts. Suits were more common than ever, with simple jackets paired with skirts that were often pencil-slim or with slight fullness, but cut on the straight grain. Jackets had a typically masculine – even uniform – flavor with boxy shapes, boleros, and waist-length military styles popular. Some suits were designed in two colors, with contrasting jackets and skirts.

Daytime dresses were usually simple. Shirtwaist looks were common, and short sleeves were often featured in the name of conserving fabric. Skirts for daytime dresses were often narrow, sometimes with inverted box pleats. Dirndl styles, with gathered or pleated fullness, provided a fuller silhouette. Plain, man-style blouses with flat collars were widespread, and peasant-style blouses were common for girls, juniors, and women. Collar and cuff sets decorated dresses and suits in an old-fashioned

A suit by Adele Simpson, as seen in *Vogue* in 1942, shows the typical trim, tailored lines of the early 1940s.

An Adele Simpson original

New suit silhouette . . . an Adele Simpson original in pure wool. Fuchsia, beige, bride blue, black, with braid buttons. Suit under seventy dollars. Blouse separate. At Saks Fifth Avenue and other leading stores.

style, stressing the conservative attitude of wartime. Sweater sets began to be popular, a trend that would increase in coming years. Slacks were offered more for leisurewear, as were overalls and coveralls.

Evening gowns continued the variety established in the mid-1930s. Columnar neoclassic styles coexisted with full-skirted 19th-century looks. For wedding clothes a romantic mood was stressed in the face of war. Dresses, frequently made of rayon satin, often used full skirts, puffed full sleeves, and sweetheart or high necklines. However, the realities and mood of the war sometimes dictated a different approach to bridal attire, with women in their best short dresses, and even suits, for hurriedly planned weddings.

Simple coats were popular. Boxy wool coats were widespread, as were simple fitted princess-line versions; both styles were also featured in short lengths. Camel, navy, gray, and plaids were popular. Fur coats remained popular at various price points, keeping them available at many levels of the market. The dominant shape was wide through the shoulder and boxy, in both hip and knee lengths. Fur pieces were also available, and fur collars and revers decorated wool coats, which were often worn with fur pillbox hats.

Tennis clothes featured simple shirtwaist styles with skirts that rose a few inches above the knee. One-piece and two-piece swimsuits were both stylish. In 1941 the West Coast Knitting Mills changed its name to Cole of California, and in 1943 introduced the two-piece "swoon suit" that featured provocative side lacing on the trunks and a tie front on the top. Other manufacturers, including Flexees and Jantzen, offered stylish swimwear. Foundation garments showed little change from the late 1930s, with slips for daytime cut to the prevailing knee length. Sleepwear remained simple, with both nightgown and pajama styles worn.

Low, stout heels were very common, suitable for walking and bicycling. Loafers, Oxfords, and low-heeled pumps were worn with daywear. Platform styles also remained popular, in a variety of materials. As leather was rationed, shoes were made in many alternative materials, including fabric, straw, woven paper, felt, and cork. Plastic was frequently used, often with a shiny finish to imitate patent leather. Wood platform soles were especially common in France. Square-style handbags were popular, but envelope (clutch) bags continued to be carried.

Bakelite jewelry was popular, and the clunky scale introduced in the 1930s continued through the war years. Often rhinestones were set into Bakelite pieces. Playful surrealist themes were present in jewelry in animal and floral forms. Plastic, bone, and wood took the place of metal in jewelry, belt buckles, cosmetic cases, and buttons.

Millinery expressed flights of fancy. Many materials commonly used for trimmings were unaffected by wartime restrictions, but the decoration of some hats was quite unconventional. Hats ranged from playful and dramatic to near-monstrosities, contrasting with simple clothing. Wool felt, affected by wool restrictions, was often replaced by other materials. One Parisian milliner created a veiled top hat covered in newspaper and net. Hat shapes ranged from Arab-style pillboxes to fedoras to pointed stocking caps. Flat berets were sometimes styled like that worn by British General Bernard Montgomery. Snoods, worn during the 1930s, became even more popular. Headscarves were worn for town and as practical headwraps for factory

Below left The Australian Women's Weekly, January 27, 1945, promotes a highly decorative, large hat that evokes turn-of-the-century millinery.

Below right Paris shoe maker Camille Di Mauro created a slingback platform shoe celebrating the Allies in 1944, decorated with the flags of France, the Soviet Union, Great Britain, and the United States.

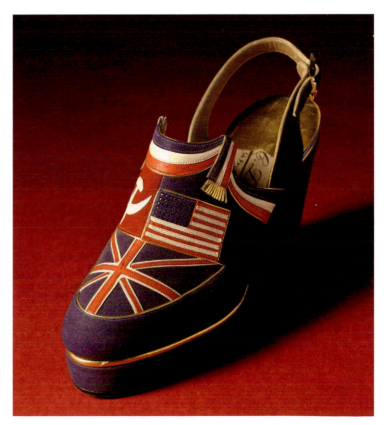

work – a style that was encouraged by workplace safety propaganda. Turbans were also popular, ranging from glamorous jersey versions, often with centered faux jewels, to simple styles such as Lilly Daché's non-flammable turban for defense workers. A striped silk turban from Schiaparelli's boutique was noted as the first hat to arrive in the United States after Paris was liberated in 1944 – sent by an Army captain to his wife in Philadelphia.

Flashlights (torches) were common and some women carried them in cylindrical cases with straps. Gas masks were considered essential, especially in wartime Britain, and were carried in small boxes with shoulder straps. Elizabeth Arden offered a waterproof velvet gas mask case for evening, with a pocket for make-up.

Hair and Beauty

Due to shortages and restrictions on hosiery, women resorted to leg make-up to achieve the look of stockings. Often called "liquid stockings" or "stockings in a bottle," leg make-up was important as trousers were still not considered appropriate for most occasions and bare legs were only acceptable for country or beach wear. In the United States, cosmetic firms started to offer leg make-up in 1942. Beauty columns were filled with advice on how to apply leg make-up. The liquid hose was available in lotion, cake, or stick form and ranged from "Leg Charm," available through Sears, to Schiaparelli's "Shocking Stocking" leg tint perfumed with her famous scent. As most stockings of the time were seamed in back, some women drew lines with eye pencils up the back

Women having their legs painted in response to the unavailability of stockings (1941).

THE PIN-UP GIRL

While Rosie the Riveter dominated the home front, servicemen at war desired drastically different views of women. Fighting men did not want to see young women in overalls, but rather scantily clad, playful girls. The term "pin-up" was derived from the act of pinning (or taping) up sexy images of women, usually in private places or in men-only domains such as clubs, locker rooms, and restrooms. The 1940s phenomenon was anticipated by images such as the *carte de visite* photographs of the late 19th century. During the 1920s and 1930s, widely distributed images of showgirls and actresses encouraged the trend. During the war servicemen used risqué pictures as reminders of the women waiting for them back home, boosting their morale to continue fighting.

Army barracks and naval ships were often decorated, if sometimes secretly, with pin-ups. Such images were adapted as "nose art" on fighter planes, furthering the use of sexy girls for the war effort. Many young actresses and models received significant boosts to their careers by posing for provocative shots. The most notable was Betty Grable, who was known for her shapely legs, usually displayed in short shorts. Her popularity as a "pin-up girl" catapulted her acting career. Other young starlets were also popular including Veronica Lake, Rita Hayworth, Lana Turner, Dorothy Dandridge, and Jane Russell – all women who figured significantly in popular culture of the decade.

The pin-up genre also included illustrations. The leading pin-up artist was Peruvian-born Alberto Vargas (1896–1982), who began his career in New York as a fashion illustrator and commercial artist during the 1910s, eventually illustrating for the Ziegfeld Follies and *Theatre* magazine. Moving to Hollywood in the mid-1930s, Vargas worked for several studios creating illustrations for film posters. Soon, he turned his talents to pin-up calendars, which led to a notable association with *Esquire* magazine (where he was published as "Varga") beginning in 1939. With *Esquire* Vargas created monthly

A typically patriotic Vargas girl.

illustrations which were among the most popular pin-ups during the war. The beach and boudoir were typical scenarios for Vargas' girls, justifying sexy and scanty clothes; often a patriotic theme was included as the girls waved flags or wore military headgear. After parting company with *Esquire*, Vargas continued illustrating, notably for *Playboy* and *Men Only*. His career continued until the late 1970s, when he created album covers for singer Bernadette Peters, and for the New Wave rock band The Cars.

Pin-up calendars and images maintained their popularity well beyond the war years, in gas stations, dormitories, and other male domains. And such provocative images helped launch the careers of actresses ranging from Marilyn Monroe during the post-war period to Farrah Fawcett in the 1970s.

of their legs to complete the illusion. In Britain, the efforts were even more desperate as women darkened their legs with gravy mix or cocoa.[8]

Throughout the decade, cosmetics and make-up were consistently referred to as "Morale-Builders." Women were told it was their duty to pay attention to their looks, to lift soldiers' spirits and keep the economy going. Factory operators were urged to make space for "powder rooms," and local retailers actively marketed make-up to female workers. Lipstick took on an especially potent role, reflected in the names of many popular shades: "Fighting Red" and "Jeep Red" from Tussy, "Emblem Red" by DuBarry, and "Mrs. Miniver Rose" by Revlon. In 1943 Constance Luft Huhn, the head of the house of Tangee, said that lipstick "symbolizes one of the reasons why we are fighting ... the precious right of women to be feminine and lovely – under any circumstances."

Hair was worn in numerous variations of softly waved styles. Many women wore shoulder-length hair partially pulled back from their foreheads and ears, sometimes pinned in place to form big curls. "Victory rolls" were formed by parting the hair in the center and rolling up the sides diagonally, to form a "V" when seen from the back. Hollywood star Veronica Lake wore her silky blonde hair draped over one eye, until the British and American governments asked Lake to change her hairdo to inspire women workers to keep their hair pinned back for safety.

The Théâtre de la Mode

Following the liberation of Paris, to revive interest in the couture industry, Lucien Lelong and Robert Ricci developed the idea for the "Théâtre de la Mode" during the winter of 1944–1945. An exhibition of more than 200 wire mannequins, each about 2 feet (61 centimeters) in height, the Théâtre de la Mode showcased the latest designs of all the major Parisian houses and opened in Paris on March 27, 1945. Designers showed fashions for each time of day: morning suits, afternoon ensembles, cocktail and dinner dresses, and evening gowns. Every piece was meticulously fabricated, made of the finest fabrics available at the time and with couture-quality finish. Miniature accessories complemented the ensembles, with hats, bags, and shoes by prestigious firms.

Lelong enlisted the aid of visual artists to create fantastic settings for the mannequins. Under the direction of Christian Bérard, thirteen leading artists provided sets that ranged from depictions of Paris parks and street scenes to Bérard's own spectacular vignette of an opening night at the Paris Opera. Jean Cocteau's surrealistic "*Ma Femme est une Sorcière*" made reference to the film *I Married a Witch* starring Veronica Lake, with long-haired mannequins in trailing evening gowns. The exhibition preparation caused excitement in Paris, still in the midst of recovery from the occupation. The Théâtre de la Mode struck a bright, optimistic note during a time when French citizens were still struggling with shortages of food, clothes, and fuel. After their debut in Paris, groups of mannequins were exhibited internationally, with showings in Europe, Britain, Brazil, and several stops in Scandinavia. Admission fees benefited the French charity Entr'aide Française.

For the exhibition in New York in April 1946, the dolls were re-dressed to promote styles for spring/summer 1946, marking the first collections designed for export since the war, and the exhibition was accompanied by an impressive illustrated catalog. Adding another layer of glamour, several dolls in eveningwear were bedecked with jewels from Boucheron, Cartier, and Van Cleef & Arpels.

Reviews of the American showings mentioned particular details: wasp waists, skirts that were either very narrow or very full, rounded shoulders, and fanciful hats. In general, coats were shapely, but some showed vestiges of the wartime shoulder line. Most day hemlines hovered just below the knee. Many evening designs featured fitted, often strapless, bodices and sweeping full skirts. Nina Ricci showed a floor-length dress of embroidered white cotton organdy with ruffled sleeves. Balenciaga's evening dress of raspberry satin was embellished with pearl and ruby beads. In addition to the established designers, younger couturiers also showed their work. Jacques Fath's

Members of the Auxiliary Territorial Service visit the London showing of the Théâtre de la Mode in 1945.

dramatic designs included a day ensemble with a three-quarter-length blouson jacket over an extremely narrow mid-calf-length skirt – a silhouette he called the *ligne stylo* or "pen line." Pierre Balmain showed a fitted two-piece black evening ensemble with black accessories and an eye-catching white fur piece. A demonstration of the creativity and vitality of the French couture industry, the Théâtre de la Mode helped re-establish the dominance of Paris and usher in the decorative, feminine fashion of the post-war era.

Christian Dior and the "New Look"

Christian Dior (1905–1957) was born in Normandy. He began working for Robert Piguet in 1938, and after a few years in the military, went to work for Lucien Lelong in 1942. After the war, Dior left Lelong and opened his own house in 1946, with financial backing from fabric manufacturer Marcel Boussac. His first collection, unveiled on a cold day in Paris (February 12, 1947), was quickly termed the "New Look," a designation attributed to *Harper's Bazaar* editor Carmel Snow. It was soon not only the talk of Paris, but also headline news throughout the fashionable world. Following directly on the heels of the Théâtre de la Mode, Dior's New Look placed Paris once again at the center of international fashion. Assessing the season's collections in April 1947, *Harper's Bazaar* declared him "agent provocateur and hero of the day."

The collection was characterized by softer, narrower shoulders, a molded torso with a cinched-in waist, emphasized hips (sometimes even padded), and very full skirts that were shockingly more than 1 foot (30 centimeters) longer than any skirt that had been seen for many years. Frequently the silhouette was teamed with a wide bergère-style hat. Named the Corolle line, the collection featured models that had the look of flowers, with long skirts using abundant amounts of fabric. *Harper's Bazaar* reported in April 1947, "The silhouette is the essence of femininity." Unabashedly

The Bar suit was one of the highlights of Christian Dior's first collection, presented in February 1947. The hourglass shape of the jacket and luxuriously long skirt help usher in a silhouette that would dominate fashion for the next decade.

romantic, the collection evoked a world of elegant fantasy that had been suppressed during the war. The collection featured the Bar suit, which teamed a black wool crepe skirt with a jacket of silk shantung featuring a shawl collar – one of the most recognizable pieces in the collection, widely photographed and illustrated. Evocative and romantic names were given to other pieces, such as Chérie, a dinner dress, and Mystère, a black coat. Following the success of the collection, a perfume, Miss Dior, was also launched in 1947.

The Envol ("Take Flight") line for spring 1948 included full skirts with drapery swagged to the side and even bustle-like fullness. Victorian-era equestrian clothes were inspirational. The Zig Zag collection that fall featured pointed collars and back-closing coats. Some body-hugging slim skirts were shown in 1949, which also brought witty touches (such as the whimsical Moulin à vent dress or the Cygne Noir ball gown). Among the most memorable and remarkable pieces of this year were the evening gowns Junon and Venus, opulent in their exquisite beaded detail and luxurious volume. Despite the historicism and luxury of his designs, Dior also embraced modern style. Some of the pieces shown – including cocktail dresses with plain shirtwaist tops and patch pockets – were notably contemporary and possibly indicated the influence of American designers, especially Valentina and McCardell.

Many aspects of the so-called "New Look" were already present in fashion. Many designers (including Lanvin, Ricci, and Rouff) had shown similar silhouettes in the late 1930s. Piguet's Amphora line and Balenciaga's Diablo line featured padded hips. Some elements of the style were already evident in the Théâtre de la Mode, including the clothes that Dior himself had designed for Lelong. Waist-nipping undergarments – such as the "Wisp" – were already widely available in the lingerie departments of stores. Traina-Norell and Valentina had both featured waist-cinching dresses with corset-inspired lacing earlier in the 1940s. Dior's 1947 Eugénie ball gown used the same Winterhalter inspirations that Norman Hartnell had mined ten years earlier with his clothes for Elizabeth, the Queen Consort. Despite these precedents, Dior's collection was nonetheless momentous. A controlled waist and torso became de rigueur for any fashionable woman, as Dior's designs did not just utilize a cinched waist and shaped bustline – they demanded them. But it was in lengthening the skirt that Dior made his most significant departure from existing styles. The return of the hemline to a longer length prompted *Harper's Bazaar*'s pronouncement that the "clearest register of the changes is in *skirt lengths*."[9]

Protests against the New Look, in both the United States and France, were widespread and often intense. Some members of the general public viewed the longer skirt lengths as a vulgar display of consumption following the war. Demonstrations in Paris included picketing at the house of Dior. The idea of covering women's legs was anathema to some members of the public, after enjoying exposed legs for several years. *Time* magazine noted the resistance:

> The furor over the new fashions rose to a fine, shrill pitch. Across the land, women by the hundreds – and city editors, too – flocked to the banners of resistance. Their stronghold was Texas and their Joan of Arc was a Dallas housewife named Mrs. Bobbie Woodward.

Mrs. Woodward, aged twenty-four, "had a nice pair of legs and a stubborn spirit," and founded the "Little Below the Knee Club" (or LBKs), which quickly developed chapters in all forty-eight states and Canada. Particularly popular in Texas, where the founder's Dallas chapter purportedly numbered more than 1,000 members, the club staged an outrageous parade and stormed Neiman Marcus crying out to keep the shorter skirts. In San Antonio, the local group declared, "The Alamo fell, but our hemlines will not." A Georgia politician attempted to introduce legislation to ban the longer skirt, and in Detroit an advisory was issued that the longer hemlines could be a hazard when boarding streetcars. As *Script* magazine declared:

> Hollywood, as Adrian would have it, continues to show the American figure au naturel with only a slight exaggeration of shoulder but with slim waist and hips. Adrian is twentieth century. Dior suggests a prosperous France of the 1890s.[10]

Although it was a hard sell in some markets, in time women adopted versions of the style at all price levels. Couture clients purchased Dior originals, and similar styles from other couturiers. Upper-middle-class women bought knock-offs at department stores or from dressmakers. And the general public began to choose longer dresses from mass-market retailers such as Macy's and Sears. Ironically, Dior received the Neiman Marcus Award in 1947.

The New Look provided fantasy at the end of the devastating years of the war. As the shortages ended and restrictions were lifted the world was ready for fashions that reveled in materials and embraced romance. The most significant aspect of the New Look was its timing. Dior, writing a few years later, suggested this reason for the triumph of the style:

> The New Look ... was a success only because it reflected the mood of the time – a mood that sought refuge from the mechanical and impersonal in a return to tradition and enduring values.[11]

The Elements of Women's Fashion 1947–1949

For the general public, the transition to the New Look was more gradual than the burst of headlines that greeted Dior in 1947. Square padded shoulders continued for some time, and other aspects of the early 1940s, including boxy fit, also lingered. With mass-market resistance to a total embrace of the New Look, dresses and suits available from mainstream retailers often showed longer skirts with shoulder pads. Other details of dress, including sweetheart necklines, continued from the war years, along with bateau styles with fichu-like collars. Cocktail dresses increased in popularity. Wedding gowns emphasized glamour and romance as a generation of young brides headed to the altar in the joyful post-war years. Day dresses usually showed increased fullness, and the fashionable longer hem. Fuller sleeves in short, three-quarter-length, and long versions were popular. Blouses, often with ethnic, Victorian, or poetic inspiration, were teamed with full skirts.

Suits were widely popular for daytime dressing, following the Paris modes. Department store versions often opted for a straighter skirt and when fullness was used the extravagant proportions of Dior were seldom achieved. Coatdresses were made as "faux suits" with peplums mimicking the bottoms of jackets. Outerwear followed the lines of popular suits, and also took on a romantic flavor. Fitted coats were often referred to by the 18th-century term "redingote," and Watteau-back styles were offered along with charming hooded capes. Fur pieces continued in popularity, and new treatments were used to make fur more water-repellent.

Shoes, hats, and handbags all showed changes. While platform styles were still worn, the general trend in shoes was toward a more feminine feeling. Open-toed pumps were common. Transparent plastic shoes were

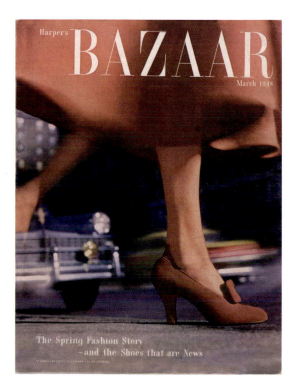

The point of view featured on the cover of *Harper's Bazaar*, March 1948, emphasized the new long skirt length.

offered. References to the past, in details such as decorative shoe buckles and Louis heels, were also seen. Casual shoes included washable styles, such as "Kedettes," with rubber soles. Hats were, in general, more subdued than during the war years (although fanciful, even outrageous styles could still be seen). Wider-brimmed styles, picture hats, and bergères were especially common. Handbags often maintained the large scale of the war years, but often with more graceful shapes, and included drawstring reticule styles. Jewelry showed a decisive elegance, and followed the general trend toward historicism seen in other accessories. The easing of wartime restrictions brought the return of a wide range of materials.

New foundation garments provided the controlled torso of the New Look. Heavily structured one-piece foundations were worn, and two-piece versions of a bra and panty girdle were also used. Petticoats were often attached to girdles. Brassieres became even more structured, with pointed cups achieved with spiral stitching. American manufacturer Maidenform unveiled its "I Dreamed …" advertising campaign in 1949, which ran for two decades. The famous lingerie retailer Frederick's of Hollywood was founded in 1947. Swimwear giant Jantzen entered the foundation garment market, claiming their girdles would "slim you, trim you, smooth you, soothe you." Nylon stockings returned, to the relief of women everywhere. Innovations included seamless stockings and new textures. Now that a woman's place was in the boudoir and not an airplane hangar, loungewear and sleepwear became more important and decorative, with negligees overtly present in the fashion media, and the old-fashioned term "tea gown" was used once again.

Denim was increasingly popular for leisurewear, especially as coveralls and playsuits. Swimwear was offered in both one- and two-piece versions; checks, dots, and floral prints – including tropicals – were all common. But the real news in swimwear, even if very few people were actually wearing it, was the bikini.

Both fashion designer Jacques Heim and automotive engineer Louis Réard have been credited with inventing the bikini. Both claimed to have introduced brief bathing suits in 1946 to the Riviera, and were probably inspired by sunbathers who rolled their suits for tanning. Heim had experimented with beach play clothes since the early 1930s, and included beach ensembles in the Théâtre de la Mode. Réard's fashion experience was limited to managing his mother's lingerie store in Paris. Heim unveiled his Atome, a suit that was very brief by the prevailing standards of the day. Réard's even skimpier version was the first to be patented and took the name "bikini" from the site of the 1946 nuclear bomb testing in the Marshall Islands. His design was composed of four triangles, and a showgirl modeled the original bikini design for the press. The suit was modeled in a swimwear show in Paris that summer. Such brief swimwear was not quickly accepted; it was considered scandalous in France, and even more scandalous in the rest of Europe. In 1947 *Harper's Bazaar* described such a brief suit as a "token sunning suit" and in America the style was not adopted into the mainstream until much later. Réard nonetheless turned the scandalous swimsuit into a success, opening a swimwear store on Avenue de l'Opéra.

Designers: France

Jacques Fath (1912–1954), a former actor and stockbroker, opened his couture house in 1937. After serving in the war, he established himself as a dynamic presence in couture. Fath was handsome and theatrical; his designs expressed drama rather than elegance. Even his impeccably tailored suits carried femme fatale undertones. In 1948 *L'Officiel* called Fath a wizard and praised the "singular beauty" of his aesthetic. Fath enjoyed contrast of shape and color, whether it was a bathing suit in stripes of bright orange and green or a high-collared, triangular red coat over a black figure-hugging "cigar" skirt. Even simple shirtwaist-style day dresses were tightly cinched at the waist. For resort wear, he showed knee-length pants in vivid prints with shapely jackets. Fath's eveningwear often made dramatic use of tulle in unusual shades. One gown combined a bodice encrusted with coral beads and a coral tulle skirt with a rosette-

shaped bustle. He counted many celebrities among his clients and his gowns were worn by Argentinian first lady Eva Perón. The wedding gown and trousseau he created for Rita Hayworth's 1949 marriage to Prince Aly Khan contributed to his fame.

Pierre Balmain (1914–1982) showed his first collection in the fall of 1945 to great acclaim. His exposure to fashion began in his childhood; his father was a textile merchant and his mother ran a boutique. Balmain studied architecture in Paris, began showing fashion design sketches to couturiers, and was hired by Molyneux in 1934. Balmain joined Lelong in 1938 but left to serve in the military. He returned to Lelong in 1941 where he worked alongside Christian Dior as a staff designer. With the establishment of his own house, Balmain made his mark as an important new name. With striking details such as a corsage of faux fruit pinned to the shoulder of a day dress, or swirls of black paillettes on a cream satin blouse, Balmain's designs were praised for their individuality. By 1946 he was promoting a rounded hipline with skirts that were full (his "cloche" line) or straight (his "sifflet" silhouette). Suits, coats, and wraps were often trimmed with exotic furs. In 1948 he showed a "sari" of black wool edged with ocelot. Balmain quickly earned an international clientele; he courted the American market with fashion shows and a ready-to-wear boutique in New York.

A Modernist during the 1930s, **Marcel Rochas** promoted a more romantic aesthetic in the post-war years. The introduction of his Femme fragrance in 1945 was followed by a period of exploration of feminine themes, perhaps inspired by his third wife, Hélène, whom he had married in 1944. He revived a corseted silhouette and became particularly celebrated for his eveningwear, often executed in black Chantilly lace, which became a signature fabric.

Mad Carpentier was founded in France in 1939 by Mad Maltezos and Suzie Carpentier, both former Vionnet employees. With Maltezos as the designer and Carpentier as the business manager, Mad Carpentier continued some of the characteristics of Vionnet's work in imaginative use of drape and piecing. They survived the occupation and participated in the Théâtre de la Mode, and became an important house during the post-war years, with notable press coverage. Romantic and historic inspiration and luxurious fabrics characterized their work. They offered evening and cocktail dresses, day dresses, and tailored ensembles, and their coats were especially admired. In 1945 American *Vogue* praised their "new shawl shoulders, draped armholes, and feminine technique."

Designers: Britain

While most leading British designers were involved in CC41, their creativity re-emerged in the post-war period, with the output of some houses rivaling that of Paris. The post-war years allowed **Norman Hartnell** to resume business as usual, creating luxurious gowns. In 1946 he embarked on a promotional tour of Brazil and Argentina; in Buenos Aires he had a successful showing at Harrods, attended by Eva Perón. For the marriage of Princess Elizabeth to Prince Philip on November 20, 1947 at Westminster Abbey, Hartnell designed Elizabeth's dress in ivory silk satin with a sweetheart neckline; its skirt was lined with taffeta and stiffened with horsehair. Hartnell's embroidery studio heavily embellished the dress with designs of lilies, orange blossoms, and roses. As many wartime restrictions were still in place in 1947, the princess had to save up ration coupons for the materials for the dress. The romantic beauty of Princess Elizabeth's dress offered a symbolic end to the deprivations of war and was copied by brides throughout the world.

After several successful years during the 1930s at the London couture house Lachasse, **Hardy Amies** (1909–2003) joined Worth in 1941. Soon, however, he was called to military service where he served in special operations in Belgium. His commanding officer evaluated him as "far tougher both physically and mentally than his rather precious appearance would suggest."[12] After the war Amies opened his own shop on Savile Row and quickly became known for quality tailored clothes for both men and women. His success was prompt and brought him notable press attention, and he became one of the most important forces in post-war British fashion. His output during these years was notable for its elegance, featuring evening gowns of luxurious material. He embraced the ideas of the New Look, but on very English terms. His tailored suits followed the general model of Dior, but he placed them within the contextual legacy of 19th-century British equestrian clothes and Redfern tailor-mades.

An avid collector of toy soldiers, **Charles Creed** designed with overt inspiration from military uniforms with braid and button details. The press described his work as "soldierly" and in the manner of a "drum major." Society women cherished his suits and wore the perennial designs season after season. **Digby Morton** (1906–1983) also specialized in tailored pieces and was known for exceptional quality. In the words of his competitor Hardy Amies, Morton could create a suit that was an "intricately cut and carefully designed garment that was so fashionable that it could be worn with confidence at the Ritz."[13] Morton offered a wider range of clothes; his dress ensembles included smart jackets, thus resembling his suits. After the conclusion of the war,

Hardy Amies applied English tailoring traditions to his version of the New Look in 1947.

Victor Stiebel began designing couture again for the Jacqmar label, continuing his affinity for designing luxurious eveningwear. Stiebel became the chairman of the Incorporated Society of London Fashion Designers in 1946. Stiebel was highly successful and his clientele included the leading actresses of the day, but also royalty and members of the aristocracy.

Designers: United States

The absence of French designers encouraged the business of **Hattie Carnegie**. Her work was highly visible in *Vogue* and *Harper's Bazaar*, and a Carnegie polka dot suit appeared on the cover of *Life* magazine in 1944, tied to an article on American fashion. Also for *Life*, in 1943 she designed an adaptable pattern for home sewing that the magazine described as the type of versatile dress that was "a mainstay of every well-dressed woman's wardrobe." As a celebrity, she was of interest to the press and the public, profiled in *Cosmopolitan* in 1942 and *Life* in 1945. While the public was interested in her opinions on taste and style, Carnegie's life story – a Jewish immigrant who rose to success and celebrity – was regarded as proof of the reality of the American dream.

As with Carnegie, **Valentina**'s business benefited greatly from the unavailability of French couture. Her stylish and idiosyncratic fashions were popular particularly in New York society where she was a fixture – dressed in her own striking creations. Ethnic and monastic themes continued to influence her designs. Her experiments with lifestyle-driven and convertible pieces applied American sportswear concepts

Hattie Carnegie's designs epitomized high-quality American fashions for several decades. This form-fitting knit dress was photographed by John Rawlings, c. 1943.

Opposite The serviceman's uniform contrasts with an elegant red dress by Valentina, accessorized with one of her signature styles, a "coolie" hat.

Above Valentina's fashion designs reflected her eccentric personal style; she was photographed in 1943 holding one of her creations.

to couture, such as practical pockets even with eveningwear. Valentina responded to the war in a wide variety of ways. She endorsed opaque rayon stockings for Gotham Hosiery, offered low-priced turban headwraps at B. Altman, and even designed coveralls for war workers. Her clever Bashlyk overcoat, designed in 1942 under L-85 restrictions, featured wrap front closure, a separate jersey hood, and a clip to hold a flashlight. Valentina followed many of the general trends of the post-war years, but maintained her own aesthetic. She offered spectacular evening gowns in luxurious taffeta and chiffon with historic references, which appealed to the customer who wanted individuality; and a remarkable use of geometry and cut permeated her work. Valentina created a Byronic blouse with poet collar and full sleeves that was featured in *Harper's Bazaar* modeled by Millicent Rogers. In the late 1940s Valentina summed up the timeless quality of her work, saying "simplicity survives the changes of fashion. Women of chic are wearing now dresses they bought from me in 1936. Fit the century, forget the year."[14]

Sophie Gimbel (1898–1981), known as **Sophie of Saks**, was the in-house designer for Saks Fifth Avenue, where her work was featured in the store's prestigious Salon Moderne. The wife of the president of the department store, she not only designed but also bought other designers' work for the boutique. Gimbel introduced a ready-to-wear line in 1943 that was sold in some branches of Saks and through other retailers. In 1947 she appeared on the cover of *Time* magazine.

Mainbocher, who had left Paris at the outbreak of the war, opened a couture house in New York with socially prominent clients who included Barbara "Babe" Paley and C. Z. Guest. His offerings included evening sweaters to be paired with long skirts, a style that followed the general trend for understated elegance. He designed uniforms for several volunteer organizations including the W.A.V.E.S. (Women Accepted for Volunteer Emergency Service) and the American Red Cross.

Charles James (1906–1978) was born in Surrey, the child of a British military instructor and a wealthy Chicago society woman. From the beginning, James established himself as an outsider who created his own rules in fashion and in business, and his personality brought him both notoriety and disrepute. During the early years of his career James moved between the United States, Britain, and Paris, opening and closing several business ventures, including millinery and custom-made apparel. He established a Paris store in 1934 and gave his first full-scale Paris showing in 1937. His early work showed experimentation with structural themes and details, including zippers; James referred to himself as a sartorial architect. With the war looming, he returned to New York in 1939 and incorporated under his own name. During the early 1940s, his friend Elizabeth Arden added a custom fashion division to her cosmetics business with James as its design director. The opening show in 1944, a gala benefit for the Red Cross, featured twenty-five of James' designs. The association was short-lived and James left Arden in 1945, opening his own salon at 699 Madison Avenue and, on his own, his fame grew in the post-war years. James showed at Hardy Amies' London salon, and shortly thereafter he presented a spectacular show at the Hôtel Plaza Athénée in Paris with assistance from some French designers, and the showing was well received. James believed that fashion was a collaboration between adventurous women of good taste and gifted designers. James presented himself as a great artist, celebrating the timeless qualities he saw in his work. His designs took on a more distinctly sculptural feel, often featuring lush fabrications and architectural drapery. James' stylistic development went hand in hand with the development of his construction techniques, with experiments in geometry, understructures, and seaming. With a few exceptions (such as a coat designed for New York coat and suit label Philip Mangone) James stuck to his custom pieces during these years. He was most famous for his stunning evening gowns, but also offered skirt and top separates for evening and cocktail wear, and smart dresses, coats, and suits for day. A 1946 late-day dress was dubbed the Infanta and strongly resembled Balenciaga's 1930s gown of the same name. His innovative short ball gowns looked forward to a style associated with the 1950s. As affluent clients donated James' dresses to museums, his work took on the mystique of fine art, and in 1949 the Brooklyn Museum presented an exhibition of James' dresses that were entirely from the wardrobe of notable client Millicent Rogers. Other customers included society women and stage celebrities, among them Barbara Paley, Marietta Tree, Gertrude Lawrence, Lily Pons, and Gypsy Rose Lee.

Norman Norell (1900–1972) became famous for applying couture quality to American ready-to-wear. After early experience in film costume design, Norell worked for Hattie Carnegie during the 1930s. In 1941 he joined the firm of manufacturer Anthony Traina. Under the label **Traina-Norell**, he imposed unusually high standards of workmanship, resulting in high-priced ready-to-wear. His designs stressed simplicity and lasting quality with lean lines and minimal detail, an aesthetic that easily conformed to the L-85 regulations. During wartime, he created figure-hugging sequined evening sheaths (sequins were not among restricted materials)

TRAINA-NORELL'S "Tango Tunic"...

superb new silhouette...
bateau necked, beaded and fringed...
exclusive with

T. A. Chapman Co.
Milwaukee

Claire McCardell's Popover, an ingenious wrapped dress that came with a matching oven mitt, was introduced in 1942 and became one of the designer's best sellers.

with thin straps, a style that became a signature design. His daytime ensembles of shirtwaist blouses and narrow skirts conveyed the versatility and comfort that were hallmarks of American fashion and made subtle references to Gibson Girl style. In 1943 he received his first (of a career five) Coty Award for excellence in design.

A great pioneer of a distinctly American aesthetic, **Claire McCardell** (1905–1958) was born in Maryland, and exhibited an early interest in fashion. During the 1920s, she attended the New York School of Fine and Applied Art (later known as Parsons) and spent her second year of school in Paris. She developed an interest in the work of Madeleine Vionnet, who was a continuing influence on McCardell throughout her career. In 1931 she went to work for Townley Frocks as assistant to designer Robert Turk, and on his unexpected death, she became the designer for Townley until 1939. At Townley, McCardell developed many of her signature ideas and details including "spaghetti" self ties, self trim, and exposed hooks and eyes. She designed her first swimsuits for the label in 1937. McCardell was fond of hoods and took influence from monastic dress, and also experimented with the idea of lifestyle-driven clothing. Her time at Townley was followed by a short stint designing for Hattie Carnegie, but she returned to Townley in 1940, now with her name on the label. Her work for Townley Frocks was prominently featured by Lord & Taylor. In 1941 she designed her "kitchen dinner dress" inspired by folk costume, with its own matching apron. Also in 1941, she showed her monastic wedding dress of white wool jersey with matching coif. In 1942 her Popover dress debuted: a wrap dress first created in blue denim but shortly available in a variety of other fabrics. One of the biggest selling designs of the decade, the Popover featured a large patch pocket and a matching oven mitt; Lord & Taylor advertised it as "The Original Utility Fashion." McCardell's collections often included pedal pushers, playsuits, and diaper-style swimwear. In 1944 she showed Capezio ballet slippers with her clothes – a stylish response to leather rationing. McCardell avoided menswear inspiration and offered a simple, feminine, youthful aesthetic. During these years, she received awards and citations from Coty, the American Fashion Critics Association, and *Mademoiselle* magazine, and her designs were on the cover of *Life* magazine in 1943. In 1945, writing in the *Washington Star*, she predicted the use of performance fabrics in the future. In the same article she also forecast changes to the prevailing silhouette, predicting a rounded shoulder and longer, fuller skirts two years before Dior's "New Look."

In February 1946 *Vogue* ran a Blumenfeld photo of Claire McCardell wearing her own "futurist dress," created entirely of triangular pieces and constructed with topstitched seams, one of her trademark details. The dress combined a relaxed sensibility with thoughtful craftsmanship, hallmarks of McCardell's style. In 1947 McCardell embraced the prevailing "New Look," but on her own terms, mixing down-to-earth fabrics with the more feminine silhouette. Longer, fuller skirts were typical, along with soft shoulders; raglan sleeves were frequently used for a rounded shoulder, and artfully manipulated stripes and plaids, often in a chevron effect, were a common design feature. McCardell also used elastic to create a flexible fit in bodices, a technique she also applied to swimwear. She often avoided zippers, and featured creative closures with hooks and lacing. Her contribution to fashion was frequently recognized in the media, and also with a Neiman Marcus Award in 1948.

Vera Maxwell (1901–1995) designed for a number of Seventh Avenue firms. Her designs, often influenced by menswear, emphasized good materials and adaptability. She designed a "weekend wardrobe" that included coordinating pieces – jacket, trousers, and two skirts – in practical woolens. She preferred soft materials and often used jersey. Even her tailored suits were less structured than those by other designers. Her background as a dancer and fashion model taught her the importance of comfort in clothing, a guiding principle throughout her career. The cotton jumpsuits she designed for women war workers at the Sperry Gyroscope Corporation strengthened her reputation as a designer who added flair to practical pieces, and were widely covered in the media.

While she continued to design for Hollywood and for department store collections, **Muriel King** was also involved with the war effort. In 1943 the Boeing Corporation asked her to design a wardrobe of work clothes for female factory workers. King's "Flying Fortress Fashions," named after Boeing's bomber aircraft, included several pieces ranging from bib overalls to a dress for office workers. With safety in mind, King designed flattering, snug-fitting silhouettes without dangling flaps or other potentially dangerous details.

Tina Leser (1910–1986) traveled the world as a child, the daughter of wealthy Philadelphia parents, and was educated at the Pennsylvania Academy of Fine Art and the Sorbonne. She settled in Hawaii after her 1931 marriage, where she opened a dress shop offering designs using native Hawaiian fabrics and fabrics from other Pacific locales. A 1940 business trip to New York led to an order from Saks and a New York branch of her business. Following the bombing of Pearl Harbor, she relocated to New York and was soon hired as designer for Foreman. Leser looked to world cultures for inspiration, continuing her Hawaiian themes, as well as utilizing inspiration from "Good Neighbor" nations, including Mexico and South American countries. Her work at Foreman was well received by the industry, and she received a Coty Award in 1945. Her post-war years were especially creative. She created a weekend travel wardrobe made of Heller jersey that even included a jersey evening gown, and created beach clothes with an Americana theme, using red and white gingham tablecloth fabric, a notion that had sprung from wartime make-do fashions. Leser used Indian inspiration for many items, applied both in cut and fabrication. On a 1948 honeymoon tour with her second husband, Leser initiated a fashion design competition in Japan encouraging modern styles derived from traditional clothing, and in 1949 the winning designs were modeled in a fashion show in Japan. Leser used kimono silks in her 1949 resort collection and was one of the first designers to utilize fabric from Jim Thompson's Thai Silk Company.

Below left Actress Barbara Britton models coveralls designed by Muriel King for female factory workers in 1942.

Below right A world traveler, Tina Leser created leisurewear with exotic inspiration, as seen in this two-piece ensemble, pictured in *Holiday* magazine, November 1949.

James Stewart, Ruth Hussey, John Howard, Katharine Hepburn, and Cary Grant in *The Philadelphia Story*. Hepburn's tiered dress by Adrian was a notable example of the designer's enthusiasm for gingham as a fashion fabric.

Pauline Trigère (1909–2002) was born in the Pigalle district of Paris of Russian parents. Her father was a tailor, and she learned the fundamentals of cut and fit at a young age. She embarked early on a long career in fashion, beginning with an apprenticeship at Martial et Armand. After working for a tailor, she opened her own Paris house with her brother, and the store was quickly recognized for its chic styles. Leaving France in 1937 with her husband and family, she settled in New York and opened a tailoring shop, but both the marriage and the business failed. After a brief period of time working for Hattie Carnegie, she embarked on her own label again in 1942, once again in partnership with her brother. Her first collections featured only small numbers of dresses, but her reputation grew quickly and she was well established by the end of the decade, winning the Coty Award in 1949.

Tom Brigance (1913–1990) studied at the Parsons School of Design and the Sorbonne, then spent time in London designing for Jaeger. By the late 1930s he was designing for Lord & Taylor, and was known especially for smart sportswear, leisurewear, and activewear. He left Lord & Taylor in 1941 to serve in the South Pacific in the US Intelligence Corps, returning in 1944 at the end of his service. **Adele Simpson** (1903–1995) trained at Brooklyn's Pratt Institute, and her career was already underway during the 1930s. Married to a textile manufacturer, Simpson designed for Mary Lee Fashions with her own name on the label during the war years, and her designs were sold by Saks Fifth Avenue and other high-end retail stores. Simpson's style, while adhering to the regulations of the time, showed marked chic and sophistication. **Clare Potter** continued to produce interesting sportswear with international inspiration and simple, elegant eveningwear. Undeterred by wartime restrictions, Potter said, "Any real

A 1948 Adrian suit from the Chicago History Museum exemplifies the designer's typical strong-shouldered silhouette and masterful use of horizontal and vertical stripes in pieced detail.

designer welcomes some limitations, since they tend to stir her imagination and her ingenuity."[15] Her innovative work was recognized with a Coty Award in 1946.

Gilbert Adrian left MGM in 1941. One of his last films, *The Philadelphia Story* (1940), starred Katharine Hepburn as a society heiress. Her wardrobe included an ensemble consisting of an organza peasant blouse and a long, tiered gingham skirt. Following in the wake of Adrian's blue gingham dress for Judy Garland in *The Wizard of Oz* (1939), Hepburn's dress helped promote gingham as a trend. Adrian's use of gingham has been attributed to his travels in Appalachia during 1938, where he saw the fabric on rural Americans.

Adrian opened his own fashion house in Beverly Hills in 1942 and concentrated primarily on fashion for the rest of his career. The strong theatrical sense that he brought to his film costumes was frequently in evidence. His eveningwear designs were particularly dramatic, often with a neoclassic sensibility, but also displayed crisp military influences and large-scale, painterly graphics. He consistently featured the broad shoulders that he helped encourage into fashion in the previous decade. Adrian's suits displayed his real genius as a fashion designer and maintained a remarkable level of quality tailoring. Striped and herringboned fabrics, often designed by textile designer Pola Stout, were frequently pieced to create remarkable geometric and chevron effects; in place of conventional darts, Adrian often used piecing and ease to mold the jacket to the shape of the torso. Stylish finishing details included self ties, military braid, and buckle closures. He received a Neiman Marcus Award in 1943 and a Coty Award in 1945. Adrian resisted the New Look, maintaining the silhouette of the early forties, especially the broad padded shoulders, but he conceded to longer hemlines. In 1946 he introduced fragrances to his offerings. In 1948 he opened a boutique in New York, and his premiere fashion shows were a great success. He also occasionally returned to film, costuming Alfred Hitchcock's thriller *Rope* (1948) and providing gowns for Joan Crawford in *Humoresque* (1946) and *Possessed* (1947). He maintained his fashion house until 1952, when he retired after suffering a heart attack.

Film and Fashion

While many European studios were brought to a near standstill, Hollywood continued to create numerous great films throughout the war years. However, costume departments were faced with many of the same sort of restrictions as the general public. Imported materials were unavailable and inferior fabrics and trims were used to substitute for more expensive materials. Color films were becoming more common, adding a new challenge to costume designers, and encouraging color trends in fashion derived from film costumes.

Costumes captured the simple forms of fashion, such as Ingrid Bergman's strikingly simple light-colored suit and angled hat (designed by Orry-Kelly) in *Casablanca* (1942), while Greer Garson in *Mrs. Miniver* (1942) epitomized both the style and the spirit of the courageous wartime woman and emerged as an Oscar winner. Gene Tierney's simple yet elegantly detailed wardrobe in *Laura* (1944), designed by Bonnie Cashin, anticipated the look of the post-war years. Glamour was still part of Hollywood's fashion message. Edith Head's varied and stylish designs for Barbara Stanwyck in *The Lady Eve* (1941) proved influential on mainstream fashion. Costume designer Helen Rose established extremes of glamour for Brazilian performer Carmen Miranda (who encouraged the continued vogue for platform shoes), and created Lena Horne's sensational gowns in *Stormy Weather* (1943).

Films of these years also encouraged, and reflected, growing interest in a full and rounded bustline. *The Outlaw* (1943), directed by aviator Howard Hughes, was shown in limited release without the approval of the Hollywood censors, enabling gratuitous glimpses of actress Jane Russell's ample bosom. In 1944 former child star Shirley Temple was cast in *I'll Be Seeing You* (at the age of fifteen), in which her wardrobe included a very tight-fitting sweater that created a stir. The look was widely copied and encouraged young women's sweater fashions into the 1950s.

Above As the title character in the 1942 film *Mrs. Miniver*, Greer Garson embodied the ideals of wartime womanhood.

Right Post-war siren Rita Hayworth in a black strapless evening gown by costume designer Jean Louis for *Gilda*, 1946.

Hollywood continued to create memorable film noir pieces that affected fashion. For *The Postman Always Rings Twice* (1946), Irene Lentz, aka Irene, costumed Lana Turner as the femme fatale in a varied, striking white wardrobe, including a two-piece playsuit. Leah Rhodes stylishly outfitted Humphrey Bogart and Lauren Bacall in *The Big Sleep* in 1946 and *Key Largo* in 1948. Ava Gardner starred in her first leading role in 1946 in *The Killers*, and established herself as a style icon. Italian actress Alida Valli provided an arresting presence in *The Paradine Case* (1947) and *The Third Man* (1949), helping to usher Italian style into North America after the war.

The French-born Jean Louis (1907–1997) developed his career as a designer for Hattie Carnegie, and came to Hollywood in 1944. In 1946 he dressed Rita Hayworth for the title role of *Gilda*. The showpiece of her stunning wardrobe was a black strapless evening gown that looked back to 19th-century styles, but also forward to the voluptuous glamour of the 1950s. The dress became one of the most notable gowns in Hollywood history.

In 1948 the first Oscar for Costume Design was presented in two categories: Roger K. Furse was honored for *Hamlet*, a black and white film, and Barbara Karinska and Dorothy Jeakins won for *Joan of Arc* in the color category. While *Hamlet* had no apparent effect on fashion, Ingrid Bergman's appearance in the title role of *Joan of Arc* helped popularize a pageboy hairstyle that was copied widely into the 1950s.

"sextette" from Jantzen

"ROMPER"   "AMPHIBIAN"   "ECSTASY"   "WATER BOY"   "ECLIPSE"   "HI-DIVER"

Jantzen
thoroughly man-tailored
sunclothes

come on you sunners...line up for the best looks of
your life! Jantzen has everything you need...the smartest,
best-fitting, best-performing man-tailored sun classics...
finest quality washable fabrics...special-for-Jantzen
wonderful-looking fast colors. Jantzen is famous
for girls' shorts...fly-front shorts of Crompton finest
cotton corduroy as in "Romper", left, 5.95...other shorts,
2.95 to 9.95. Jantzen is famous for tee shirts of finest
quality combed cotton, as the striped shirt, for men, too.

come on you swimmers...Jantzen has for you
the world's finest swim suits and swim trunks...
marvelous new exclusive Lastex-powered fabrics...
famous Jantzen girdle control and uplifting bras for
girls...flawless-fit, trim athletic lines for men. "Eclipse",
in light-as-air Cordo-Lastex, with detachable shoulder
straps is 9.95..."Ecstasy" (opposite page) finest quality
satin Lastex with terrific new Jantzen Stay-Bra 15.95
...one-piece like it 17.95...others 8.95 to 17.95.

Jantzen
Lastex-powered figure-control
swim suits

Above An ad for Jantzen shows
popular styles for sunning and
swimming for men and women.

Below Aloha shirts from Hawaii
often featured tropical motifs.
A shirt from Wong's Drapery
Shoppe in Honolulu, 1948, is
printed with a pattern of bamboo
and exotic foliage.

Menswear

The massive deployment of men meant that uniforms were part of everyday wear. Because of the lack of adult men shopping for civilian dress, manufacturers of tailored clothing targeted older men and the youth market. As in the previous war, menswear manufacturers produced uniforms; some officers had their uniforms made by tailors. Dress uniforms were often worn as formal wear; at many wartime weddings the male members of the bridal party were all in uniform.

Government restriction programs simplified menswear, as men throughout the Allied nations sacrificed vests, pockets, and trouser cuffs to the war effort. France forbade yoke backs and tunnel belt loops. Trousers could only have one hip pocket, and only false trouser cuffs (created with tucks) were allowed.[16] British Utility suit designs eliminated waistcoats, trouser cuffs, and pocket flaps. This simple styling shaped the Demobilization or "De-mob" suits issued to British troops upon their discharge from the military. In the United States, Victory suits were made without patch pockets, trouser cuffs, or pleats. Double-breasted suits consisted of matching jacket and trousers – no vest. The extra pair of trousers in two-pants suits, belts on overcoats, cutaway coats, and double-breasted tuxedo jackets were also eliminated for the duration. A maximum length of 29¾ inches (76 centimeters) was established for a size 37 jacket, with other pieces similarly limited.

Sports and work clothes were worn for outdoor activity and travel by foot or bicycle. For leisure, colorful clothes were welcomed and reflected exotic influences. In 1942 the *New York Times* reported sport shirts and socks so brightly colored they could "be seen in a blackout."[17] The aloha (or Hawaiian) shirt, a popular style since the 1930s, took on patriotic overtones related to the wartime focus on Hawaii and the South Pacific. These shirts were often made of rayon and combined botanical images with collages of island fantasies.

The zoot suit was originally associated with African American jazz musicians and entertainers. With wide-shouldered, long draped jackets, wide pegged trousers and exaggerated accessories, zoot suits, and their wearers, were self-consciously unconventional. The zoot suit was adopted by Mexican Americans in California, who wore the style as a symbol of their marginalization. During wartime, the exaggerated, flamboyant style did not conform to regulations and was consequently regarded as unpatriotic and subversive; "Zoot Suit Riots" flared between Mexican Americans and servicemen in Los Angeles in 1943. While zoot suiters and Zazous were small style groups, elements of their aesthetic influenced mainstream menswear. After wartime

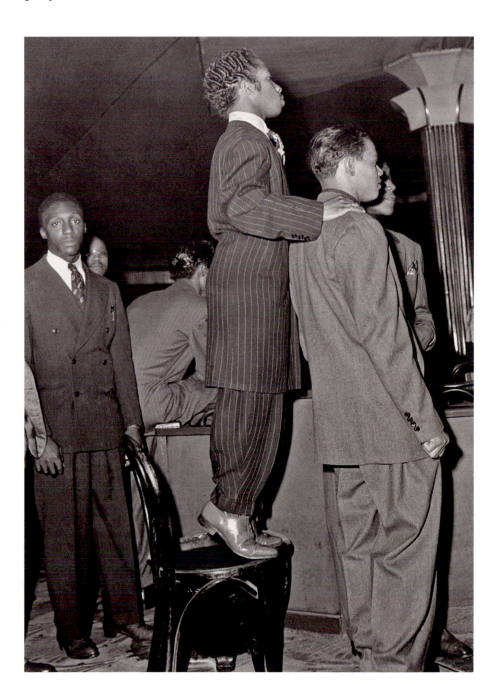

Spectators in zoot suits at the Savoy Ballroom, a famous Harlem nightclub, in the early 1940s.

The Bold Look in menswear, introduced in 1948, was characterized by broad-shouldered jackets and loose-cut pants. Neckties frequently featured large colorful geometric motifs. Advertisement for Andover from *Apparel Arts*, May 1948.

restrictions were lifted men's trousers reverted to looser styles, often amply pleated at the waistline and tapering down to narrow cuffs. Jackets were often cut longer and buttoned low, zoot-suit style.

One of the major themes in post-war menswear was the influence of military heroes. The wool duffle coat worn by Field Marshall Bernard Montgomery was enormously influential, especially on the younger generation who adopted the look as an outerwear staple. General Dwight D. Eisenhower favored a waist-length uniform jacket. This style also entered civilian wardrobes, as the Eisenhower jacket. The style was first adopted by women as a suit jacket during the war and, later, by men, for casual wear. Menswear returned to a silhouette similar to that of the 1930s, what *Esquire* magazine in 1948 called the "Bold Look." Jackets had broad shoulders and wide lapels. Trousers were pleated and high-waisted. Neckties were wide, patterned with tropical motifs, art deco-style designs and novelty prints, often in vivid colors. Other accessories completed the look including pocket squares and wide-brimmed hats. Menswear continued to evolve more relaxed versions of formal wear. Dinner jackets were increasingly and widely available in alternative colors and fabrics, worn with contrasting accessories. The trend for color and pattern extended into loungewear and sleepwear.

Colorful, bold patterns were seen in men's sports clothes, accessories, loungewear, and sleepwear, and advertising promoted a playful post-war spirit.

Children's Fashion

Practical pieces dominated childrenswear. Toddler and school-age girls continued to wear dresses, jumpers over blouses, and skirt and top combinations. Boys wore short pants or knickers with shirts and sweaters for school and play. Tailored suits for dressy occasions also included short pants or knickers.

Wartime affected children's fashion. For special occasions, some families dressed children in child-size versions of actual uniforms worn by servicemen and servicewomen. As part of the emphasis on conservation and austerity, adult clothing was often cut down or made over for kids, and home knitters and crocheters produced sweaters, caps, and mittens for children. Many of the conservation and mending campaigns included specific projects and hints for making and repairing children's clothing.

The Sears catalog offered child-sized versions of armed services uniforms during the war years, to be worn for special occasions.

An Emily Wilkens junior ensemble from 1946 features a full skirt with a fiesta look. The model also wears a charm bracelet, a popular jewelry style for women of all ages.

The junior market received increased attention. High-end stores featured junior shops, and mass-market catalogs and retailers also offered styles aimed at high school and college-age girls. American designer **Emily Wilkens** (1917–2000) was a great innovator in the development of this market. Wilkens attended the Pratt Institute and started her fashion career as an illustrator. She began designing for the teenage customer, incorporating innovations from women's fashion. She brought modernity to children's clothing, even featuring black for teenage girls' party dresses, an unusual color choice, in a 1944 collection for Bonwit Teller. Her reputation and success grew so quickly that she received a Coty Award in 1945. Her designs for teenage girls often featured dirndl skirts and other folk styles, 19th-century inspiration, and American pioneer clothing. Other typical junior looks included sportswear pieces such as skirts and sweaters (which girls sometimes wore in loose "Sloppy Joe" style), tailored suits, and dresses which ranged from simple cotton and rayon styles to "date" dresses with feminine details. Although slacks were increasingly worn, they were still considered appropriate only for casual situations and as play clothes. Available in a variety of materials, from denim to wool flannel, slacks were cut with wide legs and a high waist, and always had a side or back closure. For daily wear, children wore lace-up shoes with flat soles and low heels. Slightly older girls wore slip-on loafers, and two-tone saddle shoes were popular. Wearing higher heels was a social milestone for teenage girls and reflected changes occurring in the junior market.

The post-war turn toward more generous use of materials affected children's fashion, especially in the United States, the first major nation to end fabric restrictions. By 1946 magazines and catalogs showed trouser suits "like Dad's" for young boys who previously would have worn shorts or knickers. Girls' clothes reflected the return to femininity with more volume and details, especially for special occasions. Mother/ daughter and big and little sister looks were promoted. Another manifestation of post-war change was the expansion of designer fashions for children. In the late 1940s Townley introduced Baby McCardells and Junior Editions by Claire McCardell. At the highest level, Jacques Heim's successful Jeunes Filles line, introduced before the war, received more attention. In general, junior fashions reflected changing silhouettes with fuller skirts and lower hemlines and a renewed emphasis on romantic looks.

The End of the Decade

War brought people of different countries into contact with one another. In particular, many American, Canadian, and Australian soldiers had their first exposure to international cultures. Wartime inventions and innovations were speedily adapted for civilian use, ranging from penicillin, first used in battle in Europe, to Coppertone lotion, originally formulated as sun protection for soldiers.

The war put an enormous number of the world's men in uniforms, and those who did not go to war often made do with fashions left over from the 1930s. Post-war man, by contrast, was encouraged to be fashionable, and to assert his masculine role in civilian society. The war years required women to be thrifty, adopt practical dress, and to sometimes take a man's role in the world. Post-war values urged them to revel in their femininity, mold their bodies to a shapely silhouette, and be encumbered by longer and fuller skirts. Christian Dior's New Look, and the general aesthetic it encouraged, not only dominated fashion at the end of the decade, but also laid the foundation for the look of the 1950s. While the newly acquired might of the United States dominated world politics, the elegance of Paris dominated world fashion once again.

Maxime de la Falaise photographed by Norman Parkinson in a sumptuous, tiered Dior gown, indicates the turn toward luxury and sophistication present in fashion at the end of the decade.

The 1950s

Couture Opulence, Suburban Style

In some ways the 1950s represents fashion in stasis: the fashion vocabulary of much of the decade had already been established in the immediate post-war years. With the success of the New Look, France regained its supremacy in couture and its role as the arbiter of women's fashion. The elegant triumvirate of Dior, Fath, and Balmain created a benchmark of style that was imitated throughout the world at all market levels. The couture industry utilized luxury textiles, furs, and skilled hand-embellishment to maintain its prestige, while in mass-market fashion, easy-care synthetic fabrics promised consumers a "better life." Although France reigned supreme in fashion, the United States dominated popular culture. American film and music were widely circulated, encouraged by the United States' dominant role in world politics. However, global influences were noteworthy, and increasingly

Opposite The image of the post-war woman – as encouraged by the 1947 New Look – was amplified and emphasized during the following decade. Here an illustration by Esta captures the elegance and femininity of the 1950s ideal.

Right Family values were stressed and in many Western countries a "baby boom" resulted. The material pleasures of suburban family life were celebrated.

recognized in mainstream culture. An expanded and more affordable travel industry affected fashion: souvenir clothing was worn back at home, and regional influences continued on mainstream fashions.

Social and Economic Background

Outcomes of the war included the election of war hero General Dwight D. Eisenhower as President of the United States; the Nuremberg trials and the resulting reparations; and the establishment of new nations in Southeast Asia. With the loss of the Axis Powers as the enemy, Western Europe and the United States focused on the threat of communism and entered a period of uneasy relations with the USSR, referred to as the "Cold War." The British Empire experienced tension with communist China over the Crown colony of Hong Kong. French colonial presence in Indochina was destabilized with the growth of communism in the region. After the Korean War, fear of communism in the United States culminated with the activities of Senator Joseph McCarthy and the House Un-American Activities Committee.

After years of restraint and economizing, post-war expansion encouraged consumption in all segments of society. In Europe, rebuilding was aided by government programs that promoted purchasing and emphasized family life. Post-war recovery measures took various forms including 1951's Festival of Britain, the subsidization of the couture industry by the French government, and America's G.I. Bill of Rights. Peacetime priorities included housing and leisure, as technologies developed during the war were redeployed for civilian use. By 1950 over one million homes in the United States had television sets. This powerful new medium was instrumental in promoting the abundant consumer goods of the 1950s. On television and in print, much of the marketing was directed toward women who, re-established in the domestic sphere, were instrumental in purchasing decisions. Suburbs proliferated and many more families owned automobiles; fashion responded to the growth of "car culture." The phenomenon

Prevailing images of women were often contradictory. Tawdry seductresses in tight or revealing costume contrasted with perfect housewives in proper fashionable attire.

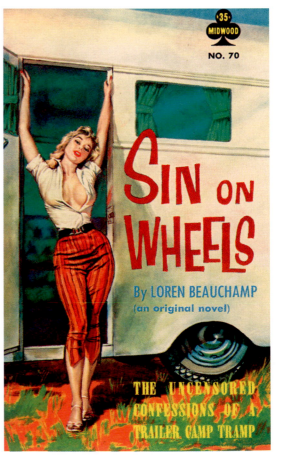

of designer maternity wear reflected the high birth rate of these years – known as the "baby boom." The 1950s man was represented as a family man, businessman, consumer, and leisure enthusiast who dressed to express his affluence and interests. However, family values and prosperity masked currents of unrest, including the beginning of the civil rights movement, which called for an end to racial segregation. Anti-fashion, often youth-driven, style statements expressed dissatisfaction with social conformity.

The Arts

Abstraction dominated painting and sculpture, as seen in the work of Europeans Jean Dubuffet and Antoni Tàpies, and the emerging New York School including Robert Motherwell and Helen Frankenthaler. Figurative art favored distortion over realism, as exemplified by Alberto Giacometti, Francis Bacon, Henry Moore, and George Tooker. Late in the decade, Pop Art evolved as Richard Hamilton and Robert Rauschenberg, among others, incorporated everyday objects and pop culture references into their artworks.

The glass walls of International Style architecture, exemplified by the work of Gordon Bunshaft, Walter Gropius, and Ludwig Mies van der Rohe, defined cityscapes. A more organic aesthetic informed work by Eero Saarinen and Le Corbusier. Decorative arts demonstrated the wide variety of styles at all price levels available to an increasingly design-conscious public. In growing suburban areas, Colonial Revival architecture and decoration contrasted with more modern styles. The emphasis on family life and informal entertaining encouraged interest in simple wood furnishings and lively textiles, such as those produced by Lucienne and Robin Day in England, and Ray and Charles Eames in the United States.

Many significant literary works reflected the restlessness of youth, including J. D. Salinger's *The Catcher in the Rye* (1951), Françoise Sagan's *Bonjour Tristesse* (1954), William Golding's *Lord of the Flies* (1954), Vladimir Nabokov's *Lolita* (1955), and Allen Ginsberg's poem *Howl* (1956). Sensational popular novels such as Herman Wouk's *Marjorie Morningstar* (1955) and Grace Metalious' *Peyton Place* (1956) proved to be best sellers. Low-priced paperbacks offered torrid stories and featured busty women on book covers in various states of undress, showcasing the decade's preoccupation with foundation garments. The challenging dramas of playwrights Arthur Miller, Tennessee Williams, John Osborne, and Harold Pinter had multiple successes on stage, as did avant-garde productions by Eugène Ionesco and Samuel Beckett.

Experimental music gained a larger public through the work of John Cage and Pierre Boulez. Operas such as *Billy Budd* (1951) by Benjamin Britten and Igor Stravinsky's *The Rake's Progress* (1951) applied modernist principles to traditional musical forms. Richard Strauss' poignantly romantic last works premiered in 1950, a year after the composer's death, as *Four Last Songs*. On the popular music scene, big bands and established vocalists, including Frank Sinatra, Ella Fitzgerald, Harry Belafonte, and Dean Martin, continued their successful careers, but they faced new competition from rock and roll performers such as Elvis Presley, Bill Haley and His Comets, and Buddy Holly.

An international group of film directors advanced cinema. Italian directors Vittorio De Sica and Federico Fellini offered gritty views of the human experience. Akira Kurosawa's influential *Rashomon* (1950) and *Seven Samurai* (1954) brought Japan's movie industry worldwide acclaim. Swedish director Ingmar Bergman produced enigmatic, artistic work such as *The Seventh Seal* (1957) and *Wild Strawberries* (1957). Satyajit Ray's films were crucial to the growth of Indian cinema. A group of young French directors, notably Jean-Luc Godard and François Truffaut, were pioneers of the "New Wave." Hollywood continued to produce movies in all the major genres. Lavish musicals included *Singing in the Rain* (1952), *An American in Paris* (1951), and *A Star is Born* (1954). War stories were portrayed in movies such as *From Here to Eternity* (1953) and *Sayonara* (1957). Westerns such as *High Noon* (1952) and *Shane* (1953) were also widely popular.

Television commanded more and more of the public's time and attention with newscasts, sports, variety shows, soap operas, and situation comedies. Comedies often centered on domestic life, and shows such as *Father Knows Best* and *Leave it to Beaver* promoted images of "ideal" families. Popular children's programs such as Britain's *Blue Peter* and America's *Howdy Doody Show* and *The Mickey Mouse Club* created opportunities for merchandise tie-ins. Fashion designers were interviewed on talk shows such as Edward R. Murrow's *Person to Person*. One of the most watched events of the decade, the television broadcast of Queen Elizabeth's coronation in 1953, reached over twenty million viewers.

Fashion Media

While great illustrators such as René Gruau, Eric, and Jacques Demachy enlivened the fashion press, photography had become the dominant visual form on both the covers and inside pages of established periodicals including *Vogue*, *Harper's Bazaar*, *Femina*, *L'Officiel* and *The Queen*. The careers of Cecil Beaton, John Rawlings, Erwin Blumenfeld, and Louise Dahl-Wolfe were still active. They were joined by a new crop of photographers, including Richard Avedon, Irving Penn, Norman Parkinson, and John French, who injected an unconventional spirit of action and technical experimentation into their fashion work. They went outside the studio to use the circus, nightclubs, and even the subway as locations for their high fashion photographs. Through their memorable images, great models such as Dovima, Barbara Goalen, and Suzy Parker became recognizable celebrities instead of anonymous "faces."

The tone of fashion writing was instructive, even high-handed. Magazines reinforced a systematic, rules-driven approach to fashion, suggesting a "blueprint" for each season, often with charts detailing wardrobe pieces, accessories, fabrics, and even make-up colors. Readers were told, for instance, that a blue suit with white blouse was perfect for committee work in the spring, a tweed coat shouldn't be worn after four o'clock, and a restaurant dinner called for a dress with a flattering neckline. Influential (mostly female) editors at major magazines included Edna Woolman Chase and Jessica Daves at American *Vogue*; Audrey Withers at British *Vogue*; and Michel de Brunhoff, succeeded by Edmonde Charles-Roux, at French *Vogue*. Carmel Snow reigned at *Harper's Bazaar* until 1957, and Diana Vreeland was also on the staff. The

Below Suburban living often included cocktail parties, with specific attire. Here embellished cardigans are worn over cocktail dresses.

Bottom France returned to dominate high fashion, clearly exemplified by this dress from Nina Ricci, seen in *L'Art et la Mode*, November 1952.

dictatorial fashion editor became a familiar character, immortalized by Kay Thompson as Miss Prescott in the 1957 film *Funny Face*, a gentle spoof of the fashion industry.

New magazines catered to individual interests and combined fashion and the arts. *Charm*, "the magazine for women who work," advised women on wardrobe as well as which vacation spots were best "to meet a man."[1] *Ebony* magazine debuted its "Fashion Fair," a traveling show of high fashion targeted to black Americans. *Gentry*, introduced in 1951, offered upscale lifestyle and fashion advice to men. *Sports Illustrated*, first published in 1954, gave a great deal of coverage to sports clothing.

The Elements of Women's Fashion

In women's fashion, two silhouettes prevailed for most of the decade in both day- and eveningwear. One featured a full skirt created by either gores or gathers and a fitted bodice, while the other combined the same bodice shape with a narrow "pencil" skirt that molded to the hips. Clothing of the decade was very specific to time of day and event, and it was important to be correct for all occasions, with not only the proper clothes, but also the proper accessories. As *Harper's Bazaar* stated in 1953, "It's a matter of immaculacy – of being well-turned-out, from smoothly shaped head to admirably shod toe."[2] Even home sewers could wear the latest looks for day or evening, as top designers' styles were available through paper patterns.

The well-dressed woman of major fashion centers often wore tailored suits in the daytime for lunch, shopping, and afternoon social engagements. Suits emphasized chic, and at the designer level were fabricated of particularly luxurious woolen fabrics, and in linen versions for summer. While the full skirt was often featured with the tailored jacket, the slim skirt was more typical. Well-chosen accessories were essential to the look of suits; gloves were usually worn to the elbow as three-quarter-length sleeves (or bracelet sleeves) allowed a woman to show off her jewelry. Necklines were often cut large enough to display pearl or jewel necklaces. Collars and cuffs added smart details, and other features included self-covered or crocheted buttons and topstitched accents. Early in the 1950s, women's suits began to prefigure the looser styles that would prevail by the end of the decade. Several designers, notably Balenciaga, encouraged this trend, as some suit jackets became boxier, leading *Harper's Bazaar* in 1953 to describe the style as "sharp, eliminated and modern."[3]

Daytime one-piece dresses also followed both silhouettes. Designers used silks, crepes, organzas, even taffetas, among their elegant fabrications, as well as a variety of cottons, such as piqué, dotted Swiss, dobby, and other novelty weaves. Despite the rather rigid choice of silhouette, a wide range of variations could be seen in necklines, sleeve styles, and dressmaker details. Sleeveless and short-sleeved dresses with matching jackets were worn for a wide range of occasions, and created a prim image. Shirtwaist styles were common, and self belts nearly always completed the look. Peter Pan collars were an especially popular detail. Summertime offerings included sleeveless styles and halterneck tops. For fall and spring, sweaters were quite often worn with skirts, with twin sets especially common. More casual daytime dressing, for the suburban lifestyle, included shirtwaist dresses in a variety of prints, especially popular in a wide range of cotton and synthetic fabrics.

Evening clothes celebrated luxury and glorified the lush materials of the time. Large volumes of fabric were used to create the fuller silhouette, while the slim shape, less common in the evening, was still used to striking effect. Evening and ball gowns were typically long and dramatic, often with draped treatments that evoked the 19th century. Shorter styles for such occasions became options at the beginning of the decade, even for ball gowns; the "ballerina" or "waltz" length (at the ankle) was common. As the social ritual of cocktail parties took on greater importance, cocktail dresses became a significant part of the wardrobe. While men sometimes arrived at cocktail parties from the office in their business clothes, women dressed in elaborate short dresses in dramatic fabrics, often beaded, and accessorized with eye-catching jewelry. Some cocktail dresses were teamed with matching or coordinating coats or

boleros. Dinner clothes included similar dresses, but designers also offered fancy dinner suits, in fabrics such as silk ottoman, matelassé and cloqué, often trimmed with fur collars and cuffs. Hostess ensembles were another important part of the market. One distinctive look combined slim pants with a divided full skirt open up the front. Decorative hostess aprons were often worn, carefully chosen to complement an ensemble.

Fitted coat styles continued from the late 1940s, but full shapes flaring from the shoulders and full through the body became very common. These frequently had loose sleeves, sometimes based on kimono shapes or with raglan cut. As with suits, three-quarter-length sleeves were sometimes seen. Dress overcoats were matched to dresses or suits worn beneath them, and the well-dressed woman owned many coats to complement her wardrobe in a variety of weights and colors. The full styles placed more importance on linings. Sometimes coat and dress or suit ensembles repeated a fabric from one piece to another. Shorter, three-quarter-length coats were worn with skirts, and followed the lines of the flared full-length styles. The term "car coat" was used for three-quarter-length coats, reflecting the lifestyle needs of many suburban women. Coats for evening typically flared to quite full proportions, and were often fabricated in satin, taffeta, moiré faille, and shantung. Fur pieces continued in popularity, with fur coats common for cold weather, and fur capelets and stoles popular for evening, especially cocktail hour. Mink, sable, and fox were common. Short fur jackets, often with three-quarter-length sleeves, were very popular. Curly pelts such as astrakhan or Persian lamb were also frequently seen as jackets, coats, and hats, and as trim on wool garments. Leopard and zebra were especially favored for both coats and trimmings.

Above Wedding dresses were especially important in the fashion industry. Hollywood contributed inspiration through both film costumes and actresses' real-life weddings. Helen Rose designed this gown for Grace Kelly's 1956 marriage to Prince Rainier of Monaco.

Below A late-decade overcoat design from a New York manufacturer reflects the silhouettes advocated by Paris designers.

Wedding dresses were usually long and romantic, using traditional bridal fabrics such as satin, tulle, and lace. Floating fabrics in pastel colors characterized bridesmaid dresses. The long voluminous skirts of wedding gowns were sometimes supported with hoop skirts. Hollywood contributed significantly to bridal fashion. But as early as 1950, shorter bridal gowns began to appear, with Balmain showing a "day-length dress with a floor-length train."[4] Audrey Hepburn's memorable Givenchy short wedding dress in *Funny Face* continued the trend.

Reproduction rates soared in the Western world and the maternity market grew substantially at all price points. Some designers included maternity styles in their collections, including Givenchy and Hartnell, and manufacturers advertised in important fashion magazines. Modest high-waisted and smock styles were the most popular, reflecting mainstream styles. Television contributed to the adoption of more stylish maternity clothes when the real-life pregnancy of Lucille Ball was incorporated into the 1952–1953 season of the show *I Love Lucy*.

Pants were increasingly common for leisurewear, even blue jeans for young women in extremely casual circumstances. In general pant legs were narrow. Very fitted "toreador" pants and cropped calf-length "Capri" pants reflected the international travel influences on fashion, as did knee-length "Bermuda" shorts. Blouses, sometimes in shirtwaist styles, sometimes in feminine versions with Peter Pan collars, were often sleeveless in white and pastel colors. Casual ensembles were topped with cardigans or short jackets. Wool plaid shirts were popular for woodsy leisure activity. Oregon's Pendleton Woolen Mills released its first women's garment, the "49er," a plaid overshirt with patch pockets inspired by their decades-old men's outdoor shirts. It took its name from the 1849 Gold Rush and its 1949 release. The style became a perennial favorite, as recreational camping grew in popularity.

Affluent, athletic women included sport activities in their lifestyles: tennis clothes were usually standardized as white; skiwear reflected developments in textile

technologies; playsuits continued to be popular; and knit polo-style shirts were adopted into feminine use. Swimwear was sometimes boned, cupped, and shaped and this was seen in both one- and two-piece suits. However, important manufacturers were introducing practical advances in swimwear that reflected textile innovations. Some notable French designers were designing swimwear for American companies, including Dior for Cole of California and Givenchy for Jantzen. Bikinis, still considered shocking, saw slow increases in acceptance. Gottex, renowned for colorful patterned swimwear, was founded in Israel by Lea Gottlieb, a Hungarian emigré, in 1956.

For day, women often wore small, shaped hats that fitted tightly to the head. Other styles included variations on berets, cloches, and small bonnets and toques. Veils were frequently featured, some in fine net but more often with thicker mesh, in black as well as light colors, and were frequently worn over the face. Cocktail hats conveyed fantasy, decorated with large flowers, arrangements of pointy feathers, and bows. Some turban-like styles completely swathed the head in tulle, lace, or fluffy wools. Wide-brimmed hats were also seen, often worn with full skirts, suggesting 18th-century styles. Prominent Parisian milliners included Paulette, Claude Saint-Cyr, and Rose Valois, but increasingly millinery trends were set by the couturiers. In London, Aage Thaarup and Rudolf both earned acclaim for their hat designs for Queen Elizabeth. American hat designers Lilly Daché and John-Frederics continued their success.

The shoulder bags of the war years were out of fashion and women typically hand-carried their purses, in a more ladylike gesture. Most bags were structured and boxy with short straps. Leather and suede were popular, but summer bags were often made of straw, raffia, or fabric in an immense range of colors to coordinate with clothing. One Hermès style, the Sac à dépêches, became famous through its association with Grace Kelly. In 1956 Kelly, by then Princess Grace of Monaco, was photographed holding the bag and the style became known as the "Kelly bag."

Prestigious shoe labels including Perugia, Ferragamo, Roger Vivier, and Delman created ornate shoes, many in luxurious silks with lavish embellishment. Evening shoes, in particular, were often made of dress fabric to create a matching ensemble.

Below left Ads for Pendleton Woolen Mills featured cheerful suburban women wearing their classic plaids for leisure activity. The woman's jacket, the "49er" (introduced in 1949), was worn by Lucille Ball on a camping episode of *I Love Lucy*.

Below right A play-clothes ensemble with a convertible top is pictured in multiple views in American magazine *Charm* in 1951.

Beginning around 1954, Vivier designed shoes with "stiletto heels," very thin heels reinforced with metal rods, influencing changes in shoe silhouette. The shape of shoes evolved over the course of the decade; the toe became pointed and less round, the vamp lowered, and heels became thinner. Many shoe styles were popular including strappy sandals for evening, ballerina flats, and, for sport and leisure, loafers and sneakers.

Gloves were worn with most daytime outfits and dresses, even those with short sleeves, year-round. Seasonal materials included suede and leather for cool weather, and cotton, including crochet and novelty prints, for summer. Printed silk scarves in all shapes were worn in a variety of ways: as an ascot or a bow at the neck, over the hair, or tied onto a handbag as a colorful accent. Colorful scarves were printed with varied designs: painterly florals, pictorial themes, dots, and geometrics. Designer scarves were popular and prestigious. Cigarette holders were revived as sophisticated accessories. Pearls were considered correct for day or evening. Fine and costume jewelry was often worn in matching sets of earrings, necklace, and bracelet. Bangle bracelets were also popular, sometimes worn in unmatched multiples. Button earrings and other close-fitting styles were appropriate for day and evening; sparkly, jeweled dangle styles were worn for evening. Rhinestone accents in jewelry, brooches, hair clips, buttons, and as buckles on shoes and bags were very popular.

Fashion Fabrics

Distinctive fabric was an important part of fashion at all price levels, from the luxurious silks of couture evening gowns to bright printed cottons on simple daywear. The opulence of the 1950s prompted a return to a pre-modern aesthetic, evoking the luxury of the 19th century. Silk brocade, warp-printed taffeta, ciselé velvet and lace were all exploited to spectacular effect. Evening textiles were often embellished with opulent embroidery or beading.

Fine fabrics came from France, Switzerland, Italy, and Britain. The long-established Lyons firms Rodier and Bianchini-Férier were still associated with high-end luxury. The London firm Ascher was popular with top designers. They produced a range of unique mohairs, and commissioned designs from leading fine artists. Many firms developed the concept of artist-designed prints, including the American company Fuller Fabrics, who launched their Modern Masters print series in 1955 with designs by top European painters that were utilized by Claire McCardell. Prints were strong in fashion year-round; the fashion press highlighted each season's new patterns and conversational prints were especially popular.

Man-made fibers were part of the post-war aspiration to a life made easier through technology. By 1955 polyester, the newest synthetic, was being commercially produced on both sides of the Atlantic. Seen as a threat to established textile industries the world over, synthetics won over consumers through aggressive marketing by manufacturers. Some of the negative qualities of manufactured fibers (a rough feel, yellowing, and the tendency to hold in perspiration) were alleviated through blends with natural fibers. As the introduction of synthetics accelerated, branding became important and wardrobes were filled with Dacron®, Crimplene, Orlon®, Fortrel®, Acrilan®, Lycra®, and other branded fibers developed by huge corporations.

Foundations and Lingerie

Highly structured bras and girdles created the fashionable body type, with pointy breasts, cinched waists and prominent hips. Many women had numerous foundation garments with variations in length, support, and color. White and pale tones

Foundations were essential to the sculpted body that fashion required through most of the decade.

were popular, but black and even animal prints were also seen. All-in-one foundations, sometimes referred to as "corselets," combined bra and girdle and often had a ruffle at the bottom, giving support to full skirts. Waist cinchers were known by a variety of names including *guêpière*, "waspie," and "waistliner." While most foundation garments produced a tight, sleek line, some girdles had articulated back panels that defined the buttocks for a more rounded look. Many bras featured circular stitching on the cups to emphasize a pointed shape, and some incorporated wires for support and structure. Many styles were strapless or convertible, and some even had straps that sat wide on the shoulders for the deep, wide necklines popular for evening. Balconnet bras, with shelf-like half cups and wide-set straps, created a high bustline that was especially attractive under low-cut necklines and visually lengthened the torso. Foundation garments

A conversational print typical of the 1950s, featuring poodles, a popular motif.

WHIMSICAL PRINTS

A taste for colorful prints characterized fashion throughout the decade, seen on everything from couture gowns to mail-order house dresses. The full, wide skirts of the period provided a perfect vehicle for interesting prints. But slimmer silhouettes were also enlivened by colorful patterns. Novelty conversational prints abounded. Food was one popular theme. In 1953 Givenchy showed prints of grapes, oysters, and red and yellow peppers on summer dresses. A year later, Adele Simpson designed dresses in silk printed with shrimp. Lobsters, cherries, corn, tomatoes, and other ingredients were fashionable on more modestly priced pieces. Clowns, cowboys, and animals – from the farm or zoo – populated prints for the important juvenile market, showing up on

shirts, pajamas, bedding, and curtains. Travel also provided inspiration; novelty prints showcased London landmarks, Chinese pagodas, and Tahitian palm trees. The Eiffel Tower and the Roman Colosseum appeared on countless dresses, blouses, and aprons.

Contemporary art influenced prints as well. Some were commissioned from fine artists, but many textile designers simply borrowed familiar elements of abstract art, such as loose brush strokes and bold colors, and applied them to fabric. Interest in scientific discoveries also inspired modern prints; molecular forms and crystalline structures appeared on clothes and furnishings. Poodles, with their suggestion of Parisian panache, were especially popular in the print parade.

were aggressively marketed. Specific models were given evocative names, including "Wonder-bra" from a Canadian company; and Maidenform's "I Dreamed" campaign reached new heights of fantasy. Foundations were marketed to juniors as well, worn by teenage models, and considered essential to proper dressing. Improvements in elasticized synthetic fabrics offered dependable stretch fit. Many girdles had zippers and elasticized panels. Lightweight and supple, nylon was popular for lingerie, even for lace. The versatile stretch fiber Lycra® was introduced in 1959.

Slips, frequently made of nylon and lace-trimmed, were usually worn under dresses over the foundation layer. Nightwear was often filmy and trimmed with lace, frequently in white, cream, and pastel colors. Full-length peignoir sets were popular, often with feminine detailing. Pajamas were also worn, for sleep- and loungewear.

Hair and Beauty

The beauty standard of the time was polished and mature. It was a look that was achieved with overt use of cosmetics – what *Vogue* in 1950 called "frankly make-believe make-up."[5] Foundation and face powder were used for a matte finish; several companies offered blends of the two in compact form. Arched brows were drawn with dark eyebrow pencil. Eyeliner was also dramatic, applied on the top lid and often extending out to make the eyes wider, and sometimes also used below the eyes. Eyeshadow was available as powder, pencil, or cream. Many colors of lipstick were worn, but shades of red dominated, including the Revlon classic "Cherries in the Snow," introduced in 1953. Long, polished nails were fashionable, and nail polish and lipstick colors matched or coordinated.

Women wore a great variety of hairstyles, most chin length or shorter and often sculpted by permanents. Hair was waved and cropped, sometimes pulled back off the forehead or cut into "pixie" styles with pointy bangs. Hair coloring was advocated as a way to update one's style and often referred to as "tint" or "rinse." Popular names for hairstyles reflected international influence, as in the short, waved "Italian bob," and "Left Bank" bangs that swept across the forehead. Late in the decade, fuller hairstyles and less severe make-up with lighter-colored lipstick presented a more youthful alternative.

Later in the decade, overt femininity was combined with strong geometric shapes often rendered in taffeta, such as this "bubble" dress with train from Maggy Rouff in 1958.

Evolution of the Silhouette in the Late Decade

Some designers departed from the prevailing silhouettes by mid-decade and had a marked impact on the later years of the 1950s, offering looser styles for daytime, often boxy or columnar, for both suits and dresses. The waist was migrating: some styles were waistless, many dresses had Empire waists, while others used a dropped waist. The word "chemise" was used to describe a number of stylistic variations on a one-piece semi-fitted sheath. The "sack" or "bag" combined a loose body with the dropped waist and recalled 1920s style, and was typically worn with an updated version of the cloche hat. Touted with much fanfare in the press, these looser styles proved unpopular, especially in the United States where many women clung to the silhouettes of the New Look. However, the look was indicative of other changes in silhouette that would gain in popularity and forecast styles of the 1960s. While the looser styles were encouraged for day, some evening clothes showed a decisively more geometric approach, as gowns became a series of architectural forms, often in taffeta and stiff satins. Bubble hems were often seen on cocktail dresses. In 1958 *L'Officiel* showed dresses for day and evening with a "modern impression" – all had hemlines at the knee and skirts that stood away from the body, ranging from A-line to bubble-shaped. Reflecting this time of transition, many dresses for evening featured trains or uneven hemlines that were much longer in back.

Designers: France

By 1950 **Christian Dior** was the most famous fashion designer in the world. *Vogue* wrote that year, "Dior is the dynamic meteoric showman of the Couture. In all his collections, there is something of the sensational, and – importantly – something that is sure to forecast a trend."[6] Dior's shows were widely covered in the press and his designs set the tone for mainstream fashion. Yet the shy and retiring Dior led a quiet life, and did not fit the mold of the flamboyant designer.

Enormously financially successful, Dior's business generated a remarkable percentage of the revenue of the French fashion industry. His licensing agreements increased, and he offered a wide variety of accessories, including lines of shoes in collaboration with designers Roger Vivier and Herbert Delman. A fur salon opened in 1951. Dior developed an unprecedented global distribution system. Following the 1948 opening of his New York boutique, Dior established several international branches and custom salons (with in-house designers) in cities including London, Caracas, Santiago, and Sydney. An agreement was made with Holt Renfrew for exclusive Canadian distribution and reproduction rights of designs from the Paris and New York salons, and similar agreements were made with El Encanto in Havana, and El Palacio de Hierro in Mexico. In 1953 Daimaru, a Japanese department store, was licensed to produce Dior fashions in Japan, and often fabricated his designs in Japanese textiles.

The house of Dior epitomized luxury and was the pinnacle of the Parisian couture aesthetic. His work made lavish use of exquisite fabrics and embellishments, often overtly resembling gowns of the great fashion houses of the late 19th century, or referencing the shepherdess styles of Marie Antoinette. The theme of the garden recurred throughout his work, as embroidered, appliquéd, flocked, and printed flowers, and the *muguet*, or lily of the valley, became a recurring motif. The motif of basket-weave appeared not only on bergère hats but also as a fabric treatment.

Below left A Roger Vivier shoe for Christian Dior typifies the diversification of the Dior brand as well as the role of fine accessories in achieving head-to-toe sophistication.

Below right By the 1950s, Dior was at the pinnacle of Paris fashion and his global distribution surpassed any prior designer. This ad for retail giant Holt Renfrew, featuring the well-known model Dovima, advertises the label's exclusive distribution in Canada.

International influences were apparent in Dior's work, with references to Mexico, South America, and Japan. He experimented with creative geometries in his piecing and drapery; for several collections he used fabric that draped from one shoulder to the opposite hip, becoming part of the skirt. His Diorama evening gown (1951) used strips of horsehair as a decorative element on the top of the skirt. Odette (1952) utilized white silk flocked with black carnations, reminiscent of the work of Jean-Philippe Worth. His Zemire evening dress (1954) featured a rounded full skirt on a simple bodice, with a matching jacket that resembled his daytime tailored pieces; the ensemble was very popular and available in licensed copies.

Dior's 1954 H line, and the A line and Y line of 1955, presented new silhouettes. The H line was straight and slender, with little shaping, and was nicknamed "the French Bean" by the press. The A line featured a wide full skirt with an elevated waist, and was most typified by the "A" ensemble, a gray silk-and-wool flannel suit. The Y line was distinguished by a wide, angled bateau neckline and a narrow silhouette through the body.

Following the success of Miss Dior and Diorama, a new fragrance, Diorissimo, was released in 1956, based on lily of the valley. Dior was pictured on the cover of *Time* magazine in 1957 brandishing a pair of oversize shears. Upon his untimely death the same year, the house continued to operate under the design direction of **Yves Saint Laurent** (1936–2008), who had been with the house since 1954. Saint Laurent presented his first collection for Dior in 1958, and transformed the A-line silhouette into the "Trapeze," which was offered in several variations, including a day version with practical patch pockets, and a cocktail version with a bubble hem. The success of this collection reassured the fashion world of the continued viability of the house of Dior.

Parisian chic was epitomized by the collections of Jacques Fath. This 1951 ensemble, photographed by Willy Maywald, includes a very full peplum over a narrow skirt.

Jacques Fath branched out into fragrance, accessories, and ready-to-wear. His designs were distributed through a boutique for scarves, ties, and other accessories including hats, muffs, and hosiery. Fath also designed the lower-priced "Fath de Fath" prêt-à-porter line and was distributed in America by Joseph Halpert, an American manufacturer, who produced dresses labeled "Designed in America by Jacques Fath." He often used materials in unusual combinations, such as jersey, lace, and sable, and added dramatic decorative details such as large bows and bouquets. Fath was particularly known for contrasting full and narrow in one ensemble: extremely fitted skirts were often combined with swing-style coats or jackets with voluminous long peplums, creating a striking silhouette. Many designs contrasted black and white, and accessories were also often oversized. Fath was known for entertaining lavishly, and for the tempestuous atmosphere of the house where the designer and his wife, both of dramatic temperament, worked together. Jacques Fath died of leukemia in 1954 and his widow, Geneviève, maintained the business until it closed in 1957.

Pierre Balmain continued his rise in the world of fashion. With an increasingly international stature, Balmain received acclaim in the fashion press, especially for his elegant, very Parisian, evening looks. In 1950 *Vogue* said his work combined wearability with "a strong touch of imagination and French subtlety."[7] A favorite with American socialites, by 1952 he had boutiques in the United States selling ready-to-wear, and he won the Neiman Marcus Award in 1955. Balmain's work showed a marked contrast in mood and aesthetic for day and night. His daywear was polished and refined, with suits that were geometric in their precision; leopard fur trim was a frequent detail. For evening, he focused on luxury and embellishment. Many cocktail and evening dresses showed influence from the 18th and 19th centuries. He conveyed historic inspiration with embroidery, bows, ruched trimming, and suggestions of

The prodigious talents of photographer Horst P. Horst and illustrator Marcel Vertès combined to create this image for a *Vogue* editorial (May 1953) featuring a floral evening gown by Pierre Balmain.

panniers as well as bustle-shaped skirts. Balmain's fragrances were very successful, especially his Jolie Madame. He designed for theater and film, ranging from Katharine Hepburn's costumes for *The Millionairess* on Broadway in 1952, to *En Cas de Malheur* (1958) starring Brigitte Bardot.

Cristóbal Balenciaga's participation in the Théâtre de la Mode helped establish his place in the spotlight. Stylistically, Balenciaga was outside the mold set by Dior, but his work was highly praised by the press and sought by discerning clients. Balenciaga excelled in evening dresses and wraps, as well as suits and outerwear for daytime. He continued themes established in the 1930s, taking inspiration from his native Spain. In addition to fitted princess-line styles inspired by flamenco, Balenciaga's evening

Above left A Cristóbal Balenciaga cocktail ensemble from 1951 illustrates his masterful manipulation of fullness for geometric effect.

Above right An illustration by Constance Wibaut for *Elseviers Weekblad*, February 1955, combines the experimentation of Balenciaga's silhouettes with an avant-garde illustration style.

and cocktail dresses often featured large volumes of fabric, frequently taffeta and gazar (silk organza), cut on the straight grain and gathered or pleated from rectangular pieces. This technique was widespread in his work, resulting in long architectural gowns, and bubble-hemmed cocktail dresses. Sometimes dresses were unadorned, while at other times profuse trimming suggested Baroque style or torero costume. He also offered a variety of evening wraps, some based on rectangular shapes and others styled along the lines of a bullfighter's cape. Customers prized his striking suits and coats, which they could wear for several seasons; they were fashion-forward but also timeless. In his suits, he experimented with fit, creative use of seaming and drapery, and unusual sleeves, and tweed was a favorite fabric. Perhaps the first to react to the hourglass form of the prevailing New Look, Balenciaga introduced a less shaped fit. His "cocoon" (or "barrel") suit with its loosely fitted jacket appeared as early as 1947, and in 1952 he featured the sack line. Balenciaga's work at the end of the 1950s showed continued innovation. His 1958 silhouettes, with loose bodies and high or low waists, forecast styles of the 1960s.

Jean Dimitre Verginie (1904–1970), known as **Jean Dessès**, was born in Egypt of Greek parentage. He went to Paris in the mid-1920s to work in haute couture, and opened his own house in 1937 on rue George V. Maintaining the business through the war years, he participated in the Théâtre de la Mode and in 1948 moved his house to Hôtel Eiffel and began selling his dresses in the United States. American *Vogue* declared in 1950, "Dessès creates with a hand that is dashing and unafraid."[8] He experienced great success in the post-war years and gained a notable clientele. Although he offered quality tailored pieces, Dessès was especially known for his cocktail and eveningwear. His signature style utilized historical inspiration from his ancestral Greece. His work featured finely pleated chiffons and georgettes with masterful drapery. Dessès' dresses were typically molded to a shapely structured torso with billowing skirts. His palette included neutrals and pastels, as well as strong saturated colors, sometimes using contrasting slips underneath sheer fabrics to create striking color effects. Like Dior, he featured a basket-weave motif on some of his dresses, where criss-crossed panels on

Above The extraordinary dressmaking of Paris couture is exemplified in this full-skirted organza cocktail dress by Jacques Griffe (*top*) and a draped chiffon evening gown with basket-weave bodice by Jean Dessès.

Opposite Sunny Harnett in an evening dress by Madame Grès at the casino at Le Touquet, France. Photographed by Richard Avedon in 1954. © The Richard Avedon Foundation.

a molded bodice flowed into the gores of the skirt. Dessès closed his Paris house in 1960, but continued designing in Greece.

Jacques Griffe (1909–1996) was born in the Languedoc region of southern France. He learned to sew as a child and trained in tailoring and dressmaking. Griffe found work in 1936 cutting for Madeleine Vionnet, who became his great mentor and gave him one of her half-scale dress forms on which to practice his draping technique. Griffe was called to fight in 1940 and was a prisoner of war for eighteen months. In 1942 he opened his first couture house in Paris. After the war, he expanded his couture business and moved into premises on rue Royale that had been previously occupied by Molyneux. Griffe created a wide variety of clothes, and added boutique and ready-to-wear lines. He was an early advocate of the looser boxy fit for suits and coats. He paid a great deal of attention to the skirt, with tucks, pleating, or ruffles often contrasting a simpler bodice. In 1952, with short ball gowns beginning to appear, Griffe created an intricately pieced tulle skirt that was hemmed higher in front, dipping low in back. Griffe maintained a very diverse career, designing costumes for theater and film, offering perfumes, and designing for Vogue Patterns.

Gabrielle Chanel returned to the world of couture after more than a decade and in February 1954 showed her comeback collection. Chanel's re-entry into the fashion industry was widely publicized. *Vogue* glossed over the designer's personal history and asserted Chanel had "retired" in 1939 before re-emerging to spread her modern ideas to a new generation. Her first collection was not well received, as the boxy, tailored Chanel look seemed out of step with the fitted silhouettes and feminine details that dominated high fashion. But quickly, Chanel's simple ensembles began to influence other designers, especially in the American career market. As *Vogue* asserted, "If the simplicity of her line was not new ... its influence is unmistakable."[9] The simple lines of her suits, with cardigan-style jackets made in richly textured bouclés and tweeds, helped develop the new silhouette of fashion in the 1960s. In 1955 she introduced the quilted handbag with a chain handle, an accessory that was to become a Chanel classic. In 1957 Chanel received the Neiman Marcus Award.

Madame Grès (Alix) was especially well known for "Grecian" evening dresses, constructed of yards of fine silk jersey or chiffon pleated into fluted columns. While many of the pieces exposed the wearer's arms, shoulders, or back, the gowns featured a hidden infrastructure of boning, bra cups, and fastenings that was greatly appreciated by clients. Despite the foundations, her designs emphasized a somewhat tubular body, in contrast to the prevailing hourglass shape of the time. Her daywear and cocktail ensembles were also highly distinctive, often featuring crisp materials such as taffeta or tweed cut on the bias, with sculptural results. Grès designed other pieces inspired by world dress including kaftans and kimonos. By the end of the decade, Grès introduced her first fragrance, Cabochard. She maintained extraordinarily high standards of workmanship and her dresses were prized by a loyal clientele that included the Duchess of Windsor and American heiress Doris Duke.

As a young man, **Hubert de Givenchy** (b. 1927) was inspired by the fashion displays at the 1937 Exposition Internationale in Paris. He trained at the Ecole des Beaux Arts and worked for Jacques Fath in 1945. After a year with Fath, Givenchy

Audrey Hepburn in a floral taffeta afternoon dress by Hubert de Givenchy in the 1957 film *Funny Face*.

moved on to Robert Piguet and shortly thereafter to Lucien Lelong. He then worked with Schiaparelli for four years. Givenchy opened his *maison* in 1952 on rue Alfred de Vigny with a collection of blouse and skirt ensembles that was hailed as "dazzling" and "youthful." His success was immediate and the young designer became known for romantic, charming styles: dresses often had wide necklines, bare shoulders, or collars that stood away from the neck, emphasizing the willowy proportions of his models. Givenchy suits were fitted, but not tight, with rounded shoulders. In 1953 he showed tight hats described as "Givenchy eggs." His style was described as discreet and elegant, with amusing touches such as contrast linings in loosely fit coats. By 1955 he made a transition to simpler, looser sheath and chemise dresses, some with higher hemlines – just below the knee – even for cocktail and evening styles. Givenchy's style became familiar to the public through the clothes he designed for Audrey Hepburn for her film roles as well as her private life. The black and white evening dress she wore in *Sabrina* (1954) was widely admired. *Funny Face* featured a complete Givenchy wardrobe – from Capri pants to traveling ensemble to wedding gown – that received a great deal of media attention and helped solidify the designer's reputation.

One of the most innovative and forward-thinking designers of the decade, **Pierre Cardin** (b. 1922) was a tailor, a costume designer, and an assistant at several couture houses before he showed his first collection in 1953. Born in Italy, Cardin began his high fashion career after the war as an assistant at Paquin. He worked at Schiaparelli, and then Dior, where he assisted with Dior's important debut collection of 1947. Cardin's tailoring skills and innovative silhouettes distinguished his work. His Bubble dress of 1954 was followed by other sculptural styles, many with striking oversize collars. By 1957 he was operating boutiques for men and women, called Adam and Eve. On a trip to Japan in 1957 Cardin met his favorite model, Hiroko, and taught a class in couture techniques to eager Japanese design students. In 1959 he presented a women's ready-to-wear collection and was temporarily expelled from the Chambre Syndicale de la Haute Couture Parisienne. By the end of the decade, the geometric emphasis, bold graphic effects, and shorter hemlines of his designs already hinted at the "futuristic" aesthetic that Cardin promoted in the 1960s.

Established houses including **Schiaparelli**, **Piguet**, **Mad Carpentier**, **Jeanne Lafaurie**, and **Marcelle Chaumont** were still active at the beginning of the decade. The house of **Nina Ricci** continued under the management of Robert Ricci, and Jules-François Crahay – a former salesman at Jane Regny and a prisoner of war during World War II – was appointed lead designer. Maison Ricci's fragrance L'Air du Temps (launched in 1948) was a best seller in the 1950s. **Jacques Heim** continued to create clothes in a variety of categories – innovative sports clothes as well as smart tailored ensembles. He opened a series of Heim boutiques, and was elected president of the Chambre Syndicale de la Haute Couture Parisienne in 1958, holding the position until 1962. **Antonio Castillo** (1908–1984), a Spaniard who moved to France to avoid the Spanish Civil War, had worked for both Robert Piguet and Elizabeth Arden during the

1940s. In 1950 he became creative director of **Lanvin**, and for a while the label's name was changed to Lanvin-Castillo. He maintained the elegant traditions of the house and produced particularly lush evening clothes. Carmen de Tommaso (b. 1909), who had opened a couture house in the mid-1940s and adopted the name **Carven**, became known for the youthful inflection of her collections, which were often inspired by her global travels, and her highly successful perfume Ma Griffe.

Designers: Britain

Wartime austerity was replaced by luxurious elegance from British houses. Although French fashion dominated media attention, British designers were creating equally sumptuous gowns and refined tailored pieces. Some firms in France and London had reciprocal arrangements for young designers and technicians, with the French learning tailoring from the British, and the British learning couture sewing techniques from the French. British fashion was usually less dramatic than French, and less relaxed than American. Its hallmark was elegance, emphasizing designs that were appropriate and correct for specific occasions. The 1953 coronation of the young queen, Elizabeth II, created the demand for vast quantities of gowns from the London couturiers – not just for the official ceremony, but for the numerous related society events – providing great financial stimulation for the houses.

The Incorporated Society of London Fashion Designers continued to promote London as a fashion center. In the manner of the Théâtre de la Mode, a touring show of dolls was organized as a benefit for the Greater London Fund for the Blind. The undisputed star of the doll show was "Miss Virginia Lachasse," a doll based on the leading model at **Lachasse**, who was displayed with a complete wardrobe, including

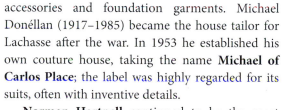

accessories and foundation garments. Michael Donéllan (1917–1985) became the house tailor for Lachasse after the war. In 1953 he established his own couture house, taking the name **Michael of Carlos Place**; the label was highly regarded for its suits, often with inventive details.

Norman Hartnell continued to be the most notable designer in British fashion. He showed his couture collection in Paris in 1951 and his work for several women of the royal family continued throughout the decade. With the death of King George VI in 1952, Princess Elizabeth became Queen of England. Following the prescribed period of mourning, the coronation was held in 1953 and Elizabeth commissioned Hartnell for her coronation dress. At the new queen's request, the gown followed the basic lines of her wedding dress, with sweetheart neckline and full skirt. The satin gown was heavily beaded, jeweled, and embroidered by Hartnell's workshops. The decoration consisted of floral and plant emblems that represented the realms of the Crown. Wales, for example, was represented by an elegantly curved leek. In addition to Queen Elizabeth's coronation gown (and accompanying wardrobe) Hartnell also designed gowns for the occasion for Elizabeth the Queen Mother, Princess Margaret, and the Duchess of Kent, and for Elizabeth's maids of honor. Hartnell's coronation-year fashion collection took inspiration from his work for the royal family and was among the most glamorous offered by a British couture house.

The design sketch for the coronation dress of Queen Elizabeth II designed by Norman Hartnell, with plants, flowers, leaves, and vegetables representing the different countries of the United Kingdom and the territories of the realm.

Photographer John French captured this theater ensemble by Digby Morton in 1952 with London's Tower Bridge in the background.

A perfectly accessorized checked coat by Pauline Trigère confirms her reputation for Seventh Avenue chic.

Victor Stiebel spent most of the decade as the house designer for Jacqmar, known for spectacular couture evening clothes. He also designed uniforms for the Women's Royal Navy Service, and the Women's Royal Air Force. He left Jacqmar in 1958 and once again established a label under his own name. **Charles Creed**'s clothes were available in limited quantities in the United States. Reacting to silhouette changes at the end of the decade, Creed advised women to dress for themselves, and to avoid new fashions unless they were truly suited to them. **Hardy Amies** received his first commission from Princess Elizabeth in 1950, and was awarded a royal warrant in 1955, which encouraged his business significantly. He published an autobiography, *Just So Far*, in 1954.

After one collection for Jacqmar in 1951, **Digby Morton** moved to the United States, where he worked with the Hathaway Shirt Company from 1955 to 1958, creating the Lady Hathaway line. When asked by *Sports Illustrated* magazine in 1956 how sports had affected fashion, he replied, "In its variations and fabrics, [the sport shirt] has become the basic style influence of this era. Because I style Lady Hathaway shirts, I'm all for this trend." In 1958 Morton merged his business with British sportswear manufacturer Reldan, forming **Reldan-Digby Morton**.

Born in Scotland, **Ronald Paterson** (1917–1993) studied design in London in the late 1930s, worked in London couture for a short time before the war, and opened his own successful house in 1947. Paterson also designed paper patterns. He insisted on a specific walk and posture from his runway models, dubbed the "Paterson Walk" by the news media in 1954. When showing the pencil-slim silhouette, he preferred very narrow "hobble" skirts and often used checked and tweed fabrics for his tailored pieces.

Irish-born **John Cavanagh** (1914–2003) worked as an assistant and secretary for Molyneux during the 1930s. During World War II, he served as an officer in the British Intelligence Corps. Following the war, he assisted Pierre Balmain from 1947 to 1952, when he returned to London to open his own house at 26 Curzon Street, famously decorated all in white. Although a new house, he experienced great success with his 1953 collection for the coronation. Throughout his career, Cavanagh was noted for his quality of cut and his delicate sense of color and, in addition to his elegant evening and cocktail dresses, featured fine tailoring.

Designers: United States

Notable designers continued innovation in sportswear and tailored pieces that were influential worldwide. Despite the pre-eminence of Parisian couture, the market for American "high couture" also continued, encouraged by the re-glamorized role of women in society. The American look was well groomed and mature, but without the exaggeration of much European fashion. In 1950 *Vogue* acknowledged the "international accent in fashion" but declared that American designers knew "the looks and likes of the American woman."[10] American designers turned out successful collections each season that maintained the "rules" of dressing yet pleased women who, increasingly, lived in the suburbs, where informality and outdoor activities affected style.

Hattie Carnegie continued to work up to her death in 1956. In 1950 she designed new uniforms for the Women's Army Corp, for which she received the Congressional Medal of Freedom in 1952. **Valentina** introduced her perfume My Own in 1950 and continued to cater to select clients until she retired in 1957. **Mainbocher** maintained his couture operation as well, with a client list as prestigious as Valentina's. In 1959 he created Mary Martin's costumes for the Broadway production of *The Sound of Music*.

Pauline Trigère, often referred to as a trendsetter and known for her personal chic, designed simple and restrained ensembles in distinct fabrications. Trigère won Coty Awards in 1951 and 1959. **Vera Maxwell**, known for adaptable ensembles, offered tweed suits, travel outfits, and dress ensembles. **Adele Simpson**'s dramatic suits, dresses, and eveningwear, often with a quite defined waist, were consistently featured in the press. Still an industry leader, by 1950 **Norman Norell** of **Traina-Norell** advocated a shaped, but waistless, chemise dress that *Vogue* described as "so

Suburban living in North America was perfectly suited to the relaxed styles of Claire McCardell, such as this halter dress photographed in 1957.

intricately cut that it suggests a tidy waistline without cleaving to one."[11] Norell's sequined evening "mermaid" sheaths remained among his most popular designs. **Nettie Rosenstein** remained well respected, as evidenced by the inaugural ball gown she designed for First Lady Mamie Eisenhower in 1953.

Claire McCardell received a degree of adulation that was virtually unprecedented for an American designer. In 1950 she was honored by the Women's Press Club and received a certificate of achievement from President Harry Truman. A Beverly Hills gallery presented a retrospective of her work in 1953. In 1955 McCardell was pictured on the cover of *Time* magazine. A *Life* magazine photo spread in 1955 pictured McCardell's designs utilizing fabrics designed by notable artists including Chagall, Dufy, Miró, Léger, and Picasso. Other accolades from the press included awards from *Sports Illustrated* and *Glamour*, both in 1956. McCardell carried on her association with Townley Frocks, becoming partner by 1952. Her fashion designs continued to build on relaxed, inventive ideas that she developed in the 1930s and 1940s. Further variations of the still popular Popover dress were offered, and her playsuits and swimwear continued to be innovative. Many of the themes she had established in her earlier work were still strongly present: self ties and piping, exposed hooks and eyes, cowl hoods, topstitching, day fabrics for evening, wrap construction, and raglan sleeves. Having recorded her design philosophy in the 1956 book *What Shall I Wear?*, McCardell died of cancer in March 1958, completing her last collection – in which she experimented with forward-thinking minimalist styles – just weeks before her death.

The 1950s proved to be the most important decade of **Charles James'** career. Themes of form and space were fully explored in some of his most celebrated creations. James prized the art of pattern making and creatively manipulated its rules, experimenting with the use of darts and shaped waistlines. While he continued to offer a variety of daytime suits and coats, often fabricated in luxurious and textured materials, it was his eveningwear that was his calling card, especially when worn by his celebrity clientele. At the beginning of the decade, James created elegantly draped gowns that often drew from the crinoline and bustle silhouettes of the 19th century. His work became increasingly sculptural; he created gowns so rigidly structured that the wearer could do little other than stand. The most famous of these was the Cloverleaf of 1953, with a skirt that projected out to resemble the shape of a four-leaf clover. The first fully realized version combined white satin with a curving band of black velvet at the mid-skirt level, and a lower section of ivory faille. The internal structure of the Cloverleaf dress was a marvel of dressmaking engineering, involving nylon mesh, taffeta, boning, and intricate seaming and piecing to create the silhouette. The asymmetrical shape was typical of James' utilization of combined concave and convex elements. James offered flamenco-style evening gowns similar to Balenciaga's. During the course of the 1950s, he entered into licensing agreements which included outerwear and suits, as well as a line of layette and toddler clothes.

New York socialite Babe Paley photographed by John Rawlings for *Vogue*, November 1, 1950, in a sculptural dress by Charles James.

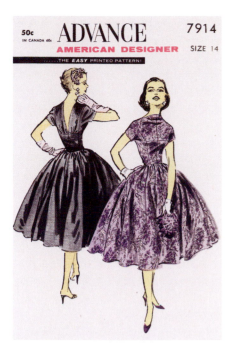

Anne Fogarty's dresses with the full-skirted "tea cosy" silhouette were available in paper patterns and popular with home sewers.

Pennsylvania native **Anne Fogarty** (1919–1980) studied theater at Carnegie Institute of Technology and went to New York City to pursue acting. A modeling job for a high-end dress house led to a career in fashion. Her first important design position came in 1948 for Youth Guild, a company that catered to the emerging junior and young adult market. In 1950 she moved to another junior label, Margot Dresses. Fogarty's success was prompt. She was recognized with a Coty Award in 1951, and the Neiman Marcus Award in 1952. Her aesthetic reflected the prevailing taste of the times: unabashedly feminine, her clothes were the type of styles that many young married women wanted. Fogarty created dresses that reveled in the post-war "New Look" trend, featuring extremely full skirts that required net petticoats to support their shape, for which Fogarty utilized new types of nylon horsehair. Her designs were given quaint names such as Tea Cozy and Paper Doll. She also featured princess lines and shirtwaist fronts. Later in the decade, she offered chemise and sheath silhouettes that followed the changes occurring in Paris. Fogarty's designs were available to home sewers with Advance Patterns' American Design collection. In 1957 she began designing for Saks Fifth Avenue and, in addition to dresses, created a line of accessories. In 1959 Fogarty wrote *Wife Dressing*, a guide for the well-dressed married woman in which she asserted that, "The clothes you choose and the way you choose them will state very clearly your outlook on life in general and your attitude toward life as a wife in particular."

Winner of a Coty Award and a Neiman Marcus Award in 1950, **Bonnie Cashin** (1907–2000) established Bonnie Cashin, Inc. in 1951, offering creative variations on sportswear pieces, distinguished by a masterful approach to materials. With plenty of pockets, her simply cut coats, suits, and jackets were favorites for travel, often made of textured tweeds, sometimes woven with metallic Lurex accents. Cashin was also known for using utilitarian metal toggle closures on outerwear. Some designs were lean, almost minimalist, such as a super-slim sheath dress in black worn with a sheer organdy apron. For skiing, she designed sleek stirrup pants with simply styled parkas and overblouses, one of which was featured on the cover of American *Vogue* in December 1952. Cashin used a lot of black and earth tones in her work. Her knits were renowned and many sweaters were designed to look hand-made. Cashin designed a knit shirtwaist dress – a jersey version of the dress that was a wardrobe staple. Cashin also favored shaggy mohairs or tweeds by renowned weaver Dorothy Liebes for hostess or "at-home" ensembles. Her work with leather and fur became an important part of her career.

Native New Yorker **Mollie Parnis** (c. 1900–1992) got her start in fashion as a saleswoman in a Seventh Avenue blouse firm during the 1920s. By the 1950s she was well established as a designer of clean-lined separates and suits; her full-skirted dresses for day and evening, many with small rhinestone accents, expressed a polished version of American ease. Parnis was among the favorite designers of American First Lady Mamie Eisenhower and was well known as an art collector and hostess.

First generation Greek American **James Galanos** (b. 1924) was born in Philadelphia and grew up in New Jersey. He attended the Traphagen School of Fashion for two semesters and then went to work for Hattie Carnegie in 1944. A chain of events took him to California where he worked as a sketch artist for Jean Louis. He went to Paris following the war where he worked for Robert Piguet, then traveled to New York in 1948, where he worked for a short time with the dress house Davidow. In 1951 he returned to California, and in 1952 launched his own line there, Galanos Originals. A New York branch came shortly afterward, as did orders from retailers Saks and Neiman Marcus, and favorable attention from the fashion press. Galanos became known for high-quality workmanship, delicate use of fabrics, and excellent taste. Some of his designs featured neoclassic inspiration while others used bold contrasting colors, perhaps reflecting the time spent working for Piguet. He used bold floral prints, cartridge pleating, and architectural forms. During the late 1950s some designs clearly foretold the look of the following decade. In addition to his collections, he provided wardrobe for female movie stars in many films, notably Rosalind Russell. Galanos received the Neiman Marcus Fashion Award in 1954, and Coty Awards in 1954, 1956, and 1959.

Arnold Scaasi (b. 1930) was born Arnold Isaacs in Montreal, the son of a furrier. Showing an interest in fashion at a young age, he began his design studies in Montreal, continuing in Paris at the school of the Chambre Syndicale de la Haute Couture Parisienne. He apprenticed at the house of Paquin, and in 1952 went to New York and began work as an assistant to Charles James. He was soon freelancing for other designers and for milliners Lilly Daché and John-Frederics. He created evening gowns that were featured in an advertising campaign for General Motors, which precipitated his name change from Isaacs to its reversed spelling "Scaasi." Leaving James' employ, he was hired to design a line of ready-to-wear by manufacturer Dressmaker Casuals, which included his name on the label. Scaasi's work was characterized by bold shapes and vibrant colors. He favored boxy, flared, and loose silhouettes for coats, and short evening ensembles. His work showed the influence of his mentor James, but also of Balenciaga. His career grew rapidly and his line was sold in a large number of stores. This success was confirmed in 1958 when Arnold Scaasi won a Coty Award, followed by the Neiman Marcus Award in 1959.

Tina Leser continued to feature Hawaiian, Asian, and other non-Western influences, encouraging the trend for internationalism. Her swimwear for the GaBar label often utilized textiles inspired by her travels. **Carolyn Schnurer** (1908–1998) began her career in the 1940s. Schnurer concentrated on sportswear for younger women, creating dresses and separates, and was well regarded for her resort wear. A world traveler like Leser, Schnurer used cultural inspirations as widespread as Provence and India. Her Flight to Japan collection in 1951 was particularly notable, and included the Rice Bowl dress that took its neckline from the back drape of a kimono and included a skirt with vertical boning inspired by parasols.

During the 1950s, the career of **Manuel Pertegaz** (1917–2014) was established on both sides of the Atlantic. Pertegaz was born in Olba, Spain, and went to Barcelona as a child, working as a tailor by his early teens. He opened his couture house in 1942 in Barcelona, then a store in Madrid in 1948. At this time he also began designing costumes for Spanish films. In 1954 he moved to the United States and presented collections in New York and other major American cities. His work was widely distributed by high-end retail stores throughout the United States, Canada, South America, Europe, and Egypt. Pertegaz's style in the 1950s was typified by feminine elegance. He took inspiration from his native culture, such as the elegant *majas* in the paintings of Francisco di Goya and the colorful dress of Spanish gypsies.

Designers: Italy

In January 1947 *Vogue* described Italian fashion using familiar generalizations: the clothes were sensual, extroverted, and dramatic, designed for (and by) sophisticated and beautiful aristocrats. Features on Italian fashion were also frequently travel articles, emphasizing Italy as a bargain destination. By the early 1950s Italy was known not just for finely made shoes and accessories, but for clothing that had European flair without being overly formal or expensive; *Vogue* praised Italy's "excellent separates ... even the cheapest sweaters have chic."[12] The looks that were initially promoted emphasized luxurious sportswear – a style that appealed to affluent Americans whose lifestyle was growing more informal. Evening gowns were also considered a specialty; *Vogue* noted in 1952, "Evening life is something the Italians understand thoroughly."[13] An important group showing of Italian designers in Florence in 1951 caught the attention of the international press.[14] **Emilio Schuberth** (1904–1972) (who had a boutique in Rome) dressed many of the stars of Hollywood and Italy's

American actress Ava Gardner wearing an ecclesiastic-inspired ensemble from the Italian house Sorelle Fontana in 1955.

Cinecittà, including Sophia Loren, Anna Magnani, and Gina Lollobrigida. **Alberto Fabiani** (1910–1987), from Rome, was praised for superlative tailoring. His wife, Countess **Simonetta Visconti** (b. 1922), was also a designer, known for her glamorous individual style. **Emilio Pucci** (1914–1992) was famed for his sportswear: striped sweaters, narrow pants, casual dresses, and ski clothes available through his boutique in Capri and at upscale retail stores. An athlete and an aristocrat, Pucci combined European prestige with comfort and ease, epitomizing the colorful and sporty spirit of Italian fashion. **Germana Marucelli** (1905–1983) gained prominence in post-war Italy creating her interpretations of Dior's New Look, but many of her designs made references to the glory of early Renaissance painting. Using the label **Sorelle Fontana** (often referred to as "Fontana" in the press), the three Fontana sisters, Zoe, Micol, and Giovanna, became famous for lavish eveningwear, wedding gowns, and their designs for films. They often designed for Ava Gardner, including her gowns for *The Barefoot Contessa* (1954), and counted international movie actresses (including Loretta Young and Elizabeth Taylor) as well as social figures among their clients. **Roberto Capucci** (b. 1930) was born in Rome and studied there at the Liceo Artistico and Accademia di Belle Arti. After he graduated from school, he worked for a short time for Emilio Schuberth, and opened his own house in Rome in 1950. Capucci quickly built a strong reputation; press attention during the 1950s focused on his bold use of color, strong geometries and amazing feats of cut. He had great success with his Box Line in 1958, a crisp and structural variation on the sack.

Film and Fashion

A less rigid studio system allowed designers and stars to move more freely from studio to studio. Hollywood designers stressed the elegance of the time by offering their own takes on Paris fashions when dressing contemporary stories. The distribution of Hollywood films spread these fashion images all over the world.

Designer William Travilla (1920–1990), billed as "Travilla," created two of the decade's most influential costume images, both for Marilyn Monroe. In *Gentlemen*

Below left William Travilla's candy pink evening gown for Marilyn Monroe's musical number "Diamonds are a Girl's Best Friend" in the film *Gentlemen Prefer Blondes* (1953) is one of the most iconic dresses of the decade.

Below right A sketch for Edith Head's design for Elizabeth Taylor in *A Place in the Sun* (1951); the dress set the tone for prom and debutante dresses.

Prefer Blondes (1953), Monroe's candy pink evening gown for the "Diamonds are a Girl's Best Friend" production number epitomized sexy glamour. In *The Seven Year Itch* (1955), the pleated skirt of Monroe's white halter dress blew in the air as she stood over a subway grate, creating one of the most memorable images in 20th-century popular culture.

Continuing her illustrious career, Edith Head created many of the most admired film costumes of the decade. In 1950 Head costumed *All About Eve* and created a striking evening gown with trapezoidal neckline – and pockets – for Bette Davis. The white gown worn by Elizabeth Taylor in *A Place in the Sun* (1951) was widely copied for the debutante market. Head was especially known for her collaborations with Alfred Hitchcock. Grace Kelly's wardrobe for *Rear Window* (1954) and *To Catch a Thief* (1955) included stylish interpretations of French couture, while Kim Novak's gray suit and black pumps in *Vertigo* (1958) reflected the taste for tailored ensembles.

Among her diverse projects, Helen Rose particularly impacted the bridal market. Elizabeth Taylor's wedding gown in *Father of the Bride* (1950) pointed out Hollywood's glorification of weddings (and their importance in society). The much copied dress was even available in an officially licensed version. Grace Kelly's real-life marriage in 1956 to Rainier III, Prince of Monaco, featured a gown designed by Rose (a wedding gift from the MGM studio) which became another of the decade's most copied dresses. Kelly's bridesmaids' dresses in beige organza were also widely copied.

Period pieces were popular on both sides of the Atlantic. Costumes by Elsa Schiaparelli and Marcel Vertès for *Moulin Rouge* (1952) and Cecil Beaton's for *Gigi* (1958) reflected the tastes of luscious Paris couture as much as they did the period settings of the films. The costumes of Bible epics such as *The Ten Commandments* (1956) often sacrificed historic accuracy for fashion relevance, as women's gowns resembled current designer styles.

Curvaceous female stars were the norm, including Monroe and Taylor, as well as Anita Ekberg, Sophia Loren, Gina Lollobrigida, and Jayne Mansfield. French model-turned-actress Brigitte Bardot presented a tousled sex kitten persona in films such as *And God Created Woman* (1956). Audrey Hepburn's lithe model-like proportions contrasted the prevailing full-figured women, beginning with *Roman Holiday* (1953). Doris Day personified the perfect American woman in vehicles such as *The Man Who Knew Too Much* (1956) and *Pillow Talk* (1959) – wholesome and perfectly turned out in high fashion or a tight-fitting knit twin set. Lucille Ball created a comedic version of this same type of woman, as her television character clumsily aspired to the chic of the day. As the hostess of a weekly drama series, Loretta Young was one of the best-dressed women on television.

Male stars provided a variety of fashion archetypes. Cary Grant and James Stewart presented individual forms of suave stylishness. Louis Jourdan and Jean Marais offered handsome elegance for European audiences. Burt Lancaster supplied an image of rugged athleticism in *From Here to Eternity*, while John Wayne and Gary Cooper provided masculine swagger in classic Westerns. Marlon Brando's working-class look in a wide range of films became iconic. Singing sensation-turned-movie star Elvis Presley alternated a more clean-cut appearance with his jeans-and-leather-jacket look, driven by the working-class roots of his music. His signature pompadour hairstyle was also widely copied. Presley became a jean-clad (and at times shirtless) movie star in vehicles such as *Jailhouse Rock* (1957) and *King Creole* (1958). James Dean's tragically short life was underscored by only three major film performances. Of these,

James Dean's red windbreaker jacket, t-shirt, and jeans, as worn in *Rebel Without a Cause* (1955), encouraged youth trends and reflected the growing Beat subculture.

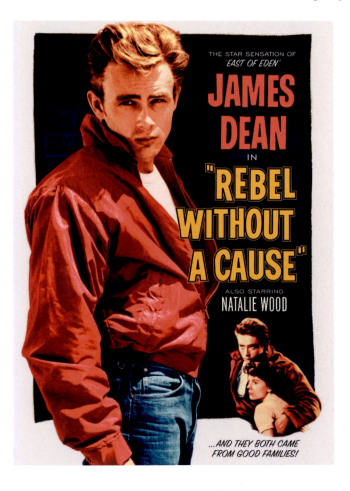

Marlon Brando in the film version of *A Streetcar Named Desire*, 1951.

BRANDO THE BAD BOY

While designing the costumes for the Broadway production of *A Streetcar Named Desire* in 1947, Lucinda Ballard found inspiration in a group of ditch-diggers she saw on the street whose work clothes were so saturated with dirt and sweat that they clung to their bodies, giving them the look of statues. The effect – both elegant and primal – was the look she sought when dressing newcomer "Method" actor Marlon Brando (1924–2004) in the role of Stanley. Brando wore a very tight, torn t-shirt. The costumers fitted his skin-tight jeans to his body while wet, insuring a snug, sculptural fit. It is with this costuming that the idea of tight jeans – so important in future decades – may have been born, as jeans made the transition from work clothes into other fashion language. Brando repeated this look (again with Ballard designing his costumes) in the 1951 film adaptation of the play, insuring its – and his – place in cultural iconography. Ballard received an Oscar nomination for Costume Design for the film. In 1953 Brando gave a similar "bad boy" performance as the leader of an outlaw motorcycle gang in *The Wild One*. He again wore tight jeans, paired with a black leather biker jacket, and topped with a military-style billed cap.

The look quickly trickled down to vernacular fashion. Brando's seminal look became a typical style of 1950s rebellious youth, including biker gangs, and was inspirational to *Les blousons noirs*, an imitative style tribe that flourished in Paris and other parts of Europe in the late 1950s. Also in the late 1950s, post-occupation Japanese youth embraced a look that combined Brando's swagger with influence from Elvis Presley and other American singers and became known as Rockabiri-zoku ("Rockabilly tribe"); such influence has recurred and continued in Asia and the West ever since. The look was often parodied, on leather-clad bullies in upbeat "Beach Party" films of the early 1960s, and the comic character Fonzie in the television series *Happy Days* (1974–1984). One of the most lasting impacts has been in gay male subculture as the "leather man," typified in the artwork of Tom of Finland and still active into the 21st century.

Rebel Without a Cause (1955), in which Dean played a troubled teen, was especially notable in solidifying his image and affecting fashion. His costumes were designed by Moss Mabry, who dressed Dean in t-shirt and jeans teamed with a red windbreaker that was widely imitated. Other actors of the time cultivated similar looks in certain film roles, including Montgomery Clift and William Holden.

Menswear

Fashionable menswear stressed quality and variety for specific occasions, with the same separation between casual and formal found in women's fashion. The desire to dress well, and dress properly, led men back to Savile Row. With fine materials available once again, some established British tailors revived an almost Edwardian formality. Slightly fitted dark suits, some with striped trousers, were worn with Chesterfield coats, bowler hats, and well-polished black Oxford shoes.

Suits remained the standard for business, and traditional cuts and colors were particularly important in corporate culture. The symbolic significance of the suit was reflected in Sloan Wilson's 1955 novel *The Man in the Gray Flannel Suit*, which described an American businessman confronting conformity and success at the expense of individuality. Gregory Peck starred in the 1956 film that dramatized Wilson's work.

The American "Bold Look" of the immediate post-war period evolved into a cut that became known as "Ivy League" by the mid-fifties. The "Ivy League" jacket was single-breasted and slightly loose, with notched lapels, lightly padded shoulders and a center back vent. Trousers were often unpleated, straight-legged, and usually cuffed. This style was associated with traditional menswear manufacturers such as Brooks Brothers. Starting in the early 1950s, peaked lapels were only seen on double-breasted jackets. Fabric included wools in light or heavier weights according to season, in flannels or worsted finishes. Solids, pinstripes and chalk stripes, tweeds, and checks

European menswear continued to define quality and conservative tastes. Here two ensembles by long-established houses Creed and Lanvin are illustrated with the accessories needed to be a complete gentleman. *Adam*, February/March 1950.

SAY IT WITH FLOWERS...

Above left During the course of the 1950s, the "Bold Look" of the late 1940s gave way to a sleeker image dubbed the "Ivy League Look" with narrower ties, lapels, shirt collars, and hat brims.

Above right Cabana sets – matching sets of swim trunks and shirts with flat collars – were particularly popular for men's leisure and resort wear.

were all popular. New types of suitings were used for business suits, including wool blended with synthetics and changeable "sharkskin" effects.

An alternative look was found in the sleeker, more fitted "Continental" style that originated in Italy. In 1952 the Italian menswear industry organized a Men's Fashion Festival in San Remo to showcase Italian design, tailoring, and fine fabrics. With a new emphasis on modern design, Italy added to its long-established reputation for excellent craftsmanship in accessories and tailoring. Prices for Italian fashion were lower than similar styles in France, adding to their appeal. Italian suits featured shorter, straighter jackets, often with two side back vents, and narrow trousers without pleats or cuffs. Thigh-length overcoats were cut to be comfortable on Vespas, the motor scooters popular in Italian cities. These streamlined suits and coats were worn with thin-soled, supple shoes. The expansion of the Italian menswear industry ushered in the "Modernist" looks that appeared late in the decade and continued into the 1960s.

One of the noticeable innovations of the post-war period was a turn toward colorful and more varied formal wear. High fashion menswear departed from tradition with styles such as a midnight blue tailcoat worn with a light gray vest and "Prince of Wales" plaid trousers. Social events featured men in dinner jackets in a range of colors and patterns including jewel tones, plaids, and iridescent effects. Musical groups, who often performed in matching colorful dinner jackets, helped popularize showy

Colorful, graphic, and playful patterns, often with surrealist influences, were typical of neckties until late in the decade. Some manufacturers such as Countess Mara, shown here, became neckwear superstars.

evening looks. For at-home entertaining, men wore less structured versions of the dinner jacket, often in velveteen in blue, maroon, or gray. In 1953 *Esquire*'s recommendation for informal gatherings was a "television coat – a loose-fitting, fingertip-length garment with large pockets."[15]

Men had many fashion choices for leisurewear, some of which were very colorful and eye-catching. Casual, waist-length jackets and open-necked shirts in lively prints were popular. Summer shirts were worn without jackets, a trend that expanded to more general casual wear year-round. Casual shirts were sometimes worn tucked into high-waisted, pleated trousers; others with straight hems and side seam vents were worn untucked. Some ended in a ribbed band at the waist. Leisure shirts were available at all price levels in bright solids, novelty prints, and plaids. Many solid-colored shirts featured contrasting yokes. Plaid shirts often had patch pockets with the plaid on diagonal. A faux vest-front look was also popular. Novelty pullovers, especially for warm weather and resort areas, were described as "Miami" or "California" style. International influences were apparent with the continued popularity of aloha shirts, and Pacific and South American looks. Western wear also influenced men's leisure clothing: cowboy-style shirts with contrast yokes, decorative stitching, and pearly snaps or buttons were a long-lasting trend. Knee-length "Bermuda" shorts were worn with blazers and ties for "casual" dress occasions. While knit swimwear was still seen, most men wore boxer-style swim trunks, often in bold patterns. Poolside, the trunks were sometimes worn with a terry-lined short-sleeved jacket, forming an ensemble known as a "cabana set." "His and hers" outfits were popular for leisurewear, reflecting the popular emphasis on togetherness and family life.

At the beginning of the decade, outerwear was generously cut but it narrowed somewhat in later years. Overcoats were typically worn loose and unbelted, often with raglan sleeves. Raincoats were available in trench styles as well as flared. Gabardine was popular, in beige and light brown and gray. Nylon was increasingly used, for anoraks and other active sportswear, as well as raincoats in business styles.

Accessories were varied. The trend for striking neckties continued; in addition to typical paisley, dots, and stripes, ties were patterned with every motif imaginable ranging from chess pieces and cocktails to landscapes and antique cars. Some ties reflected current events, with references to sports figures and the stock market. In addition to established prestige tie manufacturers such as Countess Mara, the designer necktie phenomenon gained momentum as top womenswear designers, including Dior, offered expensive silk ties in their boutiques. Hermès began marketing neckties in 1953. During the course of the decade, ties narrowed to a "skinny" width. Pocket squares often completed the look, ranging from simple white handkerchiefs to colorful patterned silks. Hats were usually worn on occasions that required a suit. Low-crowned fedoras and trilbies were popular, in felt for cooler weather and straw and other woven materials for summer and resorts. Good grooming was emphasized; most men were clean-shaven although thin mustaches were sometimes seen, and side-parted short hair was the norm.

Rayon and nylon were joined by the newest fiber, polyester, and mixed with wool for suitings, resulting in lighter-weight fabric, permanent creases in trousers, and jackets that would not wrinkle at the elbow. The modernization of menswear was satirized in the 1951 film *The Man in the White Suit*, starring Alec Guinness as a chemist who invents a synthetic fiber. In some cases, a synthetic sheen was deemed "modern." Synthetics were also used for stretch in underwear, socks, and sportswear as knit shirts became increasingly acceptable. Some styles combined knits and wovens in a colorblock effect for casual wear.

In addition to well-known tailoring houses and upscale manufacturers, leading designers started to figure prominently in menswear. Pierre Cardin was a pioneer in this market, opening his boutique Adam in 1957. Cardin's styles took the Continental aesthetic to an extreme with collarless jackets and narrow unpleated pants, which men wore with turtlenecks or round-collared shirts and narrow ties.

Children's Fashion

Children's clothing showed the same variety and abundance as adult fashions. Fashion for children was vigorously marketed and the wardrobes of young people were larger than ever before. Manufacturers appealed to mothers with easy-care fabric blends and finishes. Colorful separates were typical for all ages. For school, girls wore dresses and jumpers, or skirts with blouses or sweaters. Boys wore trousers and buttoned shirts. Striped and plaid shirts were especially popular. Jeans were not worn to school but were common for play. Movies and television influenced children's fashions. *The Roy Rogers Show* and *Davy Crockett* inspired cowboy and frontier-style play clothes – fringed pullovers and pants in sueded fabrics and "coonskin" caps – and *Flash Gordon* encouraged a Space Age look.

Childrenswear reflected the idealized version of wholesome conformity stressed in society. The illustrative style presented children in a doll-like fashion, also common in children's book illustration at the time.

Children dressed up for parties and other social occasions. Girls wore ruffly dresses and boys wore suits or jacket and trouser outfits. Girls' dance and party dresses often had very full skirts, supported by tulle crinolines, a style also favored for "flower girls" at weddings. Pastel colors and impressionistic florals were popular; party dresses were often trimmed with bows. Little boys wore shorts suits up until the age of about ten. Formal wear for older boys and teenagers followed the trends of men's formal clothing, with dinner jackets popular in a range of colors.

Girls were often dressed in matching outerwear ensembles. Coats and hats matched, and for the coldest weather some girls wore matching trousers under their dresses, removing them at their destination. Boys wore practical outerwear ranging from waist-length jackets in cool weather to thick nylon or woolen parkas with snowpants for winter. Children wore flat shoes, Oxfords, loafers and Mary Janes or ballerina flats for school, and sneakers for play. Knee socks or anklets were typical and a focus of grooming was keeping kids' socks clean. Hairstyling for pre-teen and teenage girls became more important. The pageboy was especially popular and for special occasions girls had their hair styled at the salon or at home. Boys had short, parted hair, like adult men.

Circle skirts were popular for teens, often decorated with motifs that reflected the wearer's interests, ranging from horses and poodles to musical notes and telephones. The style was encouraged when Princess Elizabeth wore it for square dancing on an official visit to Canada. The teenage market continued to expand. Junior Sophisticates, established by American designer Anne Klein in 1948, offered junior-sized versions of refined sportswear pieces, recognizing the desire of teenage and college-age girls for more adult styling. Klein's innovation in the junior market was recognized with a Coty Award in 1955. Frankie Avalon's 1959 hit "Bobby Sox to Stockings" immortalized the transformation of "bobby-soxers," girls in ankle socks, to young women in nylons. The introduction of the Barbie doll in 1959 reflected this desire for maturity. Named after the teenage daughter of toy designer Ruth Handler, Barbie was "born" with full breasts, a tiny waist, and feet shaped for high heels, and with full make-up. Envisioned as a teenage model, the doll was ironically inspired by the sexy German doll Bild Lilli, yet answered young girls' craving for sophistication.

Children at a 1956 wedding reception wearing typical special occasion outfits.

Right An ad for Coca-Cola encourages a wholesome view of teenage life.

Below Elizabeth (while still princess in 1950) wore a felt circle skirt with appliqué decoration, encouraging the popularity of the style among teenage girls.

A mainstream woman's play ensemble (*Vogue*, March 1, 1956) shows marked influence from the "beatnik" wardrobe, and even features bolster pillows inspired by bongo drums.

alex colman
C A L I F O R N I A

hats by tepoo hawes –

foreign
flavor
for suburbia

the gaiety of the tropics...by Alex Colman. Linen jacket, knit halter and gabardine pants in cotton, all washable. 8 to 18; three piece ensemble; jacket about $13; halter about $5; pants about $8 At fine stores or write Alex Colman, 409 Boyd Street, Los Angeles

Fashion and Rebellion

Teenagers and young adults asserted their independence through clothing often linked to their tastes in popular music, usually rock and roll or jazz. Countercultural influences on fashion became more pervasive, especially through depictions in film and literature. European "Existentialists," who frequented the cafes of the Boulevard Saint Germain, favored vernacular clothing: rugged sweaters, corduroy pants, and rough jackets. The artists and writers of the "Beat Generation" who espoused drug use, liberal politics, and elements from Eastern religion adopted a similar aesthetic. The clothes of "beatniks" (as they were called after 1958 – combining "Beat" and "Sputnik," the Russian satellite launched in 1957) mixed checked shirts, sweatshirts, jeans, and sweaters with ethnic styles. Beatniks often had beards or goatees – a radical grooming choice in a clean-shaven time. Beatnik women favored dance leotards and peasant-style tops with wrap skirts, Capri pants or jeans. Beatnik style was reflected in Audrey Hepburn's costumes in *Funny Face*, initially as the bookstore clerk in a shapeless jumper and then in cropped pants and flats in a Paris nightclub. Hepburn's boyish gamine look was widely imitated by young women and impacted the coming decade.

The "Teddy Boys," who emerged in London around 1954, based their rebellious aesthetic on Edwardian-style suits. Initially, the Teddy Boy or "Ted" look was a variation on a dandified style favored by certain London artists and designers including Cecil Beaton and Neil "Bunny" Roger. Long velvet-collared jackets and narrow trousers were appropriated by working-class boys, who accessorized them with thick crepe-soled shoes, skinny string ties, and greased-back "Duck's Ass" (D.A.) hairdos inspired by American rock and roll musicians. As the Teddy Boy look spread, it developed variations associated with urban gangs who distinguished themselves through specific colors and details.

The End of the Decade

Norman Norell, commenting in *Women's Wear Daily* in 1959, decried the standardization in American life and its effect on fashion. The designer blamed the American woman less than her husband: "Essentially conservative and conformist, the American husband is worried lest his wife look different from other women."[16] Norell singled out as an example the "sack" look, which did not meet with success in America. "If a woman happened to buy the new silhouette, her husband gasped, that night a TV comedian made fun of it, and the next day she brought it back to the store." The failure of the sack dress could be attributed to a resistance to depart from a comfortable status quo, and women's reluctance to hide their figures. However, decrees from Paris, which had been rigidly followed in the wake of Dior's New Look and helped create an atmosphere of conformity, began to lose their power. More individualized tastes were soon acknowledged by designers and retail alike. Counterculture fashion – largely underground but still vital to the decade – would be influential in coming years; youth, as well as groups outside the mainstream, offered opposition to the establishment.

The "sack" or "bag" dress (in this case from Givenchy) reflected experimental, fashion-forward shape and fit, but the market was reluctant to accept it. However, the style contributed to the developing aesthetic of the next decade.

Chapter 9

The 1960s

Fashion for the Future

The 1960s were a time of enormous social change throughout the world. As the first wave of post-war "baby boomers" came of age, television's expanded presence, an increased youth focus in popular music, and the introduction of the birth control pill all contributed to a visible, empowered generation that challenged existing ideas about family, education, politics, and society. A new focus on youth fashion distinguished this period, and Britain was particularly influential. Top Paris couturiers acknowledged the trend toward younger styles and changing dress codes: "The new generation is not prepared to spend precious time in endless fittings; clothes are chosen for immediate impact, not lasting value."[1] Time, always a factor in fashion, was more important than ever before: being up to the minute meant that designers and retailers actively promoted fashion that was not designed, or built, to last. The idea of "Classic" fell away, to be replaced by "Now." Advances in space travel by both the United States and the Soviet Union promised a Space Age in the foreseeable future; the theme of space travel and the future was prevalent in popular culture, ranging from science fiction films, to home product design, to fashion. The 1962 World's Fair in Seattle was dubbed "The Century 21 Exposition" and the rocket-like Space Needle

Opposite New York artist Doug Johnson illustrated the variety of menswear styles promoted during the decade, ranging from updated classics such as turtlenecks and tweeds to ruffled shirts worn with Edwardian-revival jackets.

Right The film *2001: A Space Odyssey* projected a sleek machine-made future.

267

The 1966 film *Georgy Girl* centered on freewheeling London youth culture, emphasized by the bold graphic of the poster design.

dominated the fairgrounds. The accelerated nature of the time was summed up by Andy Warhol's statement, "in the future everybody will be world famous for fifteen minutes," and celebrity culture and the cult of personality was more pronounced, and fame more fleeting, than ever before. Despite the concentration of youthful energy and optimistic visions of the future, this was a tumultuous decade; fashion, more diverse than ever, reflected all of this.

Social and Economic Background

Social and political turbulence affected the lives of millions around the globe. In China, Mao instigated the Cultural Revolution in 1966 to eliminate "bourgeois" influence in society. Throughout Africa, former colonies gained their independence. Israel's victory in the Six-Day War of 1967 asserted its importance in world affairs. In Indonesia, a 1965 coup attempt led to the death of half a million people, and race riots erupted in Malaysia in 1969. The year 1962 saw the first American combat missions in Vietnam, the start of a controversial conflict that was to last until 1975.

The 1960s were marked by continuing conflict between communism and capitalism. Tensions were underlined in 1962 as the United States confronted the Soviet Union over its construction of missiles in Cuba. The Berlin Wall, built in 1961, gave clear physical form to the "Cold War" between East and West. The conflict was aggravated by the 1968 Soviet invasion of Czechoslovakia. In 1961 technological competition between the United States and the Soviet Union reached a new level as Yuri Gagarin orbited the earth in a Russian satellite, becoming the first man in space. Each year brought new achievements in this competitive "space race," culminating in the 1969 Moon landing by Apollo 11.

The assassinations of President John F. Kennedy in 1963 and civil rights leader Martin Luther King in 1968 contributed to a sense of instability. Social protest was widespread. The civil rights movement gained steam in the United States with boycotts, sit-ins, and rallies. The 1969 Stonewall riots in New York's Greenwich Village catalyzed the gay rights movement. The later years of the decade saw violent strikes, student riots, and anti-war protests in Europe, Canada, and America. But other gatherings brought young people together in a spirit of celebration, including huge outdoor events such as the Summer of Love and Monterey Pop in 1967, the Isle of Wight festivals starting in 1968, and Woodstock in 1969.

The Arts

Pop Art emerged as an influential style as Roy Lichtenstein, James Rosenquist, and Andy Warhol among many others created art based on familiar visual elements of popular culture, such as groceries and comic books. Op Art was explored by Richard Anuszkiewicz, Bridget Riley, and Victor Vasarely. Both these movements influenced fashion and textile design. Mixed-media events and performance art – known as "Happenings" – were also important to the contemporary art scene. The psychedelic work of Peter Max, Wes Wilson, and other designers provided a graphic expression of countercultural ideas. Concert posters, advertisements, and album covers with otherworldly scenarios suggested drug-induced hallucinations. The Beatles' *Yellow Submarine* (1968) exemplified the use of psychedelic imagery in film. Revivals of vintage styles, especially art nouveau and art deco, also influenced design.

Best-selling non-fiction reflected emerging social causes, including Rachel Carson's *Silent Spring* (1962) and Betty Friedan's *The Feminine Mystique* (1963). A diverse list of best sellers included Kobo Abe's *Woman in the Dunes* (1960), Irving Stone's *The Agony and the Ecstasy* (1961), Muriel Spark's *The Prime of Miss Jean Brodie* (1961), John le Carré's *The Spy Who Came in From the Cold* (1963), and Gabriel García Márquez's *One Hundred Years of Solitude* (1967). Theatrical offerings were equally diverse and ranged from dramas such as Edward Albee's *Who's Afraid of Virginia Woolf?* (1962) and Joe Orton's *Entertaining Mr Sloane* (1964) to musicals such as *Fiddler on the Roof* (1964), *Man of La Mancha* (1965), and *Mame* (1966). The civil rights-themed *No Strings*

Above left Singer Frankie Avalon dancing with fellow cast members from the 1964 movie musical *Muscle Beach Party*, one of many films that celebrated California's surf lifestyle.

Above right The Supremes, seen here in the early 1960s, cultivated a polished, sophisticated style in their worldwide performances, often appearing in matching or coordinated dresses.

(1962), by Richard Rodgers, told the story of an interracial relationship between a novelist and a fashion model in Paris. Britain exported a number of influential films including the period pieces *Lawrence of Arabia* (1962) and *Tom Jones* (1963) and contemporary comedies *The Knack* (1965), *Alfie* (1966) and *Georgy Girl* (1966). Hollywood successes included musicals *West Side Story* (1961) and *The Sound of Music* (1965); thrillers *Psycho* (1960) and *The Manchurian Candidate* (1962); historic epics *Cleopatra* (1963) and *Anne of the Thousand Days* (1969); and contemporary stories *The Graduate* (1967) and *Midnight Cowboy* (1969). Masterpieces in European cinema included Jean-Luc Godard's *Breathless* (1960), Alain Renais' *Last Year at Marienbad* (1961), Federico Fellini's *La Dolce Vita* (1960), Luchino Visconti's *The Leopard* (1963), Roman Polanski's *Repulsion* (1965), and Franco Zeffirelli's *Romeo and Juliet* (1968).

The world of popular music continued to expand with ever more categorization of musical styles. Rock, pop, folk, jazz, and soul were popular genres. Fashion was tied to music as fans signaled their preferences through their clothes. New dance styles, particularly the Twist, the Frug, and the Monkey, emerged. Despite their brief careers, rock singer Janis Joplin and guitarist Jimi Hendrix were revered for their eccentric sartorial styles as much as their music. The "British Invasion" by groups including The Beatles, The Rolling Stones, The Who, and The Kinks inspired fashion trends and wild frenzy among their fans. Bob Dylan and Simon and Garfunkel provided a soundtrack to soul-searching youths, as did folk singers Joan Baez and Peter, Paul and Mary. Girl groups such as Martha and the Vandellas and the Supremes added glamour to Detroit's "Motown" sound. Hong Kong's Reynettes adapted the look in Asia. French "yé-yés" idolized fashionable pop singers such as Françoise Hardy and Sylvie Vartan. Television shows *American Bandstand* and Britain's *Ready Steady Go!*, with attractive hosts and youthful audiences, showcased popular bands and became important for broadcasting fashion trends.

Fashion Media

New magazines geared toward the youth market included *Honey*, launched in Britain in 1960, and the Japanese *Seventeen*, which debuted in 1967. London's venerable *The Queen* was restyled as *Queen* and redirected to "hipper" readers with younger content and brighter graphics. The fashions of young performers were showcased in music magazines such as America's *Tiger Beat*, England's *Fabulous 208*, and France's *Salut les copains*. The established magazines continued to cover fashion, lifestyle, and the arts, but also felt pressure to rejuvenate their look and message. Even in upscale publications, coverage of haute couture was matched, even exceeded, by pages devoted to ready-to-wear fashion, and "youthquake" styles received prominent coverage.

Young artists including Bobby Hillson and Caroline Smith encouraged fresh new fashion illustration styles. Junichi Nakahara's illustrations in Japan were emblematic of the developing fusion of Eastern and Western styles. New talents, including David Bailey and William Klein, joined established photographers such as Richard Avedon and Irving Penn.

A new standard of beauty, youthful and waiflike, contrasted with the womanly sophistication favored during the 1950s. Instead of haughty mature models, the press featured doe-eyed, long-legged teenagers who struck geometric poses, including Twiggy, Jean Shrimpton, and Penelope Tree. Later in the decade, Americans Lauren Hutton and Marisa Berenson (granddaughter of Elsa Schiaparelli) became successful models. Hints of ethnic and racial diversity were seen in fashion modeling. Cardin's favorite model, the Japanese Hiroko, became a recognizable face. Pauline Trigère created headline controversy when she hired Beverly Valdes, a black model, in 1961. Multiracial Donyale Luna appeared on the cover of British *Vogue* in 1966. The cover story of *Life* magazine on October 17, 1969 was entitled "Black Models Take Center Stage." Mannequin designer Adel Rootstein followed up her popular Twiggy mannequin with another inspired by Donyale Luna. Runway presentations increasingly incorporated elements of performance. Some shows mixed fashions for

Above Models often adopted geometric poses, as shown here on the cover of *L'Officiel* from June 1965, featuring dresses designed by Guy Laroche.

Below Designer Pauline Trigère fits Beverly Valdes, the first African American model hired by a major American label.

men and women, designers sent their most extreme looks down the catwalk, and accompanying soundtracks became more dominant.

Fashion and Society

Fashion setters came from all segments of society. Though still dominated by women of Western European ancestry, the list of 1960s stylish female celebrities also included Diahann Carroll, Leontyne Price, Cher, Princess Elizabeth of Toro, and Queen Sirikit of Thailand, mirroring the diversity in models. Influential singers, actresses, heiresses, and socialites typically shared one common characteristic: youth. As the *New York Times* stated, "Suddenly, the Pied Pipers of Paris and Seventh Avenue are youngsters."[2] One of the most visible trendsetters, Mrs. Leonard Holzer, sometimes known as "Baby Jane" and famous for her huge mane of blonde hair, claimed, "There is no class any more. Everybody is equal."[3] Andy Warhol's studio, known as the Factory, proved an important venue for the new society, where socialites like Holzer mingled with other upper-class rebels such as Edie Sedgwick, a media darling who was dubbed a "youthquaker." One of the most chronicled social events of the decade, Truman Capote's 1966 Black and White Ball at the Plaza Hotel in New York, exemplified the synthesis of uptown and downtown. Capote mixed established socialites with young movers and shakers, and the black and white masquerade dress-code theme reflected a favorite fashion color story.

The growth of television and media contributed strongly to the widespread awareness of celebrity weddings. For her wedding to Mohammad Reza Pahlavi, the Shah of Iran, Farah Diba wore Yves Saint Laurent. Balenciaga designed the dress for Doña Fabiola de Mora y Aragón for her wedding to King Baudouin of Belgium.

Jacqueline Kennedy on a visit to India in 1962 wearing a dress by Oleg Cassini.

Princess Margaret of Great Britain's wedding dress was designed by Norman Hartnell. Despite its full-skirted silhouette, the organza gown was streamlined in its simplicity and sharply contrasted Hartnell's design for her older sister's wedding dress of thirteen years earlier. The two dresses clearly illustrated the difference between the romantic and traditional post-war period and the emerging modernity of the 1960s. The television broadcast of Princess Margaret's wedding allowed for copies of the dress to appear for sale merely hours after the ceremony.

White House Style

Jacqueline Kennedy, the wife of American president John F. Kennedy, was an important, and imitated, fashion setter of the early 1960s. One of the youngest First Ladies in American history, Jacqueline Kennedy was popular with the public and her wardrobe choices were widely discussed. She was born Jacqueline Lee Bouvier in Southampton, New York, and her 1947 society debut was highly celebrated. For her marriage in 1953 she wore a wedding dress designed by New York-based Ann Lowe. While her husband was a senator, she favored New York custom and couture shops. For the 1960 inaugural ball, Mrs. Kennedy worked with the Bergdorf Goodman custom shop to create an evening cloak and dress ensemble inspired by a Victor Stiebel design. Mrs. Kennedy appointed American Oleg Cassini to be her official designer, and he created her off-white coat and dress for the inauguration ceremony. Cassini's work for Mrs. Kennedy featured sheath dresses, Empire strapless gowns, slim A-line shapes, geometric suits and coats with a relaxed fit and oversized buttons, clearly showing the influence of leading French couturiers. For Mrs. Kennedy's state visit to India in 1962, he created an apricot dress and coat ensemble that was widely photographed. Although his clothes for her did not invent or innovate new styles, the overall look crystallized quickly and featured her favorite color, pink, in many outfits. Even when wearing the work of other designers Kennedy maintained this look, as her own taste was fundamental to her style. In addition to Cassini, she particularly favored designs by Givenchy and American Gustave Tassell; the pink suit she wore on the day of her husband's assassination in 1963 was a Chanel "line by line" copy. The "Jackie Look" had great impact, in fashion editorials, on political wives around the globe – even on the Supremes. The *New York Times* noted Mrs. Kennedy's wide-reaching influence, saying, "Because of her, women grew bouffant hairdos and crowned them with barren pillboxes, hid their curves in little nothing dresses, their eyes behind mammoth sunglasses."[4] John F. Kennedy also contributed to fashion, if less overtly. The youthful president wore stylish suits in the Ivy League cut and his reluctance to wear hats on many occasions significantly decreased the popularity of the accessory for men in the United States and beyond. The confidence that the Kennedy administration brought to the White House was only as long-lived as his presidency, cut short by his assassination. As his administration had been compared to the fairy-tale world of the musical *Camelot*, it also ironically mirrored the show's tagline, "for one brief shining moment."

Style Tribes and the Marketing of Individual Taste

At the beginning of the 1960s, London youth subculture was influential in defining fashion. The Modernist or "Mod" lifestyle focused on music and fashion. Jazz was important, as were self-styled pop music groups including Small Faces and The Who. Mods traveled on motor scooters, with a preference for Vespas. Men wore lean Italian-style suits with narrow lapels and slim, short trousers, often crafted by tailors who specialized in the Continental look. The Mod wardrobe also included knit tops, narrow knitted ties and pointy-toed shoes. Mods took great pains with their grooming, favoring layered haircuts. By mid-decade, Mod style for men evolved to include more sporty pieces such as drawstring-waist parkas and Clarks desert boots. Although their style was less defined than their male counterparts, Mod girls often wore their hair long and straight or adopted short, geometric hairstyles. They also favored a pared-down look, wearing straight trousers, short skirts, and boots. Although it represented

Many fans who attended the Woodstock music festival in 1969 wore ethnic and bohemian-inspired clothes.

a subcultural aesthetic, the Mod lifestyle was highly dependent on consumption; the streamlined Mod image reflected other current trends including Space Age influence in high and mainstream fashion.

The hippie movement, another youth phenomenon, was based on anti-war and countercultural sentiments with roots in beatnik and bohemian styles. The epicenter of the movement was the Haight-Ashbury neighborhood of San Francisco. The hippie lifestyle, typified by "dropping out," communal living, and drug use, represented the ultimate rebellion against the conformist, family-oriented structure laid down in the 1950s. Body paint, the ironic wearing of army fatigues and vintage uniforms, denim, leather and suede, and shaggy fur were all typical components of the look. Tie-dye was highly popular and often done in one's own bathtub. Images of hippies at outdoor concerts, political demonstrations, and "love-ins" broadcast the style. The hippie lifestyle was depicted in the musical *Hair*. When prominent retailer The Gap opened in San Francisco in 1969 selling Levi's jeans and records and tapes, they used a boutique sensibility to target the youth market. The store's name referred to the "generation gap," the perceived gulf between the young people of the 1960s and their parents. Import store items found their way into a typical hippie-influenced wardrobe and the runway potential of ethnic styles was soon realized by a number of designers from Valentino and Pucci to Arnold Scaasi. The hippie movement was brought to the screen in such films as *I Love You Alice B. Toklas* (1968) and *Easy Rider* (1969) and culminated in the Woodstock music festival, which featured performances by Joplin, Hendrix and Jefferson Airplane among many others.

The Elements of Women's Fashion

While the fashionable world was still attentive to the more traditional Paris couture houses, up-to-the-minute designers such as Yves Saint Laurent and John Bates acknowledged inspiration from contemporary culture. Youthful, modern design was available to all ages and social classes. London reigned as the center of boutique culture, and California sportswear was promoted through films geared toward teenagers. A brief fad for paper dresses demonstrated the new playful spirit of fashion and the disposable focus of consumer society, as well as the ephemeral nature of fashion itself.

Although the first few years of the decade saw a carry-over of many 1950s styles – such as fitted silhouettes and stiletto heels – the 1960s quickly asserted new design

Below left An ensemble from Pierre Cardin for spring/summer 1962 shows transition from his smart ensembles of the 1950s to the futuristic looks he developed in later collections.

Below right Model Jean Shrimpton was photographed in London in 1962 in a clean-lined pink suit with simple accessories.

Above left The Finnish company Marimekko promoted progressive shapes and vibrant abstract patterns.

Above right Society photographer Slim Aarons captured two women wearing colorful printed Lilly Pulitzer dresses in Palm Beach in 1964.

Opposite Actress France Anglade in an encrusted evening gown by Marc Bohan for Dior, 1967.

ideas, and developed different and individualized looks over the course of the decade. In the early years geometric and boxy styles, as advocated by Chanel and Balenciaga in the 1950s, began to dominate silhouettes. Suits and coats followed this model, as did two-piece day ensembles with tunic tops worn over skirts. Often fabrics had substantial texture such as tweeds and bouclé. Colors were typically sophisticated neutrals and tertiary colors. Geometric details such as oversized buttons and patch pockets were common. Dresses were typically flared A-line shapes, and commonly sleeveless. Eveningwear followed the trend for simple shapes, often sleeveless, and was fabricated in luscious materials such as satins, dimensional lace, and beaded fabrics, trimmed with feathers and fur.

Colorful shift dresses were especially popular for warm weather and resort wear, even for summertime cocktail parties, and the prints often reflected the hippie idea of "flower power." The Finnish company Marimekko showed dresses in bold abstracted florals and geometric prints, and their popularity was enhanced in America when Jacqueline Kennedy wore them. American designer Lilly Pulitzer created similar simple styles. Her signature "Lilly" was a sleeveless shift, lined for women who wanted to go without underwear in casual circumstances. Pulitzer's prints were often floral, but she also offered whimsical conversational prints. Italian Emilio Pucci also used bright colors, often in psychedelic-style prints on silk jersey. In addition to white and cream, other light colors were consistently popular, including lime green, pistachio, light blue, turquoise, pale yellow, and apricot. Floral prints did not entirely disappear; geometricized daisies were a frequent motif and many prints placed flowers against a dark background.

Hemlines continued to rise and from 1962 to 1965 ascended to mid-thigh in the work of some designers. The look was particularly associated with André Courrèges, Rudi Gernreich, and Mary Quant. Once established it continued until the end of the decade, lingering into the next, even when challenged by other hemlines. Older and more conservative women seldom adopted thigh-length skirts and kept their hems at

PAPER FASHION

Around 1967, when "disposable" signified modern (rather than wasteful), a brief but intense fad for paper clothing rocked fashion. Like Kleenex tissues, called "paper handkerchiefs," paper clothing was a novelty. But unlike tissues, paper clothes never replaced cloth and the focus was on fashion, not hygiene. Manufacturers experimented with various paper-based materials. Some resembled paper toweling, while others were similar to felted nonwoven interfacing. No single company or person claims to have "invented" paper clothes, but many jumped on the cellulose bandwagon. Most paper dresses were mass-produced shifts printed with eye-catching designs. Op Art patterns were popular, as were stripes, dots, paisleys, and psychedelic designs, and some dresses featured crinkled and creased textures. Several major designers, including Ossie Clark and Paco Rabanne, saw paper as a perfect extension of their experiments with materials and produced colorful dresses. Some paper dresses bore pop culture references – a famous style by Harry Gordon featured a photo of Bob Dylan, and Campbell's offered "The Souper Dress," printed with a pattern of soup cans for $1 plus two soup labels, embracing Pop Art imagery and literally giving their product legs. The prevailing simple silhouette naturally suited fabrication in paper and it proved the perfect medium to express the spirit of fashion: lightweight, light-hearted, and of the moment. In addition to dresses, paper hats were also produced, and, ironically, rainwear – with a plastic coating. Vividly colorful paper shirts for men were also available, suited to the new swinging "peacock" male. Paper clothes were especially popular for parties. One company offered a kit that included matching tablecloth, paper cups and plates, a centerpiece, and a paper dress for the hostess. London journalist Prudence Glynn extolled the practical virtues of paper clothes for children: "The brightest idea yet. Cheap, pretty, flare-proof, chocolate cake and banana ice cream can be tipped down the front with impunity ... and mother will not say a word."[5] But Glynn also appreciated the advantages for adults:

> Why carry a diary when you can write on your hem? Why tote a notebook when you can record your impressions of one couturier straight on the work of another? Don't worry if you forget your hanky, just rip a piece off the bottom of your dress.

A paper shirt, made in Germany in the late 1960s, now in the collection of the Philadelphia Museum.

the knee, while more trendy and youthful women embraced the miniskirt. The short lengths were also common for eveningwear for cocktails and dancing.

Great experimentation in materials characterized fashion at all price levels, from handcrafted plastic and metal dresses by Paco Rabanne to vinyl raincoats in mass-market retail. Plastic was a favorite; ciré, glossy vinyl, and softer polyvinyl chloride (PVC) were used for jackets, skirts and dresses, and accessories. Other stylistic innovations included the frequent use of lamé, synthetic knits, plastics, and vinyl, encouraged by the Space Age influences. Synthetic fibers were still considered fashion-forward; their ability to take brilliant dyes made them suitable for Op Art- and Pop Art-influenced styles. Even the old guard embraced the synthetic trend, as when First Lady Claudia "Lady Bird" Johnson wore a "wrinkle-resistant" Adele Simpson ensemble in 1966 to her daughter's wedding. No longer limited to sportswear, knits were increasingly used in high fashion, for dresses and ensembles. Double knits of wool or synthetics were popular for simple shifts and other untailored pieces. Tight ribbed "poor boy" sweaters in both short- and long-sleeved styles were also popular, worn with miniskirts or slim trousers. Corduroy was used for everything from casual skirts to full-length coats, often in vivid paisley prints.

Pants for women, while still the object of much controversy, became more common. Several designers featured pantsuits and culotte suits in their collections, as well as vest and pant combinations. Pant ensembles became increasingly popular even for evening wear toward the later years of the decade, in the form of tuxedo styles (encouraged by Yves Saint Laurent), pajama sets, and harem pants. By mid-decade, low-rise "hip huggers" became popular, as did sailor-inspired bell bottoms. Jumpsuits, encouraged by Mod styles, were popularized, especially by actress Diana Rigg on *The Avengers*, with fitted stretch versions known as "catsuits." The style affected skiwear as one-piece ski suits replaced two-piece styles.

Below left Dresses from Sears catalog, spring/summer 1969, show how youthful styles were adapted for women and demonstrate the widespread acceptance of short hemlines.

Below right Vinyl raincoats reflect the bright colors and straight silhouette of fashion.

THE MINISKIRT

Miniskirts are such a part of the image of the 1960s that it is hard to believe the style did not really take hold until mid-decade. *Vogue* clearly decreed "NO" on March 15, 1962 to "a skirt three or four inches above the knee" and to "… the fashion proposals for the Twist,"[6] indicating that the struggle for dominance had begun: status quo versus youth. By the mid-sixties, in terms of mainstream fashion, youth and the miniskirt had clearly won. Fashion historians often like to find "ground zero" moments for styles, when in reality virtually everything throughout fashion history is an extension of what has come before. The year 1965 is typically pinpointed as a moment when suddenly skirts shot up, and designers Mary Quant and André Courrèges commonly share the credit for the "invention." Quant is likely responsible for the term "miniskirt" as she purportedly marketed short skirts named after her favorite car, the Mini Cooper. But the creation myth for the miniskirt, and the attribution of the invention, breaks down upon closer inspection. John Bates showed such short skirts a year prior to Quant, and consequently some sources credit him with debuting the garment. But the development of the mini can be tied to sources even in the 1950s, and earlier. Arnold Scaasi and James Galanos both showed above-the-knee dresses in the late 1950s. Costume design also foretold the trend: Helen Rose's design for Anne Francis in *Forbidden Planet* (1956) predicted both the hemline and the silhouette of the mid-1960s – her sci-fi frock would have looked at home on the runway ten years after its design. Years earlier, late-1930s tennis dresses for women were typically thigh length, and in the 1920s, such hem lengths for Jazz Age showgirl costumes were common. The most notable example of a thigh-length hemline came when Alla Nazimova wore Natacha Rambova's rubber dress in the 1923 screen adaptation of *Salome*. Whatever the source of the fashion, the path up the leg was inevitable. By 1966 the previously nay-saying *Vogue* declared that the "miniskirt is the snippiest bit of fashion today." Just as the path up was inevitable, the path back down the leg in the late 1960s and early 1970s was inevitable as well.

A mini dress by designer John Bates.

Longer hems offered competition to the miniskirt as the decade drew on, and became more asserted toward the end of the decade. As the miniskirt became commonplace and almost obsolete, tops were an increased point of interest, with full and flounced sleeves, layered with vests, and scarves a common accessory. According to the London *Times* in 1968:

> For the first time since the advent of the miniskirt, the top half of the female wardrobe has become more interesting than the hemline. Suddenly no one cares if a skirt is short, maxi, divided, or whether it is not a skirt at all, but trousers. The fashion interest lies in what you wear with your chosen bottom half.[7]

Ethnic and peasant looks began to influence fashion as hippies and other counterculture movements became more visible. Retro styles, inspired by fashions from the turn of the century through the 1940s, were popular and instigated a more fitted silhouette in reaction to the Space Age styles of the decade's middle years.

Couture bridal designs went to extremes, from miniskirts and lace playsuits to revealing tribal-inspired pieces and even bikinis. Saint Laurent's 1965 hand-knit wedding dress – covered in cables and bobbles, and adorned with ribbon bows – reflected trends toward folk art, and encased the bride in a hooded tube. Balenciaga's 1967 conical satin dress was completed with a matching headpiece that resembled both a space helmet and a nun's headdress. While stiff full-skirted styles continued from the late 1950s into mid-decade, narrower silhouettes with Empire waistlines were also common as early as 1960. For her 1967 wedding, Lynda Bird Johnson, daughter of the United States president, wore a narrow Geoffrey Beene design with detachable Watteau train, Empire waist, long sleeves and a mock turtleneck collar, graphically trimmed with bold dimensional lace.

Short wedding dresses made of eyelet or large-scale lace were popular with Mods, and other trendy brides often followed edgy Paris looks, even teaming short hems with white go-go boots. As the decade drew to a close, the hippie fashion aesthetic had made its way to the altar; bridal options included bohemian medieval styles. Pillbox hats with veils were popular, as were small shaped veils on stiffened frames, and even large crisp satin bows. By mid-decade, helmet-like bonnets were fashionable; wreaths of flowers complemented hippie dress styles. Bridesmaids were typically in bright or pastel colors, ranging in length from mini to floor. Paper patterns for home sewers offered companion dresses for bridesmaids that could be made in long and short versions.

Lightweight nylon lingerie was decorated with colorful, sometimes psychedelic, patterns.

Patent leather shoes by Charles Jourdan exemplify a popular shape: square-toed with chunky heels and geometric decoration.

Foundations and Lingerie

The revolution in dressing affected underwear as well, as women moved away from sculpting foundations. Rudi Gernreich's "No-bra," introduced in 1964 by Exquisite Form, consisted of two triangles of lightweight nylon with shoulder straps and one slender strap around the body. It was simultaneously denounced as immodest and celebrated as liberating and set a new model for lingerie. Straight slips in short lengths were worn under dresses and skirts, sometimes known as "demi-slips" and "chemises." Pettipants, resembling the tap pants of the 1920s and 1930s, served as panty and slip. One-piece, flesh-colored body stockings were worn under peekaboo clothes and sheer bodices and blouses. Nightwear also reflected fashion trends with harem pant-style pajamas; "shortie" nightgowns followed the mini hemlines of daywear.

Hosiery took on increasing importance and a wide variety of colors and textures were available. Ribbing, diamond patterns, and lace were all popular, as were flat opaque knits, floral patterns, checks, and stripes. Some hosiery had shimmery effects for evening. By 1964 stockings were being abandoned in favor of tights and "panti-legs" (stocking-weight tights). But the transition to pantyhose took several years, during which manufacturers and consumers devised interesting ways to bridge the gap between hosiery and rising hemlines. Some hosiery makers offered longer stockings; Kayser made extra-long stockings that were to be worn inside a special "pantee belt."[8] Women sometimes wore their hosiery under panty girdles so they continued to have the support of a girdle along with the leg coverage provided by the new hosiery styles. "Hiphose" by Sunerama was another option: each leg was a separate piece and they fastened together at the waist so, in the event of a tear or "ladder," the wearer could replace a single leg. Another effect of the shorter hemline was that knee socks returned to fashion.

Accessories

Elaborate hairstyles, often stiffened with spray and embellished with hairpieces, began to take the place of hats. However, the millinery industry continued to promote hats, and leading designers set the pace. Tight hats, referred to as "helmets" and "baby bonnets," were shown as early as 1961. The bonnet trend accelerated and became particularly associated with Courrèges, who often showed face-framing bonnets that tied under the chin. Other popular styles included variations on the fedora, some with domed crowns, others miniature versions with short brims. Later in the decade, berets and wide-brimmed felt hats reflected new trends.

By 1961 square-toed, low-heeled shoes were starting to be featured in Paris collections. Still quite narrow, shoes became clunkier through the decade. Slingbacks were popular for spring and summer. Shoes were often decorated with buckles, buttons, flowers, and other geometric details. The two-tone shoes from Chanel were influential on mainstream styles. Boots became extremely popular. Courrèges showed slim flat-soled white leather boots that reached to the lower calf. Their distinctive proportion and squared, slightly open, toe were widely copied. Other styles of boots included knee-high styles made of tight leather or vinyl and low ankle boots. Some shoe styles referenced boots, with lacing up the leg ending just below the knee. The popularity of lower-heeled shoes was encouraged by rising hemlines, creating a more pleasing and youthful proportion. Handbags and shoulder bags were both carried. Many were structured, often in straw, woven plastic, or vinyl, sometimes hung from the shoulder on a chain. Many accessories were decorated with Pop Art, geometric motifs, and stylized flowers. Daisies were especially common. Long earrings, oversized hoops, and plastic teardrop shapes were seen. Colorful brooches were very common. Kenneth Jay Lane was among the prominent creators of costume jewelry. Long strings of "love beads" reflected countercultural influence. Sunglasses became an important accessory, some bizarre and graphic in shape, with patterned frames, others futuristic. Some small eyeglasses, known as "granny glasses," had wire frames and oval, round or rectangular lenses.

The Boutique

Boutique fashion from adventuresome designers and small specialty shops targeted younger, more daring customers with less expensive clothing – available in junior sizes – and witty accessories. "The boutique idea? The fun idea – all over the map."[9] New styles were made in small quantities and not repeated, and service was often casual (even disdainful). Contemporary music was an important part of the ambience and the soundtracks were related to the styles each store promoted. Some boutiques also featured cafes and bars, combining shopping and socializing and transforming the store into a "scene."

Several designers including Mary Quant and Barbara Hulanicki were pioneers in the boutique concept. Other notable London boutiques included Annacat, Carrot On Wheels, and Harriet. Realizing the importance of the trend, department stores established in-store boutiques for individual designers and opened thematic shops

Boutique pioneer Mary Quant, with a geometric Vidal Sassoon haircut, in her store with two young women wearing her trendy, youthful styles.

on their selling floors. Peter Robinson launched Topshop, a basement department catering to young customers, in 1964. The Cardin Shop in Selfridges opened in 1966 and Harrods' "Way In" department, which debuted in 1967 featuring fashion for men and women, was arranged like small stores on a shopping street.

New York's Paraphernalia, which opened on Madison Avenue in 1965, offered eye-catching clothes by young designers in a sleek white and chrome decor. In the words of designer Betsey Johnson, "All the clothes at Paraphernalia were experimental. Always changing. It had nothing to do with the customer. It had everything to do with the time, the moment."[10] Customers included a mix of socialites, performers, and unknowns. Actress Julie Christie was photographed in a miniskirt at the store. The founder, Paul Young, started the store as a division of Puritan, a major New York manufacturer. He imported fashions by well-known designers including Ossie Clark and Mary Quant and promoted experimental New York designers including Johnson and Diana Dew, who was known for battery-powered dresses that lit up the dance floors of Max's Kansas City and other New York nightclubs.

Designers: France

Paris couture saw a changing of the guard. Established houses including **Jean Dessès**, **Jacques Heim**, **Carven**, and **Rouff** continued to represent Parisian elegance but a younger generation of designers acknowledged the importance of youthful customers and more casual style. Couture was still prized by loyal clients, but designer ready-to-wear was increasingly accepted and received press attention. **Pierre Balmain** was particularly praised for luxurious eveningwear that often displayed historic inspiration. Balmain designed for an extremely select clientele that included Queen Sirikit of Thailand. **Chanel** continued to assert the relevance of her signature style and updated her classic cardigan suits in brighter colors. In 1960 she showed a suit with a bouclé pullover and pleated skirt that was an imaginative revisiting of her early pullover ensembles. Even though his designs of the 1950s clearly prefigured those of the new decade, **Cristóbal Balenciaga** was not interested in the youthful trends that pervaded fashion. However, despite his resistance to trends, Balenciaga was among the first to show see-through and peekaboo styles and also featured designs in a 1920s-inspired silhouette. His experiments with form, space, and cut continued, creating extraordinary dresses with minimal seams and often featuring silk gazar. Unwavering in his high standards, up through his last collections Balenciaga was hailed as showing "the best clothes in the world from a technical point of view."[11] Balenciaga closed his house suddenly in 1968, disillusioned with what had become of the fashion industry. **Jules-François Crahay** (1917–1988) presented his "tomboy" collection for Nina Ricci in 1962, building on the *garçonne* image of the 1920s; he received a Neiman Marcus Award the same year. He also created a ready-to-wear line, "Mademoiselle Ricci," for the American market. In 1963 Crahay left Ricci to replace Antonio Castillo as the designer for Lanvin, where his first collection "sizzled with ideas."[12] Throughout his long tenure with the house, he maintained elegance and traditional couture standards.

A 1963 suit by Jules-François Crahay for Nina Ricci features a luxurious chinchilla collar and recalls styles of the 1920s.

Above left to right Designs from Yves Saint Laurent: a tuxedo-like pantsuit for women introduced in 1966 called "Le Smoking"; a Pop Art-inspired dress from 1966; and three models in dresses from his 1967 "African" collection.

Yves Saint Laurent solidified his central role in fashion, dressing many of the most important women in the world. Saint Laurent's inspirations were varied and included "street" style, a relationship that was clearly stated when he featured beatnik style in his fall 1960 collection for the house of Dior, including black turtlenecks, leather trench coats, berets, and knit caps, worn by "zombie-faced models." The controversial collection caused displeasure among the conservative management at Dior, who were relieved when the young designer was drafted into the army later that year, and severed their relationship with him. Saint Laurent was soon hospitalized, and later discharged from the army. Successfully suing the house of Dior for breach of contract, Saint Laurent set up his own house with partner Pierre Bergé. He showed his first collection under his own name in 1962, including suits that the press compared to Chanel. His fall and winter collection of the same year featured looks that became Saint Laurent classics: tunics over slim skirts, the peasant smock, and the pea coat. He also advocated pantsuits for women in these early collections, and featured little black dresses with white collars. Saint Laurent quickly became a darling of the press (particularly *Vogue*'s Diana Vreeland) and firmly established at the vanguard of Paris fashion. In 1965 his wool jersey, color-blocked "Mondrian" dresses were acclaimed as "the dress of tomorrow,"[13] and came to be considered among the most iconic fashion designs of the decade.

His 1966 collections included witty Pop Art-inspired dresses, some reflecting the Surrealist effects created by Schiaparelli and Jean Cocteau in the late 1930s. He also showed his first "Le Smoking" tuxedo for women, building on the aesthetic of the 1920s underground. Also in 1966, he opened the first of his Rive Gauche prêt-a-porter boutiques at 21 rue de Tournon. His 1967 collection included his highly celebrated "African" dresses. They combined African tribal inspiration with a 1920s-style sheath, fabricated in a combination of wooden beads, plastic beads, shells, bold prints, and straw, and were dubbed "a fantasy of primitive gems."[14] The following year brought further classic designs, including his infamous "see-through" dresses and his safari look. During these years, Saint Laurent also worked frequently as a theatrical costume and set designer, and contributed wardrobe for several films, most notably for his friend, actress Catherine Deneuve, in *Belle de Jour* (1967) and *La Sirène du Mississippi* (1969).

Paris-born and educated, **Marc Bohan** (b. 1926) began his career with Robert Piguet, and during the following years was employed by Edward Molyneux and by Maison Patou. In 1958 Bohan became the designer at Dior's London house. Following Yves Saint Laurent's controversial 1960 collection, Maison Dior appointed Bohan designer and creative director at the Paris house. His first collection featured a sleek 1920s-inspired silhouette; dubbed the "slim look," its impact was compared to the house's 1947 and 1958 showings and declared "A smash hit" by journalist Carrie Donovan:

> This morning the shouting, clapping, surging mob ... caused chaos in the elegant salon. M. Bohan was pushed up against the boiserie, kissed, mauled, and congratulated. Chairs were toppled. Champagne glasses were broken. People were knocked down. It was a complete triumph for the designer ...[15]

As the decade unfolded, Bohan provided sophisticated and chic designs for a discerning clientele. His work maintained relevance in the fashion press, but continued the couture standards of the 1950s, and did not succumb to the swinging young styles of the time. Bohan was praised for being a master at every category of a collection, from eveningwear, to daywear, to outerwear; among the diffusion products, he even created skiwear with the Dior Sport label. His two 1965 showings drew particular praise; Asian and historic references were teamed with sophisticated color, fabric, cut, and drape, leading a fashion reporter to declare that Bohan "continues to prove he can make the prettiest clothes in Paris."[16]

Unlike some of the new couturiers who aimed to shock, **Hubert de Givenchy** maintained his unique combination of youth and elegance. His designs showed a softer version of the prevailing geometric lines of fashion; dresses and ensembles were spare but never harsh. In his day- and eveningwear, Givenchy emphasized beautiful material and skillful cut over surface embellishment. Givenchy's association with Audrey Hepburn continued to enhance his reputation. Other noteworthy Givenchy clients included Diana Vreeland, Jacqueline Kennedy, and actresses Jean Seberg and Lauren Bacall.

By 1960, **Pierre Cardin**'s increasingly geometric aesthetic was described as "stark, almost surrealist."[17] He showed clean, straight coats, often accessorized with close-fitting helmet-like felt hats. Cardin's "futuristic" designs for men, women, and children combined immaculate tailoring with youthful styles, such as straight dresses in wool knits that resembled schoolgirl jumpers and well-tailored suits worn with turtlenecks. Committed to diversification, Cardin also offered accessories and was one of the first couturiers to feature dark, textured pantyhose on his models. He showed his first children's collection in 1966 and opened a children's boutique in 1968. Cardin often designed in solid colors with little embellishment, but beginning in 1965 some styles included Space Age icons or "PC" (the designer's initials) as appliqués or on belt buckles. His Cosmos line, which debuted in 1966, featured simple pieces for the whole family. While clean-cut and practical, the Cosmos styles, especially when accessorized with some of Cardin's more outrageous hats and boots, were considered too outré for most customers. In 1968 Cardin teamed with Union Carbide to produce "Cardine," a moldable synthetic fabric he used to make seamless dresses. His solution for the hemline transitions of the late 1960s was to offer ensembles that mixed hemlines, pairing miniskirts with maxi coats and offering pieces in midi length.

The first collection by **André Courrèges** (b. 1923) in 1961 was an immediate success. Courrèges' focus on precision tailoring and the structural details of clothes revealed his training with Balenciaga, for whom he worked from 1950 to 1961. He was often called "an architect" in fashion and attained a cult-like following among fashion-forward women, including Jane Holzer and Françoise Hardy (who wore a

Pierre Cardin with a group of models in London in 1966, typifying his ultra-modern aesthetic.

Courrèges ensemble in Godard's 1966 film *Masculin Féminin*). He produced simple A-line dresses, tunics, and coats, often with bound edges at necks and armholes. Courrèges was a proponent of clean-lined trouser suits for women, even for dressy occasions. He offered trouser ensembles in many variations, pairing narrow trousers with short jackets and tunics, and under ankle-length evening coats. Courrèges was one of the first to promote short skirts. By 1963 his skirts hovered at knee length but a year later he raised hemlines well above the knee. The *New York Times* declared that, "for the first time in many years, the widely copied fashion 'Ford' was not a Chanel suit but Courrèges' neat little chemise dress."[18] For spring 1965 he combined Space Age and Western references, showing dresses, pantsuits, and coats in combinations of white and bright colors, as well as stripes and checks. Modernized cowboy hats, some edged with colored binding, completed the look. He sometimes (like Cardin) used his initials as a decorative detail. His clients included the Duchess of Windsor and Baronne Guy de Rothschild. In mid-1965, Courrèges closed his house to reorganize and reopened in 1967 with "Couture Future," a ready-to-wear line. Toward the end of the decade he promoted knits, especially for body suits, in keeping with his emphasis on youth and mobility.

Another Balenciaga alumnus, **Emanuel Ungaro** (b. 1933), opened his couture house in 1965 and quickly gained a reputation as an "ultra-modern" designer, one of the new group of edgy young French couturiers. His work was marked by shocking

André Courrèges promoted a refined, well-tailored version of Space Age style, often featuring trouser ensembles.

color combinations and hard lines. In his first few seasons, Ungaro emphasized geometric shaping with dresses that were almost triangular from shoulder to hem in full-bodied fabrics that stood away from the body. Ungaro promoted very short skirts and even showed ensembles composed of tunics with matching shorts, often accompanied with shiny boots or over-the-knee socks. His version of "modern" was decidedly sexy, a theme that became a hallmark of his work.

Born in Spain, **Paco Rabanne** (b. 1934) trained in architecture in Paris and began working in fashion designing and fabricating jewelry. Rabanne presented his first apparel collection in 1966, entitled "12 Unwearable Dresses in Contemporary Materials" – dresses made of plastic disks held together by metal links, some in fluorescent colors. Rabanne epitomized the experimental spirit of the time and referred to himself as an "*accessoriste*." He designed metal dresses, tunics, bra tops, and other pieces in a technique that resembled chain mail, making designs suitable for modern warrior princesses. He also crafted provocative fringed dresses from metal ball chain. Rabanne's spectacular (and, reportedly, uncomfortable) work received impressive media coverage, especially in the United States, and spawned many imitations. His costume designs for the 1968 film *Barbarella* emphasized the futuristic influence in his styles. Late in the decade he used other materials, notably fur, leather, molded plastic, and metallic lace and tulle, to convey his distinctive aesthetic.

One of the most experimental designers of the time, **Jacques Esterel** (1917–1974) was born Charles-Henri Martin, trained as an engineer, and considered fashion "a game." Although he established his couture house in the mid-1950s, a simple pink

Paco Rabanne used unconventional materials including metal, pieced leather, and plastic disks, as shown here.

gingham dress he designed for Brigitte Bardot's 1959 wedding to Jacques Charrier helped launch his career. Esterel was also a songwriter and performer and his collections often included theatrical elements. In addition to Op Art-patterned dresses, he showed pieces with built-in lights and accessories made of kitchen utensils, and later promoted unisex styles.

After a start in millinery and almost ten years with Jean Dessès, **Guy Laroche** (1921–1989) opened his own fashion house in 1957. In 1961 he moved to larger quarters, started to design ready-to-wear, and opened a boutique. Like Cardin and Courrèges, Laroche promoted a modern, sometimes futuristic, aesthetic. However, he was known for vivid colors and more sensual styles. Although his clientele was international, Laroche was particularly appreciated by Parisian women and his fashions were often held up as the epitome of French chic. In 1966 Laroche ventured into menswear with ready-to-wear and a boutique.

Designers: Britain

Savile Row continued to be the world leader in conservative, classic tailoring, and Norman Hartnell's gowns epitomized traditional elegance. But some of the established names made steps toward a more contemporary outlook. **Hardy Amies** continued to design for Queen Elizabeth, and maintained his successful women's and menswear lines. But he reflected fresher styles in his costumes for *2001: A Space Odyssey* and also uniforms for the 1966 English World Cup team. **Edward Molyneux** came out of retirement and operated the ready-to-wear Studio Molyneux, which opened in 1964. However, young designers working out of small ateliers and boutiques in Soho, Carnaby Street, and other London neighborhoods offered youth-oriented looks that were influential worldwide. Design team **Foale & Tuffin** (Marion Foale and Sally Tuffin) were among the first to offer startling dresses and ensembles, many with trousers, for an adventurous clientele. Their colorful shop on Carnaby Street featured Op Art-inspired pieces, many in black and white knits, and they also sold their designs through other stores as diverse as Paraphernalia and J. C. Penney.

Mary Quant (b. 1934) opened her boutique, Bazaar, in 1955 on the King's Road in London's artsy Chelsea neighborhood in partnership with her husband, Alexander Plunket Greene, and a friend, Archie McNair. A London native, Quant attended Goldsmiths College of Art and briefly worked as a milliner before opening Bazaar. The shop's party-like atmosphere and window displays, some featuring live mannequins, drew crowds and many pieces sold out quickly. At the height of Bazaar's popularity, there were three stores, all of which closed in 1968. Quant was especially known for her promotion of high hemlines, and used the term "miniskirt" to describe short skirts. Quant never established a signature style; her designs ranged from pinafores to rugby-inspired dresses to form-fitting PVC trench coats. The pieces were produced in small quantities that, at the boutique level, did not generate a profit. The formation of her wholesale division, Ginger Group, in 1963 enabled wider distribution and corporate partnerships, including Quant's work for American retailer J. C. Penney. By mid-decade, Quant was viewed as a respected authority on fashion and her designs were ubiquitous: in addition to youthful ready-to-wear, her stylized daisy logo was found on everything from tote bags to aprons. Quant was an innovator in the marketing of popular cosmetics, including lip gloss and false eyelashes, and with her bobbed haircut by Vidal Sassoon she came to represent the new spirit in British fashion. She was appointed an OBE in 1966 and wore a miniskirt to accept the prestigious award.

Designing under his label "John Bates for Jean Varon," **John Bates** (b. 1938) showed two distinct visions. The sharp, geometric clothes he designed for Diana Rigg in her role on *The Avengers*, many in black or white leather, contrasted with Bates' romantic side, exemplified by straight shift or Empire-waisted dresses, many in lace, panné velvet, and chiffon. A great experimenter, Bates used plastic and vinyl freely, and was an early advocate of short skirts. In a fashion editorial featuring his lightweight evening dresses in 1964, American *Vogue* declared Bates represented London fashion that was "larky, romantic, British to the core."[19] A linen dress with a nylon mesh midriff was named "Dress of the Year" in 1965.

Born in Warsaw, **Barbara Hulanicki** (b. 1936) attended the Brighton School of Art, and worked as a fashion illustrator. She developed a mail-order business, "Biba's Postal Boutique," in 1964 with her husband Stephen Fitz-Simon. One of their first notable successes was a gingham shift. That same year Hulanicki and Fitz-Simon opened a boutique, Biba, on Abingdon Road; it too was quickly successful. Targeting women in their late teens and twenties, the store sold fun, trendy designs at affordable prices. With casual and eclectic merchandising, products were displayed from antique bentwood hat stands, and the store was decorated with second-hand Victorian furniture. Hulanicki dressed television personality Cathy McGowan, a key figure in the Mod scene, encouraging the popularity of the Biba line. While the mail order expanded into a large catalog business, the store soon moved to larger premises on Kensington Church Street, decorated with a kitschy mix of art nouveau and art deco. Clients, who ranged from rock stars to shop girls, waited in line for the communal dressing room. An early advocate of the emerging "retro" aesthetic, Hulanicki took inspiration from a wide variety of influences, including period styles from the 1890s through World War II, especially Hollywood glamour of the 1910s, 1920s, and 1930s.

Below left A jumpsuit from Biba illustrates the prevalence of Op Art influence. The carefree look of the model posed outside the boutique captures the essence of "Swinging London."

Below right An Ossie Clark dress made of fabric designed by Celia Birtwell from 1968 with a handkerchief hem, as fashion transitioned into longer lengths.

The Biba label and hangtag featured an art nouveau graphic motif. Hulanicki often favored dark tertiary colors including purplish hues such as aubergine, mulberry, and plum, which she described as "Auntie colors." Her early designs favored the prevailing miniskirt styles of the mid-decade – one skirt was only 10 inches (less than 26 centimeters) long – but she soon became an advocate of the longer midi and maxi lengths. Biba offered long overvests in old-fashioned brocade fabrics; soft velvets and lyrical prints were common for both dresses and pantsuits, and accessories such as wide-brimmed hats, feather boas, scarves, and costume jewelry were offered. Hulanicki's style was an important factor in the development of the look of the early 1970s, and her retail presence continued to expand into the new decade.

Ossie Clark (1942–1996) was born Raymond Clark in Liverpool, but the family moved to Oswaldtwistle in Lancashire during the war, and the town became the source of his nickname. Clark sewed clothes as a child, with the help of his mother, and in 1958 began his studies at the Regional College of Art in Manchester. There he befriended the young artist David Hockney and met Celia Birtwell (b. 1941), who would later become his collaborator and wife. Beginning in 1962, Clark studied at the Royal College of Art; his 1965 graduation collection was so successful it was featured in British *Vogue*. From this collection forward, Clark showed his affinity for fluid, body-conscious construction, vintage glamour, and bold use of color. The following year, Clark's work was featured in the trendy London boutique Quorum, owned by designer Alice Pollock, and Clark began creating designs that utilized Birtwell's fabrics. Soon the clothes were available in Europe, and at Bendel's in New York, and became popular with well-known music performers including Mick Jagger and Marianne Faithfull. Quorum was sold to Radley Gowns in 1967, and the new company expanded the Ossie Clark brand.

Clark's work showed great skill with cut, and his softer, sometimes dance-inspired, designs contrasted the prevailing crisp Space Age styles popular mid-decade, helping set the style of the 1970s. Clark often used piecing to feature parti-colored treatments, a technique he used to bold effect with exotic leather coats. Borrowing from the 1920s and 1930s, his retro sensibility was often combined with peasant inspiration. Clark showed full skirts, handkerchief hems, puffy sleeves, and soft pant ensembles. Frequently his clothes utilized Birtwell's fabrics – often engineered floral or conversational prints with art deco inspiration – throughout the collections, even on overcoats. In 1969 Clark and Birtwell were married, and the same year a printed chiffon pajama set they designed was named "Dress of the Year" by the Museum of Costume in Bath.

Designers: Italy

Italian fashion continued to be presented in terms that mixed ease and prestige, typified by "palazzo pajamas," a popular style for luxurious, yet informal, eveningwear. The Italian fashion industry was split between Rome, Florence, and Milan, and early in the decade several established Italian fashion houses moved to Paris. The "parade from the Tiber to the Seine"[20] included Roberto Capucci, Patrick de Barentzen, and husband and wife designers Alberto Fabiani and Simonetta Visconti.

After a start selling sketches to other designers, **Pino Lancetti** (1928–2007) opened his fashion house in Rome in 1961. Devoted to the tradition of fine craftsmanship, Lancetti often used textiles of his own design inspired by major modern artists. His international clientele included Italian film stars Silvana Mangano and Monica Vitti. In 1966 **Mila Schön** (1916–2008), who was born in Yugoslavia and moved to Milan upon her marriage, established a business on the city's chic Via Montenapoleone. Although her beautifully constructed and somewhat serious clothes did not receive major fanfare, her illustrious clientele included Marella Agnelli, wife of the president of Fiat, Lee Radziwill, and Farah Diba, then Queen of Iran.

Light, colorful dresses and separates by **Emilio Pucci** were prized by women who saw themselves as modern and young in spirit. Pucci's printed silk jersey dresses

(signed "Emilio") were popular for travel, and full-length skirts and palazzo pajama sets were favorites for entertaining. Pucci designs were available at in-store boutiques of large department stores and via his many licensing agreements in sports apparel, accessories, and home furnishings. The distinctive Pucci prints were featured on hosiery and handbags. A former Olympic skier, Pucci had an affinity for skiwear and the printed jackets were particularly attractive. As air travel became simultaneously more accessible and more glamorous, Pucci not only outfitted sophisticated travelers, but also designed uniforms and accessories for Braniff air hostesses.

Roberto Capucci opened a Paris atelier in 1962 on rue Cambon. Capucci's Optical Line for fall and winter 1965/1966 featured Op Art-inspired fabrics by Italian textile designer Luciano Forneris. His "Homage to Vasarely" visually pulsated with black and white lines and shapes; the long dress was also trimmed with ostrich feathers. This was followed by experiments in plastic garments with space helmet-like hats. In 1967 he showed more fluid dresses with below-the-knee hems worn with boots, and was dubbed by the press "the bravest designer in all of Paris."[21] Although successful in Paris, Capucci returned to Rome in 1968.

Husband and wife Alberto Fabiani and Simonetta Visconti combined their talents and in 1962 launched **Simonetta et Fabiani** in Paris, where they also opened a boutique. Their collections displayed the hallmarks of the two designers: Fabiani's skill with tailoring and outerwear and Simonetta's emphasis on volume and drama in eveningwear. The joint venture lasted several years until Fabiani returned to Rome and resumed his work there. Simonetta continued to design high fashion through the 1960s and then turned her attention to spiritual and humanitarian activities.

Princess Irene Galitzine (1916–2006), known for superb tailoring, also offered colorful beachwear and evening looks. Galitzine's aesthetic, like that of other Italian designers, combined beauty and informality. Her evening ensembles were often variations on palazzo pajamas. Galitzine also designed pajama ensembles with trim, tapered trousers that were worn with tops ranging from hip to floor length.

The couture career of **Valentino** Garavani (b. 1932) began in 1959 when he opened his house on Rome's fashionable Via Condotti, after several years working for Jean

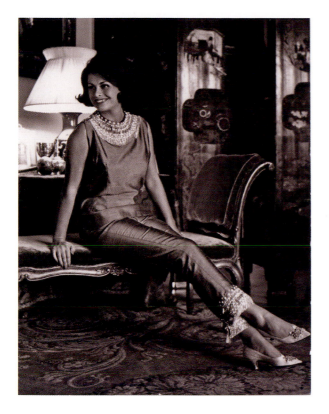 

Above left Princess Irene Galitzine modeling one of her signature pants ensembles, a glamorous but modern option for evening.

Above right A dashing white ensemble by Valentino includes a Russian-inspired fur hat, laced boots, and dramatic cape over a mini dress.

Dessès and then Guy Laroche. In 1960 Giancarlo Giammetti became his partner and his business acumen was important to Valentino's success. Valentino presented his first couture collection at the Palazzo Pitti in 1962 and was immediately hailed as a rising star. In 1966 he started to show in Rome. Valentino often showed eveningwear in a vibrant tomato red, a color that became a signature and often identified as "Valentino red." He frequently presented ensembles that mixed black and white to great effect. For summer 1968 all the evening looks were white. Valentino found inspiration from a variety of times and places, merging silhouette and details from the 17th and 18th centuries with motifs borrowed from such diverse sources as Persian carpets and Delft pottery. By mid-decade, he was respected and admired as a leading designer known for magnificent, beautifully made clothes that were also lively and flattering. In 1967 he received the Neiman Marcus Award. Valentino counted among his celebrity clientele some of the most visible women in the world, including Elizabeth Taylor and Jacqueline Kennedy.

Designers: United States

The American fashion industry encompassed a variety of viewpoints. Some American designers looked to British and Parisian high fashion, following trends set by leading designers. Others embraced the tradition of sportswear that was already a hallmark of American fashion, but in very contemporary terms.

Models in ensembles by **Pauline Trigère** were often featured in advertisements for other prestigious products ranging from cosmetics to private jets. Trigère favored textural, sophisticated fabrics for dresses and her work was consistently mature and elegant. Building on the success of her junior line, **Anne Klein** continued to be a force in the American fashion industry, establishing her own label in 1968. She received the Coty and Neiman Marcus Awards in 1969. **John Weitz** was known for practical but well-designed wardrobe basics that were often featured as perfect travel clothes. His name appeared on a wide array of products for men, women, and children. After designing for several Seventh Avenue firms, **Chester Weinberg** established his own label in 1966.

Barbra Streisand wore a chiffon Arnold Scaasi pants ensemble when she received an Oscar in 1969, demonstrating evolving attitudes toward pants, even for formal occasions.

Oleg Cassini (1913–2006) was born in Paris, the son of Russian and Italian aristocrats. Encouraged by his mother, who worked in fashion, Cassini studied fashion and opened his own store in Rome. The young designer moved to the United States, ending up in Hollywood, where he designed for Paramount Pictures and Twentieth Century Fox. Cassini maintained a successful costume design career, dressing such notable stars as Veronica Lake and Rita Hayworth. After serving in the United States Army, Cassini moved to New York in the early 1950s where he launched his own womenswear collection, its success aided by favorable merchandising at Lord & Taylor. With his designs for Jacqueline Kennedy, Cassini was catapulted to fame throughout the world. Cassini also developed a menswear line that was often known for its vibrant fashion-forward look, such as Nehru jackets and colored shirts. He provided suits for American television talk-show host Johnny Carson. His many licensing agreements added to his name recognition and celebrity.

James Galanos maintained a devoted society following (dubbed "Galanos Girls") and the quality of his clothing was among the highest in the world. His conservative yet daring designs did not closely follow trends: "always a man to go his own way, usually 'upstream' against the rest of the fashion world" but "a man whose influence is strong on other American designers."[22] Galanos showed intricately embellished clothes; his evening gowns featured such styles as one-shoulder necklines and lace hoods. He created a cocktail dress of woven ribbon, and his above-the-ankle jersey evening dresses in 1964 startled the press. The recipient of several awards, he received the Sunday Times (London) International Award in 1968, and was honored in his home town with awards from The Fashion Group of Philadelphia and Drexel Institute of Technology.

Already well established by the early sixties, the young **Arnold Scaasi** had success with several different lines. In 1964 he concentrated on his couture salon, showing lavishly embellished eveningwear hailed for its high quality. In 1969 Barbra Streisand wore a Scaasi pajama set to accept the Academy Award for Best Actress. The controversial beaded see-through black chiffon bell-bottom pants and tunic top featured a large white collar and cuffs, with a nude-colored lining that was so subtle the provocative ensemble caused much speculation. The media attention added greatly to Scaasi's celebrity.

Bonnie Cashin continued to be known for her work in leather. She designed for leather goods company Coach beginning in 1962 and for knitwear firm Ballantyne in 1964. She orchestrated imaginative pairings of leather with other materials. Where other designers might offer a leather skirt with a wool jacket, Cashin did the opposite, showing soft kid, chamois, and suede shirts and jackets with wool skirts or pants. Her cloth coats and dresses, even shorts ensembles, were often trimmed in leather. Her work ranged from tailored and fitted to loose and natural. At mid-decade, Cashin interpreted the fashion for tubular cut and pale colors into remarkable white leather tunics, and by the end of the decade her fringed suede dresses captured the hippie look for high fashion. She received a Coty Award in 1968.

Rudi Gernreich (1922–1985) was born in Vienna. Fleeing Austria in 1938, Gernreich and his mother went to Los Angeles. He studied art at Los Angeles City College, and eventually worked as a dancer and costume designer for modern dance. This early experience informed the sensibility of his later fashion designs. Making the move to fabric design, then fashion design, in the 1940s, he worked for several different companies during the 1950s, in both California and New York. Both Hattie Carnegie and Diana Vreeland encouraged the young designer. Gernreich began a partnership with manufacturer Walter Bass and designed relaxed clothes that reflected the American sportswear tradition. He began designing swimwear, both for the Bass label and also for Westwood Knitting Mills; his swimwear designs earned him an award from *Sports Illustrated* magazine. He founded his own lines in Los Angeles, GR Designs in 1960 and Rudi Gernreich Inc. in 1964. Gernreich won numerous awards throughout the decade, including the Neiman Marcus Award in 1961 and four Coty Awards.

Gernreich developed an association with model Peggy Moffitt, who became his muse and longtime friend, and her husband, photographer William Claxton. Sometimes he presented a futuristic aesthetic through knitted bodysuits, and inventive use of vinyl and plastics, including bonnet-shaped visors. Ethnic influences were present with Nehru suits and turbans, gaucho pants, and sarongs. He embraced a vibrant and free-spirited use of color, mixing prints, showing dots and stripes together, and using boldly rendered animal patterns. He featured unexpected views of the body with cut-outs and clear plastic insets. Gernreich's inventive hosiery often matched and completed an ensemble, sometimes even a striped or parti-colored motif on the main garment continued on the legwear. At the end of the decade, Gernreich began to experiment with androgynous and unisex styles. Concerned with the sociological statements in his clothes, particularly issues of gender and modesty, he showed his infamous topless bathing suit in 1964 on Peggy Moffitt. Many of his designs, such as the topless, were more important for their shock value than for their popular appeal (especially sales). Nonetheless, his ideological impact on the world of fashion was significant, and with his loosely fitted shift silhouettes and body-conscious design sensibility, Gernreich was among the most influential designers of the decade.

Bill Blass (1922–2002) had an interest in fashion starting in childhood in Indiana. Blass sold fashion sketches as an adolescent and went right from high school to Seventh Avenue where he began his career at David Crystal sportswear. After serving in World War II, Blass worked for Anne Klein and then moved to Maurice Rentner, establishing his sportswear-inflected American look. Blass found success in upscale ready-to-wear designs, characterized by simple shapes and quality materials, deemed "good investments" by the fashion press. Blass brought menswear influence into his women's fashions, creating well-tailored suits, ensembles, and dresses that could be personalized with accessories. Blass reinvigorated classics such as shirtwaist dresses and sheaths for day and evening and produced striking swimwear. He received two

Below left A 1964 sketch by Bonnie Cashin of a simple pink suede suit illustrates her continued expertise in leather sportswear.

Below right Rudi Gernreich, seen here with his favorite model Peggy Moffitt, espoused an extremely forward-thinking look for both men and women.

Opposite Two models in long dresses by Geoffrey Beene featured in *Vogue*, March 1965, show extremely high fashion hairstyles and illustrate the burgeoning art nouveau revival. Photograph by Gordon Parks.

Right Betsey Johnson's designs for the Paraphernalia line included the dresses in bold graphic prints seen here from 1966.

Coty Awards, in 1961 and 1963. Venturing into menswear, he introduced a line in 1967 and won the first Coty Award for menswear the following year.

Enrolled in a pre-medical program in the 1940s, **Geoffrey Beene** (1927–2004) displayed an interest in clothes, doodling fashion sketches on the bodies in his anatomy textbook. Dropping out of pre-med, Beene studied in New York at Traphagan then moved to Paris in 1948 and studied at the Ecole de la Chambre Syndicale de la Couture Parisienne and privately with one of Molyneux's tailors. When he returned to New York in 1951, Beene had comprehensive knowledge of design and construction. By 1960 he was a featured designer for Teal Traina in New York. Beene established his own company in 1963 and consistently received positive press coverage. Easy-fitting silhouettes rendered in unusual materials characterized Beene's work during the 1960s. In 1965 he showed simple columnar dresses made of silk panels in engineered prints with no repeat. Evening looks were often playful, including satin babydoll dresses with fully beaded bodices, sequined "football jerseys" of 1967, and gingham gowns in 1968. Beene received the Coty Award in 1964 and the Neiman Marcus Award in 1965.

After being educated in both costume design and fashion design at several prestigious schools, Connecticut-born **Donald Brooks** (1928–2005) worked for Lord & Taylor as a window designer, and for several ready-to-wear lines. He became the designer for Townley after the death of Claire McCardell, and created a custom line for the store Henri Bendel's. Brooks opened his own store in 1964, but also had success as a costume designer, including Broadway musicals *Promises, Promises* and *No Strings*, and the films *Star* and *The Cardinal*. He received both Oscar and Tony nominations. In 1967 *Life* magazine featured a photograph of his sinuous black and white evening dress modeled in front of a blow-up of an Aubrey Beardsley illustration, an emblematic moment in the revival of art nouveau.

Oscar de la Renta (1932–2014) was born in the Dominican Republic, where he studied art as a teenager. His fashion career began in Madrid, where he sold sketches to fashion houses including Balenciaga's Eisa. De la Renta traveled to Paris and assisted Antonio Castillo at Lanvin-Castillo. In 1962 he took a job at Elizabeth Arden as head designer and his work was immediately successful. Coats in full-bodied fabrics revealed an emphasis on structured silhouette. For evening, he showed short dresses in soft lace and transparent layers as well as gala styles in thicker silks with sophisticated colorations. He was known for using ruffles, small bows, flower details, and a luscious color palette. In 1965 de la Renta left Arden and started a ready-to-wear label, which went public in 1969. He won two Coty Awards during the decade, in 1967 and 1968.

Connecticut native **Betsey Johnson** (b. 1942) developed an interest in dance and costuming as a child, and attended Pratt Institute and Syracuse University. After interning at *Mademoiselle* magazine, Johnson went to work as designer for the New York boutique Paraphernalia, where her offbeat aesthetic developed. She became the most visible American designer of cutting-edge fashion trends. Johnson designed clear plastic sleeveless dresses, with opaque stick-on pieces that the wearer could place. She also featured lamé shifts: "It was all very spaceship. 'What would you wear on the Moon?' This was the big question of the Sixties."[23] In 1969 Johnson opened a boutique called Betsey Bunky Nini with two other owners. Socialite-turned-underground celebrity Edie Sedgwick was Johnson's first fit model, and wore the designer's clothes in Andy Warhol's film *Ciao! Manhattan*.

Giorgio di Sant'Angelo (1933–1989) was born in Florence, and grew up in Argentina. He was educated in Florence, Barcelona, and Paris. Arriving in the United States in 1962, he worked in a variety of other applied arts, including jewelry design, before working as a fashion stylist for *Vogue*, where he created many well-known images with body paint on models Twiggy and Veruschka. Launching his own clothing line in the late 1960s, Sant'Angelo's look was described as "rich hippie," which represented the zenith of high fashion hippie style. Sant'Angelo typically mixed a variety of inspirational sources in one ensemble, combining, for example, American Indian clothing, European folk costume, and the Middle Ages, to create a fantasy, fairy-tale effect. Floral and paisley prints, fringe, ruffles, suede, tie-dye, and embroidery were typical features of his work. The designer captivated the press: "if there are such things as fashion geniuses, Giorgio di Sant'Angelo is one."[24]

Film and Television and Fashion

Film and television continued to affect the diffusion of fashion. *Breakfast at Tiffany's* (1961) featured Audrey Hepburn once again in Givenchy; her famous black sheath evening dress was widely copied, and provided one of the decade's most memorable fashion moments. Hepburn's co-star, Patricia Neal, also sported a chic wardrobe, provided by Pauline Trigère. The British television show *The Avengers* (1961–1969), starring Patrick Macnee and several leading ladies including Honor Blackman and Diana Rigg, provided fashion-forward inspiration. Some of Rigg's costumes were designed by John Bates and Alun Hughes, while Pierre Cardin contributed to Macnee's wardrobe. The television series was so popular it inspired several lines of clothes for men and women. Many junior styles were also driven by television shows; *The Patty Duke Show* and *Gidget* were particularly influential.

Geraldine Chaplin and Omar Sharif in costume for *Doctor Zhivago*. The furs and outerwear featured in the 1965 film were especially influential on fashion.

Period films influenced current styles. *My Fair Lady* (1963), with costumes designed by Cecil Beaton, included the famous black and white "Ascot Gavotte," which reflected the taste for black and white present in the arts and in many fashion collections. *Doctor Zhivago* (1965), starring Omar Sharif and Julie Christie, with costumes designed by Phyllis Dalton, influenced Marc Bohan, Yves Saint Laurent, and Valentino to create Russian-inspired clothing. Images of Sharif in a pea coat helped establish it as a classic for years to come. *Thoroughly Modern Millie* (1967) featured designs by Jean Louis and mirrored ersatz "flapper" styles being offered by high fashion designers ranging from Crahay to Quant. Other period films propelled the trend for "retro" style. For *Bonnie and Clyde* (1967), designer Theadora Van Runkle dressed Faye Dunaway in early 1930s fashions, including a Norfolk-style jacket, yellow sweater, and beret that were widely copied. *Life* ran a cover on January 12, 1968 with the headline "Bonnie: Fashion's New Darling" and *Vogue* featured Dunaway in Bonnie-inspired fashions. Other films, importantly *Funny Girl* (1968) with Barbra Streisand as Fanny Brice, dressed by Irene Sharaff, and *They Shoot Horses, Don't They?* (1969), a tale of 1930s dance marathons costumed by Donfeld, also encouraged the retro trend.

Science fiction films such as *Journey to the Seventh Planet* (1962) and *Fantastic Voyage* (1966) both encouraged and reflected the futuristic trends in fashion. The characters on television cartoon *The Jetsons* (1962–1963) wore clothes that prefigured the space-inspired fashion of the following years. *2001: A Space Odyssey* (1968) featured costumes designed by Hardy Amies, including space-station stewardess uniforms reflecting current offerings by London's Mod designers and the Paris avant-garde. Television's *Star Trek* (1966–1969) included costumes designed by William Ware Theiss that strongly resembled the work of Cardin and Courrèges. Prehistory figured almost as importantly as the future, with vehicles such as *One Million Years BC* (1966), with Raquel Welch dressed in an improbable doeskin bikini designed by Carl Toms.

Above Faye Dunaway's costumes in *Bonnie and Clyde* (1967) contributed to fashion's retro trend.

Below The impact of the 1963 film *Cleopatra* extended to make-up, such as Revlon's promotion of "Sphinx Pink" lipstick.

Sean Connery as James Bond.

Ursula Andress as Honey Ryder in *Dr. No* (1962).

JAMES BOND – FASHION ICON

As menswear started to become more informal and subject to the whims of fashion – with changing silhouettes and trendy accessories – the breakdown of existing traditions was confusing for many men. The screen version of James Bond appeared just in time to remind men that it was possible to act tough and look good. Although several actors have portrayed 007, Sean Connery (b. 1930) set the standard for masculine elegance in six Bond films starting with *Dr. No* in 1962. Asked who fitted him for his gun, he replied, "my tailor, on Savile Row," stressing prestige, even in dangerous circumstances. Connery wore a white dinner jacket like no one else, reinvigorating the style and erasing any hint of effeminacy associated with dressing up. His customary outfit was a well-tailored suit, but Bond also appeared in swim trunks, scuba gear, safari jackets, and bathrobes (a logical follow-up to his many romantic interludes). He even sported a remarkably fashion-forward outfit in *Dr. No* – a shantung Mandarin-style jacket that prefigured the exotic styling of menswear later in the decade.

The Bond movies were not just influential on men's fashion. Various female characters, always attractive and frequently deadly, became collectively known as "Bond Girls" and were also inspirational; Ursula Andress' white bikini in *Dr. No* helped the style gather steam. While futuristic gadgets and sexy cars added sophistication to the atmosphere, James Bond's sharp suits and immaculate accessories defined the character. Whether outfitted in a tuxedo for an evening at the casino or an open-necked polo shirt for secret reconnaissance, James Bond remains the model for the modern man, dressed to kill.

A 1964 Saint Tropez street scene shows a couple in Continental leisurewear.

The fashion industry itself provided narrative inspiration. *Darling* (1965) depicted Julie Christie as a model climbing her way up the profession. *Qui êtes-vous, Polly Maggoo?* (1966), directed by fashion photographer William Klein, offered a satire of the current Paris fashion scene including send-ups of designs by Rabanne and Esterel. The murder mystery *Blow-Up* (1966) featured top models – such as Peggy Moffitt and Veruschka – playing top models.

Hair and Beauty

Eyes became a fashion focus, brought into prominence by heavy eyeliner, thick mascara, and false eyelashes sometimes applied both above and below the eyes. The 1963 film *Cleopatra*, starring Elizabeth Taylor with dramatic kohl-lined eyes, had an influence on eye make-up styles, culminating in Revlon's "Cleopatra Look" which, in addition to heavy eyeliner, also included "Sphinx Pink" lipstick. Big eyes contrasted with pale, even-toned faces to produce a doll-like image, a look that was associated with model Jean Shrimpton. Pale lipstick, a major change from the red lips of previous years, was already popular at the beginning of the decade and shades lightened almost to white, sometimes with frosted effects. Nails followed the same palette and were often painted to match the lips. Fashion models emphasized their wide-eyed looks with striking eye make-up, especially Penelope Tree and Peggy Moffitt. Pablo, a make-up artist at the Elizabeth Arden salon in Rome, was known for creating memorable effects using jewels, lace, and feathers. Particularly wild eye make-up and body paint became common in fashion images, especially associated with Veruschka.

Several major trends in hairstyling were seen. Bouffant or "beehive" hairdos, especially popular at the beginning of the decade, required backcombing and teasing, setting, and hairspray to achieve the height and volume of styles such as Dusty Springfield's bouffant. London hairdresser Vidal Sassoon promoted short, geometric haircuts that needed no hairspray. The style was also popularized by Mary Quant, American actress Nancy Kwan, and model Grace Coddington. Very short hair was another option; Twiggy and Mia Farrow were known for their cropped hairstyles. During its five years on television, *That Girl*, which premiered in 1966, promoted Marlo Thomas' "flip" hairstyle as an all-American look. Long straight hair also became fashionable as the decade progressed. Women with natural curls and waves used large rollers to achieve the smooth, swinging hair of singers Mary Travers and Françoise Hardy.

As hats went out of fashion, some hairstylists used wire and extreme lacquering in high fashion grooming. Frankly fake hairpieces – ponytails, falls, braids, and "wiglets" – were worn for fun. Dynel, a synthetic fiber, was used to make wigs in a range of colors and styles, perfect for "a girl who wants to create a stir at winter parties."[25] Some falls were attached to a wide headband, and turbans with fake hair at the top were also available. Another colorful option was glow-in-the-dark hairspray.

Menswear

For the first time since the 1920s, menswear encouraged variety and personal style and contemporary films reflected this diversity. The actor Alain Delon embodied Continental cool in 1960's *Plein Soleil* (also known as *Purple Noon*). Frank Sinatra, Sammy Davis Jr., and other members of Hollywood's "Rat Pack" were influential on

The Beatles' fashion style evolved along with their music. Here they are seen in trim Mod-style suits in a still from *A Hard Day's Night* (1964).

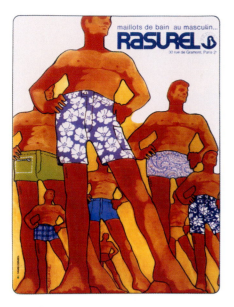

Boldly patterned swim trunks in a variety of lengths from the French firm Rasurel, 1969.

Dresses from Pierre Cardin's 1968 collection feature his Space Age aesthetic even for little girls.

men's fashion. Sean Connery as James Bond provided an example of suave dressing for every occasion.

The so-called "Peacock Revolution" began, as men enjoyed a new freedom in dress. The Beatles exemplified the experimental approach as they moved from a Mod look in the early years of the decade through a psychedelic period to Indian-influenced styles; and their fans followed suit. As in the past, London set the standard for traditional men's fashion, but the new "London Look" offered surprises and originality. Carnaby Street was the center of innovation and became synonymous with "swinging" styles for men. John Stephen opened his boutique called His Clothes there in 1958 and during the 1960s established himself as an important name in men's fashion. Soho was also a fashion center with many shops for men, as was Piccadilly, where Michael Fish, who was trained as a shirt maker, established his boutique Mr. Fish in 1966. The Mr. Fish aesthetic was decorative, even exotic, and featured unorthodox materials such as flowered Liberty prints for menswear. While many of the most daring styles sprang from an urban homosexual aesthetic, straight men embraced trends such as hip-hugging pants, colorful shirts, and fitted jackets. Traditional British elements including tartan, waistcoats, and ascots were reinterpreted in brighter colors and exaggerated fit to appeal to the youth market. The boutique ideal also infiltrated the traditional menswear trade. In 1967 century-old clothier Aquascutum opened Club 92, offering newly styled, bold-colored versions of the jackets, trousers, and outerwear for which the firm was known.

While the early years of the decade continued Continental and Ivy League suit styles, the suit became the focus of experimentation. Early in the decade, jackets were short and tight, buttoned high with narrow lapels. Trousers were tight and narrow. In later years, jackets lengthened, lapels widened – especially on double-breasted styles – and the waist was strongly nipped in. As the decade progressed, neckties widened in tandem with lapels. A great variety of materials was used for suits; in addition to the usual range of solids and tweeds, wool checks and stripes, patterned corduroy, velvet, and brocade were all seen. Trousers evolved into a bell-bottom shape. Shirts were often equally bold, in stripes, dots, paisleys, and Op Art-inspired prints. British tailor Tommy Nutter offered shaped jackets, often with wide lapels, in bold and colorful patterns. Trained in a Savile Row firm, Nutter counted many musicians, including Mick Jagger and the Beatles, among his clients even before he opened his own shop, Nutters of Savile Row, in 1969. The exoticism and historic inspiration that influenced women's clothing also affected menswear. With shaped suits and ruffled shirts, some men presented a romantic appearance. Others adopted ethnic influences such as the fitted Nehru jacket with standing collar, often made in silk, or colorful African-style dashikis.

Designers increasingly entered the menswear market, including Oleg Cassini, Guy Laroche, and Ted Lapidus. Pierre Cardin in particular was a great innovator in menswear. He showed his first men's collection in 1960, using college students as models, and opened a ready-to-wear department one year later. Cardin's designs showed an extreme version of Mod style. He eliminated traditional tailoring details including lapels, pocket flaps, and sleeve buttons. Collarless round-necked jackets and narrow trousers were initially shown with white shirts and ties. Later collections continued the slim, tubular silhouette with tapered shirts and low-waisted trousers, with no back pockets, in stretchy synthetics

Top Girls' separates from Sears, spring/summer 1968, in bright colors with stylish accessories, showing the similarity between junior and adult markets.

Above A sewing pattern offers multiple variations on the Nehru jacket for boys, as well as an updated version of a belted Norfolk style.

and blends. As with his womenswear, Cardin promoted Space Age styling for men, offering zippered jumpsuits worn with turtlenecks and ribbed boots.

By the end of the decade, hippie styles influenced menswear. Young men adopted fringed jackets and vests, and Afghan-style jackets with embroidery and shaggy fur edging. Denim jackets were customized with embroidery, patches, and appliqués. Flags and flag motifs were frequently worn as an ironic statement on politics and conformity. Pete Townshend, guitarist for The Who, wore a tailored jacket based on the Union Jack in 1966. In the 1969 film *Easy Rider*, Peter Fonda wore a leather jacket with an American flag sewn on the back. Denim jeans became almost a uniform. Many men "aged" their jeans, purposely fraying the hems, removing pockets, and using bleach to achieve a washed or spattered effect.

The diversity of grooming styles for men mirrored an increasingly wide spectrum of fashion ideals and reflected influence from actors and musicians. At the beginning of their careers, the Beatles' neat haircuts with longer bangs and sides were widely influential. As the decade progressed, they grew their hair to shoulder length and sported mustaches and beards, reflecting countercultural trends. Other performers, such as Roger Daltrey, grew out their layered Mod cuts into longer styles that prefigured "glam rock." Robert Redford, Paul Newman, and Ryan O'Neal presented a clean-cut look that contrasted with the androgyny of Donovan or Mick Jagger.

Reflecting the growing ethnic diversity seen among female style icons, men also emulated more diverse role models. The elegant Egyptian-born Omar Sharif starred in several major feature films; African American rock guitarist Jimi Hendrix promoted flamboyant hippie styles; and martial arts star Bruce Lee was the first Chinese American male sex symbol.

While the general population did not fully embrace collarless Mod looks or Nehru jackets for business wear, mainstream menswear showed influences from these alternative aesthetics and the trend toward informality progressed as rigid rules of dressing were relaxed, even discarded. Some men adopted evening suits made of velveteen in place of standard tuxedos, while others opted for suits instead of formal wear for their weddings. Ascots and even turtlenecks worn with jackets provided alternatives to the necktie. Manufacturers continued to promote synthetics as modern, exemplified in the 1963 film *Charade* in which Cary Grant took a shower in his suit, emerging to "drip dry" – soaking wet but dapper as ever.

Children's Fashion

The general categories of children's clothing were largely unchanged from earlier years. One of the major stories in childrenswear was the importance of media tie-ins. Cartoon characters from television and film provided a steady stream of inspiration and revenue for manufacturers. Popular programs including *Batman*, *The Green Hornet* and *The Jetsons* inspired licensed clothes and accessories, as did musical groups. Astronauts were widely admired and little boys often wore space-themed play clothes and pajamas. Zipped jumpsuits, like miniature flight suits, were decorated with "planet" and "atomic" patches. Conversational prints for shirts and sleepwear featured rockets, spacemen, stars, and similar motifs. Girls' fashion expressed the Space Age look through narrow nylon pants worn with tunic-length tops. A-line jumpers (pinafore dresses) were popular over turtlenecks or blouses. Like their mothers, young girls wore boots, sometimes reaching to mid-calf or to the knee. While the concept of mother–daughter fashion was not new, the youthful look of much of women's fashion prompted press commentary on the similarities of style for women and young girls. Straight lines, flat-soled shoes, above-the-knee hemlines, and pale and bright colors characterized fashion for both age groups.

By the end of the decade, retro and romantic styling affected children's clothes as well. Boys increasingly wore long hair, and for special occasions some were dressed in miniature versions of the Nehru jackets or velveteen suits worn by their fathers. Some girls were dressed in folk styles, often with kerchiefs.

The End of the Decade

Skirt length was both big news and a great debate at the end of the 1960s. With hemlines in flux the decade ended with no decisive length, and skirts in the 1969 Paris collections were anywhere and everywhere on the leg. This variety represented a choice, but also confusion for women. Writing in the London *Times*, Prudence Glynn identified no less than five lengths, "the mini, the norm, the midi, the mixi and the maxi," and said of the midi:

> Depending on the curve of your calves it is either young, witty and alluring, or old, fussy and male deterring. Probably the most important thing to do if you adopt this length is to look as though you meant to. The new midi skirts are slightly A line and hang very flat. Your old 1950s pencil slim model with the pleat at the back simply will not do. [26]

The writer also added advice to women to try the "norm" length, defined as 2 inches (5 centimeters) above the knee, over trousers to give it a fresh look! The various lengths did not just apply to skirts but to coats, scarves, and waistcoats. Designers sometimes embraced the confusion with mixed hemlines, such as maxi coats over miniskirts.

With hippie and retro looks in the mix, a clear fashion viewpoint for both men and women could not be discerned, as a variety of tastes and looks were available. Hippie styles were well assimilated into the mainstream, but ironically devoid of their earlier meaning. Ethnic styles, once embraced for a sense of global awareness, were adopted merely for fashion, and other trends, such as Victorian and retro, rooted in the past, perhaps appealed to a public disenchanted with a volatile and uncertain present.

Colorful London fashions from late in the decade showing influence from hippie and bohemian styles anticipate the layered, retro feeling that opened the 1970s.

Chapter 10

The 1970s

Revivals and Individuality

The major theme of fashion in the 1970s was variety. The late 1960s established fashion genres that were explored further by designers in the 1970s. Vintage styles and international costume, experiments with length and shape, and hints of cross-dressing were some of the features of fashion. Film and television were crucial influences on style for both men and women. The women's liberation, gay rights, and "Black Power" movements all considered the importance of appearance in the development and presentation of their respective agendas. Style tribes continued to develop as both politics and music influenced the eclectic nature of fashion in this particularly politicized decade. The designer's touch was increasingly valued across all segments of the fashion industry. Top designers presented diffusion lines and licensing was widespread. Even moderately priced sportswear and jeans carried the imprimatur of leading names – creating the new category of designer jeans. The evolution of fashion during this decade reflected the coming of age of the baby boom generation, moving from playful individualism in the early years to a more materialistic maturity.

Opposite An illustration by Steven Stipelman of loungewear for *Women's Wear Daily* conveys a folkloric mood, one of the many themes of fashion during the 1970s.

Right Yves Saint Laurent with models from a 1972 collection. Longer hems and a smoother fit on the body were indicative of the new decade.

Social and Economic Background

The effects of a lingering and unpopular war in Southeast Asia, economic instability, and the recent memory of assassinations of prominent American leaders dampened the social and political climate of the United States in the early 1970s. The Wounded Knee incident in 1973, when followers of the American Indian Movement occupied the South Dakota town for seventy-one days, crystallized tensions between Native American populations and the US government. The Watergate scandal led to the resignation of American president Richard Nixon in 1974 and by the time the Vietnam War ended in 1975, the optimism and trust in the future that had characterized much of the previous decade had worn off. The OPEC (Organization of Petroleum Exporting Countries) oil embargo that began in 1973 caused economic difficulties throughout much of the industrialized world and culminated in gas rationing in Europe and North America in the late 1970s. Conflicts in the Middle East were frequent, and the 1972 summer Olympics in Munich were stained by the murder of eleven Israeli athletes by Palestinian terrorists. In 1978 the leaders of Egypt and Israel signed the Camp David Accords, promising peace in the region. Iran's 1979 revolution installed a new leader, the Ayatollah Ruhollah Khomeini, and an extremist Islamist government. Around the globe, a series of high-profile actions by revolutionary groups – Symbionese Liberation Army, Brigate Rosse (Red Brigades), Baader-Meinhof group, Basque Separatist ETA (Euskadi Ta Askatasuna) group, IRA (Irish Republican Army), Front de libération du Québec (Quebec Liberation Front) – included kidnappings and murders. With the death of Mao and international recognition of the People's Republic, including the historic visit by Richard Nixon, China took steps toward modernization. The communist revolution in Cambodia installed the Khmer Rouge government and brought about widespread famine and the death of tens of thousands of citizens. Expansion of apartheid restrictions in South Africa deprived the non-white majority of civil rights. The 1975 death of Francisco Franco resulted in more social freedoms for the Spanish population. The "Winter of Discontent" in the United Kingdom led to a series of strikes against the Labour government's attempts at wage-freezing in 1978–1979. Aptly dubbed the "Me decade" by writer Tom Wolfe, this period was marked by various special interest groups demanding political and economic voice and visibility – adding to the sense of cultural disunity. This image of a society in flux was powerfully mirrored in the diverse, expressive fashion of the time.

The Arts

Artists including Vito Acconci, John Baldessari, and Joseph Beuys explored ideas through writing, performance, and other ephemeral actions and their work was labeled "conceptual art." More permanent artistic monuments took the form of large-scale projects such as Christo's *Valley Curtains* and earthworks such as Robert Smithson's *Spiral Jetty* and Walter De Maria's *Lightning Field*. Photorealist painters such as Richard Estes produced detailed images of modern life and Pop Art was still vital in the hands of David Hockney and Wayne Thiebaud. Feminist art offered alternative views and critiqued the predominantly male art establishment. Judy Chicago's *The Dinner Party* presented a colossal display of overt feminist fervor. Graphic styles varied widely as many posters, album covers, and advertisements conveyed movement with flowing script and rainbow colors. Others featured an "Old West" aesthetic with muted earth tones. The first Earth Day was held on April 22, 1970 and the back-to-the-earth mentality was embodied by the ecology movement, which had its own flag and logo. Expo '74 in Spokane, Washington, had an environmental theme, as opposed to other world's fairs which emphasized technology. A handcraft revival, mixed with global sensibilities, contributed to the popularity of crafts such as macramé and batik and the continued use of tie-dye. But it was also the dawn of the computer age, as IBM's innovations for business and Apple's personal computers made the emerging technology a factor in design. Other new technologies that had an impact on daily life included pocket calculators, microwave ovens, and telephone

Paul Davis' poster for Ntozake Shange's 1976 stage play *For Colored Girls …* reflects the vogue for headscarves and the overall impact of African American style on mainstream fashion.

answering machines. Interior decoration and furniture design reflected both prevailing trends: a craft aesthetic was seen in abundant use of wood, shaggy rugs, and muted color schemes, while lacquered or molded plastic furniture in bold colors expressed the emerging high-tech look. A futuristic style pervaded the architecture of retail spaces. Skyscrapers thrust higher than ever, as the World Trade Center in New York, Chicago's Sears Tower, and the CN Tower in Toronto were all completed. The high-tech aesthetic of Renzo Piano and Richard Rogers' Centre Georges Pompidou, Paris, was influential on later projects.

Major exhibitions brought new audiences to museums and were influential on fashion. The elaborate, theatrical shows of historic and international dress mounted by former fashion editor Diana Vreeland at the Costume Institute of the Metropolitan Museum were very popular. Highlights included *Romantic and Glamorous Hollywood Design* (1974) and *The Glory of Russian Costume* (1976). Treasures from the tomb of Tutankhamun, which toured internationally from 1972 to 1979, were repeatedly referenced throughout fashion, design, and popular culture, creating the second "Egyptomania" of the century.

The spirit of the "Me decade" permeated best-seller lists. The self-help genre exploded with titles such as *How to Be Your Own Best Friend* (1971) and *Looking Out for #1* (1977). One of the best-selling books of the decade was *Jonathan Livingston Seagull* (1970), Richard Bach's motivational parable. Many popular works of fiction went quickly into film including William P. Blatty's *The Exorcist* (1971), Peter Benchley's *Jaws* (1974), Stephen King's *Carrie* (1974), and Alex Haley's *Roots: the Saga of an American Family* (1976). A particularly rich period in British fiction included continuing output from Muriel Spark and Graham Greene as well as works from new talent such as John Fowles' *The French Lieutenant's Woman* (1970), Mary Renault's *The Persian Boy* (1972), Richard Adams' *Watership Down* (1975) and Iris Murdoch's *The Sea, The Sea* (1977).

On the musical stage important works included *Jesus Christ Superstar*, which premiered on Broadway in 1971 and received many global productions during the decade, as did *Godspell*, another New Testament reimagining. The long-running and influential *A Chorus Line* opened in 1975 and *Annie* in 1977. 1978's *On the Twentieth Century* strongly reflected the taste for art deco revival. The New York Shakespeare Festival's production of *The Threepenny Opera* encouraged revival of Kurt Weill and Bertolt Brecht's work. *Evita* premiered in London in 1978. The 1975 Broadway musical *The Wiz* was made into a film shortly after. Award-winning dramas included *Travesties* by Tom Stoppard (1974), Peter Shaffer's *Equus* (1975), *For Colored Girls Who Have Considered Suicide When the Rainbow is Enuf* (1977) by Ntozake Shange, and Harold Pinter's *Betrayal* (1978).

A new generation of film directors pursued individual visions, including Woody Allen, Robert Altman, Peter Bogdanovich, Francis Ford Coppola, Brian De Palma, George Lucas, Martin Scorsese, Ridley Scott, and François Truffaut. Significant films reflected diverse subjects and moods including period pieces, nostalgia, and gritty contemporary realism. Landmark movies included *Ryan's Daughter* (1970), *The Last Picture Show* (1971), *A Clockwork Orange* (1971), *Day for Night* (1973), *Enter the Dragon* (1973), *Murder on the Orient Express* (1974), *Barry Lyndon* (1975), *Cousin Cousine* (1975), *Taxi Driver* (1976), *The Man Who Fell to Earth* (1976), *Allegro Non Troppo* (1976), *Star Wars* (1977), and *Alien* (1979). However, new entertainment options challenged film as never before, most notably cable television, videocassette recorders, and video games.

The association of popular music styles with fashion was particularly important. The American television show *Soul Train* premiered in 1971. It showcased dance music for a black audience and highlighted individual dance and fashion styles. The emergence of disco in the middle of the decade revived both partner and line dancing. At nightclubs such as New York's Studio 54, Trocadero Transfer in San Francisco, Le Palace in Paris, or Montreal's Lime Light, DJs mixed music to create endless dance sets

The Jackson 5's fashion-forward outfits c. 1970, including bright shirts layered under hippie-inspired vests, were typical of the styling of Motown label acts.

enhanced by gigantic sound systems and spectacular lighting effects. The permissive disco scene often involved heavy alcohol and drug use and a freewheeling attitude toward sexuality. The disco aesthetic was glamorous and dressy, sometimes tending toward futuristic, as seen in nightclub decor and the costume of some performers such as "Eurodisco" sensations Boney M. and Abba. Even the theme from *Star Wars* got a disco remix. Donna Summer, The Queen of Disco, scored major success with dance hits such as "I Feel Love" and "Last Dance"; her hit "Bad Girls" included whistles and a repeated "beep-beep" that captured life on the street.

Other clothing trends were reflected in musical styles. American Judy Collins and British Cleo Laine maintained an artistic, bohemian look. Retro styling was embraced in the costuming, staging, and music of Liza Minnelli, The Manhattan Transfer, and The Pointer Sisters; retro icon Bette Midler even remade the Andrews Sisters' wartime hit "Boogie Woogie Bugle Boy." Racial diversity was celebrated in the career of Cherokee singer Rita Coolidge and Cher's mixed heritage was reflected in her hit song "Half Breed"; their performance wardrobe reflected their American Indian backgrounds. Fashion trends toward exotic orientalism were mirrored in the lyrics of songs such as Maria Muldaur's "Midnight at the Oasis" and Amanda Lear's "Queen of Chinatown."

Punk music emerged around 1974 in Britain in an atmosphere of revolt against mainstream conformity and popular music. Important British punk bands included Sex Pistols, The Clash, and Siouxsie and the Banshees. In the United States, The Ramones and Richard Hell and the Voidoids were among the best-known punk groups. The discordant music and nihilistic lyrics of songs such as the Sex Pistols' "Anarchy in the U.K." or Richard Hell's "Blank Generation" were reinforced by punk's visual message.

Fashion Media

New magazines that increased the spread of fashion included the celebrity-focused *People*, which debuted in 1974, and *Essence*, targeted at black women, which began in 1970. A number of prominent models pursued acting careers, including Twiggy and Marisa Berenson. Important faces included Lauren Hutton who, with her gap-toothed smile, projected a quirky glamour. Overall, the demeanor of models was happy, animated, and physically fit. Name recognition for models became more important and fresh-faced Americans, mostly blondes, dominated fashion media including Cybill Shepherd, Christie Brinkley, and Patti Hansen. Dayle Haddon, Shelley Hack, and Margaux Hemingway were especially known for their work with cosmetic companies. Following the groundbreaking career of Naomi Sims, other African American models gained prominence, including Pat Cleveland and Beverly Johnson, who became *Vogue*'s first black cover girl in 1974. They were followed by Somalian model Iman, who began modeling for *Vogue* in 1976. Diana Ross' starring role in *Mahogany* (1975), the story of an African American woman who becomes a fashion designer, presented the world of fashion as accessible to black women.

A new aesthetic in fashion photography was initially embraced by European magazines but infiltrated American and British publications by mid-decade. Images such as Helmut Newton's photo of a model in a Saint Laurent tuxedo in a dark alley challenged the elegant look that had defined fashion. Newton's work, like the photography of Guy Bourdin and Chris von Wangenheim, often included suggestions of violence and sadomasochistic sexuality and served as the inspiration for the film

The Jamaican German disco act Boney M. perform their hit "Rasputin" in "à la Russe"-style costumes for a 1979 concert.

CHIC ETHNIQUE

As the 1970s began the Western world was captivated with global styles in a way that far surpassed the orientalist trends of previous decades and centuries. *National Geographic* and similar periodicals fed Western imaginations with images of exotic cultures. Hippie chic had blossomed into the couture ethnic and peasant styles of Thea Porter (with her glorious kaftans) and Giorgio di Sant'Angelo (and his rich gypsy chic). Mary McFadden, after living in Africa during the 1960s, was a keen collector of African art, and Zandra Rhodes visited Australia for the first time in 1971 and created the "Ayers Rock" print.

By mid-decade "ethnic" and "peasant" styles were readily available throughout different market levels and in many variations. Peasant blouses teamed with flounced skirts were a fashion staple, and import clothing stores overflowed with options. Imported costume jewelry was absolutely essential to the look. Shifting international influences included Russia and China (particularly asserted by Yves Saint Laurent) and glamorous folkloric looks sent women to the workplace as "citified peasants." Russian influence was seen in side-buttoning, band collars, and tunic-length tops bloused over pants. Ponchos and culottes, often teamed with suede boots, presented numerous women and schoolgirls as South American gauchos. The decade's men would also have their share of such costumey styles. Blousy gauze and muslin shirts continued a bohemian hippie aesthetic, along with the ongoing popularity of dashikis. Djellabas were an option, even in long loungewear styles. The Russian influence was seen in silk "Cossack" shirts for evening or, for the most adventurous, worn belted during the day. Indian paisley patterns were more pronounced than ever before on neckties and adorned numerous shirts.

Retail devoted to goods imported from Africa, India, and the Far East offered consumers a wide array of housewares. Western culture embraced global cultures in ways far beyond fashion and design. Spiritual movements, such as Transcendental Meditation and Krishna Consciousness, sprang forth from India along with yoga and paisley gauze bedspreads. Mainstream appetites in the West were also affected by a global mentality, as many tried such exotica as tabouli, baba ganoush, pita bread, sushi, and even curry for the first time.

While the fashionable Western world was embracing global styles, other parts of the world were reacting to issues of traditional dress in distinct and different ways. During the course of the 1960s Queen Sirikit of Thailand promoted the adoption of a newly designed national costume for the Thai people, as the traditional styles had been virtually eradicated by the edicts of Prime Minister Phibunsongkhram in 1938. Drawing inspiration back to the Ayutthaya period, she and her dressmakers developed a variety of looks worn for diplomatic and festival occasions and she abandoned her chic Western wardrobe in favor of the "new" traditional. Other women of Thai society followed the queen's example and adopted such fashions. Other countries strove to modernize their populations to keep up with a continuously developing world, with attempts at legislating many customary adornment practices. Some tribal men in New Guinea, Indonesia, wore little more than the codpieces made of gourds (*koteka*) that had been part of their traditional attire for generations. The Islamic majority government based in Jakarta, nearly 2,500 miles (4,000 kilometers) away, sought to eliminate the indigenous, if immodest, style and launched *Operasi Koteka* ("Operation Penis Gourd") in 1971. *Operasi Koteka* debuted with great fanfare in a ceremony attended by Indonesian First Lady Ibu Tien. Government workers went to the tribes and distributed t-shirts and shorts to the male natives, hoping to transform their wardrobes. But the men kept wearing the *koteka* and even purportedly fashioned the newly acquired shorts into turbans; *Operasi Koteka* was abandoned the following year.

Eyes of Laura Mars (1978). An alternative, more ethereal, mood was exemplified in other photographic work. Photographers Sarah Moon and Deborah Turbeville created mysterious, soft-focus images of distant and aloof models. Steven Stipelman, Kenneth Paul Block and Joe Eula breathed continued life into fashion illustration.

The Elements of Women's Fashion

Boutiques and smaller retail stores continued to thrive, and were selling more individualized clothing to smaller market segments. The acceptance of individualized tastes had become permanently established. Several trends that emerged in the late 1960s, including hippie, peasant and ethnic, retro, and unisex styles, dominated the fashion scene throughout the early and middle years of the 1970s. Rules of dressing that were established in the post-war period and challenged by the 1960s were now virtually eliminated. Casual dressing grew and divisions between afternoon and dinner or cocktail dressing all but disappeared. For the average woman, evening clothes became less formal; only the most important of social occasions called for designer glamour. Pants were more and more prevalent in a variety of circumstances. Along with the more widespread acceptance of women in pants came new, relaxed protocols of dressing and standards of modesty. Showing the continued influence of the youthful spirit and free-love ideals of the 1960s, t-shirts and tank tops became acceptable streetwear. For women, halter tops, crop tops, and tube tops without brassieres were accepted for leisure attire.

The midi and maxi were slow to be adopted. They were initially rejected by women, who saw them as dowdy and matronly, and the mini lingered as retailers found the new lengths a hard sell. Unlike the 1947 edict of Paris for longer hems, this change was much more gradual and slower to be adopted by a reluctant public. The midi did not dominate until mid-decade, and the miniskirt, while waning, still clung to a place in the vernacular wardrobe. Hot pants, the shorts equivalent of the miniskirt, prolonged focus on the legs. For a few years, long and short coexisted; long sweaters and slim coats were worn over short skirts or hot pants. But by the middle of the decade the midi was established as the prevailing length, and the maxi was common for casual evening, holiday, and special occasion.

The boxy silhouette of the mid-1960s was still available at a vernacular level, but the truly fashionable silhouette was softer, sleek, and closer to the body. Gores were sometimes used in the construction of the new longer skirts, giving the lower body a definition that had been missing from fashion since the pencil silhouette of the 1950s. Calvin Klein articulated a popular sentiment, saying clothes should be "easy and free, not stiff. When clothes are simple and beautiful, they permit the sense of the woman wearing them to come through."[1]

In general, fashion was fluid and body-skimming with a fit defined by softness. Soft fit was sometimes controlled by cinched-in waistlines. Wrap construction was another important component to the sleeker fit, with wrap dresses and wrap skirts worn with contrasting tops. Many bias-cut skirts used stripes and the stripes formed a chevron. Sunray pleated styles were popular. Knit t-shirt-style and shirtwaist dresses were popular at all levels of fashion.

Trousers, in many variations, provided more fashionable options for women. Leading the way for other designers, Yves Saint Laurent continued to offer menswear-inspired pantsuits for women at the couture level, settling once and for all the question of the appropriateness of trousers in refined social settings. Pants styles included wide-legged bell bottoms, knickers, and gauchos, and, by decade's end, narrow cigarette cut. Pajama sets were

Opposite Emerging Korean designer André Kim is shown here with two of his models in 1979; Kim's diaphanous dresses are typical of the overtly romantic trends embraced by Yves Saint Laurent, Oscar de la Renta, and many other designers.

Below A *Life* magazine cover photo from 1970 caught an important moment of transition in fashion. The shopper – in her psychedelic print Pucci mini dress – contemplates a midi-length peasant-style suede skirt, in an earth tone typical of the early 1970s.

common for cocktail and evening. By the end of the decade, pants were wider at the top and often pleated, gathered or wrapped and narrowed at the ankle.

In addition to the popularity of pantsuits, the skirt suit continued to maintain its place as a wardrobe staple. Often the styling of the jacket was quite masculine. In the later years, a wider shoulder line appeared in tailored jackets. Blouses were varied. In addition to fitted shirtwaist styles, many had cowl necklines or jabot tied bow fronts. Turtlenecks were also very popular.

Along with the overt peasant styles, by 1976 more volume appeared in fashion. Fuller skirts were sometimes gathered, often tiered, or made with soft, unpressed pleats. Tops gathered more volume as well. Oversized tops and blouson styles were worn belted or sashed. Fuller sleeves were seen. Some smock styles were belted at the waist in soft materials such as cotton eyelet and challis.

Knits were important in fashion and were frequently worn in layered combinations. Low belts and tight sleeves lent a slinky appeal to lean knits. As part of the move to more volume, thicker knits were featured after 1975, including thick ribbing, horizontal textures, cabling, and novelty stitches. For fall 1978, emerging Italian designer Gianni Versace even showed cable-knit trousers.

Contrasts in color and fabric also displayed the contradictions and variety of the era. Under the influence of an ecological consciousness, one part of fashion moved into a period of earth tones, denim, darker hues, and heathered effects. However, brightly colored synthetic materials also continued in favor. Surface detail was profuse; oversized buttons and zippers, topstitching (sometimes called "jeans stitching"), ribbing, and patch pockets were prevalent.

Trim, princess-line coats reflected the slender shape of fashion. Other options included man-tailored greatcoats, sometimes with wide lapels that showed early 19th-century influence. Car coats, knee-length coats and maxi coats were all worn. Belted trench coats took influence from vintage styles and were often worn with the belts tied rather than buckled. Shawls and ponchos were popular and showed ethnic influences. Patch pockets and piping were common details. The volume and variety of dress silhouettes after mid-decade spawned capes, burnooses, and other wraps. By the last years of the decade, more traditional coats reappeared such as polo coats, and double-breasted and single-breasted reefer styles. Leather and suede were particularly important both for casual styles and dressier looks. Some coats and jackets were trimmed in fur; fur bands at cuff and hemline evoked vintage and Russian inspirations. Fur was consistently fashionable, from short "chubbies" to long luxurious coats that were very full. Long-haired furs were especially popular and were dyed and tinted in a wide palette.

Lingerie and Loungewear

A trend for going bra-less was noted, but even for those who still wanted support and/or a layer under their clothes, foundations were increasingly abbreviated and lightweight and often available in wide color ranges. Many styles had minimal seams to reduce visibility under clinging knit tops. Women's underpants were available in brief, bikini, and high-cut styles. The "visible panty line" or "vpl" – a phrase referenced in the 1977 film *Annie Hall* – was a fashion faux pas. Tap pants were also worn, often with matching camisoles, with a vintage flavor. Bras, slips, and nightwear also often

German illustrator Hannelore Brüderlin depicted dress and vest ensembles in this 1976 fashion plate; the gored construction was a notable element of fashion.

had a 1920s or 1930s look in pastel shades with bias cut, lace trim, and lace inserts. Slinky charmeuse lingerie camisoles with spaghetti straps were even worn as evening tops. Lingerie and loungewear represented an important fashion category. Kayser-Roth's "King Tut" nightgowns (inspired by the Tutankhamun exhibition) and Emilio Pucci's continuing designs for Formfit Rogers were accessible and distinctive examples of fashionable lingerie.

Accessories

The individualism of fashion was often conveyed through accessories. Boots, shoulder bags, and wide belts with hardware and lacing were among the most popular accessories. Wearing a hat had become a fashion decision instead of a social requirement. Hats in every conceivable shape were seen: berets and tams, masculine fedoras and trilbies, soft felt hats with wide brims, cloches, tight knit caps, even brocade Mongolian styles with pointed crowns and wide bands of fur.

Shoes and boots were also very varied. Platform shoes and boots were often square- or round-toed but sleeker 1940s-influenced styles were also seen. Other popular styles included clogs, rope-soled wedgies, and espadrilles. Thin-soled boots sometimes showed Edwardian influence with lacing up the front. Several shoe brands emerged that exemplified ideas about ecology and ergonomics, including Earth shoes and Famolares. Frye boots, a traditional workwear style, were also widely worn. These eclectic and very casual styles gave way to more refined looks mid-decade including sleek flats and slingbacks with slender two-inch heels, and the pump re-emerged. Wider, more voluminous skirts and dresses called for a narrower, more feminine foot.

Above Knit dresses reflect a relaxed quality; both feature a full sleeve gathered to a cuff.

Right An ad for French hosiery not only exhibits chic stocking colors, but also depicts fashionable shoes, skirts, and hairstyles of the time, reflecting a 1930s-revival aesthetic.

Sautez à toutes jambes dans les nouvelles couleurs de la Rentrée.

Above left Qiana nylon blouses from 1977 exhibit two notable neck treatments of the mid- to late decade: the cowl neckline, and the jabot, or "tie neck," style.

Above right Three of the most emulated women of the decade, Farrah Fawcett, Kate Jackson, and Jaclyn Smith, the cast of *Charlie's Angels* in its 1976 premier season. Fawcett's feathered hairstyle was particularly influential.

Early in the decade, legwear was textured and colorful. Legwarmers were sometimes worn as an element in knitted ensembles or with hot pants, even over jeans. Socks were worn rolled down, or visible under rolled-up pants with short boots. Anklets, some trimmed with lace, were worn with skirts.

Bags ranged from large, soft shoulder bags to sculptured clutch bags, some with an art deco influence. Disco bags, small and often very decorative with metallic braid or tassels, carried evening necessities and were often worn on long straps slung across the body. Belts were sometimes worn loose around the waist, or below the waist at hip level, often used to form a blouson look. Sometimes worn in multiples, many had oversize grommets, studs, tooling, or fringe. Thin stretch metal belts defined the waist. Later in the decade, wide cummerbund styles and obi-like double wraps came into style.

Scarves were worn in all shapes and sizes: long knitted mufflers, often with deep fringe; small silk squares knotted around the throat or worn as headwraps; big printed squares worn as shawls, sarongs, and bra tops. Gloves were decorative or worn for warmth but, as with hats, were no longer required for proper dressing. Jewelry was sometimes piled on in gypsy style with stacked bangles, multiple necklaces, and swinging earrings. Other jewelry showed the art deco revival or Egyptian influence, and a vogue for velvet chokers revealed Belle Epoque inspirations. Designing for Tiffany, Elsa Peretti espoused a cleaner aesthetic. She designed a minimalist gold mesh bra in 1975 that she said "is worn as a jewel, it has a good feeling on the body and it is amusing."[2] Digital watches introduced a new look and technology to timepieces. Eyeglasses and sunglasses were often extremely large, in circular, square, and oval shapes. Aviator frames were enormously popular.

Hair and Beauty

Early in the decade, the emphasis of make-up was to achieve a "natural" look. Lips were tinted and glossy, and powder eyeshadow was seen in many colors ranging from frosty blues to reddish and coppery browns. Eyelashes were not styled to the artificial look of the 1960s – a more spiky look was favored. Eyebrows were either plucked to thin arches, reflecting the 1930s influence, or worn thick and natural in the style of actress Ali MacGraw. Past mid-decade, more contrast was favored in make-up, with darker, smoky eyes, cheekbones defined by heavy applications of blush, and deeper colors for the mouth. New trends in fragrance emphasized decadence and sexuality, such as Yves Saint Laurent's Opium and the many musk-based perfumes popular for men and women, such as Halston's signature fragrance introduced in 1975.

Hair was a major component of style and celebrity hairstyles were of particular importance. At the beginning of the decade, short gamine styles were banished as previously cropped models, such as Twiggy, appeared with flowing Pre-Raphaelite locks. Ali MacGraw's long, straight, center-parted hairstyle in the movie *Love Story* (1970) was widely imitated. In the early 1970s, civil rights activist Angela Davis became an accidental fashion icon as her Afro (or "natural") hairstyle became widely copied. The shag haircut, as seen on Jane Fonda and Judy Carne, was popular in the early years of the decade. Figure skater Dorothy Hamill popularized the "wedge" among young women all over the world when she won an Olympic gold medal in 1976. Farrah Fawcett sported her signature blow-dried feathered mane on the television show *Charlie's Angels*. Shorter versions of feathered looks were also well established by mid-decade. Cornrows were already a fashion staple for black women, but when the white actress Bo Derek wore them adorned with beads in the 1979 film *10*, she created a fad for the style among women and girls of all ethnicities. Gibson Girl-inspired top knots were also popular, often accessorized with combs or chopsticks. By the end of the decade, several styles were in fashion. Hair was often sleekly pulled back in a variety of chignons; permed curls became widespread, often side-parted, hiding half the face.

Denim in Fashion

Denim increasingly carried multiple messages and existed at all market levels. Jeans were worn by young people everywhere; they embraced the democratic message of the style. *Vogue* declared, "Levi's, a pullover, marvelous belts, it's the uniform of the world, the way we all want to look when we're feeling easy, moving fast – a way of life."[3] Because they were worn by both men and women, jeans also represented sexual equality and cut across social classes. And as the fit evolved from workwear to fashionable cuts, this implication extended to sexual liberation. Hip-hugging styles emphasized crotch, thigh, and rear end, and jeans became an overtly sexy garment. Bell bottoms, sometimes so wide at the hem they were referred to as "elephant" pants, were worn long and trailed under heels. Some styles were extremely low-rise.

The denim aesthetic evolved during the decade, moving way beyond blue denim trousers. Head-to-toe denim was one option: jeans were often paired with a waist-length denim jacket or worn with a matching denim shirt. Bib overalls were popular for men and women, often decorated and embellished. Denim was used for every conceivable wardrobe item, including boots in cowboy or laced knee-high styles that hugged the calf. For those who required a more "dressed" look but still wanted to participate in the trend, Yves Saint Laurent created a denim suit for his Rive Gauche men's boutique in 1970, and Bill Blass and Oscar de la Renta also offered tailored denim menswear. Jeans embellishment was seen as an art form, celebrated in numerous books and gallery exhibitions. Tie-dyeing, bleaching, embroidery, patches, beading, and studding were initially popular effects but individually embellished denims gave way to expensive, status-symbol designer jeans. Partnering with manufacturer Murjani, socialite and artist Gloria Vanderbilt was a pioneer in this market. Calvin Klein added denim to his repertoire by 1976 but his real jeans success came two years later when 200,000 pairs of "Calvins" were sold within a week of arriving in stores. Even Studio 54 licensed a line, with its logo embroidered on a back pocket. By the end of the decade the fit had become so tight that some wearers went without underwear, throwing genitals and buttocks into focus. Other prominent brands included Jordache, Sasson, and Sisley – who all used edgy advertising campaigns and provocatively posed models to add excitement to the designer denim phenomenon.

Swimwear by Halston was particularly chic, such as this asymmetrical style from 1977.

Active Sportswear

A focus on fitness and exercise helped expand the market for active sportswear. Jogging suits and warm-up suits, often in cotton knit or velour, were popular with both men and women. Many people wore short shorts with elastic waists and contrast edging for sports, a style known as "gym shorts." Athletic shoes started to emerge as fashion items, gaining momentum as celebrity athletes endorsed specific styles. Basketball player Walt Frazier endorsed the Clyde style by Puma, and tennis champion Stan Smith endorsed an Adidas model. Tennis wear was still predominantly white and, with its tight fit, reflected the lines of fashion. A number of prominent tennis stars provided fashion influence, especially Chris Evert, known for her polished fingernails and diamond bracelets. Blond and handsome, Björn Borg wore long hair with a headband and played in close-fitting knit shirts and very short shorts.

Styles from hiking and outdoor sports entered the general wardrobe. Flannel shirts and canvas field coats were very frequently worn. Nylon down-filled jackets and vests were popular and several companies sold kits for home sewers to make these garments. The Army Navy surplus store became trendy and shoppers found practical pieces such as parkas, paratroopers' pants, and jumpsuits. Skiwear still followed the general lines established in earlier decades, with improvements seen in synthetic fabric technology.

Rudi Gernreich proposed thong swimsuit styles for men and women, and the string bikini made its debut, but most swimwear provided a bit more

Above Unisex looks from many designers and manufacturers were popular; the "unisex" image was usually created by adding masculine elements to women's clothing, with little change to menswear, as in these leisure suits from Marimekko from 1972.

Opposite Vivienne Westwood, c. 1977, wearing a plaid bondage suit of her own design, accompanied by two London punk devotees.

Below Jane Fonda in the 1971 film *Klute* with costume design by Ann Roth. Fonda's role as a call girl inspired the identification "hooker boot" for her over-the-knee footwear style, and her shag haircut was widely copied.

coverage. Halston created striking one-piece swimsuits, often with an asymmetrical cut. Dancewear giant Danskin began offering swimwear in 1976 in a nylon–spandex blend that was especially clingy. Men's swimsuits were available in many styles, some quite abbreviated. Bikinis and short trunks, some with laced-up fronts or sides, were available. Photos of Olympic gold medalist Mark Spitz wearing a stars-and-stripes Speedo swimsuit helped popularize the style. Tanning was still fashionable, but skincare was also a concern and the sun protection factor (SPF) index was introduced.

The Unisex Style

Emerging in the 1960s, the unisex style truly came to fruition during the early 1970s; what was considered "unisex" was usually based on masculine dress. Yves Saint Laurent, whose pantsuits were instrumental to setting the trend in motion in the 1960s, continued to promote menswear styling for women. Rudi Gernreich boldly predicted in a magazine interview in 1970 that clothing would cease to be a function of gender; his unisex collection of that year included skirts, bikinis, and catsuits, even pasties, for both men and women. His kaftans, emblazoned with bold prints, looked not only futuristic but also, ironically, recalled T-shaped gowns of Jaeger and the loungewear offered by the Wiener Werkstätte. Finnish clothing and textile designer Armi Ratia at Marimekko featured "his and hers" leisure suits in vivid colors. Celebrity couples appeared in his and hers suits, and kilts available for both men and women took on a new mystique in this context. Socialite Bianca Jagger was associated with cross-gender styles. A French runway show at the Porte de Versailles in 1970 took the trend to an extreme, going so far as to send a man and a woman down the runway simultaneously in the same midi dress and matching heeled boots.

Punk Fashion

Male and female punk fans created a distinctive style. Both sexes combined elements of 1950s greaser styles – jeans, tank tops, work boots, leather jackets – made more aggressive through slashing, rips, and studs. Some clothing, especially t-shirts, displayed provocative, even obscene, images and slogans that expressed the hostile aspect of the punk movement, often rendered in a graffiti-like style. Sexual provocation was important to the look. Sadomasochistic references were common and garments included styles such as bondage pants and leather and vinyl apparel. The punk aesthetic also included extreme hairstyles, often spiky and disheveled, and multiple piercings and tattoos. New York-based band Blondie, with attractive lead singer Deborah Harry, offered a slicker, pop-infused version of punk style in music and fashion. The British designer Vivienne Westwood worked with early punk bands as the movement developed. While authentic punk was a street style, the look was rapidly adopted by fashion at all levels from the high style interpretations of Zandra Rhodes to mass-marketed t-shirts featuring bands including the Sex Pistols.

Film and Fashion

A wide range of films affected fashion. Ann Roth costumed Jane Fonda as a prostitute in *Klute* (1971), encouraging high "hooker" boots into the mainstream. The "Blaxploitation" films of the 1970s had strong impact, including Tamara Dobson's stunning Giorgio di Sant'Angelo wardrobe in *Cleopatra Jones* (1973). The genre also encouraged African American male fashion icons. *The Rocky Horror Picture Show* (1975) reflected punk and glam rock trends, and made its star Tim Curry an icon of gender-bending with fishnet stockings, corset, and provocative pearl necklace. Disco was glorified in *Saturday Night Fever* (1977); designer Patrizia von Brandenstein provided a white three-piece suit with open-necked black shirt for John Travolta that became one of the most emblematic fashion images of the era. The red dress worn by actress Karen Lynn Gorney featured a convertible neckline popular in fashion at the time. For *Alien* in 1979, John Mollo costumed Sigourney Weaver in a utilitarian jumpsuit that mirrored the garment's crossover into fashion.

Right Tamara Dobson as Cleopatra Jones, with a vibrant film wardrobe by Giorgio di Sant'Angelo, helped sustain the continued popularity of the Afro hairstyle.

Far right For Saturday Night Fever (1977), John Travolta wore one of the most iconic film costumes of the decade.

Many period films encouraged retro fashion. Among the first was *The Boyfriend* (1971), a faux 1920s-style musical starring Twiggy, designed by Shirley Russell, which included "flapper"-style dresses and wild production numbers. *Cabaret* (1972), designed by Charlotte Flemming, provided decadent fashions of Weimar Republic Germany, and underscored the similarity between that time and the self-indulgent 1970s; images of a bowler-clad Liza Minnelli inspired fashion photographs and editorials. Smart 1930s fashions were featured by designer Polly Platt in *Paper Moon* (1974), and Anthea Sylbert in *Chinatown* (1974), and Edith Head in *The Sting* (1973) continued that decade's influence on fashion design. In *Lady Sings the Blues* (1972) Bob Mackie and Ray Aghayan provided 1930s and 1940s period costumes for Diana Ross. A 1950s revival in youth fashion was encouraged by several films including *American Graffiti* (1973) by Aggie Guerard Rodgers, and *Grease* (1978) by Albert Wolsky, which provided inspiration for teenagers to dress for 1950s days in high schools and at college

Mia Farrow and Robert Redford, in Theoni V. Aldredge's picturesque versions of 1920s styles for *The Great Gatsby* (1974), encouraged continued retro sensibilities in fashion.

campuses. The revival was reinforced by the television series *Happy Days* (1974–1984) with its comedic 1950s setting. For *Animal House* (1978), set in 1962, Deborah Nadoolman Landis dressed a toga party, and spawned copycat toga parties among young people worldwide.

Theoni V. Aldredge (1922–2011) was the most celebrated costume designer of the decade. *The Great Gatsby* (1974) provided men in white flannel suits, and women in beaded sheath dresses, and cinematic images that reveled in the clothes for their own sake; the film won Aldredge the Academy Award for costume design. For *Network* (1976), Aldredge costumed Faye Dunaway in sexy silk blouses that anticipated trends of the 1980s. *Eyes of Laura Mars* (1978) was

THE "ANNIE HALL LOOK"

Woody Allen's *Annie Hall* was released in April 1977. The film provided the career-defining role for actress Diane Keaton, who took home a "Best Actress" Academy Award for her performance, one of the most engaging female screen characterizations of the decade. The film itself achieved classic status, winning three other Oscars, including Best Picture, and Keaton was awarded several other best actress citations including the Golden Globe and the British Academy Award.

Keaton had performed on Broadway in *Hair*, and was known for her supporting role in the 1972 film *The Godfather*, but her appearance in the title role of *Annie Hall* made her a household name. Keaton wore distinctive clothing in the film, primarily outfits put together from menswear pieces. In floppy men's pants, jackets, and ties, Keaton conjured an image of the tomboy-next-door. Keaton wore many of her own clothes, and the "Annie Hall Look" was primarily derived from her offbeat fashion sense (just as the character was inspired by Keaton herself). Keaton followed the loose casual style of the bohemian denizens of New York's Soho neighborhood; the oversized man's fedora she wore in the film was borrowed from an actress friend. For her personal look Keaton cobbled together vintage and thrift store pieces, often menswear, including vests, dress shirts, baggy khakis, boots, and neckties, sometimes worn with long skirts. Keaton's shy, enigmatic, self-effacing, and often reclusive personality contributed to the mystique of the look.

In the film, both Keaton and Allen wore pieces from their own closets by American designer Ralph Lauren, and Lauren was given a screen credit acknowledging his clothes. This prompted the fashion press of the time to erroneously credit Lauren as the "creator" of the look, neglecting Ruth Morley, the film's costume designer, and Keaton's contributions. Whatever its genesis, the Annie Hall Look had a huge impact on fashion as young women aped the style, even parroting Annie's catchphrase "la-di-da," and high school girls wore their fathers' neckties to class. Magazines, store windows and catalog styling marketed the trend as it was embraced as a commodity by the fashion industry. The Annie Hall Look continues to inspire international runway collections and fashion editorials, referred to as "El Estilo Annie Hall" and "Le Look Annie Hall" among many other designations. New generations of female celebrities sporting quirky menswear-inflected outfits are compared to her, while Keaton herself has become a perennial style setter, maintaining much of the spirit of the original Annie Hall Look.

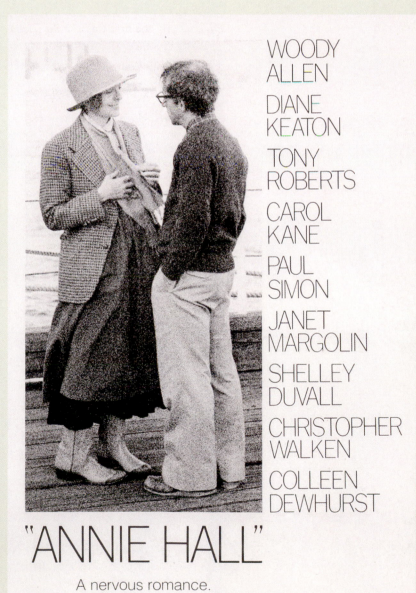

WOODY ALLEN

DIANE KEATON

TONY ROBERTS

CAROL KANE

PAUL SIMON

JANET MARGOLIN

SHELLEY DUVALL

CHRISTOPHER WALKEN

COLLEEN DEWHURST

"ANNIE HALL"

A nervous romance.

The "Annie Hall Look" as worn by Diane Keaton on the film's poster.

a quintessential film about fashion. The murder mystery thriller featured Dunaway as a fashion photographer whose violence-charged photographs included lavish high fashion clothes. Aldredge was also prominently featured on Broadway, and her costumes for *A Chorus Line* (1975) encouraged the trend for dance rehearsal clothes as street style and disco wear.

Designers: France

An era came to an end with the death of Coco Chanel in 1971. While Parisian couture continued to provide exclusive day ensembles and special occasion dresses to a rarefied clientele, much of the excitement in fashion came from new talents who emphasized a livelier, more diverse aesthetic. Increasingly, the focus was on ready-to-wear and boutique brands.

A much publicized fashion show at Versailles in November 1973 brought together five French houses (Saint Laurent, Dior, Givenchy, Ungaro, and Cardin) and five American designers (Bill Blass, Stephen Burrows, Halston, Anne Klein, and Oscar de la Renta) in a fund-raising effort for the restoration of the palace. The venerable but exclusive Parisian haute couture contrasted with lively American ready-to-wear and (perhaps unintentionally) helped build global interest in American design. Reflecting the new order, the models in the show presented a diversity previously unseen in high fashion.

Ungaro, **Givenchy**, and **Marc Bohan** for **Dior** all maintained high standards and their collections received attention. **André Courrèges** offered updates of his futuristic looks, with a softer focus, and began to design menswear. **Pierre Cardin** successfully navigated fashion's transition toward eclecticism and variety. He enthusiastically embraced knitwear and varied lengths, creating ensembles that attractively combined

Below *Vogue* described Yves Saint Laurent's fall/winter 1976–1977 collection as "*the* most appetite-whetting collection – not that a whole lot of women can afford to dress this way. But a whole lot of women are going to start *thinking* this way."

Opposite Yves Saint Laurent's glamorous folkloric look was quickly adapted for the vernacular market, pictured here in a 1977 catalog.

short and long. While his aesthetic was still quite experimental, Cardin's emphasis on fluidity and inventive proportions kept his designs relevant. His brand exposure continued to increase through licensing and his signature men's fragrance, with its phallic packaging, proved a best seller.

"Saint Laurent Leads the Way" proclaimed *Vogue* in March 1973, and indeed **Yves Saint Laurent** was perhaps the single most important designer of the decade, influencing other major designers and the mass market alike. The 1971 collection inspired by the early 1940s included brightly colored fur "chubbies," derived from the style of Parisian streetwalkers. The collection met with criticism, both for the references to prostitution, but also for the reference to the World War II years, a time that was still clearly a bad memory for many Parisians. Nonetheless the chubby emerged as a fashion staple. Several eclectic fashion elements converged in Saint Laurent's winter 1970–1971 collection that included midi-length suede coats with folk art-inspired appliqués, Edwardian lace-up boots, and masculine hats. Saint Laurent's 1974 smock coat and "naïve chemise" followed bohemian trends and were also widely copied.

Saint Laurent's highly influential 1976 fall/winter collection mixed a variety of ethnic inspirations, including Russian, Mongolian, North African, Gypsy, and Persian, with full skirts and sleeves, corset belts, turbans, and voluminous cloaks in luxurious fabrics, profusely trimmed:

> After years of beguiling women into austerely tailored pantsuits, now, in the cool age of less is more and casual is all, the world's most influential couturier has stopped the parade with a collection of high-camp peasant fashions that are impractical, fantastical, and egotistical. They are also subtle, sumptuous, sensual and jubilantly feminine. The overwhelming first response … let the costume ball begin.[4]

While ethnic inspirations had been in the fashion vocabulary steadily for several years, Saint Laurent presented the ethnic mode at its glamorous zenith, and by keeping the look alive, provided a foil for the more streamlined and simplified aesthetic that had developed in the decade. The impact of this collection was reinforced the following year with one of equal glamour inspired by Imperial China, with vibrant colors and luxurious silk, lamé, brocade, and fur, along with tasseled accessories and conical hats. The chinoiserie continued in the 1977 release of the provocatively named fragrance Opium, which was launched in an outrageous Asiatic theme party at Studio 54. Although only a few couture clients wore the actual runway looks, the companion Rive Gauche collections were popular, and Saint Laurent's impact on mainstream taste was enormous. Living up to Saint Laurent's philosophy that "women become beautiful when the artifice begins," trends in make-up became more exotic with smoky metallic eyeshadow, and tassels decorated disco bags on dance floors. Mass-market retail and catalogs featured corselet-style bodices, bolero-shaped vests over peasant blouses, satin and brocade mandarin jackets, even frog closures on housecoats. Saint Laurent finished the 1970s showing a variety of inspirations, including Victorian and Edwardian looks, even Pierrot and Pierrette clowns (a popular decorative motif of the decade). His last collection of the decade was inspired by Picasso, with silhouettes that shaped the 1980s.

Karl Lagerfeld (b. 1935) broke into fashion as a winner of a design competition sponsored by the International Wool Secretariat in 1954. Born in Hamburg, he was fascinated by fashion from an early age and went to live in Paris while still in his teens. He was hired by the house of Balmain and then worked at Patou. By the early sixties, he left couture and became a freelance designer for several ready-to-wear labels. Lagerfeld was named head designer for the French line **Chloé** in 1966, providing an update to their *haute bohème* style. Founded in 1952 by Gaby Aghion, the Chloé label emphasized free-spirited clothes. Stylish women ranging from Brigitte Bardot to Maria Callas wore the longer skirts, wide-legged pants and sophisticated peasant

Dapper Karl Lagerfeld is shown here in 1973 with a model wearing a dress from his collection for Chloé, maintaining the label's typical bohemian aesthetic.

looks, making Chloé one of the chicest brands of the 1970s. Lagerfeld also designed for other clients, including Fendi, and became known as a multi-talented designer who repeatedly found inspiration in the history of art.

Knitwear featured prominently in the development of important new French brands. Parisian-born **Sonia Rykiel** (b. 1930) built her reputation with luxurious but unconventional knitwear, earning her the title "Queen of Knits." During the 1960s, she designed for the Laura boutique and established her own label in 1968. She promoted adaptable layering pieces. Signature details included poorboy ribbing and seams on the outside of garments. Many ensembles were monochrome, in a sophisticated color palette of black, grays, and unconventional colors. A former couture model, **Emmanuelle Khanh** (born Renée Mezière, 1937) was a freelance designer during the 1960s who counted Missoni and Cacharel among her clients. She launched her own label in 1971 and opened a Paris boutique in 1977. Khanh offered a full range of clothing from slim knitwear to embellished peasant-style ensembles. Another important Paris-based brand, **Dorothée Bis**, was an offshoot of Dorothée, a trendy boutique established by Elie and Jacqueline Jacobson. Known for knit pieces during the 1960s, the label continued to produce distinctive knitwear often featuring layered ensembles that combined lengths and textures. The chain of Dorothée Bis boutiques focused on contemporary, often playful, interpretations of sportswear. **Cacharel**, founded by Jean Bousquet in the 1960s, established itself as a major label with soft blouses and dresses made of Liberty prints and feminine knits in the early 1970s. The romantic style of Cacharel was enhanced by its advertising, especially Sarah Moon's photographs for the introduction of the fragrance Anaïs Anaïs in 1978.

Two Japanese-born and trained designers were integral to Parisian fashion. One of the first male students at Tokyo's prestigious Bunka Fashion College, **Kenzo Takada** (b. 1939) prefigured Japan's influence on global fashion when he arrived in Paris in 1964. Designing as **Kenzo**, he opened his boutique Jungle Jap in 1970 featuring colorful, playful clothes. Some silhouettes were based on kimono and other Japanese styles, but Kenzo mixed patterns, colors, and textures freely, and experimented with knits. In creative mixes such as lean olive suede pants worn with a bright pink wool tunic, he achieved a style that fused elements of Japanese tradition and European high fashion.

Below left Sonia Rykiel's inventive use of knits can be seen in the sweater and cap of this ensemble featured in *Vogue*, March 1973, worn with three-quarter-length pants with oversize pockets.

Below right The playful enthusiasm of this cowl-necked polka dot dress with its pannier-draped skirt from 1977 is typical of the energetic output of Kenzo Takada. Newsboy cap, wide belt, and crushed boots complete the look.

Issey Miyake (b. 1938) studied graphic arts in Tokyo at Tama Arts University and later in Paris at the Ecole de la Chambre Syndicale de la Couture Parisienne. He worked for Guy Laroche and later at Givenchy. Miyake went to New York in 1969 and worked as an assistant to Geoffrey Beene, but returned to Tokyo one year later where he opened his design studio. Miyake showed collections in New York and Tokyo in 1971 and in Paris in 1973, which brought him international renown. From the early days of his career, Miyake established a unique style based on his exploration of materials. His work often involved wrapping and tying and interpretations of traditional dress from around the world, such as a wrapped "cheongsam" dress and burnoose-style outerwear. Late in the decade, he pioneered the look of oversized tops over very narrow pants and leggings, with some pants bound at the ankle. Independent and original, Miyake asserted he designed clothes "to do whatever the wearer wants."[5]

Designers: Britain

The vibrant fashion scene of London benefited from the creativity of several outstanding designers. **Mary Quant**'s achievements in fashion were celebrated in a 1973–1974 exhibition at the London Museum entitled *Mary Quant's London*. At its height, the scope of her business included fashion, fragrance and cosmetics for men and women, toys, and even wine. **Ossie Clark**'s career continued until the middle of the decade and he retained his focus on innovative cut and often daring combinations of materials. In addition to ongoing work for Quorum he also designed for a French firm and for private clients including Mick and Bianca Jagger, and branched out into menswear. **John Bates** was one of the best-established designers in London. He managed to maintain a reputation for originality despite his commercial success. Another noted design talent, **Bill Gibb** (1943–1988), was credited with dresses that made his customers feel "enhanced and radiant"[6] and espoused a very eclectic aesthetic.

The success of **Biba**, established in the 1960s by Barbara Hulanicki, grew notably during the early 1970s. Biba's advertising continued to play with the iconography of classic femmes fatales, and the clothing also continued its retro themes, with dramatic picture hats and gored skirts offered in a variety of lengths. The 1972 collection included an all-white wardrobe that conjured images of the 1930s "silver

Below left An early 1970s photograph by Herb Schmitz depicts model Ika Hindley in a typical dress from Ossie Clark, utilizing one of Celia Birtwell's tulip-inspired prints. The style of the dress, the model's hair, the long pearls, and platform shoes all make retro references to the 1920s, 1930s, and 1940s.

Below right A Biba fashion shoot, c. 1970, illustrates many of the label's aesthetics: vintage inspiration, along with rich, dark "auntie" colors.

Twiggy, a prominent model of the 1960s and early 1970s, is pictured here in 1971 at Big Biba. The luxurious and striking art deco interior was widely copied in retail spaces during the decade, as the retro sensibility in fashion was mirrored by a retro sensibility in merchandising.

screen." Whimsical pajama sets were available, such as the "cats pajamas," a set printed with cats that played on 1920s slang. The 1969 move to more stylish quarters on Kensington High Street was followed by another move, in 1974, to a seven-story former department store on the same street, built in the early 1930s in the art deco style. The Biba brand utilized the 400,000 square foot (37,000 square meter) space to expand to a department store concept: "Big Biba." Women's clothing, accessories, and cosmetics were offered along with menswear and childrenswear, housewares, books, and a restaurant. A roof deck was populated with live pink flamingos, and a theater presented glamorous superstar musical groups. The evocative "Casbah" floor featured Middle Eastern wares. Much of the store was decorated in a 1930s style, with vintage mannequins and mirrored surfaces, curved sectional sofas, potted palms, art deco figurines, and atmospheric lighting. The impact of Big Biba could clearly be detected in other parts of the world, such as the theatrical retail "happenings" at New York's Bloomingdale's, or the art deco interior design of the Galleria, an urban mall in Portland, Oregon (itself created from a vintage department store). The success of Big Biba was short lived as Hulanicki and Fitz-Simon's business partners sold their interest, and the couple was edged out, as the new partners degraded the store's look and vision, leading to its demise.

Half-French and half-English, **Thea Porter** (1927–2000) was born in Jerusalem and grew up in Damascus. Her childhood in Syria, time spent in Lebanon as a young adult, and further travels in the area developed her deep appreciation for art and design of the Levant and the Middle East. Porter began her design career as a decorator,

opening her shop in London's Soho in 1966, selling exotic Eastern fabrics. She imported kaftans to cut up for throw pillows, but kaftans soon became fashionable in the wave of the ethnic clothing trends of the late 1960s. As her business grew, a Paris boutique was added. Her exotic expensive creations suited the decadent jet set of the 1970s and her varied clients included Elizabeth Taylor, Princess Margaret, Mick and Bianca Jagger, Begum Aga Khan, Jane Holzer, and Elsa Peretti. Her clothes were available in the United States at I. Magnin, Neiman Marcus, and Giorgio of Beverly Hills. She opened her own boutique in 1971 in New York's Upper East Side, featuring kaftan-shaped gowns in rich colors and luscious fabrics, printed or brocaded in traditional motifs. Her interpretation of Eastern style included Asiatic jewelry and head ornaments, with cultural twists such as rendering an Islamic *abaya* in black chiffon.

Laura Ashley (née Mountney, 1925–1985) was born in Wales and served in the Women's Royal Naval Service during World War II. She began her business during the 1950s with her husband Bernard, working out of their home. Inspired by handcrafts that she had seen at the Victoria and Albert Museum, they hand-printed collections of headscarves and household linens. The print designs included geometrics, conversationals, and the florals that became the company's signature style. The Laura Ashley brand expanded into clothing with smocks and full dresses that recalled Regency and Edwardian England, and bohemian "milkmaid" styles, usually in cotton. During the 1970s the expansion of the company was rapid and global, with stores in Canada, Australia, Japan, and France. A San Francisco store opened in 1974, followed by a New York store in 1977. The same year, the company received the Queen's Award for Export, and by the end of the decade the brand expanded into fragrance. Ashley's styles influenced a wide range of designers, from Yves Saint Laurent to Jessica McClintock.

Jean Muir (1928–1995) was born in London of Scottish heritage and showed an aptitude for needlework and art at a young age. Her earliest jobs in fashion were for some of Britain's most historic fashion companies, sketching for Liberty of London, and developing a junior label for Jaeger. From 1962 to 1966 she designed the Jane & Jane label, where her jersey dresses were so successful that one was honored with the

Above A fanciful ensemble by Thea Porter from 1971 mixes eclectic elements, including Central Asian ikat fabric.

Right A frilly cotton dress and straw hat from Laura Ashley, 1974, are exemplary of Ashley's 18th- and 19th-century inflected "milkmaid" styles.

Far right A 1979 Jean Muir two-piece dress, with matching hat by British milliner Graham Smith and black pumps from Manolo Blahnik.

Dress of the Year award from the Fashion Museum at Bath. She created her own label, Jean Muir Ltd., with her husband Harry Leuckert as partner, in 1966. The focus of Jean Muir Ltd. was simple svelte silhouettes created with high-quality materials and construction, and subtle dressmaker details, frequently described as timeless, classic, and elegant. Muir did not slavishly follow trends, but rather her own restrained aesthetic. Her fluid designs suited the sleek mode of the 1970s; she showed in Paris, and Muir designs were available in paper patterns from Vogue and Butterick. Well known for dresses in black and neutrals, she also possessed a keen sense of color. Muir's house model was the actress Joanna Lumley, and her celebrity clientele included notable actresses Diana Rigg and Charlotte Rampling. The Bath Fashion Museum honored her again in 1968 and 1979, and Muir received the Neiman Marcus Fashion Award in 1973.

Turning street fashion into boutique business, **Vivienne Westwood** (b. 1941) embodied the increasingly important links between music and fashion. With her partner Malcolm McLaren, who served as manager for the Sex Pistols, Westwood operated a shop that evolved through the decade according to changing trends. It opened in 1971 under the name Let It Rock and focused on 1950s records and retro-inspired fashion. In 1972 McLaren and Westwood renamed the boutique Too Fast to Live, Too Young to Die. By 1974 the shop was rechristened SEX and sold leather and rubber S&M clothing and pieces with "punk" details such as intentional rips, violent imagery, and provocative slogans. When the shop was renamed Seditionaries in 1976, it was well known for punk style. By the end of the decade, the boutique was known as World's End and offered clothes and accessories related to the emerging New Romantic music trend which would flourish in the 1980s. **Zandra Rhodes** (b. 1940) studied printed textile design at Medway College and the Royal College of Art. From the presentation of her first collection in 1968, Rhodes emphasized textile design as the basis of her fashion. In the 1970s her ethereal, flowing dresses displayed motifs based on travel, poetry, and history, drawing upon multi-ethnic influences for her fabric design, including folk art patterns and Aboriginal Australian art. She was named Designer of the Year in 1972 and in 1975 she opened a shop in London.

Above A midi-length chiffon dress from Zandra Rhodes reflects her use of ethnographic patterns, and her love of saturated colors.

Right The rock music scene is celebrated in a t-shirt by Vivienne Westwood and Malcolm McLaren from the late decade.

A 1975 Missoni knit ensemble with stripes and bargello patterns typical of their distinctive style. The pillows are covered with Missoni fabric as well.

Rhodes also designed costumes for the British rock group Queen. Zandra Rhodes unveiled her "Conceptual Chic" collection in 1977, a subverted high style take on punk with brightly colored jersey, slashing, and jeweled safety pins.

Designers: Italy

A number of Italian design houses were particularly renowned for high fashion, knitwear, leather apparel and accessories, and other luxury goods. **Valentino**'s career continued to grow with his romantic designs that were prized by his elite clientele but did not necessarily reflect widespread trends. He was an early fan of the midi length, saying it was more elegant than the mini. The Valentino empire developed further with the introduction of ready-to-wear, a home line, fragrance, and a more international presence including a Tokyo boutique. Throughout this expansion, Valentino maintained high levels of craftsmanship and an emphasis on luxury.

Tai and Rosita Missoni established their label in 1958 in Milan. They opened an in-store boutique at Bloomingdale's in 1968, leading to their success in the American market, and were honored with a Neiman Marcus Award in 1973. **Missoni** offered completely knitted outfits that layered pieces such as vests or pullovers over turtlenecks, and knit skirts or trousers in distinctive, instantly recognizable patterns that mixed zigzags, flame stitches, and stripes in a range of colors. Fluid, textural and adaptable, Missoni knitwear expressed major themes in fashion of the time. **Krizia**, founded by Mariuccia Mandelli in the 1950s, grew into a firm producing a full range of high-end fashion and noted for distinctive knitwear ranging from textural sweater coats to clinging metallic knit maillots. Born into a family dressmaking business, Roman native **Laura Biagiotti** (b. 1943) presented her first women's collection in Florence in 1972. Biagiotti became known for the innovative use of cashmere, and her ensembles often layered cashmere pieces including dresses, jumpsuits, and accessories.

The **Fendi** company, operated by several daughters of the founders, pioneered innovations in fur. With house designer Karl Lagerfeld, the Fendi sisters treated fur like fabric, reinterpreting the material to produce lighter, more supple fur pieces. They also developed "ready-to-wear" techniques for fur that greatly expanded the market for their work and, in 1977, branched out into ready-to-wear apparel. **Roberto Cavalli** (b. 1940) showed ensembles, often jacket and pants, in patterned and patchwork suede and leather, treated to create unique surface textures and colors. The careers of **Gianni Versace** (1946–1997) and **Giorgio Armani** (b. 1934) began. Versace received acclaim for his designs for Complice and Callaghan and established his own label in 1978. Armani's fluid but impeccable sportswear was featured at the selective store Barney's New York, paving the way for his success in the following years.

Designers: United States

The 1970s saw significant output from a number of great American designers; it was the most important period for American design since the 1940s. The Versailles fashion show markedly raised the international profile of the five American designers who showed there. **Bill Blass**, known for dressing some of America's most visible women, accommodated modern ideas of career and leisure but always maintained a high society focus and a classic aesthetic. In 1970 Blass bought Rentner (the firm for which he had been working for over a decade) and changed its name to Bill Blass Ltd. That same year, he won a Coty Award for womenswear and was admitted to the Coty Hall of Fame. Countering trends toward casualness, Blass promoted the revival of the cocktail dress mid-decade. **Anne Klein**'s showing in Versailles proved to be the last major event of her career as she died suddenly in 1974. Klein's assistants, Louis Dell'Olio and Donna Karan, took over as designers and maintained the aesthetic and reputation of the firm, creating polished, urban coordinates and winning a Coty Award in 1977. **Oscar de la Renta** continued his reign as "The King of Evening," dressing an international group of prominent women. His first fragrance, Oscar, launched in 1977 to enormous success. While de la Renta found inspiration from travel and history – such as his use of China and the Belle Epoque – he was known for consistently offering beautiful, flattering clothes to a loyal clientele.

A graduate of New York's Fashion Institute of Technology, **Stephen Burrows** (b. 1943) had a boutique in Greenwich Village in the late 1960s. His first ready-to-wear collection for Bonwit Teller was very successful, and was followed by a long-term exclusive merchandising agreement with Henri Bendel. With unstructured body-conscious silhouettes, witty details, and eye-catching color combinations, Burrows dressed independent-minded women. He often used a "lettuce edge" finish, which became a signature detail. Burrows used traditional fabrics in playful new ways – such as producing lamé trousers perfect for disco evenings. Sexy, leggy looks such as skirts with high slits, or asymmetrical or handkerchief hems, were favorites with his clientele, which included model Jerry Hall, and entertainers Cher, Diana Ross, and Barbra Streisand. Burrows won three Coty Awards during the decade.

Halston (born Roy Halston Frowick, 1932–1990) began his career as a milliner. After working for Lilly Daché in the late 1950s he designed hats for the millinery salon of Bergdorf Goodman, including Jacqueline Kennedy's pillbox worn for the 1961 presidential inauguration. Halston carried his architectural approach to hats into apparel design, opening Halston Ltd. in 1968. His clothes were promoted by Bloomingdale's in New York and by 1972 Halston Ltd. occupied several floors of a building on Madison Avenue that contained a retail boutique and made-to-order salon. The Halston style was very sophisticated and urban and his life and work were intertwined with the disco scene. Frequent collaborators were jewelry designer Elsa Peretti and illustrator Joe Eula, while his friends, an international group of "jet set" celebrities, included Andy Warhol, Bianca Jagger, and entertainers Elizabeth Taylor

The lion motif became a signature for Anne Klein's line. This scarf, a popular accessory late in the decade, typifies the trend for prominent logos on designer fashion.

and Liza Minnelli (he designed costumes for the 1977 Broadway production of *The Act* starring Minnelli). Halston worked in a limited palette, favoring solid colors; his best designs were minimal in styling and luxurious in fabrication. While his aesthetic was precise, Halston's range was extensive. In addition to luxuriously draped jersey pieces, he created clean-lined day separates, tie-dyed cashmere turtlenecks, and flowing silk kaftans and pajamas for evening. Halston designed Ultrasuede shirtwaist dresses in 1972, and the style became a classic. His prowess at cut approached that of Vionnet and Grès, and although his own work was rooted in the American sportswear tradition, Halston was an admirer of Charles James' designs. His contributions to the American fashion industry were recognized with four Coty Awards during the decade.

New York native **Calvin Klein** (b. 1942) was trained at the Fashion Institute of Technology. After graduating, he found work as a coat designer at two different labels. Going into business on his own in 1967 with financial help from friend Barry Schwarz (who later became his official business partner), Klein created a collection of three dresses and six coats that was ordered by Bonwit Teller. The group sold well and was followed by his first complete collection of ready-to-wear in 1968. He promptly made a notable showing in the press and *Vogue* featured one of his wool coats on the cover of the September 1969 issue. Klein found ready support from New York retailers and the fashion press for sportswear and separates that were elegant and simple, polished but easy-fitting. Klein offered a softer, less structured version of tailoring and became known for styles that *Vogue* described as "American Casual at the top of its form!"[7] In Klein's own words:

> The American woman has had enough gimmicky overdesigned clothes. Now she is
> interested in beautiful fabrics, subtle colors and simpler things. It's not easy to design or
> to make simple clothes, but that's what one has to do today. Besides, it's what I like to do.[8]

© Mellon Tyrell 2014

Klein received three consecutive Coty Awards beginning in 1973. While his well-made sportswear drew praise from an upscale clientele, Klein became a household name through the wide distribution of his signature line of women's jeans, prized for their fit. A successful menswear line launched at the end of the decade was instantly popular, and featured the newer sleek and narrow proportions of the late 1970s with a focus on lush earth tones and natural fibers. Klein's charisma, good looks, and lifestyle made him a natural celebrity in a decade where designers began to achieve media star status.

In an age when more and more designers were creating clothes for both men and women, those who did usually began working in womenswear and expanded into menswear. **Ralph Lauren** (b. 1939) went in the opposite direction, to become one of the decade's most celebrated designers. Born Ralph Lifshitz in Bronx, New York, he began his career with a line of neckties created for the manufacturer Beau Brummell in 1968. Riding the trend of the "peacock male," Lauren's ties were wider than most others on the market and inaugurated his Polo label. The ties sold well at high-end menswear shops and provided impetus for Lauren's next step. He opened a menswear boutique in Bloomingdale's and received a Coty Award in 1970. The 1972 introduction of the cotton piqué knit polo shirt with embroidered polo player logo created a sportswear sensation. He introduced women's clothing the same year, much of which was menswear-inspired. Lauren quickly established his aesthetic, offering smartly tailored pieces and sportswear that evoked styles of the 1920s, 1930s and 1940s. Often men and women were shown in his advertising in companion ensembles. After he constructed menswear for Theoni V. Aldredge's designs for *The Great Gatsby*, he promoted his own "Gatsby" look. Lauren's expansion into fragrance, childrenswear, and home furnishings provided the opportunity for the customer to obtain and experience a complete Ralph Lauren lifestyle. Eschewing the sexy, provocative advertising of many of his competitors, Lauren showed established-looking men, women, and families wearing his conservative pieces in genteel settings, evoking the leisurely and moneyed world of Britain and "Waspy" East Coast America.

Geoffrey Beene's career continued to build momentum, based on his reputation for cut that was architectural but never stiff. The movement of clothes on the body was important to him and he experimented with a variety of materials, often favoring jersey, in step with the widespread popularity of knits. In 1971 he launched his lower-priced Beene Bag label. In 1976, in an unusual step for an American designer, Beene began showing his ready-to-wear collections in Europe. His men's fragrance Grey Flannel was launched in 1975; the name evoked one of Beene's signature fabrics, popular for both clothing and decor.

Born in Belgium, **Diane von Furstenberg** (b. 1946) married a prince yet was determined to have a career. She learned about fashion in Italy working at the factory of a friend and moved to New York with her husband in 1970. In 1974 she introduced a printed jersey wrap dress with a deep V-neck and narrow sleeves that became a best-selling style. While wrap dresses were already part of the vocabulary of American fashion, Von Furstenberg's jersey version perfectly suited the time. The wrap dress provided a sexy but "dressed" look that could go from day to evening, an aspect that was emphasized in promotion of the style. While sales of Von Furstenberg's wrap dress peaked quickly, the designer also began offering shirtwaist dresses, scarves, and other accessories and fragrance, establishing herself as a legitimate force in New York fashion.

Mary McFadden (b. 1938) was educated in her native New York and in Paris. She began her career in fashion during the 1960s working in public relations and fashion journalism. By the 1970s she was working in fashion and jewelry design. The label Mary McFadden was incorporated in 1976. Success was immediate, as Henri Bendel gave her clothes favorable merchandising, and editorial coverage was generous. From 1976 to 1980 McFadden won three Coty Awards. McFadden's work was characterized by great creativity and exotic glamour. Inspiration came from a

Above Designer Mary McFadden leads a conga line of exotic McFadden-clad models through New York City traffic in 1977.

Opposite top Model and actress Lauren Hutton in a relaxed ensemble from Calvin Klein. Photographed by Francesco Scavullo in 1974.

Opposite center Smartly tailored suits for men and women by Ralph Lauren from fall 1973 evoke the soigné look of 1930s style, and fashion icons such as the Duke and Duchess of Windsor.

Opposite bottom The popularity of Diane von Furstenberg's wrap dress made it one of the signature looks of the late 1970s, and a popular style for home sewing.

wide variety of sources, including regional styles (notably Asia, the Middle East, and Africa), the ancient world, and fashion designers Poiret and Fortuny. The latter was especially inspirational to McFadden's pleated fabrics. She created notable textile designs, including hand-painted treatments, and striking prints often inspired by the artist Gustav Klimt. McFadden's designs featured sweeping draped layers, trapunto, metallic fabrics, braided tied belts, tasseled trims, and turbans. She included scarves in her fashion output, and her business expanded into interior fabrics. With her attenuated frame and glossy dark hair, McFadden was her own best model and frequently appeared in her advertising.

Adolfo (born Adolfo Sardina, 1933) produced elegant but individualistic clothes, including special knit suits that were favorites of socialites such as Mrs. William F. (Pat) Buckley and Mrs. Winston (C. Z.) Guest. Known for his gracious manner, Adolfo declared it the "designer's duty to take care of the size four as well as the size eighteen woman."[9] Tall, lanky Adrienne Seckling (1934–2006), who designed as **Adri**, was also committed to making fashion flattering to all figures. Known for her emphasis on comfort and adaptability, Adri was described as the conceptual successor to Claire McCardell. A leader in knitwear, **Clovis Ruffin** (1946–1992) was credited with promoting the "t-shirt dress." **Scott Barrie** (1946–1993) was known for his matte jersey dresses and included menswear in his collections. **Carol Horn** (b. 1936) saw freedom in clothing as an aspect of women's liberation. Her inspiration came from travel and sources as diverse as India and Native American design and her creative dresses and separates exemplified a downtown, artistic look. **Perry Ellis** (1940–1986) began his career in retailing, and moved to designing sportswear; in 1976 he debuted his own line for his employer, Portfolio. The success of that venture led to the founding of his own company, Perry Ellis International, which would flourish in the coming decade. When he was only thirty-one, **Albert Capraro** (b. 1943), a former assistant to Oscar de la Renta, caught the eye of First Lady Betty Ford, who admired his attractive designs and commissioned him to create clothing for her. Capraro's work for Mrs. Ford and her daughter, Susan, raised the designer's profile and expanded the market for his suits and dresses that were classic yet feminine.

Designers: Japan

Japan was increasingly important to world fashion. Economic prosperity kindled consumer awareness of fashion and went hand in hand with the decline of traditional dress. The new generation of designers (including Kenzo Takada and Issey Miyake) mostly worked overseas, but there were also indications of a burgeoning fashion scene in Tokyo. **Hanae Mori** (b. 1926) established herself in Tokyo during the 1950s working for the film industry and showed ready-to-wear in the United States in 1965. She opened a salon in Paris in 1976 and began showing couture in 1977. After studying fine arts and literature at Keio University in Tokyo, **Rei Kawakubo** (b. 1942) worked in public relations for a chemical company that produced synthetic fibers. During the 1960s, she became a freelance stylist, which led to her design career. She started using the **Comme des Garçons** label in Tokyo in 1969 and formally incorporated the firm in 1973. Kawakubo began with womenswear and started designing menswear in 1978.

Kansai Yamamoto (b. 1944) was born in Yokohama. He studied at the Bunka College of Fashion in Tokyo, and opened his first boutique in the city in 1968. He first

A Kansai Yamamoto design from the Philadelphia Museum of Art, c. 1974, shows his inventive use of form, shape, color, and traditional Japanese elements.

Walt "Clyde" Frazier in 1974.

GET IT ON

Major fashion inspiration in the 1970s came from prominent African American men, particularly in entertainment and sports. As private detective John Shaft in *Shaft* (1971), Richard Roundtree's wardrobe, designed by Joseph Aulisi, exuded cool. A black leather calf-length trench coat worn over turtleneck and trim pants became a signature look. All his clothes had a sleek cut, minimalist and smooth-surfaced – armor for an urban warrior. In a well-groomed "natural" hairstyle with full sideburns and a mustache, Roundtree was in sync with current fashion, but established a look that would be much imitated.

Brazilian soccer star Pelé was an international ambassador for the game and a proponent of eye-catching menswear. Off the field he favored showy looks, often three-piece suits in wide stripes, and sometimes leisure suits worn with prominent jewelry for his many press appearances. Walt Frazier dazzled basketball fans, but also scored fashion points for his flamboyant personal style. Frazier was nicknamed "Clyde" for his preference for fashions that reminded his teammates of Warren Beatty's costumes in *Bonnie and Clyde*. Frazier's custom-made suits, often with contrasting lapels and yokes, worn with wide ties and broad-brimmed Borsalino hats, created an indelible image for the 6 foot 4 inch (1.95 meter) all-star. His predilection for full-length fur coats also helped establish fur as a fashion choice for the sartorially confident man.

Performers including Marvin Gaye and Barry White brought funk and fashion together. The Isley Brothers were particularly important to the image of the black peacock male – they were often photographed in elaborate open-necked leisure suits and jumpsuits, with wide bell pants and platform shoes. They sported major gold jewelry – prefiguring the style's association with rap musicians – and amazing headgear, ranging from metallic headbands to cowboy hats. From their early tailored looks to their fancy funk-glam dandy style, the Isley Brothers modeled the most extreme fashions of the decade while retaining their masculine mojo. Performers Rick James and Prince extended the reach of the extreme styles into coming decades. The synchronized dance moves and matching costumes of the Jackson 5 helped the musical group achieve major pop music stardom. Their upbeat energetic family vibe even inspired a television cartoon show. In Afro hairstyles and wearing vivid and pastel colors, the Jacksons inspired extreme youth fashions of the decade. With his high-pitched voice and stage charisma, young Michael became especially popular. As his solo career skyrocketed, Michael Jackson's impact on fashion soared as well.

On the other side of the style spectrum, Arthur Ashe emerged as the first prominent black man in tennis. Lean, graceful, and stylish on the court, Ashe was an activist on a number of important issues. In his wire-framed aviator glasses, Arthur Ashe diligently worked to make tennis accessible to all, and the image of a black man in tennis whites helped change the color palette of the game.

An acetate tie from mid-decade displays the "Ecology" symbol in a repeat pattern.

showed in the United States in 1971 at Hess, a department store known for promoting avant-garde fashions, in Allentown, Pennsylvania. He also showed in London the same year, the first Japanese designer to do so. In 1973 he debuted in New York City at an Asian fashion show at the World Trade Center, and then in Paris in 1975. Yamamoto took great inspiration from traditional Japanese forms, including kabuki, traditional clothing, historic painting and printing, and irezumi tattoos, mixing these sources with a contemporary Pop Art aesthetic and remarkable experimentation with form and shape. Yamamoto created outrageous stage costumes for David Bowie for his stage alter ego, Ziggy Stardust.

Menswear

The "Peacock Revolution" which had started in the mid-1960s continued as men experimented with diverse styles. By the 1970s the role of name designers in men's fashion was firmly established, beginning to match their importance for women. Music and musicians were particularly influential, including glam rock (David Bowie, Marc Bolan); funk (George Clinton and Parliament Funkadelic); disco (The Bee Gees, Sylvester); and punk (The Ramones, Sex Pistols).

In general, the fit of clothing was quite lean and body-conscious. Suit jackets were cut long and shaped with a defined waist. Lapels were wide, especially for double-breasted styles, and many jackets were double-vented in back. Variations on Norfolk and safari jackets were popular, available in a wide range of fabrics including corduroy, denim, twill, and synthetic double knits. Trousers were often flat-front, low-rise styles called "hip huggers." "Sansabelt" trousers were manufactured with a lapped waistband and no belt loops. Toward the end of the decade, the waistline rose and pleats were common. Even with the higher waist, the fit remained tight. As with women's fashion, denim was a favorite fabric and was used for much more than pants. Trousers cut like jeans were made of leather, suede, heavy knits, and textured wovens including tweed. Jean-cut corduroys were especially popular and known as "cords." The leisure suit originated in the early 1970s and combined a casual jacket, sometimes shirt-like and often with patch pockets, and matching trousers. Leisure suits offered a casual, but matched, look and were usually worn without ties, even in the workplace and for special occasions.

Shirts were mostly fitted, with wide collars and often deep cuffs. In addition to traditional shirting materials, synthetics and blends in a rainbow of colors and patterns were used including bold geometrics, florals, paisleys, and abstracts. Patchwork effects were another popular motif. Knit shirts were often worn open-necked or with solid-color ties, which were also often made of textured polyester. Rugby-striped shirts with white collars provided a casual option. A revival of aloha shirts was encouraged as part of the retro sensibility. Vests were very popular and were worn as part of a three-piece suit or in many variations, including safari, biker, or cowboy style, or thigh-length and boxy with a low belt. Knits were incorporated into men's wardrobes as pullovers, vests, and accessories; multicolored stripes were especially popular. The color palette of men's fashion was very inclusive but, as with womenswear, deep colors and earth tones were popular.

Unless black tie was required, many men adopted velvet suits for evening or wore velvet jackets with jeans – especially popular for host's attire. Men relaxed in long robes, or in silk dressing gowns, in the style of *Playboy* publisher Hugh Hefner. Outerwear was very varied and included many double-breasted greatcoat styles, often with wide lapels. Length varied from the traditional three-quarter and knee length to more trendy styles that reached mid- to low calf. In perhaps the ultimate "Peacock" statement, fur for men was promoted and American football player Joe Namath and Russian ballet star Rudolf Nureyev were widely photographed wearing fur coats. The fashion for fur also included shearling and faux fur in full-length, three-quarter and jacket styles.

Neckties remained wide until around 1978 and then retreated during the later years of the decade. Other neckwear options included knotted kerchiefs and ascots worn with

An advertisement for h.i.s. illustrates some of the trendy extremes of 1970s menswear, and also reflects the diversity of models used in advertising by this time.

For whom the bells toll.

Ask not. They're for you. Our swinging bells have an ultra-slim fit, low rise and come in a ring-a-ding assortment of colors and fabrics. They're definitely becoming a novel American great. Talon zipper. $6 to $12. Apache shirts from $6. Shoes from $12. Higher in West. For retailers, write h.i.s, 16 E. 34 Street, N.Y. 10016. Available in Canada. Boys' sizes, too.

h.i.s

open-neck shirts. Hats were no longer considered an essential part of the wardrobe but were treated as fashion accessories. Many styles of hats were worn including wide-brimmed Italian styles, cowboy hats, slouchy newsboy types, and knitted watch caps. The silhouette of shoes evolved over the course of the decade, moving from chunky and round-toed to a more sleek line. In addition to the traditional shoe styles (loafers, Oxfords, wingtips) that were still worn by older men and for business, boots of all kinds were popular. Styles frequently seen included ankle-height slip-on boots, chukka and desert boots, and Western styles. Platform shoes, clogs, and Earth shoes were worn by both sexes. Shoulder bags for men, while not widely accepted, were carried by the most fashion-forward. Some were soft, ethnic styles, made of hand-woven wool or cotton, or fringed suede. Others were more structured, resembling plain, square leather purses. The range of acceptable jewelry for men expanded quite a bit. Some men wore simple chain necklaces and bracelets, while others opted for more elaborate pieces with medallions or beads. Distinctive rings with knot patterns, ethnic inspiration, and other motifs were widely seen. Other surprising accessories were available; in 1978 *GQ* promoted a gold eyepatch with pavé diamond accents, deemed perfect for eveningwear.

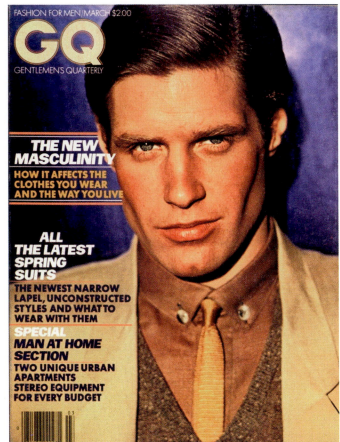

Underwear also reflected the slim cut of fashion and many men opted for knitted briefs or low-cut bikini styles rather than boxer shorts. Men's underwear became more varied and decorative, sometimes offered in bold solid colors, patterns such as stripes or animal prints, or trimmed with contrast edging, and were more than ever overtly linked with sex appeal. Undershirts in crew-neck, V-neck and singlet styles were all worn, in tightly fitting knits, ribbing, or mesh.

Distinctive hairstyling was an integral part of fashion for men. Side- or center-parted, hair was worn long over the ears and shaped in back, usually no longer than the collar. Sideburns were de rigueur and mustaches and well-trimmed beards and goatees were all very fashionable. Warren Beatty's longer locks in *Shampoo* (1975) were inspirational to those who maintained a longer hairstyle. Many men started to patronize stylists instead of barbers; traditional barbershops became salons and many top women's salons opened facilities for men. Haircare products were openly adopted, including Gillette's "Dry Look" line and other hairsprays. Treatments for thinning hair were widely promoted. Skincare products for men were gaining acceptance, and fragrances were more aggressively advertised. Moisturizers formulated for men were marketed and some men applied cosmetic bronzer to achieve a tanned-looking face.

Gay culture produced several fashion archetypes including the "Castro clone" look derived from working-class clothing such as flannel shirts, jeans, tank tops, and leather jackets, typically worn with sideburns and mustaches. Accessories including colored bandanas and keys were used to signal sexual preferences. The disco group Village People embodied a variety of stereotypical looks, cementing gay archetypes in the popular imagination.

By the late years of the decade, tradition and seriousness returned to men's fashion. In 1973 *Esquire's Fashions for Today* advised a man interviewing for a job to wear a suit or "a blazer jacket with solid-color or patterned slacks" and a "pair of slip-ons or demi-boots" and counseled that if you found a company that required more formality, "it's unlikely you'd want to work there anyway."[10] But only two years later, John Molloy's book *Dress for Success* advised that "every item of clothing and every accessory must be conservative, traditional and conventional."[11] The emphasis in menswear switched from experimental to classic. Instead of keeping up with trends, men dressed to convey affluence and maturity. By 1978 pinstriped suits, yachting blazers, country tweeds, and argyle sweaters reappeared as major elements of menswear. Two other important themes emerged that would prove significant in coming years: sophisticated Western wear and a revival of fine Italian tailoring. While retro influences were still present, the prevailing reference shifted from romanticism to well-groomed 1920s dandyism. The fashion press rediscovered the Arrow Collar Man, Edward, Prince of Wales, and even Rudolph Valentino, and styled models with slicked-back hair.

Children's Fashion

Children's clothes shared in many of the general trends of fashion. Ethnic and gypsy styles were easily adapted for the young and were seen as peasant-style tops and dresses and tiered skirts for girls. Wrap skirts and smock-style dresses were often worn, many

A German fashion photograph from 1970 features stylish children's outerwear options.

made in cotton paisley from Indian import shops. Vests were very popular for both boys and girls. A great many styles were seen, ranging from short bolero styles to tunic length, often fringed or with oversized buttons, ornamental chain, or lacing. Clogs, sandals, and many styles of boots also expressed the gypsy look. Knits were very fashionable. The renewed popularity of hand-knitting and crocheting produced crocheted vests for girls (sometimes with pom-poms), and textured pullovers for boys. Both sexes wore ponchos and long mufflers, knitted caps, mittens, and gloves.

As dress codes for children were relaxed in some areas, girls were allowed to wear pants to school in many regions, leading to the introduction of pants ensembles and pantsuits for young girls. Many such ensembles teamed pants with a tunic or vest and some girls wore dresses over pants. Denim was very popular for children, used in jeans, overalls, jumper (pinafore) dresses, jackets, and accessories. The progression of denim styles for kids mirrored that of adults as hippie looks gave way to designer jeans. The popular Garanimals line of children's clothing was introduced in 1972. The mix-and-match separates (with animal logo coding) were intended to make it easier for children to choose their outfits, dress themselves, and be happy with the results.

A retro mood influenced dressy clothing. Suits for boys reflected earlier modes: collarless Eton jackets were paired with shorts for little boys while older boys and teenagers wore shaped Edwardian-style three-piece suits, often with contrasting lapels. For girls, maxiskirts were often seen for special occasions. Quilted maxis with sashes were especially popular for winter holidays. Laura Ashley and the Gunne Sax line by Jessica McClintock were instrumental in popularizing romantic looks. Their Victorian and frontier-style dresses were often worn by teenage girls for special occasions, including the prom.

Like those of their parents, children's hairstyles varied widely. Many girls adopted the long looks of the early years of the decade, then chose "wedge" haircuts or feathered styles as those looks emerged by 1976. Boys often wore their hair collar length, sometimes reminiscent of medieval or Victorian styles, emphasizing natural curls and waves. Many black children wore Afros or had their hair styled in African-influenced braids and cornrows.

The End of the Decade

The 1970s saw the continued development of individuality as a fashion philosophy; the uniform edicts of high fashion had been challenged. If one woman dressed as an

Yves Saint Laurent Mongol and another as Annie Hall, no one found it odd. However, in some respects, this eclecticism in fashion revealed a lack of sartorial originality. The major themes of the decade had already been established by the late 1960s; revival of pre-war styles was also constant. Perhaps music best encouraged what was innovative in the 1970s as punk and disco both emerged as original styles. Each had a fashion repertoire and a distinct style tribe to promote it. Whereas punk assembled an eclectic collage of improbable pieces and outlandish grooming only to be embraced by designers as the movement grew, disco dressing, with its body-skimming sleekness, had the stamp of approval of top designers from its inception. Fanciful menswear, fulfilling the promise of the Peacock Revolution, was replaced by classic subtlety and conformity by the end of the decade. Synthetic materials lost their allure and natural fibers were aggressively reasserted at the decade's end.

Youthful hedonism was being replaced by a new set of priorities, conservative and status-conscious. A letter to the editor in *Vogue* in 1977 reflected the sea change:

> Youth was on our side back in the 'sixties and early 'seventies, and we needed only to whimper a bit in order to have our smallest whims satisfied ... Back then it was nifty to pooh-pooh the Establishment, which we all did, without tact or eloquence. How embarrassing it is now – looking back at the impudent fools we were. Yes, the age of the teenage tyrant has seen its last sunset. Now we all want high-powered jobs and Cartier watches. Since Getting Back to Nature didn't work, we're trading in our denim for three-piece grey flannel suits.

By 1979 the silhouette had evolved into a leaner line with a crisp shoulder, ushering in the shape of the 1980s. "Seventh Avenue" designers, including (left to right) Ralph Lauren, Anne Klein, Oscar de la Renta, Bill Kaiserman, and Mady Gerrard, were illustrated in *McCall's* magazine, August 1979.

Chapter 11

The 1980s

Power Dressing and Postmodernism

Status, glamour, and materialism dominated fashion consciousness, prompting a revival of interest in established luxury brands, haute couture, and the return of the idea of "dressing up." Conservative political ideals encouraged traditional styles for preppies, Sloane Rangers, and BCBGs, while the status consciousness of the decade contributed to a renewed interest in European royals as many took center stage as fashion setters. Prosperity in the business world promoted "dress for success" principles for men and women. Yuppies (Young Urban Professionals) dedicated equal attention to their jobs and their lifestyle, defined in large part through their possessions. However, not everyone adopted the mandate for suits, power ties, and expensive watches: "identity politics" were played out through the adoption of styles that ranged from rebellious, to arty, to "fabulous." Countertrends around the world, often music-driven – from London to New York to Sydney – embraced post-punk and "New Wave" styles. Japanese expatriate designers offered alternative design aesthetics. Fashion had entered a postmodern age in which, despite a conformist mainstream

Opposite Patrick Nagel's slick graphic illustration conveyed the hard-edged chic of 1980s fashion, hair, and make-up. His work was seen on album covers and in numerous advertisements and limited-edition prints.

Right An image of turn-of-the-century beauty Lina Cavalieri provided the motif for many designs by Piero Fornasetti, including this fabric used in Perry Ellis' spring 1986 collection.

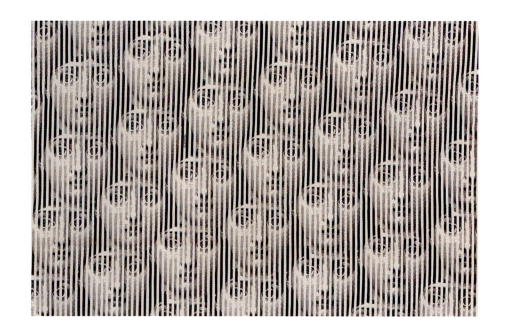

aesthetic, a multiplicity of looks was available, distributed globally via the fashion press, television, film, and the new medium of music videos.

Social and Economic Background

The 1980s saw a return to conservative politics in many countries. Economic prosperity seemed to validate the free market policies of world leaders such as Ronald Reagan and Margaret Thatcher. Financial markets, real estate, and the fashion and fine art sectors of the economy were especially buoyant during the 1980s. Indeed, their status was intertwined as fortunes made on Wall Street supported speculation in real estate and led to conspicuous consumption of fashion and art. Simultaneously, society experienced a retrenchment in attitudes toward sexuality as HIV/AIDS, identified in 1981, became a threat to the permissiveness of the previous decade. Response to the AIDS crisis was acute in the fashion industry, precipitated by the loss of prominent fashion figures such as designers Halston and Perry Ellis and model Gia Carangi.

In the Philippines, the 1983 assassination of Senator Benigno Aquino by the military reinforced perceptions of the corruption of Ferdinand Marcos' regime; after the People Power Revolution deposed Marcos in 1986, Aquino's widow, Corazon, became the first female president of an East Asian country. "Black Monday," a stock market crash that began in Hong Kong on the morning of October 19, 1987, caused a ripple effect through markets around the world, dampening the jubilant, affluent spirit of the decade. The end of the decade was further marked by political upheavals, with violent protests in Beijing's Tiananmen Square and the fall of the Berlin Wall, both in 1989.

Computers were becoming more common tools in both the workplace and the home. The fashion industry started to adopt computer technology, especially for knitwear and textile design. The compact disc debuted in 1982, making music more portable than ever. World's Fairs in Knoxville (1982), Tsukuba (1985), Vancouver (1986), and Brisbane (1988) showcased new technologies, such as touchscreens and high-definition television, anticipating the technology boom of the 1990s.

The Arts

Artwork in many media was characterized by visual and conceptual aspects often termed postmodernist: exuberant juxtapositions of color and surface, humorous reworkings of classic forms, and an unprecedented mixing of media. The postmodern aesthetic was first identified in architecture. Major monuments in the style included Philip Johnson's AT&T Building in New York City, Michael Graves' Portland Building, and Tomás Taveira's Amoreiras Towers in Lisbon. "Sampling" and "appropriation" became common in art, music, architecture, and fashion, as artists explored sources that ranged from classical sculpture to cartoons. A number of painters rediscovered and reinterpreted the figure as subject matter, including Julian Schnabel, Sandro Chia, Francis Bacon, and Robert Longo. Other artists, such as Jenny Holzer and Barbara Kruger, focused on text as a medium. The work of Gilbert & George ranged from performance to collage. Richard Long and Andy Goldsworthy incorporated natural materials, and sometimes land itself, in sculpture and installations. Graffiti was celebrated as an art style: Futura 2000, Keith Haring, and Jean-Michel Basquiat all started as street artists but soon found international success in established galleries and museums. Graffiti style was especially influential on fashion and was inspirational to designers Vivienne Westwood and Stephen Sprouse. Other artists, including Anselm Kiefer, Gerhard Richter, David Wojnarowicz, and Robert Mapplethorpe, explored more challenging themes such as the Holocaust and AIDS. Performance art developed further as an important medium with a number of outstanding artists. Leigh

A 1980 teapot by Peter Shire exemplifies the colorful, humorous side of the postmodern aesthetic.

STYLE TRIBES OF AFFLUENCE

Three closely related style tribes emerged during the decade, each related to affluence, tradition, and status. The "preppy" look was a significant mainstream trend coming into the 1980s, reflecting a return to a classic, moneyed style. The name derived from the prep-school education of elite Americans. With the 1980 publication of best seller *The Official Preppy Handbook*, edited by Lisa Birnbach, the movement had its bible, and a dress code associated with the Northeastern Establishment was explained to the general public. The preppy aesthetic stressed natural fibers, tartan plaid, button-down shirts, and such details and accessories as monogramming, school ties, and pearls. Birnbach's book included diagrams for proper prep dressing, and a glossary of prep slang phrases. Across the Atlantic, a very similar group, the Sloane Rangers, had developed, taking their name from London's Sloane Square. The clothes were traditional and a bit dull. The most notable exemplar of this style was Lady Diana Spencer, in the rather dowdy look that she maintained before her marriage to Prince Charles. Typically educated in select schools, Sloanes enjoyed country living, conservative Tory politics, and the sporting life. Guidelines for the lifestyle were published in 1982 in *The Official Sloane Ranger Handbook*, by Peter York and Ann Barr. Meanwhile in Paris, elite BCBGs ("*bon chic, bon genre*") were known by their clothes of restrained, often Anglophile, chic. Wealthy and conventional, "*les BCBGs*" glorified French elitism. They, too, had their own handbook when Thierry Mantoux published *BCBG: le guide du bon chic, bon genre* in 1986. Certain retailers and designers contributed to – and benefited from – these tastes, including Lacoste, Ralph Lauren, Jaeger, Burberry, Hermès, and Brooks Brothers.

A 1981 cartoon by Christine Meyers dissects the "preppy" look.

Bowery, who designed the flamboyant costumes integral to his performances, was immortalized in paintings by Francis Bacon. Countertenor Klaus Nomi was noted for his unique vocal and visual styles. Experimental musician Laurie Anderson offered genre-crossing work that also found mainstream success.

The art market ran at a fever pitch, and auction records were set every season. Works by Van Gogh and Picasso were particularly in demand, but prices even for young artists reached record highs. Status-conscious middle-class art consumers collected limited edition graphics by blue-chip names as well as more popular artists such as Thomas McKnight and Patrick Nagel. Memphis, an international design collective founded by Ettore Sottsass, produced colorful furniture and lighting fixtures in plastic laminate and sheet metal, materials previously considered strictly utilitarian and industrial. On the other hand, popular period films inspired a revival of the eclectic grandeur of English country house style, and Laura Ashley home furnishings enjoyed renewed popularity. Ralph Lauren was a pioneer in designer home furnishings, promoting the aspirational aesthetic that characterized his clothing.

Outstanding films included *Raging Bull* (1980), *Fanny and Alexander* (1982), *Gandhi* (1982), *Tampopo* (1985), *A Better Tomorrow* (1986), *Hannah and her Sisters* (1986), *Au revoir les enfants* (1987), *The Last Emperor* (1987), and *Jesus of Montreal* (1989). *Amadeus* (1984), *Dangerous Liaisons* (1988), and a number of films from the team of Merchant Ivory proved highly influential on trends in fashion and decor.

Internationally best-selling books ranged from Jean M. Auel's prehistoric sagas to Umberto Eco's *The Name of the Rose*, and to Gabriel García Márquez's *Love in the Time of Cholera*, Margaret Atwood's *The Handmaid's Tale*, Martin Amis' *London Fields*, and Salman Rushdie's controversial *The Satanic Verses*. Isabel Allende's magic realist *The House of the Spirits* and Peter Mayle's *A Year in Provence* also saw international success. Romances by Judith Krantz and Danielle Steel were extremely popular and newcomers Jay McInerney and Bret Easton Ellis explored contemporary urban themes.

A number of outstanding theatrical pieces debuted, including *Nine*, *Les Misérables*, *La Cage aux Folles*, and *Sunday in the Park with George*. Andrew Lloyd Webber's musicals *Cats* and *Phantom of the Opera* had lasting appeal. Important dramatic works included Mark Medoff's *Children of a Lesser God*, *"Master Harold" … and the Boys* by Athol Fugard, Tom Stoppard's *The Real Thing*, Wendy Wasserstein's *The Heidi Chronicles*, and *M. Butterfly* by David Henry Hwang.

Fashion and Society

The decade was characterized by a renewed emphasis on high-society style. At a 1982 party on Long Island's moneyed North Shore, a young guest quipped:

> I think it's great that we're all dressing up again. We're all kind of reacting to the generation who came before us. Besides, it's more exciting to dress. When you do, you make sure you're going to have a good time.[1]

Society rituals were revived, including ballroom dancing and debutante parties. Cornelia Guest, the daughter of C. Z. Guest (and god-daughter of the Duke of Windsor), provided fodder for the society gossip columns and was declared "Deb of the Year" in 1982, prompting comparisons to the "celebutantes" of earlier decades. Style groups flourished, including preppies, Sloane Rangers and BCBGs, embracing new traditionalism. Style setters were not only found among the young. Ronald and Nancy Reagan, both former Hollywood actors, brought star power to the White House. Perfectly coiffed Mrs. Reagan openly enjoyed high fashion; James Galanos and Adolfo were among her favorite designers and the color she preferred for clothes and interiors became known as "Reagan red." Prime Minister Margaret Thatcher served as a model of traditional British style in pearls and richly hued tailored suits. Paloma Picasso and Tina Chow were admired for their precise, cosmopolitan chic.

Lady Diana Spencer reinvigorated royalty-watching and other European royals also captivated public interest. German Princess Gloria von Thurn und Taxis (known in the press as "Princess TNT") was renowned for her eye-catching fashion sense – combining couture evening dresses with mohawk hairdos – as well as numerous lavish parties. Prince Albert and Princesses Caroline and Stéphanie of Monaco, the children of Rainier III and Grace Kelly, were also in the spotlight; lifestyle magazines frequently covered the exploits of bachelor-about-town and Olympic bobsledder Albert, Caroline's equestrian triumphs, and Stéphanie's career as a fashion model and pop singer.

The Diana Phenomenon

Lady Diana Spencer (1961–1997) captivated the world when she became engaged to Charles, Prince of Wales, in 1981. Born of an aristocratic British family, Diana was working as a preschool attendant in 1981, and dressed in the "Sloane Ranger" style. Early photographs in the media showed a shy, awkward young woman; however, she transformed into one of the 1980s' (and the century's) most notable fashion icons. Mere weeks after her twentieth birthday, Diana wore a spectacular dress for her wedding on July 21, 1981. Designed by husband and wife design team David and Elizabeth Emanuel, the ivory silk taffeta gown was encrusted with pearls and sequins and included a 25-foot (7.6-meter) train. The dress featured a very full skirt, ruffled neckline, and puffed sleeves, with strong allusions to the 17th, 18th, and 19th centuries. Copies of the dress appeared in store windows later that same day, and full skirts, taffeta fabric, and puffed sleeves were encouraged in eveningwear fashions worldwide. Shortly afterwards, Diana made her first appearance on a *Vogue* cover when she was photographed by the Earl of Snowdon (Antony Armstrong-Jones) for the August 1981 British issue. Magazine covers became a regular habitat for the princess. Throughout the 1980s, Diana's style was widely imitated, and reflected her generation; she was often seen in laid-back casual styles, but looked sleek and elegant in formal evening clothes. For daytime occasions she wore well-matched ensembles paying close attention to hat, shoes, jewelry, and bag. Diana

Above Punk/rock vocalist Siouxsie Sioux of Siouxsie and the Banshees appeared on the cover of *The Face* (August 1980), an influential music and style magazine.

Below Madonna and Rosanna Arquette helped popularize thrift shop "bricolage" in the 1985 film *Desperately Seeking Susan*.

often favored coatdress styles, and encouraged military and sailor looks. She showed a fondness for the bold, large-scale prints and dots popular at the time. Young women copied her various feathered hairstyles and her make-up. Much of the wardrobe that defined her cool elegance was provided by Catherine Walker; another favored supplier was the well-established house of Belleville Sassoon, and Diana continued to wear dresses from the Emanuels. Media coverage was so persistent that "Diana Style" became a global phenomenon.

Fashion Media

Fashion information was conveyed in a wide variety of publications. The venerable but faded British society magazine *Tatler* received a makeover in 1979, launching the career of editor Tina Brown. Its American counterpart, *Town & Country*, focused on privileged lifestyles. *Connoisseur* and the luxuriously produced *FMR* covered art and design for a discerning and aspirational audience. *Interview* offered an inside view of New York's art and fashion lifestyles. Two British magazines, *i-D* and *The Face*, both launched in 1980, featured a street-style focus and proved influential on emerging styles of fashion photography.

The young women who became known as "supermodels" walked the runway and were featured on magazine covers, in advertisements, and in fashion editorials. While international top models were more ethnically diverse than in previous decades, the prevailing beauty standard emphasized height and a physically fit look. Favorites included Anna Bayle, Naomi Campbell, Cindy Crawford, Linda Evangelista, Jerry Hall, Iman, Elle Macpherson, Paulina Porizkova, Claudia Schiffer, and Christy Turlington. Fourteen-year-old Brooke Shields began modeling Calvin Klein jeans in 1980 and was featured on the cover of American *Vogue*. Illustrations from Antonio Lopez and Michael Vollbracht graced the pages of newspapers and magazines, while photographers including Arthur Elgort, Herb Ritts, Francesco Scavullo, Victor Skrebneski, and Bruce Weber contributed to the high style of the decade in women's fashion and menswear.

Music and Fashion

Pop, New Wave, arena rock, and rap were among the many styles which provided significant fashion inspiration. Music styles were increasingly specific and created fevered followings with highly detailed fashion agendas. Music videos, especially via the music television channel MTV that was launched in 1981, provided more exposure than ever before for fashion associated with the music industry. Glam rock entered a more mainstream phase but also influenced the emerging Goth aesthetic. London's Batcave club, showcasing bands such as The Damned, was the epicenter of the developing Goth scene. Important New Wave acts came directly from the earlier punk movement and included Siouxsie and the Banshees, Joan Jett and the Blackhearts, and Blondie. Devo, The Eurythmics, Elvis Costello and the Attractions, and The Pretenders, among many others, all inspired young people through hairstyles and make-up. Most of these performers were lean and angular, and their clothing mixed futuristic looks with retro styles. Fans of ska adopted the short trousers, trim shirts, and pork pie hats of popular bands such as The Specials.

The New Romantics also emerged in London. With his heavy eye make-up, long hair, and layered ensembles, the look of "gender-bending" Boy George embodied the movement's message. The Thompson Twins and Bow Wow Wow also adopted distinctive hairstyles and costumes. Adam Ant and Ivan Doroschuk (lead singer of Quebec's Men Without Hats) displayed a swashbuckling style. On their 1982 album *Rio*, British heart-throbs Duran Duran featured a Patrick Nagel illustration of a dark-haired woman, one of the most iconic (and fashion-related) graphic images of the decade. The young men of A Flock of Seagulls became better known for their upswept hairstyles than for their music. Fans imitated the streaked, feathered haircut of George Michael of Wham. And with the release of his solo debut, *Faith*, they also imitated the hyper-masculinity of his biker jacket, stubble, and torn jeans. Brosettes – fans of the British band Bros – followed "a strict dress code" that included ripped jeans and Dr. Martens. The large hairdos of Kate Pierson and Cindy Wilson of the B-52s brought elaborate bouffants back into fashion. Girl groups such as The GoGos and Bananarama adopted an intentionally vapid style.

Madonna and Cindy Lauper helped popularize postmodern "bricolage" with a stylistic mix of elements such as vintage gowns and thrift store petticoats with bustiers and costume jewelry. The look was epitomized in Lauper's "Girls Just Want to Have Fun" video and the 1985 film *Desperately Seeking Susan*. By the end of the decade, Madonna took on a 1930s Hollywood glamour look, the first of her many "reinventions." Pat Benatar's mix of punk and activewear inspired many imitators. Tina Turner, a rhythm and blues star of the 1960s and 1970s, crossed over into rock and roll; her spiky haircut and long legs, accentuated by high heels, created a signature look. Grace Jones offered a cool androgyny, with her flat-top hair and lean figure. Gloria Estefan of The Miami Sound Machine developed a Latina party-girl image, while petite and curvaceous Paula Abdul combined sporty and feminine elements.

Rockabilly bands such as The Stray Cats sported an updated "greaser" look with elaborate "duck's ass" hairstyles, pegged pants, boots, and work shirts, in the style of 1950s country musicians. Arena rock acts such as Journey, Styx, Toto, and Loverboy promoted large-scale stadium spectaculars and large hairstyles, including mullets and bleached blonde locks. Van Halen front man David Lee Roth was an excellent example, as he tossed his long hair for the camera in their 1983 "Jump" video. Lita Ford represented a female version of the look. The hard rock image often merged with

Below left Rockabilly style, as embodied by The Stray Cats, included references to the greasers of the 1950s with pegged pants and elaborate "duck's ass" or "quiff" hairdos.

Below right The New York-based trio Run DMC was among the first rap acts to enjoy mainstream success. Their fashion choices included Kangol caps, big gold jewelry and Adidas footwear.

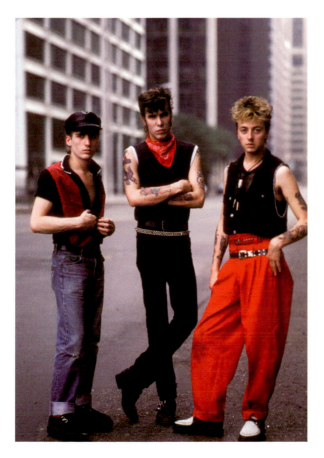

Sean Young's costumes in *Blade Runner* (1982), by Michael Kaplan and Charles Knode, featured a broad-shouldered silhouette that reprised the 1940s but also encouraged developing trends.

Right American Gigolo (1980) enhanced Richard Gere's star status and cemented the reputation of Giorgio Armani, who provided Gere's wardrobe.

Opposite left Jeremy Irons and Anthony Andrews in the 1981 series *Brideshead Revisited*, one of many films and television productions that celebrated vintage British sportswear styles.

Opposite center Miami Vice promoted a relaxed, tropical menswear style, as seen on stars Don Johnson and Philip Michael Thomas.

Opposite right Teenagers found fashion inspiration in many films about adolescent life, including *Pretty in Pink* (1986), starring Jon Cryer as a quirky high-school student with a flair for accessorizing.

glam, as seen in the style adopted by Heart in the late 1980s. Debonair Robert Palmer was backed by a group of women who became known as the Palmer Girls: their tightly pulled-back hair, form-fitting dresses and severe make-up were widely imitated from masquerade parties to the fashion runway.

Michael Jackson was among the most influential performers of the decade. His clothing and grooming were copied by young people of all races around the world, especially his frequently changing hairdos and distinctive jackets. The fashion style of rap and hip hop, inspired by black urban street dress, combined name-brand athletic shoes and running suits with Kangol caps and chunky gold jewelry. African-inspired details, such as kente cloth, often completed the look. The bands Run DMC and Salt-N-Pepa particularly influenced style. Fashion was so important to rap and hip hop that song lyrics often made reference to favorite brands and designers.

Toward the end of the decade, a new genre and counterculture emerged in Seattle, Washington: grunge. An independent record label began recording local acts, including Nirvana. Street fashion worn in Seattle's University District would influence mainstream style throughout the following decade.

Film and Television and Fashion

The filmmaking world continued frequent tie-ins with fashion designers. For *American Gigolo* (1980), Giorgio Armani provided the costumes for lead actor Richard Gere, catapulting Armani to major North American success. Gere's clothes, showing the narrow proportions and smoky colors typical of the early decade, were prominently featured in the storyline and were well represented in the fashion press. The film also featured fashion model-turned-actress Lauren Hutton. Armani also provided wardrobe assistance to designer Marilyn Vance for the Depression-era menswear in *The Untouchables* (1987); and 1930s styles appeared in his own collections.

The "white flannel" film genre was important to style, as exemplified by Merchant Ivory productions *A Room With a View* (1985) and *Maurice* (1987), as well as *Another Country* (1984) and *A Handful of Dust* (1988). The early 20th-century settings inspired classic looks celebrated in fashion. Perhaps the most important production of this ilk was the 1981 British television series *Brideshead Revisited*, which proved influential on preppy style, designer collections, and fashion editorials. Aloysius, the teddy bear carried by the character Sebastian, encouraged a teddy bear mania: bears were featured in fashion merchandising, and young gay men held teddy bears as an accessory; even Moschino satirized the trend with his teddy bear dress.

Joan Collins and Diahann Carroll in costume for the long-running television show *Dynasty*, which featured assertively glamorous designs by Nolan Miller.

For *Blade Runner* (1982), director Ridley Scott conceived Sean Young's character as a futuristic film noir siren, and designers Michael Kaplan and Charles Knode looked to Adrian's 1940s silhouette for inspiration; Young's broad-shouldered suits helped encourage a developing trend in fashion. Big shoulders were also glorified by the costumes for American television show *Dynasty*, where designer Nolan Miller dressed actresses Joan Collins, Linda Evans, and Diahann Carroll in luxurious beaded gowns with massive shoulder pads or leg-of-mutton sleeves combined with nipped waists and sleek torsos. The look of the show was so celebrated that Miller created his own fashion line, and Miller's *Dynasty* styles were available to home sewers through paper patterns. The costumes for the movie *Wall Street* (1987) were designed as exaggerations of financial industry style, but the look of character Gordon Gekko, with suspenders and contrasting white collars, was soon emulated by financial workers. Television's *L.A. Law* also encouraged designer power dressing via the show's well-costumed male cast, with wardrobe assistance provided by Hugo Boss. The television series *Miami Vice* featured Don Johnson and Philip Michael Thomas in pastel-colored sportswear and unconstructed suits (often with rolled-up sleeves) that complemented their art deco surroundings. American television contributed further to style setting in a variety of markets. *The Golden Girls* presented assertive style for mature women, while *Designing Women* showcased well-dressed career women. Jasmine Guy in *A Different World* presented designer style as something accessible to young African American women, and co-star Kadeem Hardison displayed quirky hip-hop fashion.

Jennifer Beals' torn sweatshirts and leg warmers in *Flashdance* (1983) provided inspiration for dance and exercise wear to be worn as street clothes, continuing trends encouraged by *A Chorus Line* in the previous decade. A number of films directed by John Hughes, including *The Breakfast Club* (1985) and *Ferris Bueller's Day Off* (1986), featured costumes designed by Marilyn Vance, and included eclectic, individualized looks for teens that were widely emulated. Winona Ryder's costumes in *Beetlejuice* (1988), designed by Aggie Guerard Rodgers, reflected the developing Goth style.

Perhaps the most notable film costume designer of the decade was Milena Canonero (b. 1946). She established herself in the 1970s, and her first major work of the 1980s was *Chariots of Fire* (1981), one of the major films in the "white flannel" mode; the film won the Academy Award and BAFTA Award for Best Picture, and costume design awards from both for Canonero. Other period films followed. *The Cotton Club* (1984), with its 1920s Harlem Renaissance setting, featured tailored suits

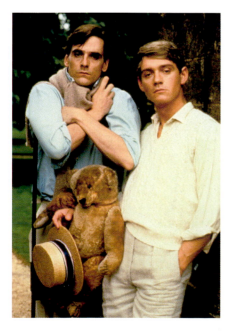

and "flapper" styles that influenced contemporary fashion editorials. The restrained safari and Edwardian looks of *Out of Africa* (1985) were strongly reflected in the market, including the J. Peterman catalog and Ralph Lauren. For *The Hunger* (1983), Canonero dressed Catherine Deneuve and David Bowie as chic vampires (with wardrobing assistance for Deneuve from Yves Saint Laurent). In 1986 Canonero was retained to revamp the look of television's *Miami Vice*, adding pieces by trendy designers to the actors' wardrobes, and replacing "the famous *Vice* pastels with a selection of orchids, blacks, and grays."[2]

The film work of Deborah Nadoolman Landis also showed strong ties to fashion. *The Blues Brothers* (1980) featured John Belushi and Dan Aykroyd in black suits, white shirts, black ties, black Ray-Ban sunglasses, and black fedoras – a look that inspired countless masquerade costumes. *Raiders of the Lost Ark* (1981) starred Harrison Ford in a brown fedora and leather bomber jacket, a style that was widely imitated by (among others) Giorgio Armani and New York outerwear label Andrew Marc, as well as at other price points. Nadoolman Landis followed this with Michael Jackson's *Thriller* video (1983), featuring the iconic trapunto-decorated red leather jacket. For *Coming to America* (1988), Nadoolman Landis' costumes for a fictitious African kingdom both reflected and encouraged the use of kente cloth.

The Elements of Women's Fashion

Fashion in the 1980s was especially indicative of social status. The fashionable person used his or her appearance to signal economic achievement, cultural affiliations, lifestyle preferences, even taste in music. A number of important looks coexisted and overlapped during this period, including: preppy (and its equivalents); "power dressing"; avant-garde Japanese; and numerous subcultural styles. "Art-to-wear," one-of-a-kind clothing, jewelry and accessories, was available from specialty galleries that offered exclusive pieces, often created with a modernist sensibility.

Retro influence continued in the form of a pronounced 1940s revival, particularly expressed with the V-shaped silhouette that dominated women's fashion. The wide shoulder and narrow skirt that Adrian and Schiaparelli had championed was once again fashionable. But in contrast to the retro styles of the late 1960s and the 1970s, the 1980s displayed a more disciplined approach to mining the past. Volume was key, seen in shoulder, sleeve, skirt, or the generous shape of sweaters and coats. Oversized jackets, including vintage menswear pieces, were often worn with rolled-up sleeves and described as "boyfriend" style.

While the mid-calf length continued from the previous decade, skirt lengths varied from very short (often worn over leggings or eye-catching tights) to ankle length. Long knitted tube skirts were very popular. Knee length was common for business. Some designers featured a variety of hemlines in one collection. Pants had a high waistline, sometimes a wide waistband, and were usually pleated. Very tight jeans continued from the late 1970s but soon fuller, pegged styles became common. Jeans were sometimes decorated with slashing to provocative effect. Leggings were worn as a trouser alternative, often with tunics or long jackets. Jumpsuits enjoyed great popularity, as did short playsuits, especially for young women.

Romantic white blouses, some with standing collars, lace insets, or back buttons, were worn with full skirts. Silk shirtwaists with shoulder pads were often worn with knee-length pencil skirts. For casual wear, polo shirts were paired with khaki skirts.

Black and neutrals returned to fashion, strongly encouraged by French, American, and Japanese designers. Unusual, tertiary colors were often contrasted with black or vied with jewel tones. Vivid royal blue, magenta, and emerald green remained popular throughout the decade, even for outerwear. Italian designers' variations of gray, taupe, and tawny shades set a new standard for fashionable neutrals. Neon brights were seen across fashion from swimsuits to body-hugging knits to accessories.

Crisp linens, fine woven cottons, and full-bodied wools (often borrowed from menswear) were typical for career dressing. Natural fibers continued to be essential to

Below A 1986 advertisement for Yves Saint Laurent's Rive Gauche line demonstrates a typically hard mid-decade silhouette with bold, graphic color scheme.

Bottom Classic knitwear from the British brand Jaeger – celebrating its centennial in 1984 – was in keeping with the assertion of traditional style for men and women.

This ready-to-wear ensemble, an oversized top and black harem pants, is worn with high-heeled pumps, large earrings and a hat – all popular accessories.

fashion, though some synthetics were encouraged for specific uses, namely activewear. Many knits were highly textural. Sweatshirt fleece was explored for fashion. Popular surface ornamentation included studding, beading, rhinestones, and other sparkly embellishments.

Celebrity influence on activewear trends was strong, with fitness videos encouraging aerobic exercise. Australian pop star Olivia Newton-John modeled current trends in her video *Let's Get Physical*. American runner Florence Griffith Joyner favored high-cut legs on her running gear, influencing activewear design.

Dusters, loose unconstructed coats, were especially popular for transition seasons or over tailored suits. Many overcoats were mid-calf length, with an oversize cut, strong shoulder lines and deep armholes. Some were belted. Graphic plaids and tweeds were popular. Blouson jackets were often made of leather, and frequently trimmed with fur collars.

Occasion dressing was important. Cocktail dresses were an essential feature of fashion, and the short dress for evening, sometimes worn with a hat, was an important concept. Silk taffeta made a comeback for dramatic evening looks, used in full skirts, leg-of-mutton sleeves and volumetric ruffles and peplums. Some evening dresses combined a full taffeta skirt with velvet bodice. Other evening and special occasion options included tuxedo-inspired pantsuits and dresses, strapless and one-shouldered gowns, and glamorous evening jumpsuits. Couture strongly reasserted the role of trim and embellishment for status-conscious dressing.

After mid-decade, designers including Romeo Gigli, Christian Lacroix, and Emanuel Ungaro promoted a new look, and an aggressive return to a softer, less rigid style with more body definition. The fashion press inflated these new styles into another "New Look":

> Most women of the baby boom generation went from blue jeans to blue suits. They went from one uniform to another. They've spent years competing in a man's world and now they're rediscovering their femininity.[3]

But, as with many such changes in the past, the public adopted the styles in a gradual way; boxy shoulder-padded silhouettes continued to linger into the early 1990s.

Accessories

Accessories were very important as fashion accents and status symbols. Many hat styles were in vogue. Berets were popular, often decorated with brooches. Felt gaucho hats and fedora variations were also worn. Black headwear was especially popular. Some versatile felt and fabric hats folded up at front or side, or all the way around, for a dramatic crown-like silhouette. Stephen Jones created some of the decade's most creative pieces for individual clients as well as runway showings. Surrealism was an important influence on millinery, especially at the couture level.

Pumps returned to fashion; most were slender with thin soles, pointy or almond-shaped toes, and conical heels. Some had very high-cut vamps, leaving a narrow opening for the foot. For evening, lower vamps exposed the instep and "toe cleavage" and these shoes generally had higher heels. Some evening shoes were decorated with bows and other details; shoe clips were sold to dress up plain shoes. "Tuxedo pumps," low-heeled black patent pumps with flat black bows, were also worn for evening. Daytime pumps were considered standard for work, usually in dark-colored leather, suede, or reptile. In a unique twist on workwear, many American women wore sneakers during their commute – a style said to have begun during the New York City transit strike in 1980 – and then changed into pumps at the office, as highlighted

KRIZIA

SHADES OF FASHION

Corey Hart had his first hit single, "Sunglasses at Night," in 1983 from his debut album *First Offense*, with a film noir-style music video that featured a sunglass-wearing Hart and sunglass-wearing extras. Sunglasses were, of course, nothing new and the trend for their increased high fashion presence can be detected by the late 1970s. Ray-Ban Wayfarers, first introduced in the 1950s, were catapulted to renewed popularity when Tom Cruise wore the style in *Risky Business* in 1983 – and again in *Rain Man* (1988). Aviator-style glasses, another Ray-Ban design (dating back to the 1930s and worn by General Douglas MacArthur during World War II) were very popular and widely copied throughout the 1980s, often with mirrored lenses; another Cruise film, *Top Gun* (1986), encouraged their continued popularity into late in the decade. Vuarnet, a decades-old French company, was another brand with remarkable appeal. The renewed interest in these classic manufacturers is a good example of the decade's taste for established high-status brands. In addition, stylish new manufacturers such as Sanford Hutton Colors in Optics were well asserted in the marketplace. 1950s-style "cat-eye" shapes, such as those worn by Catherine Deneuve in *The Hunger*, also enjoyed widespread popularity. Frames in various pastel shades were available to match fashionable, playful, colorful clothing. Counterfeit knockoffs of high-end sunglasses were widely available, often stamped with phony names such as "Ban Ray." Fashion editorials and advertisements – even runway shows – featured models wearing sunglasses to a degree not seen before, including such brands as Calvin Klein, Krizia, Emanuel Ungaro, and Giorgio Armani, among many others. During the 1980s, virtually no daytime outfits (and even some for evening) were truly complete without sunglasses.

Judith Leiber's opulently decorated minaudières hold just enough for a gala evening.

in the 1988 film *Working Girl*. Other popular shoe styles included streamlined loafers, ghillies, Oxfords, and, for summer, fisherman sandals and plastic "jellies." Shoes from French designers Charles Jourdan and Maud Frizon were particularly desirable. Boots ranged from ankle to knee height. Many boots were cuffed or worn slouched down, creating volume around the ankle. Legwear was very varied; lace, fishnet, and other patterns were extremely popular for pantyhose and tights. Seamed stockings and pantyhose were seen for evening. Some women wore patterns over solids, creating a layered look. Ankle socks were also worn in layers, sometimes in contrasting colors such as neon brights or black and white.

Handbags were as varied as shoes, with the same separation between day and evening. Bags from Coach and from Louis Vuitton, with the company's distinctive quatrefoil pattern, were particularly prestigious. Many daytime shoulder bags had equestrian details, and room for leather-bound datebooks from Filofax. Envelope bags and clutches were also popular, sometimes decorated with leather bows or art deco-style accents. Some small shoulder bags had very long, thin straps that were sometimes worn across the body. Boxy, structured handbags were also seen, especially with tailored daywear. Minaudières by Judith Leiber, prized for evenings out, were "just big enough to accommodate a lipstick, a comb, and a one-hundred dollar bill," according to socialite Pat Buckley.[4]

Jewelry was often large, or worn in multiples. A pronounced historic influence was seen in jewelry design. Pearls, real or faux, were fashionable, as were oversize crosses and rosaries and brooches; the style was encouraged by Madonna. High-collared blouses were often accented with cameos or other Victorian-inspired pieces at the neck. Bold costume jewelry was promoted by Karl Lagerfeld's revitalization of the Chanel style. Other prominent designers included Isabel Canovas, Paloma Picasso, and Angela Cummings. Earrings were large, sometimes reaching almost to the shoulder in chandelier-like forms or long, spiky shapes. Button earrings were also popular. Fingerless gloves were another fashionable accessory – available at the designer level, such as those by Gaultier, in artfully ragged versions from Comme des Garçons, and in more mainstream lacy styles. Hermès scarves were seen as the perfect accessory, worn at the neck, as belts or hairbands, or even as short skirts.

Designers: France

Leading names at the ready-to-wear level included **Jean-Charles de Castelbajac** (b. 1949), **Agnès B.** (b. 1941), **Daniel Hechter** (b. 1938), and knitwear leader **Sonia Rykiel**. However, much attention was directed to top designers, those working in ready-to-wear and couture. The birth of a new couture house – Christian Lacroix – and the revitalization of the Chanel brand added excitement to the Paris fashion scene.

Yves Saint Laurent celebrated the twentieth anniversary of his house in 1982, and the following year was the subject of a retrospective exhibition at the Metropolitan Museum of Art curated by Diana Vreeland. Saint Laurent's work continued to show varied inspirations, maintaining his orientalist themes of the late 1970s, such as his black sheath evening ensemble with massive projecting Siamese-style shoulders in 1980. He explored diverse inspirational sources ranging from Monet to Schiaparelli, and including unabashedly romantic and historic themes. His luxurious designs of the early 1980s contributed strongly to the development of the glamour of the decade, and encouraged the new silhouette. His Rive Gauche boutique and menswear line continued to be highly successful. Two new fragrances were launched, Kouros for men in 1981, and Paris in 1983. As the decade went on, Saint Laurent's role as a trendsetter diminished, and his pre-eminence in French couture declined in the wake

of newer, celebrated talents. Nonetheless, he continued to dress many of the world's most fashionable, elite women.

Despite minimal formal training in fashion, **Claude Montana** (b. 1949) founded a ready-to-wear company in 1979, and launched his menswear line, Montana Hommes, in 1981. He immediately became known for innovative designs in leather that ranged from waist-length biker jackets to full-length trench coats to swirling capes. For his own label and for the Italian brand Complice, Montana promoted a wide-shouldered, hourglass silhouette. His designs mixed luxury materials with S&M references to produce a powerful glamour. Architectural hats and details such as metal studs and oversize lapels reinforced Montana's hard-edged look.

Thierry Mugler (b. 1948) had training in dance and experience in the corps de ballet of a regional company, a focus that informed his theatrical, body-conscious fashions. He worked in a trendy Paris boutique and as a freelance designer for several fashion houses. After success with his Café de Paris line, he established his own house in 1974. His aesthetic was dramatic, at times even campy. He was one of the first to advocate the strong-shouldered silhouette; by 1980 Mugler was already showing futuristic jumpsuits with sharp padded shoulders and cinched waists. Mugler's work showed influence from the 1940s with details such as narrow skirts, swing-style coats, and peplums.

The opening of **Christian Lacroix**'s (b. 1951) couture house in 1987 indicated the renewed interest in haute couture, as it was the first new house to open since Saint Laurent in 1961. A native of the south of France, Lacroix studied literature and art history before moving to Paris in 1973. He worked for a public relations firm, then became assistant designer at Hermès where he stayed until 1981. That year he joined the house of Patou, soon becoming head designer. At Patou he developed his aesthetic of daring color combinations and historic silhouettes, revitalizing the venerable establishment. When he opened his own house, Lacroix was already an acclaimed designer. He received France's Golden Thimble (*Dé d'or*) award in 1986 and 1988. He became particularly renowned for his frivolous evening looks, often inspired by the past – especially the 18th century – and colorful regional pieces from the south of France and Spain. Lacroix emphasized luxurious materials and used silk taffeta, lace, and fur lavishly. His "pouf" dresses, with very short bouffant skirts, epitomized the extravagance of the era: admired and widely imitated when they were first introduced, and then condemned at the end of the decade, after the fashion for fantasy had passed.

Emanuel Ungaro enjoyed a return to the forefront of fashion late in the decade, after several years outside of the spotlight. His 1987 and 1988 work represented the return to femininity that had been missing in the V-shaped hard chic popular since the beginning of the decade. Publisher John Fairchild exclaimed, "Ungaro is the most daring designer in Paris," and the press was quick to lavish praise, ironically making the long-established designer an overnight triumph:

There is no designer in Paris who endorses dressing up the way Emanuel Ungaro does. The long-reigning master of the female form is once again a springtime sensation: his bright pretty clothes express today's fashion mood, invite his wealthy customers to part with thousands of dollars and inspire American knockoff artists to create more affordable copies for everyone else.[5]

His short, draped silk "wrap" dresses were best sellers. A sexy body-hugging fit was prominent in his work. Ungaro favored vivid jewel tones and black. Frequently prints were seen, from rococo florals, to black and white abstracts and flamenco polka dots. Ruffles and shirring were common details, and evening gowns featured large bows and puffy sleeves; sometimes sleeves blossomed like roses on a woman's shoulder. Particularly striking were his floral silk evening suits of cocktail dress and matching coat with black velvet facings.

Interested in fashion since his childhood in a suburb of Paris, **Jean Paul Gaultier** (b. 1952) began his career at Cardin when he was just eighteen. He briefly worked for Jacques Esterel, then moved to Patou. He returned to Cardin for about two years before launching his own collection in 1976 – a group of woven straw dresses that established his experimental approach to fashion. Often referred to as an *enfant terrible*, Gaultier continually challenged convention, featuring form-fitting dresses with cone-shaped bra bodices, corsets and bustiers, unisex looks, and witty variations on French staples such as the beret and sailor jersey. Beginning in 1985, he offered skirts for men – a recurring theme in his work. Gaultier's brash fashion was favored by an avant-garde clientele, as well as performers ranging from David Bowie to French accordionist Yvette Horner.

In 1983 **Karl Lagerfeld** became artistic director at **Chanel**, at that time a languishing fashion house. Lagerfeld had had years of experience at Chloé and Fendi, and his revitalization of the brand included an ironic examination and re-presentation of iconic Chanel elements such as chain trim, quilting, and patent leather. Lagerfeld said his aim was to let Chanel "come from the house of Chanel, not from copiers and those who render homage to her."[6] One of the standout pieces in his debut couture collection, a long black dress decorated with rows of *trompe l'œil* "jewels" sewn around the neck and wrists, alluded to Coco Chanel's jewelry collection. Archetypal tweed suits were updated in bolder tweeds, narrower cuts, and exaggerations of detail such as multiple pocket flaps. The initial collection was hailed as a triumph for Lagerfeld and the house enjoyed increased visibility and renewed prestige, even among young customers. Two Chanel models were instrumental in promoting the updated image: slim brunette Inès de la Fressange, and Carole Bouquet, who was also a Bond girl in *For Your Eyes Only* (1981). Lagerfeld's strategy, combining judicious use of the house's archives with a nod to current trends, set a standard for the numerous brand makeovers that affected the fashion industry in coming years.

Azzedine Alaïa (b. 1940) was born in Tunisia, and attended the Ecole des Beaux-Arts in Tunis; after moving to Paris in 1957 he worked briefly for Christian Dior, and then for Guy Laroche. Striking out on his own in the 1970s as a private dressmaker, he launched his first ready-to-wear collection in 1980. Prominent editorial coverage soon followed, and success came very quickly, as his collections were sold in major exclusive department stores. In 1984 he won two awards at the newly created French "Oscars de la Mode." In addition to his Paris boutique, he opened stores in New York and Beverly Hills. Alaïa was the master of drape and cut, often working directly on the body to achieve the finely tuned fit of his sleek, figure-hugging, draped clothes. He took great inspiration from Madeleine Vionnet, as well

Azzedine Alaïa fits performer Grace Jones, a frequent client, in one of his signature body-hugging dresses in 1985.

as from the spandex activewear popular in the decade, and his tightly fitting clothes earned him the nickname "king of cling." Alaïa also featured crisp boxy silhouettes, and an inventive use of materials, utilizing denim with diagonal zippers, and leather with grommets as a decorative element. *Connoisseur* argued that:

> His clothes call for women who can comfortably renounce established ideas of "dressing up" and who at the same time are beyond wearing the uniform of someone or other's fashion "revolution."[7]

His celebrity clientele was notable, from French aristocrats to American rock divas: according to British *Vogue*, Alaïa aimed to make his diverse "customers look almost as sensational as his models."[8] Grace Jones, a frequent client, showcased his draped designs beautifully on her statuesque figure.

The first African American designer to establish a successful business in Paris, **Patrick Kelly** (1954–1990) was born in Mississippi, attended Parsons in New York, and started his design career in France. During his brief but successful career, Kelly rapidly earned a reputation for crisp clothes with witty details. He often decorated simple dresses and suits, even gloves, with colorful buttons and bows. Exclusive boutiques and department stores carried his work. Celebrity clients, including Madonna and Isabella Rossellini, appreciated daywear as simple as his solid-color tank dresses, and lively evening pieces such as a black wool bustier dress printed with red hearts, stars, and lips.

Several Japanese designers in Paris provoked the fashion establishment with their avant-garde aesthetic. While these designers resisted being labeled as "the Japanese," they were all known for unusual – often oversized – silhouettes, highly textural fabrics and artistic store decor and merchandising. The similarity between their designs for both sexes and their tendency to offer clothes only in one size perplexed customers. Although early in the decade many questioned their relevance and wearability, the Japanese designers proved their staying power. Their influence on emerging designers, especially in Belgium, was significant.

Seen here with a group of models in 1987, Patrick Kelly designed exuberant, colorful clothes, often adding masses of bows and plastic buttons as embellishment.

Issey Miyake continued to show in Paris. His collections were often marked by experimentation with materials and an architectural approach. His outerwear was especially striking, ranging from wide blanket coats to futuristic nylon ponchos. Miyake's designs varied considerably; standout designs included simple printed cotton dresses inspired by global textiles, wide parachute-style pants gathered at the ankle, crinkled cotton separates, and unique accessories, including a wool hat with felted "dreadlocks." The 1989 publication of a book of Irving Penn photographs of Miyake's work reinforced his image as a creator of sculptural clothing.

The work of **Rei Kawakubo** featured slashes and cut-outs, asymmetry, and creative fabric treatments. Jackets and tops were often oversized with wide sleeves and deep armholes. Kawakubo used wrapping and tying for skirts, trousers, and even booties. She showed her collections on models in flat shoes, wearing no make-up or with unusual face painting. Kawakubo consistently pursued an individual aesthetic, saying that her designs were for a woman who "is not swayed by what her husband thinks. One who can stand by herself."[9] Her work ran counter to prevailing designer trends and was embraced by young women and the artistic avant-garde. Kawakubo's Comme des Garçons boutiques were known for their minimalist interiors, with merchandise displayed as in an art gallery.

The son of a dressmaker, **Yohji Yamamoto** (b. 1943) studied law before attending Bunka Fashion College. When he began designing fashion in the late 1970s, he said it was just to be able to work in his mother's shop. But after success in Tokyo, he showed a collection in Paris in 1981 with Rei Kawakubo, his then partner, where his work was simultaneously described as shocking and inspirational. Ensembles combined traditional Japanese elements such as kimono sleeves, quilting, and indigo with layering and menswear details. Yamamoto's use of head-to-toe black was seen as a particular challenge in an era of decorative fashion.

Born into a family in the kimono business, **Mitsuhiro Matsuda** (1934–2008), who also studied at Bunka, designed under the label Nicole as well as his own name. Much of Matsuda's work was distinguished by a minimalist aesthetic and quirky detailing. His suits for men and women applied a softer aesthetic to traditional tailoring and were much appreciated by customers in creative industries. Matsuda was also a pioneer in designer eyewear, applying his architectural sensibility to frames and sunglasses.

Designers: Britain

Established designers coexisted with new talents. **Jean Muir** continued to pursue her relaxed sensibility, offering pieces in a variety of materials including soft suede and tweeds. **Zandra Rhodes** excelled at creating theatrical cocktail and evening dresses in lightweight silk jersey, lamé, and layers of colored chiffon. Distinctive details included frayed hems, feather edging, and scattered beading. Rhodes became a fixture of London style and also found success among North American customers. **Alistair Blair** (b. 1956) trained in Paris and worked with Dior, Givenchy, and Chloé. He presented his first collection under his own name in 1986, showing New Look-inspired dresses in assertive colors. **Bruce Oldfield** (b. 1950) was celebrated for his special occasion clothes and included Princess Diana among his prominent clientele. He opened his first shop in 1984.

Particularly notable in London fashion during the decade was **Catherine Walker** (1945–2010). Born Catherine Baheux in northern France, and educated at the University of Lille and the University of Aix-en-Provence, she went to Britain during the 1960s. She opened her own shop, the Chelsea Design Company, with her husband Saïd Ismael as partner, in 1976. She offered smart childrenswear, often based on classic sailor middies, and then added maternity wear. By 1981, a women's dress collection was offered. The company grew rapidly and began to be featured in fashion editorials. It was the maternity clothes that first attracted Walker's most notable client, Diana, Princess of Wales, when she was pregnant with Prince William. In 1982, after William's birth, Diana began wearing a wider range of Walker designs, and it was

Princess Diana at Ascot in 1988 wearing a smart daytime formal ensemble by Catherine Walker, with carefully coordinated accessories.

when the princess requested coats that Walker expanded her business into tailored pieces. For Diana – and in her work in general – Walker looked to classic styles for inspiration, often the 1940s, and was captivated with the idea of the elongation of the silhouette, placing great attention on the treatment of the waistline. The shy Walker eschewed the spotlight of celebrity designer status; she did not stage fashion shows, once telling a reporter she only wanted to sell her designs and not perfume. Walker made several hundred dresses and ensembles for the princess, and she looked to traditions of the royal family, including the pastel colors favored by Queen Alexandra, and to military inspiration. Her evening clothes for Diana were frequently decorated in lavish couture details, such as passementerie, embroidery, and beading. Among her most notable designs for Diana was the so-called "Elvis" dress, a white gown heavily embellished with pearls, with a matching bolero with stand collar, which Diana wore on an official visit to Hong Kong in 1989, and also to the British Fashion Awards the same year.

From her roots as a punk provocateur, **Vivienne Westwood** grew into an important fashion designer. Still working with Malcolm McLaren, she presented her first collection in 1981, entitled "Pirates." The runway show included clothes with romantic, historical inspiration set to a rap soundtrack. Westwood said, "We wanted to see a pageant, so we looked back into history, extracting the most emotional, comic book kinds of themes."[10] After separating from McLaren, Westwood continued to offer juxtapositions of old and new with a global flavor. Her "Buffalo Girls" collection for autumn/winter 1982–1983 featured a Peruvian look (full skirts and bowler hats) and bras worn as outerwear. "Mini-Crini" (1985) included short, full skirts in Harris tweed, launching Westwood's ongoing exploration of British traditions. Often inspired by fine art, Westwood referenced sources as diverse as 18th-century decorative arts, African prints, and contemporary graffiti as her designs captured a wider audience.

Born in Istanbul in 1953, **Rifat Ozbek** (b. 1953) graduated from Central Saint Martin's School of Art in London. After several years working for the Monsoon company, he began designing under his own name in 1984. Ozbek became known for exotic styling and details influenced by his Turkish heritage, including velvets, ogival cut-outs, embroidered moon and stars, and deep color combinations. Other locations, including Mexico, also provided inspiration. A secondary line, Future Ozbek, was launched in 1987. He was named British Designer of the Year in 1988.

Katharine Hamnett (b. 1947) was educated at Central Saint Martin's and started her company in 1979. She featured smart and inventive fashion for men and women, and was particularly known for her t-shirts that featured slogans linked to political and social causes, frequently worn by celebrities. Her London boutique was celebrated for its cutting-edge design. In 1989 she became involved in labor ethics and awareness of the dangers of pesticides used on cotton, prefiguring the sustainability concepts of the 2000s.

Below left Boy George in a Vivienne Westwood shirt, c. 1982. Westwood's influences included graffiti and African textiles.

Below right Among the first designers to call attention to social justice issues, Katharine Hamnett wears one of her slogan t-shirts in 1987.

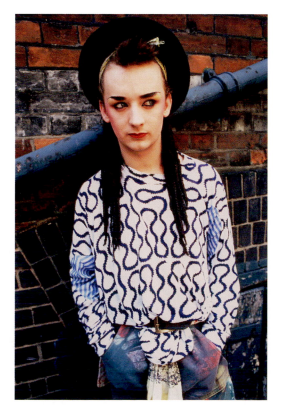

Below Giorgio Armani's suits, for both men and women – refined yet often less constructed than other brands' tailored pieces – represented the ultimate in prestige "power dressing."

Opposite top Brooke Shields in an evening dress by Gianni Versace made of metallic mesh Oroton, photographed in 1983.

Opposite bottom An ensemble by Romeo Gigli, shown in 1989, exemplifies his luxurious use of fabrics and inspiration from Byzantine and medieval sources.

Designers: Italy

The influence of Italian fashion was significant at all levels. The **Missonis** continued their focus on innovative knitwear. **Etro**, another family-owned company, promoted a range of apparel, leather goods, and home furnishings with ethnographic inspiration. Mariuccia Mandelli of **Krizia** offered slinky evening gowns and graphic separates alongside the amusing knits for which she was known. Under the direction of young British co-designers Keith Varty and Alan Cleaver, **Byblos** offered clothes with a youthful focus ranging from bright tartan wool dresses to colorful "gypsy" ensembles, often with interesting surface detail. The company was also successful with updated menswear. **Benetton** grew from a family-owned knitting business to a highly visible international empire. As they expanded throughout Europe into North America and Asia, Benetton also diversified their products by adding sportswear, sporting goods, homewares and watches, becoming one of the largest fashion manufacturers in the world. In the late years of the decade, they debuted their controversial United Colors of Benetton advertisements which addressed social issues.

Giorgio Armani (b. 1934) became the foremost Italian designer of this decade, rising from a little-known suit designer to a household name. A cover story in *Time* magazine

in 1982 credited the designer with popularizing "elegance without stricture" and "tailoring of a kind thought possible only when done by hand."[11] Excellence in both menswear and women's fashion was important to his success. While his women's collections included separates and dresses, it was the tailored pieces that made his reputation. He offered tailored clothing to women at a time when professional dressing was important but women did not want to feel constrained by their clothing. The "Armani attitude" expressed relaxed elegance, marked by unusual color combinations and a fit that was comfortable without being sloppy. Clients repeatedly spoke of the perfect curve of armholes, angle of pockets and placement of pleats. While the designer consistently pursued his individual aesthetic he was not immune to popular culture; early in the decade his clothes for women showed an "Annie Hall" influence and men's outerwear suggested inspiration from Indiana Jones. As the decade wore on, he advocated more restraint in color and a narrower silhouette. Renowned for his work ethic and business focus (he once said, "I cannot allow myself the luxury of waiting for 'the moment of inspiration'"[12]), Armani established several lower-priced lines including Armani Jeans and Emporio Armani; and diverse product offerings, including prestigious eyewear, contributed to his global success.

Having opened his own boutique in 1978, **Gianni Versace**'s swift success led to a global presence: by 1980 the line was available throughout Europe, the United States, and Asia. Versace's clothes could be aggressive yet playful, featuring bold use of color and stripes, uneven hemlines, piecing, and color blocking. He featured influences from regional dress, often Central Asian, and from historic sources, playing with drapery and blouson, tassels and fringe. His menswear experimented with shape and proportion while his womenswear was dramatic and seductive. Versace also worked as a costume designer, notably in ballet. In his much heralded 1982 women's collection presented at the Paris Opera, Versace began to experiment with a metal mesh fabric that he developed named "Oroton." Its outstanding draping capabilities created remarkably sexy, lustrous, and sleek dresses, combining the warrior effects of Paco Rabanne with the fluidity of Vionnet. He began collaborating with photographer Richard Avedon in 1979, and the arresting photographs in his advertising campaigns strongly contributed to the success of many emerging supermodels.

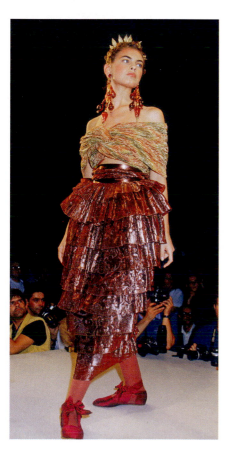

Romeo Gigli (b. 1949) was born in Castel Bolognese, Italy, and studied architecture before working in fashion. He held a variety of fashion-related jobs in the 1970s and debuted his own label in 1983. He established himself as a genuine force in Italian fashion mid-decade, designing under his own name and for Callaghan. His new softer styles prompted the *Los Angeles Times* to declare rhapsodically in 1987:

> It's rare that a single designer, especially a newcomer, can change the course of fashion. But Romeo Gigli, who emerged as a design star last season, has apparently carried it off. Gigli's soft look, body-hugging dresses with draped bubble shaped skirts have influenced the Establishment here. And Milan, usually a bastion of hard edge, sophisticated tailoring, has capitulated to a fall fashion look that is surprisingly rounded and soft.[13]

Gigli's effect on Milan was comparable to Ungaro's in Paris: the herald of new, softer shapes. Inspirations ranged from counterculture street fashion to a myriad of historical, romantic themes, including Byzantine Christianity and Pre-Raphaelite style. Fabrics were luxurious and the use of color sophisticated. Gigli's designs were outside the mainstream and appealed to a selective, individualistic customer.

Franco Moschino (1950–1994) created remarkably witty clothing, combining an appreciation for Surrealism with a sense of humor about the fashion industry. After starting his career as a fashion illustrator and designing for a sportswear company, he showed his first women's collection in 1984. Moschino's company grew rapidly to include menswear, jeans, fragrance, and the lower-priced Cheap and Chic line. He offered well-tailored silhouettes enlivened with comical details such as oversize gloves as pockets, prints based on other designers' logos, and clustered teddy bears as a neckline treatment. Clients such as Princess Gloria von Thurn und Taxis appreciated the designer's antics and his witty advertising campaigns. Although his designs were too eccentric to appeal to a mainstream customer, Moschino created some of the most striking fashion images of the decade.

Gianfranco Ferré (1944–2007) was born in Legnano, and like his countrymen Gianni Versace and Romeo Gigli he trained as an architect before embarking on a fashion career. He began as an accessories designer, then launched his first label, Baila, in 1974. He added menswear in 1982 and debuted Ferré, a fragrance for women, in 1984. He was well respected in the Italian fashion industry, earning the Occhio d'Oro award several times. Ferré assumed the creative directorship of Christian Dior in 1989, while continuing his own label in Milan. His designs were dramatic, frequently opulent, and sometimes witty. Architectural structure and geometric details were common, and he often utilized overt historic inspirations and borrowings from menswear. Sculptural evening gowns were often detailed with couture flights of fancy such as elaborate gardens of fabric leaves and flowers.

Valentino's career continued to build, as the dramatic elegance of his designs perfectly suited the prevailing tastes of the decade, and provided the prestige that the wealthy sought. His established product catered to the middle-aged wealthy woman who eschewed more experimental styles. Evening gowns in his signature Valentino red were mainstays for well-dressed society women, and he often showed diaphanous florals and unabashed historical references. An energetic advertising campaign featured models leaping through the air in his elegant evening gowns or tailored ensembles. His menswear was equally refined. Valentino's cut was often a bit narrower than that of other designers with precise details such as sharply peaked jacket lapels and reduced trouser pleats.

Roberto Capucci combined a highly developed skill for cut (reminiscent of Charles James and Cristóbal Balenciaga) with a vivid color sense. Genuinely going to extremes, Capucci created gowns that sometimes resembled origami or paper lanterns, and often featured a profusion of sun-ray pleats. The complex and voluminous evening gowns provided a whiff of escapade to adventurous customers.

Designers: United States

A number of well-established American designers saw continued success, including **Bill Blass**, **Arnold Scaasi**, and **Oscar de la Renta**. Their high-quality, wearable designs for day and evening were in demand by major socialites, political figures, and celebrities including American First Ladies Nancy Reagan and Barbara Bush and television personality Barbara Walters. **Geoffrey Beene**'s designs took on a new wit and geometry, with curved seams and panels of contrasting fabric, and won him a new audience. Always innovative with materials, Beene had begun designing for men. Comfort was a priority; he even foresaw the possibility of evening sweaters for men, worn with his signature gray flannel trousers.

Top Franco Moschino's theatrical runway presentations showcased his witty fashions, as seen in this ensemble from fall/winter 1988, featuring "fur" trim made of teddy bears.

Above Gianfranco Ferré's elegant ball gown from 1988 exemplifies his dramatic design sense and masterful construction skills.

James Galanos, "the keeper of the couture flame in America,"[14] enjoyed renewed interest in his prestige label, in large part because he was a favorite designer of Nancy Reagan; she wore Galanos gowns on many important occasions, including the 1980 presidential inaugural gala. Galanos maintained a following among women of the United States' economic elite. His exquisitely detailed gowns displayed inventive but restrained chic, favoring timeless style over trend, and his construction standards were perhaps the finest in the nation.

Victor Costa (b. 1935) was the "King of the Copycats" who made very near knockoffs of couture gowns. He offered the look of Ungaro or Lacroix to socialites on a budget and celebrities who required numerous party dresses. Born in Houston, Costa was educated at Pratt Institute, and L'Ecole Chambre Syndicale de la Haute Couture (where his classmates included Yves Saint Laurent and Karl Lagerfeld). He began his career in bridalwear during the late 1950s and early 1960s. By the late sixties, he was specializing in Paris copies, and created his own label in 1975. During the affluent and aspirational 1980s, his dresses enjoyed great popularity. The decline in the economy late in the decade actually encouraged his business, as many society women needed to tighten their belts and substituted Costa's products for their previous Paris purchases. His work was often used by costume designers in American "Night Time" soap operas, and a black and white Costa gown was worn by Holly Hunter in the film *Broadcast News*. *Newsweek* observed in 1988, "Victor Costa … is officially in vogue. Offering low prices in the world of high fashion, the affable Texan has found his way into the closets of women on the best dressed lists," and he included Ivana Trump and Betsy Bloomingdale among his clients.

Above A red dress with a dropped waist from 1980 by Oscar de la Renta, a designer favored by the international social set, especially for evening and formal occasions.

Below Ralph Lauren reinvigorated American classics, here mixing patterned knits and buffalo checked flannel.

Calvin Klein was at the forefront of American fashion as the decade began; he maintained his relaxed good taste and continued his updated takes on the great American sportswear traditions with elegance and his characteristic sense of restrained chic. "Klein has an extraordinary knack for anticipating what people will want to wear," declared the fashion author Bernadine Morris in 1980.[15] He received the Council of Fashion Designers of America (CFDA) award in both 1981 and 1983. Calvin Klein Jeans became a fixture of popular culture with the introduction of Brooke Shields as his spokesmodel in television advertisements asking, "You wanna know what comes between me and my Calvin's? Nothing." The success of his menswear lines grew, and he debuted his men's underwear in 1982, with provocative advertising photographed by Bruce Weber. Designer underwear was a new, notable development in men's underwear history. Klein's entrance into the fragrance market created best sellers including Obsession (1985), Obsession for Men (1986), Eternity (1988), and Eternity for Men (1989).

Ralph Lauren continued to build on his patrician theme and added Western and prairie influence and Victorian style. Markedly apt for the status-conscious 1980s, "his clothes appeal to a fantasy of belonging: to clubs, boards, cliques, and ultimately to a former aristocracy."[16] Inspiration from sport was essential, including the continued success of his polo shirts for both men and women. His equestrian logo was emblazoned on shirts as well as neckties, scarves, and a wide variety of other accessories, as well as his men's cologne, Polo (which debuted in 1978). His business grew substantially, and in 1981 Lauren opened a store in London. In 1984, he moved his flagship retail operation into the former Rhinelander mansion on Madison Avenue in New York. The new store strongly emphasized Lauren's overall elite lifestyle-driven approach, merchandising the clothes within a store decorated with oriental rugs, equestrian oil paintings and leather-upholstered furniture. Diffusion continued, and was significant. Lauren founded Ralph Lauren Home in 1983, and offered a lower-priced menswear label, Chaps.

Perry Ellis was born in Virginia and studied at William & Mary, then studied retailing at New York University. He began his career in department stores as a buyer and merchandiser in the 1960s. With the launch of his labels Portfolio in 1976 and Perry Ellis International in 1978 he grabbed immediate attention, prompting comments such as "Perry Ellis is likely to be one of the names to be reckoned with in the 1980s."[17] A success in both menswear and womenswear, he branched out into a variety of accessories and housewares. Ellis' clothes were relaxed and sexy, and he took traditional styles and gave them an offbeat, often playful twist. His designs often featured full skirts with wide waistbands, or a loose, dropped-waist silhouette. He was particularly known for his sweaters which were frequently long and baggy, as well as short bolero styles, often with color blocking in unusual color combinations and a variety of textural stitches. In 1984 he started Perry Ellis America with Levi Strauss, and his underwear for men competed with Calvin Klein with similarly erotic advertising. Ellis won eight Coty Awards from 1979 to 1984, and a CFDA award in 1983. His premature death in 1986 shocked the fashion industry.

Donna Karan (b. 1948) left Anne Klein in 1984 and established her own line of womenswear. She showed her first collection the following year and immediately received praise for her relevant, sophisticated designs. She offered career wear with a distinctly urban sensibility and promoted black as a fashion color. She advocated bodysuits as a stylish and practical concept. Karan believed in "strong basics" and versatility, saying she used her own wardrobe needs as a benchmark for her customers. Perennial key pieces in her collections included slim black skirts and shapely black sweaters, accented with brightly colored jackets. Luxurious overcoats were another specialty, often paired with dramatic hats. She emphasized wrapping, showing surplice tops and sarong skirts. By the end of the decade, Karan launched her lower-priced DKNY line and was considered the "Queen of Seventh Avenue."

New talent **Stephen Sprouse** (1953–2004) briefly interned for Bill Blass and spent several years working for Halston. He first gained recognition with his designs for Debbie Harry of the group Blondie. His rise to prominence was rapid with a *Vogue* cover in 1982 and a Coty Award in 1983. Sprouse's modernist aesthetic of bright colors, hints of androgyny, and punk-influenced details appealed to an art-world clientele. He closed his business in 1985 but reopened in 1987 with backing and established three lines at different price levels. Despite notoriety gained from pieces such as camouflage mini dresses and orange sequined jeans, Sprouse closed his business again in 1988.

Native New Yorker **Norma Kamali** (b. 1945) graduated from the Fashion Institute of Technology. By 1978 she was designing for her own boutique, OMO ("On My Own"), and by 1980 had a licensing agreement with Jones Apparel, a major Seventh Avenue firm. Her designs ranged from full-length down coats to revealing swimsuits. Kamali was especially well known for spandex bodywear suitable for exercise or as one layer in an ensemble. Sweatshirt fleece became another signature fabric, used for tunics, knickers, and blousons, as well as shapely shoulder-padded dresses. She also designed for children. Kamali launched a fragrance line in 1985 and OMO Home in 1988. She received Coty Awards in 1981, 1982, and 1983 and CFDA Awards in 1982 and 1985, and she was also recognized by the American Institute of Architects for the design of her building on West 56th Street.

Sandra Garratt (b. 1954) grew up in California's Malibu Valley. After schooling at the Fashion Institute of Design and Merchandising in Los Angeles (FIDM-LA), she worked in New York in the fashion industry. Garratt moved to Dallas and began to create "modular" clothing that had quick local success under the label Units. In 1989 she debuted Multiples, a line of one-size poly-cotton jersey mix-and-match pieces that could be worn multiple ways, as each piece in the collection could be transformed. For

Above Renowned for her use of sweatshirt fleece, Norma Kamali brought an activewear influence to her fashion collections. Photograph © Steve Landis 1981

Right Sandra Garratt's Multiples offered versatile, simple but striking jersey pieces that could be worn in a variety of combinations.

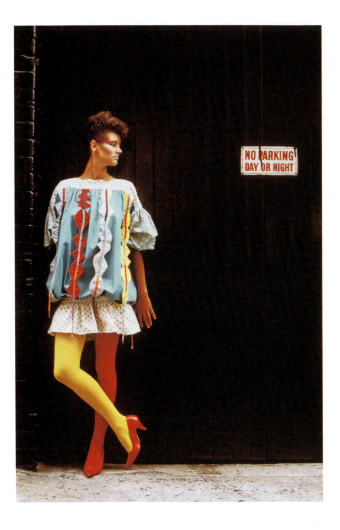

Australian designer Katie Pye used innovative fabric treatments to express her art-driven sensibility, as in this appliquéd dress from c. 1981.

example a tube of fabric could be a strapless dress, a long skirt, or, rolled up at the waist, a short skirt. "It's not just style, it's concept."[18] With striking packaging, sleek in-store display and salespeople trained to demonstrate the versatility of the pieces, Multiples was a fashion expression of the emerging techno-pop aesthetic. Garratt introduced a children's line, and Multiples boutiques were in department stores across the United States, Europe, Australia, and Japan.

Designers: Australia

Australian culture achieved a wider global presence through the work of filmmakers Peter Weir and George Miller, and actors such as Mel Gibson, Rachel Ward, and Judy Davis. The exhibition *Australian Visions* at New York's Guggenheim Museum in 1984 presented the work of contemporary Australian artists. As a counterculture scene in Sydney embraced punk and New Wave aesthetics, the venerable Art Gallery of New South Wales presented the 1980 exhibition *Art Clothes*, featuring the work of eight avant-garde Australian fashion designers. It showcased work that went outside the confines of mainstream dress, and included emerging designer **Katie Pye** (b. 1952).

After art school Pye opened her first boutique, Duzzn't Madder, in Sydney in 1976, selling highly conceptual clothing. She formed Katie Pye Studio in 1979, became involved in costume design, and staged a performance art piece that attracted great notoriety. Pye's clothing was a distinct expression of the post-punk aesthetic, straddling the worlds of performance and fashion. Her inspirations ranged from urban street life to Asian traditional dress; her clothes often made political statements. Some pieces in the 1980 exhibition included sexual and religious imagery and attracted controversy. But the same year some of her designs received retail distribution. In 1982, she received the Australian Council Arts Grant and traveled to Europe and India. Upon returning to Sydney, she staged her 1983 multi-media event, "The Ascension": part fashion show, part theater. Her collection showed influence from Vivienne Westwood and historic elements gleaned from her travels. This was followed by her "Desperados" collection, with primitive and apocalyptic inspiration that earned comparison with the movie *Mad Max*. In an interview in 1983, Pye declared, "What you call fashion, I call product. What I call fashion is art."[19] Although she positioned herself outside of the fashion mainstream, the industry embraced her; Pye won the Australian Fashion Industry New Wave Award in 1984, and their Signet Award in 1985 and counted among her clients fashion model Penelope Tree.

Sydney's avant-garde **Flamingo Park** boutique gained marked recognition when Princess Diana wore their koala bear "Blinky Bill" knit pullover in 1982. The sweater had been a wedding present to the princess from the daughter of the Premier of New South Wales and a variation, "Blinky Di," was soon available as a knit pattern in *Australian Women's Weekly*. The overtly rugged Outback look embodied by Paul Hogan in the Crocodile Dundee films was available from **R. M. Williams**, founded in 1932 by Reginald Murray Williams. **Country Road**, founded in 1975 as a women's shirt company, grew rapidly into a global presence. With stores in the United States by 1988, their version of Australian outdoor style was appreciated by a larger audience.

Hair and Beauty

Hairstyles were often linked to music personalities and other celebrities. Contrast between day and evening looks was important, often achieved with the same haircut styled differently. A woman could wear her hair smooth for day, Princess Diana-style,

Above Deborah Nadoolman Landis' costume for Harrison Ford as Indiana Jones in *Raiders of the Lost Ark* (1981) prompted imitation by many designers and labels, including Armani and Andrew Marc.

Right A bold silhouette combined with refined neutral colors typified the menswear from prestigious label Hugo Boss.

yet be moussed and spiked for evening, like Pat Benatar. Many women wore their hair sleekly brushed back and held in place by a bow at the nape of the neck, a hairband, or a rolled scarf or bandana. Blonde highlights accented shaped, layered haircuts, a style favored by conservative yuppie types. Curly permanents were also popular. Both straight and wavy styles were often chin to shoulder length, worn with a side part. French braids were popular, often ending in low ponytails ornamented with large bows. Countercultural styles included partially shaved hairdos and dreadlocks.

A made-up face was fashionable with distinct looks for day and evening. Eyes were emphasized with shadow and mascara; a smoky eye prevailed for night. Heavy eyebrows – à la Brooke Shields and Princess Caroline of Monaco – were cultivated. Blusher was used to define cheekbones and a renewed focus on lips brought out lipstick in a range of colors from mauve to deep red.

The use of tanning salons grew. Cosmetic surgery became more popular, but was still not openly discussed as a fashionable practice. Multiple ear piercings became more common in mainstream style.

Menswear

Menswear received major attention in the 1980s and many top designers were successful in women's and menswear. As *Vogue* asserted in 1983, "fashion thoughts, these days, bounce back and forth from men's and women's collections."[20] Continental elegance characterized menswear from Saint Laurent, Valentino, and Ferré. Montana, Byblos, and Moschino offered edgier styles, often with exaggeration of silhouette and vivid

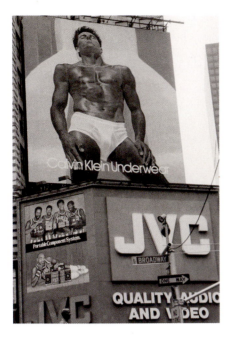

Above Calvin Klein's provocative advertising campaigns included a huge outdoor billboard in New York's Times Square, markedly sexualizing the promotion of menswear.

Below Sportswear with a nautical theme for all ages from Ralph Lauren's Polo line evokes a leisured, upper-class lifestyle.

colors. Traditional looks were revalidated as part of the "dress for success" ideology. Revivals of the 1920s and 1930s, encouraged by film, were especially influential and took many forms; men wore dapper vests, sweaters around their shoulders, neckties as belts, driving caps, and dusters. Country tweeds and blazers with crests were popular. Striped seersucker for summer suits made a comeback. Another retro trend revived 1950s style and men wore iridescent shawl-collared jackets with narrow pants, skinny ties, and abstract print shirts.

Distinctions between Italian and Anglo-American tailoring still existed. Italian styling featured wider shoulders and looser trousers and was consistently described as "elegant but easy." British style was associated with business wear and gentrified leisure. But high fashion menswear often blurred the boundary as designers expressed their individual visions. The Italians, especially Armani and Versace, were renowned for subtle, smoky coloring and tactile fabrications – using lightweight wools, linens, and even silk. More structured suits, often with extremely broad shoulders, from the long-established Italian company Ermenegildo Zegna and venerable German label Hugo Boss, were particularly prestigious. London designer Paul Smith updated English classics, often showing ensembles that combined sophisticated colors and creative patterns to produce an artistic, almost bohemian, effect. American designer Alexander Julian focused on a colorful interpretation of collegiate style. Other influential names included Daniel Hechter and Nino Cerruti. Marithé + François Girbaud were successful in jeans and casual wear. The media presented varied role models for men. Known for his tailored suits and narrow ties, singer Bryan Ferry promoted a moody elegance. Photographs of Olympic pole vaulter Tom Hintnaus in Calvin Klein underwear provided a new chiseled standard of masculine beauty. Charismatic Olympic skier Alberto Tomba showed flair on and off the slopes.

Suits were the dominant look for business and evening. In the early years of the decade, jackets were fitted with natural shoulders and narrow lapels. But they soon widened at the shoulder, reaching extremes in the work of some designers. By mid-decade, the V silhouette of menswear mirrored women's fashion; both emphasized a wide shoulder line tapering down to a narrow waist. Lapels tended to be medium-wide, and many jackets buttoned quite low. The two-button option was popular, exposing a lot of tie or vest. Single- and double-breasted styles were both worn and three-piece suits enjoyed a revival. Formal wear followed the same silhouette as business suits. Vests became a new fashion focus, sometimes made of contrasting suiting fabric, but also seen in silk foulard prints and piqué, ribbed, or cabled knits. Trousers were almost uniformly worn at waist height, or even slightly above. Legs were wide. Pleated-front pants were most common; pleats, including inverted box pleats, were often very deep, even on denim, and multiple pleats produced a very baggy profile. This silhouette narrowed by the end of the decade.

Shirts were frequently cut rather full with a deep armhole – a move away from the body-conscious tapering of the previous decade – and details were important. Perry Ellis' shirts were known for a shoulder-line pleat on each sleeve. Small collars, sometimes held around a tie with a collar pin, were popular. Many men favored solid-colored or striped shirts with contrasting white collars.

A wide range of knits was promoted. Increasingly cotton knits vied with wool in the sweater market. Popular styles included fisherman sweaters; Fair Isles; argyles and similar patterns; ribbed, cabled and flat knit cardigans (some with lapels); crew necks; and V-necks. Knit categories included Italian styles – often wide-necked with low armholes and

Above An African barbershop sign from Togo advertises an array of fashionable hairstyles, each a variation on the popular "fade" cut.

Below An affected bad-boy image, as exemplified by celebrities such as George Michael, impacted even the styling of childrenswear advertising.

distinctive surface texture – and more traditional British/American preppy looks. While many men regarded Japanese suits and jackets as too avant-garde for most occasions, oversized, textural knits from Japanese designers were more easily integrated into the wardrobe. Designer Jhane Barnes, a pioneer in the use of technology in fashion, created computer-generated patterns for her distinctive knits and wovens.

Outerwear options included topcoats, heavier overcoats, often in tweed, and gabardine and poplin raincoats. Waist-length leather blouson jackets were often seen, frequently in black but available in many colors, even white and light tones – a look that was popular in warm weather areas.

Wide-shouldered, low-buttoning jackets made neckties a focal point. Traditional patterns such as paisleys, foulard prints, and wide striped "school" ties in silk repp were all popular. But ties were available in a rainbow of colors and assorted printed and woven patterns including tropical florals, animal motifs, and art deco-inspired geometrics. Ties by Ferré, Fendi, Boss, and Armani were particularly desirable. Very narrow ties, a style often referred to as "New Wave," were seen in black and retro patterns inspired by the 1950s. Ties worn with polo shirts were another version of a New Wave look. Knit ties of silk or lightweight wool, very narrow with a squared-off end, were also popular. Some men wore their ties casually knotted with open-necked shirts, reflecting Italian influence. Pocket squares returned to fashion, sometimes matching the tie but often contrasting. Other important accessories included cufflinks, money clips, and smoking sets. Eyeglasses often showed retro influence; frames in tortoiseshell and a variety of colors were popular. Late in the decade, a fashion for severe steel rims in architectural shapes emerged.

Trends in footwear emphasized quality and many traditional styles were brought into focus including wingtip and two-tone Oxfords and loafers, in tasseled, plain, and "penny" styles. Light-colored suede shoes and "white bucks" – cream-colored nubuck Oxfords with red rubber soles – were promoted for summer wear. Boating shoes (such as Sperry Topsiders) and rugged outdoor boots (L. L. Bean style) were worn for country and outdoor activities. Athletic shoes made a transition from sports to fashion and sneakers were more accepted for general wear. Style groups favored specific brands. Many rap fans favored Adidas; Converse Chuck Taylors were a more New Wave option. Black fabric slip-ons with rubber soles were often worn (with white or bright socks) by young designers to accessorize ensembles. A trend for soft leather Oxfords with paper-thin soles, like those worn by dancers, was seen in the mid-decade.

Hair was often side-parted, slicked back Gatsby-style, or with a slightly wedged look reminiscent of Britain in the 1930s. Men's grooming emphasized neatness and an Establishment look. *Gentleman's Quarterly* addressed this issue in January 1983: "Black men's hair, no longer a political badge, now demonstrates a personal style. The clean-cut versatile looks available for 1983 are suited for business and pleasure."[21] Another trend, attributed to the influence of Michael Jackson, produced more curly styles with a curly forelock on the forehead. White men with curly and wavy hair wore a variation with full, long hair on the forehead, the waves tousled or defined by gel or mousse, with the rest of the hair cut rather close to the head. Graduated "fade" haircuts were seen in the late years of the decade. Men's skin-care products were heavily advertised. The importance of a clean-shaven look was emphasized with promotions of old-fashioned bristle shaving brushes and high-quality razors. Early hints at a revival of tattooing were seen in certain locations, particularly Amsterdam, Tokyo, and San Francisco – even some women were taking to the practice.

Children's Fashion

Major trends in adult fashion were seen in children's clothes as well. The preppy look greatly affected children's fashion. The popularity of cotton piqué polo shirts extended to the young. Children wore miniature blazers, tartan skirts, and other traditional styles on both sides of the Atlantic. The trend for dressing up was reflected in a strong focus on young girls' party dresses, which often resembled their mothers' full-skirted looks. The backlash against synthetic fibers also affected children's clothing. After decades of

Right Advertisements for Italian knitwear company Benetton conveyed a global message and often included international, multi-ethnic groupings.

Below left A German illustration from 1988 shows the traditional styling of much children's fashion, including fair isle knits and jackets in tartan and tweed.

Below right The curly hairstyles, felt hat and beret, large hoop earrings, layering and knits all represent popular styling choices for young women as seen in this ad for junior fashions.

embracing wash and wear, parents returned to the ironing board, laboriously pressing cotton button-down shirts and smocked dresses to achieve a new traditional look.

New Wave and rock influence was also significant as kids were outfitted in leather and leather-look jackets, narrow pants or leggings, and dark sunglasses. Teen boy bands New Kids on the Block and Menudo contributed to youth styles. Popular prints of the time were brightly colored and mixed many elements including geometrics and graffiti. Many children's clothes, especially t-shirts and pajamas, showed imagery from films and television shows, such as *Star Wars* and the Smurfs. Teenage girls imitated Cindy Lauper's thrift shop look and the colorful "Valley Girl" style inspired by the 1983 movie of that name. Hairstyling was equally trendy and salons for children proliferated.

Many brands, including Brooks Brothers and Ralph Lauren, featured children in their advertising, endorsing the idea of family tradition and heritage as consumable values. Benetton's advertising assertively promoted the idea of fashion for all ages. Designer children clothing continued to expand. Established brands were joined by new designers such as Norma Kamali, who was recognized by the industry for her outstanding children's sportswear. As adults began wearing sneakers for street wear, children did too, and athletic shoes started to replace other styles for all but dressy occasions.

The End of the Decade

The economic crash of 1987 and its subsequent ricochet effect set the economic tone for the coming years in much of the world. The decline in wealth-inspired glamour encouraged the growth of "casualization" in dress for the general population; however, many customers were reluctant to give up their status-symbol clothes and accessories, clinging to the jubilee years of the economic bubble. Greater prosperity was developing in Asia, particularly in Japan. As the decade wound to a close, the press observed:

> The new status symbol trend in fashion is being fueled by a rapidly expanding Japanese market that is now buying more "haute" ready to wear than Americans are (Lacroix has just opened four boutiques in Japan); by huge financial conglomerates that now run many fashion houses and know very little about fashion but know big yen; and above all a high fashion buying public that has been confused by wishy-washy journalism: women now prefer to don an Hermès scarf over an old raincoat so that everyone will think they are rich.[22]

In addition to the increasingly international consumer base, design influence was also coming from a new quarter. An important group of young designers emerged from Belgium promoting alternative aesthetics that would become influential on fashion. Changes in economics, shopping habits, technology, and corporate management pointed toward a new configuration for the fashion industry in the coming years.

Despite economic changes approaching the 1990s, luxury accessories such as scarves by Hermès retained status-symbol desirability.

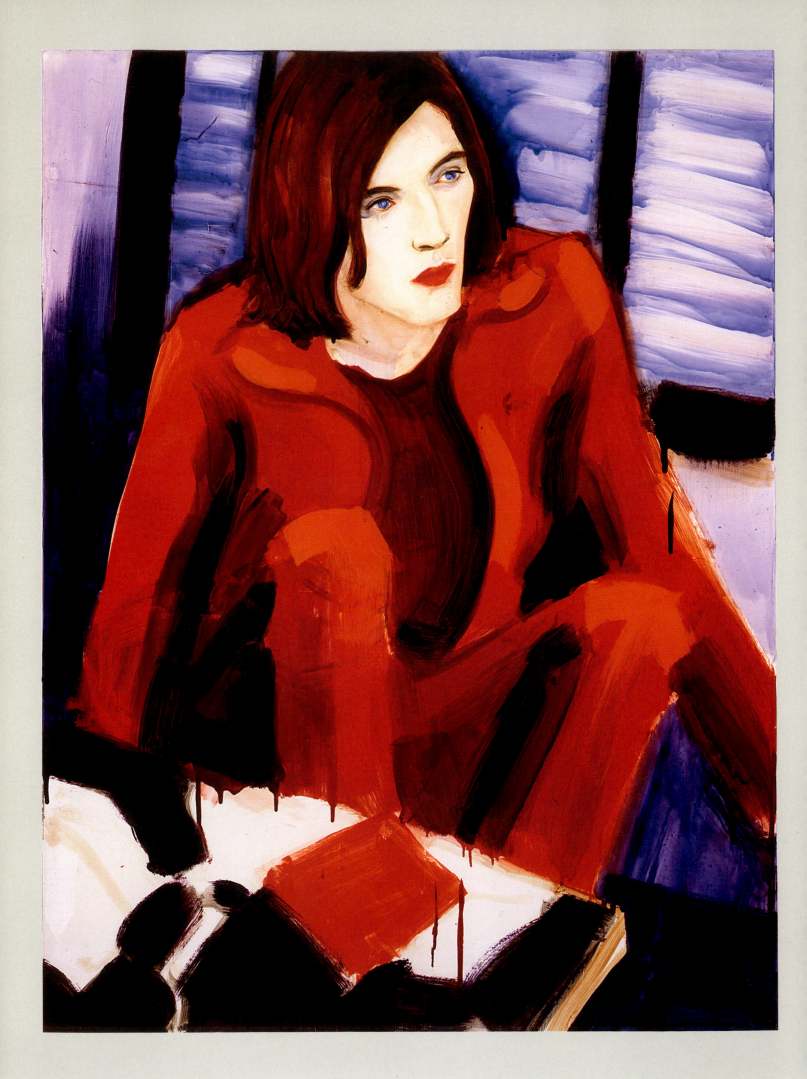

Chapter 12

The 1990s

Subcultures and Supermodels

The 1990s was a decade of extremes and contradictions, a mixture of new ideas and familiar names. High-end stores catered to a variety of niche tastes as sartorial expressions were more fragmented and individualized. Subcultural influences were increasingly asserted, even at the mainstream level. Supermodels embodied glamour and awards shows featured extravagant gowns, while the workplace was more casual and dressing up became a rare occurrence for most people. A number of designers embraced a minimalist aesthetic. The phrase "biker jacket and ball gown" was used to evoke the schizophrenia of fashion, and some designers (and "fashion victims") did indeed combine the two. Britain exerted a strong influence on fashion and the arts, and many of the new talents in fashion design began their careers in London. Runways became theatrical spectacles used to create excitement for selling diffusion products, as brand awareness and the mass marketing of designer trends were extremely acute. The general public aspired to elite style and luxury, but a new definition of luxury had less to do with fine materials and craftsmanship than with recognizable branding. Off-price retail outlets, even counterfeit merchandise,

Opposite Evan reviewing singles of the week for the Melody Maker, a 1997 oil on canvas by Elizabeth Peyton, conveys the androgynous air of much fashion of the decade.

Right Torn and distressed jeans brought the highbrow concept of "deconstruction" to the vernacular level.

abounded for the luxury brand aspirant on a budget. The role of media, while always important to fashion, greatly expanded as more information was conveyed through different forms, augmenting, and even supplanting at times, designers' shows and fashion magazines. The public turned to the entertainment media to find out about fashion and designers and, in turn, the media's obsession with fashion continued to grow.

Social and Economic Background

The beginning of the decade was marked by a recession in many parts of the world, which was largely remedied by 1995. However, financial instability troubled Asia, Japan in particular, toward the end of the decade. The world map changed substantially. In the aftermath of the fall of the Berlin Wall, East and West Germany were reunified. In 1991 the Union of Soviet Socialist Republics split into smaller independent nations. Formerly part of Yugoslavia, Slovenia and Croatia declared their independence in 1991 and other territories soon followed; hostilities between former Yugoslav states continued throughout the decade. During the first Gulf War (1990–1991), an international military coalition liberated Kuwait from occupying Iraqi forces. Leadership instabilities in Haiti and civil war in Somalia demonstrated the extent of unrest in both hemispheres. Tensions continued in China in the aftermath of the 1989 Tiananmen Square massacre, prompting global reaction and protest.

Computer use entered daily life as people increasingly relied on technology for work, communication, and leisure. Online forums, email, and early social networking sites created new "communities," and allowed consumers to shop the global marketplace without leaving their homes. Amazon.com Inc., a pioneer in online shopping, was founded in 1994. The potential of the internet started to transform the fashion industry. Along with this enthusiasm came unease and paranoia as the Y2K scenario suggested the possibility of worldwide computer malfunctions as the end of the millennium approached.

The Arts

The sensationalism of fashion runway shows was paralleled by developments in contemporary art. Several young British artists (sometimes referred to as YBAs), including Damien Hirst, Tracey Emin, and Jake and Dinos Chapman, presented works calculated to shock. Performance art reached an extreme in the body manipulations of Orlan, and Rirkrit Tiravanija transformed galleries into dinner parties. Their work was promoted by an influential art-world circle. A number of exhibitions acknowledged the symbiosis between art and fashion. The 1996 Florence Biennale included work by an international group of artists alongside projects by major fashion designers. Other collaborations encouraged blurring of boundaries, such as Jürgen Teller's photos for Marc Jacobs' advertising campaigns and Prada's contemporary art space. Museum buildings were among the most significant architectural achievements, including Daniel Libeskind's Jewish Museum in Berlin and the Guggenheim Museum in Bilbao designed by Frank Gehry. The shimmery Petronas Twin Towers in Kuala Lumpur were the tallest buildings in the world upon their completion in 1998.

A variety of styles coexisted in interior design. The minimalist aesthetic promoted a revival of clean-lined mid-20th-century furniture and was often favored for urban apartments and retail environments. The principles of feng shui captured the Western public's imagination – clutter was condemned, mirrors repositioned, and walls repainted in more "harmonious" colors. A romantic "Shabby Chic" look was expressed through purposefully faded chintz and distressed paint, encouraged by British television personality Rachel Ashwell. However, opulent glamour was also promoted, for example through the Versace home collection launched in 1992. American tastemaker Martha Stewart expanded her business into a media empire.

Several influential filmmakers, including Ang Lee, Pedro Almodóvar, Yimou Zhang, and the Coen brothers, turned out multiple successes. An international group

Film posters for Pedro Almodóvar's *Kika* (1993) and the Wachowskis' *The Matrix* (1999) reflect trends in graphic design and, with their focus on clothing, demonstrate each film's relation to fashion.

of notable films explored a great range of genres and themes. A dark sensibility was conveyed by *The Silence of the Lambs* (1991) and *Heavenly Creatures* (1994). *Schindler's List* (1993), *Farewell My Concubine* (1993), *La vita è bella* (1997), and *Titanic* (1997) presented history in epic form. The *Three Colors* trilogy (1993–1994) and *The Crying Game* (1992) explored complex human relationships. *La Femme Nikita* (1990), *Pulp Fiction* (1994), *Se7en* (1995), and *Trainspotting* (1996) combined visual sophistication with gritty and violent storylines. Important works of animation included *Beauty and the Beast* (1991) and *Toy Story* (1995). *The Matrix* (1999) and *Star Wars: The Phantom Menace* (1999) set a new standard for science fiction imagery.

Science fiction and fantasy were notable in television programs produced around the globe, including new shows from the *Star Trek* franchise, along with legendary tales such as *Hercules*, *Xena: Warrior Princess*, and *Beastmaster*, and present-day supernatural dramas *Charmed* and *The X Files*. Both sides of the law were represented in police dramas such as *Law and Order* and *Prime Suspect* and the mafia soap opera *The Sopranos*; the fascination with life-or-death medical situations was typified by *ER*.

Best-selling books were equally international and included Helen Fielding's *Bridget Jones's Diary*, Frank McCourt's *Angela's Ashes*, Amy Tan's *The Kitchen God's Wife*, John Berendt's *Midnight in the Garden of Good and Evil*, Robert James Waller's *The Bridges of Madison County*, and Kazuo Ishiguro's *The Unconsoled*. Madonna's 1992 book *Sex* became a controversial best seller, and the first of J. K. Rowling's Harry Potter books was published in 1997.

Many significant theatrical dramas debuted including John Guare's *Six Degrees of Separation*, Tony Kushner's *Angels in America*, and Tom Stoppard's *Arcadia*; David Hare and Martin McDonagh were among the decade's most honored playwrights. Outstanding musicals included *Sunset Boulevard* and *The Lion King*. *Rent* presented

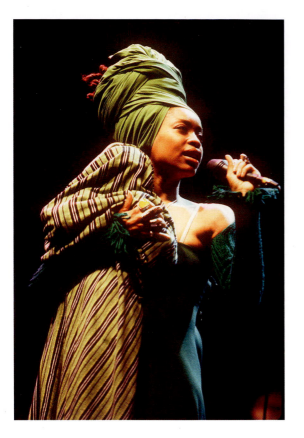

Singer Erykah Badu performs at the 1998 Lilith Fair concert in Pasadena, adorned in one of her dramatic headwraps.

an updated retelling of *La Bohème* set in New York's East Village, with themes of AIDS and drug abuse. *Elisabeth*, the tragic story of Elisabeth of Austria, became the most successful German-language musical of all time.

Popular music genres were more varied than ever, with marked classifications and sub-classifications of music continuing to inspire fashions and style tribes. Nirvana's *Nevermind*, first released in 1991, was arguably the most influential album of the decade, and its tracks became anthems for a generation. Varied genres of popular music were strongly encouraged by festivals and special-event benefit concerts such as Lollapalooza, Lilith Fair, Rock in Rio, and Woodstock '94. Charity musical events were also important including Live Aid, the Tibetan Freedom Concerts in San Francisco, and the Freddie Mercury tribute concerts in London for AIDS-related charities. The Rock and Roll Hall of Fame opened in 1995 in Cleveland. MTV continued its dominant position in the music media, with new international branches of the network throughout Asia, Europe, and South America. Concert tours by North American and European artists became more global in their scope. Latin American music gained a wider audience and tango music was revived.

Composers including Arvo Pärt and John Adams contributed new works to classical music idioms. Aggressively advertised, "The Three Tenors" became a popular sensation, playing stadium venues to capacity audiences. In similar attempts to revive classical music for new audiences, record companies portrayed artists in more youthful and sexy marketing, a trend that perhaps reached its most extreme when French–Italian tenor Roberto Alagna appeared shirtless on the cover of his *Verdi Arias* album.

Fashion Media

British editor Anna Wintour's revamping of American *Vogue* began in late 1988. Wintour's preference for celebrity covers grew but did not completely dominate fashion magazines until the end of the decade. Having launched British *Marie Claire* in 1988, Glenda Bailey was appointed to the American edition in 1996, positioning the magazine as a source for serious journalism as well as fashion information. Other influential journalists included Suzy Menkes, fashion editor of the *International Herald Tribune*, as well as Isabella Blow, Iain Webb, and André Leon Talley.

Supermodels truly gained celebrity status, and the term became even more common in popular culture. The cover of American *Vogue*'s 100th anniversary special issue (April 1992) featured a group photograph by Patrick Demarchelier of the leading supermodels of the time: Christy Turlington, Linda Evangelista, Cindy Crawford, Karen Mulder, Elaine Irwin, Niki Taylor, Yasmeen Ghauri, Claudia Schiffer, Naomi Campbell, and Tatjana Patitz. Other well-known faces (and figures) included Tyra Banks, Carla Bruni, Helena Christensen, Shalom Harlow, Stephanie Seymour, Amber Valletta, and Alek Wek. Tall, aristocratic Stella Tennant was a catwalk favorite and also became the face of Chanel mid-decade. The unconventional looks of Kate Moss and Kristen McMenamy made them favorites with photographers who promoted the anti-glamour aesthetic of the mid-1990s that, at its most extreme, was referred to as "heroin chic." The emergence of Brazilian beauty Gisele Bündchen at the end of the decade marked a return to a curvaceous beauty standard. Prominent photographers included Mario Testino, Nick Knight, Peter Lindbergh, Craig McDean, and Steven Meisel. Independent magazines gained a following among young readers. *Dazed & Confused*, first published in 1992 in London, grew from a one-page fold-out to a professionally produced monthly. *Wallpaper*, another British magazine, debuted in 1996, demonstrating the successful crossover between fashion and the arts.

Stars such as Cate Blanchett, Gwyneth Paltrow, George Clooney, and Pierce Brosnan were featured in the fashion press as "icons" when the phrase "well dressed" was perhaps more appropriate. The arrival of the celebrities at major awards shows, especially the Academy Awards, became prominently featured in telecast pre-shows and the clothing worn by the stars provided opportunities for very visible product placement by designers. The emergence of the internet challenged fashion publications and traditional retail methods. By the end of the decade several sites were offering fashion content, with coverage of runway shows, and many individual designers used their websites to show their collections directly to the public, bypassing the press.

Heroin Chic
The aesthetic of "heroin chic" was related to anti-glamour posturing, and was as much a fashion media construct as it was a bona fide style. It emerged from a number of sources including punk, the grunge aesthetic, and the presence of HIV. Named for its evocation of the worn-out look of drug culture – and reflecting the upsurge in heroin use in the second half of the decade – this photographic style in the fashion press was ubiquitous mid-decade and featured expensive designer clothing on emaciated

Jodie Kidd brought the "heroin chic" look to the catwalk in 1995.

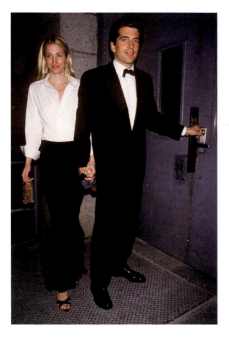

Above John F. Kennedy Jr. and Carolyn Bessette Kennedy caught by photographer Arnaldo Magnani in 1999; her relaxed, minimalist approach to eveningwear is typified by a plain white shirt teamed with a simple black skirt.

Below Julia Roberts and Richard Gere in *Pretty Woman* (1990), with Roberts in the widely copied brown polka dot dress by costume designer Marilyn Vance.

models in dingy settings. Models associated with the style were so extremely thin that they projected a near androgynous as well as unhealthy look, particularly Kate Moss, Jodie Kidd, and Jaime "James" King (herself a heroin abuser at the time). The style emerged and was often seen in independent publications such as *i.D.*, but the aesthetic extended to the mainstream; Calvin Klein's advertisements were often cited as influential examples, including a campaign with Moss and Vincent Gallo. The look became so publicized that it was even lampooned in pop culture, for instance in an episode of the television comedy *Seinfeld*. Those that embraced the style – skinny jeans, worn t-shirts, and dirty sneakers – were often drug addicts who arrived at the look circumstantially. A variety of films, including *Pulp Fiction* and *High Art*, vividly depicted drug abuse. The mainstream news media condemned the fashion industry for its glorification of a drug-abusing lifestyle; even President Bill Clinton denounced it in 1997 as "glorifying death."[1] Such negative criticism was underscored by the death of fashion photographer Davide Sorrenti, boyfriend of James King, at age twenty from complications of heroin abuse, prompting King to enter rehab.

Fashion and Society

Diana, Princess of Wales, fascinated the world as she completed her transformation from Sloane Ranger to princess to best-dressed divorcée. Although she continued to wear the clothes of British designers, Diana began to display a more international flair. In 1997 Diana put seventy-nine of her gowns up for auction at Christie's in New York to benefit AIDS and cancer charities; it was one of the most important society events of the decade. Her life continued to fill the pages of tabloids and the intense media pressure and scrutiny was cited as a contributing factor to her tragic death in Paris on August 31, 1997.

America produced its own brand of "royalty" from members of high society. Chief among these were the Miller sisters, Pia, Marie-Chantal, and Alexandra, the daughters of duty-free tycoon Robert Miller and his Ecuadorean wife. The sisters were constant fodder for the society columns, and appeared in numerous fashion editorials, including shoots for *Vogue* and *Vanity Fair*, which celebrated them as classic beauties, noting "those duty-free dimples, those champagne complexions, those pink Miller manicures, and that fine photographable nose."[2] Also ranking with "American Royalty" was lawyer and magazine publisher John F. Kennedy, Jr., the son of President John F. Kennedy and Jacqueline Bouvier Kennedy. The handsome and athletic Kennedy was a star of popular culture, and a fixture on "eligible bachelor" lists. Kennedy met Carolyn Bessette, a Calvin Klein publicist, and the couple was hounded by paparazzi, so much so that their 1996 wedding in Georgia was kept secret from the media. Bessette wore a strikingly simple wedding dress from **Narciso Rodriguez** (b. 1961) that was widely copied. The 1999 death of the couple, along with Bessette's sister Lauren, in a small-plane crash, was widely covered in the media.

Film and Fashion

Film provided many memorable costumes that had widespread impact on fashion. 1990's *Pretty Woman*, designed by Marilyn Vance, dressed Julia Roberts in ensembles ranging from thigh-high "hooker" boots paired with a vintage band jacket, to a red Valentino-like evening gown. Roberts' brown silk polka dot dress was copied at several price points, including a knock-off available from Victoria's Secret. *Clueless* (1995), designed by Mona May, featured entitled Beverly Hills teenagers with extraordinary designer wardrobes, using tartan plaid (a staple of grunge and punk) to high fashion effect. Helen Hunt's vintage-style red shirtwaist dress by Molly Maginnis in *As Good as It Gets* (1997) was another influential film costume. Michael Kaplan's costumes for *Fight Club* (1999) included thrift

store chic on Brad Pitt that inspired high fashion collections, and was also imitated by young men with an eye for vintage shopping. Kym Barrett's monastic sci-fi costumes for *The Matrix* (1999) spawned imitations at all levels from runway to mass market. Renée Zellweger's black dress in *Jerry Maguire* (1996), by Betsy Heimann, reflected the renewed taste for black dresses in fashion.

Several designers' careers were strongly asserted in the 1990s with films that had important impact on both fashion and visual culture. Richard Hornung's costuming provided sleek sunglassed chic for *The Grifters* (1990), and gave audiences another take on outlaw style in *Natural Born Killers* (1994), mixing skinhead, rock and roll, and Southwestern aesthetics in his designs for the serial-killer couple. Sandy Powell created costumes for a variety of films ranging from influential period pieces – *Interview with the Vampire* (1994), *Shakespeare in Love* (1998) – to the 1970s glam rock styles of *Velvet Goldmine* (1998). Japanese multi-media artist and costume designer Eiko Ishioka won numerous awards for her eclectic costumes for *Bram Stoker's Dracula* (1992), which reflected both the film's Victorian setting and Ishioka's Japanese aesthetic, and were influential on romantic Goth styles and the emerging Steampunk ethos.

Other beautifully costumed, award-winning period dramas were fuel for numerous fashion editorials, and inspirational to designers. The 16th and 17th centuries were represented with highly stylized costuming in *La Reine Margot* (1994), *Restoration* (1995), and *Elizabeth* (1998). The early 19th century was depicted in *Sense and Sensibility* (1995) and *Emma* (1996) – which strongly encouraged Empire silhouettes in eveningwear – and *The Age of Innocence* (1993) and *Anna Karenina* (1997) provided lavish bustle styles. *Howards End* (1992) continued the white flannel aesthetic into the 1990s. The 1912 styles of *Titanic* (1997) were used as inspiration to fashion designers, and the gowns worn by Kate Winslet were widely imitated; clothing catalog retailer J. Peterman even contributed to the hype by selling memorabilia of the film along with knock-offs of the costumes. The 1920s period costumes for *Bullets Over Broadway* (1994) encouraged yet another resurgence of editorial interest in Jazz Age fashions. Several films set in the 1930s and 1940s made their contribution to fashion as well, including *Bugsy* (1991) and *The English Patient* (1996). *Evita* (1996) spawned a resurgence of interest in Eva Perón as a fashion icon and *L.A. Confidential* (1997) offered an update of mid-century film noir style. *Malcolm X* (1992) generated renewed interest in the civil rights leader, but also led to a widespread revival of his signature black "browline" glasses; a variety of other apparel, from belts to t-shirts

FASHION-ATION

In the increasingly media-saturated *fin de siècle*, the fashion runway extended into living rooms and theaters around the world. The public developed an insatiable hunger for fashion – its products, processes, and personalities – and eagerly followed every step (and misstep) of Linda and Naomi, Karl and Marc. Media representations of the fashion industry multiplied and the industry was portrayed as the most exciting, creative, demanding, and dream-fulfilling world imaginable.

Television shows dealing with fashion ranged from critiques of celebrity outfits to sitcoms with fashion themes. Fashion critics, previously known only through their writing, became television personalities. Carrie Donovan, a veteran editor with years at major publications, became a spokesperson for Old Navy, offering pronouncements on low-cost sportswear like a latter-day Miss Prescott from *Funny Face*. The formidable Elsa Klensch also made a transition from print journalism to television as the host of the long-running *Style with Elsa Klensch* on Cable News Network. Canadian journalist Jeanne Beker covered fashion from the trenches for *Fashion Television* and the BBC's *The Clothes Show* reported on current trends. *Models Inc.*, a salacious television drama about a Los Angeles modeling agency, aired mid-decade. The American comedy *Veronica's Closet* ran for three years and starred Kirstie Alley as the owner of a New York lingerie company. *Absolutely Fabulous,* a British series that aired from 1992 to 1995, starred Jennifer Saunders and Joanna Lumley. "*Ab Fab*" chronicled the antics of two middle-aged women, one a public relations executive and the other a fashion writer, who madly sampled every fashion and lifestyle trend while consuming notable quantities of alcohol and pills. Their chant of "Lacroix, sweetie, Lacroix!" became shorthand for fashion's irresistible folly.

Robert Altman's 1994 film *Prêt-à-Porter* interpreted Parisian high fashion with an illustrious cast playing designers, clients, and various hangers-on, alongside designers and models who portrayed themselves. The final scene – a fashion show with no clothes – presented a cynical view of fashion that was largely responsible for the film's poor critical reception. In contrast, Douglas Keeve's *Unzipped* (1995) offered a "behind-the-seams" peek at the preparation of Isaac Mizrahi's fall 1994 collection. Mizrahi came off as creative, neurotic, and committed – just what the public expected of a fashion designer – and appearances by top models in states of undress added spice to the production.

The catwalk itself was also a popular fixation. Right Said Fred's "I'm Too Sexy" gently spoofed fashion and fashion models and became a dance-music hit, as did RuPaul's "Supermodel (You Better Work)." Voguing, a performance style that combined fashion, dance, and modeling moves, emerged from the Harlem gay community in the 1980s and received wider exposure through Madonna's song and video "Vogue" and Jennie Livingston's 1990 documentary *Paris is Burning*. Voguers found inspiration in high fashion but it was individual flair and dedication that made their performances so compelling. Voguing provided access to the fantasy of fashion for marginalized social groups. Its subsequent embrace by the mainstream set the stage for even more inclusive media representations of fashion in the 2000s, such as the *Ugly Betty* series, and *Project Runway*, where fantasy met reality.

The ladies of *Absolutely Fabulous* shopping for (what else?) Lacroix.

to hats, were marked with an "X" in tribute. Mike Myers revisited Mod and Peacock Revolution menswear in the *Austin Powers* films, influencing both fashion trends and scores of masquerade costumes. Revival of 1970s styles in fashion were both mirrored and encouraged by films as diverse as *Boogie Nights* (1997) and *The Ice Storm* (1997).

With some producers prioritizing designer style over character content in film costumes, a trend developed for hiring fashion editorial stylists as film costume designers. Model-turned-celebrity magazine stylist Kate Herrington was typical of the trend, and became a film costume designer with projects such as the remake of *The Thomas Crown Affair* (1999). The film industry's fascination with fashion designers continued: for instance, Gianni Versace's and Jean Paul Gaultier's contributions to Pedro Almodóvar's *Kika* (1993) were prominently noted in the opening credits, and *The Fifth Element* (1997) featured colorful, futuristic costumes also by Gaultier.

Television and Fashion

Television exerted a profound impact on fashion in the decade. *Baywatch*, an international success, premiered in 1989 and ran throughout the decade. Its scantily clad and attractive cast encouraged gym-toned bodies and large breasts. Fashion was notably influenced by *Friends*, which debuted in 1994 and had global impact; although the style of characters Ross (David Schwimmer) and Rachel (Jennifer

The *Friends* phenomenon became a worldwide sensation, as seen in this French fashion editorial, "Let's be Friends," shot by Robert Lakow for *Madame Figaro*, which mimics the look of the show's cast and includes fashions and accessories from H&M, Monoprix, Kookaï, Miss Sixty, Replay Blue, Façonnable, and Kenzo.

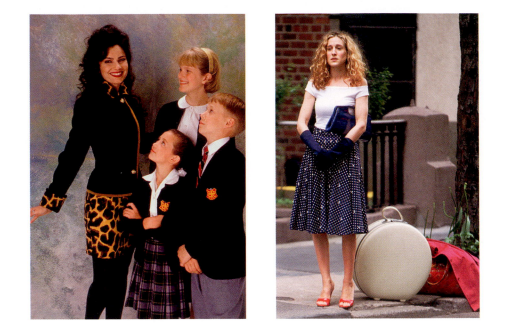

Aniston) were especially noted in the media, each of the show's six leading cast members was influential on youth fashion. The impact of *Friends* was anticipated by the earlier French college life comedy *Hélène et les garçons*, starring an ensemble cast led by French pop singer Hélène Rollès. Television shows with high school settings, including *Saved by the Bell*, *Boy Meets World*, and *Beverly Hills 90210*, also proved notable influences on junior styles.

The extremes in womenswear were clearly illustrated by *The Nanny*; Fran, the title character, wore colorful, tight styles, often from Todd Oldham and Moschino; her rival C. C. wore classic tailored styles in the manner of Armani and Calvin Klein. *Ally McBeal* premiered in 1997, presenting sexy women lawyers in miniskirted business suits. *Sex and the City* debuted in 1998. Each of its four lead actresses became a style setter to some degree, particularly Sarah Jessica Parker. The wardrobe for the show was styled by costume designer and boutique owner Patricia Field and showcased noteworthy luxury brands. The 1999 Colombian telenovela *Yo soy Betty, la fea*, with its title character working as a secretary for a large fashion house, encouraged the fashion industry as a dramatic topic, and spawned remakes in the coming decade.

Music and Fashion

Prominent music magazines including *Rolling Stone*, *Spin*, and *New Musical Express* contributed to fashion trends in their coverage of performers. Music videos displayed greatly enhanced production values, and were even more influential in spreading fashion information.

Female vocalists presented a broad range of styles, from the offbeat glamour of Gwen Stefani of No Doubt and the hostile anti-fashion of Sinead O'Connor, to the gamine look of Lisa Stansfield and the eccentric eclecticism of Shania Twain. Admirers of Erykah Badu imitated her striking headwraps. Madonna continued to reinvent herself on a regular basis, espousing intense sadomasochistic styles; with her leading role in the film *Evita* she incorporated some of Eva Perón's look into her maturing style. After her appearance in *The Bodyguard*, Whitney Houston's Hollywood-infused look was widely imitated. Australian Kylie Minogue grew from wholesome to glamorous during the decade, and experimented with Pre-Raphaelite and Japanese aesthetics in her videos. Britney Spears transformed a schoolgirl uniform into a provocative ensemble in her break-out song, "Baby One More Time," which marked the seventeen year old as an underage temptress; Spears became known for her exposed midriff and helped encourage the fad for pigtails. Janet Jackson's cool uniform in the "Rhythm

Nation" video at the beginning of the decade reflected androgynous styles, and also a vogue for uniform-inspired womenswear. The Tejano star Selena was often dressed in tight pants with skimpy tops and oversized newsboy caps, frequently bejeweled and decorated, and created her own line of clothing. The film biography of Selena that followed her 1995 murder encouraged her music and her style posthumously, and advanced the career of the new Latin American star who portrayed her, Jennifer Lopez. Lopez's own style often mixed high fashion with street trends from her native Bronx. Her curvaceous figure contributed to a new body image that was being exalted in fashion and media. Riot Grrrl fashion combined vintage looks with a feminist message. The Spice Girls, driven by their self-proclaimed "Girl Power," used their style to express adolescent naughtiness and disregard for authority, further conveyed in their "Wannabe" song and video and well-publicized (often inappropriate) antics. The "Union Jack" mini dress that "Ginger Spice" Geri Halliwell wore to the 1997 Brit Awards made headlines.

Much of the most widely copied male clothing from the musical world came from grunge, Goth, and heavy metal acts established by the end of the 1980s. Elegant style on popular music's leading men was strongly encouraged by Latin artists. Luis

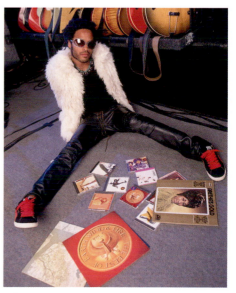

Miguel, nicknamed "El Sol de México," was a best seller in several markets; the former teen pop sensation reached adulthood and typically performed in well-cut suits and ties, sometimes with 1920s-style slicked-back hair. Coverage in the fashion press was widespread. Marc Anthony displayed a similar dapper, suited style mixed with the aesthetic of his native Spanish Harlem, with his undone shirts and round, often dark, glasses. Ricky Martin, a graduate of the Puerto Rican boy band Menudo, became an overnight sensation in 1999 performing on the Grammy Awards; his leather pants, sexy shirts, and pelvic gyrations became his trademark. Lenny Kravitz had his own distinct, heavily accessorized style, with piercings, denim, and dreadlocks. He frequently reinvented himself, always with great stylistic aplomb, often reflecting his multi-ethnic heritage. Boy bands were powerful contributors to young men's styles, including the Backstreet Boys and NSync from the United States, and Take That from Britain.

Grunge

A do-it-yourself style that relied on vernacular American staples such as flannel shirts, thermal underwear, jeans, and stocking caps, grunge was a significant trend for the first few years of the decade, especially embraced by Generation X (those born after the baby boom). The grunge aesthetic combined improbable elements such as floral-print dresses with Dr. Marten boots, and layered pieces such as pajamas under ragged jeans or Henleys under shirts with short or cut-off sleeves, often realized from the thrift shop or garage sale. Several Seattle-based bands, including Nirvana and Pearl Jam, rejected the slick looks of 1980s musicians, and their respective lead singers, Kurt Cobain and Eddie Vedder, became potent style setters. The film *Singles* (1992), with its Seattle setting, exemplified the grunge look, and on television *My So Called Life* featured the style on actress Claire Danes. Perhaps the high point of the style came in December 1992, when *Vogue* presented a fashion editorial entitled "Grunge and Glory" and the same month Italian *Glamour* presented "Mix di abiti: Grunge Style" as its cover editorial. The look made it to the cover of most other major fashion magazines that same season, in both North America and Europe. Marc Jacobs for Perry Ellis and Anna Sui both sent grunge-inspired collections down the runway. Even Donna Karan showed its influence in a DKNY advertising campaign. Cobain's wife Courtney Love, actress and lead singer of Hole, contributed her own take on grunge style. Cobain's suicide in 1994 at age twenty-seven hastened the decline of the movement; but elements of grunge – and the term itself – entered the fashion lexicon.

Fantastic, morbid-themed jewelry, limp dark hair, and often extreme pallor characterize the Goth aesthetic.

Goth

The rebellious stance of Goth in the 1980s took on a higher degree of artifice in the 1990s. Goth fashion was macabre and melancholy. British musicians Bauhaus and Siouxsie Sioux were particularly influential. Black was the core of the Goth look from head to toe:

Carefully powdered faces and heavy, precise black eyeliner represent hundreds of hours in front of the mirror. Gender is irrelevant: men as well as women sport tight patent-leather bodices, leather trousers and tresses of black or bleached white hair.[3]

Black lipstick and nail polish completed the look, and lace was common. The aesthetic was often Victorian, but included inspiration from the Middle Ages and other eras. Religious imagery – both pagan and Christian – provided important motifs. Reveling in the graveyard and the funerary, Goths were highly inspired by Victorian mourning customs. They often wore black coats and veils, and authentic 19th-century mourning jewelry was a prized Goth accessory.

The look of the subculture took great inspiration from the dark fiction of Mary Shelley and Edgar Allan Poe and the contemporary author Anne Rice. Celebrities ranging from Lord Byron to Sarah Bernhardt to Carolyn Jones were also inspirational. Film and television contributed to the aesthetic, including classics such as *Nosferatu* (1922), *Dracula* (1931), and *Edward Scissorhands* (1990). *The Crow* (1994) took on morbid significance with the accidental death of lead actor Brandon Lee during its filming. Popular music acts contributed to the look in performance clothing that was widely emulated, notably Marilyn Manson, Nine Inch Nails, Sisters of Mercy, and the neoclassic act Rasputina. Goth maintained an overlap with sadomasochistic subcultures, and the use of 19th-century-style corsetry was related to "tightlacer" fetishists. The look spread and grew in major urban centers throughout the world, and Goth taste had a strong impact on style tribes in Japan. The Goth aesthetic also wielded a strong effect on leading designers of the decade, including emerging talent Olivier Theyskens (b. 1977).

Hip-hop Style

Hip-hop performers promoted a fashion aesthetic that eventually had global and multi-racial impact. Magazines including *Vibe* chronicled and spread the development of the style, and it also embraced more traditional R & B performers. *Ebony* declared in 1991:

The new Black style consists of doorknocker earrings, vibrant Moroccan beads, loose-fitting pants, wildly painted jeans, Ghanaian cloth wrap-around skirts, and other Afrocentric attire. It's Kente cloth crowns atop Reggae-inspired dreadlocks or fade hair cuts, with creative lines shaved into the hair or eyebrows.[4]

Hip-hop artists and fans often favored oversized t-shirts, hoodies, sports jerseys, and pants with dropped waists exposing underpants. Clothing manufacturers catered to the style with oversized print and logos. FUBU, Cross Colours, Timberland, and even Lagerfeld for Chanel were among the most desired brands. Vintage-style suits and accessories, especially from the 1920s and 1930s, inspired "gangster" looks. Suits were sometimes worn with the brand label at the bottom of the sleeve (usually removed after purchase) left visible as a mark of status. Such looks were often accessorized with baseball caps, worn backward, sideways, or angled, do-rags, bandanas, and large items of jewelry commonly called "bling." Many rappers and followers decorated their teeth with gold and platinum caps called "grills" or "fronts." Hip-hop style placed continued premium attention on sneakers, strongly contributing to "sneaker culture."

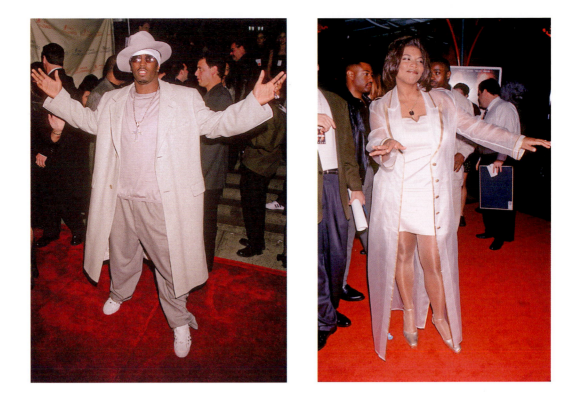

Leading figures in hip hop Sean "Puffy" Combs and Queen Latifah transcended street style and were often clad in elegant white for public events.

M.C. Hammer's loose-fitting trousers, known as "Hammer pants," were widely copied by the fashion industry. Rapper and actor Will Smith, also known as The Fresh Prince, was also influential, especially through his television show *The Fresh Prince of Bel-Air*. Artists Ice-T, Ice Cube, Snoop Dogg, Tupac Shakur, and Biggie Smalls each made his own contribution to the style. Sean Combs, operating under aliases including Puff Daddy and P. Diddy, imbued the hip-hop style with street chic combined with cool designer elegance. Boyz II Men, whose music mixed hip-hop, R & B and boy-band styles, were dapper fashion chameleons, mixing preppy and elegant *GQ* Casanova looks with more street hip-hop styles. Mary J. Blige and Lauryn Hill both mixed hip-hop street style with designer cool. Queen Latifah often adopted a harder, more masculine edge, but also sometimes favored African-inspired looks. In her television and film appearances Latifah became an exemplar for attractive plus-size women. The hip-hop girl group TLC experimented with many looks from Afrocentric to a rave sensibility. White artists Vanilla Ice, Marky Mark, and Eminem encouraged the idiom beyond racial lines, contributing to the musical and fashion aesthetics of the movement. The Wu-Tang Clan from Staten Island mixed Asian martial arts with hip hop, a combination that was mirrored in the Japanese manga magazine serial *Afro Samurai*. Hip-hop style and its cross-cultural influence became the focus of scholarship and serious research including the Brooklyn Museum's exhibition *Hip-Hop Nation* in 2000.

Fashion Trends

Fashion in the 1990s was eclectic and segmented, but a number of general trends influenced the clothing of both men and women. Despite repeated assertions about its irrelevance, couture continued to excite and inspire with runway spectacles and a constantly evolving list of "hot" designers. Popular fashion reflected influences from music, movies, fashion history, and subcultures. Postmodernism was still in play while a new term, "deconstruction," came into usage in the fashion world. Also called "*la mode destroy*," deconstruction was expressed as unfinished-looking garments with torn edges and exposed seams, along with distressed finishes, and tears and holes. Another new mode, "minimalism," rejected the artifice of postmodernism in favor of simple clean lines and solid, often neutral, colors.

The designation "business casual" revolutionized dressing for the workplace. While the definition of business casual was often dictated by regional tastes – in a New York brokerage house the term meant a button-down shirt worn with khakis and dress shoes, while at Seattle software companies cut-off jeans and flip-flops were acceptable – the move toward informality was important. Khaki trousers from the Levi's brand Dockers were strongly associated with a business casual aesthetic for men and women. In 1992 the company published a brochure about casual business style and in 1993 Dockers expanded to Europe.

A major revival of 1970s styles included low-rise flared trousers for men and women, tie-dye, and body-hugging silhouettes. The color palette of popular fashion – green, mustard, eggplant – reflected a 1970s influence, albeit with new names (sage, curry, aubergine) for these familiar hues. The popularity of 1970s styling indicated a compression of the fashion trend cycle, as looks from only twenty years earlier (or less) were already considered retro. One manifestation of this revival was a trend toward transparency in dress and an emphasis on toplessness and displaying nipples through sheer or tight clothing, for both men and women. While most average fashion consumers did not adopt this trend, nipples were routinely exposed at designer shows and nightclubs.

Denim continued to be important and was available in many finishes at all price levels. Distressed denim jeans, skirts, dresses, and jackets were fashionable. The popularity of cargo pants for men and women toward the end of the decade reflected two cultural developments. Conceptually, cargo pants (and also cargo shorts and skirts) conveyed an attitude of democratization. But, in practical terms, the added pockets accommodated new electronic devices, beginning with pagers and CD players, and later including cell phones. Cashmere was increasingly popular as a fashion fiber. As China emerged as a major clothing manufacturing center, cashmere was available at lower price points from mass-market stores, competing with more prestigious labels such as TSE.

Levi's Dockers line became a leading contributor to the "business casual" boom of the 1990s, and were known especially for their workplace-appropriate khaki trousers.

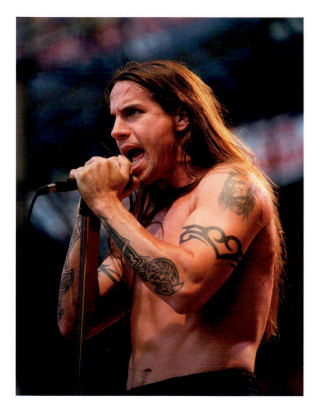

Singer Anthony Kiedis of the Red Hot Chili Peppers performs at the Tibetan Freedom concert in 1998. Tattoos had become nearly ubiquitous in the music industry, and among the younger generation in general.

Body Modification

During the 1980s, several books on body art were published, as both scholarly and general interest in these practices increased. A tattooing subculture was highly developed, and artists such as Leo Zulueta, Ed Hardy, and Horyoshi III had cult followings. Other forms of body modification – including scarification, piercing, and manipulation – were the object of growing attention and practice. During the 1990s numerous periodicals emerged devoted to these topics, while mainstream women's fashion magazines discussed "appropriate tattoos" for women. Neighborhoods in several international cities eventually developed body art districts, such as the Castro in San Francisco, Ximending in Taipei, and the Rosse Buurt in Amsterdam. The Lollapalooza music festivals, beginning in 1991, were often strongly credited with propelling the popularity of tattooing and other body arts, because they made heavily tattooed and pierced performers widely visible to music fans. Body art was embraced as a form of anti-fashion with much the same attitudes that fueled the initial popularity of grunge and Goth, and while developing its own subculture it overlapped with others. Nose piercings and multiple ear piercings, while eye-catching if not jarring in the 1970s and 1980s, became commonplace, nearly mainstream, in the 1990s. Stretched earlobes, commonly referred to as "gauged," became popular. Other practices included bifurcated tongues, brands, and transdermal and subdermal implants, along with extreme cosmetic surgery practices. The tightlacer subculture included men and women who wore corsetry and waist restraints to create abnormally small waists.

The Elements of Women's Fashion

Women's fashion was very diverse and eclectic, as designers, stylists, and consumers almost perversely mixed clothing genres. Many styles showed a 1970s inspiration. During the course of the decade there were extreme highs and lows in hem length, and sexuality was emphasized through "underwear as outerwear" and the widespread use of transparent materials. While the color story was varied, the widespread use of black and neutrals often created the impression of uniforms.

A slender cut characterized clothing and many styles emphasized a small waist. Skirts were often long and narrow during the early and middle years of the decade, some even reaching the ankle. Pantsuits were extremely popular. Jackets tended toward a long, shaped cut, sometimes showing a 1970s-inflected interpretation of Edwardian style. Many designers offered shapely pinstripe suits which were feminized with filmy or silky blouses, strongly referencing Saint Laurent's pantsuits. Trousers were narrow, sometimes cut like jeans, sometimes flared, often cuffed. Knock-offs of classic Chanel-style skirt suits were popular, but were often updated with bright colors and a tighter fit. Youthful interpretations of the skirt suit paired a classic jacket – such as a cardigan or blazer style – with a very short skirt, as hemlines rose mid-decade. Many skirts had a low waistline with no waistband, riding on the hips. Most short skirts were straight-cut with no pleats or gathers, but some young women wore short pleated skirts resembling mini kilts. Bias-cut skirts, often in crepes and other fluid fabrics, were worn at knee length. Such skirts were sometimes paired with ribbed tops and thin belts. T-shirts, slim sweaters, and other knit tops were often very short, revealing skin or underwear. Blouses and shirts were often quite fitted; popular details included deep cuffs and ties at the neck. Catsuits were worn for day or evening.

While separates and layers offered variety, dresses were also worn. Loose, high-waisted babydoll dresses with short sleeves, often made in retro patterned silk, cotton, or rayon, were popular with young women. Body-skimming slip dresses with thin straps were in fashion for a number of years. Available in a vast array of fabrics and

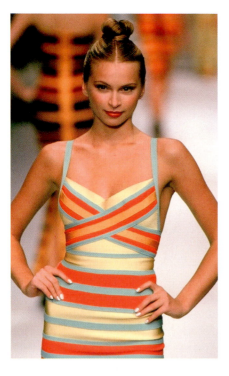

Above left **A Hervé Léger wrapped "bandage dress" on the runway shows the continued taste for cling established in the late 1980s, with a "Glamazon" modeling the dress.**

Above right **Repeating frogs, a 1990s interpretation of the conversational print, were available in this colorful crepe. Prints in a variety of whimsical motifs were popular with a wide range of designers, from Gianni Versace to Nicole Miller.**

colors, slip dresses were worn for all occasions, and were often covered with fitted cardigans for a more modest look. "Fit and flare" short-sleeved shirt-style dresses were also seen, sometimes evoking cowboy-style shirts, with snaps and Western pockets, often made in satin or other lustrous materials. Simple but shapely jumpers, often with zip fronts, were worn over knit tops and t-shirts. By the end of the decade, sleeveless sheaths emerged as an alternative to slip dresses, offering a more tailored and sophisticated look, and dresses were often promoted over suits and separates for professional and dressy wear.

Leather and snakeskin were popular for pants at the designer level. Advances in synthetic fibers resulted in a more upscale reputation for synthetics; some microfibers had the look and feel of silk, and stretch materials such as spandex were used to enhance the fit of clothes from the couture level to mass market. Matte-finish synthetic crepe was especially common in suitings and matte jersey was often used for dresses even for evening, although satin was increasingly worn for day. Animal print motifs, especially leopard spots, were popular for clothing as well as accessories.

Casual clothing and active sportswear were influenced by a number of factors. In contrast to the slim-fitting trousers that dominated fashion, some young women adopted loose jeans like those worn by skateboarders and rap artists. Rave music enthusiasts wore pants with extremely wide legs. The category of performance sportswear was increasingly important as specific sports and activities were associated with particular styles and materials; the debut of the X Games in 1995 influenced sportswear styles.

At the beginning of the decade, a wide silhouette was popular for outerwear, as were double-breasted greatcoats. By mid-decade, outerwear often echoed the slim fit of clothing and above-the-knee wool coats were worn. Many coats were belted. Short trench coats were popular in traditional beige as well as many other fabrics and patterns including checked and brightly colored poplin. Short satin trenches were worn for evening. Despite protests by animal rights activists (including a celebrity-filled campaign by PETA), fur and fur-trimmed jackets and coats were promoted; the silhouette of fur coats often evoked glamorous pieces from the 1920s and 1930s with wide shawl collars and fur cuffs. Shearling was popular, in natural brown and other colors. Hip-length blanket plaid jackets were seen for casual wear, as were down jackets, often styled in candy colors and metallics.

Evening and special occasion dressing especially showed the polar extremes of fashion. Versace's bondage-inspired dresses influenced legions of partygoers to step out in strappy bra-like tops, often paired with long, full skirts. Lacroix offered evening t-shirts in sheer chiffon embellished with gold sequins. In a well-publicized "anything goes" moment, Sharon Stone wore a dark gray Gap turtleneck to the Oscars in 1996 with a designer skirt. Other eveningwear styles recalled the slinky looks of the 1930s; John Galliano's bias-cut silk dresses were widely imitated. Calvin Klein's metallic lace slip dresses were popular and inspired many copies. Long, lean matte jersey evening dresses such as Tom Ford's for Gucci and Donna Karan's styles offered another evening option, and another 1970s reference.

Accessories

Many designer runway shows featured spectacular hats, including millinery by Philip Treacy and Stephen Jones. Vivienne Westwood showed tams with extra-long pheasant feathers; Donna Karan showed high-crowned styles in dark colors, like witches' hats. Top hat variations were particularly fashion-forward. Popular mainstream styles included berets in many variations and newsboy caps; baseball caps were seen everywhere, in many fabrics from sequined satin to leather.

In addition to shoes by top designers and established luxury brands, other labels were especially popular, including Manolo Blahnik and Jimmy Choo. The prevailing high fashion silhouette was slender and pointy, although significant variations on the stiletto shape were seen, including high-heeled Mary Janes, T-straps, and other styles with instep-crossing straps. Young women sometimes opted for chunkier styles, some with square toes and buckles, resembling Pilgrim shoes. Platform shoes with heavy heels were revived. Some high-heeled sandals featured straps around the foot and going up the leg, gladiator style. Mules were very popular in a wide range of heel heights and shapes and ranged from casual leather clog types to glamorous evening styles. After mid-decade, mid-height "kitten" and "Louis" heels were popular for pumps, mules, and sandals. Boots of all shapes and styles were fashionable: chunky motorcycle types, laced-up granny styles, streamlined ankle boots with pointy toes and slender heels, even over-the-knee boots and thigh-highs. Reptile and suede were popular. Casual shoes included Dr. Martens and round-toed Oxfords. Birkenstock sandals were available in a range of colors and materials and became increasingly mainstream.

Legwear was a fashion focus. Pantyhose and tights were available in a rainbow of colors and many patterns including stripes, cables, and lace. European prestige hosiery brands Wolford and Fogal led the market. Opaque tights were often worn in the same color as shoes. Hosiery frequently featured slenderizing control tops. Knee socks were worn as part of a retro look.

Each season ushered a specific handbag into must-have status. The roster of fashion favorites included the Birkin and Kelly bags by Hermès, Fendi's "baguette," and many styles from Vuitton. Designers realized the earning potential of accessories; *Vogue* called the handbag "fashion's biggest breadwinner."[5] Some were unusually small, such as Chanel's quilted bags with chain straps or Lulu Guinness' whimsical clutches, thus creating the need for an additional tote bag. Even Chinese take-out containers served as inspiration for small purses. Backpacks were particularly fashionable. Miniature versions served as purses, often available in fine leather or fabrics. Larger, more utilitarian backpacks complemented the casual and somewhat military look of youth fashion. Prada's backpacks and totes became staples and were often counterfeited. Handbag design began to accommodate electronic gadgets.

Fashionable jewelry pieces included very long necklaces, strings of small beads, or long pendants that sometimes reached almost to the waist. Some long necklaces were worn with chokers or lockets. Striking cuff bracelets were also popular. Body piercings were accentuated with jewelry. Pashmina shawls were considered essential accessories, available in every color and worn for day and evening.

Martin Margiela's eccentric individuality is seen in his split toe "Tabi" shoe, a recurring style for Maison Margiela.

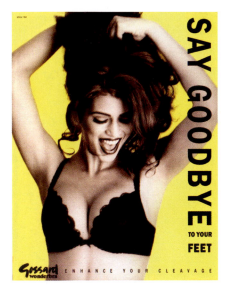

The Wonderbra, which enjoyed great success during the 1990s, featured a provocative and joyous ad campaign.

Foundations and Lingerie

The lean lines of fashion motivated consumers to adopt modern foundation garments, now quite lightweight and increasingly known as "shapewear." Several manufacturers were prominent in the shapewear market, including Nancy Ganz, whose Hip Slip was especially popular. Thong underwear became more acceptable and was worn under low-rise pants. The Wonderbra offered a pushed-up look that became the standard bust shape. The Victoria's Secret company, long considered a déclassé catalog brand, revamped its image, establishing retail stores worldwide and staging extravagant televised runway shows that reached millions of viewers.

Designers: France

For fashion spectators, the late 1990s presented a game of "musical chairs" as new designers – often quite young – moved rapidly and internationally between name-brand houses and their own independent labels. In 1995 John Galliano was hired by Bernard Arnault of LVMH to rejuvenate Givenchy, becoming the first British designer to head a French couture house. After only a year there, he moved to Dior, also a LVMH brand, taking the place of Gianfranco Ferré. Galliano's replacement at Givenchy was another British upstart, twenty-seven-year-old Alexander McQueen. The American designer Tom Ford was hired by Gucci in 1990 and, after Gucci's acquisition of the house of Yves Saint Laurent, designed for YSL as well, where he replaced Alber Elbaz.

Thierry Mugler presented his first couture collection in 1992, mixing custom pieces and ready-to-wear on the runway, and insisting that there was little difference between the two. In the same year he introduced his fragrance Angel and during the decade Mugler expanded his menswear offerings. **Claude Montana** designed for Lanvin from 1990 to 1992 then concentrated on his own house until 1997. Body-

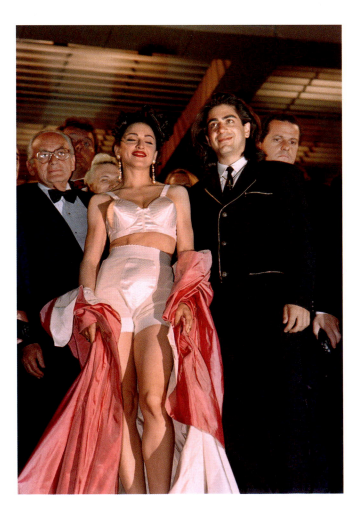

conscious dressing kept focus on **Azzedine Alaïa** and his work remained in high demand, especially dresses made of strips of elasticized material that clung to the body and provided glimpses of skin between. Bold combinations of color and pattern characterized **Emanuel Ungaro**'s collections as he continued to show couture and ready-to-wear and introduced several new fragrances.

Jean Paul Gaultier explored a range of themes that further cemented his reputation for wit and invention. In 1991 he focused on Rastafarian style. In 1994 he found inspiration in the clothing of Hasidic Jews; his "Tatouages" collection of the same year included flesh-colored pieces printed with tattoo designs. Other influences came from regional styles, especially Asian. His fascination with foundation garments resulted in striking dresses with the look of girdles and his costumes for Madonna's 1990 "Blond Ambition" tour, which revisited the cone-shaped bra, had worldwide impact.

Christian Lacroix opened the decade with the launch of his fragrance C'est la Vie and expansion into a full range of accessories. His more casual Bazar line was introduced in 1995, as was a home division. His love of embellishment and vivid color combinations found expression in signature details such as ruffles and jeweled embroidery. Lacroix designed eye-catching costumes for figure skater Surya Bonaly for the 1992 Winter Olympics, which she wore to compete against the more reserved Nancy Kerrigan, costumed by Vera Wang, prompting press quips that women's figure skating had become a fashion show on ice.

Karl Lagerfeld for **Chanel** kept the brand visible and relevant, churning through multiple inspirations that utilized and exaggerated Chanel motifs including pearls, camellias, and black. The overt use of logos was one way the house kept pace with popular culture. Lagerfeld showed biker-style leather jackets and caps with oversize jewelry for day. Other examples actually anticipated trends, such as Lagerfeld's "moon boots" offered in the early 1990s that included many familiar Chanel details (including chains and quilting) but introduced shoes that would become popular in the next decade.

Viktor Horsting (b. 1969) and Rolf Snoeren (b. 1969) met at art school in Amsterdam. Designing as **Viktor & Rolf**, they presented their first collection in 1993 in Hyères, France, consisting of reconstructed vintage garments. The initial press reaction to their eccentric designs encouraged them to continue working in France and they showed several collections in Paris, sometimes as installations in which garments were displayed like artworks. Their first couture collection was presented in 1998 at a contemporary art gallery. The following season they proposed an "Atomic" silhouette, with exaggerated volume around the neck and shoulders. Their foray into fragrance offered perfume bottles with no perfume inside.

Helmut Lang (b. 1956) was born in Vienna and operated a fashion business there in the late 1970s. He presented his first women's collection in Paris in 1986 as part of a celebration of Viennese design at the Pompidou Centre. The following year Lang introduced a menswear line and showed both womenswear and menswear on the official Paris fashion calendar. In the late 1980s he shied away from runway spectacle, preferring to present his collections via quiet shows he called *séances de travail* or working sessions. Lang's work in the 1990s crystallized his signature style: spare silhouettes and a limited palette dominated by darks and neutrals that often included unexpected pieces in bright colors. Narrow trousers for both men and women were worn with equally slim jackets, coats, and tunics, all refined to the point of severity. Although

Opposite bottom left Madonna wears an underwear-inspired ensemble from Jean Paul Gaultier, one of her favorite designers, at the Cannes film festival in 1991.

Opposite bottom right A Christian Lacroix costume for French national champion figure skater Surya Bonaly, inspired by Spanish toreros. The *New York Times* dubbed the trend for top designers creating skating costumes "couture eveningwear on ice."

Below Lagerfeld for Chanel sent these plaid ensembles down the runway, providing cafe society with exaggerated versions of core Chanel elements.

he was known for the use of "hard" materials such as leather and rubber, by the end of the decade Lang featured softer fabrics. Through collaborations with photographer Jürgen Teller on advertising and artist Jenny Holzer on store design, Lang was strongly associated with, even embraced by, the contemporary art world. In 1998, instead of staging a runway show, Lang showed his collection on the internet, establishing a new model for fashion without borders.

Issey Miyake introduced his first fragrance, L'eau d'Issey, in 1992 and in 1993 launched his Pleats Please label, which featured permanently pleated garments. His APOC ("A Piece of Cloth") line, which debuted in 1997, sought to eliminate material waste from clothing production by knitting or weaving pieces to the exact specifications of the wearer. In a particularly striking collection for spring/summer 1997, **Rei Kawakubo** departed from the dark, loose garments she often showed with a series of stretch gingham pieces with internal padding. Kawakubo's collection once again challenged conventional silhouettes; the dresses were padded not at bust or hipline but formed bumps at shoulders, backs, and other unexpected, "unfashionable" areas. **Junya Watanabe** (b. 1961) was the designer of the Tricot line at Kawakubo's Comme des Garçons for several years. In 1992 he began designing under his own name at the company and in 1994 launched his own label, showing in Paris. Like Kawakubo, Watanabe maintained a distance from prevailing trends, instead concentrating on his experimentation with textiles on the body. A Bunka graduate, **Yoshiki Hishinuma** (b. 1958) showed in both Paris and Japan and utilized contemporary and traditional fabric effects, sometimes with a Goth aesthetic.

For her spring/summer 1997 collection, Rei Kawakubo proposed altered body shapes rendered in a familiar fabric, stretch gingham.

Designers: Britain

British designers exerted international influence and several design schools, especially Central Saint Martin's, nurtured revolutionary talents. Established designers and brands continued to offer refined, elegant fashion. **Vivienne Westwood**'s collections deepened her identification with British traditions. "Anglomania" for fall/winter 1993 featured a radical reworking of tartans, tweeds, argyle, and other elements of British style. Westwood often combined fine tailoring details with an exaggerated, hyper-feminine silhouette. For "Cut, Slash and Pull" (spring/summer 1991), she slashed garments in the manner of the 16th century; other collections included ruffs and panniers, and corsetry was repeatedly revisited. Westwood introduced a menswear line in 1996, based in Milan. She was named Fashion Designer of the Year by the British Fashion Council in 1990 and 1991, and received an OBE in 1992. **Rifat Ozbek**'s work showed a variety of influences ranging from Native American jewelry to the rainbow-colored styles worn by rave music fans. Ozbek's output was varied and sophisticated, usually based on a body-conscious fit. French-born **Nicole Farhi** (b. 1946), a former designer for French Connection, eschewed theatricality in favor of consistent elegance and showed body-skimming slip dresses and simply cut pieces in sensual fabrics that were popular with a wide range of customers.

Alexander McQueen (1969–2010) graduated from Central Saint Martin's College of Art and Design and gained immediate attention for his 1992 graduation show, which was purchased by Isabella Blow. Before attending school, McQueen had worked at two Savile Row firms and at a theatrical costume company, experiences that honed his tailoring expertise and his knowledge of fashion history. He also worked for a short time with Romeo Gigli. In 1993 McQueen established his own label. His controversial presentations included the 1995 "Highland Rape" collection that featured bedraggled models in torn clothing and was the designer's comment on the British treatment of Highland Scots. His "bumster" trousers, which put buttock cleavage on display, also contributed to McQueen's reputation as the "bad boy" of British fashion. Despite (or perhaps because of) his youth and notoriety, McQueen was appointed chief designer at Givenchy, where he worked from 1996 to 2000 while also designing for his own label. McQueen was renowned for his exacting knowledge of tailoring, pattern making and mastery of the fitting process and, unlike many other designers who relied on their ateliers to realize their sketches, could create clothes directly on the model. He was named British Designer of the Year in 1996, 1997, and 2000. The theatrical runway shows were important to the realization of his ideas; his spring/summer 1999 show featured an industrial paint sprayer that embellished a dress while the model danced on the runway. McQueen closed the decade in memorable form; for the fall/winter 1999 show he created a snowstorm and sent models out in furs and ice skates.

Born in Gibraltar, **John Galliano** (b. 1960) was raised in London. He attended Central Saint Martin's and graduated in 1984 with a show entitled "Les Incroyables," which evoked the French Revolution and went on display in the windows of the London boutique Browns. The pieces quickly sold out and helped launch Galliano's career. Despite recognition and awards, including British Designer of the Year in

Opposite bottom Alexander McQueen's breakthrough fall/winter 1995 "Highland Rape" collection made reference to the violent history of English domination in Scotland, a benchmark of conceptual thinking in fashion collections.

Right A 1992 ensemble by John Galliano exhibits his typical whimsy with a combination of 18th- and 19th-century inspirations mixed with burlesque elements. An oversized hat of "Merry Widow" proportions is teamed with a peplum metallic jacket, and panties.

Above Popular with stylish young women, Stella McCartney perpetuated the feminine Chloé image, offering urban elegance such as this dress from 1998.

Below Renowned for his experimental approach to materials and techniques, Hussein Chalayan presented a wooden corset at London Fashion Week in 1995.

1987, Galliano had continual financial difficulties and moved to Paris in 1990, where he found financial backing and encouragement from Anna Wintour. Shortly after his move to Givenchy, he created a memorable dress for Princess Diana in 1996. In his work for Dior, Galliano achieved a significant revitalization of the house. His designs combined historical references with impressive craftsmanship and re-established the allure of Dior. In 1997 he interpreted Christian Dior's Bar suit with a peplum jacket made of leather "lace" over a short bias-cut skirt. Galliano returned several times to the Empire theme, but also explored the Belle Epoque, chinoiserie, and the 1940s, among many other influences. His collections were often staged in memorable locations, including the Gare d'Austerlitz and a riding stable in the Bois de Boulogne. Galliano's love of drama extended to his personal styling; he often appeared at his runway shows in outfits that ranged from astronaut to pigtailed pirate to shirtless.

The daughter of Paul and Linda McCartney, **Stella McCartney** (b. 1971) cited her parents' seventies-style suits among the influences for her early collections. Her impact on the fashion industry began with her graduation show at Central Saint Martin's, where Naomi Campbell, Yasmin Le Bon, and Kate Moss modeled her clothes. Her skills were honed with internships at Lacroix and with Edward Sexton, a Savile Row tailor. From the beginning of her career, McCartney's style was marked by quirky but wearable combinations that appealed to young customers. In 1996 she showed crisply tailored blazers over light, feminine camisoles, some of which incorporated pieces of antique lace. In 1997 McCartney's appointment to the French label Chloé, where she succeeded the much more established Karl Lagerfeld, made waves. But the young designer's reputation for youthful, hip style with romantic details proved to be a good fit for the label and its *haute bohème* heritage, and she continued at Chloé until 2001.

Hussein Chalayan (b. 1970) emerged as an interesting new talent. Born in Nicosia, Cyprus, Chalayan graduated from Central Saint Martins in 1993 with an outstanding graduation collection entitled "The Tangent Flows," which included garments he buried in soil with iron filings to produce a rusty surface. After launching his own label the next year, Chalayan presented themes of time, movement, and cultural ideas of modesty within a predominantly minimalist aesthetic, such as his "airmail" clothing made of white Tyvek with red and blue stripes (1994). Chalayan's explorations of corsetry ranged from a surgical corset (spring/summer 1996) to a beautiful polished wood piece from fall/winter 1995, in which the curving grain echoes the wearer's body beneath. His final collection of the decade, "Echoform" from fall/winter 1999, was inspired by plane and automobile interiors. The Airplane dress, made of fiberglass, had segments that opened and closed electronically. Only five years into his career, Chalayan received the British Fashion Award for Designer of the Year in 1999.

Designers: United States

Several designers who came to prominence during the 1970s and 1980s continued to dominate American fashion and, through the development of diffusion lines and licensing, enabled their brands to reach a huge public. Donna Karan, Calvin Klein, and Ralph Lauren were particularly well established with multiple lines at a range of price points. Using a similar strategy, mega-retailer The Gap, having acquired Banana Republic, reinvented it as its upscale line, and later opened Old Navy stores as its lower-priced brand.

Donna Karan continued to build on her success and her DKNY brand became particularly visible. Her offerings expanded to include DKNY Jeans in 1990, the Signature collection for men in 1991, DKNY for men in 1992 and her eponymous fragrance the same year. Karan designed clothes she wanted to wear: flattering separates, often in black, that were versatile and fitted well. One of her designs, the Cold Shoulder dress, with long sleeves and cut-outs at the shoulders, was a best seller that was seen on celebrities including actress Candice Bergen and First Lady Hillary Clinton. Despite Karan's 1996 public stock offering that was initially unsuccessful, the designer continued to receive awards and recognition within the industry, including her third Council of Fashion Designers of America (CFDA) Award in 1997.

Several aspects of **Calvin Klein**'s business reflected important trends of the 1990s: minimalism, lean fit, and provocative advertising. Despite success during the previous decade, the company was on an insecure financial footing by 1992, but returned to profitability within the next several years, due in part to the scope of Klein's diversification. The upscale lines for men and women perpetuated Klein's limited palette and sharp tailoring; the lower-priced CK line, jeans, underwear, and homewares reached a wider public. Klein's fragrance line grew through the introduction of Escape and the unisex scent cKone. After photographs of young models in 1995 advertisements for CK Jeans were heavily criticized as being exploitative, even pornographic, the company withdrew many images from circulation. Advertisements for another Klein fragrance, cKbe, featured photographs of semi-dressed teenagers, many with tattoos and piercings, that offended many viewers. Rapper Marky Mark posed in a memorable series of advertisements for Klein underwear grabbing his crotch, a move from hip-hop culture.

This period was marked by expansion, industry recognition, and financial success for **Ralph Lauren**. His growing roster of brands reflected the interests of his broad customer base, with a focus on sports and outdoor wear. Lauren also established his Purple Label, offering higher-priced tailored clothing and formal wear. Lauren received the Lifetime Achievement Award from the CFDA in 1991. His varied interpretations of a military look won praise during the Gulf War, ranging from ornate versions of 19th-century officers' jackets to utilitarian zipped jumpsuits. A successful public offering in 1997 further solidified Lauren's standing in the business of fashion.

Tom Ford (b. 1961) began his career at Cathy Hardwick, briefly worked for Chloé and Perry Ellis, and went to Gucci in 1990. He was brought into Gucci by creative director Dawn Mello, who had been charged with reigniting the brand. While at Gucci, Ford rekindled the sexy aspects of the house, often favoring a disco-inflected yet minimalist aesthetic that was reminiscent of Halston. Form-fitting dresses with metal accents offered a sophisticated reference to the Gucci tradition of equestrian details; revealing cuts and sensuous materials recalled the brand's glory years in the late 1960s and 1970s. Ford was instrumental in re-establishing Gucci as a desirable luxury name.

Marc Jacobs (b. 1963) graduated from Parsons School of Design in 1984 and directly after graduation began designing a line of sweaters for the New York boutique Charivari. He launched his own label in 1986 and received the CFDA's Perry Ellis Award for New Fashion Talent only one year later. Jacobs went to work for Perry Ellis in 1988 and rose to head designer quickly. His controversial 1992 "grunge" collection ended Jacobs' association with Ellis and he revived his own label, presenting a comeback collection in 1994. Jacobs accepted a position with Louis Vuitton, and his contract provided financing for his own business. His mission at Vuitton was to launch a women's ready-to-wear collection. The move to place a young, iconoclastic designer at the helm of a classic leather goods company was controversial, but Jacobs succeeded and his work received consistent praise and major awards for womenswear and accessories.

Another Parsons graduate, **Isaac Mizrahi** (b. 1961) worked for several designers including Perry Ellis and Calvin Klein before opening his own business in Manhattan's SoHo neighborhood in 1987 in partnership with Sarah Haddad-Cheney, a family friend. The early lines were successful and Mizrahi expanded into menswear in 1990. The same year he received the CFDA

Tom Ford designed minimalist matte jersey dresses for his fall 1996 collection for Gucci that revisited the elegance of Halston in the 1970s.

Designer of the Year Award for womenswear. His collections concentrated on wearable separates that acknowledged mid-century American sportswear. Mizrahi's career gained momentum very quickly. He was extremely visible in the 1990s, with wide retail distribution in North America and Asia and cameo appearances on television, and was also the subject of a 1995 documentary.

A number of emerging designers working in New York offered fashion with a colorful, young focus. **Anna Sui** (b. around 1960) was born in Michigan, and attended Parsons School of Design in New York. She launched her own business in 1991 with a show of pieces worn by top models who walked the runway in exchange for clothes. The famous models added visibility to the event, but Sui's colorful versions of fashion classics established her as a designer with an original vision. While some of her designs showed influence from a grunge and rave aesthetic, Sui's interpretation of the style was more optimistic, with a colorful, retro mood. Sui became known for a style that mixed elements from many sources including global ethnic traditions and popular music to produce dresses and ensembles favored by "club kids" looking for fun evening styles. She introduced cosmetics and fragrance in 1998. Born in China, **Vivienne Tam** (b. 1957) moved to Hong Kong as a young child and studied fashion there. She arrived in New York in 1981 and began her own label the following year. Her first runway show was presented in 1993 at New York's "7th on Sixth" fashion week. Her 1995 "Mao" collection, which featured images of the Chinese leader on dresses and suits, was met with acclaim and controversy and several pieces entered museum collections. Tam's fashion enterprise also included the East Wind Code label. She served as a consultant in other industries including automobile manufacture, and was actively involved in the rapidly growing Asian fashion market, with several stores in Japan by the end of the

Below left Anna Sui's aesthetic playfully combined classic rock and roll, Carnaby Street, and grunge, among many other inspirations.

Below right Wedding dresses decorate the showroom windows at Vera Wang's bridal salon in the Carlyle Hotel on New York's Madison Avenue in 1990.

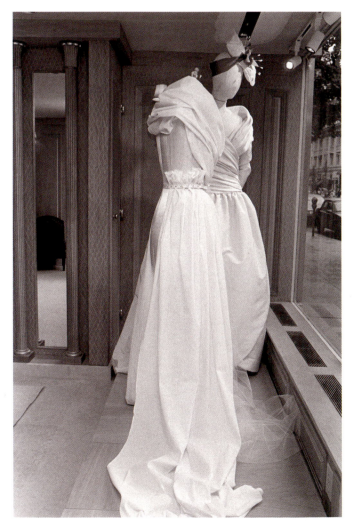

decade. **Todd Oldham** (b. 1961) grew up in Texas and produced a fashion collection in 1981 that was sold at Neiman Marcus. After his move to New York in 1988, he launched a womenswear line characterized by colorful pieces with whimsical touches. Oldham's taste for eye-catching, almost surrealistic, surface effects, short skirts, and playful details earned him a young following. A strong animal rights activist, Oldham refused to use animal products in his clothing and was a pioneer in the use of "pleather," a synthetic with the look and feel of leather. **Cynthia Rowley** (b. 1958) launched her fashion company in 1988. Often inspired by vintage style, including Claire McCardell, Rowley authored a lifestyle and fashion guide, *Swell*, in 1999. New Yorker **Christian Francis Roth** (b. 1969) was hailed for his small collections of witty designs, some with cut-out shapes and *trompe l'œil* details such as collars and cuffs. He began showing in 1990, closed his custom design business in 1995, and then reorganized toward the end of the decade to produce lower-priced clothes.

Vera Wang (b. 1949) grew up on Manhattan's Upper East Side and became a competitive ice skater in her childhood. After college, she worked at *Vogue* as a fashion editor and stylist, and then at Ralph Lauren as a design director for accessories before opening Vera Wang Bridal House in 1990. The by-appointment salon offered upscale wedding dresses from a number of designers, including Wang's own line, and soon included evening and cocktail dresses. Wang explained her approach to bridal as "not thinking bridal formulas but fashion."[6] **Michael Kors** (b. 1959) expanded the womenswear line he launched in 1981 to include menswear, with his characteristic focus on well-fitting separates in quality materials that were sold in in-store boutiques in exclusive department stores. Kors was hired by the French label Céline as creative director and he received acclaim for his polished and luxurious sportswear. **Randolph Duke** (b. around 1955), the son of a former Las Vegas showgirl, began his career as a swimwear designer. In 1996 he was contracted to re-establish the Halston brand. Duke debuted an eveningwear line in Los Angeles in 1998 that earned him a devoted celebrity clientele. **Pamela Dennis** (b. 1966) gowned celebrities and top models in columnar evening dresses, and her after-five looks were carried by department stores and boutiques. **Richard Tyler**'s (b. 1946) career took him from Melbourne, Australia, to Los Angeles where his meticulously tailored clothing became a favorite with entertainers. From 1993 to 1994, he was head designer for Anne Klein, and shortly thereafter design director at Byblos. Tyler won multiple awards for his couture-level collections, all produced in California.

Designers: Italy

Ever the master of understatement, **Giorgio Armani** continued to show deceptively simple clothes that maintained the Armani "illusion of weightlessness" so important to his international clientele. He also maintained business independence, refusing an acquisition offer from LVMH. Armani added new lines to an already impressive fashion empire: A/X Armani Exchange, offering lower-priced casual clothing, launched in 1991, and accessories, watches, and home furnishings followed. In 1995 he offered skiwear for men and women and in 1998 he opened an Armani store in Beijing, China.

Gianni Versace continued to build his empire with several labels and diffusion lines, swimwear, denim, underwear, fragrance, and home. Versace's advertising continued the promotion of the supermodel; and he typically used the same women in his print advertisements as on the runway. His work in the 1990s was simultaneously derided for objectifying women and praised for empowering their sexuality. His 1992 collection of leather dresses with inspiration from S&M and gladiators was highly controversial. Other highlights of these years included short evening dresses based on lingerie and corsetry, leather jackets adorned with studs and trapunto, and Christian imagery including crosses and the Virgin Mary. An Andy Warhol-inspired dress that featured beaded faces of Marilyn Monroe and James Dean was memorable. A 1994 collection featured broad slashing and slits held together by oversized safety pins;

Below An extremely sexy but wearable ensemble from Gianni Versace is representative of his iconoclastic approach to fashion. The vivid colors, oversized Greek key motif and fitted denim are all among Versace's favorite design elements.

Opposite top The bold sophistication of the Italian aesthetic was epitomized by this pantsuit from Dolce & Gabbana, as modeled by Yasmeen Ghauri in Milan in 1992.

Opposite bottom Classic and cutting edge often combined in the work of Miuccia Prada, as seen in this ensemble from 1998.

a dress from this collection was worn by actress Elizabeth Hurley to the premiere of *Four Weddings and a Funeral* (1994), and the shocking style brought attention to both Hurley and Versace. His continued love of the classical world was shown with his signature Medusa head as well as his frequent use of Greek keys in his design. He continued his use of metal mesh and experimented with new materials. His menswear included bold printed shirts in leopard or paisley designs, neoclassic images, and even whimsical animal repeats such as frogs. His menswear advertising often featured half-dressed leather-clad models, a sort of couture biker gang. Versace continued to design theater costumes, and also provided numerous rock stars with performance clothes, and his pieces were in the wardrobe of Princess Diana. He published several well-illustrated books of his work that enhanced his image as a pre-eminent style setter, including *Vanitas*, *Signatures*, *Men Without Ties*, and *Rock and Royalty*. His murder in 1997 at the height of his fame sent shockwaves through the fashion world. After his death, Versace's sister Donatella took over the creative directorship of the company. A major retrospective exhibition was mounted at the Metropolitan Museum of Art the year following his death.

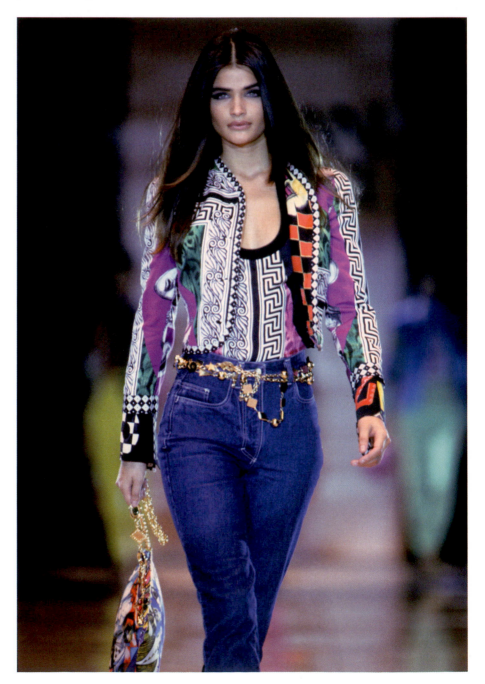

Domenico Dolce (b. 1958) and Stefano Gabbana (b. 1962), who designed under the name **Dolce & Gabbana**, launched their brand in 1985 with a show in the New Talents section of the Milan showings. They expanded their label into knitwear, lingerie, and beachwear, and showed their first menswear in 1990. Their lower-priced D&G line debuted in 1994. The duo also designed for the Complice label for several years. Early collections were described as "cinematic," often based as much on styling as on the clothes: supermodels Linda Evangelista and others were posed and made-up to resemble Italian movie stars of the 1950s. The titles of their collections revealed their inspirations, including "Little Italy" (fall/winter 1990) and "La Dolce Vita" (spring/summer 1992). They also found inspiration in Sicily, exploring the eroticism of religion and repression and the sense of seduction inherent in black dresses worn by widows. Dolce & Gabbana unabashedly incorporated retro references into their collections, creating cross-dressed zoot suit looks for women as well as corseted 19th-century-influenced styles. The actress Isabella Rossellini frequently appeared in their clothes, creating a physical link between the past and present of Italian cinema. They costumed Madonna for her 1993 world tour and their theatrical fashions were popular with musicians and entertainers, including the tobacco-brown gown worn by Susan Sarandon when she received the Best Actress Academy Award for *Dead Man Walking* in 1996. As Brooke Shields said the same year, "Somewhere between Baudelaire and Brenda Starr these two sweet boys have created a great place to dwell."[7]

Prada, a luxury goods firm established in Milan in 1913, underwent a major expansion and greatly increased visibility in the hands of Miuccia Prada (b. 1949), granddaughter of the firm's founder, Mario Prada. She inherited the family business in 1978. In the late 1980s, Prada introduced a simple black nylon tote bag and small backpacks to the existing line of fine leathers. With a distinctive triangular logo, the Prada bag became an international must-have accessory. Prada launched a women's ready-to-wear collection in 1989, followed by menswear in 1993, and introduced the lower-priced line Miu Miu the same year. By the end of the decade, Prada had joined the ranks of major international fashion corporations, with accessory and eyewear lines and shares in other fashion houses. From the outset, Miuccia Prada's aesthetic was challenging, even contrary, as she experimented with proportions and color combinations that were at odds with prevailing taste. Prada's association with artists was important to the brand; in 1993 Prada and her husband Patrizio Bertelli founded a contemporary art exhibition space in Milan which grew into the Fondazione Prada. Prada's collaborations with avant-garde architects for her boutiques also added intellectual cachet to the label.

Although her company headquarters were located in Hamburg, **Jil Sander** (b. 1943) showed her collections in Milan for most of the decade. A graduate of the Krefeld School of Textiles, Sander worked as a fashion journalist and began her design career with a boutique in Hamburg in 1968. As her business grew during the 1970s and 1980s, Sander began to design collections and added furs, cosmetics, and accessories. She opened a Paris boutique in 1993 and debuted a menswear line the same year. Sander took a strict approach to fashion with a design aesthetic that was sometimes described as "sensual solemnity." Her trouser suits were especially appreciated for a unique blend of menswear detailing and realistic, feminine cut. The same principles informed her unadorned dresses: "Ms. Sander pays close attention to fabric and cut. This is an absurd observation to be forced to make about a fashion collection: every designer should care about these ... many don't."[8]

Designers: Belgium

In 1986 six young designers, all graduates of Antwerp's Royal Academy of Fine Arts, emerged on the international fashion scene with a group showing at London's British Designer Show. Showing under the collective name "The Antwerp Six," Walter Van Beirendonck, Dirk Bikkembergs, Ann Demeulemeester, Dries Van Noten, Dirk Van Saene, and Marina Yee offered striking, and strikingly individual, fashion that

Below Dries Van Noten's relaxed look on the runway in 1999 anticipates the "Boho" look that would dominate young women's fashion early in the coming decade.

Opposite A 1998 runway image from Ann Demeulemeester encapsulates many of the elements of the designer's romantic deconstructed aesthetic.

established Belgium as a source of avant-garde design. As Van Noten said, "We don't want to become a little Paris. We want to stick to Antwerp."[9] While no signature aesthetic unified the group, the Belgian designers prioritized concept over market appeal, asserting that clothing should be "read" like art. The deconstructed aesthetic was in evidence, and several acknowledged the influence of Rei Kawakubo and other Japanese designers. Within a year of their initial showing in London, the Antwerp designers had received major press coverage and their work was in select stores.

Of the original six, some went on to establish important international careers. **Walter Van Beirendonck** (b. 1957) designed under his own name, produced the W. & L.T. (Wild and Lethal Trash) line, and designed for the German jeans company Mustang. His work was characterized by bright, often fluorescent, colors and willful exaggeration of silhouette. A fluorescent yellow plastic jacket from spring/summer 1996 featured inflatable "pecs." Van Beirendonck's collections of the mid- to late 1990s combined retro references to futuristic style, such as molecular shapes, Mod snowflakes, and flower-power daisies, with the candy-colored aesthetic of rave subculture and the emerging visual vocabulary of computer graphics. Fittingly, his collection for fall/winter 1997 was entitled "Avatar." Van Beirendonck also experimented with holographic fabrics, garments that generated sound, and printed textiles impregnated with scent.

After success at the London showing, **Ann Demeulemeester** (b. 1959), who had established a company called bvba 32 in Antwerp in 1985, offered a line of accessories and then started showing in Paris in 1992. From the start of her career, Demeulemeester used strong tailoring and luxury materials to produce an elegant version of the deconstructionist aesthetic. She favored a slim, disciplined silhouette with surprise elements such as frayed seams and asymmetry. While certain collections were understood and accepted only by a limited group of fashion insiders, other aspects of Demeulemeester's aesthetic were more readily adapted to mainstream fashion, for instance white shirts worn with shirt tails out, and extra-long sleeves covering the hands. Demeulemeester launched a menswear line in 1996 and established a flagship store in Antwerp in 1999.

Dries Van Noten (b. 1958) opened a store in Antwerp in 1987 and began showing in Paris four years later. He quickly gained renown for both his menswear and women's collections. Van Noten's work was especially distinguished for the international scope of the textiles he chose. His designs incorporated batiks, woven paisleys, prints, and embroidery in an era that often emphasized minimalism and neutral color. Van Noten's emphasis on layering was also important; some ensembles layered jackets over dresses over pants, each piece in a carefully considered, but not matching, fabric. Of all the Belgian designers who came to prominence in the early 1990s, Van Noten was perhaps the most accessible.

Although not part of the original "Antwerp Six," **Martin Margiela** (b. 1957) also graduated from the Royal Academy. He worked for Gaultier for several years and showed his first solo collection in 1988. Margiela incorporated vintage pieces into many of his collections, layering or altering them to give them a new life. His aesthetic of deconstruction was expressed with unfinished seams, frayed areas, and some pieces subjected to mold and rust. A designer who famously stayed behind the scenes at presentations, he refused to be photographed. Margiela was appointed the director of the women's line at Hermès in 1997, a move that surprised many in the fashion industry.

The leading ladies of *Friends*, Courtney Cox, Jennifer Aniston, and Lisa Kudrow, were especially noted as hair and fashion style setters, perhaps the 1990s equivalent of *Charlie's Angels*. Aniston's hairstyle, named the "Rachel" after her character, became especially popular.

Hair and Beauty

Many hairstyles were inspired by film and television, including the layered "Rachel" worn by Jennifer Aniston on *Friends*. Smooth bobs and chin- to shoulder-length blunt cuts were particularly popular, often with zigzag parts. Up-dos, chignons, and French twists, often with face-framing tendrils, were also fashionable. Many black women adopted very short hairstyles, often with areas of straightened hair. Women of all ages experimented with hair coloring, achieving effects that ranged from subtle blonde highlights to vivid, and frankly fake, shades from aubergine to blue. Wide, high-contrast highlights were known as "skunk stripes." Hair extensions were greatly popular. A number of celebrities, including model Lucie de la Falaise, adopted short haircuts, prompting converts to the "gamine" look.

Strong brows were still in fashion, but were more tweezed and shaped than the style of the 1980s. Make-up was balanced, with no particular feature emphasized. Eye make-up was refined, somewhat smoky. Lipstick colors were often very saturated and plums and earth tones were popular for several seasons. Matte lipstick came into fashion mid-decade. Nails were an important part of the beauty story as low-cost nail salons sprung up in urban centers and the manicure began to be regarded as a grooming necessity. While many women indulged their preference for long, brightly painted nails, the most fashion-forward look was seen on Uma Thurman in *Pulp Fiction* – short, dark nails. Chanel's black-red "Vamp" nail polish and "Vixen," a lower-priced imitation from Revlon, were among the most popular shades of the decade. Like Thurman, Patricia Arquette in *Lost Highway* (1997) popularized dark-painted nails and a hairstyle with bangs – expressions of "bad girl" style influenced by 1940s film noir as well as the look of 1950s pin-up Bettie Page. Actress Elizabeth Taylor's best-selling fragrance White Diamonds debuted in 1991, launching a series of gem-titled scents from her perfume company.

Menswear

Menswear was very designer-driven and, like women's fashion, reflected influence from the 1970s, subcultures, film, and television. It was also similarly segmented as designers and brands offered something for every taste. Dress codes continued to relax and one of the main stories of the period was the personal styling of the suit. Prestige brands including Armani, Ermenegildo Zegna, and Valentino continued to be important. Calvin Klein and Donna Karan were also well recognized for their contemporary tailored designs. Paul Smith offered creative variations of the classics, emphasizing color and details. Joseph Abboud presented casual elegance in refined materials. Hugo Boss was a major name in menswear; the company launched two additional lines in 1993, the trend-driven Hugo brand, and Baldessarini, its premium line, named for lead house designer Werner Baldassarini. The company also became known as a prominent sponsor of exhibitions and began awarding the Hugo Boss prize for contemporary art in 1996.

Through the course of the decade, high fashion moved toward a narrow silhouette for tailored clothes. Single-breasted suits dominated, usually three-button styles. Four-button styles were worn by fashion-forward men. Some jackets with five, even ten, buttons were available, showing influence from Victorian, Edwardian, even Mod, modes. Lapels were medium width, sometimes tending toward narrow, resembling menswear from the mid-1950s. Dark three- or four-button jackets (with white shirts and black ties), as seen in *Men in Black* (1997), were popular. Calvin Klein produced suits reflecting this influence that were described as "Amish." Pleated trousers were common at the start of the decade, but flat-front trousers began to be seen widely by mid-decade.

Below left A 1997 ensemble by Daniel Hechter combines a rich eggplant jacket, plaid trousers, changeant shirt, and a green tie, typical of the unusual tertiary shades favored by menswear in this decade.

Below right The peacock male sensibility of the late 1960s and early 1970s had a strong impact on the runway late in the decade.

MOMMY TRACK

The August 1991 cover of *Vanity Fair*, featuring a very pregnant Demi Moore, nude but for her diamond jewelry, signaled the dawn of a new motherhood-obsessed era. Mindful of the ticking of their "biological clocks," millions of women born at the tail-end of the baby boom rushed into parenthood, creating a boomlet of their own. They brought with them heightened expectations for motherhood: seamless integration of work and family, intellectually optimized offspring, and stylish apparel to wear "while waiting."

Dressing during pregnancy was of course an age-old issue, one that often involved altering existing garments and grimly accepting several months of dowdiness or isolation. Ready-to-wear for pregnancy had been available since the early 20th century and designer maternity was notably promoted during the 1950s. Seemingly oblivious to fashion trends, the maternity market often seemed to channel an inner child, putting pregnant women in smocked tops and Peter Pan collars – unacceptable choices for a generation weaned on designer jeans. In the 1990s, maternity clothing evolved into a significant market niche. High-style maternity labels acknowledged that modern expectant mothers worked, played, and wanted to look trendy, even sexy.

Gap's maternity line brought a sportswear sensibility to a previously matronly product. The aesthetic of maternity changed as the belly became a cultural obsession, rather than a site of embarrassment: celebrated instead of camouflaged. The American company Belly Basics debuted The Pregnancy Survival Kit, consisting of dress, tunic, skirt, and leggings – a versatile wardrobe in a box. Unlike maternity styles of previous eras, the jersey pieces did not add bulk to a woman's already blooming figure but offered comfortable body-skimming styles that worked for all occasions and were easily accessorized. Some women took body-consciousness to an extreme, showing off their contours as late-pregnancy bellies (and distended belly buttons) became socially acceptable. Prefiguring the contemporary pop culture obsession with spotting celebrity "baby bumps," a number of high-profile celebrities took their place on the mommy track with well-documented pregnancies and births during this decade, including Madonna and Sarah, the Duchess of York.

Pregnant supermodel Yasmin Le Bon, photographed in 1998 outside a posh Manhattan baby store.

Rugged outdoorsy style meets dandyism in this 1993 ensemble from Sonia Rykiel.

The suit was still the basis of the business wardrobe, but with changing dress standards, many men accessorized with more freedom. Some eliminated ties; the suit worn with an open-necked shirt became an acceptable look in creative industries and for casual Fridays. It was also popular for eveningwear as formal evening looks had significantly declined. Others wore a t-shirt or polo shirt with a suit, or sometimes with trousers and blazer; a look that had previously been acceptable only for informal occasions found its way to business settings. Footwear options changed as well and some men paired their fashionable suits with high-style sneakers.

Shirts were often tapered with a higher armhole and narrower sleeves than in previous years. While standard colors such as white and light blue were popular, dark tones were also worn, even with suits. A smooth finish was desirable and many shirts had a polished look; some men even wore silk. Collar shapes were quite varied. The "mafia" styles of films such as *Goodfellas* and *Casino* encouraged an elongated collar shape. Dark and bright colors were also favored for sport shirts. The golfer Tiger Woods brought new attention to his sport, making golf wear trendy. Skateboarding and surfing also received greater attention and renewed the popularity of California-style sportswear, raising the profile of brands such as Vans, Volcom, and Quiksilver. Knit shirts and sweaters also followed the lean silhouette. Commando sweaters were worn, both the army surplus versions and designer interpretations. Overcoats frequently had a vintage flair and harkened back to the "Bold Look" of the 1950s. Fine fabrics such as mohair, bouclé, and plush were frequently used. Raincoats maintained a classic, even minimalist, style. Hip-length barn jackets, blanket coats, car coats, peacoats and parkas were also worn, even over suits.

High-status underwear was aggressively marketed. Calvin Klein briefs were sold in provocative packaging. Versace produced sexy underwear that often included a Greek key design on the waistband. Boxer shorts, especially in retro prints, and boxer briefs (knit underpants with longer legs) were popular. Many ties were wide, at 1970s proportions. While brocades and other woven patterns were widespread, prestige prints such as Hermès and Fendi were also desirable. Footwear showed a clunkier proportion; even some dress shoes had wide welted soles. Sneakers were more widely worn than ever and some even became collectors' items.

Perhaps as a result of the aging of the baby boom generation, and probably influenced by gay culture and an athletic aesthetic, the shaved head became more common and signified a new masculinity; men in urban centers around the world resembled the bald cartoon mascot Mr. Clean. In general, body hair was discouraged and many men underwent waxing and other depilation, especially for chest and backs. The male body image continued to transform as more and more men went to the gym. Muscled men adorned advertisements – for instance, holding up microwave ovens in much the same way that buxom women stood next to cars in 1950s advertising. A new version of the peacock male developed in the gay subculture and quickly entered the mainstream. Muscular men wore snug spandex t-shirts, and tight-fitting, mid-thigh short pants combined with Dr. Marten boots. Social commentators noted that men had become the new victims of the "beauty myth" and steroid abuse created unnaturally shaped bodies. Obsessive bodybuilding became classified as a psychological disorder termed "bigorexia," making linguistic reference to the eating disorder anorexia.

Above left A 1997 advertisement shows the prevalence of denim in the children's market for both boys and girls.

Above right Child star Mayim Bialik as Blossom in 1994 shows her sophisticated side. Style setters such as Fran Drescher were important to junior fashion, as seen here with the upswept hair, tight-fitting dress, and black hose.

Children's Fashion

Continuing the social trend toward informality apparent since the 1960s, most children dressed in casual attire for all but the most formal occasions. There was little separation between clothes for school and for play. The pieces and silhouettes were largely unchanged and included dresses and jumpers (pinafores) for girls of all ages, and t-shirts, pullovers, and jeans and other trousers for both sexes. In the wake of the Gulf War, a pronounced military styling influenced both boys' and girls' clothing. For young children, classics such as smocked dresses, nautical styles, and tartan outfits coexisted with more trend-driven options. Brand awareness strongly affected children's clothing and identifiable logos were prominent. Many major labels, including Armani, Krizia, Moschino, and Charvet, offered children's fashion. As with the adult market, denim was a fashion focus. Most major denim brands had childrenswear divisions, such as Baby Guess and Little Levis, offering stylish jeans and jackets.

Professional sports were particularly influential on sportswear. Licensed football and soccer jerseys in small sizes reflected team loyalty. Michael Jordan and the Chicago Bulls made basketball jerseys a wardrobe staple; Air Jordan sneakers by Nike were extremely popular, even for babies. The baggy look favored by snowboarders entered the mainstream and influenced children's sports clothes.

Several color trends stood out including the predominance of bright colors and the very pronounced gendering of colors: shades of pink and purple dominated girls' clothing while boys' apparel was offered in a palette based on blue, green, and neutrals. Camouflage was a popular motif and was recolored without regard to its military associations, in shades of pink and multicolors for girls, dark blues and greens for boys, and neon mixes for both genders. Pop culture imagery decorated t-shirts, pajamas and other pieces. Children could choose from characters such as Teenage Mutant Ninja Turtles, the Simpsons, Doraemon, Smurfs, and Peanuts.

Name-brand athletic shoes were status items; popular brands included Converse, Etnies, Fila, and Pelle Pelle. Sneakers often had a high-tech look with high-contrast color schemes, shaped soles, mesh, and Velcro straps. Child-size Timberland and Dr. Marten boots were also available. Backpacks were very popular and ranged from large, functional styles to miniature handbag-sized versions. Boys of all ages wore baseball caps, often with the brims to the back. Many young girls wore flower-trimmed hats in imitation of Mayim Bialik of the popular television series *Blossom*.

Asian Style

In addition to the Asian designers established and enjoying great success in both New York and Paris markets, Asian style and style setters were more prominent than ever before in Western consciousness. Asian consumers were increasingly important to Western luxury brands, while Asia also enjoyed a more significant influence on fashion and style. Fashion weeks developed in many major Asian cities while the use of traditional dress styles declined further throughout the continent. Asian-based designers, such as Taiwanese Wang Chen Tsai-Hsia of the label Shiatzy Chen, grew in significance. David Tang launched the line Shanghai Tang in 1994 and soon established retail stores in cities in Asia, North America, and Europe. Biyan Wanaatmadja established his own line, Biyan, in Jakarta after more than a decade working in Europe. André Kim was the leading Korean fashion designer, operating Salon André in Seoul; he had shown in Paris as early as 1966. In 1997 he received the Presidential Culture and Art Medal.

Japanese popular culture exerted a marked influence on fashion. The strong stylization of anime presented striking images of fashion in graphic novels and in television cartoons, influencing street style. A highly developed street fashion scene, populated by teenage adherents of a number of subcultures including "Lolita," "Ganguro," and "Gothic Lolita" began late in the decade in Tokyo, each with its own subset of devotees. "Lolita" style often involved doll-like proportions and make-up, frequently utilizing lace and ribbon, along with short, stiffened, full skirts; "Gothic Lolita" realized Lolita style in black with inspiration from Victorian mourning attire. "Ganguro" girls favored a tanned complexion and candy-colored hair. For men, the Victorian "Aristocrat" style was closely related to Lolita girls, as was the Elvis-inspired Rockabilly look. Much of this activity was centered on the Harajuku district of Tokyo. Japanese popular music encouraged these styles. The rock guitarist Mana, with his own personal aesthetic, operated his clothing and accessories company, Moi-même-Moitié, beginning in 1999. Groups including The 5.6.7.8's and L'Arc-en-Ciel also promoted global awareness of Japanese popular culture.

Above Lolita became a popular style tribe in Japan and was later copied in other parts of the world. Here a "sweet Lolita" is typified by her doll-like demeanor, pastel colors, and Victorian frills.

Below Hong Kong-based Shanghai Tang combined traditional Chinese style with a *Matrix*-inflected cool in this modernized take on the traditional cheongsam.

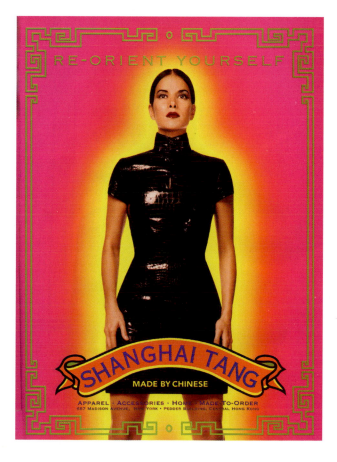

Above left Film director John Woo at the MTV Movie Awards with actor Andy Lau. Woo's red ribbon, worn to promote AIDS awareness, was typical of the use of different colored ribbons to make socially conscious statements.

Above right Film star Gong Li wears a gown with traditional Chinese elements before crowds of fans at the Cannes Film Festival in 1997.

While the successful film careers of Jackie Chan and Jet Li represented the continuing importance of action heroes, a new group of performers demonstrated a wider view of Asian influence in movies and music. In John Woo's *Hard Boiled*, Chow Yun-Fat, Anthony Wong, and Tony Leung wore costumes that continued a *Miami Vice* look, including jackets in saturated or pastel colors, and shirts worn open to reveal athletic singlets. Hong Kong-born singer and actor Leslie Cheung, a founder of the "Cantopop" style of music and star of the film *Farewell My Concubine* (1993), was one of Asia's most important stars. In addition to his performing, Cheung, the son of a leading Hong Kong tailor, was celebrated for his elegant style and was repeatedly featured in notable fashion magazines. "The Four Heavenly Kings" of Cantopop (Jacky Cheung, Aaron Kwok, Leon Lai, and Andy Lau) all had similar impact on men's style; female singing stars Faye Wong and Anita Mui contributed to women's looks. Gong Li's appearances in numerous Chinese films with global distribution led the international press to make comparisons to glamorous movie stars of Hollywood's golden age. Michelle Yeoh, a former Miss Malaysia and established Hong Kong action star, became the first Asian leading "Bond Girl" in *Tomorrow Never Dies* opposite Pierce Brosnan. The 1997 film thrust Yeoh into the international spotlight, and gained her the distinction of being named one of the "50 Most Beautiful People in the World" by *People* magazine in that same year.

Malay singer Anuar Zain modeled for Dockers in Malaysian advertising, and performed wearing khakis and shirts in his 1998 music video "Bila Resah," along with a dozen Dockers-clad extras. Filipina singers Lea Salonga and Regine Velasquez reached global audiences; Indonesian singer Ruth Sahanaya won major awards in European cities, while her compatriot Anggun Cipta Sasmi (known as "Anggun") enjoyed the status of international style setter.

Simultaneously with this assertion of Asian style and Asian celebrities, Westerners of Asian descent became more prominently placed in the mainstream media, and "glass ceilings" were broken. Figure-skating champions Japanese American Kristi Yamaguchi and Chinese American Michelle Kwan were both notably featured as product spokesmodels and in fashion advertisements. Taiwanese American Lucy Liu joined the cast of *Ally McBeal* in its second season and contributed strongly to the style of the show with her chicly venomous character. Korean American actor and model Rick Yune was the first Asian man to appear in advertisements for Ralph Lauren and Versace.

The End of the Decade

Despite fragmented stylistic options, fashion was available through so many sources and offered so many possibilities that the fashion system could seem massive and monolithic. As Guy Trebay wrote in 1999, "Something's changed about fashion. It's nobody's groovy little secret anymore, any more than McDonald's is. Once the province of women (and a certain sector of the gay male population), fashion has been supersized."[10] Fashion had become more democratized and phenomena such as fast fashion would soon permeate the market, producing a truly globalized fashion outlook. New factors in the fashion equation included increased use of the internet, mobile technologies, textile advances, rampant individuality, and the adoption of the euro by the European Union in 1999. Helmut Lang's fall/winter 1999 collection offered a compelling view of possibilities: subtle references to unisex dressing and science fiction without any suggestion of kitsch or costume. As the turn of the millennium loomed, glimmers of fashion's future shone through.

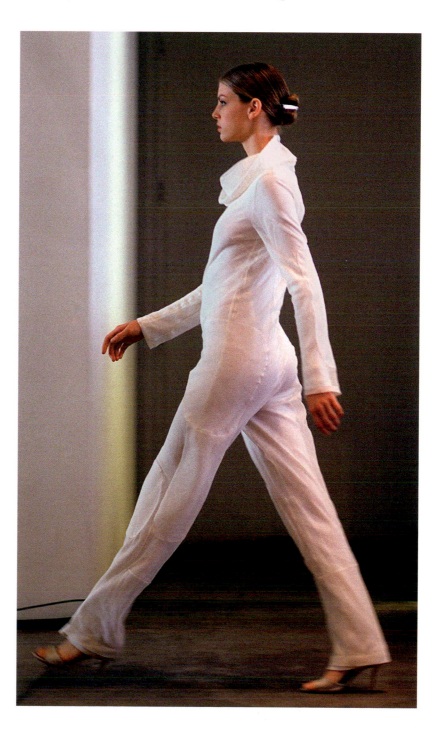

The simple and forward-thinking elegance of Helmut Lang provided very wearable versions of the minimalist aesthetic, an idea that would continue into the 2000s.

Chapter 13

The 2000s

Mixed Messages

Shopping at a mainstream retailer in 2009, a consumer could find nearly the same looks as in 2000, or even 1995. Perhaps to offset global turmoil and rapid innovation, people were "clinging as never before to the familiar in matters of style and culture," observed Kurt Andersen in *Vanity Fair*. He continued, "The future has arrived and it's all about dreaming of the past." Meanwhile, fashion designers presented ever more outrageous "theme" collections, described by the press as "masquerade ball" or "under the big top." Galliano's version of Egypt for the spring 2004 Dior collection, or Lagerfeld's "over the top ode to Russia"[1] for Chanel pre-fall 2009, made for eye-catching press, but had little relevance to ready-to-wear. During much of the 20th century, collections from different fashion houses often showed a consistent seasonal aesthetic. But by 2000, such cohesion had ceased to exist and individualism was stressed all the more. With nothing ever *truly* out of style, garments and accessories that once

Opposite Rebecca Westcott's 2003 painting of fellow artist Isaac Tin Wei Lin captures the ubiquitous hoodie and a "fauxhawk" hairstyle, elevating Isaac's paint-stained casual look into the context of fine art portraiture.

Right The popular television show *Project Runway* gave aspiring fashion designers the opportunity to show their work to industry professionals. With numerous international editions, the show became a global phenomenon as catchphrases like "make it work" and "one day you're in, the next you're out" became vernacular expressions.

would have been considered seasonal or easily dated were soon absorbed into the realm of "seasonless fashion basics." Despite unrest throughout much of the world – and the mixed messages coming from the fashion industry – fashion continued to be more globalized, with Asia an especially important participant. As luxury brands became part of everyday jargon, the demand for branded items increased and, priced high enough, anything could attain "luxury" status. The public fascination with the fashion industry grew even further, as fashion-oriented television programs turned fashion terms – such as "red carpet," "couture," and "make it work" – into vernacular expressions.

Social and Economic Background

"The Decade From Hell" proclaimed *Time* in December 2009:

> Bookended by 9/11 at the start and a financial wipeout at the end, the first 10 years of this century will very likely go down as the most dispiriting and disillusioning decade in the post-World War II era.[2]

The world held its breath as, time zone by time zone, digital clocks turned from 1999 to 2000. While the transition did not produce the feared "Y2K" effects, the mood of the decade would soon be defined by acts of terrorism. The September 11, 2001 attacks on the World Trade Center in New York and the US Pentagon were followed by the Moscow Theater hostage crisis of 2002, the Madrid train bombings of 2004, the 2005 London bombings, the hotel bombing in Islamabad in 2008, and a series of terrorist bombings in Indonesia; the world was set on edge as each incident was linked to religious or nationalist extremism. Conflicts in the Middle East in response to September 11 involved armed forces from the United States, the United Kingdom, and their allies, led by George W. Bush and Tony Blair. Extremist groups were also responsible for the 2007 assassination of Pakistani Prime Minister Benazir Bhutto. These tragedies were dwarfed by the Indian Ocean tsunami of 2004, which claimed more than 150,000 lives, and a catastrophic earthquake in Sichuan, China, in 2008.

Influential heads of state included British Prime Minister Gordon Brown and France's President Jacques Chirac, who was followed by Nicolas Sarkozy. In the United States, Barack Obama was elected President in 2008, the first man of African descent to hold the office. Vladimir Putin of Russia set an agenda that helped the nation out of its financial troubles but was seen as authoritarian and alienated historic allies. Premier Wen Jiabao was fundamental to China's rise as an economic power.

Despite friction between countries, global trade flourished, encouraged by the adoption of the euro as a common currency across most of the European Union. Western companies and products expanded their presence in previously underdeveloped markets. Large cities all over the world filled with branches of Starbucks, Gap, and Louis Vuitton. Another aspect of the "shrinking" world was the increase in portable technology. By 2003 smartphone users could email and browse the internet from a hand-held device. Soon users had constant access to news, entertainment, communication, and shopping via countless applications. Social media sites such as MySpace, Friendster, Facebook, and Twitter created global online communities while users created individual websites to showcase themselves.

The Arts

While New York and London remained important art centers, international exhibitions brought attention to other regions. African artists were increasingly represented in Europe and North America. Contemporary art flourished in mainland China and India, while art fairs multiplied around the world. Major museum expansions included London's Tate Modern, the Museum of Contemporary Art in Taipei, and the Ian Potter Center of the National Gallery of Victoria in Australia. Among the most publicized works of the decade were Damien Hirst's diamond-encrusted skull and the

Damien Hirst's controversial sculpture *For the Love of God* incorporates diamonds and platinum and human teeth. Emblematic of the taste for spectacle in the arts, it also reflects the vogue for skulls as a fashion motif.

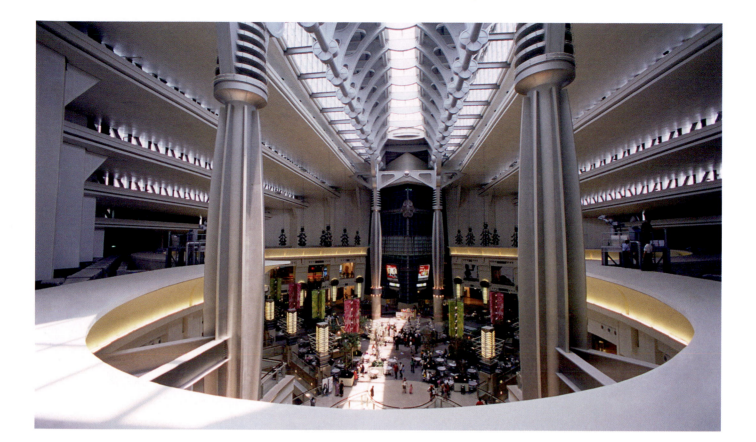

The colossal skyscraper Taipei 101 held the distinction of being the world's tallest building for much of the decade. The tower's base contains a multi-level shopping complex, seen here, primarily devoted to luxury brand merchandise.

large-scale installations of Icelandic artist Olafur Eliasson. Several touring exhibitions, including *Bodies, Tutankhamun,* and *Titanic,* became mass-market spectacles. The annual Burning Man art event in the Black Rock Desert, Nevada, was increasingly visible and commercialized.

Monumental architectural projects included Taipei 101, the tallest building in the world when completed in 2004. The 101-floor tower incorporated "green" building methods and a postmodern Asian aesthetic. The Taipei 101 mall, at the building's base, offered several floors of high-end stores. Dubai's Palm Islands, a lavish residential development, were the largest man-made islands in the world. By contrast, the "Small House" movement in domestic architecture emerged in North America, the United Kingdom, Japan, and other areas. Eclecticism in interior design paralleled individualism in fashion. Top fashion designers collaborated with retailers to produce limited-edition home goods. The concept of good design for the public continued to grow and was the basis of brands such as IKEA and Design Within Reach.

DVDs drastically reduced movie theater attendance, and services such as Netflix brought easier access to movies. Hand-held devices were commonly used to view movies, bringing the "big screen" art form into progressively smaller screens. Computer-generated effects raised audiences' expectations. The "franchise" concept became pervasive as movies generated sequels, spin-offs, and video games. International films were more popular than ever before in Western markets. Important films included such diverse releases as *Traffic* (2000), *Letters from Iwo Jima* (2006), *The Queen* (2006), *La Vie en Rose* (2007), and *Slumdog Millionaire* (2008). The variety of human experience was explored in *In the Mood for Love* (2000), *Eternal Sunshine of the Spotless Mind* (2004), and *The Lives of Others* (2006). Films with a historical setting varied widely in locale and time period and included *Gladiator* (2000), *Red Cliff* (2008), and *The Young Victoria* (2009), while apocalyptic visions of the future were presented in such films as *28 Days Later* (2002) and *Children of Men* (2006). Animation enjoyed continued popularity with films including *Shrek* (2001) and *Kung Fu Panda* (2008). Asian films dominated the action genre with varied offerings including *Hero* (2002), *Infernal Affairs* (2002), and *Ong-bak* (2003). Fantasies *Pan's*

Eiko Ishioka's costume designs for *The Cell* (2000) were no more bizarre than those shown on the fashion runways. The headpiece worn by Jennifer Lopez suggested similar styles by McQueen or Galliano.

Labyrinth (2006), *Transformers* (2007), and *Avatar* (2009) captivated audiences, and a number of fantasy films generated sequels; some were based on literary series, including *The Lord of the Rings* and *Harry Potter*.

"Reality" television threatened to dominate the medium and was a potent vehicle for creating celebrity. Despite a mixed reception to their reality "stardom," hotel heiress Paris Hilton and Kim Kardashian, the daughter of a Los Angeles attorney, emerged from reality television as style setters and subsequently launched fashion lines. Makeover shows such as *Ambush Makeover* and *What Not to Wear* were extremely popular. Talent competitions such as *Britain's Got Talent* and *American Idol* were copied the world over, from Brunei's *Passport to Fame* to *Iceland Idol* to Brazil's *Ídolos*. However, dramas and comedies were still widely popular. Shows with paranormal themes were popular. *Being Human* prompted the widespread observation that "zombies were the new vampires." But vampires maintained a loyal following, as evidenced by *True Blood* and *The Vampire Diaries*. Medical and crime dramas retained their appeal. Workplace sitcoms were also audience favorites, especially *The Office*, in its British and American versions.

Best-selling books by international authors included *The Kite Runner* by Khaled Hosseini, *The Shadow of the Wind* by Carlos Ruiz Zafón, Yann Martel's *Life of Pi*, *The Time Traveler's Wife* by Audrey Niffenegger, Elizabeth Gilbert's *Eat, Pray, Love*, and Joan Didion's *The Year of Magical Thinking*. Japanese manga comics became widely popular, and the stature of the graphic novel was upgraded with serious subjects. Portable reading devices proliferated and e-books became popular.

Stage productions were as varied as fashion looks. Numerous adaptations from films included *The Producers*, *Spamalot*, and *Billy Elliot*. *Avenue Q* presented a *Sesame Street*-style show, with actors and puppets intermingled discussing racism and pornography, while *The Light in the Piazza* explored new musical forms. Dramas including David Auburn's *Proof*, Edward Albee's *The Goat*, and John Patrick Shanley's *Doubt* explored complex themes. Nilo Cruz earned the first Pulitzer Prize awarded to a Latino playwright for *Anna in the Tropics*. Tom Stoppard's award-winning trilogy *The Coast of Utopia* was presented in several languages, while Yasmina Reza's French-language *Le Dieu du Carnage* enjoyed success in English translation as *God of Carnage* on Broadway and the West End. Other performance genres displayed a retro sensibility, including neo-burlesque and the Roller Derby revival.

Popular music encompassed a wide range of styles, each with its own fashion influence. Long-established bands including The Rolling Stones and Red Hot Chili Peppers continued to fill large arenas. The fan base of rap and hip hop expanded globally. Techno was a favorite for nightclubs, and country music produced a number of charismatic singers. The careers of Charlotte Church and Andrea Bocelli demonstrated classical music's continued turn toward pop.

Fashion Media

Online sources became increasingly important for fashion information. Many blogs concentrated on "real people" through street photography and bloggers' own wardrobe posts, encouraging a personal relationship between writers and readers. An international group of pioneering fashion bloggers included Scott Schuman of *The Sartorialist*, Tavi Gevinson of *The Style Rookie*, Bryan Grey Yambao of *Bryanboy*, Yvan Rodic of *FaceHunter*, and Susanna Lau of *Style Bubble*. As the fashion industry and mainstream media acknowledged their influence, bloggers obtained front-row seats at fashion shows, served as guest editors, curated exhibitions, and judged competitions. *Vogue*, *L'Officiel*, *Harper's Bazaar*, and *Elle* launched editions in several Asian markets and developed websites and mobile applications. Celebrities consistently appeared on covers, displacing models. Digital manipulation of images became common but the use of heavy retouching on some models' faces and bodies was controversial. Fashion shows were frequently broadcast live on the internet so that viewers could see the show direct from the runway. Music and lifestyle magazines and websites also relayed fashion information, often targeting specific groups. The US television series *Project Runway* generated numerous international spin-offs including *Project Catwalk* in the United Kingdom, *Proyekt Maslul* in Israel, Portugal's *Projecto Moda*, and Norway's *Designerspirene*. Video games such as *Imagine: Fashion Designer* and Facebook's *Fashion World* reflected the media's obsession. In 2006 Robin Givhan, fashion writer for *The Washington Post*, won a Pulitzer Prize for criticism; the award recognized that writing on fashion was important cultural commentary.

As the apparel and cosmetics industries recognized the advantage of broader marketing, standards of beauty continued to expand to include a variety of ethnicities and body types. Vanity sizing, such as size zero, appeared in ready-to-wear, but plus-sized models were promoted; full-figured Sophie Dahl and Anna Nicole Smith were among the few exceptions to the established trend for extremely thin fashion models. In addition to familiar faces such as Gisele Bündchen, Kate Moss, and Alek Wek, international favorites included Joan Smalls, Catherine McNeil, Coco Rocha, and Sasha Pivovarova.

Designers as Celebrities, Celebrities as Designers

The place of fashion in the media – and in the public imagination – was so large that many designers became celebrities, as details of their personal lives became newsworthy. Valentino, on the verge of retirement, was the subject of a 2008 documentary that recapped his career but focused mainly on the designer's de luxe lifestyle. One of the most exposed design celebrities, Marc Jacobs, was profiled in *The New Yorker* in 2008 in an article that detailed his personal struggles and included a photograph of the designer posing on a balcony in his underwear; Jacobs' work at Vuitton was the subject of a television documentary. Many designers exerted authority outside fashion; *bon vivant* Roberto Cavalli introduced a premium vodka and opened several nightclubs, one in a revamped 15th-century church in Florence. Tom Ford ventured into movie-making, financing and directing *A Single Man* (2009), and appeared naked in *Out* magazine in 2007.

Valentino at an exhibition of his red dresses in celebration of *The Last Emperor*, the 2008 documentary film about his career.

Many celebrities, most with little or no training, established fashion lines and brands. In 2001 Jennifer Lopez launched her J.Lo by Jennifer Lopez line, targeted to voluptuous women, saying, "Just because you dress sexy doesn't mean you're a bad girl, it just means you know how to dress."[3] Singer and actress Jessica Simpson was extremely successful with a shoe line, followed by affordable clothing and accessories, while actress Chloë Sevigny was briefly creative director at the edgy label Imitation of Christ. With numerous product endorsements under their belts, twin actresses Mary-Kate and Ashley Olsen launched two fashion lines, The Row, offering upscale basics, and Elizabeth and James, a lower-priced contemporary line. Former Spice Girl Victoria Beckham showed her first dress collection, for spring/summer 2009, at New York Fashion Week. Sean Combs debuted his Sean John men's sportswear label in 1999; named Menswear Designer of the Year by the Council of Fashion Designers of America (CFDA) in 2004, Combs expanded into a full range of clothing. Jay-Z's preference for fashion basics inspired him to launch his Rocawear line. Rapper Pharrell Williams launched two fashion lines, Billionaire Boys Club and Icecream, and singer Beyoncé Knowles founded House of Deréon in 2006 in collaboration with her mother, a fashion stylist. Real estate magnate Donald Trump hopped onto the fashion bandwagon with his Signature Collection of menswear; his daughter Ivanka ventured into jewelry and accessories. Controversial former Philippine First Lady Imelda Marcos debuted a jewelry line in 2006 that included butterflies and shoes as recurring motifs, referencing her nickname "The Iron Butterfly" and her immense shoe collection.

Fashion and Society

American First Lady Michelle Obama emerged as an important style setter. She was in the public eye from the beginning of her husband's campaign, and her wardrobe choices were heavily scrutinized. Mrs. Obama consistently displayed an independent attitude toward fashion and helped advance the careers of several young or unsung designers. Among her favorites were Isabel Toledo, Jason Wu, Sophie Theallet, Rodarte, and Duro Olowu, but she mixed designer looks with clothes from Gap, J. Crew, and

Below left Michelle Obama and Carla Bruni-Sarkozy in one of their much publicized "fashion face-offs" on April 4, 2009. Obama wears an Alaïa jacket, while Bruni-Sarkozy wears a Dior coat and carries a Chanel bag.

Below right At the 2008 wedding of Ellen DeGeneres and Portia de Rossi, both brides wore Zac Posen designs.

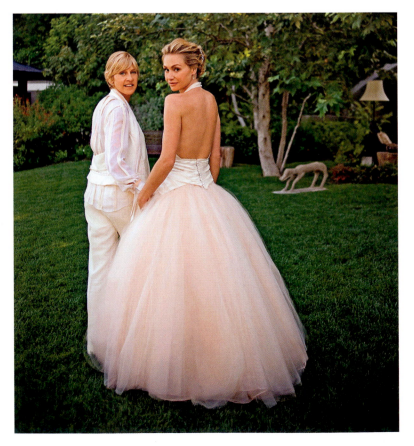

In March 2009, *Women's Wear Daily* featured a photo editorial, including this cover image, inspired by Edie Beale and styled by Catherine Marie Thomas, the costume designer of the television adaptation of the "Grey Gardens" story.

Target. Some of her fashion choices were controversial, including her sleeveless dress on the cover of *Vogue*. Her first four years in the White House coincided with former fashion model Carla Bruni-Sarkozy's term as First Lady of France, and the press manufactured an ongoing sartorial competition between the two. When they met in Paris in April 2009, the meeting was described as a "fashion face-off."

Argentinean Máxima Zorreguieta Cerruti wed the prince of the Netherlands, Willem-Alexander of Orange, in 2002 wearing Valentino, while television journalist Letizia Ortiz wore a dress by venerable Spanish designer Manuel Pertegaz – then in his late eighties – for her wedding to Spain's Prince Felipe of Asturias. The 2008 wedding of Ellen DeGeneres and Portia de Rossi, with both women in Zac Posen designs, set the tone for the growing number of same-sex weddings being performed in different parts of the world.

With the constant desire of the press to dub the latest acting or music personality a "fashion icon," curators and authors reinforced fashion legacies. Wardrobes of society celebrities on display in major museums included Jacqueline Kennedy's at the Metropolitan Museum of Art in New York and Anna Piaggi's at the Victoria and Albert Museum in London, as well as exhibitions devoted to Iris Apfel, Nan Kempner, and Grace Kelly. Exhibition openings became "red carpet" events, covered in the fashion press like awards shows, especially the Metropolitan Museum Costume Institute opening, which was dubbed "the Party of the Year." The Heart Truth®, a North American organization devoted to women's cardiovascular health, used red dresses as their symbol and staged fashion shows of elegant red dresses modeled by diverse celebrities; in 2005 they mounted the First Ladies' Red Dress exhibition.

Edith Ewing Bouvier Beale, the cousin of Jacqueline Kennedy and the subject of a 1975 documentary film, *Grey Gardens*, became an accidental icon. "Little Edie's" bizarre and improvisational personal style included wrapped short skirts along with headscarves and hoods adorned with vintage brooches. Her story was retold as a Broadway musical in 2007 and was adapted for television in 2009. Little Edie's eccentric look influenced several designers, including Phillip Lim in 2007, and Marc Jacobs created the "Little Edie" bag. Among the many editorials imitating her look was a March 31, 2009 *Women's Wear Daily* cover story guest-styled by the costume designer for the television version, Catherine Marie Thomas.

Film, Television, Stage, and Fashion

In *The Devil Wears Prada* (2006), costumed by Patricia Field, the fashion media was the subject of the film, while *Zoolander* (2001) presented the fashion industry in outrageous parody. In *Legally Blonde* (2001) Reese Witherspoon's character mirrored the fashion consumer with her love of "It" bags and designer shoes, while in *Confessions of a Shopaholic* (2009), shopping was the story. *The Royal Tenenbaums* (2001) featured Gwyneth Paltrow with heavy eyeliner, bobbed hair, and childish plastic barrette, which were much imitated; and in *The Dukes of Hazzard* (2005), Jessica Simpson introduced "Daisy Dukes" (very short shorts) to a new generation. In *The Tuxedo* (2002), Jackie Chan gained superpowers when wearing a tuxedo equipped with built-in smart technology, a prediction of fashion's future.

Period films had considerable impact on fashion press, trends, and style tribes. Productions with an 18th-century setting such as *Marie Antoinette* (2006) and *The Duchess* (2008) were particularly influential. *Pride and Prejudice* (2005) presented romanticized versions of Regency fashions by Jacqueline Durran. The manipulated late 19th-century styles created by Catherine Martin and Angus Strathie for *Moulin Rouge!* (2001) were imitated in music videos, fashion magazines, and burlesque costumes. *The Prestige* (2006) and *Sherlock Holmes* (2009) encouraged period details in men's fashions.

Films with a 20th-century period setting were also very important. In *Coco avant Chanel* (2009), Catherine Leterrier's costumes traversed several decades while the film itself contributed to the Gabrielle Chanel mystique. *Frida* (2002), with costumes by Julie Weiss, renewed interest in the artist Frida Kahlo, with the film asserting a fictitious edition of *Vogue* with Kahlo on the cover. For *Chicago* (2002), Colleen Atwood created slick, widely imitated late 1920s looks, while for *Idlewild* (2006) Shawn Barton blended Prohibition-era styles with a hip-hop aesthetic. Keira Knightley's provocative green dress by Jacqueline Durran in *Atonement* (2007) spawned numerous imitations. Post-war 1950s styles were celebrated in Sandy Powell's romantic clothes in *Far From Heaven* (2002) and Albert Wolsky's more naturalistic styles in *Revolutionary Road* (2008), encouraging vintage enthusiasts to seek out 1950s finds, while Marit Allen's

The reach of *Moulin Rouge!* (2001) extended to television advertising, fashion editorials, and merchandising, as seen in this store window at Bloomingdale's in New York inspired by the film.

Kirsten Dunst in *Marie Antoinette* (2006)

QUEEN OF FASHION

In 2000 John Galliano created his "Masquerade and Bondage" collection, which included a characteristically costumey "Marie Antoinette" dress. It had an 18th-century pannier silhouette and *engageant* sleeve ruffles, and was embroidered with depictions of Marie's life and the guillotine. An analysis of Galliano's dress opened Carolyn Weber's 2006 book, *Queen of Fashion: What Marie Antoinette Wore to the Revolution*. With such attention from Galliano, Weber, and many others, the 2000s proved to be the best decade in Marie Antoinette's fashion career since the 1780s. Although Madonna had dabbled in Marie Antoinette style back in 1990, it was the 2000s that really solidified Marie as a pop culture icon. The decade began with the 2001 film *The Affair of the Necklace*, with Hilary Swank as a scheming noblewoman at the court of Marie, played by Joely Richardson, costumed by Milena Canonero. The same year Antonia Fraser published the biography *Marie Antoinette: The Journey*, in which she called into question some of the longstanding negative assumptions about Marie. Many film productions were forthcoming, including a French television movie in 2005 and a Canadian television movie in 2006.

The most notable production was Sofia Coppola's adaptation of Fraser's biography. Shot on location at the Palace of Versailles, the film captured the transformation of Marie's style during her years as princess and then queen. Canonero (again the costume designer) earned the Academy Award, along with nominations from the British Academy of Film and Television Arts (BAFTA) and the Costume Designers Guild. The film's transgressive style – post-punk soundtrack, a shot of red high-top sneakers, and sequences resembling music videos – increased its cool factor. Kirsten Dunst, the film's star, was soon the darling of the fashion media. Her *Vogue* cover in September 2006 accompanied an opulent editorial shot by Annie Leibovitz, with Dunst modeling 18th-century-inspired gowns by such designers as McQueen and Galliano for Dior, and also including some of Canonero's costumes. Macarons, heavily consumed by Marie in the film, became a fashionable treat once again, particularly from the French confectioner Ladurée. Runways and retail were filled with 18th-century-inspired fashion products, and Marie Antoinette's peasant-derived "shepherdess" style was linked to boho-chic.

Meanwhile, the 2001 biography *Georgiana: Duchess of Devonshire* was adapted for the big screen in *The Duchess* (2008), a vehicle for Keira Knightley. The costumes, by Michael O'Connor, were awarded both the Academy Award and the BAFTA Award. Georgiana generated the same public fascination as Marie Antoinette, and was even referred to in such terms as "The British Marie"; Knightley graced magazine covers and the film inspired its own fashion editorials, including one in *Vogue* in 2008 showing designs modeled by Stella Tennant, a descendant of the duchess.

Following the popularity of Coppola's *Marie Antoinette*, John Corigliano's 1991 opera *The Ghosts of Versailles*, with Marie its protagonist, experienced several revivals, and an important exhibition about the queen was shown at the Paris Grand Palais in 2008. By the end of the decade she was fully ensconced as a fashion icon, and her popularity showed no signs of waning, with several film and television productions emerging in the early 2010s, notably *Farewell My Queen*, with former fashion model Diane Kruger as the doomed Marie.

Above left Anne Hathaway, Meryl Streep, and Stanley Tucci portrayed fashion-press insiders in the 2006 film version of *The Devil Wears Prada*, an adaptation of Lauren Weisberger's novel.

Above right Uma Thurman's slick yellow tracksuit in *Kill Bill: Vol. I* (2003) not only referred to a costume worn by Bruce Lee in *Game of Death* (1973) but also showed the influence of a manga aesthetic on activewear.

costumes for *Brokeback Mountain* (2005) encouraged Western wear for men and women. *Down With Love* (2003) was described in the press as a "nonstop fashion show"[4] thanks to Daniel Orlandi's lavish early 1960s costumes, while Colleen Atwood's glamorous mid-1960s costumes for *Nine* (2009) provided inspiration for fashion editorials. *Factory Girl* (2006) solidified Edie Sedgwick's posthumous fashion influence. Betsy Heimann's costumes for *Almost Famous* (2000), Sharen Davis' for *Dreamgirls* (2006), and Albert Wolsky's for *Across the Universe* (2007) also encouraged continued interest in 1960s and 1970s styles.

Fantasy films provided inspiration as well. The *Pirates of the Caribbean* films included swashbuckling ensembles by Penny Rose that were widely influential from masquerade to vernacular fashion, and reinforced the vogue for skulls as a motif – from prints to t-shirts to belt buckles. With *Spiderman* (2002) and its sequels, costume designer James Acheson stimulated the continuation of superhero influences on fashion, furthered by Lindy Hemming's costumes for *Batman Begins* (2005) and *The Dark Knight* (2008). *Twilight* (2008) and its sequels were widely covered in the fashion press, fashion blogs, and fan sites, as young people emulated the look of its protagonists. For *Harry Potter and the Philosopher's Stone* (2001) and its sequels, Judianna Makovsky's costumes encouraged school insignias as a fashion trend, and school scarves with stripes for tweens.

Crouching Tiger, Hidden Dragon (2000) and *Curse of the Golden Flower* (2006) reinforced interest in Asian style. Colleen Atwood's costumes for *Memoirs of a Geisha* (2005) were inspirational to numerous designers, cosmetic companies, and editorials. The film's leading ladies – Michelle Yeoh, Gong Li, and Ziyi Zhang – were featured in magazines modeling clothing similar to their costumes. Asian martial arts inspired the *Kill Bill* movies (2003, 2004), in which the costumes included a bright yellow jumpsuit on Uma Thurman, inspired by actor and martial artist Bruce Lee.

On television *Sex and the City* continued to air for several seasons, with ensembles styled by Patricia Field. While the influence of the sartorially confused Carrie, played by Sarah Jessica Parker, was debated, Parker and her co-stars became fixtures in fashion magazines. The series hammered brand names into the minds of the general public, making Manolo Blahnik a household name all over the world. *Ugly Betty* premiered in 2006 (based on the Colombian telenovela *Yo soy Betty, la Fea*), and took as its setting the world of the fashion press. The teen drama *Gossip Girl*, which debuted in 2007, presented prep-school teenagers clad in designer clothing, and their look was widely covered in the press and on fashion blogs; a variety of styles was encouraged, such as blazers with contrasting trim, bow ties, headbands, colorful hosiery, and designer bags. *Mad Men*, which debuted in 2007, inspired fashion editorials and further interest in vintage pieces; costume designer Janie Bryant enjoyed significant press coverage.

A spate of reality shows contributed to the media obsession with luxury style. *Real Housewives of Orange County* showed wealthy women with luxury brands and cosmetic procedures; the fashion relevance of the show and its spin-offs was reinforced in the press, including a feature on the New York wives in *Harper's Bazaar* in July 2008.

A few theatrical productions also had a bearing on fashion. For *Spring Awakening*, the reimagining of Frank Wedekind's 1891 novel, designer Susan Hilferty provided an edgy postmodern update on period clothes that was widely imitated by artistic young people. Hilferty was also known for her costumes for *Wicked*, creating a much publicized dress for the good witch Glinda inspired by Dior's 1947 "Junon." Martin Pakledinaz's costumes for *Thoroughly Modern Millie* (2002) encouraged the continued taste for 1920s flapper styles. On stage at the Salzburg Music Festival and the Metropolitan Opera, a contemporary-styled production of *La Traviata* included soprano Anna Netrebko clad in a knee-length red cocktail dress. The widespread exposure of Netrebko's dress in the fashion press perpetuated the popularity of the "little red dress."

Music and Fashion

Female performers were influential fashion figures, onstage and off. Madonna's looks included bohemian and disco. Jennifer Lopez's most memorable fashion statement was a green dress by Donatella Versace, open to the navel, worn to the 2000 Grammy Awards. Continuing the trend for exposure, Toni Braxton chose a white dress by Richard Tyler completely open on both sides for the 2001 Grammy Awards. Janet Jackson's key fashion moment was her "wardrobe malfunction" during her performance at the 2004 Superbowl, which exposed one breast. Lady Gaga's outré outfits were an essential part

The diverse fashion statements made by female vocalists such as (left to right) Avril Lavigne, Shakira, and Britney Spears mirrored the diversity in fashion (as well as reflecting their distinct styles).

Right Many fans imitated the vintage-inspired style of Amy Winehouse, particularly her beehive hairdo, cat-eye make-up, and tattoos.

Opposite below Sportswear from Ed Hardy/Christian Audigier exemplifies the casual turn of mainstream fashion. Embellishments and patterns were derived from tattoo motifs.

of her performances and provocative videos. She patronized an international group of designers, notably Alexander McQueen. Curvaceous Christina Aguilera's girl power inspired imitation with fans "decked out in pastel tank tops and denim cutoffs, and armed with pink frosted lipstick."[5] Gwen Stefani's strong look combined a post-punk allure with a sinewy physique. Alicia Keys and Nelly Furtado were often seen with long hair and large earrings, and Jewel transcended the casual image associated with other singer–songwriters, often appearing in glamorous low-cut gowns. Björk's idiosyncratic fashion choices ranged from a swan-inspired dress for the 2001 Academy Awards to a performance wardrobe from Eiko Ishioka. Amy Winehouse created a diva persona, channeling great performers of the past, including Ronnie Spector's beehive hairdo and Maria Callas' cat-eye make-up.

Influential bands, including Creed, Coldplay, Linkin Park, and Radiohead often adhered to a post-grunge aesthetic with casual clothes, quasi-uniform ensembles, and unstyled hair. The Killers moved through several phases, transitioning from an early New Wave look to a more rugged eclectic style, often showing elements of Teddy Boy influence. Fans imitated the ska-inflected look of Sugar Ray and the California post-punk styling of Green Day. The fresh-faced boys of Liverpool's BBMak helped popularize a hip clean-cut look. Rappers were influential in fashion, through their

own wardrobe choices and the brands and designers mentioned in their songs and videos. Diamond studs in both ears were worn by many rappers and quickly transferred into mainstream style. Heavily tattooed Soulja Boy set styles in eyewear and popularized long bead necklaces. Nelly's Band-Aid, originally worn to cover a basketball injury, prompted many fans to imitate the quirky accessory. Kanye West's style ranged from oversized preppy basics worn with flashy jewelry to precisely tailored white suits. LL Cool J, 50 Cent, and Ludacris were all known for their contributions to hip-hop style.

Male solo performers reflected and perpetuated trends in menswear, including Josh Groban's tousled hairstyle and untucked shirts worn with a tailored jacket. Michael Bublé's look combined a narrowly cut suit, loosened tie, and well-groomed stubble. Jason Mraz reflected a hipster aesthetic; Justin Bieber influenced young men's hairstyling. The death of Michael Jackson in 2009 generated enormous amounts of merchandise as commemorative t-shirts and collectables were promoted at major retailers.

Fashion Trends

A number of trends were common throughout men's, women's, and children's clothing. Sources of inspiration included a random mix of fashion history, world dress, and a century's worth of subcultural styles, rehashed or revamped. Fashion staples were reinvented, such as brightly colored trench coats at car coat length, or denim jackets with ruffles. Despite periodic calls by designers and the press for "dressing up," informality prevailed. Mainstream "fast fashion" offered democratized style and low prices, encouraging consumers to regard garments as disposable. Teenagers and twenty-somethings (known as Millennials or Generation Y) displayed changed ideas about modesty, wearing very low-cut pants that revealed underwear, midriff-baring crop tops, and exposed cleavage in the workplace. T-shirts and denim continued to be central to most wardrobes. Jeans were available in many finishes such as "whisker washed" and dark "hard denim." The premium denim market expanded. Jeans were purposely slit, frayed, or shredded, sometimes appliquéd, embroidered, or graffitied. Pocket variations were common; often the rear pockets were lowered and embellished. Pants that were very tight on the calf sometimes had zippered, even laced-up, ankles. Cargo pockets had become firmly established in the fashion repertoire.

Hooded jackets and sweatshirts were so popular that the "hoodie" became a wardrobe staple. Originally associated with active sportswear, then adopted into hip-hop style, it expanded to include versions in a variety of materials, often featuring bold graphics, all-over prints, and patterns based on designer logos. While utilitarian cotton jersey hoodies continued to be worn, the hoodie was fabricated in such far-flung materials as cashmere and upholstery brocade. Sleeveless hoodies were popular during the decade, with style compromising function.

By the 2000s camouflage was firmly ensconced in the general fashion story, strongly encouraged by the spring 2001 collection from John Galliano for Dior. The wars in Iraq and Afghanistan further popularized the pattern's relevance. In womenswear, menswear, and childrenswear, the print was widespread in a variety of colorways, including grayscale, pink, blue, orange, and mixed colors. Camo accessories, including shoes, bags, scarves, and wallets were common, as were camo home products. Camouflage's meaning was so diluted that it became a perennial print, like polka dots or stripes.

General trends in embellishment included slashing, popular early in the decade, with cuts strategically placed to expose underwear, body parts, and tattoos. Frayed

Above Perry Farrell of Jane's Addiction performs during the 2003 Lollapalooza festival. The group was known for flamboyant costumes; here Farrell's patchwork ensemble shows the influence of a deconstructed designer aesthetic.

Above Cargo pants became a wardrobe staple for both men and women; their multiple pockets were put to use as electronic gadgets such as cell phones and MP3 players became widespread.

Right Competitive swimwear incorporated textile innovations and fuller body coverage, such as Speedo's Fastskin swimsuits.

edges and unraveling were common. Beading and sequins were frequently applied to daytime garments, even in menswear. Along with the many embellishments used on jeans, embroidered patches, stones, and studs were common. Oversized or obvious zippers were used for decorative effects. Amulet symbols were seen as jewelry, t-shirt motifs and tattoos; popular symbols included the Egyptian *ankh*, Arabic *hamsa*, and Norse *aegishjalmur*. Earbuds and headphones took on the role of accessories and were available in many colors and styles.

Innovations from competitive sports were adapted for consumers, including anti-bacterial finishes, UV blocking, and bonded seams. Speedo's Fastskin, a fabric inspired by sharkskin and designed to reduce drag, revolutionized performance swimwear. Eiko Ishioka's hooded speedskating unitards continued the superhero aesthetic. Shoes with articulated toes appeared as an alternative to conventional sneakers.

The body modification vogue that began in the 1990s continued to grow significantly. Tattooing in particular was widespread and de-stigmatized. New technologies included white tattoos, fluorescent tattoos, and some that were easily removable. Tattoos, piercings, and other modifications such as stretched earlobes and scarification became visible even in the business world. Several reality television shows focused on tattooing, including *Miami Ink* and its Los Angeles, London, New York, and Madrid spin-offs.

Responsible Fashion

The fashion industry began to address sustainability in various ways. Taking inspiration from the ecology movement of the 1970s, and later products such as Sally Fox's color-grown cotton (Fox Fibre®) and the organic materials of Sandra Garratt's New Tee Inc., an alternative fashion movement developed. Michael Braungart and William McDonough's 2009 book *Cradle to Cradle* set the tone for the development of "green fashion," "eco fashion," or "slow fashion." Hemp, bamboo, and corn-based fibers were promoted, and fiber content often became a selling point. Some designers and manufacturers emphasized the use of artisanal practices, such as Natalie Chanin's Alabama Chanin company. Rogan Gregory of Loomstate and Phillip Lim's "Go Green Go" line focused on the use of organic materials. Outdoor clothing company Patagonia

Reflecting increased focus on sustainability in fashion, an organic cotton skirt and sweater by Patagonia are shown against a backdrop of bamboo, a material also used as an alternative fiber for apparel.

was one of the first mainstream brands to make a commitment to sustainable practices part of their mission, while Brooklyn Industries was founded on recycling. Designers examined indigenous cultures as sustainability prototypes. Magazines published "green issues" and industry associations, including the Sustainable Style Foundation, were formed. Vintage and do-it-yourself were touted as sustainable fashion practices, an idea that gained traction especially among the young and hip. But some high-end designers also incorporated vintage pieces into their designs, notably Martin Margiela, and Tara Subkoff of Imitation of Christ. Some fashion followers even justified their short shorts and other scanty clothing as using less fabric and therefore being "sustainable," suggesting one of the ironies of the popular phrase, "green is the new black."

While the design centers of fashion were mostly located in major cities in Europe and North America, much of the manufacturing took place in developing countries in Asia, Africa, and South America. Several high-profile cases brought to light child labor and exploitative working conditions. Major companies including Gap and Wal-Mart were found to have used factories where children were virtually enslaved; athletic shoe manufacturers were frequently cited in labor violations. As organizations such as Human Rights Watch brought attention to the problem, corporations responded with "social responsibility" pledges. Like eco fashion, "responsible" fashion became a distinction. Brands such as People Tree and Edun promoted their commitment to fair-trade fashion and some labels went so far as to include information with garments about the workers involved in the production of each piece.

Style Tribes

In lifestyle and fashion, hipsters affected an urban pastiche that was heavily influenced by past subcultures including bohemians, beatniks, and hippies. The reuse of the word "hipster," part of the vocabulary of Greenwich Village and Harlem's jazz scene as far back as the 1940s, was an ironic indication of the recycled ethos of the contemporary hipster:

> The hipster is that person, overlapping with the intentional dropout or the unintentionally declassed individual – the neo-bohemian, the vegan or bicyclist or skatepunk, the would-be blue-collar or postracial twentysomething, the starving artist or graduate student – who in fact aligns himself both with rebel subculture and with the dominant class, and thus opens up a poisonous conduit between the two.[6]

Particular neighborhoods were known as hipster hotspots, in cities including Brooklyn, Chicago, Seattle, Los Angeles, and San Francisco. But the style also thrived, with local variations, in London, Berlin, Moscow, Sydney, Prague, Paris, and in Asia. "Indie rock" was fundamental to the hipster ethos. The emergence of Hipster Rap demonstrated how the movement went beyond its white roots to embrace a wider racial and economic sweep. The self-consciously shabby apparel that many hipsters adopted signified their mixing of anti-establishment sentiment and cultural elitism, encouraging *Details* to dub them the "poor-geosie." Male hipsters wore plaid shirts or t-shirts with retro or satirical logos, with jeans or cut-off shorts. Fit was either baggy or shrunken. Common accessories included truckers' caps, and pork pie and snap-brim hat styles. Female hipsters layered t-shirts with open shirts, vests, and sweaters with skinny jeans, or wore droopy vintage dresses. Both men and women wore Keds and Converse sneakers, Dr. Martens, and other heavy shoes, preferably scuffed. Vintage or retro eyeglasses and childlike accessories such as cartoon lunchboxes and backpacks completed the look. For men, ironic facial hair, such as mutton-chop

whiskers and bushy beards, were common; physical fitness was not stressed and a "beer belly" attested to hipster embrace of artisanal brews. Women preferred casual, undone hair or blunt-cut, obviously dyed, styles; many wore floppy knit stocking caps. Body modifications were essential and many hipsters became walking galleries of tattoos and piercings. Humorous publications including *A Field Guide to the Urban Hipster* and *The Hipster Handbook* defined and illustrated the movement. Thoroughly commercialized by the end of the decade, ready-to-wear hipster fashion was available from youth-oriented brands such as American Apparel and Urban Outfitters.

The term "geek chic," used to describe both men and women, played on the assumption that "techies" were too busy or too brainy to care about fashion. The widespread popularity of geek chic acknowledged the influence of computer technology and offered an alternative fashion that combined elements of retro styles with an adolescent or college-age sensibility. The *Times* of London quipped, "It's cool to be uncool."[7] The style existed at all price levels. Viktor & Rolf's 2003 menswear show – featuring tight sweaters with collegiate-style lettering, plaid jackets, and knotted mufflers – was tied to the style. The popular television comedy *The Big Bang Theory* debuted in 2007 and showcased the nerdy wardrobes of four young physicists: *Star Wars* t-shirts, fatigue jackets, 1970s-style hip huggers, and sneakers. The characters Betty and Henry from *Ugly Betty* also embodied the look. Specific items earned the "geek chic" description, particularly Penguin-brand knit shirts, and heavy dark eyeglass frames.

The Steampunk aesthetic emerged from 19th-century science fiction such as Jules Verne's *20,000 Leagues Under the Sea*, and H. G. Wells' *The Time Machine*, with significant input from films such as *Metropolis* and *Brazil*. Steampunk style visualized a future derived from pre-digital technology, typically with steam-driven machines; it was reinforced by several films during the decade, including *Sky Captain and the World of Tomorrow* and the Japanese animated film *Steamboy*. The look of *Lemony Snicket's Series of Unfortunate Events*, with costumes by Colleen Atwood and set design by Rich Heinrichs, was perhaps the on-screen pinnacle of Steampunk. The style affected fine art and home decor as well as fashion; Steampunk conventions and trade shows were organized. The fashion expression showed influence from a variety of sources including Goth and Japanese street style, and bore a relationship to cosplay. Steampunk fashion mixed improbable and anachronistic elements, such as Victorian corsetry with goggles, or frock coats and top hats with ray guns and gas masks.

The Elements of Women's Fashion

In a time when many divergent – even contradictory – fashion niches were encouraged, "boho-chic" was perhaps the most prevalent style for young women. Tied to revivalism, regionalism, and a strong reaction to minimalism, the "boho-chic" aesthetic derived from a wide range of sources, including the Middle Ages, Pre-Raphaelites, bohemians, gypsies, and the multicultural chic of the early 1970s. Indian influences were strong, encouraged by the international popularity of Bollywood films, and general "tribal" details were also an important part of the look. Tops were often camisoles and tank tops, and frequently peasant blouses. Sometimes layers were added, such as oversized tunic tops, often diaphanous, and vests, ranging from fur and skins to peasant-inspired. Gauzy babydoll dresses were popular. Full skirts, often dubbed "floaty," were integral to the look, often tiered, or gored, or with large billowing godets. Skirts were often layered, mixing opaque with sheer, and hems were often uneven, scalloped, or handkerchief. Tie-dye and paisley were typical patterns, and embellishment included fringe, embroidery, sequins, and coins. Boots were popular, including cowboy as well as suede and fringed styles. Oversized scarves, floppy wide-brimmed hats, and large shapeless shoulder bags, along with braided or tousled hair, often completed the look. Vintage elements were integral to the style.

British actress Sienna Miller was so strongly associated with the look that young

New York burlesque performer Lily Faye wearing a Steampunk ensemble, photographed by Babette Daniels.

London women were noted for their "Sienna-ishness" in the *Sunday Times*. Mary-Kate and Ashley Olsen embraced a disordered variation, dubbed "hobo-chic." The boho look was supported throughout the market. High fashion versions were provided by Roberto Cavalli and Catherine Malandrino; peasant blouses and tiered skirts were aggressively encouraged by mass-market retail, with Old Navy promoting the full gypsy styles as "super skirts." Despite press declarations that the look had peaked mid-decade and was denounced as "over" by some fashion writers, the style continued to thrive, with German *Vogue*'s "Haute Bohème" editorial in 2009, and Macy's hippie-derived "Summer of Love" collection the same year.

The revival of "boyfriend" style is attributed to a moment in 2008 when paparazzi-stalked actress Katie Holmes was spotted wearing jeans that belonged to her husband Tom Cruise: "Menswear is back in a very basic way, and straight from his closet! Katie Holmes has literally been wearing Tom's jeans!" extolled *Today Style Buzz*.[8] Boyfriend jeans were baggy, usually cuffed, often torn, the waist cinched in with a big belt. Soon oversized t-shirts, jackets, and overcoats were common; Holmes herself was often seen in Levi jean jackets. Retailers and manufacturers offered "boyfriend khakis" and "boyfriend cardigans" along with blazers and neckties.

Long skirts and dresses were frequently worn for day. Jersey dresses with spaghetti straps or halter necklines, frequently with a narrow skirt shape, were sometimes called "patio dresses" but were worn in urban settings as well. The press and designers placed emphasis on dresses (over separates) and promoted many styles: shirtwaists, sheaths, safari looks, and wrap dresses, often with thin belts and a slightly elevated waistline. The Empire waistline was very important for day dresses, evening and special occasions, and even for casual tops.

Skirt suits and pantsuits continued to be popular. Some skirt suits featured boxy jackets with three-quarter-length sleeves, suggesting a late 1950s influence. Designers showed wider shoulders and shoulder pads in 2008, but generally jackets maintained a lean line. Oversized hooks and eyes, eyelets, and grommets were sometimes used both as design and functional details. Skirt length varied from mini to knee length to mid-calf. Gored skirts often emphasized construction, with piping between the gores or the use of contrasting fabrics. Spiral gores, bias-cut and trumpet skirts were popular. Some skirts and dresses were longer in back than in front, diagonally cut to be longer on one side, or uneven side to side. Lean, low-cut pants were stylish; the term "muffin top" described the effect resulting from low pants worn too tight. While some trousers were flared or boot-cut, many were extremely narrow on hips and legs. Tight, thin jersey leggings were extremely popular and "jeggings," leggings with jeans details, emerged. High-waisted pants were seen late in the decade in many variations, some with wide legs but others continuing the prevailing lean silhouette.

Poet blouses and turtlenecks were as popular as classic buttoned styles. Knits ranged from extremely lightweight devoré t-shirts to chunky cardigans and long sweater coats. Many sweaters and tops featured overly long sleeves. Tops with peekaboo shoulders were seen and many women wore wide-necked shirts off one shoulder. Empire-waisted babydoll dresses were worn as tops over jeans and leggings. Ruffles were used widely, from blouses to purses to coats, as details on otherwise basic clothes.

Many coats were quite tight-fitting, often belted or with a slightly high waistline. Trench coat variations were popular, especially three-quarter length. Satin and lamé trench coats were worn for evening. More loosely fitting, oversized coats were also seen, including square-cut jackets and coats that continued the early 1960s influence. Ponchos were also very popular.

Special occasion dressing was greatly varied. Goth inspiration was seen at all levels, from avant-garde designers to mainstream styles. Classically inspired dresses, marked by a slender silhouette, small pleats, and draped cowl necklines, were often termed "goddess" dresses; Versace, Marchesa, Blumarine, and many other labels promoted the look. Nude tones and pastels were often used. One-shouldered dresses and cascade drapes and ruffles were often seen for special occasions.

While black, gray, and other neutrals were popular, bright bold colors were also seen, often in the form of color blocking or as accents, or "pops," of color in otherwise neutral ensembles. Animal prints were extremely popular, as were vintage-looking florals. The increased use of digital printing created new effects; printing on crinkled fabric produced random-looking (but intentional) blank areas. Futuristic-looking fabrics, vinyl, and other materials with a shiny finish, were in widespread use.

Swimwear showed varied inspiration. Neoprene tank suits, some with large zippers, resembled abbreviated wetsuits. Two-color florals and bright prints suggested Hawaiian and surfing influence. Retro-style one- and two-piece suits featured shirring, structured bras, and high-waisted bottoms. But many swimsuits were extremely scanty; thong bikinis totally exposed the buttocks and tanga bikinis featured half coverage. Other categories of activewear continued to develop, especially yoga clothing; lululemon and Athleta were leading brands in activewear.

Above Two models in boho style pose with a chihuahua in 2005. The red dress is by Burberry Prorsum and the gray dress is by Paul & Joe. Textured accessories including the hand-stitched shoulder bag and knit cap and scarf provide contrast with the sleek headphones and cell phone.

Opposite A 2009 concept sketch by illustrator Renaldo Barnette for an urban sportswear line demonstrates popular fashion elements including princess-line dress, shapely jeans, and a faux fur shrug – all worn with stiletto heels.

Body Suit of Matte Jersey and Satin worn with Rhinestone & Chain Mail Belt and Stretch Wool Pants

Patent Leather & Chain Mail Bag

Chinchilla Shrug over Silk Chiffon Dress

Matte Jersey Dress w/ Rhinestone Buttons and Green Goat Skin Scarf

Ranaldo Barnett

"IT"

Midway through the decade, the *New York Times* asked, "Who pays $1,200 for a handbag, and why?"[9] The article reported on shoppers' "infatuation" with handbags, naming pieces from Marc Jacobs, Prada, and Hermès as current best sellers. But $1,200 was actually a modest amount considering that certain bags from Mulberry, Vuitton, Chanel, and others were priced upward of $2,000, often pushing into the *tens* of thousands for very limited-edition models or those made of exotic leathers. As fashion consumers redirected their attention and money from status-symbol shoes to "It Bags," designers and brands focused on the profit potential of bags, even including handbags in runway presentations. This was in contrast to earlier decades, when accessories had been considered important to the bottom line but peripheral to seasonal spectacles. Department stores expanded selling areas for handbags and boutiques cashed in on the trend, exploiting the perception of exclusivity that fed public desire. Waiting lists formed, and retailers reported desperate customers weeping because they were unable to acquire Fendi's "Spy" or the "Paddington" from Chloé.

The "It Bag" phenomenon coincided with an early to mid-decade trend for especially ornate bags. Logos and distinctive hardware were important and made certain bags instantly recognizable. Many handbags were heavily decorated with fringe, chains, grommets, and padlocks. The size and prominence of handbags prompted comparisons to luggage, and inspired humorous cartoons; the heaviest bags were carried in the crook of the elbow, provoking satirical references to the "teapot" stance with one arm out and the other on the hip. Many top designer styles inspired imitations at all market levels, including counterfeit copies. In 2003 Dooney & Bourke offered a bag that closely resembled a Vuitton. An ensuing court case decided that the Dooney & Bourke style was indeed a copy, but was within the acceptable practices of the "knock-off." Ironically, Dooney & Bourke's product, advertised as a "multi-color signature satchel," was named the "It Bag." By 2008 the fashion press declared the end of the transient "It" and promoted "classic luxury." The following year brought reports of "It-bag backlash." But the frenzied rise and fall of expensive, well-publicized accessories epitomized by the handbag craze was established as a central aspect of 21st-century fashion.

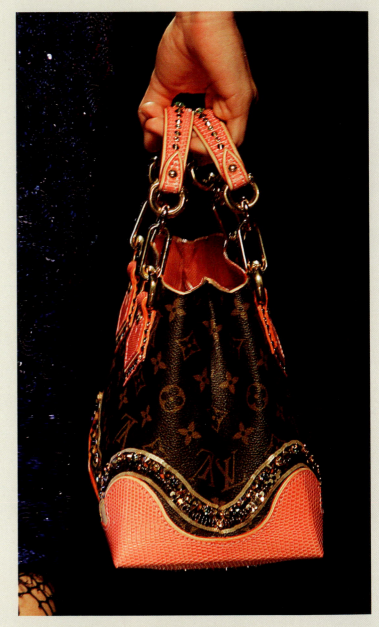

Marc Jacobs for Louis Vuitton, spring/summer 2005

Accessories

Handbags and shoes were important accessories and represented one area in which high fashion wielded significant influence. Accessories were shown on the runway, and details from collections that were deemed otherwise unwearable found their way to handbags, shoes, and other accessories. The press went to great lengths to include as many accessories as possible in photographs, sometimes showing improbable uses, such as shoes as hats and handbags with bathing suits. As *Harper's Bazaar* declared in January 2009, "Show stopping accessories are a must this season!" Bags were often large and very ornate and ranged in materials from smooth leather to lamé. Early in the decade, very pointy toes and stiletto heels were stylish. Platform shoes became fashionable; in contrast to the platforms of previous eras, many styles combined a platform sole with very high thin heels. Some styles extended the vamp material over a "hidden" platform; others used a wedge-shaped silhouette. Especially mid- to late decade, many shoes were very elaborately decorated, featuring fringe, studs, and other

A witty 2009 runway look from Isaac Mizrahi featured a handbag as a hat, reflecting fashion's obsession with that particular accessory.

hardware details. Boots of every shape were seen, many with fringe and studding, some with a crushed look. Christian Louboutin emerged as an important and much copied designer. His signature lacquer-red soles were immediately recognizable. Influential styles also came from Prada, Alexander McQueen, Tory Burch, and other designers. Popular casual styles included UGG boots and Crocs; some Crocs fans decorated their shoes with small charms. Ballerina flats continued to be popular, as did gladiator sandals, flip-flops, and other very bare sandals. Some shoes had lace-up ballerina-style ribbons. Bright colors and animal patterns were frequently used for shoes, bags, and other accessories including legwear. Purposely shredded tights were also fashionable.

A fashion for wearing large plastic eyeglasses with no lenses was present by the end of the decade. Probably having its roots in 1990s Japanese street style, the trend reflected the geek chic aesthetic. Fashionable with both young men and women, the frames were often black (sometimes repurposed 3D-movie specs) but often also in white or colors; the trend encouraged prescription eyewear with larger frames and a revival of Ray-Bans. Most major designers had eyewear lines and imitation of celebrities led to fads in eyewear, such as the frenzy for US politician Sarah Palin's rimless Kawasaki glasses. Popular sunglass styles included aviator shapes, dark rectangles, and oversized ovals, associated with many celebrities including Victoria Beckham and the Olsen twins. Hooded scarves were also popular toward the end of the decade. Vintage costume jewelry, especially brooches, became very fashionable. Large, elaborate necklaces were also popular. Alber Elbaz's ribbon necklaces for Lanvin were widely imitated.

Foundations and Lingerie

Shapewear became an even more important category of lingerie. One of the leading brands, Spanx, was created when company founder Sara Blakely cut the feet off a pair of pantyhose to create a smooth effect under white pants. The line expanded to include control camisoles, bodysuits, and a range of shorts and panties. Other lines included Flexees and Heather Thomson's Yummie Tummie line. Some shapewear labels even offered control garments for upper arms. Women wore gel-filled bras to achieve deep cleavage. Some front-closure bras had several settings to create varying degrees of cleavage. Although bra straps were often exposed casually or, with more decorative

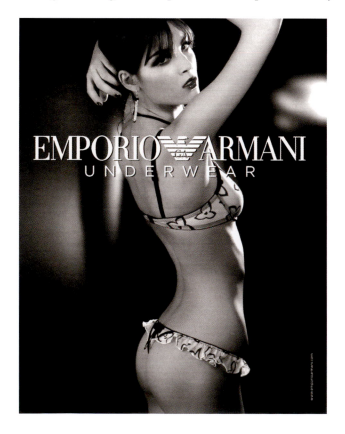

Right Lingerie from Emporio Armani features a matched set of bra and thong panties, a style no longer seen as risqué.

Opposite bottom The revival of the Balenciaga label was exemplary of marketing trends of the early 21st century. In designs such as this 2005 coat, designer Nicolas Ghesquière made reference to the striking aesthetic associated with the house.

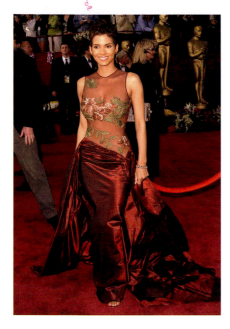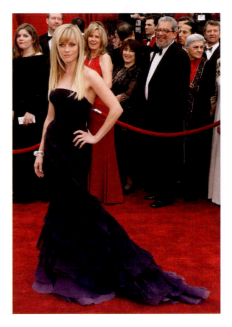

lingerie, on purpose, some women purchased bra-strap adjusters to hold their straps in place. Similarly, modesty panels were available to fill in deep necklines that were "not safe for work." The popularity of thong underwear was celebrated in Sisqó's "The Thong Song," with a video that featured gyrating thong-bikini-clad female dancers. Thong fever reached all levels of fashion and "whale tails" (thongs visible above low-cut pants) showed the range available: from lacey versions from brands such as Agent Provocateur to souvenir thongs decorated with Disney characters.

Designers and Brands

Many established designers expanded their lower-priced lines; several venerable houses and brands were updated; and a number of young designers emerged. A defining strategy was the proliferation of "fast fashion/high fashion" partnerships – sometimes termed "masstige" fashion. H&M, Topshop, and Target were especially active in this market. Starting with a 2002 collection by Isaac Mizrahi, Target developed collaborations with a wide range of designers, including Stella McCartney and Rodarte. The 2004 Karl Lagerfeld collection for H&M sold out within hours of reaching the stores. Model Kate Moss' collaboration with Topshop, begun in 2007, generated excitement for the mainstream store. Temporary "pop-up" shops were often used to promote such projects. Several labels grew in size and stature, truly becoming global brands; Zara and Uniqlo were among the leaders in "fast fashion." The expansion of designers' diffusion brands, "pre-season" showings, and the concept of "demi-couture" all contributed to the atmosphere of constant activity and increased accessibility.

Red carpet exposure continued to be important; film premieres, large galas, and award ceremonies were crucial for both emerging and established designers – even collaboration lines. Leaders in the special occasion market included **Reem Acra**, **Marchesa**, **J. Mendel**, **Zac Posen**, and **Narciso Rodriguez**. **Elie Saab**'s dark red gown for Halle Berry's Oscar win in 2002 was one of the most commented-upon dresses of the decade, and **Vera Wang** repeatedly offered red carpet favorites.

Numerous existing designers and brands were revived or reasserted, ranging from **Roberto Cavalli**, newly appreciated for his extravagant and luxurious styles, to **Lilly Pulitzer** and **Lacoste**, whose bright sportswear fitted with the return of the preppy theme, to **Diane von Furstenberg**, whose dresses experienced renewed popularity. **Balenciaga** underwent a major revival when Nicolas Ghesquière (b. 1971) was appointed creative director in 1997, and led the house into a period of growth. A young French designer who had been at the house since 1995, Ghesquière was lauded

for his masterful, but not imitative, use of the Balenciaga archives. He produced collections within the tradition of geometry and impeccable tailoring associated with the founder but offered innovations, such as extremely narrow trousers, which appealed to young customers. Balenciaga Edition, a line based on pieces in the archive, debuted in 2004. Menswear, accessories, and fragrance were added to the brand. Shaw-Lan Wang, a Chinese entrepreneur, purchased a majority stake in **Lanvin** and installed Alber Elbaz (b. 1961) as creative director in 2001. Consistently described as personable and unpretentious, Elbaz won acclaim for his refined, feminine update of the elegant Lanvin style and was awarded the *Légion d'honneur* in 2007. When **Jil Sander** departed from her company in 2005, Belgian designer Raf Simons (b. 1968) was appointed design director. While staying true to the brand's reputation for modern, minimalist style, Simons introduced more detailed, feminine looks. There was a rapid turnover of designers at **Chloé**: Phoebe Philo from 2002 to 2006, Paulo Melim Andersson from 2007 to 2008, Hannah MacGibbon from 2009 to 2011. Still, the brand continued to be a favorite among fashionable young women. Following her stint at Chloé, Phoebe Philo moved to **Céline**, re-energizing the label. Other long-established brands that enjoyed increased visibility included **Bottega Veneta**, **MaxMara**, **Fendi**, **Aquascutum**, and **Akris**.

IMPURE COUTURE

One consequence of major upheavals in the fashion system was the ubiquitous and perverse misuse of the term "couture." While the Chambre Syndicale de la Haute Couture Parisienne continued to regulate seasonal showings by the likes of Lanvin, Dior, and Chanel, for the general population just about anything remotely special was deemed "couture." Pampered millennial pets romped in species-specific collars, sweaters, and tiaras – dubbed Canine or Kitty Couture. Born 4 Couture supplied car seat covers and "blinged out pacifiers" for lucky little ones and Couture Pops featured crystal-covered sticks and round candy lollipop heads.

Despite the small size of the actual couture industry – one report in *Vogue* in 2008 estimated the number of regular customers at merely 200 – its psychological influence was immense. *The Secret World of Haute Couture*, a 2007 BBC documentary, and *Signé Chanel*, a mini-series from 2005, offered television viewers an entrée into the privileged world. Emphasizing the high-quality craft involved in true couture, and featuring behind-the-scenes views of the workshops and peeks into clients' closets, both programs fed the public's desire to join, and perhaps served as a virtual initiation into, the couture club.

The highly successful mainstream brand Juicy Couture is perhaps the best example of the public seizure of the word "couture." Founded in 1997 by Gela Nash-Taylor and Pamela Skaist-Levy, two self-described "girly" Californians, Juicy Couture shot to fame with form-fitting velour tracksuits introduced in 2001 that quickly became favorites of celebrities including Jennifer Lopez and Cameron Diaz. Nash-Taylor and Skaist-Levy focused on colorful clothing with a feminine fit, including shapely V-necked t-shirts, with a very low V. With "Juicy" emblazoned across the rear, their provocative low-cut sweatpants contributed to the demise of "couture" as an exclusive concept. When the company was sold to mainstream Seventh Avenue giant Liz Claiborne, Inc., in 2003 the deal was juicy indeed.

Further proof of couture's devaluation came with the 2010 debut of *Jersey Couture*. The reality television show followed the wildly popular (and similarly titled) *Jersey Shore*, and featured a New Jersey dress-shop owner and her boldly decorated daughters as they enthusiastically outfitted an endless stream of grateful customers for special occasions, sounding the death knell for "couture" as a synonym for prestige and exclusivity.

An advertisement for fragrance from Juicy Couture.

Designers: France

With **Yves Saint Laurent** in poor health, his business entered the new century under the design direction of Tom Ford, who was replaced by Stefano Pilati (b. 1965) in 2004. Pilati successfully paired references from the past with trend-inspiring silhouettes and produced profitable accessories. The overflow crowds at Saint Laurent's funeral in Paris in 2008, and numerous homages in the press, reconfirmed his pre-eminent position in French culture. At his death, the brand was strong and relevant with an updated image and a celebrity clientele.

Chanel offered a steady parade of new fragrances (and new "faces" including Nicole Kidman, Keira Knightley, Audrey Tatou, and Vanessa Paradis), sold-out cosmetics (such as the Jade nail polish that caused waiting lists in 2009), and equally covetable accessories. Under **Karl Lagerfeld**'s continued direction, Chanel also expanded fine jewelry offerings and opened boutiques worldwide, including a ten-story "megaboutique" in Tokyo and a Moscow flagship store. A 2005 exhibition at the Metropolitan Museum of Art and the 2006 documentary *Signé Chanel*, chronicling the creation of a couture collection, underlined the significance of the brand.

John Galliano continued to reinvigorate **Dior**, expanding product lines and offering theatrical runway shows, while also designing his eponymous collections.

The tremendous diversification of designers and houses extended to cars, home products, and even sports equipment, as exemplified by a snowboard from Chanel.

While his 2000 "Clochards" collection for Dior shocked audiences, Galliano was named Commander of the British Empire in 2001, and received his award wearing a suit without a shirt. Dior's 60th anniversary couture showing in 2007, held at Versailles, included updates of Christian Dior's famous 1947 Bar suit, and conjured the aesthetic of the post-war era.

Ever versatile and iconoclastic, yet a respected fixture of Paris fashion, **Jean Paul Gaultier** received the *Légion d'honneur* in 2001 and was named artistic director of women's ready-to-wear by Hermès in 2003, where he stayed through the decade. He continued to design his own collections, counting award-winning actress Marion Cotillard among his most prominent clients. Gaultier continued to create performance clothes for popular music stars including such diverse artists as Marilyn Manson, Kylie Minogue, and Leslie Cheung.

Born in Brussels and educated there at the visual arts school La Cambre, **Olivier Theyskens** began his own brand in 1997 with a collection, made from vintage sheets, that he did not intend to sell. His career was advanced when Madonna wore a black satin Theyskens gown to the 1998 Academy Awards. He was named Artistic Director at Rochas in 2002 and moved to Nina Ricci in 2006. Theyskens' Goth-inflected romanticism represented an exciting aesthetic development for both of the venerable French houses; but his use of couture-type details in his ready-to-wear lines resulted in high prices that limited his clientele. At the end of the decade he was appointed artistic director of Theory, where he designed Theyskens' Theory collections.

Wang Chen Tsai-Hsia (b. 1951) markedly expanded her label **Shiatzy Chen** when it debuted in Paris in 2008, presenting her signature restrained and elegant styles that mixed Eastern and Western influences. "If someone looks at a piece of clothing and is able to tell at once that it is a Shiatzy Chen piece, then I know I have succeeded," said the designer in 2008.[10] The label gained membership in the Chambre Syndicale de la

Taiwanese label Shiatzy Chen showed this ready-to-wear collection in Paris in October 2009.

Dutch design duo Viktor & Rolf challenged conventions of taste and beauty. This ensemble from their fall/winter 2006–2007 women's collection combines familiar shapes for blouse and skirt with an outré mesh face covering for the runway presentation.

Haute Couture in 2009, and offered a wider range of accessories and furniture, and by 2010 had expanded to teahouses in both Taipei and Paris.

Viktor & Rolf abandoned couture in 2000 and launched a ready-to-wear line. Their first (actual) fragrance, Flowerbomb, debuted in 2005. While the duo still excelled at original designs such as blue-screen dresses with projected images, they also took on more conventional projects that included the wedding dress for Mabel Wisse Smit's marriage to Prince Johan Friso of Orange-Nassau, and a luggage collection for Samsonite. After his departure from Hermès in 2003, **Martin Margiela** continued to challenge the fashion world with collections made of recycled materials and conceptual presentations, and was invited by the Chambre Syndicale to show haute couture in 2006. Margiela maintained a cultish following of fashion insiders who could recognize his work by the four white stitches visible at the neckline anchoring the (blank) Margiela label. Margiela left the business in 2009, leaving Maison Margiela in the hands of a design team. With experience at a number of top fashion houses, including Capucci and Ungaro, **Giambattista Valli** (b. 1966) launched his own label in 2005. Especially renowned for his elegant eveningwear with hints of mid-20th-century structure, Valli said his "clothes are for the international jet set,"[11] a claim that was supported by admirers such as actress Katie Holmes and Queen Rania of Jordan.

Designers: Britain

After almost 150 years in business, **Burberry** updated its image with the appointment of Christopher Bailey (b. 1971) as design director in 2001. Under Bailey the brand expanded from classic outerwear to fashion, promoted with memorable advertising campaigns. Their "Art of the Trench" website, inaugurated in 2009, invited customers to contribute photos of individually styled Burberry trench coats to an online gallery, harnessing the new focus on street photography and "crowdsourcing" in fashion.

Parting ways with Givenchy in 2000, **Alexander McQueen** obtained backing from Gucci Group that enabled him to expand with international boutiques, and branch out into fragrances and accessories. He debuted a menswear line in 2004 and a lower-priced line, McQ, in 2006. The drama and creativity that marked his early years continued full force; runway shows were especially elaborate with models dressed as mental patients or chess pieces, or sent down the catwalk in 12-inch (30-centimeter) "Armadillo" shoes. His 2009 "Horn of Plenty" collection offered recycled glamour

with a pastiche of references to landmarks of 20th-century couture, the designer's statement on the quick turnover of fashion. As his associate Sarah Burton later said, "Each of his shows was like ten of anyone else's."[12] His suicide in February 2010 seemed especially tragic given his rapid upward trajectory and undeniable talent. Among the many awards he received during the decade were the CFDA's International Designer of the Year (2003), *GQ* Menswear Designer of the Year (2007), and Commander of the British Empire (2003).

Collections featuring pieces as diverse as wood skirts and laser-firing dresses reinforced **Hussein Chalayan**'s reputation for innovation. His artistic use of technology offered possibilities for fashion's future. Although he did not officially launch his business until 2006, **Gareth Pugh** (b. 1981) was already known in the London fashion scene through his styling work and collaborations with artists and musicians. His background in theatrical costumes came through in his collections with futuristic silhouettes and Gothic references.

Designers: Italy

When Julia Roberts wore vintage Valentino in 2001 to collect her Oscar for Best Actress for *Erin Brockovich*, her choice not only validated the trend for vintage but signaled the continuing demand for Valentino. After staging a massive celebration of his forty-five years in fashion, **Valentino** retired in 2007. His house continued under creative directors Maria Grazia Chiuri and Pierpaolo Piccioli, who maintained the Valentino reputation for high style and fine craftsmanship but were able to appeal to younger clients as well.

Celebrating his thirty years in fashion, **Giorgio Armani** was the subject of an exhibition at New York's Guggenheim Museum in 2000–2001; the show was controversial because of Armani's financial support of his own retrospective. While Armani's numerous lines at varying price levels enjoyed continued success, his couture collection, Armani Privé, was especially notable and Privé gowns were favorites with actresses including Anne Hathaway and Cate Blanchett.

Donatella Versace (b. 1955) continued the aesthetic associated with the label: bold, sexy, and colorful. Capitalizing on its name recognition, Versace expanded further in menswear with Collezione and added Versace Sport, Home Couture, and luxury hotels. Versace's very visible entertainment-world clientele included Jennifer Lopez, Elizabeth Hurley, Angelina Jolie, and Lucy Liu, who all kept the brand in the spotlight. High-profile customers including Kylie Minogue, Madonna, Scarlett Johansson, and Penélope Cruz chose **Dolce & Gabbana** for public events and performances. Brazilian model Gisele Bündchen wore D&G for her 2009 wedding. The design duo underlined their commitment to expansion with new headquarters in Milan and a variety of collaborations and licensing, including a make-up line, uniforms for a soccer team, and a cell phone with a disco ringtone. Despite her often quirky and challenging aesthetic, **Miuccia Prada** was regarded as a fashion seer and a leading trendsetter with her main brand and the Miu Miu line. Prada became a major financial player in the fashion industry and the name of the brand, nearly a household word, became a shorthand term for "high fashion."

Designers: United States

The stalwarts of American fashion, **Calvin Klein**, **Ralph Lauren**, and **Donna Karan**, continued to diversify, adding collections at both high and low price points. As with established European houses, accessories proved profitable and served as a medium for promoting the brands to wider audiences. Unlike European fashion leaders, the American designers stuck to straightforward seasonal presentations, showing clothes that were hanger-ready and concentrating on bottom-line viability rather than runway theatrics. **Michael Kors**, **Nanette Lepore** (b. 1964), and **Catherine Malandrino** (b. 1963) concentrated on more individualistic looks. Kors' luxurious sportswear pieces suggested continental flair. Lepore's easy to wear, feminine styles were favorites with a wide range of customers. Transplanted Frenchwoman Malandrino's red, white, and blue American-flag dresses received significant attention when she first showed them in 2001 and on their relaunch in 2009.

Designing for Louis Vuitton in Paris and his own line in New York, **Marc Jacobs** was one of the most visible designers in the world. His lower-priced Marc line debuted in 2001. He expanded overseas with his first freestanding European store in Paris in 2006, followed by London in 2007; he introduced childrenswear the same year. His work for Vuitton was marked by a bold reimagining of the house's tradition. Jacobs initiated collaborations with artists to restyle Vuitton products. For example, Takashi Murakami replaced the brown and gold of the house monogram with brightly colored letters on white or black, creating a new status accessory line that developed a cult following and high sales.

Tom Ford expanded his influence through his work at Gucci, YSL Rive Gauche (after its acquisition by Gucci), and for his own line established in 2005. Ford's reputation for a highly sexualized version of luxury was underscored with lavish runway shows,

Right A dress from Chado Ralph
Rucci for spring/summer 2004
shows Rucci's concentration on
structural details and painterly
decorative elements.

Far right Rodarte's eclectic
aesthetic and innovative use
of materials is expressed in
this 2008 dress.

chic retail design, and provocative advertising. Perfume advertisements featuring fully nude female and male models were refused by many publications. Ford's New York flagship store on Madison Avenue opened in 2007, devoted to extremely expensive menswear including made-to-measure suits. Ford was recognized with numerous CFDA awards.

Born in Philadelphia, **Ralph Rucci** (b. 1957) attended Temple University and the Fashion Institute of Technology. He worked for Halston for a short time, then went into business on his own, with a women's collection inspired by Madame Grès, that helped to establish his business in custom-designed pieces. In 1984 he launched a ready-to-wear company. In 1994 Rucci reorganized, calling his business "Chado Ralph Rucci" (referring to the Japanese tea ceremony). His work was lauded for its technical finesse and restrained aesthetic. In 2002 Rucci was invited to show couture in Paris, the first American since Mainbocher to be so honored. His couture line featured innovative construction such as his "suspension" technique, in which pieces of fabric were held together by knotted threads, creating visible openings in the surface of the garment, and extremely luxurious materials including cashmere and reptile; some garments were trimmed with semi-precious stones. His work was featured in many exhibitions and a 2008 documentary.

Sisters Kate (b. 1972) and Laura Mulleavy (b. 1974) named their company **Rodarte** after their mother's maiden name. Raised in California, both attended Berkeley and received no formal training in fashion. Based in Pasadena, they showed their first collection in 2005 and their unique approach to materials caught the attention of the press and fashion-forward clients, after which they opened a studio in Los Angeles and began to show in New York. Rodarte became known for artistic, often fearless, manipulation of materials that produced shredded, webby effects and unexpected juxtapositions that were striking on the runway but often less than wearable. The Mulleavy sisters expanded the brand's appeal after several years in fashion, showing more separates; a collection for Target solidified their name recognition and market reputation.

A new wave of designers with individualistic styles made headlines and won celebrity fans. **Derek Lam** (b. 1967), whose family owned a fashion business, worked for Michael Kors before launching his label in 2003. Lam quickly became known for

collections with a feminine flavor and fine construction details. San Francisco-born **Peter Som** (b. 1970) created chic American clothes for his own line and served as creative director at Bill Blass. After various jobs in the fashion industry, **Phillip Lim** (b. 1973) founded his own line, 3.1 Phillip Lim, in 2004 with a mission to produce affordable, contemporary women's clothes. Within five years, Lim had expanded into accessories, childrenswear, and menswear, and completed collaborations with Gap and Birkenstock. **Thakoon Panichgul** (b. 1974) was born in Thailand and moved to the United States in 1985. He showed his first collection at New York Fashion Week in 2004. Reviews stressed the elegance of Thakoon's aesthetic and *Vogue* became an enthusiastic supporter. New Yorker **Alice Roi** (b. 1976) established a career as a designer with a distinctive downtown sensibility. Her 2007 collaboration with Uniqlo was one of the company's first invitational collections. New York-based **Proenza Schouler** was founded in 2002 by Jack McCollough (b. 1978) and Lazaro Hernandez (b. 1978), who met studying fashion at Parsons School of Design. They rapidly acquired a clientele of celebrities and socialites and support from the fashion industry, winning numerous awards within eight years. Their distinctive aesthetic was often described as a colorful mix of traditional and modern and their astute licensing made the brand a model of 21st-century success. Born in Taipei, **Jason Wu** (b. 1982) grew up in Canada and the United States and began designing dolls as a teenager; a RuPaul doll he designed was featured in *Women's Wear Daily* in 2005. His association with Michelle Obama ignited Wu's career. The First Lady wore his ivory and black sheath on television in 2008 and chose Wu's one-shouldered silk chiffon gown for the Inaugural Ball in 2009. Featuring a cool, relaxed look influenced by his California upbringing, **Alexander Wang** (b. 1983) launched his label in 2007 with a collection of interesting sweaters, leather pants, knit dresses, and other pieces, all designed to mix and layer – high fashion variations of familiar basics.

Hair and Beauty and Body Modification

The prevailing hairdo of the decade consisted of long straight or slightly waved hair, center-parted or side-parted. Bangs were often worn very long but a fashion for short bangs continued. Other trends included bobs, as seen on Victoria Beckham and Katie Holmes, and ponytails, worn casually and for special occasions. Women with

As fingernails became an important fashion focus, increasingly elaborate manicures not only offered a variety of colors and finishes but often included decals and sculptural details.

very curly hair often cultivated a natural look, with generous volume. Some black women wore braids, often in elaborate patterns, and extensions remained fashionable. Highlights were popular, often more subtle than the thick stripes of previous years; colorful streaks were also widely seen. Some women combined thin headbands and ponytails or chignons for a Greek look. Feathered hairbands, decorated barrettes, and other accessories were popular.

Many make-up trends focused on the eyes, including a "smoky" look, cat eyes drawn with eyeliner, and prominent eyeshadow in blue and other pastel colors (a style propelled by the 2000 film *Charlie's Angels*). Brow shaping was important and threading salons proliferated. Some people, both men and women, cut stripes into their eyebrows. Eyelashes became a fashion focus and long lashes were achieved through Latisse, a lash-growing drug, extensions, and false eyelashes, in many colors and metallic variations. Tattooing was also used as permanent make-up to enhance eyebrows, eyelashes, and other features. Lipstick shades were very varied, with a revival of prominent lip liner. Viva Glam by MAC continued to be a popular shade of lipstick with an evolving list of spokesmodels. Mineral-based powders caught on as an alternative to liquid foundation and many make-up products incorporated skin treatments. A trend for natural cosmetics was part of the eco-fashion movement. Developments in manicure included a wide range of colors including dark hues, blues, greens, and yellows. Decals, jewels, and sculptural details were used to accessorize nails; while many manicures were purely decorative, some women used their nails to express their interests or make political statements. Best-selling fragrances came from leading cosmetic houses and designers. But many top fragrances were introduced by celebrities as diverse as singers Renée Fleming and Mariah Carey, and event designer Robert Isabell. The Demeter Fragrance Library offered unconventional single-note scents ranging from Birthday Cake to Poison Ivy.

Pubic grooming also took on importance; Brazilian waxes were common and many women had pubic hair waxed or shaved into shapes. Betty™ dye, "for the hair down there," was available in a range of colors from natural shades to bright blue and hot pink. "Vajazzling," the decorative application of jewels and other embellishments to the waxed pubic area, was another aesthetic option.

The use of cosmetic surgery and injectables increased among women as well as men around the globe. Cosmetic surgery entered the public consciousness to the extent that several television shows centered on procedures, including *Nip Tuck* and *Extreme Makeover*. Celebrities' weight-loss surgeries received widespread attention including those of opera singer Deborah Voigt and writer and designer Star Jones. The press commented on the overinflated lips, or "trout pout," seen on many celebrities. Before and after images were readily available showing the effects of multiple procedures; a new aesthetic of frankly fake faces and bodies emerged.

Menswear

General trends in menswear included continued influence from the 1970s and 1980s. Looks ranged from a revival of preppy to futuristic biker. Minimalism was asserted, especially via designers Helmut Lang, Prada, and Calvin Klein. As with women's fashion, individual styling was emphasized. Many top fashion houses sent exotic looks down the runways – inspired by everything from Lawrence of Arabia to Op Art. Support for skirt-wearing among men grew, bolstered by the *Men in Skirts* exhibition seen in London and New York as well as companies such as Seattle's Utilikilts. But the staples of men's wardrobes remained consistent.

Male style setters were varied. Justin Timberlake, often seen in three-piece suits, brought sex appeal to the traditional look; new 007 Daniel Craig maintained James Bond's swank standard, wearing Brioni in *Casino Royale* (2006); Beck and Johnny Depp were cited as examples of male boho style, while Will Smith offered athletic elegance. The term "metrosexual" was used to describe well-dressed, well-groomed men who also displayed interest in stylish living, a trend that was encouraged by the

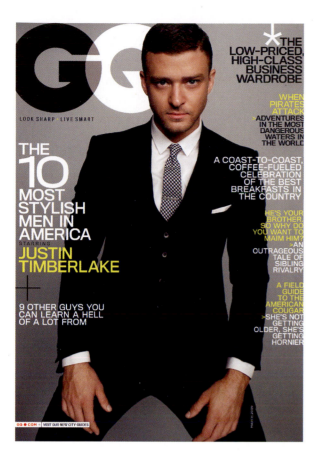

The March 2009 cover of *Gentleman's Quarterly* featured Justin Timberlake in a suit by Dolce & Gabbana. The tight fit of the suit, crisp accessories, and Timberlake's well-tended stubble exemplify male style of the late decade.

television show *Queer Eye for the Straight Guy*. The metrosexual ethos was aspirational and related to the 19th-century dandy ideal.

Suit variations included long jackets buttoned high, with four or more buttons, traditional double-breasted styles with structured shoulders, and single-breasted two- or three-button types. The two-button styles became more widespread as the years progressed. A "shrunken" look became popular, featuring a tight fit, high armhole, slightly short length and sleeves; designer Hedi Slimane, among others, promoted this style. After several years at Yves Saint Laurent, where he updated the menswear collection with a younger, leaner silhouette, Slimane became the head designer for Dior Homme from 2001 to 2007. Thom Browne also encouraged the "shrunken" style through his menswear line and his collaboration with Black Fleece for Brooks Brothers. In a period of widespread informality in dress, Browne declared that "jeans and a t-shirt have become Establishment … So actually putting on a jacket is the anti-Establishment stance."[13] With almost twenty years of experience with Ralph Lauren and Calvin Klein, John Varvatos launched his own company in 2000. His menswear collections exemplified the mixing of genres that pervaded fashion. He often showed tailored jackets and logo t-shirts worn with distressed jeans and boots or sneakers. His business was rapidly successful and recognized with several awards.

Other suit and jacket styles offered variations on menswear traditions, including updates of school blazers, with piped edges, and Norfolk styles. Reflecting different options for formal wear, black tie was often replaced by a dark suit. Patchwork madras was revived, often seen in jackets, trousers, and especially shorts. The battle between pleated and flat front trousers became a matter of personal taste. This applied to leg width as well. In general, the trouser silhouette evolved from baggy to lean during the decade; designers often showed styles at one extreme or the other. Shorts were often worn long and capri-length pants were available. Duffle coats, pea jackets, and trench coats were also fashionable, in various lengths and fabrics. Shearling jackets were popular. There was a revival of vintage waist-length Members Only jackets and similar styles. The renewed fashion status of the suit contributed to a revival of the topcoat.

Shirts generally adhered to a traditional cut or were tapered with slightly high armholes and narrow sleeves. Classically cut button-front shirts in solid colors or patterns, from companies such as Bugatchi Uomo, Façonnable, and Ben Sherman, often had contrasting collar bands, cuff facings or plackets. Some shirts featured diagonal stripes. Many men wore untucked shirt tails even with suit jackets (dubbed the "flyaway" look); when wearing an expensive belt buckle men often tucked in only the center front of the shirt or t-shirt. T-shirts were more popular than ever, often with logos, slogans, and embellished with other decoration, and were even worn with suits. V-necked t-shirts often featured deep necklines and sleeveless t-shirts were common. T-shirts were often layered, sometimes with a light color over a darker shade. Renowned tattoo artist Don Ed Hardy and entrepreneur Christian Audigier launched the Ed Hardy fashion brand in 2004, offering clothing and accessories decorated with tattoo-inspired motifs. Superdry, a British sportswear brand, featured Japanese script and "Tokyo" or "Osaka" printed on t-shirts, hoodies, and messenger bags. Henleys were extremely popular and were often layered under t-shirts, a look that was popularized by Brad Pitt in *The Mexican* (2001). Denim remained a vital wardrobe component. Popular brands Diesel, 7 For All Mankind, True Religion, and many others competed with established labels. Jeans were available in a variety of fits and cuts from super-skinny to loose.

Men's swimwear styles ranged from small briefs to baggy boxers and longer board shorts. Short trunks reminiscent of 1960s style were popular, especially those from

Vilebrequin. Celebrity athletes influenced sportswear styling; Target offered a line of clothes endorsed by snowboarder Shaun White, and soccer star David Beckham's move to Los Angeles encouraged a vogue for colorful soccer jerseys in the United States. With the fashion for low-rise trousers, underwear waistbands were often on display showing prominent logos. Boxer briefs and low-rise boxer briefs were popular. Shapewear for men was increasingly available, often promoted using terms related to athletic wear such as "compression shirts." Many men went without socks for leisure and, in high fashion looks, even with suits. Socks were available in a wide variety of colors and patterns including polka dots, stripes, and argyles. Sock styles were also varied, including ankle height, a type previously only worn for active sports but now even worn with dress shoes for a fashionably naked ankle.

Neckties became optional as men wore open-collared shirts in business settings. Most neckties were medium to wide width, but designers and stylish younger men sometimes favored quite narrow ties, and the prevailing tie width narrowed during the decade. Scarves of all sorts emerged as important accessories, ranging from thick rib knit and British "school striped" mufflers to fringed cotton squares looped loosely around the neck. Some men wore soft scarves knotted as neckties. Traditional footwear styles, especially Oxfords, boat shoes, moccasins, and desert boots were available in variations with squared or pointed toes. Pointy "winklepicker"-style ankle boots were also worn, especially by those who favored a vintage aesthetic. Tougher-looking knee-high boots were also seen; laced-up boots and motorcycle styles were particularly popular. In the early to mid-decade, sneaker-like shoes were stylish. Sneakers continued to be popular for casual wear. Certain styles and brands were extremely sought after; some brands offered special editions that resulted from partnerships with designers or celebrities. Most major athletic shoe companies offered consumers the opportunity to create unique customized looks, a direct result of the increase in online shopping.

While backpacks were a wardrobe standard, large hand-held "status bags," sometimes the size of weekenders, were seen frequently, even carried on the runway. Gym bags ranged from inexpensive pieces from athletic wear companies to high style versions from luxury houses. Baseball-style caps with trucking logos, team or place names, or retro insignia were fashionable; brims were either worn severely arched or perfectly flat and caps were tilted at extreme angles. Stocking caps, renamed beanies, became a ubiquitous fashion statement, in all weather. Peruvian-style caps and faux-fur "bomber" hats were also common. Many men wore long belts with the ends hanging, a style that derived from hip-hop clothing. Oversized prayer beads were often worn with informal clothing. Other important accessories included bold wristwatches and wallet chains, which were available at every price from luxury to mainstream.

Male grooming and body image received a lot of attention. Hairstyles were eclectic and ranged from long and shaggy to tousled to close-cropped. The "fauxhawk" featured a row of hair held upright by gel. The shaved head remained fashionable. While many idols and icons were youthful, white-haired television personality Anderson Cooper, visibly graying actor George Clooney, and former Olympic swimmer Mark Foster offered models of mature sophistication. A clean-shaven look prevailed; however, some men wore goatees and well-groomed stubble was fashionable. By contrast, many men had their eyebrows trimmed, plucked, or waxed, and continued to eliminate unwanted body hair. Emphasis on body toning and grooming extended to legs and feet. Toes became a new erogenous zone as by mid-decade it became popular to wear flip-flops with trousers.

Heraldic-style emblems and ornate gothic filigree – encouraged by such diverse sources as Harry Potter, *The Da Vinci Code*, and Goth fashion – were typical motifs on t-shirts, Henleys, jeans, and other sportswear.

Children's Fashion

Children's fashion was a blend of diverse influences. Inspiration from the 1970s and 1980s continued in the form of flared and embellished jeans and t-shirts with retro rock and roll images. The scholarly look of geek chic influenced the styling of fashion for children. Back-to-school clothes were often accessorized with dark-framed eyeglasses and children were posed pigeon-toed, in "nerdy" postures. School uniforms were revived as many communities sought to establish a serious atmosphere in the classroom.

For both girls and boys, jeans and other pants, knit tops and sweaters were the basis of their wardrobes. Logos and licensed images served to distinguish brands in the sportswear market. In addition to brand logos, children's clothing was also decorated with television and movie references, cartoon characters, sports insignia, and popular slogans. While children's everyday dress remained casual, special occasions brought out princess looks and ballerina-inspired pieces for girls and mini three-piece suits and preppy blazers for boys.

General trends for boys included the continuation of khakis and neutral colors and camouflage. Pants and shorts were very baggy until the late years of the decade when "skinny" pants became fashionable. Pants that zipped around the leg to become shorts were popular. Knit tops and sweaters often had horizontal stripes across the chest. Plaid shirts were popular. The skull and crossbones motif was widely used in boys' clothing and was often restyled to resemble less sinister images, such as the smiley face or jack-o'-lantern. General trends in girls' fashion included the "flashdance" look with wide-necked tops over camisoles, worn with leggings, jeans, or shorts. Bleached denim, neon, and animal prints provided a vivid color story. Many girls wore multiple accessories, including jewelry, hair ornaments, and colorful socks and shoes.

Above Camouflage was pervasive across fashion in nearly all markets – even couture – and was especially popular in different color ways for children's and junior markets.

Below Foul weather gear such as raincoats and rubber boots were available in fashionable bright colors and patterns, reflecting increased design emphasis even for practical wardrobe pieces.

Celebrity inspiration that characterized adult fashion was seen in children's clothing. The Obama girls' inauguration outfits in 2008 brought increased attention to Crewcuts, the children's line of J. Crew. Childrenswear boutiques, such as Lucky Wang, focused on fun and creative design, for parents who wanted their children to reflect their own stylish aesthetic. Children, "tweens," and teenagers looked to young celebrities including Miley Cyrus, Lauren Conrad, Ashlee Simpson, Zac Efron, and Corbin Bleu for fashion inspiration.

Children's outerwear trends included trench coats, ponchos, snorkel jackets with fur-edged hoods, down jackets, and duffle coats. High-top sneakers were seen in a multitude of colors and patterns. Fashionable shoes for girls included ballerina flats and flip-flops. UGG boots were widely desirable and many girls wore them in pink. Boat shoes were popular with both girls and boys.

Even young children experimented with cosmetics and hair coloring. Young girls and boys used colored gels or sported colorfully streaked hair. Grooming was emphasized at increasingly younger ages; many young girls received salon treatments and in some areas mani/pedi parties for children became common. Children's nail polishes, such as Piggy Paint, were specially formulated with fewer harsh chemicals and were available in a wide range of colors, reflecting adult cosmetics.

Traditional Dress, Modern World

While fashion was steadily becoming global, strongholds of traditional dress worn daily still existed, particularly in South Asia, the Islamic world, and Africa. Global political events brought greater awareness in the Western media of traditional Islamic dress, and hijabs, burqas, niqabs, and chadors were commonly noted. Following the removal of the Taliban regime, Afghanistan's president Hamid Karzai was frequently seen in traditional styles, often an astrakhan Karukul and T-shaped *chapan* (traditional coat). Fashion thrived in the Arabian peninsula, with local designers

A young man in Malaysia, is dressed in traditional *baju melayu* to celebrate the *Idul Fitri* holiday.

creating custom special occasion wear. European prestige labels, taking advantage of the concentration of wealth and acknowledging regional preferences, created *abayat* (women's overgarments). Handbags from luxury brands were sold in special regional versions, more heavily embellished than the European or North American editions. Dubai was a shopping destination while Abu Dhabi Fashion Week was an important style event. Arab *keffiyeh* scarves, which had been associated with Palestinian nationalism, were marketed outside of the region as fashion accessories. When celebrity chef Rachael Ray appeared in a television commercial with a paisley scarf that merely resembled a *keffiyeh*, she drew ire from conservative groups who denounced her as glorifying terrorism. However, the *keffiyeh* widened its appeal and was worn by Japanese youth and hipsters, and found its way into the boho-chic repertoire, even draped as a miniskirt. Religious communities clung to traditions in dress, including Orthodox Jews, the Amish, Sikhs, and sects such as The Yearning for Zion Ranch community, whose old-fashioned shirtwaist dresses were widely seen when the group made headline news in 2008.

Above Lie Sang Bong (a favorite of Lady Gaga) sent this striking look down the runway in 2009, suggestive of inspiration from both the ancient world and the future.

Below The members of Girls' Generation mix grunge and hipster style in this publicity shot, photographed in Seoul in 2009.

Some sub-Saharan Africans often wore *mitumba* – second-hand clothing – that came from Western countries, mixing it with indigenous garments. Nonetheless African designers enjoyed success both on their own continent and in Europe, including Xuly Bët (founded by Lamine Badian Kouyaté) and Alphadi (born Sidahmed Seidnaly). Style tribes were strongly asserted, such as the metrosexual Sapeurs in the Congo, or the heavy metal advocates in Botswana. In India, native-inflected high fashion thrived with local designers presenting at fashion shows including the "Lakmé" Fashion Week in Mumbai. But in cities of the world with large South Asian populations – such as Toronto, New York, London, and Kuala Lumpur – women still often dressed in *shalwar kameez,* the traditional tunic and trousers, while men were often more assimilated into Western fashion. Most of the rest of the world had adopted Western styles, except for special occasions when traditional dress was still worn: a young man in Borneo, for instance, might wear French Connection or Guess on a daily basis, but traditional *baju melayu* shirt and trousers for a special event.

Asian Style

East Asia and Southeast Asia were firmly positioned in the global fashion scene – both as consumers and contributors. Throughout East Asia mainstream Western brands were more available, while individual countries and cities applied their own regional interpretations. The entertainment industry was strongly linked to the promotion of fashion trends, and the fashion press grew notably. MTV's presence in Asian markets reinforced the media and fashion profiles of many stars. A peacock male aesthetic mirrored the metrosexual trend in Western countries, and boy bands were highly influential. Hairstyling was an important part of the fashion story for both sexes, and a variety of hair color treatments were common.

André Kim remained the elder statesman of Korean fashion and an important designer for international beauty pageants. Actress Kim Min Jung and actor Kim Rae Won modeled in fashion shows for Kim, who often included a celebrity finale in his runway spectacles. Kim's eccentric personality was so well known that he was parodied on Korean television. Lie Sang Bong first showed in Paris in 2002; his customers included Lady Gaga, Beyoncé Knowles, and Rihanna, and he marketed a wide range of diffusion products. The leather goods brand MCM was reasserted when

Korean businesswoman Sung Joo Kim purchased the company in 2005. Kim opened a flagship store in Seoul and new boutiques in Europe, and increased distribution in the United States; an MCM bag was featured on the television series *Gossip Girl*. Kim strove to create understated bags for elegant businesswomen, and stressed she did not create overly embellished pieces for "concubines of rich men."[14] Television and film actor – and hip-hop performer – So Ji Sub also worked as a model, as did singer–actors such as Hong Kwang Ho, Yoo Seung Woo, and Oh Ji Ho. Korean pop music, "K-Pop," had a strong impact on fashion, combining stylistic influences ranging from Japanese street to American hip hop. Female looks were reinforced by popular girl groups such as Jewelry and Girls' Generation, and notably in the look of Lee Hyori, who left girl group Fin.K.L. to pursue a solo career, naming her first album "Stylish." Influential boy bands included Super Junior and SS501, whose front man Kim Hyun-Joong was spokesmodel for The Face Shop (a notable percentage of the male population wore make-up on a daily basis). Big Bang were particularly known for their clothing and hairstyles, epitomizing K-pop fashion ranging from bubblegum to sporty to bad boy. Singer Jung Ji-Hoon, known by the stage name "Rain," was featured in American *People* magazine in 2007 as one of the world's most beautiful people, which, along with sell-out performances in the United States, raised the international profile of Korean cultural exports. Champion figure skater Kim Yuna created a sensation with her Bond Girl persona for her "007 Medley" short program, wearing a stunning off-one-shoulder black beaded dress. Korea's edition of *Project Runway* debuted in 2009.

Mainland China grew enormously as a world power with the implementation of more free-market economic policies, and increased its production of manufacturing for export. A new elite developed, built on entrepreneurship, and wielded more purchasing power. More shopping malls and megastores supplied the developing market. Established entertainers endorsed luxury brands, and performers such as Ziyi Zhang and Han Geng modeled in magazines. The Chinese fashion industry was the subject of a 2007 documentary, *Useless*, directed by Jia Zhangke. Designers Guo Pei and Ma Ke led the industry. Major Chinese cities, especially Shanghai, nourished street styles. Wei Wei and Huang Yixin, two art students, became an internet sensation in 2005 as the "Back Dorm Boys," shooting lip-synched versions of pop songs – often by the Backstreet Boys – in their dorm room. Their videos found their way onto YouTube and television, and as their fame became global, fans imitated Wei and Huang's hip-hop-derived fashion – usually matching athletic wear, including Yao Ming's Houston Rockets jerseys. With performances, modeling, and product endorsements, the Back

K-Pop boy band Big Bang display their enthusiasm for the latest cell phones, and their colorful sartorial sensibility.

Taiwanese singer Jay Chou in concert in Shenyang in 2009, his matinee-idol charisma enhanced by fashionable costume choices.

Below Maggie Cheung and Tony Leung in a scene from *In the Mood for Love* (2000), an example of the growing presence of Chinese films in Western markets. The film's costuming encouraged continued interest in the cheongsam as a fashionable option.

Dorm Boys were a potent example of the power of the internet to create international celebrities out of unknowns.

Hong Kong continued to be prominent in film and music, as well as fashion. Designer Barney Cheng created cheongsam designs for celebrities including actress Michelle Yeoh. Charismatic performers, including Stephen Chow and Maggie Cheung, set beauty standards, and "Canto-pop" singers, such as the girl duo Twins, strongly contributed to style. Canadian-born Hong Kong actor and singer Edison Chen followed the example of celebrities involved with fashion lines, with his partnership in the CLOT Inc. label. Actor and style icon Tony Leung asserted, "The beauty of Hong Kong is that people are not just Chinese. They are a hybrid of West and East. They know how to dress. Casual elegant."[15]

The international high-profile successes of the Shiatzy Chen label and Taiwan-born Jason Wu encouraged awareness of Taiwanese fashion. Taiwanese "Mando-pop" contributed to the boy band craze, with F4, Fahrenheit, and Tension strongly encouraging hair and fashion trends. Actors Jay Chou and American-born Leehom Wang had diversified careers, including singing, acting, and modeling, and worked in many markets within the Chinese-speaking world. Singer Jolin Tsai, "Asia's Dancing Queen," and Singaporean transplant Stefanie Sun invigorated feminine style. Young people in Taiwan embraced nerd chic and adapted American hipster fashion into an Asian hipster style.

Japanese style continued to encourage street looks, some of which had a strong reciprocal relationship with Steampunk. The practice of *kosupure* or "cosplay" (short for "costume play") was strongly encouraged by these style tribes, especially the historic and fantasy elements of groups such as Gothic Lolitas and Aristocrats. Manga and anime also influenced the trend for cosplay, which

grew quickly in the Western world, reflected in a new subculture of re-enactors and fetishists. "J-pop" exerted its own brand of style, with bands Arashi, KAT-TUN, and AKB48 being especially influential.

The Philippines debuted their edition of *Project Runway* in 2008, and "Pinoy-pop" was strongly represented by XLR8. Philippine Fashion Week became an important event in the Asia/Pacific scene. Philippine-born Monique Lhuillier, the daughter of a fashion model, relocated to the United States, and enjoyed success as a special occasion designer; in 2006 Lhuillier received the Medal of Honor from the Philippine president. In Vietnam design talents including Minh Hanh and Vo Viet Chung were showcased in the Vietnam Collection Grand Prix. Thailand offered expanded luxury shopping and a highly developed fashion press. Designer Nagara Sambandaraksa catered to elite customers and frequently utilized Thai silks from Jim Thompson. Princess Sirivannavari Nariratana, granddaughter of King Rama IX and Queen Sirikit, showed her designs in both Bangkok and Paris. Malaysia stepped further into the fashion arena, with the first East Asian edition of *Project Runway* in 2007. The same year, the Pavilion Kuala Lumpur opened, a mall dedicated to Western luxury brands and designer collections. Singer and model Ziana Zain was a notable style setter for women, seen on the cover of *Glam* Malaysia in 2008 with the caption "My Life, My It Bags & My Chinese Fashion Escapade."[16] Her brother, singer Anuar Zain, added cool factor to suits in his maturing style, and his oft-changing hairstyles were noted on hair blogs. Singer and television host Aznil Nawawi embodied Malaysia's version of metrosexual. Indonesia's "Indo-pop" featured stylish rock bands including Ungu and Samsons, whose looks reflected grunge and hipster elements. At Jakarta Fashion Week some designers mixed Western looks with more traditional and Islamic styles, while many designers incorporated diverse local textile traditions – including batik and ikat – into fashion-forward designs. Award-winning Stanley Gunawan led the field, designing evening and bridal wear along with childrenswear, as well as pieces for the traditional Islamic market.

HAUTE HOMELESS

Zoolander (2001), the outrageous send-up of the fashion industry, included a tour-de-force runway sequence in which fictitious designer Jacobim Mugatu presented his "Derelicte" collection, a line of trash fashion inspired by "the homeless, the vagrants, the crack whores." Mugatu's "Derelicte" bore an uncanny resemblance to the spring/summer 2000 "Clochards" collection at the house of Dior, designed by John Galliano, which drew mixed reactions and was dubbed "Haute Homeless":

> Dior models who starve themselves posed as the starving. They came down the runway raggedy and baggy, some swathed in newspapers, with torn linings and inside-out labels, accessorized with empty little green J&B whiskey bottles, tin cups dangling from the derriere, bottle caps, plastic clothespins and safety pins. The fashion designer said he was inspired by the French homeless as well as the mentally ill. French homeless advocates were appalled ... Our giddy gilded age is stretching the chasm – and perhaps also the tensions – between the haves and have-nots.[17]

Brother Sharp wandering the streets of Ningbo.

In 2004 doe-eyed twins and former child stars Mary-Kate and Ashley Olsen moved to New York City to attend college. Mary-Kate's recent treatment for anorexia made her of particular interest to paparazzi, and her ad hoc collegiate wardrobe came under great scrutiny. Ripped jeans were combined with baggy sweaters and shirts, billowing scarves, plaid shirts tied around the waist as makeshift kilts, and floppy fedoras, often with some part of the ensemble dragging on the ground – a calculated randomness. Olsen's look resembled hippie, grunge, heroin chic, even Annie Hall, and initially was described as "Boho-chic." However, the fashion press seemed determined to toss Olsen into the ashcan of Haute Homeless, dubbing her style "Bag-Lady look" and "Dumpster Chic."

Not long after Mary-Kate chicly walked the streets of New York, a mentally ill homeless man in his mid-thirties began wandering the streets of Ningbo, China. The man attracted attention among locals by 2008 for his tattered and eclectic sartorial sensibility. He sometimes incorporated women's pieces into otherwise masculine ensembles, or wore overtly manly layered looks (such as a long parka over a leather biker jacket), makeshift tied belts, and tousled long hair. Photographs of the man were posted on the internet in the early weeks of 2010 and his "hobo chic" became a viral sensation, first in China and then the world. His lanky frame and distant demeanor were likened to that of a fashion model; his strikingly handsome looks earned comparison with actors Takeshi Kaneshiro and Chang Chen – while he still ate from garbage cans. His deep, penetrating gaze earned him the nickname Xi Li Ge, "Brother Sharp," and he was romanticized as a "beggar prince." His most famous layered ensemble drew comparison to a look from a

Dolce & Gabbana menswear collection, and soon young Chinese men were imitating Brother Sharp's style. As netizens flocked to Ningbo to catch a photograph of him, the attention confused the disturbed man, unaware of his overnight fame. The rabid media attention reached a fever pitch and the ethics of the situation came into question. However, the intense media attention was instrumental in revealing the man's identity as Cheng Guorong, who had been missing from his family for eleven years.

As Brother Sharp's story was unfolding in China, Vivienne Westwood made a January 2010 menswear showing of yet another homeless-inspired collection that included models emerging from cardboard boxes, pushing shopping carts, and carrying bed rolls, wearing looks composed of mismatched collaged elements. While some interpreted the collection as a social commentary, the general reaction was to scoff at Westwood's work, with words such as "tasteless" and "desperate." The correlation to Galliano's "Clochards" and *Zoolander*'s "Derelicte" was pointed out by numerous journalists and the overall reaction was one of ridicule, with *The Guardian* proclaiming: "Homeless Chic? It's so last decade."[18] With the aberrant fame of Brother Sharp uncannily reaching its apex merely days after Westwood's show, the correlation was vividly reinforced and the infamy of her collection was prolonged in the media. On a more positive note, Cheng Guorong was reunited with his family and received treatment for his mental illness. He also modeled in a fashion show, and inspired a Chinese clothing line. Countless others in Ningbo – as well as in Galliano's Paris, Olsen's New York, and Westwood's London – remained homeless.

New Millennium, Global Watch

Eclecticism, choice, and variety characterized fashion. The defining silhouette, fabrics, and color palette of the season, as dictated by designers of the past, were replaced by a multiplicity of trends suggested by retailers, modeled by celebrities, and driven by developments in technology, further enhanced by fashion's wider geographic reach. As Western fashion became global fashion, by the end of the decade billions of people felt they had a stake in fashion, whether through purchasing their own wardrobes or "visually consuming" clothes created by their favorite designers or worn by celebrities. While fashion insiders might recognize Margiela's discreet white threads as an exclusive "label," bold graphic branding such as "Superdry" and "Juicy" had significant visual impact on the world at large.

Despite a global outlook, regional styles and preferences still affected fashion. In New York City, a woman could wear a black cocktail dress to an evening wedding, but such somber color sense would be unlikely in Atlanta or even in Los Angeles. In France, a slender Parisienne might choose a short skirt and high heels, while women in the Netherlands wore print jersey dresses from King Louie and white leggings. A woman in Jakarta would be sure to match her hijab to her designer bag and shoes. Because of the diversity and reach of fashion, and the absence of a dictated point of view, was anything really out of fashion? While *Vogue* might report that wide-legged jeans were the look of the season, an informal survey of the streets could prove that skinny jeans were still favored. Even in an era that privileged individual choice, fashion still depended on the cycle of desire and disdain, or else "fashion" would cease to exist.

Like the models in this Lacoste sportswear ad, fashion was up in the air as it entered the 2010s.

Notes

Chapter 1
1850–1890: The Dawn of Modern Clothing

1   Norman Lebrecht, *Who Killed Classical Music?: Maestros, Managers, and Corporate Politics* (New York: Citadel Press, 1997), p. 40.
2   "Dress Improvers Downed," *The Daily Telegraph* (November 2, 1888), p. 2.
3   Princess Pauline Metternich, *My Years in Paris* (London: Eveleigh Nash & Grayson, 1922), p. 58.
4   Sara Elisabeth Hume, "Charles Frederick Worth: A Study in the Relationship between the Parisian Fashion Industry and the Lyonnais Silk Industry 1858–1889." Unpublished Master of Arts thesis (SUNY Fashion Institute of Technology, 2003), p. 10.
5   "Empress Elizabeth [*sic*], Her Tragic Death Last Summer – New Light on Her Life," *The New York Times* (March 18, 1899), p. 23.
6   "Many Women in Mourning – Closing of Mr. Felix's Dress-Making Establishment the Cause," *The Pittsburgh Press* (June 30, 1901), p. 15.
7   Alison Matthews David and Elizabeth Semmelhack, *Fashion Victims: The Pleasures and Perils of Dress in the 19th Century*, exh. cat. (Toronto: Bata Shoe Museum, 2014), p. 14.
8   Exhibition signage, *Reveal or Conceal?/ Dévoiler ou Dissimuler?* (Montreal: McCord Museum/Musee McCord, February 22, 2008–January 18, 2009). See also www.musee-mccord.qc.ca/expositions/expositionsXSL.php?lang=1&expold=47&currSectionId=2

Chapter 2
The 1890s: Extremes of the Gilded Age

1   Elizabeth Ann Coleman, *The Opulent Era: Fashions of Worth, Doucet and Pingat* (New York and London: Brooklyn Museum with Thames & Hudson, 1989), p. 29.
2   *Standard Designer* (November 1896), p. 78.
3   Lourdes Font, "International couture: The opportunities and challenges of expansion, 1880–1920," *Business History* 54:1 (2012), p. 31.
4   Coleman, p. 146.
5   Sandra Barwick, *A Century of Style* (London: George Allen & Unwin, 1984), p. 53.

Chapter 3
The 1900s: A New Century

1   Frederic Lees, "The Evolution of Paris Fashions: An Inquiry," *The Pall Mall Magazine*, vol. XXVII (May–August 1902), p. 116.
2   Advertisement for Berthe May's Maternity Corset, *Harper's Bazar* (January 1910), p. 29.
3   Font, p. 31.
4   Robert Forrest Wilson, "The House of Drecoll," *Vogue* (November 15, 1925), p. 34.
5   Paul Poiret, *King of Fashion: The Autobiography of Paul Poiret*, transl. by Stephen Haden Guest (Philadelphia & London: J.B. Lippincott Company, 1931), p. 93.
6   Font, pp. 35–36.
7   Ella Adelia Fletcher, *The Woman Beautiful: A Practical Treatise on the Development and Preservation of Woman's Health and Beauty, and the Principles of Taste in Dress* (New York: Brentano's, 1901), p. 410.

Chapter 4
The 1910s: Exotic Fantasy, Wartime Reality

1   "Worth Allows Styles of the Days of Empress Eugenie to Suggest Leading Silhouette and Control Richness of Fabrics Used," *The New York Times* (March 19, 1916), p. X3.
2   Lady Duff Gordon, *Discretions and Indiscretions* (New York: Frederick A. Stokes Company, 1932), p. 205.
3   Lees, p. 121.
4   "Cheruit Features the Full Skirt, Which, It Is Prophesied, Will be as Successful as Was the Pannier Skirt," *The New York Times* (March 15, 1914), p. X2.
5   Guillermo De Osma, *Mariano Fortuny: His Life and Work* (New York: Rizzoli, 1980), p. 138.
6   Quoted in Stephen Howarth, *Henry Poole: Founders of Savile Row* (London: Bene Factum Publishing, 2003), p. 90.
7   Major Gen. Sir Frederick Maurice, "Contrasts Signing with 1870 Ceremony," *The New York Times* (June 29, 1919), p. 3.

Chapter 5
The 1920s: *Les Années Folles*

1   Valerie Steele, in exhibition brochure for *Fashioning the Modern Woman: The Art of the Couturière, 1919–1939* (New York: The Museum at FIT, February 10–April 10, 2004), p. 9.
2   "Bedford Women Vainly Ask For New Style Long Skirts," *The New York Times* (August 21, 1922), p. 9.
3   "Revolt Against Long Skirts Starts Among Montreal Girls," *The New York Times* (August 30, 1922), p. 13.
4   Farid Chenoune, *A History of Men's Fashion*, transl. by Deke Dusinberre (Paris: Flammarion, 1993), p. 156.

Chapter 6
The 1930s: Aspirations of Glamour

1   "Woman of the World: The Spirit of the Paris Openings," *Vogue* (September 15, 1937), p. 79.
2   "Business: Haute Couture," *Time* (August 13, 1934), p. 55.
3   "Négligés Come Down to Dinner," *Vogue* (April 15, 1931), p. 65.
4   *L'Officiel* (May 1930), p. 34.
5   "The Dressmakers of France," *Fortune* (August 1932), p. 75.
6   "Miss June Collyer," *Vogue* (November 1, 1934), p. 77.
7   *Fashions Art*, 1:1 (Fall 1934), p. 16.
8   "The Dressmakers of France," *Fortune* (August 1932), p. 75.
9   Marjorie Howard, "Of This and That," *Harpers Bazaar* (February 1933), p. 59.
10   Michael Pick, *Be Dazzled! Norman Hartnell, Sixty Years of Glamour and Fashion* (New York: Pointed Leaf Press, 2007), p. 10.
11   "A Revival of 'Lakme'," *The New York Times* (February 14, 1932), p. X7.

Chapter 7
The 1940s: War and Recovery

1 "London ... War Notes," *Vogue* (November 1, 1939), p. 71.
2 "Soutenir le commerce de luxe est le devoir de tous les Français," *L'Art et la Mode* (May 1940), p. 11.
3 Lou Taylor, "Paris Couture 1940–1944," in Juliet Ash and Elizabeth Wilson (eds), *Chic Thrills* (Berkeley and Los Angeles: University of California Press, 1993), p. 130.
4 See "Disciplining the Body, Language and Style," in Eugenia Paulicelli, *Fashion Under Fascism, Beyond the Black Shirt* (Oxford and New York: Berg, 2004), pp. 57–67.
5 Robert Daoust, *Fashion or ration: Hartnell, Amies and dressing for the Blitz*, podcast link at www.nationalarchives.gov.uk/podcasts/fashion-or-ration.htm.
6 *Ibid.*
7 "Fashion is Colour," *Vogue* (March 1, 1941), pp. 49–56.
8 Daoust.
9 "The Measure of the Hem Line," *Harper's Bazaar* (March 1947), p. 188.
10 "Fashion," *Script* (May 1947), p. 33.
11 Quoted in Richard Martin and Harold Koda, *Christian Dior* (New York: The Metropolitan Museum of Art, 1996), p. 13.
12 1939–1946 Special Operations Executive: Personnel Files – Edwin Hardy Amies, doc. ref. HS 9 29/2. www.nationalarchives.gov.uk/releases/2003/april28/popup/hs9_29_2a.htm
13 Hardy Amies, *Just So Far* (London: Collins, 1954), p. 54.
14 Bernadine Morris, "Valentina, a Designer of Clothes For Stars in the Theater, Dies at 90," *The New York Times* (September 15, 1989), p. B5.
15 "Coat and Suit Recovery Board, N.Y. Dress Institute, NRDGA, Union Officials and Others Pledge Cooperation," *Women's Wear Daily* (April 8, 1942), p. 4.
16 Chenoune, p. 204.
17 "Styles for Men Far from Somber," *The New York Times* (September 24, 1942), p. 29.

Chapter 8
The 1950s: Couture Opulence, Suburban Style

1 Lee Rhodes, "Where Can I Go To Meet a Man?," *Charm* (May 1951), p. 136.
2 "The Well-Turned Look," *Harper's Bazaar* (October 1953), p. 197.
3 "Suits with Their Own Winter Coats," *Harper's Bazaar* (September 1953), p. 237.
4 "Essence of a Wedding," *Vogue* (May 1, 1950), p. 100.
5 "And So On into the Fifties," *Vogue* (February 1, 1950), p. 204.
6 "Paris Directory: Names in the News," *Vogue* (March 1, 1950). p. 5.
7 *Ibid.*, p. 4.
8 *Ibid.*
9 "Paris Collections: One Easy Lesson," *Vogue* (March 1, 1954), p. 101.
10 "They See You This Way," *Vogue* (September 1, 1950), p. 155.
11 *Ibid.*
12 "From the Italian Collections, Casual Clothes," *Vogue* (September 1, 1951), p. 247.
13 "Italian Collections Notebook," *Vogue* (September 15, 1952), p. 154.
14 See, for example, "Italy Gets Dressed Up," *Life* (August 20, 1951), pp. 104–112.
15 *Esquire's Handbook for Hosts* (New York: Grosset & Dunlap, 1953), p. 278.
16 Bernadine Taub, "Norell Says Conformity is a Drag on Fashion," *Women's Wear Daily* (April 21, 1959), pp. 1 and 5.

Chapter 9
The 1960s: Fashion for the Future

1 "Fashion Extra," *The Times* (January 20, 1967), p. 13.
2 Marylin Bender, "The New Society, Young and Daring, Swings Into Style," *The New York Times* (December 14, 1964), p. 47.
3 *Ibid.*
4 Marylin Bender, "The Fashion Decade: As Hems Rose, Barriers Fell," *The New York Times* (December 9, 1969), p. 63.
5 Prudence Glynn, "A Throw-Away Line," *The Times* (February 7, 1967), p. 13.
6 Jessica Daves, "Paris: Yes-s and No-s in the spring collections," *Vogue* (March 15, 1962), p. 93.
7 "Top Halves," *The Times* (May 6, 1968), p. 7.
8 "Ever-rising skirts," *The Times* (January 6, 1967), p. 13.
9 "The Boutique Idea in America," *Vogue* (March 15, 1964), p. 122.
10 Quoted in Jean Stein with George Plimpton (eds), *Edie: An American Biography* (New York: Knopf, 1982), p. 296.
11 Gloria Emerson, "Balenciaga's Techniques Art Still Unmatched," *The New York Times* (February 3, 1968), p. 18.
12 "Crahay's First Collection For Lanvin Is a Success," *The New York Times* (January 30, 1964), p. 21.
13 "This Woman Is You," *Harper's Bazaar* (September 1965), p. 250.
14 "Where is Paris Going?," *Harpers Bazaar* (March 1967), p. 165.
15 Carrie Donovan, "Dior Collection by Marc Bohan, Successor to St. Laurent, Is a Hit," *The New York Times* (January 27, 1961), p. 1.
16 Gloria Emerson, "Prettiest Clothes in Paris By Marc Bohan for Dior," *The New York Times* (July 30, 1965), p. 28.
17 Jessica Daves, "Paris light-struck," *Vogue* (March 1, 1960), p. 116.
18 Angela Taylor, "1964 – The Year When Everyone Had Fun With Fashion," *The New York Times* (January 1, 1965), p. 23.
19 "Sarah Miles," *Vogue* (August 1, 1964), p. 63.
20 Robert Alden, "French Are Welcoming New Italian Designers," *The New York Times* (May 12, 1962), p. 12.
21 Gloria Emerson, "Capucci: the Bravest Designer in All of Paris," *The New York Times* (July 31, 1967), p. 31.
22 Carrie Donovan, "American Collections for Spring," *The New York Times* (December 10, 1960), p. 16.
23 Stein, p. 296.
24 "New York: What a joy is Giorgio!," *Vogue* (April 1, 1969), p. 254.
25 "The lengths the wig craze can go to ...," *The Times* (October 28, 1966), p. 13.
26 Prudence Glynn, "A wardrobe of lengths," *The Times* (October 14, 1969), p. 13.

Chapter 10
The 1970s: Revivals and Individuality

1 Bernadine Morris and Barbra Walz, *The Fashion Makers: An Inside Look at America's Leading Designers* (New York: Random House, 1978), p. 145.
2 "Modern Living: Karat Top," *Time* (May 19, 1975), p. 61.
3 "Belts and the Blue Denim Look," *Vogue* (January 15, 1971), p. 33.
4 "Modern Living: Let the Costume Ball Begin," *Time* (August 16, 1976).
5 Mary Russell, "Paris Signals: New Designers, New Ideas," *Vogue* (July 1977), p. 150.
6 Prudence Glynn, "English Collection," *The Times* (October 19, 1971), p. 13.
7 "American Fashion – The Movers," *Vogue* (February 1975), p. 107.

8 Morris and Walz, p. 145.
9 *Ibid.*, p. 16.
10 Bill Gale and the Editors of *Esquire* Magazine, *Esquire's Fashions for Today* (New York: Harper and Row, 1973), p. 188.
11 John T. Molloy, *Dress for Success* (New York: Peter H. Wyden Publisher, 1975), p. 230.

Chapter 11
The 1980s: Power Dressing and Postmodernism

1 John Duka, "A Black-Tie Debutante Party on the North Shore," *The New York Times* (June 21, 1982), p. A17.
2 Jeanie Kasindorf, "New Uniforms for the Vice Squad," *The New York Magazine* (September 1, 1986), p. 11.
3 Jennet Conant, "The Heat is On," *Newsweek* (April 4, 1988), p. 55.
4 "Judith Leiber Offers More Than 'Mere Bagatelles,' at the Jewish Center of The Hamptons, June 2011," www.leibermuseum.org/?p=665
5 Conant.
6 Mary Russell, "Vogue's View: Chanel ... Life after Coco ...," *Vogue* (May 1, 1983), p. 230.
7 G. Y. Dryansky, "An Eye for Allure," *Connoisseur* (August 1986), p. 74.
8 Caroline Kellett, "Body Talks," *Vogue* (British edition, May 1983), p. 94.
9 Bernadine Morris, "From Japan, New Faces, New Shapes," *The New York Times* (December 14, 1982), p. C10.
10 "Vivienne Westwood: Shock Treatments," *GQ* (January 1983), p. 132.
11 Jay Cocks, "Giorgio Armani: Suiting Up For Easy Street," *Time* (April 5, 1982), p. 60.
12 *Ibid.*
13 Bettijane Levine, "In Milan, One Designer Captures Fashion Scene," *Los Angeles Times* (March 11, 1987), p. F1.
14 Morris and Walz, p. 76.
15 Bernadine Morris, "The Best Clothes in the World," *United Mainliner* (March 1980), p. 82.
16 Caroline Rennolds Milbank, *Couture, The Great Designers* (New York and London: Thames & Hudson and Stewart, Tabori and Chang, 1985), p. 398.
17 Morris and Walz, p. 68.
18 Harriet Shapiro, "Off Her Knees and Out of the Red, Sandra Garratt Strikes It rich with Mix-and-Match Multiples," *People* (June 20, 1988), retrieved at people.com.
19 1983 interview for ABC TV "Nationwide," quoted in *Katie Pye: Clothes for Modern Lovers*, exh. cat. (Melbourne: National Gallery of Victoria, 2007), p. 11.
20 Mary Russell, "Backstage, Paris/Milan: spring–summer '84 in the making," *Vogue* (November 1, 1983), p. 304.
21 Camille Duhé, "A Head for Business," *GQ* (January 1983), p. 114.
22 Diane Rafferty, "The Many Faces of Yves: The Designer of the Half Century," *Connoisseur* (February 1990), p. 61.

Chapter 12
The 1990s: Subcultures and Supermodels

1 Christopher S. Wren, "Clinton Calls Fashion Ads' 'Heroin Chic' Deplorable," *The New York Times* (May 22, 1997), p. A22.
2 Laura Jacobs, "The Millers' Tale," *Vanity Fair* (June 1995), p. 140.
3 Courtney Weaver, "Paint it Black: London Goes Goth, Again," *The New York Times* (February 22, 1998), p. 421.

4 Renée D. Turner, "The High-Five Revolution," *Ebony* (August 1991), p. 29.

5 Mimi Spencer, "Handbag Mania," *Vogue* (February 1, 1998), p. 243.

6 Alex Witchel, "Vera Wang," *New York Times Magazine* (June 19, 1994), p. 25.

7 Quoted in I. Rosselli, *10 Years of Dolce & Gabbana* (New York: Abbeville Press, 1996), p. 41.

8 Amy M. Spindler, "A Few Artisans Try to Blow the Socks Off," *The New York Times* (October 6, 1993), p. C12.

9 Anne Bogart, "The Antwerp Six," *Elle* (May 1988), p. 288.

10 Guy Trebay, "Death of the Fashion Groupie," *The New York Times* (August 22, 1999), p. FT108.

Chapter 13
The 2000s: Mixed Messages

1 Cover of *Women's Wear Daily* (December 4, 2008).

2 Andy Serwer, "The '00s: Goodbye (at Last) to the Decade from Hell," *Time* (December 7, 2009), http://content.time.com/time/subscriber/article/0,33009,1942973,00.html.

3 Sarah Tippit, "Jennifer Lopez, Hilfiger Unveil 'J.Lo' Fashions," *Puerto Rico Herald* (April 26, 2001), http://www.puertorico-herald.org/issues/2001/vol5n19/JLoClothes-en.html.

4 Kelly Carter, "'Down With Love' makes a fashion statement," *USA Today* (May 27, 2003), http://usatoday30.usatoday.com/life/movies/news/2003-05-19-love_x.htm.

5 Jennifer Mathieu, "Christina Aguilera August 11, 2000," *Spin* (November 2000), p. 80.

6 Mark Greif, "What Was the Hipster?," *New York Magazine* (October 24, 2010), http://nymag.com/news/features/69129/.

7 Carol Midgley and Stefanie Marsh, "The A–Z of Cool," *The Times* (October 28, 2002), p. 5 S1.

8 Bobbie Thomas, "Katie's latest fashion steal: Tom Cruise's jeans," *Today Style Buzz* (August 24, 2008), http://www.today.com/id/26330879/ns/today-today_style/t/katies-latest-fashion-steal-tom-cruises-jeans/#.VQeDR2TF-cl.

9 Ruth La Ferla, "Over the Shoulder, Over the Top," *The New York Times* (October 6, 2005), p. G1.

10 Catherine Shu, "Threading tradition and modernity together," *Taipei Times* (August 27, 2008), p. 14.

11 Robert Murphy, "The Latest from Paris," *Women's Wear Daily* (February 24, 2005), p. 15.

12 Sarah Mower, "Alexander the Great," *Vogue* (May 1, 2011), p. 246.

13 Amy Larocca, "The Dapper Mr. Browne," *New York Magazine* (August 20, 2006), http://nymag.com/fashion/06/fall/19389/.

14 Elva Ramirez, "MCM's Eastern Makeover – An ambitious South Korean businesswoman attempts to resurrect the faded luxury brand," *The Wall Street Journal* (March 13–14, 2010), p. W4.

15 *New York Magazine* (August 15, 2005), http://nymag.com/nymetro/news/people/features/12392/index1.html.

16 Cover of *Glam* (Malaysian edition, February 2008).

17 Maureen Dowd, "Haute Homeless," *The New York Times* (January 23, 2000), p. WK 15.

18 "Homeless chic? It's so last decade," *The Guardian* (January 18, 2010), http://www.theguardian.com/lifeandstyle/2010/jan/19/homeless-chic-is-so-last-decade.

Glossary

abaya (pl. **abayat**) A long and loosely fit women's dress, typically black, worn in the Islamic world.

aegishjalmur An ancient Viking symbol, often called the helm of awe, typically with eight decorated spokes radiating from a joined center.

aigrette A long feather or bunch of feathers, usually pointing up, as decoration on a hat. Often made of egret feathers, an aigrette usually has a medallion or ribbon rosette as a mounting at its base. The term also can refer to a piece of jewelry of similar shape worn on a hat or headdress.

ankh An ancient Egyptian symbol representing the life force and eternity, in the shape of a cross with a looped top section.

ascot A long rectangular necktie that is worn simply looped and usually secured with a decorative stick pin through both ends. The tie takes its name from the Ascot horse races in Britain, where it was often worn as a common piece of men's daytime formal wear.

baju melayu Literally "clothing of the Malay," the term refers to the traditional wear of Malaysian men, consisting of shirt, pajama trousers, and sarong.

Bakelite A brand name for a type of plastic created from heat-set resin, first developed in 1907. Bakelite was used for a variety of household products such as radios and kitchenware, and was a common material for costume jewelry.

ball fringe A type of fringe where balls or pom-poms of yarn are equally spaced along the edge.

barn jacket A hip-length wool or canvas jacket in the style of farm workers typical of western North America and Australia.

bateau neckline A wide and shallow neckline, usually as wide as shoulder to shoulder, and not much deeper than the collar bone. Also called "boat neckline."

batik A fabric technique that creates pattern with applied wax as a dye resist, originated in Indonesia.

bergère style In the style of a shepherdess, in reference to Marie Antoinette fashions and other country French styles.

bertha collar An oversized collar that drapes down over the shoulder point, originating in women's fashions in the 17th century.

bias cut Construction method that involves cutting garment pieces diagonally across the grain of fabric.

bishop sleeve A long sleeve that gets fuller toward the bottom, gathered into a cuff at the wrist. The name is probably derived from the full sleeves on a bishop's vestment.

blouson Having fullness that blouses up over the waist; can also describe fullness in general, such as a "blouson sleeve." In French, used to refer to a waist-length leather jacket, as in the Blouson noir subculture.

boat shoe A flat, rubber-soled shoe with leather or suede upper, laced with leather, and often prominently topstitched. Originally associated with boating activities, now more generally worn as informal footwear.

bobbinet Machine-made hexagonal mesh, softer than conventional tulle.

bomber hat Warm headgear, often made of fur or faux fur, with flaps at ears and forehead that can be worn down or up. Derived from styles worn by aviators.

bouclé From the French word for "curled," novelty yarn with looped components. Also the fabric, often tweed, made from such yarn.

bracelet sleeves Women's sleeves that are approximately three-quarter length, allowing for the display of bracelets.

bricolage The French word for "tinkering"; in English-language usage refers to a combination of improbable or jarring elements.

bugle beads Tubular glass beads typically used for decorating women's clothing. The beads are applied with thread through a channel running lengthwise through the center of the bead.

burnoose A full cloak with a large hood, traditional dress for Berber and Arab men in North Africa.

burqa A mask related to female-modesty customs in Islamic culture, often made of fabric, metal, papier mâché, or mesh. The term is also sometimes used to describe full-body coverings with a face-mask component (see **chador**).

busk A stiff piece of wood or bone placed down the center front of a corset to encourage rigid posture. Such busks were the likely source of center front boning on early forms of the brassiere in the 1910s.

chador A full-body covering for women in Middle Eastern Islamic cultures, often with a face opening. With an enclosed face it is sometimes referred to as a **burqa**, a word typically describing a face mask.

chalk stripe A light- to medium-weight wool flannel or worsted suiting fabric, often navy blue or dark grey, distinguished by a pattern of light-colored woven stripes that resemble chalk lines.

chapan A loosely cut man's coat of Central Asian origin, often worn hanging from the shoulders without the arms through the sleeves.

charmeuse Lightweight, drapeable warp-faced satin weave fabric with a lustrous face and a matte reverse side. Originally made of silk, now available in a variety of fibers.

chemise Derived from the Latin *camisa*, the word chemise has acquired several meanings in English-language usage. Used to indicate a woman's undergarment, the word also describes dresses with soft cotton fabrication, dresses with elevated Empire waistlines, and also loose-fitted dresses.

cheongsam A Cantonese term (known as *qipao* in Mandarin), the cheongsam is a smooth-fitting sheath dress traditional to Chinese culture, frequently with short sleeves and a small stand-up collar. The fitted form of the cheongsam developed in the 1920s from fuller-style gowns.

chubby A waist-length jacket, usually for women, that is full in silhouette, often made of fur or down-filled.

ciré satin From the French for "waxed," a sturdy satin with an especially glossy finish.

ciselé velvet Figured velvet that combines areas of cut and uncut pile. May also have a voided ground.

clocks (on stockings) Designs placed typically on the outer side of stockings, usually created with embroidery or knitted in.

cloqué Textile having a puffed or blistered effect.

cocoon coat A full and rounded coat, narrowing to the hem, resembling a cocoon. It is usually created by simple drapery of straight-grain fabric folded into two opposing diagonal folds to form sleeves. The style was particularly common in the 1910s and associated with the work of Paquin, Poiret, and others. Sometimes the term is used to describe more closely fitted, tubular-shaped coats.

combination Woman's undergarment that joins a camisole to knickers or tap pants. Can also be used to describe a one-piece undergarment for men.

crinoline Originally used to describe woven horsehair (*crin*), the word is also used to describe stiff netting, as well as cage-style hooped underskirts.

cuirasse style A bodice molded to the torso in the manner of a *cuirasse*, a man's armor breastplate.

dagging A cut-edge detail in the shape of a repeating triangle, initially common to styles of the early 15th century.

Daisy Dukes Very short cut-off jeans, as popularized by the costuming of Catherine Bach in the television series *The Dukes of Hazzard*, which aired from 1979 to 1985.

dickey Neckline filler that intentionally resembles the top of a shirt or turtleneck.

décolletage A cutaway neckline; also often refers to the expanse of chest and cleavage revealed by such a neckline.

demimondaine European, particularly French, term for a woman outside of "respectable society" because of her position as the mistress of a prominent or wealthy man, or of a series of such men. Some *demimondaines* were also singers and actresses.

devoré A method of producing a surface pattern whereby a fabric consisting of two fibers is treated with chemicals that "devour" or etch one of the component fibers without affecting the other.

Directoire In the style of the Directoire (or "Directory") period of French history following the French Revolution.

dirndl Traditional dress of Germany (and other German-language-speaking countries), consisting of a sleeveless bodice that laces up the front, attached to a gathered skirt. Sometimes the term refers to the skirt only, and such a skirt is made of straight-grained panels gathered or pleated into a waistband.

dobby Simple, geometric woven pattern often used in shirting for textural contrast.

dolman (cloak) A long, full robe of Turkish origin, the term became common in the 19th century to describe full overcoats with an orientalist flavor, as well as military coats.

dolman (sleeve) A sleeve that is cut in one with the body of the garment, usually tapering up from the waist to the wrist; also sometimes referred to as a "magyar" sleeve or a batwing sleeve.

dotted Swiss Lightweight cotton fabric that features rows of raised dots formed in the weaving process or added later with flocking.

dress shield A piece of fabric or lightweight pad attached under the arm to protect a garment from moisture and staining caused by perspiration.

duster Similar to a raincoat, the duster was created to keep dust off the wearer, and was usually used by cowboys in North America and Australia. The style was also worn for driving in the early 20th century, and was a fashionable style in the 1980s.

engageantes Undersleeves that emerge from the sleeves of an overgarment; often they were strictly decorative pieces and not a complete undersleeve.

envelope bag A clutch purse in the shape of an envelope.

espadrilles Canvas shoes with jute soles. Usually flat but sometimes wedged, the style derives from vernacular footwear of France and Spain.

Fauvism Taking its name from *fauve*, the French word for "wild beast," Fauvism was an artistic movement following Impressionism and Post-impressionism known for its gestural forms and vivid, "wild" colors.

fedora A man's hat with a peaked crown and wide-angled brim, originating in the early 20th century.

fichu A large scarf, typically white and worn tucked into a neckline, resembling a small shawl. The style originated in the late 17th century and was often revived in later periods.

fisherman sandal A low-heeled shoe with several horizontal straps attached to a central piece and a closed or open back. A casual footwear style worn by both men and women.

foulard pattern Woven or printed design, such as a small geometric or other repeated motif, typical of neckties or scarves, often used on silk or silk-like fabric.

four-in-hand tie A necktie in its standard 20th-century form, often simply referred to as a "tie." Commonly made of bias-cut silk, the four-in-hand tie consists of a "blade" (the front part) that typically tapers to the neckband and the "under end" or tail.

French cuffs Shirt cuffs on men's dress shirts and women's blouses that are double length and are worn folded back, usually secured with cufflinks.

galoshes Short boots for rain or slush that are worn over another pair of shoes, typically fastening with snaps, hooks, or buttons.

gaucho hat A wide-brimmed felt or leather hat, typical of the gauchos (cowboys) of the South American pampas.

gazar A sheer but sturdy fabric, made of silk or silk-like fiber, with a smooth, crisp texture, often used for special occasion and bridal apparel.

ghillie Shoe with crossed lacing over the otherwise open instep, based on styles worn for traditional Celtic dance.

gigot sleeve A sleeve style popular in the 1830s and 1890s, with a full puffed top portion which (with either piecing or tapering) tightened at the forearm and wrist. Also known as a "leg-of-mutton" sleeve.

gladiator sandal Sandal for either men or women that laces up the ankle in imitation of ancient Roman styles.

godet An inset of fabric, usually triangular in shape, typically at the bottom of a skirt or sleeve cuff, which increases the fullness with a flare at the hem.

gore A skirt panel, usually angled so that when all gores are sewn together an A-line shape is created.

"Greenaway" dress A dress for girls with an Empire waistline and full skirt in the style of illustrations by Kate Greenaway.

grommet Metal ring used to reinforce an eyelet for lacing, such as on shoes or corsets.

guilloché Repeating curved pattern formed by a spirograph or similar means.

hamsa Arabic for the numeral five, the term refers to an amulet depicting the hand of God with five fingers, and often with the eye of God in the center. Common in usage in the Middle East and Judaic culture, it is used in some Islamic sects that allow amulets and is usually referred to as the "Hand of Fatima."

Henley A long-sleeved jersey knit shirt, usually with a short placket at center front and no collar, sometimes called a "foreign legion shirt."

hijab Islamic headscarf; the term can also refer to a more generalized concept of modesty and body coverage. A woman who wears a hijab is known as a *hijabi*.

hoodie Late 20th-century/early 21st-century term for a hooded sweatshirt.

huarache Flat, woven leather slip-on shoe characteristic of Central America.

jabot Of late 17th-century origin, the term jabot usually refers to a long and narrow rectangular lace simply tied around the neck and hanging down in front. The term can also refer to tie necklines that resemble an ascot.

jellies Soft plastic sandals, manufactured in a wide range of colors, often imitating the style of fisherman sandals.

jewel neckline A round neckline that circles the base of the neck.

jumper In American usage, a sleeveless dress, like a pinafore, usually worn over a blouse. In British English, a pullover sweater.

Karukul A hat made of astrakhan or fur from the Karukul lamb, commonly used in Central Asia. The Karukul-style hat is brimless and typically comes to a point in the front.

keffiyeh A traditional scarf in the Middle East, typically worn by men, with a checked pattern. Frequently associated with Arab peoples and Islam, the *keffiyeh* scarf was adopted as a symbol of Palestinian liberation.

knickerbockers Knee-length pants for men, worn for recreational activities such as golfing, hunting, and bicycling, especially during the 1890s and early decades of the 20th century. The style was essentially a return to the knee breeches of the 17th and 18th centuries, albeit in a casual context. Boys in the late 19th and early 20th centuries wore the style on a regular basis until they were mature enough for long trousers. The term was shortened to knickers, a word also used in British English to describe women's underpants.

lamé Fabric that is woven or knitted with metallic yarn.

Lastex An elastic yarn with a latex core and an outer wrapping of another fiber. Typically used to provide stretch to foundation garments and activewear.

Louis heel A medium-height heel for women's shoes with a distinctive concave curve at its front, and a shallower curve at its back. The style was first popularized in the 18th century when women's skirts were worn short enough to expose the heel.

Lycra® Brand name of spandex, an elastic fiber developed by DuPont, now a trademark of INVISTA.

macramé Decorative lace-like work created with knotting of many strings, yarns, or cords. Used both for clothing trim and decorative applications.

madras Fabric named after a city in southern India, originally the source of this yarn-dyed plaid, usually cotton, often characterized by a subtle color palette.

maillot From the French, a term for a one-piece swimsuit or, in performance sportswear, a tightly fitting jersey.

mannequin Originally denoted a live female model, often used at couture houses to show prospective clients the firm's dresses. Later usage of the term indicated a display form for merchandising menswear, womenswear, and childrenswear, usually in the realistic image of a human figure.

Mannerism An artistic movement of the 16th century that followed the High Renaissance, noteworthy for artifice, tension, and gesture. The name likely derived from the Italian word *maniera*. The term has been adapted to mean superficial or emphasizing form over content.

marabou Small fluffy feathers harvested from various birds and used as trim for apparel and millinery.

Mary Jane Black patent leather shoe for women and girls with rounded toe and a strap across the instep. Can also be used to describe a shoe in the same style but made of other materials.

matelassé Fabric with prominent puffed or pocketed areas. Similar to cloqué, but more highly textured.

middy Sailor-style blouse, especially common for children but also popular for women, taking its name from the naval term "midshipman."

moccasin Soft leather slipper derived from American Indian footwear.

moiré faille A medium-weight fabric with crosswise ribs with a wavy pattern pressed into the surface.

mousseline Lightweight fabric made of either cotton or silk (*mousseline de soie*), similar to cotton voile or silk organza but softer.

muffler A wool scarf worn for warmth in cold weather.

mullet A popular layered hairstyle of the 1980s for both men and women, with a short crown and bangs and longer hair in back, notably similar to the "à la Titus" hairstyle of the 1790s.

niqab A face veil hanging from below eye level, worn combined with a hijab or chador in Islamic dress.

nubuck Leather that has been sanded to produce a velvety surface, similar to suede but less textured.

ogival In the shape of a pointed arch. Often used as a repeat pattern.

organza Plain weave cotton fabric that is sheer and crisp. Often used for blouses, dresses, and trim, especially collars and cuffs.

ottoman A fabric with prominent crosswise ribs, similar to grosgrain, often used in women's special occasion apparel.

Oxford A low-heeled shoe that laces up. The term is used to describe shoes for both men and women, with many variations including laced tabs and details such as cap toes and wingtips.

paillette A small metal sequin.

paisley A motif derived from the Indian and Persian *boteh*, often described as having a teardrop or mango shape and used widely for apparel and interior design.

panné velvet A velvet with short pile that has been pressed down to produce variation in luster.

pannier drapery Fabric drapery that emphasizes the hips. The term takes its name from the pannier understructure of 18th-century womenswear; the word *panier* is French for basket.

passementerie Elaborate trimming for womenswear, usually made of braid, cording, and ribbons. The term can also have broader meaning including decorative trims such as tassels and upholstery trimmings.

pegged Term used to describe trousers that narrow at the ankle.

peignoir A woman's dressing gown or robe, typically of a soft, often sheer, fabric.

pelerine A small capelet for women that resembles an oversized bertha collar, usually of matching fabric with a dress. The pelerine was typically detachable from the dress to be convertible for varying weather conditions.

pendant sleeve A detail from medieval clothing, revived in 19th- and 20th-century fashions, featuring panels hanging typically from mid-arm. Another form includes oversleeves that hang from the armhole.

peplum A small skirt-like tier attached to the bottom of a bodice, jacket, or blouse.

Phrygian cap Derived from ancient Anatolian dress and worn as a symbol of liberty in the French Revolution, the Phrygian cap is a soft hat which comes to a point that typically flops forward. The shape is periodically revived in millinery.

pinstripe A light- to medium-weight wool flannel or worsted suiting fabric, often navy blue or dark grey, distinguished by a pattern of narrow, light-colored woven stripes that resemble lines of pin dots (for comparison see **chalk stripe**).

piqué Compound woven cloth with a bird's-eye or waffled look often used for shirting and other apparel. Term also applies to knits with the same surface texture.

placket A garment opening that is typically closed with buttons or a zipper.

plastron Originating as a stiffened front panel of a surcote during the Middle Ages (named for the front of an armored breastplate), the later usage of the term includes a large appliquéd panel on men's formal shirts with center back closures, as well as a decorative center front panel of a woman's bodice.

plissé Lightweight fabric with a crinkled surface used especially for summer apparel.

plush Pile woven fabric, often heavyweight, frequently used for outerwear.

princess line Construction method that utilizes vertical seams running down the apex of the chest.

poet blouse Loose-fitting blouse with a turned-back open collar.

polonaise A style of looping up a woman's skirt to expose an underskirt or petticoat that originated in the 1770s, was endorsed by Marie Antoinette, and was revived during the 1860s, 1870s, and 1880s.

poncho Typically a large rectangle of fabric with a neck hole in the center, derived from traditional South American dress.

pouter pigeon style Placing emphasis on an enlarged chest for women. The style was achieved with puffy draped fichus and ruffles across the bust and was sometimes enhanced by corsetry.

reefer A slim-fitting, below knee-length coat, single- or double-breasted, usually with a center back vent, worn by men and women.

repp Crosswise ribbed fabric, frequently made of silk, often used for neckwear.

reticule A woman's small handbag, often with a drawstring or "reticulated" closure at the top.

revers Often describing lapels of a jacket front, the term can refer to any part of the garment that is turned back to reveal a contrasting or self facing.

rhinestone A glass ornament in the shape and color of a precious or semi-precious gemstone.

robe tailleur A dress with elements of tailor-made costume.

scalloping A cut-edge detail in the shape of a repeating half circle, initially common to styles of the early 15th century.

self Term used to indicate a detail made with the same fabric as the body of a garment, such as "self piping" or "self-covered buttons."

shalwar kameez An ensemble of tunic top and pajama-style trousers commonly worn in South Asian countries, including India, Pakistan, Bangladesh, and Afghanistan.

shantung Lightweight silk, or silk-like, fabric with noticeable slubs.

sheath A dress with a fitted silhouette, usually narrow to the hem and sleeveless.

shirring Gathering formed by pulling fabric along stitching lines. Used as a decorative detail.

shirtwaist A woman's blouse in the style of a man's shirt, especially with a center front placket.

snood A headdress of open net, typically made of yarn, worn on the back of the head to contain the hair. In contemporary 21st-century usage, the term also describes a hooded scarf.

soutache A flat, narrow trim often used to define edges or create scrollwork designs.

spandex, see **Lycra**®

spats Abbreviated from "spatterdashes," spats partially cover shoes, revealing only the toes and heels. They are worn over shoes both for protection from mud and rain and as a decorative accessory.

Spencer A short, fitted, waist-length jacket for both men and women, purportedly named for Lord George Spencer.

stock Rectangular neckwear that is wrapped around the neck at least twice and knotted in front; sometimes worn with a pin through the knot.

stole A shawl or wrap; often used to describe a fur piece.

straight grain The lengthwise direction of fabric, parallel to the selvedges.

superfine A category of extremely fine wool used in men's tailoring. Superfine usually consists of wool from Merino sheep, although sometimes cashmere is also included in a blend.

surplice front A wrapped front, where two sides of the garment overlap across the center front. The term can be used to describe both actual wrapping and a faux wrap effect.

Symbolism An artistic movement of the late 19th century that emerged from styles of fiction and poetry, and the earlier Romantic movement. Symbolist art often featured decadent, erotic, and morbid themes, and anticipated aspects of the later style Surrealism.

tap pants A type of shorts for women, the term is often used to describe underwear in this shape. Sometimes with a flare on the outseam side of each leg, the term tap pants is derived from the 1920s and 1930s, when the style was used by female tap dancers for rehearsal wear.

tertiary colors Colors that are neither primary nor secondary, but fall between the two (such as "blue-green"), extending to a variety of shades and tones of colors.

tie-dye A resist dye technique where the resist is created by tying up various sections of the fabric, preventing the tied areas from absorbing the dye, creating patterns on the fabric.

toilette 19th- and early 20th-century term for a woman's ensemble.

trapunto Quilting with high relief achieved with topstitching over padded linings.

tricorne A three-cornered hat, in the style of the 18th century.

trompe l'œil From the French for "fool the eye," a visual effect that provides the illusion of reality.

trumpet skirt A variation on the gored skirt with additional flare at the hem, created by widening the gores or inserting godets, which has the appearance of a trumpet.

tulle Netting with a hexagonal mesh and a somewhat stiff hand, used extensively in special occasion and bridal apparel.

Ulster A practical overcoat of wool fabric for daytime wear, usually with an attached self cape.

Ultrasuede A suede-like fabric made of polyester.

unitard A one-piece body-hugging garment that extends from the neck to the legs or feet.

vamp (of shoe) The upper front part of a shoe that covers the toes to the instep.

vest In American usage, a waistcoat or sleeveless jacket. In British English, an undershirt.

warp-printed A method by which warps are printed before a fabric is woven, resulting in a slightly blurred effect.

whisker washed Term applied to a method of distressing denim to achieve the look of permanent creases and bleaching across the hips.

windowpane check A fabric pattern of lines in a check or plaid on a solid background so that the evenly spaced lines resemble a window.

Bibliography

GENERAL SOURCES AND DESIGNER MONOGRAPHS

Alaïa, Azzedine. *Azzedine Alaïa in the 21st century*. Belgium BAI, 2011.

Amory, Cleveland et al. (eds) *Vanity Fair: Selections from America's Most Memorable Magazine: A Cavalcade of the 1920s and 1930s*. New York: Viking Press, 1970.

Anthony, Carl Sferrazza. *America's First Families*. New York: Touchstone, 2000.

Arnold, Janet. *Patterns of Fashion 2, Englishwomen's Dresses and their Construction c. 1860–1940*. New York: Drama Book Specialists, 1977.

Ash, Juliet and Elizabeth Wilson. *Chic Thrills: A Fashion Reader*. Berkeley and Los Angeles: University of California Press, 1993.

Banks, Jeffrey and Erica Lennard. *Perry Ellis: An American Original*. New York: Rizzoli, 2013.

Barwick, Sandra. *A Century of Style*. London: Unwin Hyman, 1984.

Battersby, Martin. *Art Deco Fashion: French Designers, 1908–1925*. New York: St. Martin's Press, 1974.

Beard, Geoffrey W. *The Complete Gentleman*. New York: Rizzoli, 1992.

Beaton, Cecil. *The Glass of Fashion*. Garden City, NY: Doubleday, 1954.

Beene, Geoffrey. *Beene by Beene*. New York: Vendome Press, 2005.

Beirendonck, Walter van. *Walter van Beirendonck: dream the world awake*. Tielt: Lannoo, 2011.

La Belle Epoque (exhibition brochure with an essay by Philippe Jullian). New York: The Metropolitan Museum of Art, 1982.

Blackman, Cally. *100 Years of Fashion Illustration*. London: Laurence King Publishing, 2007.

—. *100 Years of Menswear*. London: Laurence King Publishing, 2009.

Blum, Dilys E. *Roberto Capucci: Art Into Fashion*. Philadelphia: Philadelphia Museum of Art, 2011.

—. *Shocking! The Art and Fashion of Elsa Schiaparelli*. New Haven: Yale University Press, 2003.

Blume, Mary. *The master of us all: Balenciaga, his workrooms, his world*. New York: Farrar, Straus and Giroux, 2013.

Bott, Danièle. *Thierry Mugler*. London and New York: Thames & Hudson, 2010.

Bowles, Hamish (ed.). *Jacqueline Kennedy: the White House Years*. New York: The Metropolitan Museum of Art and Boston: Bulfinch Press, 2001.

Bradley, Barry W. *Galanos*. Cleveland: The Western Reserve Historical Society, 1996.

Breward, Christopher. *Fashion (Oxford History of Art)*. Oxford: Oxford University Press, 2003.

—. *Fashioning London: Clothing and the Modern Metropolis*. London: Bloomsbury Academic, 2004.

Brown, Sass. *Eco fashion*. London: Laurence King Publishing, 2010.

Bryant, Michele Wesen. *WWD Illustrated: 1960s–1990s*. New York: Fairchild, 2004.

Calahan, April D. *Tina Leser: designs for escape*. (MA Thesis), SUNY Fashion Institute of Technology, New York, 2009.

Calloway, Stephen and Stephen Jones. *Royal Style: Five Centuries of Influence and Fashion*. Boston: Little, Brown and Company, 1991.

Casadio, Mariuccia. *Missoni*. London: Thames & Hudson, 1997.

—. *Moschino*. London: Thames & Hudson, 1997.

Cashin, Bonnie. *Bonnie Cashin, practical dreamer* New York: Museum at the Fashion Institute of Technology, 2000.

Cassini, Oleg. *In my own fashion: an autobiography*. London: Simon & Schuster, 1987.

Cavaliero, Roderick. *Ottomania: The Romantics and the Myth of the Islamic Orient*. London: I. B. Tauris Publishing, 2010.

Chaille, Francois. *La Grande Histoire de la Cravate*. Paris: Flammarion, 1994.

Chenoune, Farid. *A History of Men's Fashion*. Transl. Deke Dusinberre. Paris: Flammarion, 1993.

Chierichetti, David. *Hollywood Costume Design*. New York: Harmony Books, 1976.

Cole, Daniel James. "Heritage and Innovation: Charles Frederick Worth, John Redfern, and the Dawn of Modern Fashion," *Mode de recherche*. Institut Français de la Mode, June 2011.

—. "Asiatic Trends in 1930s Styles and the Icons that Promoted Them." *The Business and Marketing of Icons*. Los Angeles: IFFTI/FIDM, 2013.

Coleman, Elizabeth Ann. *The Opulent Era: Fashions of Worth, Doucet, and Pingat*. London and New York: Thames & Hudson, 1989.

—. *The Genius of Charles James*. Brooklyn: Brooklyn Museum and New York: Holt, Rinehart, and Winston, 1982.

Cox, Caroline. *I Do: 100 years of Wedding Fashion*. New York: Amphoto Books, 2002.

Craughwell-Varda, Kathleen. *Looking for Jackie: American Fashion Icons*. New York: Hearst Books, 1999.

Creed, Charles *Maid to measure*. London: Jarrolds, 1961.

Davis, Mary E. *Ballets Russes Style: Diaghilev's Dancers and Paris Fashion*. London: Reaktion Books, 2010.

de la Haye, Amy. *The Cutting Edge: 50 Years of British Fashion, 1947–1997*. London: V & A Publications, 1997.

de la Haye, Amy and Cathie Dingwall. *Surfers, Soulies, Skinheads and Skaters: Subcultural Style from the Forties to the Nineties*. London: V & A Publications, 1996.

de la Haye, Amy and Elizabeth Wilson (eds.). *Defining Dress: Dress as Object, Meaning and Identity*. Manchester: Manchester University Press, 2000.

de la Haye, Amy, and Shelley Tobin. *Chanel: The Couturière at Work*. New York: The Overlook Press, 1995.

De Marly, Diana. *Worth: Father of Haute Couture*. London: Elm Tree Books, 1980.

Demornex, Jacqueline. *Lucien Lelong*. London: Thames & Hudson, 2008.

—. *Madeleine Vionnet*. New York: Rizzoli, 1991.

Demeulemeester, Ann and Patti Smith. *Ann Demeulemeester*. New York: Rizzoli, 2014.

Designing the It Girl: Lucile and Her Style (exhibition catalogue with essay by Rebecca Jumper Matheson and Molly Frances Sorkin). New York: The Museum at FIT, 2005.

Deslandres, Yvonne: *Poiret*. New York: Rizzoli, 1987.

Di Trocchio, Paola et al. *Black in Fashion: Mourning to Night*. Melbourne: National Gallery of Victoria, 2008.

Druesedow, Jean L. *In Style: Celebrating Fifty Years of the Costume Institute*. New York: Metropolitan Museum of Art, 1987.

Ehrman, Edwina. *The Wedding Dress: 300 Years of Bridal Fashions*. London: V & A Publishing, 2011.

English, Bonnie. *Japanese fashion designers: the work and influence of Issey Miyake, Yohji Yamamoto and Rei Kawakubo*. Oxford and New York: Berg, 2011.

Etherington-Smith, Meredith. *Patou*. New York: St. Martin's Press, 1983.

Evans, Caroline and Susannah Frankel. *The House of Viktor & Rolf*. London, New York: Merrell, 2008.

Farrell-Beck, Jane and Jean Parsons. *Twentieth Century Dress in the United States*. New York: Fairchild, 2007.

Ferragamo, Salvatore. *Shoemaker of dreams: the autobiography of Salvatore Ferragamo*. Florence: Centro Di, 1985.

FIDM Museum Blog. Los Angeles: Fashion Institute of Design and Merchandising, 2009 http://blog.fidmmuseum.org/

Finamore, Michelle Tolini. *Hollywood before glamour: fashion in American silent film*. New York: Palgrave Macmillan, 2013.

Flusser, Alan J. *Style and the man*. New York: HarperStyle, 1996.

The Foundation Pierre Berger and Yves Saint Laurent. *Yves Saint Laurent: Style*. New York: Abrams, 2008.

Friedel, Robert. *Zipper: an exploration in novelty*. New York: W. W. Norton, 1994.

Fukai, Akiko et al. *Collection of the Kyoto Costume Institute. Fashion: A History from the 18th to the 20th Century*. Köln: Taschen, 2002.

Garner, Philippe. *The world of Edwardiana*. London and New York: Hamlyn, 1974.

Gavenas, Mary Lisa. *The Fairchild Encyclopedia of Menswear*. New York: Fairchild, 2008.

Gilman, Sander. *Making the Body Beautiful: A Cultural History of Aesthetic Surgery*. Princeton: Princeton University Press, 1999.

Giorgetti, Cristina. *Brioni, fifty years of style*. Firenze: Octavo, 1995.

Giroud, Françoise. *Dior: Christian Dior 1905–1957*. Paris: Editions du Regard, 1987.

Givhan, Robin. *The Battle of Versailles: the night American fashion stumbled into the spotlight and made history*. New York: Flatiron Books, 2015.

Goldstein, Gabriel and Elizabeth Greenberg. *A Perfect Fit: The Garment Industry and American Jewry (1860–1960)*. Lubbock, TX: Texas Tech University Press, 2012. Published for Yeshiva University Museum.

Gordon, Lady Duff. *Discretions and Indiscretions*. New York: Frederick A. Stokes Company, 1932.

Golbin, Pamela (ed.). *Madeleine Vionnet*. New York: Rizzoli, 2009.

Grimaud, Pamela. *Vera Maxwell: Timely and Timeless, An Examination of the Designs of Vera Maxwell from the 1930s to the 1950s* (MA Thesis). New York University, New York, 2002.

Grove Art Online. Oxford Art Online. Oxford University Press.

Gross, Elaine and Fred Rottman. *Halston: An American Original*, New York: Harper Collins, 1999.

Guillaume, Valérie. *Courrèges*. New York: Assouline, 2004.

—. *Jacques Fath*. Paris: Adam Biro, Paris-Musées, 1993.

Gutner, Howard. *Gowns by Adrian: the MGM years 1928–1941*. New York: Abrams, 2001.

Haiken, Elizabeth. *Venus Envy: a history of cosmetic surgery*. Baltimore: Johns Hopkins University Press, 1997.

Hall, Lee. *Common Threads: A Parade of American Clothing*. Boston: Little, Brown and Company, 1992.

Hanley, Susan B. *Everyday Things in Premodern Japan: The Hidden Legacy of Material Culture*. Berkeley: University of California Press, 1997.

Head, Edith and Paddy Calistro. *Edith Head's Hollywood*. New York: Dutton, 1983.

Heilbrunn Timeline of Art History. New York: The Metropolitan Museum of Art, 2000--http://www.metmuseum.org/toah/hi/te_index.asp

Hesse, Jean-Pascal. *Pierre Cardin: 60 years of innovation*. New York: Assouline, 2010.

Hilfiger, Tommy with Anthony DeCurtis. *Rock style: how fashion moves to music*. New York: Universe, 1999.

Hollander, Anne. *Seeing Through Clothes*. Berkeley: University of California Press, 1993.

Holme, Bryan et al. *The World in Vogue*. New York: Viking Press, 1963.

Horwood, Catherine. *Keeping up Appearances: Fashion and Class Between the Wars*. Stroud, Gloucestershire: The History Press, 2011.

IMDb – Internet Movie Database. www.imdb.com.

Jorgensen, Jay. *Edith Head: The Fifty-Year Career of Hollywood's Greatest Costume Designer*. Philadelphia: Running Press, 2010.

Jouve, Marie-Andrée and Jacqueline Demornex. *Balenciaga*, New York: Rizzoli, 1989.

Kamitsis, Lydia. *Rabanne, les sens de la recherché*. Paris: Editions M. Lafon, 1996.

Kirichenko, Evgenia. *Russian Design and the Fine Arts 1750–1917*. New York: Harry N. Abrams, 1991.

Kirke, Betty and Issey Miyake. *Madeleine Vionnet*. (3rd ed.) San Francisco: Chronicle Books, 2012.

Keenan, Brigid. *The Women We Wanted to Look Like*. New York: St. Martin's Press, 1978.

Kjellberg, Anne and Susan North. *Style & Splendor: The Wardrobe of Queen Maud of Norway, 1896–1938*. London: V & A Publications, 2005.

Kobal, John. *Hollywood Color Portraits*. New York: William Morrow & Company, 1981.

Kochno, Boris. *Christian Bérard*. London: Thames and Hudson, 1988.

Koda, Harold. *Extreme Beauty: the body transformed*. New York: The Metropolitan Museum of Art and New Haven: Yale University Press, 2001.

Koda, Harold and Andrew Bolton. *Poiret*. New York: The Metropolitan Museum of Art and New Haven: Yale University Press, 2007.

Koda, Harold and Jan Glier Reeder. *Charles James: beyond fashion*. New York: The Metropolitan Museum of Art and New Haven: Yale University Press, 2014.

Landis, Deborah Nadoolman. (ed.) *Hollywood Costume*. London: Victoria & Albert Museum, 2012.

Lansdell, Avril. *Fashion à la carte, 1860–1900: a study of fashion through cartes-de-visite*. Princes Risborough, Aylesbury, Bucks, UK: Shire Publications, 1985.

Lauren, Ralph. *Ralph Lauren*. New York: Rizzoli, 2007.

Lee, Sarah Tomerlin. *American Fashion: the life and lines of Adrian, Mainbocher, McCardell, Norell and Trigère*. New York: Quadrangle/New York Times Book Co., 1975.

de Leeuw-de Monti, Matteo and Petra Timmer. *Color Moves: Art & Fashion by Sonia Delaunay*. (exhibition catalogue) New York: Cooper-Hewitt, National Design Museum, Smithsonian Institution, 2011.

Lepicard, José Marie and Susan Train. *Givenchy: 40 years of creation*. Paris: Paris-Musées, 1991.

Lewenhaupt, Tony and Claës Lewenhaupt. *Crosscurrents: Art, Fashion, Design, 1890–1989*. New York: Rizzoli, 1989.

Lloyd, Valerie. *The Art of Vogue Photographic Covers*. New York: Harmony Books, 1986.

Loriot, Thierry-Maxime. *The fashion world of Jean Paul Gaultier: from the sidewalk to the catwalk*. (exhibition catalogue). Montreal: Museum of Fine Arts and New York: Abrams, 2011.

Maison Martin Margiela. With contributions by Jean-Paul Gaultier, Susannah Frankel, Andrée Putman and Vanessa Beecroft. New York: Rizzoli, 2009.

Majer, Michele (ed.). *Staging fashion, 1880–1920: Jane Hading, Lily Elsie, Billie Burke*. New York: Bard Graduate Center and New Haven: Yale University Press, 2012.

Martin, Richard. *American Ingenuity: Sportwear 1930s–1970s*. New York: The Metropolitan Museum of Art, 1998.

—. *Cubism and Fashion*. New York: The Metropolitan Museum of Art, 1998.

—. *Fashion and Surrealism*. New York: Rizzoli, 1987.

—. *Orientalism: Visions of the East in Western Dress*. New York: The Metropolitan Museum of Art, 1994

Martin, Richard and Harold Koda. *Christian Dior*. New York: The Metropolitan Museum of Art, 1996.

—. *Giorgio Armani: Images of man*. New York: Rizzoli, 1990.

—. *Haute Couture*. New York: The Metropolitan Museum of Art, 1995.

Martorelli, Barbara. *George Barbier: The Birth of Art Deco.* New York: Marsilio Publishers, 2009.

Mauriès, Patrick. *Christian Lacroix: the diary of a collection.* New York: Simon & Schuster Editons, 1996.

Mayer, Martin. *The Met: One Hundred Years of Grand Opera.* New York: Simon and Schuster, 1983.

McDermott, Catherine. *Street style: British design in the 80s.* New York: Rizzoli, 1987.

McFadden, Mary and Ruta Saliklis. *Mary McFadden: High Priestess of Fashion.* Charlestown, MA: Bunker Hill Publishing Inc. in association with Allentown Art Museum, 2004.

Mears, Patricia. *American beauty: aesthetics and innovation in fashion.* New Haven: Yale University Press in association with the Fashion Institute of Technology, 2009.

—. *Madame Grès: sphinx of fashion.* New Haven: Yale University Press in association with the Fashion Institute of Technology, 2007.

Mendes, Valerie and Amy de la Haye. *Fashion Since 1900.* London and New York: Thames and Hudson, 2010.

Merceron, Dean L. *Lanvin.* New York: Rizzoli, 2007.

Milbank, Caroline Rennolds. *Couture, The Great Designers.* New York and London: Thames & Hudson and Stewart, Tabori and Chang, 1985.

Modern Master: Lucien Lelong Couturier 1918–1948. (exhibition catalogue with essay by Sonya Mooney and Sarah Scaturro). New York: The Museum at FIT, 2006.

Morris, Bernadine. *Scaasi: a cut above.* New York: Rizzoli, 1996.

Mower, Sarah. *Oscar: the style, inspiration and life of Oscar de la Renta.* New York: Assouline, 2002.

Müller, Florence. *Inspiration Dior.* New York: Abrams, 2011.

Muriel King, Artist of Fashion (exhibition brochure with essay by April Calahan). New York: The Museum at FIT, 2009.

North, Susan. "John Redfern and Sons, 1847 to 1892," *Costume,* vol. 42, 2008.

—. "Redfern Ltd., 1892 to 1940," *Costume,* vol. 43, 2009.

Noten, Dries Van. *Dries Van Noten* (exhibition catalogue). Tielt: Lannoo, 2014.

O'Hagan, Helen with Kathleen Rowold and Michael Vollbracht. *Bill Blass: an American designer.* New York: Harry N. Abrams in association with Elizabeth Sage Historic Costume Collection, Indiana University, 2002.

de Osma, Guillermo. *Fortuny: Mariano Fortuny, his life and work.* New York: Rizzoli, 1980.

Packer, William. *The Art of Vogue Covers.* London: Octopus/Chancellor Books, 1983.

Palmer, Alexandra (ed.). *Fashion: A Canadian Perspective.* Toronto: University of Toronto Press, 2004.

Pannunzio, Gabriella. *"Made in Italy" – Unique Synergies at Work* (MA Thesis). New York University, New York, 2009.

Payne, Blanche. *History of Costume: From the ancient Egyptians to the twentieth century.* New York: Harper & Row, 1965.

Pellé, Marie-Paule and Patrick Mauriès. *Valentino: Thirty Years of Magic.* New York: Abbeville Press, 1990.

Penn, Irving. *Irving Penn regards the work of Issey Miyake: photographs, 1975–1998.* Boston: Little, Brown and Co., 1999.

Perrot, Philippe. *Fashioning the Bourgeoisie: A history of clothing in the nineteenth century.* Princeton: Princeton University Press, 1994.

Pick, Michael. *Be Dazzled! Norman Hartnell, Sixty Years of Glamour and Fashion.* New York: Pointed Leaf Press, 2007.

Pochna, Marie France. *Nina Ricci.* Paris: Editions de Regard, 1992.

Poiret, Paul. *King of Fashion: The Autobiography of Paul Poiret.* trans. by Stephen Haden Guest. Philadelphia & London: J.B. Lippincott Company, 1931.

Polhemus, Ted. *Streetstyle: from sidewalk to catwalk.* New York: Thames & Hudson, 1994.

Proddow, Penny, with Deborah Healy and Marion Fasel. *Hollywood Jewels: Movies, Jewelry, Stars.* New York: Abradale Press/Abrams, 1996.

Pruzhan, Irina. *Léon Bakst: Set and Costume Designs, Book Illustrations, Paintings and Graphic Works.* St. Petersburg, Russia: Aurora Art Publishers, 1986.

Quant, Mary. *Quant by Quant.* London: Cassell, 1966.

Reeder, Jan Glier. *High Style: Masterworks from the Brooklyn Museum Collection at the Metropolitan Museum of Art/* New York: The Metropolitan Museum of Art and New Haven: Yale University Press, 2010.

—. *The Touch of Paquin: 1891–1920* (MA Thesis), SUNY Fashion Institute of Technology, New York, 1990.

Rhodes, Zandra. *Zandra Rhodes: a lifelong love affair with textiles.* Woodbridge: Antique Collectors' Club and Camberley: Zandra Rhodes Publications Ltd., 2005.

Ribeiro, Aileen. *The Gallery of Fashion.* Princeton: Princeton University Press, 2000.

Ricci, Stefania (ed.). *Salvatore Ferragamo: inspiration and vision.* Milan: Skira, 2011.

Riordan, Teresa. *Inventing Beauty: A History of the Innovations That Have Made Us Beautiful.* New York: Broadway Books, 2004.

Ross, Josephine. *Society in Vogue: the international set between the wars.* New York: Vendome Press, 1992.

Rossellini, Isabella (intr.). *10 Years of Dolce & Gabbana.* New York: Abbeville Press, 1996.

Rothstein, Natalie (ed.). *Four Hundred Years of Fashion.* London: Victoria & Albert Museum, 1992.

Ruane, Christine. *The Empire's New Clothes: A History of the Russian Fashion Industry 1700–1917.* New Haven: Yale University Press, 2009.

Rubin, Arnold (ed.). *Marks of Civilization: artistic transformations of the human body.* Los Angeles: Museum of Cultural History, UCLA, 1988.

Rudoe, Judy. *Cartier, 1900–1939.* New York: Abrams and The Metropolitan Museum of Art, 1997.

Rudofsky, Bernard. *The Unfashionable Human Body.* Garden City, NY: Doubleday and Company, 1971.

Saint Laurent, Yves. *Yves Saint Laurent par Yves Saint Laurent.* Paris: Herscher, 1986.

Salvy, Gérard-Julien. *Balmain.* Paris: Regard, 1995.

Scherman, David E. (ed.) *The Best of Life.* New York: Avon Books, 1973.

Semmelhack, Elizabeth. *Icons of Elegance: The Most Influential Shoe Designers of the 20th Century.* Toronto: Bata Shoe Museum, 2005.

Schweitzer, Marlis. *When Broadway Was the Runway: Theater, Fashion, and American Culture.* Philadelphia: University of Pennsylvania Press, 2011.

Small, Lisa. *A Distant Muse: Orientalist Works from the Dahesh Museum of Art.* New York: Dahesh Museum of Art, 2000.

Sorkin, Molly and Jennifer Park (eds.). *Fortuny y Madrazo: An Artistic Legacy.* New York: Queen Sofia Spanish Institute, 2012.

Steele, Valerie. *The Corset: a cultural history.* New Haven: Yale University Press, 2001.

—. *Fashion, Italian style.* New Haven: Yale University Press, 2003.

—. *Fashioning the modern woman: the art of the couturière, 1919–1939.* (exhibition brochure). New York: The Museum at FIT, 2004.

—. *Fifty Years of Fashion: New Look to Now.* New Haven: Yale University Press, 1997.

—. *Japan Fashion Now.* New Haven: Yale University Press in association with the Fashion Institute of Technology, 2010.

—. *Paris Fashion: A Cultural History.* New York: Oxford University Press, New York, 1988.

—. *Women of Fashion: twentieth-century designers.* New York: Rizzoli, 1991.

Steele, Valerie and Jennifer Park. *Gothic: dark glamour.* New Haven: Yale University Press in association with the Fashion Institute of Technology, 2008.

Steele, Valerie and John S. Major. *China Chic: East Meets West.* New Haven: Yale University Press, 1999.

Steele, Valerie with Patricia Mears and Clare Sauro. *Ralph Rucci: the art of weightlessness.* New Haven: Yale University Press in association with the Fashion Institute of Technology, 2007.

Strizhenova, Tatiana. *Soviet Costume and Textiles 1917–1945.* Paris: Flammarion, 1991.

Sullivan, James. *Jeans: A Cultural History of an American Icon.* New York: Gotham, 2006.

Tam, Vivienne. *China Chic.* New York: Regan Books, 2000.

Trahey, Jane (ed.). *Harper's Bazaar: 100 Years of the American Female.* New York: Random House, 1967.

Thieme, Otto Charles (ed.). *With Grace & Favour: Victorian and Edwardian Fashion in America.* Cincinnati: Cincinnati Art Museum, 1993.

Thomas, Steven and Alwyn W. Turner. *Big Biba.* Woodbridge, U.K., Easthampton, MA: Antique Collectors' Club, 2006.

Three Women: Madeleine Vionnet, Claire McCardell, and Rei Kawakubo (exhibition brochure). New York: Fashion Institute of Technology, 1987.

Troy, Nancy J. *Couture Culture: A Study in Modern Art and Fashion.* Cambridge, MA: MIT Press, 2003.

Turner, Alwyn W. *Biba: the Biba experience.* Woodbridge, U.K., Easthampton, MA: Antique Collectors' Club, 2004.

V & A Fashion. London: Victoria and Albert Museum. http://www.vam.ac.uk/page/f/fashion/

Vassiliev, Alexandre. *Beauty in Exile: The Artists, Models and Nobility who Fled the Russian Revolution and Influenced the World of Fashion.* New York: Harry N. Abrams, 2000.

Violette, Robert (ed.). *Hussein Chalayan*. New York: Rizzoli, 2011.

Von Eckardt, Wolf and Sander L. Gilman. *Bertolt Brecht's Berlin: A Scrapbook of the Twenties*. Garden City, NY: Anchor Press, 1975.

Vreeland, Diana. *American Women of Style*. New York: Metropolitan Museum of Art, 1975.

Vreeland, Diana et al. *Yves Saint Laurent*. New York: The Metropolitan Museum of Art, 1983.

Wackerl, Luise. *Royal Style: A History of Aristocratic Fashion Icons*. New York: Prestel Publishing, 2012.

Waissenberger, Robert (ed.). *Vienna, 1890–1920*. New York: Rizzoli, 1984.

Watt, Judith. *Ossie Clark, 1965–74*. London: V&A Publications, 2003.

Welters, Linda and Patricia A. Cunningham (eds.). *Twentieth-century American Fashion*. Oxford, UK and New York: Berg, 2005.

Wichmann, Siegfried. *Japonisme: The Japanese Influence on Western Art Since 1858*. London and New York: Thames & Hudson, 1999.

Wilcox, Claire (ed.). *The Golden Age of Haute Couture: Paris and London 1947–1957*. London: V & A Publications, 2007.

—. *Radical Fashion*. London: V & A Publications, 2001.

—. *Vivienne Westwood*. London: V&A, 2004.

Wilcox, Claire and Valerie Mendes and Chiara Buss. *The art and craft of Gianni Versace*. London: V&A Publications, 2002.

Wollen, Peter and Fiona Bradley. *Addressing the century: 100 years of art & fashion*. (exhibition catalogue) London: Hayward Gallery, 1998.

Woodham, Jonathan M. *Twentieth Century Design*. Oxford: Oxford University Press, 1997.

Worth, Gaston. *La Couture et la Confection des vêtements de femme*. Paris: Chaix, 1895.

Worth, Jean-Philippe. *A Century of Fashion*. Translated by Ruth Scott Miller. Boston: Little, Brown and Co., 1928.

Yohannan, Kohle. *Valentina: American Couture and the Cult of Celebrity*. New York: Rizzoli, 2009.

Yohannan, Kohle and Nancy Nolf. *Claire McCardell: Redefining Modernism*. New York: Harry N. Abrams, 1998.

1850–1890

Apraxine, Pierre et al. *La Divine Comtesse: Photographs of the Countess de Castiglione*. Metropolitan Museum of Art/Yale University Press, New York and New Haven, 2000.

Arnold, Janet. "Dashing Amazons: The Development of Women's Riding Dress," in Amy de la Haye and Elizabeth Wilson (eds.) *Defining Dress: Dress as Object, Meaning, and Identity* Manchester: University of Manchester Press, 1999.

Beatty, Laura. *Lillie Langtry: Manners, Masks and Morals*, London: Chatto & Windus, 1999.

Cherry, Robin. *Catalogue: An Illustrated History of Mail-Order Shopping*. New York: Princeton Architectural Press, 2008.

Cone, Polly (ed.). *The Imperial Style: Fashion in the Age of the Hapsburgs*, Metropolitan Museum of Art, New York, 1980.

Cooper, Grace Rogers. *The Sewing Machine: its invention and development*. Washington, D.C.: Smithsonian Institution, 1976.

Cunningham, Patricia A. *Reforming Women's Fashion, 1850–1920*. Kent: The Kent State University Press, 2003.

Cunnington, C. Willett. *English Women's Clothing in the Nineteenth Century*. London: Faber and Faber, 1937.

Cunnington, Phillis Emily. *English Costume for Sports and Outdoor Recreation*. New York: Barnes and Noble, 1970.

David, Alison Matthews and Elizabeth Semmelhack. *Fashion Victims: The Pleasures and Perils of Dress in the 19th Century* (exhibition catalogue). Toronto: Bata Shoe Museum, 2014.

Woolson, Abba Goold (ed.) *Dress-Reform: A Series of Lectures Delivered in Boston, on Dress as it Affects the Health of Women*. Boston: Roberts Brothers, 1874.

Ferry, John William. *A History of the Department Store*. New York: Macmillan, 1960.

Goldthorpe, Caroline. *From Queen to Empress: Victorian Dress 1837–1877*. New York: The Metropolitan Museum of Art, 1989.

Harvey, John. *Men in Black*. Chicago: University of Chicago Press, 1995.

Hollander, Anne. "When Mr. Worth was King," *Connoisseur*, December 1982, 114–120.

Hume, Sara Elisabeth. *Charles Frederick Worth: A Study in the Relationship between the Parisian Fashion Industry and the Lyonnais Silk Industry 1858–1889* (MA Thesis), SUNY Fashion Institute of Technology, New York, 2003.

Johnston, Lucy. *Nineteenth Century Fashion in Detail*, London: V&A Publications, 2005.

Lambert, Miles. *Fashion in Photographs 1860–1880*. London: B.T. Batsford, 1991.

Lebrecht, Norman. *Who Killed Classical Music?* New York: Birch Lane Press, 1997.

Levitt, Sarah. *Fashion in Photographs 1880–1900*. London: B.T. Batsford, 1991.

von Metternich-Winnenberg, Pauline. *My Years in Paris*. London: E. Nash & Grayson, Ltd., 1922.

Ribeiro, Aileen. "Fashion in the Work of Winterhalter," in *Franz Xaver Winterhalter and the Courts of Europe* (ed. Richard Ormond and Carol Blackett-Ord). London; New York: National Portrait Gallery; Harry Abrams, 1992.

—. *Ingres in Fashion: Representations of Dress and Appearance in Ingres' Images of Women*. New Haven: Yale University Press, 1999.

Robar, Stephen F. *Frances Clara Folsom Cleveland*. New York: Nova History Publications, 2004.

Severa, Joan L. *Dressed for the Photographer: Ordinary Americans & Fashion, 1840–1900*. Kent: Kent State University, 1995.

Taylor, Lou. "Wool cloth and gender: the use of woolen cloth in women's dress in Britain, 1865–85" in Amy de la Haye and Elizabeth Wilson (eds.), *Defining Dress: Dress as object, meaning and identity*. Manchester: Manchester University Dress, 1999.

Waugh, Norah. *Corsets and Crinolines*. London: Routledge, 1954.

1890s

Font, Lourdes. "International couture: The opportunities and challenges of expansion, 1880–1920." *Business History*, 54:1, 2012, 30–47.

Jowett, George F. "Eugene Sandow," *Strength*, March 1927.

Bernhardt, Sarah. *My Double Life: The Memoirs of Sarah Bernhardt*, London: Heinemann, 1907.

Blainey, Ann. *Marvelous Melba: The Extraordinary Life of a Great Diva*. Chicago: Ivan R. Dee, 2009

Ockman, Carol and Kenneth E. Silver. *Sarah Bernhardt: The Art of High Drama*. New York: Jewish Museum, 2005.

Parry, Albert. *Tattoo: Secrets of a Strange Art*. New York: Simon and Schuster, 1933.

Vincent, W.D.F. *The Cutters' Practical Guide to Cutting Every Kind of Garment Made by Tailors with copious hints on their production*. London: The John Williamson Company, 1889.

1900s

Lees, Frederick. "The Evolution of Paris Fashions: An Enquiry," *Pall Mall Magazine*, 1903, 113–122.

Mendes, Valerie and Amy de la Haye. *Lucile Ltd: London, Paris, New York and Chicago 1890s – 1930s*. London: V& A Publications, 2009.

Ewing, Elizabeth. *Fur in Dress*. London: Harper Collins, 1981.

Exposition universelle internationale de 1900 – Les toilettes de la Collectivité de la couture. Paris: Société de publications d'art, 1900.

Fletcher, Ella Adelia. *The Woman Beautiful: A Practical Treatise on the Development and Preservation of Woman's Health and Beatuty, and the Principles of Taste in Dress*. New York: Brentano's, 1901.

1910s

Bass-Krueger, Maude. "From the 'union parfaite' to the 'union brisée': The French Couture Industry and the *midinettes* during the Great War." *Costume*, 47:1, 2013.

Burbank, Emily. *Woman as Decoration*. New York: Dodd, Mead and Company, 1917.

Golden, Eve. *Vamp: The Rise and Fall of Theda Bara*. New York: Vestal Press, 1998.

Howarth, Stephen. *Henry Poole: Founders of Savile Row*. London: Bene Factum Publishing, 2003.

Martin, Richard. "Fundamental Icon: J.C. Leyendecker's Male Underwear Imagery, *Textile & Text*, 15:1, 1992.

Palais Galliera. *Europe: 1910–1939, Quand l'art habillait le vêtement*. Paris: Paris-Musées, 1997.

1920s

Battersby, Martin. *The Decorative Twenties*, London: Herbert Press, 1988.

Churchill, Allen. *The Theatrical Twenties*. New York: McGraw Hill, 1975.

Ginsburg, Madeleine. *Paris Fashion: The Art Deco Style of the 1920s*. New York: Gallery Books, 1989.

Lipmann, Anthony. *Divinely Elegant: The World of Ernst Dryden*, London: Pavilion Books in association with Michael Joseph, 1989.

Morano, Elizabeth. *Sonia Delaunay: Art into Fashion*. New York: G. Braziller, 1986.

Scruggs-Seaman, Margo. *The Formation of a Distinctive Style: Childrenswear 1895–1925*. Master of Arts Thesis, SUNY Fashion Institute of Technology, 1993.

Shapiro, Suzanne. *Nails: The Story of the Modern Manicure*. New York: Prestel USA, 2014.

Steele, Valerie. *Fashioning the Modern Woman: The Art of the Couturière, 1919–1939* (exhibition brochure). New York: The Museum at FIT, 2004.

1930s

Battersby, Martin. *The Decorative Thirties*. New York: Whitney Library of Design, 1988.

Blum, Stella. *Everyday Fashions of the Thirties as Pictured in Sears Catalogs*. New York: Dover Publications, 1986.

Brawley, Sean and Chris Dixon. *Hollywood's South Seas and the Pacific War: Searching for Dorothy Lamour*. New York: Palgrave Macmillan, 2012.

Crosbie, Lynn. *Dorothy L'Amour*. Toronto: Harper Flamingo Canada, 1999.

Drake, James A. and Kristin Beall Ludecke. *Lily Pons: A Centennial Portrait*. Milwaukee, WI, Amadeus Press: 2003.

Hawes, Elizabeth. *Fashion is Spinach*. New York: Random House, 1938.

Hodges, Graham Russell. *Anna May Wong: From Laundryman's Daughter to Hollywood Legend*. New York: Palgrave McMillan, 2004.

Leibfried, Philip and Chei Mi Lane. *Anna May Wong: A Complete Guide to Her Film, Stage, Radio and Television Work*. Jefferson, N.C.: McFarland, 2004.

Martin, Richard and Harold Koda, "Jockey: The Invention of the Classic Brief," *Textile & Text*, 15:2, 1992.

Windsor, Edward, Duke of. *A Family Album*. London: Cassell, 1960.

1940s

Amies, Hardy. *Just So Far*. London: Collins, 1954.

Daoust, Robert. *Fashion or ration: Hartnell, Amies and dressing for the Blitz*. http://www.nationalarchives.gov.uk/podcasts/fashion-or-ration.htm.

Dower, John W. and Jacqueline M. Atkins. *Wearing Propaganda: Textiles on the Home Front in Japan, Britain, and the United States, 1931–1945*. New Haven, Conn.: Published for the Bard Graduate Center for Studies in the Decorative Arts, Design and Culture by Yale University Press, 2005.

"Fashion." *Robert Wagner's Script Magazine*, May 1947.

Guenther, Irene. *Nazi Chic? : fashioning women in the Third Reich*. Oxford; New York: Berg, 2004.

Paulicelli, Eugenia. *Fashion under Fascism, Beyond the Black Shirt*. Oxford and New York: Berg, 2004.

Peiss, Kathy. *Zoot Suit: The Enigmatic Career of an Extreme Style*. Philadelphia: University of Pennsylvania Press, 2014.

Théâtre de la Mode. With contributions by Edmonde Charles-Roux, Herbert R. Lottman, Stanley Garfinkel, Nadine Gasc, Katell le Bourhis. New York: Rizzoli, 1991.

Walford, Jonathan. *Forties Fashion: from Siren Suits to The New Look*. New York: Thames & Hudson, 2008.

1950s

Esquire's Handbook for Hosts. New York: Grosset & Dunlap, 1953.

Handley, Susannah. *Nylon: The Story of a Fashion Revolution*. Baltimore, Maryland: The Johns Hopkins University Press, 1999.

Fogarty, Anne. *Wife Dressing: The Fine Art of being a Well-Dressed Wife*. New York: J. Messner, 1959.

Haugland, Kristina. *Grace Kelly: Icon of Style to Royal Bride*. New Haven: Yale University Press in association with the Philadelphia Museum of Art, 2006.

1960s

Davis, Deborah. *Party of the Century: the fabulous story of Truman Capote and his black and white ball*. Hoboken, N.J.: John Wiley, 2006.

Drake, Nicholas. *The Sixties: A Decade in Vogue*. New York: Prentice Hall Press, 1988.

Fashion Flashbacks (videorecording). New York: Vidcat, 1995.

Lester, Richard. *John Bates: Fashion Designer*. Woodbridge, Suffolk: ACC Editions, 2008.

Lobenthal, Joel. *Radical Rags: Fashions of the Sixties*. New York: Abbeville Press, 1990.

Ozzard, Janet. "Retailing in the 1960s: The Phenomenon of the Boutique," *Textile & Text*, 12:3, 1990.

Stein, Jean and Plimpton, George. *Edie: American Girl*. New York: Grove Press, 1994.

1970s

Drake, Alicia. *The Beautiful Fall: Fashion, Genius, and Glorious Excess in 1970s Paris*. New York: Back Bay Books, 2007 (reprint).

Gale, Bill and the Editors of *Esquire* Magazine. *Esquire's Fashions for Today*. New York: Harper and Row, 1973.

LaBarre, Harriet. *Plastic Surgery: Beauty You Can Buy*. New York: Dell, 1970.

Lambert, Eleanor. *World of Fashion: People, Places, Resources*. New York: R. R. Bowker Co., 1976.

Morris, Bernadine and Barbra Walz. *The Fashion Makers: An Inside Look at America's Leading Designers*. New York: Random House, 1978.

Molloy, John T. *Dress for Success*. New York: Peter H. Wyden Publisher, 1975.

Trachtenberg, Jeffrey A. *Ralph Lauren: the man behind the mystique*. Boston: Little, Brown, 1988.

1980s

Barr, Ann and Peter York. *The Official Sloan Ranger Handbook: the guide to what really matters in life*. London: Ebury Press, 1982.

Birnbach, Lisa. *The Official Preppy Handbook*. New York: Workman Publishing, 1981.

Colacello, Bob and Kirby Hanson. *Nancy Reagan: a first lady's style*. Simi Valley, Calif.: Ronald Reagan Presidential Library Foundation, 2007.

Heimel, Cynthia. *Sex Tips for Girls: Lust, Love and Romance from the Lives of Single Women*. New York: Schuster & Schuster, 1983.

Jackson, Carole. *Color Me Beautiful*. New York: Ballantine, 1987.

Katie Pye: Clothes for Modern Lovers (exhibition brochure). Melbourne: National Gallery of Victoria, 2007.

Kawamura, Yuniya. *The Japanese Revolution in Paris Fashion*. London: Bloomsbury Academic, 2004.

Mantoux, Thierry. *BCBG: Le Guide du bon chic bon genre*. Paris: Seuil, 1986.

Nemy, Enid. *Judith Leiber: The Artful Handbag*. New York: Harry N, Abrams, Inc., 1995.

Walker, Catherine. *An Autobiography by the Private Couturier to Diana, Princess of Wales*. New York: Universe, 1998.

1990s

Agins, Teri. *The End of Fashion: How Marketing Changed the Clothing Business Forever*. New York: William Morrow, 2000.

Kawamura, Yuniya. *Fashioning Japanese Subcultures*. London: Bloomsbury, 2012.

Light, Alan (ed.). *The Vibe History of Hip Hop*. New York: Three Rivers Press, 1999.

Vale, V. and Andrea Juno. *Modern Primitives: tattoo, piercing, scarification: an investigation of contemporary adornment & ritual*. San Francisco: Re/Search, 1989.

A Guide To Casual Business Wear. San Francisco: Levi Strauss and Co., 1992.

2000s

Hethorn, Janet and Connie Ulasewicz. *Sustainable Fashion: Why Now? A conversation exploring issues, practices, and possibilities*. New York: Fairchild, 2008.

Jones, Terry and Susie Rushton. *Fashion Now*. Köln: Taschen, 2006.

Kuczynski, Alex. *Beauty Junkies: Inside Our $15 Billion Obsession with Plastic Surgery*. New York: Doubleday, 2006.

Taschen, Angelika (ed.). *Aesthetic Surgery*. Köln: Taschen, 2005.

Thurman, Judith. "The Misfit," *The New Yorker*, July 4, 2005.

EXHIBITIONS

Chanel, The Metropolitan Museum of Art, New York. May 5–August 7, 2005.

Lilly Daché: Glamour at the Drop of a Hat, The Museum at FIT. March 13–April 21, 2007.

Reveal or Conceal?/Dévoiler ou Dissimuler?, McCord Museum/Musée McCord, Quebec. February 22, 2008–January 18, 2009.

Yves Saint Laurent: The Retrospective. Montreal Museum of Fine Arts, Montreal. May 29–September 28, 2008.

Shopping in Paris: French Fashion 1850–1925, Philadelphia Museum of Art. April 11–November 1, 2009.

On Stage In Fashion: Design for Theater, Opera, and Dance, The New York Public Library for the Performing Arts. New York October 14, 2010–January 22, 2011.

The Peacock Male: Exuberance and Extremes in Masculine Dress, Philadelphia Museum of Art. January 22–September 18, 2011.

Alexander McQueen: Savage Beauty, The Metropolitan Museum of Art, New York. May 4–August 7, 2011.

Punk: Chaos to Couture, The Metropolitan Museum of Art, New York. May 9–August 14, 2013.

The Fashion World of Jean Paul Gaultier: From the Sidewalk to the Catwalk. Brooklyn Museum, October 25, 2013–February 23, 2014.

Patrick Kelly: Runway of Love, Philadelphia Museum of Art. April 27–December 7, 2014.

PERIODICALS

Adam: La Revue de l'Homme
Apparel Arts
Art Goût Beauté
L'Art et la Mode
ARTnews
Der Bazar
Bomb
Charm
Chicago Tribune
Connoisseur
Daily Telegraph
Die Dame
The Delineator
Demorest's Family Magazine
Details
Earnshaw's Magazine
Elegante Welt
Elle
Les Enfants très Parisiens
Esquire
European Fashion Service
The Face
Façon Tailleur
Fashions Art
Femina
Fortune
La Gazette du bon ton
Gentleman's Quarterly
Gentry
Godey's Lady's Book
La Guirlande des mois
Harper's Bazaar
L'Iris
Interview
Journal des Demoiselles et Petit
    Courrier des Dames Réunis
Junior Bazaar
Ladies' Home Journal
Life
London Times
Los Angeles Times
Man and His Clothes
Marie Claire
McCall's
La Mode Enfantine
La Mode Illustrée
La Mode Pratique
Les Modes
Les Modes Parisiennes Peterson's Magazine
Modes et Manières d'Aujourd'hui
Le Moniteur de la Mode
Monsieur
Motion Picture Magazine
New Straits Times
New York Magazine
New York Times
Newsweek
L'Officiel de la couture et de la mode de Paris
The Oregonian
Pall Mall
People
The Pittsburgh Press

La Revue de la Mode; Gazette de la Famille
Rolling Stone
The Queen
The Seattle Times
Seventeen
Der Silberspiegel
Spin
Standard Designer
Textile & Text
Time
Town and Country
USA Today
United Mainliner Magazine
Vanity Fair
Vogue
W
Wall Street Journal
Washington Post
Women's Wear Daily

Index

Picture Credits

Every effort has been made to contact the copyright holders of the illustrations, but should there be any errors or omissions, Laurence King Publishing would be pleased to insert the appropriate acknowledgement in any subsequent printing of this publication.

CHAPTER 1: 12 Art Gallery of Ontario, Toronto, Canada / Bridgeman Images **15** © Image courtesy of Fashion Institute of Technology/SUNY, Gladys Marcus Library Department of Special Collections **16** Courtesy Trustees of the Boston Public Library **20** © The Art Archive/Corbis **21** © adoc-photos/Corbis **22 (bottom)** Fotosearch/Getty Images **23 (top)** © National Portrait Gallery, London **23 (bottom)** © Bettmann/CORBIS **25 (top left)** Author's own collection **25 (top center)** Private Collection / Bridgeman Images **25 (top right)** © The Metropolitan Museum of Art/Art Resource/Scala, Florence **25 (bottom)** Wisconsin Historical Society **27** The Art Archive / Kharbine-Tapabor / Collection IM **28 (top left)** Image courtesy of Fashion Institute of Technology/SUNY, Gladys Marcus Library Department of Special Collections **28 (top right)** © McCord Museum M6327.1-3 **28 (bottom)** Courtesy of The Spurlock Museum, University of Illinois at Urbana-Champaign **29 (left)** © McCord / M14797.1-2 **29 (right)** © Amoret Tanner **30 (left)** Private Collection / Peter Newark Pictures / Bridgeman Images **30 (right)** © LACMA - The Los Angeles County Museum of Art **31** © Photo Scala Florence/Heritage Images **32, 33 (top left and bottom)** Images courtesy of Fashion Institute of Technology/SUNY, Gladys Marcus Library Department of Special Collections **35** Western Reserve Historical Society Permanent Collection. 59.909 **36** akg-images **38** Image courtesy of Fashion Institute of Technology/SUNY, Gladys Marcus Library Department of Special Collections **39** National Gallery of Victoria, Melbourne **40 (top)** Image courtesy of Fashion Institute of Technology/SUNY, Gladys Marcus Library Department of Special Collections **41 (top)** © INTERFOTO / Alamy **41 (bottom left)** Courtesy of Nancy E. Rexford **41 (bottom right)** Image courtesy of Fashion Institute of Technology/SUNY, Gladys Marcus Library Department of Special Collections **42** Hulton Archive/Getty Images **43 (left)** National Gallery of Victoria, Melbourne. The Joseph Brown Collection **43 (right)** © Corbis **44 (top)** © Fine Art Photographic Library/CORBIS **44 (bottom), 45** Images courtesy of Fashion Institute of Technology/SUNY, Gladys Marcus Library Department of Special Collections **46** akg-images **47** Images courtesy of Fashion Institute of Technology/SUNY, Gladys Marcus Library Department of Special Collections **48** Photo by DeAgostini/Getty Images **49** © Mary Evans Picture Library **50 (bottom)** Author's own collection **51 (left)** Hulton Archive/Getty Images **51 (right)** Author's own collection **52** Image courtesy of Fashion Institute of Technology/SUNY, Gladys Marcus Library Department of Special Collections **53** Scripps College, Claremont, California, USA

CHAPTER 2: 54 Mucha Trust / Bridgeman Images **56** © McCord Museum / Detail M970.25.1 **57 (left)** Library of Congress, Prints and Photographs Division, William McKenzie Morrison, LC-USZ62-58386 **57 (right)** Spencer Arnold/Getty Images **59 (left)** Private collection / Bridgeman Images **60, 61** Images courtesy of Fashion Institute of Technology/SUNY, Gladys Marcus Library Department of Special Collections **62 (top)** Library of Congress, Prints and Photographs Division, Thomas E. Askew, LC-USZ62-114272 **63 (left)** Ella Strong Denison Library, Scripps College **63 (right)** Image courtesy of Fashion Institute of Technology/SUNY, Gladys Marcus Library Department of Special Collections **64** Author's own collection **65 (top)** Image courtesy of Fashion Institute of Technology/SUNY, Gladys Marcus Library Department of Special Collections **65 (bottom)** akg-images **66** © The Metropolitan Museum of Art/Art Resource New York/Scala, Florence **67 (left)** Philadelphia Museum of Art / Bridgeman Images **67 (right)** © The Metropolitan Museum of Art/Art Resource New York/Scala, Florence **68** Library of Congress, Prints and Photographs Division, Napoleon Sarony, LC-USZ62-104487 **69 (top)** © The Metropolitan Museum of Art/Art Resource New York/Scala, Florence **69 (center)** Image courtesy of Fashion Institute of Technology/SUNY, Gladys Marcus Library Department of Special Collections **69 (bottom)** Author's own collection **70** Images courtesy of Fashion Institute of Technology/SUNY, Gladys Marcus Library Department of Special Collections **71** Mansell/The LIFE Picture Collection/Getty Images **72, 73** Images courtesy of Fashion Institute of Technology/SUNY, Gladys Marcus Library Department of Special Collections **74** The Art Archive / Kharbine-Tapabor / Collection IM

CHAPTER 3: 76 Courtesy Archives of American Illustrators Gallery, New York, NY **78 (top)** © Succession Picasso/DACS, London 2015 **78 (bottom)** © Hessische Hausstiftung, Kronberg im Taunus, Germany **79 (top)** © The Art Archive / Alamy **80 (bottom)** Archive Photos/Getty Images **81** Library of Congress, Prints and Photographs Division, LC-USZ62-13520 **82** Images courtesy of Fashion Institute of Technology/SUNY, Gladys Marcus Library Department of Special Collections **83** Author's own collection **84 (top)** Tim Graham Picture Library/Getty Images **84 (bottom left)** Image courtesy of Fashion Institute of Technology/SUNY, Gladys Marcus Library Department of Special Collections **84 (bottom right), 85 (top)** Author's own collection **85 (bottom), 86 (top and bottom)** Images courtesy of Fashion Institute of Technology/SUNY, Gladys Marcus Library Department of Special Collections **86 (center)** akg-images **87 (left)** © The Metropolitan Museum of Art/Art Resource New York/Scala, Florence **87 (right)** Philadelphia Museum of Art / Bridgeman Images **88 (top)** © Victoria and Albert Museum, London **88 (bottom)** Images courtesy of Fashion Institute of Technology/SUNY, Gladys Marcus Library Department of Special Collections **89** Westminster City Archives and Liberty Ltd **90** Courtesy of the FIDM Museum at the Fashion Institute of Design & Merchandising, Los Angeles, CA. Accession #: 99.274.99. Photo: Brian Sanderson **91 (left)** Image courtesy of Fashion Institute of Technology/SUNY, Gladys Marcus Library Department of Special Collections **91 (right)** 2014 © Fondi Fotografici del Museo Fortuny - FMCV Photo Archive **92 (top)** Courtesy Bard Graduate Center: Decorative Arts, Design History, Material Culture **92 (bottom), 93 (bottom)** Images courtesy of Fashion Institute of Technology/SUNY, Gladys Marcus Library Department of Special Collections **93 (top)** FPG/Hulton Archive/Getty Images **94 (left)** Images courtesy of Fashion Institute of Technology/SUNY, Gladys Marcus Library Department of Special Collections **94 (right)** John Swartz/American Stock/Getty Images **95** © 2014 by The National Museum of American Illustration, Newport, RI **96, 97** Images courtesy of Fashion Institute of Technology/SUNY, Gladys Marcus Library Department of Special Collections

CHAPTER 4: 98 akg-images **99** Image courtesy of Fashion Institute of Technology/SUNY, Gladys Marcus Library Department of Special Collections **100 (left)** LSE Library's collections, TWL.2009.03.12 **100 (right)** Interim Archives/Getty Images **101** Christie's Images/Bridgeman **103** Image courtesy of Fashion Institute of Technology/SUNY, Gladys Marcus Library Department of Special Collections **104 (left)** Hulton Archive / Getty Images **104 (right)** American Stock/Getty Images **105 (left)** Image courtesy of Fashion Institute of Technology/SUNY, Gladys Marcus Library Department of Special Collections **105 (right), 107** Conde Nast Publications **108, 109** Images courtesy of Fashion Institute of Technology/SUNY, Gladys Marcus Library Department of Special Collections **110 (top)** Conde Nast Publications **110 (bottom left)** The Art Archive / Kharbine-Tapabor / Collection IM **111** Courtesy Drexel University Historic Fashion Collection **112 (left)** Courtesy Western Reserve Historical Society **112 (right)** Image courtesy of Fashion Institute of Technology/SUNY, Gladys Marcus Library Department of Special Collections **113 (top)** Author's own collection **113 (bottom), 114, 115** Images courtesy of Fashion Institute of Technology/SUNY, Gladys Marcus Library Department of Special Collections **116 (left)** © Hulton-Deutsch Collection/CORBIS **116 (right)** Ira L. Hill/FPG/Getty Images **117** © L'Illustration **118** AP/Press Association Images **119, 120, 121, 122 (bottom)** Images courtesy of Fashion Institute of Technology/SUNY, Gladys Marcus Library Department of Special Collections **122 (top)** Imagno/Getty **123 (top)** Images Buyenlarge/Getty Images **123 (bottom)** MPI/Getty Images **124 (bottom)** Image courtesy of Fashion Institute of Technology/SUNY, Gladys Marcus Library Department of Special Collections **125 (left)** The Art Archive / Kharbine-Tapabor / Jean Vigne **125 (right)** Collection of David Roberts **126 (top left)** Image courtesy of Fashion Institute of Technology/SUNY, Gladys Marcus Library Department of Special Collections **126 (top right and bottom)** Author's own collection **127** © ADAGP, Paris and DACS, London 2015

CHAPTER 5: 128 Conde Nast Publications **129** Private collection / The Stapleton Collection / Bridgeman Images **131 (left)** © Ullsteinbild / Topfoto **131 (right)** Library of Congress, M1630.2.F Performing Arts Reading Room (Madison, LM113 **132 (left)** © The Print Collector / Alamy **132 (right)** akg-images / Album / GEORGE HURRELL **133 (bottom)** © Victoria and Albert Museum, London **134** © 2014. Photo Scala, Florence **135 (left)** Courtesy Everett Collection/REX **136 (top)** STARSTOCK/Photoshot **136 (bottom)** Courtesy Advertising Archives **137 (left)** © Illustrated London News Ltd / Mary Evans **137 (right)** Helen Dryden / Conde Nast Publications **138** Pierre Mourgue / Conde Nast Publications **139** Topical Press Agency / Getty Images **140 (left)** Image courtesy of Fashion Institute of Technology/SUNY, Gladys Marcus Library Department of Special Collections **140 (right)** © Victoria and Albert Museum, London **141 (left)** Fox Photos / Getty Images **141 (right)** © The Estate of Edward Steichen/ARS, NY and DACS, London **143 (left)** © Amoret Tanner / Alamy **143 (right)** The Art Archive / Kharbine-Tapabor **144 (left)** © Bettmann/CORBIS **144 (right)** © Roger Viollet / Topfoto **145 (left)** © ADAGP, Paris and DACS, London 2015 **145 (right)** © Mary Evans Picture Library **146 (top)** Les Arts décoratifs - Musée de la Mode et du Textile, Paris **146 (bottom)** National Gallery of Victoria **147** UPPA/Photoshot **149 (top)** © 2014 Image copyright The Metropolitan Museum of Art / Art Resource / Scala, Florence **149 (bottom)** Edward Steichen / Conde Nast Publications **150** Luigi Diaz/Getty Images **152** UNITED ARTISTS / THE KOBAL COLLECTION / RICE **154 (left)** Topical Press Agency / Getty Images **154 (right)** George Hoyningen-Huene / Conde Nast Publications **155 (top)** Image courtesy of Fashion Institute of Technology/SUNY, Gladys Marcus Library Department of Special Collections **155 (bottom)** Ronald Grant Archive **156 (left)** UPPA/Photoshot **156 (right)** © John Springer Collection/CORBIS **157** Courtesy Advertising Archives **158** Images courtesy of Fashion Institute of Technology/SUNY, Gladys Marcus Library Department of Special Collections **159** © McCord Museum

CHAPTER 6: 160 © Sevenarts Ltd/DACS 2015 **161** Conde Nast Publications **162** Haags Gemeentemuseum, The Hague, Netherlands / Bridgeman Images **163** Author's own collection **164** Popperfoto/Getty Images **165** Georges Lepape / Conde Nast Publications **166 (top)** Author's own collection **166 (bottom)** Image courtesy of Fashion Institute of Technology/SUNY, Gladys Marcus Library Department of Special Collections **167 (top)** Bob Thomas/Popperfoto/Getty Images **167 (bottom left)** Conde Nast Publications **167 (bottom right)** A Hudson/Getty Images **168** Image courtesy of Fashion Institute of Technology/SUNY, Gladys Marcus Library Department of Special Collections **169** Conde Nast Publications **170 (left)** Mary Evans Picture Library **170 (right)** © Imagno/Getty Images **172** Leicestershire County Council Museums Service: The Symington Collection **173** Author's own collection **174 (left)** George Hoyningen-Huene / Conde Nast Publications **174 (right)** Courtesy Hearst Magazines UK **175** Courtesy L'Officiel **176** Courtesy Hearst Magazines UK **177 (left)** © Man Ray Trust/ADAGP, Paris and DACS, London 2015 **177 (right)** © Horst - Photo courtesy Staley/Wise Gallery **178 (left)** Courtesy Hearst Magazines UK **178 (right)** Lipnitzki/Roger Viollet/Getty Images **179** © Victoria and Albert Museum, London **180** Courtesy Conde Nast Publications **181** Courtesy Metropolitan Opera Archives **182** Image courtesy of Fashion Institute of Technology/SUNY, Gladys Marcus Library Department of Special Collections **183** John Kobal Foundation/Getty Images **184 (left)** George Hurrell/John Kobal Foundation/Getty Images **184 (right)** THE KOBAL COLLECTION / MGM / HURRELL, GEORGE **185 (left)** Alfred Eisenstaedt/Pix Inc./Time Life Pictures/Getty Images **185 (right)** Imagno/Getty Images **186** United Artists / The Kobal Collection **187 (top)** Popperfoto/Getty Images **187 (bottom)** Silver Screen Collection/Hulton Archive/Getty Images **188–191** Images courtesy of Fashion Institute of Technology/SUNY, Gladys Marcus Library Department of Special Collections

CHAPTER 7: 193 © Mirrorpix **195** Warner Bros./Courtesy of Getty Images **197** Courtesy Harper's Bazaar/Hearst Communications Inc **198** Courtesy Advertising Archives **199 (left)** Roger Viollet/REX **199 (right)** Albert Harlingue/Roger Viollet/Getty Images **200** akg-images / ullstein bild / Sonja Georgi **201** James Jarche/Popperfoto/Getty Images **202** Courtesy Conde Nast Publications **203** Author's own collection **204** Image courtesy of Fashion Institute of Technology/SUNY, Gladys Marcus Library Department of Special Collections **205 (left)** With kind permission of the Australian Consolidated Press / Image courtesy National Library of Australia **205 (right)** © Roger Viollet / Topfoto **206** G W Hales/Getty Images **207** Alberto Vargas/Getty Images **209** Reg Speller/Getty Images **210** Courtesy Conde Nast Publications **211** Courtesy Harper's Bazaar/Hearst Magazines UK **213** The Art Archive / Kharbine-Tapabor **214** © Victoria and Albert Museum, London **215** Courtesy Conde Nast Publications **216** By kind permission of Manya Drobnack

217 George Karger/Pix Inc./The LIFE Images Collection/Getty Images **218** Author's own collection **219** © The Metropolitan Museum of Art/Art Resource/Scala, Florence **220 (left)** Walter Sanders/The LIFE Picture Collection/Getty Images **221** © Moviestore collection Ltd / Alamy **222** Chicago History Museum/Getty Images **223 (left)** SNAP/REX **223 (right)** Robert Coburn Sr./John Kobal Foundation/Getty Images **224 (top)** Courtesy Advertising Archives **224 (bottom)** Courtesy Department of Family & Consumer Sciences Apparel Product Development & Merchandising, University of Hawai'i at Manoa **225** FPG/Getty Images **226** Author's own collection **227 (top)** Courtesy Advertising Archives **227 (bottom)** Image courtesy of Fashion Institute of Technology/SUNY, Gladys Marcus Library Department of Special Collections **228** Herbert Gehr/The LIFE Picture Collection/Getty Images **229** © Norman Parkinson/Corbis

CHAPTER 8: 230 Image courtesy of Fashion Institute of Technology/SUNY, Gladys Marcus Library Department of Special Collections **231** © H. Armstrong Roberts/ClassicStock/Corbis **232 (left)** Courtesy Advertising Archives **232 (right)** Pulp Image © 1998 Jeffrey Luther/PC Design. www.pulpcards.com. All Rights Reserved. Publisher's name and logo are trademark of their respective owner **234 (top)** John Rodgers/Redferns/Getty Images **234 (bottom)** Courtesy Conde Nast Publications **235 (top)** Nina Leen/The LIFE Picture Collection/Getty Images **235 (bottom)** Image courtesy of Fashion Institute of Technology/SUNY, Gladys Marcus Library Department of Special Collections **236 (top)** Sipa Press/REX **236 (bottom)** Image courtesy of Fashion Institute of Technology/SUNY, Gladys Marcus Library Department of Special Collections **238** Courtesy Advertising Archives **240** Courtesy L'Officiel **241 (right)** Courtesy Holt Renfrew **242 (left)** Courtesy Conde Nast Publications **242 (right)** Courtesy L'Officiel **243** © Association Willy Maywald/ADAGP, Paris and DACS, London 2015 **244, 245 (left)** Courtesy Conde Nast Publications **245 (right)** © DACS 2015 **246 (top)** Bibliothèque nationale de France **246 (bottom)** Courtesy L'Officiel **247** © The Richard Avedon Foundation **248** Silver Screen Collection/Getty Images **249** Mary Evans Picture Library / Hardy Amies London **250 (top)** © Victoria and Albert Museum, London **250 (bottom)** Gjon Mili/The LIFE Picture Collection/Getty Images **251, 252** Courtesy Conde Nast Publications **254** Olycom SPA/REX **255 (left)** Courtesy Everett Collection/REX **255 (right)** Courtesy Iconothèque de la Cinémathèque française **256** Warner Bros / The Kobal Collection **257** Courtesy Everett Collection/REX **258** Image courtesy of Fashion Institute of Technology/SUNY, Gladys Marcus Library Department of Special Collections **259, 260** Courtesy Advertising Archives **261** Image courtesy of Fashion Institute of Technology/SUNY, Gladys Marcus Library Department of Special Collections **262** Margaret Bourke-White/The LIFE Picture Collection/Getty Images **263 (top)** Courtesy Advertising Archives **263 (bottom)** Time Life Pictures/Pix Inc./The LIFE Picture Collection/Getty Images **264** Image courtesy of Fashion Institute of Technology/SUNY, Gladys Marcus Library Department of Special Collections **265** Yale Joel/The LIFE Picture Collection/Getty Images

CHAPTER 9: 266 Image courtesy of Fashion Institute of Technology/SUNY, Gladys Marcus Library Department of Special Collections **267** © Sunset Boulevard/Corbis **268** Everett Collection/REX **269 (left)** Alan Band/Keystone/Getty Images **269 (right)** Michael Ochs Archives/Getty Images **270 (left)** Courtesy L'Officiel **270 (right)** Gordon Parks/The LIFE Images Collection/Getty Images **271** Art Rickerby/The LIFE Picture Collection/Getty Images **272** Bill Eppridge/The LIFE Picture Collection/Getty Images **273 (left)** Keystone-France/Gamma-Keystone via Getty Images **273 (right)** Paul Popper/Popperfoto/Getty Images **274** Jean-Pierre BONNOTTE/Gamma-Rapho via Getty Images **275 (left)** Courtesy Marimekko / Photo Design Museum, Finland **275 (right)** Slim Aarons/Hulton Archive/Getty Images **276** © Art Resource, New York Scala, Florence **277 (right)** Popperfoto/Getty Images **278** Linen Mini John Bates for Jean Varon 1967 **279 (left)** © Pictorial Press Ltd / Alamy **279 (right)** Keystone/Getty Images **280 (top)** Courtesy Advertising Archives **280 (bottom)** Courtesy Hearst Magazines UK **281** Mario De Biasi/Mondadori Portfolio via Getty Images **282** © Association Willy Maywald/ADAGP, Paris and DACS, London 2015 **283 (left)** © Fondation Pierre Bergé - Yves Saint Laurent **283 (center)** © Topham / AP **283 (right)** © Topfoto **285** RDA/AGIP/Getty Images **286** Courtesy L'Officiel **287** David McCabe / Condé Nast Publications **288 (left)** David Graves/REX **288 (right)** Keystone/Hulton Archive/Getty Images **290 (left)** Franco Rubartelli / Condé Nast Publications **290 (right)** Keystone/Getty Images **291 (left)** Princess Irene Galitzine wearing Palazzo pajamas, courtesy the Historical Archive, Maison Galitzine **291 (right)** Henry Clarke / Condé Nast Publications **292** George Birth / AP/Press Association Images **293 (left)** Image courtesy of Fashion Institute of Technology/SUNY, Gladys Marcus Library Department of Special Collections **293 (right)** Courtesy Conde Nast Publications **294** Conde Nast Publications **295** David McCabe / Condé Nast Publications **296** Gianni Ferrari/Cover/Getty Images **297 (top)** © Moviestore collection Ltd / Alamy **297 (bottom)** Courtesy Advertising Archives **298 (left)** © Sunset Boulevard/Corbis **298 (right)** Everett Collection/REX **299** Roger Viollet/Getty Images **300** Michael Ochs Archives/Getty Images **301 (top)** The Art Archive / Kharbine-Tapabor **301 (bottom)** Keystone-France/Gamma-Keystone via Getty Images **303** Philippe Le Tellier/Paris Match via Getty Images

CHAPTER 10: 304 Art by Steven Stipelman **305** Conde Nast Publications **306** Library of Congress (LC-USZC4-2429) **308** RB/Redferns/Getty Images **309** Peter Bischoff/Getty Images **310** John Dominis/The LIFE Picture Collection/Getty Images **311 (top)** H. Edward Kim/National Geographic/Getty Images **311 (bottom)** akg-images / E. Mierendorff **312 (top)** Jerry Salvati / Condé Nast Publications **312 (bottom)** Les Arts Décoratifs, Paris / Laurent Sully Jaulmes / akg-images **313 (right)** Photoshot/Getty Images **315** Lynn Karlin / Condé Nast Publications **316 (top)** Courtesy Marimekko / Photo Design Museum, Finland **316 (bottom)** © Cat's Collection/Corbis **317** Tim Jenkins / Condé Nast Publications **318 (top left)** Everett Collection/REX **318 (top right)** © Sunset Boulevard/Corbis **318 (bottom)** Moviestore Collection/REX **319** Everett Collection/REX **320** By kind permission of Duane Michals **322** Reginald Gray / Condé Nast Publications **323 (left)** Courtesy Conde Nast Publications **323 (right)** Ken Towner /Associated News / Rex **324 (left)** © Herb Schmitz **324 (right)** Duffy/Getty Images **325** Justin de Villeneuve/Getty Images **326 (top)** Courtesy Conde Nast Publications **326 (bottom)** Chris Barham / Associated News / Rex **327 (top)** © Zandra Rhodes / zandrarhodes.ucreative.ac.uk **327 (bottom)** © Victoria and Albert Museum, London **328** Hulton Archive/Getty Images **330, 331** Conde Nast Publications **332 (top)** Francesco Scavullo / Condé Nast Publications **332 (center)** © Mellon Tytell 2014 **332 (bottom)** Courtesy Advertising Archives **333** Oliviero Toscani/Conde Nast Publications **334** Philadelphia Museum of Art, Pennsylvania, PA, USA / Gift of Hess's Department Store, Allentown, 1974 / Bridgeman Images **335** Suzanne Vlamis/AP/Press Association Images **336** Author's own collection **337** Courtesy Advertising Archives **338 (left)** Robert Riger/Getty Images **338 (right)** Condé Nast Publications **339** akg-images / Günter Rubitzsch **340 (left)** © Ted Streshinsky/CORBIS **340 (right)** Roland and Sabrina Michaud / akg-images

CHAPTER 11: 342 © Estate of Patrick Nagel / ARS, NY and DACS, London 2015 **343** Courtesy Fornasetti **344** Courtesy Peter Shire / Photo William Nettles **345** Christine Meyers for The Seattle Times **347 (top)** Mai/Mai/The LIFE Images Collection/Getty Images **347 (bottom)** Anwar Hussein/Getty Images **348 (bottom)** © Orion/Everett/REX **349 (left)** Ebet Roberts / Redferns / Getty Images **349 (right)** © Pictorial Press Ltd / Alamy **350 (top)** © Warner Br/Everett/REX **350 (bottom)** © AF archive / Alamy **351 (top)** REX/Everett Collection **351 (bottom left)** ITV/REX **351 (bottom center)** Silver Screen Collection/Getty Images **351 (bottom right)** Paramount/Getty Images **352 (top)** Courtesy Advertising Archives **352 (bottom)** City of Westminster Archives Centre and Jaeger Ltd **353** akg-images / Interfoto / George Ksandr **354** Courtesy Krizia **355** Courtesy The Leiber Collection **356 (top left)** catwalking.com **356 (top right)** Niall McInerney/Bloomsbury **356 (bottom)** Daniel SIMON/Gamma-Rapho via Getty Images **357** © David Montgomery **358** Sharok Hatami/REX **359** © Julio Donoso/Sygma/Corbis **360** Daniel SIMON/Gamma-Rapho via Getty Images **362** Jayne Fincher/Getty Images **363 (left)** © Laura Levine/Corbis **363 (right)** David Corio/Redferns/Getty Images **364** Courtesy Giorgio Armani **365 (top)** Corbis **365 (bottom)** © Pierre Vauthey/Sygma/Corbis **366 (top)** © Anthea Simms **366 (bottom)** Courtesy Fondazione Gianfranco Ferré **367 (top)** Courtesy Conde Nast Publications **367 (bottom)** Courtesy Advertising Archives **368** Images courtesy of Fashion Institute of Technology/SUNY, Gladys Marcus Library Department of Special Collections **369 (top)** © Steve Landis 1981 **369 (bottom)** Courtesy Sandra Garratt **370** Courtesy Katie Pye, photography by Geoff Kleem **371 (top)** © AF archive / Alamy **371 (bottom)** Keith Beaty/Toronto Star via Getty Images **372 (top)** © Bettmann/CORBIS **372 (bottom)** Courtesy Advertising Archives **373 (top)** © Imagestate Media Partners Limited - Impact Photos / Alamy **373 (bottom)** © Beezer/YouthClub **374 (top)** Courtesy Advertising Archives **374 (bottom left)** akg-images / E. Mierendorff **374 (bottom right)** © Courtesy Advertising Archives **375** Courtesy Hearst Magazines

CHAPTER 12: 376 © Elizabeth Peyton, courtesy Sadie Coles HQ, London **377** © Catherine Karnow/Corbis **379 (right)** © AF archive / Alamy **380** S Granitz/Wireimage/Getty Images **381** © Rex Features **382 (top)** Arnaldo Magnani/Liaison/Getty Images **382 (bottom)** © Moviestore collection Ltd / Alamy **383** Paramount Pictures/Getty Images **384** Edward Hirst/REX **385** Camera Press/ Figarophoto/ Robert Lakow **386 (left)** CBS via Getty Images **386 (right)** © Mitchell Gerber/Corbis **387 (top left)** Dave Einsel/AP/Press Association Images **387 (top right)** JMInternational/Redferns/Getty Images **387 (bottom left)** © Frank Trapper/Sygma/Corbis **387 (bottom right)** © Neal Preston/Corbis **388** Paul Bergen/Redferns/Getty Images **389** © The Condé Nast Publications **390** Terry Doyle/Getty Images **391 (left)** © Mitchell Gerber/Corbis **391 (right)** The LIFE Picture Collection/Getty Images **393** ERIK C PENDZICH/REX **394 (left)** catwalking.com **394 (right)** Author's own collection **395** © Les Arts Décoratifs, Paris / Jean Tholance / akg-images **396 (top)** Courtesy Advertising Archives **396 (bottom left)** GERARD JULIEN/AFP/Getty Images **396 (bottom right)** © Neal Preston/Corbis **397** akg-images / Interfoto / amw **398 (top)** © Frederique Dumoulin/Corbis **398 (bottom)** Charles Knight/REX **399** © Julio Donoso/Sygma/Corbis **400 (top)** Ken Towner/Evening Standard/REX **400 (bottom)** Alex Lentati/Associated News/REX **401** Ken Towner/Associated News/REX **402 (left)** Kyle Ericksen/The Condé Nast Publications **402 (right)** © Fairchild Photo Service/Condé Nast/Corbis **404** © Anthea Simms **405 (top)** Neville Marriner/Associated/REX **405 (bottom)** Ken Towner/Evening Standard /REX **406** WOOD/REX **407** Courtesy Ann Demeulemeester **408** NBC/NBCU Photo Bank via Getty Images/© [January 01, 1995] NBCUniversal/Getty Images **409** William STEVENS/Gamma-Rapho via Getty Images **410** Keith Butler/Getty Images **411** PIERRE VERDY/AFP/Getty Images **412 (right)** ©1994, Touchstone Television/Getty Images **413 (top)** Photo Courtesy of Misako Aoki, Former Kawaii Ambassador **414 (left)** Joyce Silverstein/REX **414 (right)** ANDRE DURAND/AFP/Getty Images **415** STAN HONDA/AFP/Getty Images

CHAPTER 13: 416 Photo Adam Wallacavage, collection of Max Lawrence **417** © BRENDAN MCDERMID/Reuters/Corbis **418** © HO/Reuters/Corbis **419** © Louie Psihoyos/Corbis **420** REX/Moviestore Collection **421** © ALESSANDRO BIANCHI/Reuters/Corbis **422 (left)** © ULI DECK/epa/Corbis **422 (right)** Lara Porzak Photography via Getty Images **423** Kyle Ericksen/Conde Nast Publications **424** REX/Mychal Watts/BEI **425** REX/©Sony Pictures/Everett **426 (left)** REX/©20thC.Fox/Everett **426 (right)** REX/Snap Stills **427 (left)** © Startraks Photo/REX **427 (center)** © John Rogers/Getty Images **427 (right)** © Picture Perfect/REX **428** REX/David Fisher **429 (top)** Tim Mosenfelder/Getty Images **429 (bottom)** Don Arnold/Wireimage/Getty Images **430 (top)** © Laurence Mouton/PhotoAlto/Corbis **430 (bottom)** Getty Images for Speedo **431** Rich Sugg/Kansas City Star/MCT via Getty Images **432 (left)** © Kari Medig/Aurora Photos/Corbis **432 (right)** Neilson Barnard/Getty Images **433** Model Krystal Fernandez / Photography by Babette **434** Camera Press/ Figarophoto/ Donja Pitsch **435** © Renaldo Barnette **436** © Stephane Cardinale/People Avenue/Corbis **437** John Aquino / Condé Nast Publications **438** Courtesy Advertising Archives **439 (top left)** Sgranitz/Wireimage/Getty Images **439 (top center)** REX/James McCauley **439 (top right)** © Lucas Jackson/Reuters/Corbis **439 (bottom)** Rex Features **440** Courtesy Juicy Couture **441** Camera Press/ Figarophoto/ David Benchitrit **442** PIERRE VERDY/AFP/Getty Images **443** © CHARLES PLATIAU/Reuters/Corbis **444** © Surachai Saengsuwan. Photographer: Surachai Saengsuwan; stylist: Nichakul Kitayanubongse; makeup: Wirat Leemakul; model: Ludmilla **445 (top)** © Andreea Angelescu/Corbis **445 (bottom)** Ralph Lauer/Fort Worth Star-Telegram/MCT via Getty Images **446 (left)** Myrna Suarez/Getty Images **446 (right)** JP Yim/Wireimage/Getty Images **447 (left)** Scott Gries/Getty Images **447 (center)** catwalking.com **447 (right)** © Karen Collins / Creative Exchange Agency **448** © KIYOSHI OTA/X02055/Reuters/Corbis **449** Conde Nast Publications **450** catwalking.com **451** Author's own collection **452 (top)** PYMCA/UIG via Getty Images **452 (bottom)** Jamie Kristine/Getty Images **453** Photography by Jaydee Wahid **454 (top)** Six 6 Photography/Getty Images **454 (bottom)** Ten Asia/Multi-Bits via Getty Images **455** Courtesy LG Electronics **456 (top)** Wang Jiang/ChinaFotoPress/Getty Images **456 (bottom)** REX/©Miramax/Everett **457 (left)** © Christian Kober/Robert Harding World Imagery/Corbis **457 (right)** Tony Barson/Wireimage/Getty Images **459** Courtesy Advertising Archives